REVISITING THOMAS F. O'DEA'S *THE MORMONS*

Revisiting Thomas F. O'Dea's

The Mormons

Contemporary Perspectives

Edited by

Cardell K. Jacobson,

John P. Hoffmann, and Tim B. Heaton

THE UNIVERSITY OF UTAH PRESS
Salt Lake City

To Rosanne, Lynn, and Tammy

 The Defiance House Man colophon is a registered trademark of the University of Utah Press. It is based upon a four-foot-tall, Ancient Puebloan pictograph (late PIII) near Glen Canyon, Utah.

12 11 10 09 08   1 2 3 4 5

LIBRARY OF CONGRESS CATALOGING-IN-PUBLICATION DATA

Revisiting Thomas F. O'Dea's The Mormons : contemporary perspectives / edited by Cardell K. Jacobson, John P. Hoffmann, and Tim B. Heaton.
    p. cm.
  Includes bibliographical references and index.
  ISBN 978-0-87480-920-6 (cloth : alk. paper) 1. O'Dea, Thomas F. 2. Mormons.
3. Mormon Church. I. Jacobson, Cardell K., 1941- II. Hoffmann, John P.
(John Patrick), 1962- III. Heaton, Tim B.
  BX8611.R45 2008
  289.3—dc22

                    2007034626

Printed and bound by Sheridan Books, Inc., Ann Arbor, Michigan

Contents

Situating O'Dea among *The Mormons*

~ CARDELL K. JACOBSON, JOHN P. HOFFMANN, AND TIM B. HEATON ~

> Mormonism retains much of its old peculiarity and Mormondom remains in many respects a society in its own right and, as such, has been subject to a number of stresses and strains within its own structure.... [S]ome of them are even now capable of severe threats to its welfare.
>
> — THOMAS F. O'DEA, *The Mormons*

THIS BOOK IS ABOUT THE PAST AND THE PRESENT. It is about a man and the landmark study he made of the Church of Jesus Christ of Latter-day Saints (also referred to as the LDS Church or Mormon Church), a work he simply called *The Mormons,* published in 1957. This book presents work by sociologists and other scholars who examine the place and contributions of Thomas F. O'Dea in and to the study of Mormonism. O'Dea was prescient in his analysis, but he failed to anticipate issues that have arisen since the middle of the twentieth century. As with any sociological analysis, O'Dea's work was grounded in the philosophical, methodological, and theoretical orientations present when he was writing. Thus, in addition to being an assessment of O'Dea's contribution to the literature on the LDS Church and the sociological study of religion, the present work is an assessment of important issues in the LDS Church today.

The LDS Church has been the object of study since its formation. Early reactions were perhaps predictably apologetic or inflammatory and demeaning. The extraordinary claims of new revelations, the emergence of the Book of Mormon, and the rapid number of converts required public explanation. This same bimodal distribution of popular treatises on the LDS Church continued through much of the nineteenth century to the middle of the twentieth century when O'Dea was working on *The Mormons*.

O'Dea brought together several intertwining threads of social research in *The Mormons*. The first thread was the popular and historical writing that was available at that time. In addition to historical treatises, O'Dea examined community studies and the controversial writings by both apologists and critics, including those who had left the LDS Church. A second thread in O'Dea's work was the dominant sociological perspective of the time, functionalism. The third thread involved community studies conducted in the United States.

O'Dea's sociological introduction to Mormonism came as part of his doctoral dissertation. His fieldwork was part of the Harvard Comparative Study of Values in Five Cultures that examined the Hopi, the Navajo, Mexican Americans, white Texas settlers, and the Mormons. O'Dea's assignment and focus in the project were the Mormon community, though he eventually left the project and completed *The Mormons* as an independent study. He later taught at the University of Utah from 1959 to 1964. His research in Utah and elsewhere resulted in numerous publications that included themes from his research on the LDS Church.

O'Dea's subsequent work was centered in the sociology of religion and included work on Catholicism, Judaism, and Islam. Among his most notable works were *American Catholic Dilemma: An Inquiry into the Intellectual Life* (1958), *The Sociology of Religion* (1966), and *The Catholic Crisis* (1968).[1]

Bruce Karlenzig (1998) notes that O'Dea, utilizing the dominant theoretical perspective of the time, was particularly interested in how religious functions could turn dysfunctional at a later time. This focus on functionalism led O'Dea to examine the "sources of strain and conflict" in Mormonism. O'Dea also used Ernst Troeltsch's church-sect typology, but found the LDS Church to be neither a church nor a sect, but rather a near nation, or a "quasi-ethnic" group in the isolated Intermountain West. He later applied similar functional analyses to Catholicism and other religious traditions.

The Mormons, his first book, remained important in part because it was insightful and cogent, and its focus was a group that had not received thorough attention by social scientists. O'Dea's background included reading the controversial writings about Mormons, including Fawn M. Brodie's *No Man Knows My History: The Life of Joseph Smith, the Mormon Prophet* (1945). A granddaughter of George H. Brimhall, a prior president of Brigham Young University, Brodie had written a vituperative essay about the early church and its founder, Joseph Smith. She also garnered attention because her uncle David O. McKay was a member of the Quorum of Twelve Apostles and later became the ninth president of the church. A decade later, Kimball Young, a grandson of Brigham Young and a graduate of the institution bearing his grandfather's name, wrote a critical review of polygamy, *Isn't One Wife Enough? The Story of Mormon Polygamy* (1954). Young, who had been president of the American Sociological Society, provided interesting sociological insights about the previous practice of polygamy in the LDS Church, but the tone of his work was clearly critical and contemptuous. O'Dea also drew on numerous other historical treatises written by both LDS and non-LDS authors (see Chapter 1 by Lynn England in this volume for a more detailed historical context of O'Dea's work).

Though historians had found Mormon history to be fertile territory, social scientists, some with backgrounds in the rural LDS communities, also found abundant material for analysis. Community studies were important at the time in both sociology and anthropology. Anthropologists followed the conventional path of studying "primitive peoples" or relatively unknown cultures around the world. But they also focused on unusual communities within the United States.

A variant of the anthropological model was used in sociology, mostly in community studies. W. Lloyd Warner, an anthropologist who had taught at the University of Chicago, was influential in establishing these studies within the United States, and he and his team produced several volumes about Yankee City (Newburyport, Massachusetts).

Other community researchers included Robert S. Lynd and Helen M. Lynd who spent several years studying Muncie, Indiana, a town they thought typified small-town USA. They produced two volumes on "Middletown": *Middletown: A Study in Modern American Culture* (1929) and *Middletown in Transition* (1937). Later, Floyd Hunter studied the power structure in Atlanta in *Community Power Structure: A Study of Decision Makers* (1953), and Robert A. Dahl, a political scientist, studied political power in New Haven, Connecticut, in *Who Governs?* (1961). Other notable community studies included John Dollard's *Caste and Class in a Southern Town* (1937) and *Deep South: A Social Anthropological Study of Caste and Class* (1941) by Allison Davis, Burleigh B. Gardner, and Mary R. Gardner, which was conducted under the direction of W. Lloyd Warner.

It was out of these traditions that researchers at Harvard University proposed the study of the five cultures in the Southwest, more specifically the Rimrock area of western New Mexico (see Vogt and Albert 1966). Community studies had already been conducted in LDS communities by

Ephraim E. Ericksen who traced the responses of Mormons to critical conflicts between Mormons and non-Mormons in *The Psychological and Ethical Aspects of Mormon Group Life* (1922). Lowry Nelson later produced a series of articles and pamphlets that, when combined, were published as *The Mormon Village: A Pattern and Technique of Land Settlement* (1952). Ronald W. Walker, David J. Whittaker, and James B. Allen (2001, chap. 2) note that *The Mormon Village* became an important resource for anthropologists, folklorists, geographers, historians, and sociologists. Nels Anderson, a sociologist employed by the Works Progress Administration during WWII, published *Desert Saints: The Mormon Frontier in Utah* in 1942.

The Harvard five-cultures project was planned in 1948 and 1949 and initiated in June 1949. The community studies influenced the Harvard researchers, who decided to include Mormons in the five-cultures project. O'Dea, then a graduate student at Harvard, was invited to participate and was assigned to study Mormons.

Talcott Parsons's influence is also evident in O'Dea's work. Parsons, one of the most influential sociologists of the mid-twentieth century, was well known for his focus on values and their relationship to the social structure. O'Dea combined the study of values with his interest on functions to examine strains and conflicts in both his work on *The Mormons* and his writings on Catholicism. Thus, on Mormonism O'Dea wrote that it "retains much of its old peculiarity and Mormondom remains in many respects a society in its own rights and, as such, has been subject to a number of stresses and strains within its own structure" (1957, 222). For O'Dea, the question was how the LDS Church could retain its own uniqueness as it confronted the larger society. He noted that this confrontation had produced "grave" problems in the past and would continue to produce stresses and strains. He further argued that some of the ideas and values themselves contained elements of conflict. The most significant of these, O'Dea believed, was the "encounter with modern secular thought." He foresaw a conflict between the church's encouragement of education and the exposure that it would inevitably bring to secular thought and church teachings on a variety of topics. Closely related, he thought, was the potential conflict between the "implicit rationality" of the church's tenets and its focus on the charisma of its leaders. The third conflict he foresaw was between concern for authority and individualism and what Mormons refer to as free agency.

Society and the sociological study of society have changed since O'Dea's time, however. Sociologists are less likely to write expansively about a group, culture, or community in general. Further, although O'Dea's was a prescient examination of Mormonism at the middle of the twentieth century, the church and the society in which it is embedded have changed dramatically over the past fifty years. Some of these changes O'Dea anticipated; others he did not.

The essays in this volume examine where O'Dea "got it right" as well as where tensions remain. The educational attainment of Americans has increased dramatically over the past half century, as have the educational levels of LDS Church members. Thus, this critical test, the potential conflict with modern secular thought, remains. Several of the essays in this volume address this issue in one way or another. Perhaps one surprise is that this dilemma has not been as salient among the members as O'Dea might have seen. As Stan Albrecht and Tim B. Heaton (1984) have shown, educated Mormons tend to be more highly involved than less educated Mormons in the LDS Church.

O'Dea was not referring to mere educational attainment, however. He thought that exposure to secular ideas in general would conflict with church doctrine and members' ascription of charisma to church leaders. Modern secular thought in a more general sense, however, also resulted in several societal changes that O'Dea failed to anticipate. Among the more salient issues addressed by the authors of the chapters are the rise of the civil rights movement, the emergence of the women's movement, the increase in tolerance of homosexuality in society, and the development of the LDS Church internationally.

The civil rights movement and the women's movement produced major conflicts for the institutional church as well as discomfort among many members. The church reached an accommodation with the civil rights movement by endorsing it, though struggles and embarrassments for individuals remained for some time. Eventually, the conflicts were further reduced by the Priesthood Revelation in 1978. Armand L. Mauss (2004) and Cardell K. Jacobson (2004) have shown that current LDS members do not differ greatly from other Americans on national surveys, though some LDS members as well as Americans in general still harbor prejudices.

In addition to social changes in the United States, the expansion of the church into the less developed parts of the world created a new set of challenges for the LDS Church. These challenges include new cultural contexts, governmental restrictions, and sometimes impoverished populations.

O'Dea's work was important at its time, and it continues to be a significant analysis for students of Mormonism. Nevertheless, the continuing changes call for an update on the sociology of Mormonism and the sociological work done since O'Dea. This volume attempts to contribute to such an update.

THE GENESIS OF THIS EVALUATION:
THE MORMONS AT FIFTY YEARS

The initial seed for the project that culminates in this book began during meetings of the Mormon Social Science Association (MSSA). Several individuals, Rick Phillips, Ryan Cragun, Armand Mauss, and others, began discussions in 2003 and 2004 about developing a volume of readings on contemporary Mormon studies. They agreed that a valuable contribution to the social science literature on Mormonism would be a revisiting of O'Dea's treatise *The Mormons* on its fiftieth anniversary. They recognized that O'Dea's thorough sociological treatment of Mormon life has influenced at least two generations of scholarship, but they thought that subsequent changes, such as an expanding international church, left important areas unexplored. These scholars, with MSSA sponsorship, sent out a call for editors to develop a volume to revisit and reevaluate *The Mormons* in light of contemporary scholarship.

A subcommittee of MSSA members appointed the present editors— Cardell Jacobson, John Hoffmann, and Tim Heaton—to develop this volume. The result has been a fruitful collaboration among many scholars, those whose work appears in this volume but also several others, such as Ryan Cragun, Lynn Payne, Rick Phillips, and Daryl White, without whom our consideration of O'Dea's work would not be complete. The editorial team then sent out a request for chapter proposals to about thirty scholars who had contributed to the social science literature on Mormonism. Following a careful evaluation of about twenty proposals, we selected the fifteen essays present in this volume. We believe they provide a sound assessment of O'Dea's essential contributions. We also believe they present novel information and methods of inquiry that will further advance the cause of Mormon studies.

THE ESSAYS

We have grouped the essays into three parts. The first we call "Engaging O'Dea." The first two chapters are written by students of O'Dea, people who knew him personally. The other two essays address O'Dea in other ways.

The second part includes essays about contemporary social issues and Mormonism. Though all of the authors address O'Dea, and all present contemporary issues, the chapters in this section examine the interplay between changing social issues and the LDS Church. The demand by African Americans for full civil rights and the women's movement were dramatic sea changes that occurred primarily after O'Dea's analysis in *The Mormons*. Likewise, a number of issues on which the church has taken stands arose. These issues include not only changes in heterosexual norms and practices and increasing tolerance of homosexuals but also the increase in the divorce rate, delay of marriage, and childbirth outside of marriage. These chapters address the relationship between these issues and the LDS Church. The last essay in this section discusses the church's relationship to the nation as a state.

The final section of the book discusses the international church. Armand Mauss provides a theoretical overview of why the church has continued to be successful, whereas David Stewart provides more of a descriptive overview of where the church has been successful internationally. Henri Gooren and David Knowlton each assess aspects of the church's growth in Latin America, while Sarah Busse Spencer examines aspects of the LDS Church in Russia.

ENGAGING O'DEA

As noted earlier, O'Dea's work is grounded in the prevailing philosophical, methodological, and theoretical orientations of his time. Lynn England elucidates the sociological tradition in which O'Dea was trained and which guided the five-cultures study where O'Dea began fieldwork for his dissertation. England also provides important background information about extant studies of Mormon history, theology, and community. He ends with a call for a new synthesis, one informed by theoretical and methodological developments since O'Dea's time and one that incorporates the dramatic changes in LDS membership. Later chapters in this volume address some of the most significant changes in composition and the emergence of new issues and demonstrate that a variety of theoretical approaches can be used to understand the Mormons as a people and the LDS Church as an institution.

O. Kendall White Jr. provides a nuanced analysis of O'Dea's views of Mormon intellectualism. Having completed his master's thesis under the tutelage of O'Dea and other prominent University of Utah figures (such as Lowell Bennion and Sterling McMurrin), White was concerned with intellectual strains in Mormonism during the 1960s, an interest that continues to this day. However, his chapter addresses primarily O'Dea's views of Mormon intellectual life and his conclusions about Mormonism's theological naïveté. After reviewing some of the aspects of Mormon culture that affect or perhaps attenuate its members' intellectual tendencies (including centralized authority and trickle-down revelation), White turns to the theological acumen of its leaders. Consistent with O'Dea, White finds limited theological development or erudition among LDS Church officials. However, he is optimistic about the "sophisticated" theological contributions of some church members who study and teach religion. White then provides a useful discussion of his continuum of Mormon intelligentsia, from those who remain staunch defenders of the faith to those who are commonly termed "cultural Mormons." Although O'Dea may have been critical of the theological sophistication of church leaders, White points out that O'Dea was also intrigued by Mormonism's "new religious doctrine" and "new worldview" that culminated in the notion of eternal progression. Perhaps this was not a full-blown theological contribution to Christian thought, but it was, to O'Dea, a remarkable result of Mormon thought. Like Douglas J. Davies (also in this volume), White is critical of O'Dea's use of dichotomies to represent Mormonism, in this case the notion of the polar extremes of apostate versus apologist. White contends that his continuum better represents the contemporary intellectual strains in the Mormon Church.

In his chapter, Douglas J. Davies focuses on the twin themes of mastery and mystery, both as engaged by O'Dea and as seen from his contemporary theological viewpoint. He finds that the mastery-mystery motif introduced by O'Dea in later chapters of *The Mormons* is a valuable interpretive frame for the earlier chapters on the history of the LDS Church and the values of its members. Various aspects of mastery included mastery of the self, of nature, of social development, and of an urban environment. O'Dea discussed both the more benign as well as the negative aspects of mastery in the early church. The negative mastery was manifested in polygamy, the concept of blood atonement, and the Mountain Meadows massacre. Yet mastery took on a more positive value when O'Dea considered the tremendous agricultural and urban progress of the Utah pioneers. Davies then transitions from mastery to mystery by addressing the prophetic mantle that passed from Joseph Smith to Brigham Young. Beginning with Joseph Smith's presumed interaction with the divine, mastery and mystery became "embodied in the prophet-founder" and continued through prophetic lines of succession. Yet many other aspects of Mormondom also exemplified the mastery-mystery motif, including baptism for the dead, endowments for the dead and the living, a "Mormon God" who is the master of natural law, and a Christ who masters human sin through a mysterious and engaging event in a Middle Eastern garden. According to Davies, this motif is embodied in a most fascinating way when one considers the Mormon approach to the individual as a "god in embryo"; this clearly requires both mastery of self and mystery of the divine. Davies, however, disapproves of O'Dea's emphasis on rationality versus charisma. He argues that this conflates principles and individuals. Charisma is used, whereas the miraculous is conceptualized. Davies also criticizes O'Dea's tendency to use oppositional categories (for example,

"consent versus coercion") and the strain between them when a more parsi-
monious account would use the unifying concept of mastery (for instance,
mastery of self implies obedience, thus explaining both consent and coercion). Davies's contribution thus demonstrates both the limitations and the
value of O'Dea's conceptual analysis.

Terryl L. Givens provides an excellent analysis of O'Dea's literary approach to the Book of Mormon. He approaches O'Dea carefully by trying
to understand how a 1950s scholar might see such a book. O'Dea seemed
less hostile than others, such as Fawn M. Brodie, who dismissed it based on
a "commonsense," naturalistic explanation. O'Dea clearly falls within this
camp, including a tendency to focus on the book's New England sentiments,
New York revivalism, Arminianism, Freemasonry, and hermeticism. After
debating some of O'Dea's ideas through an analysis of the burgeoning field
of Book of Mormon scholarship, Givens admits that there are still unex-
plained parallels with cultural scripts prevalent in early-nineteenth-century
America, such as "echoes of folk magic, anti-Catholicism," and others. Yet,
for Givens, this does not minimize the significance of the text—through its
various machinations—as a lens through which to explore how these various
concepts continue to intrigue those who read it as history, or even as myth.
His conclusion speaks volumes not only about O'Dea's interpretations but
also about the benefit of fifty subsequent years of literary scholarship: "The
Book of Mormon revealed a great deal...about the boisterous interplay of
democratic yearnings and covenantal elitism; of visionary utterance with
its promise and danger; of the longing for religious tradition, stability, and
boundaries; and of the appeal of religious dynamism and exceptionalism."

CONTEMPORARY SOCIAL ISSUES

Thomas O'Dea was an astute observer of human behavior and religious institutions. Looking back, O'Dea was prescient, insightful, and sanguine
about much of the unusual culture and religious institution, the incipient
nation, he encountered in the Intermountain West. As noted earlier, he
nevertheless failed to anticipate several developments that affected the LDS
Church during the fifty years that followed his innovative and important
study. Among these are the rise of the civil rights movement and the wom-
en's movement and changing sexual mores.

O'Dea considered the possible conflict between Mormon belief in the
equality of women and the patriarchal family structure but concluded that
this discrepancy did not pose a major problem. In her chapter, Carrie A.
Miles addresses social changes that have made the conflict between gender
equality and patriarchy "one of the more pressing issues facing the church."

Increased female educational attainment and labor force participation in combination with growing social acceptance of gender equality directly challenged the LDS position that women's primary roles were to be mothers and homemakers. The LDS response to national trends was multifaceted. Initial resistance gave way to some accommodation, but the church has continued to reaffirm its position that men and women have different roles. Her chapter provides an intriguing example of the dilemma the church faces in maintaining core beliefs in the face of profound social transformation.

Janet Bennion carries these themes further by arguing that O'Dea, along with many other social scientists, failed to anticipate several trends related to women's roles in society. The trends include the women's movement, a dramatic increase in the divorced population in the church, and increases in the postponement of marriage and sexual relationships outside of marriage. The changes and conflicts engendered by these trends would become especially evident in the LDS Church because of its traditional emphasis on men being dominant in the home and the church. She argues that O'Dea was more keenly aware of the male world than the female world and felt genuinely that men and women in society were equal. Today, by contrast, women's needs have become increasingly diverse. Bennion focuses specifically on four groups: career and professional women, single and divorced women, polygamous women, and lesbians. She argues further, however, that the idealized woman, married with children and well off economically, does not describe many women in the current church.

The second social issue, the emergence of the race issue, is addressed by Armand L. Mauss, arguably the best chronicler of minority relationships in the LDS Church. Mauss notes that O'Dea completely overlooked an important potential conflict that was to arise in the last half of the twentieth century—the ban against priesthood ordination and temple privileges for those of African descent. Indeed, fifteen years later O'Dea himself acknowledged that the race issue was likely to become a "diagnostic issue" that would portend the future of the LDS Church. In this chapter Mauss considers three primary questions. The first is how O'Dea could have missed this issue as he envisioned the conflicts the LDS Church was facing. His short answer, which is much more nuanced in the chapter, is that the race issue was not prominent either in Utah, the center of the LDS Church, or in the nation as a whole in the 1950s when O'Dea was conducting his research on the LDS Church. Second, Mauss considers whether it would be a "diagnostic issue" that would speak to the future success of the LDS Church. Mauss presents evidence that the church was already grappling with the issue, and O'Dea, having left the intensive study of the church, missed it. Finally,

Mauss examines how well the LDS Church responded to the crisis over the race issue. He believes O'Dea, if he were examining the issue today, would find a very mixed record, with surprising success in some arenas at the same time that some members of the church retain prejudices and biases.

A third social issue that all churches have had to confront is changes in sexual mores. O'Dea completed *The Mormons* before the sexual revolution dramatically transformed the connection between sexual intimacy and marriage in Western society. Melvyn Hammarberg describes LDS theology regarding sexual relationships and marriage, noting that the sexual revolution has created a crisis in the formation and regulation of Mormon sexual identity. He interprets official responses in terms of the juxtaposition between changing national norms and LDS beliefs. He gives particular attention to same-sex attraction and homosexuality. His comparison of official statements, scholarly analysis, and the experience of homosexual members of the LDS faith provides an insightful picture of challenges facing both members and church officials.

The final two essays in this section are concerned with other social issues. Michael Nielsen and Barry Balleck describe the LDS Church's uneasy fit within its host country, the United States. They note that for much of its history the LDS Church has had strong tensions with the larger society. Conflicts included block voting and the presence of federal troops stationed in Utah little more than a decade after the "saints" had fled there from persecution in Ohio, Missouri, and Illinois. Difficulties over the LDS practice of polygamy persisted during the last half of the nineteenth century. Ironically, the LDS Church became aligned with conservative elements in the latter part of the twentieth century. Nielsen and Balleck end with a discussion of the ambivalent and sometimes contradictory stances of some church leaders on war and other issues.

In the last essay in this section, Loren Marks and Brent D. Beal examine how Mormons remain distinctive as a people, even as membership is no longer exclusively or even mainly an American phenomenon. As they point out, O'Dea was particularly intrigued by the contrasting behaviors and beliefs of members of the Mormon Church and others in the United States: his book is "not only a scholarly report ... but also a narrative that clearly (if unintentionally) reflects O'Dea's fascination with the peculiarities of a peculiar people." Marks and Beal evaluate some of the ways that Mormons have remained peculiar in terms of lived values and the organizational structure of their church. Their generous analysis examines the dietary mandates of the Word of Wisdom and the behavioral restrictions of the Law of Chastity, in both cases finding that highly active Mormons embrace both.

Turning to the distinctiveness of the church's organizational structure, Marks and Beal suggest that it is based primarily in five programs or practices: missionary work, lay priesthood, unpaid clergy, church service callings, and participation in temple rituals. In each case, they argue that there is something unique, something that although it does not guarantee distinctiveness makes key contributions to it. To give just one example from their chapter, the strict requirements for temple entry and the sacred and secret ceremonies that take place there serve as touchstones for differentiating active Mormons from all others. They conclude that, although the fifty years since *The Mormons* may appear to have diminished their sense of being one "people," there is still much to distinguish Mormons from others, especially when considering those engaged in "temple Mormonism."

THE LDS CHURCH IN THE INTERNATIONAL CHURCH

In the final section of the book authors address the internationalization of the LDS Church. In his second chapter for this volume, Armand L. Mauss argues that O'Dea examined the LDS Church through the traditional lens that others had used to characterize religious groups, namely, the sect-church dichotomy. In the decades after *The Mormons* appeared, analysts shifted to the framework of new religious movements—movements that set themselves apart from the more traditional religious groups as well as the larger society. Such movements must maintain a certain degree of tension with society to be successful. If they are too stringent and separatist, they will stagnate and shrink. If they accommodate too much to the larger society, they lose their organizational vitality. Mauss notes that O'Dea "fretted" about the success of the LDS Church in the decades ahead as it would confront modern secular thought. Mauss contends, however, that O'Dea did not have the use of the new religious movements perspective to explain the success the LDS Church has had in becoming an international church, perhaps even a new world religion. Where O'Dea foresaw difficulties as the church moved ahead, Mauss argues that the church's "retrenchment" of the 1970s and 1980s actually helped maintain the vitality needed to move the church ahead. Mauss acknowledges that the encounter with modern secular thought remains problematic for some members of the LDS Church. He also points to other potential strains and contradictions, including those between rationality and charisma, obedience and individualism, and the increasing acceptance of premarital and same-sex relationships and the traditional teachings of the church.

In a related chapter, David G. Stewart Jr. provides a detailed analysis of growth and retention of members, demonstrating how the missionary efforts and other processes are reshaping the international composition of the LDS population. Rodney Stark's bold prediction that the Mormon Church would become the next major world religion has been popular among Mormons. Stewart offers a more complete and nuanced analysis. Growth is uneven in different regions of the world. Although growth in membership and organizational units such as congregations is evident, rates of growth have declined. Failure to retain new converts, declining fertility, and cultural conflicts are all impediments to rapid growth.

The two following chapters address the LDS Church in Latin America. Henri Gooren contributes to the growing scholarship on the LDS Church in Latin America, which was very small fifty years ago when O'Dea published *The Mormons*. Gooren asks two questions. First, what is the meaning of church membership for Latin American Mormon converts? Second, what does having a majority of members outside the United States mean for the LDS Church? After discussing the top-down bureaucracy of the church, Gooren turns his attention to LDS growth in Central America by drawing on his field studies in Nicaragua, Guatemala, and Costa Rica. He suggests that most converts, especially since 1990, have come from the upper-lower and lower-middle classes, with a majority being female. Gooren finds that many accepted the missionaries' teachings at face value because they provided an intellectually appealing message. Converts did not often subject the teachings to critical examination, however. The result, Gooren argues, was that up to half of the converts left the church within a year of their baptism. Gooren notes that the Pentecostal Church, despite claims about its high rate of success in Latin America, has similar disaffiliation rates as the LDS Church. Using O'Dea as a starting point, he examines some of the sources of strain and conflict for the church in Latin America, focusing particularly on callings, machismo, and inactivity. Using his qualitative interviews for support, Gooren suggests that the LDS leadership is more authoritarian in Latin America than in the United States, that male machismo leads to family problems for many members, and that many members find the church's demands on their time to be too onerous. Taken together, Gooren's evidence indicates that only a minority, perhaps as few as one-quarter, of Central American converts become core members; most either disaffiliate or transform into marginal members.

David Clark Knowlton also provides an in-depth analysis of LDS Church growth in an international context and specifically Latin America. He argues that the interaction between LDS models of organizational structure, increasing international support for religious tolerance, and local conditions account for characteristics of LDS congregations outside the United

States. For example, there is a substantial discrepancy between the size of the LDS membership as reported by the church and as reported by the national census in Mexico. Moreover, other groups such as Seventh-Day Adventists and Jehovah's Witnesses have higher rates of growth (though Gooren's chapter suggests that disaffiliation rates may be similar). Knowlton argues that the prevailing model of organizational leadership in the United States at the time when rapid expansion began had a profound influence on the nature of growth in countries such as Mexico. His analysis encourages the reader to consider the interaction of organizational structure, local conditions, and proselytizing techniques.

In the volume's final chapter, Sarah Busse Spencer provides an assessment of the LDS Church in Russia. Spencer notes that O'Dea described the "typical American quality" of Mormonism. How can such an American church become an international one? Her answer, drawn from O'Dea, is that a gradual conception developed—that one could adopt a Mormon way of life without physically removing oneself to the land of gathering. Spencer illustrates ways in which such spiritual gatherings or clustering can present tensions in the international church. She also discusses the tensions specific to the introduction of Mormonism to the Russian Federation, where religion had been suppressed until the collapse of the Soviet Union. Further, the Russian social context provides a much different experience for members of the LDS Church. The culture and the social context provide different tensions there than exist for the church in other countries.

Conclusion

Taken as a whole, these essays by distinguished scholars of Mormonism reinforce the value of O'Dea's *The Mormons* even as new social issues have emerged and as the LDS Church has grown and changed. O'Dea's work continues to engage and provoke thought about a new American religion that seeks to become a true global faith. His attention to stresses and strains, though it may have been incomplete, is an important model for examining how the LDS Church—a faith founded on New and Old World ideas and principles—might face expansion or stagnation in the coming years. Can a "peculiar people" engage and attract a sufficient number of outsiders in the United States and abroad to remain both vibrant and peculiar? Can this church that achieved "near nation" status within a limited geographical area of the United States become a world faith? Or does peculiarity come at a cost as the strains of building a church in a postmodern world confront diminution, reconstitution, and transformation of faith and supernatural beliefs across the globe? The chapters in this volume, written by contemporary scholars of religion, address issues that were salient in O'Dea's time. Many issues remain significant as the LDS Church expands globally in the twenty-first century.

Nevertheless, at the risk of overspeculation and misplaced prescience, we suggest that O'Dea would have written a much different book had he been writing about the LDS Church today, at the beginning of the twenty-first century. We have already discussed O'Dea's failure (not unique among social scientists writing at midcentury) to anticipate the women's movement, the changes in race relations in the LDS Church and society more generally, and the internationalization of the LDS Church. Several other issues deserve comment here.

One involves the shifts in the theoretical emphases of the social sciences. Although some of O'Dea's analysis might be similar if done today, it is unlikely that either the conceptual framework or the empirical observations would be the same. The brand of functionalism made popular by O'Dea's teacher Talcott Parsons is no longer a dominant paradigm in sociology. This is especially true when considering the prominent role that values played in the theory. That functional aspects can turn dysfunctional is no longer the domain of functionalist thought, but rather has been co-opted by conflict theories of social order and behavior. Moreover, social scientists emphasize values much less today and focus more on macrostructures and economic interactions as motivators and impediments to human behavior.

Thus, given his emphasis on the stresses and strains of Mormonism, if O'Dea were writing today he would likely adopt a conflict-theory explanation of how Mormonism negotiates the modern world. For example, he might see the Mormon ideal of the family as the norm to be in conflict with the movement toward gender equality, or he might examine competing groups within society that address various aspects of family, gender, and sexuality. One useful model from social psychology is how strain outside a group (for example, a push toward gender equality or women's rights) often motivates holding on to an opposing tradition or school of thought within a particular group. Such conflicting processes may help us understand why well-educated Mormons are among the most active participants.

In addition, O'Dea may have utilized the rational-choice paradigm that has been developed to explain the persistence of religious participation in the United States and the emergence of new religious groups. He likely would have given more attention to the costs and benefits of being a Mormon and speculated about how rational decision making would affect the growth of the LDS Church in the United States and in other nations. Utilizing the empirical observation that second-generation members of new religious movements often become disengaged from their parents' religious faith for presumably rational reasons, O'Dea may have found it unremarkable that the church has high inactivity levels in Latin American countries or in other parts of the world.

The influence of prominent Mormons in the U.S. political system is another important area that was unanticipated by O'Dea. It may not be clear what he thought of George Romney's primary run for the presidency of the United States in the late 1960s, but it is clearly an overly speculative enterprise to imagine what he would have thought about Harry Reid's ascendance to the leadership of the U.S. Senate or Mitt Romney's run for the presidency in 2008. Whatever its geographic limitations, Mormonism has made significant inroads in American politics since O'Dea's time. There is little reason, given the relatively high education levels of Mormons and the church's increasing wealth, to think that the political influence of members of the church will not continue to increase.

Issues involving sexuality were clearly within O'Dea's sphere of interest. He did not, however, anticipate the gay marriage movement or the gay rights movement in contemporary America. The LDS Church is not at the forefront of opposition to these movements, but it has been involved behind the scenes (in California, for example). It is interesting to speculate how this stress and strain will affect the LDS Church in the future. The external pressures may lead to an accentuation of norms and beliefs, which suggests that there will be little softening of the church's stance anytime in the near future.

At the same time, an interview with Dallin Oaks of the Quorum of the Twelve was posted in the "Newsroom" portion of the church's Web site in 2006. In it, he and Lance B. Wickham offered a gentler position on homosexuals than some earlier leaders had taken. Nevertheless, for all the talk of "hate the sin and not the sinner," the presumed "threat" that homosexuality has on the "traditional" family and the consistent opposition to political measures designed to move society toward accepting gay rights suggest that the LDS Church will not greatly shift its positions on gay rights and marriage in the near future.

Perhaps the most salient issue for the LDS Church, one that is described selectively in this volume, is its international growth. Substantial work has been devoted to it already, and we suspect that if O'Dea were writing today he would devote substantial analysis to the issue. The specific treatment of international growth is what remains unclear, however. From our vantage point, it is likely that O'Dea would have paid the most attention to Latin America. The competition with other new movements in

Latin America provides a fascinating social laboratory in which to examine contemporary patterns of sacralization. However, an intriguing issue that is not addressed enough is the growth and potential for the LDS Church in areas of the world that do not have a strong Christian history (see, for instance, Hoffmann 2007). O'Dea might have addressed questions such as who joins, who continues to participate, which countries are most likely to sustain increased membership, and what tensions emerge when a hierarchical organization centered in the western United States exports a particular organizational model.

The chapters in this volume demonstrate the innovative and insightful research approaches that are currently being utilized to study Mormons and the LDS Church. At the same time, the volume pays tribute to O'Dea's seminal work. But we also hope it helps foster the application of new approaches to the understanding of long-standing questions and emerging issues created by growth and change in the LDS faith.

Notes

1. A listing of O'Dea's work is provided in the appendix to this volume.

References

Albrecht, Stan, and Tim B. Heaton. 1984. "Secularization, Higher Education, and Religiosity." *Review of Religious Research* 26: 43–58.

Anderson, Nels. 1942. *Desert Saints: The Mormon Frontier in Utah.* Reprint, Chicago: University of Chicago Press, 1966.

Brodie, Fawn M. 1945. *No Man Knows My History: The Life of Joseph Smith, the Mormon Prophet.* New York: Alfred A. Knopf.

Dahl, Robert A. 1961. *Who Governs?* New Haven: Yale University Press.

Davis, Allison, Burleigh B. Gardner, and Mary R. Gardner. 1941. *Deep South: A Social Anthropological Study of Caste and Class.* Chicago: University of Chicago Press.

Dollard, John. 1937. *Caste and Class in a Southern Town.* Reprint, Garden City, N.Y.: Doubleday, 1949.

Ericksen, Ephraim E. 1922. *The Psychological and Ethical Aspects of Mormon Group Life.* Salt Lake City: University of Utah Press, 1975.

Hoffmann, John P. 2007. *Japanese Saints.* Lanham, Md.: Lexington Books.

Hunter, Floyd. 1953. *Community Power Structure: A Study of Decision Makers.* Garden City, N.Y.: Anchor Books.

Jacobson, Cardell K. 2004. "African American Latter-day Saints: A Sociological Perspective." In *Black and Mormon,* ed. Newell G. Bringhurst and Darron T. Smith, 116–31. Urbana: University of Illinois Press.

Karlenzig, Bruce. 1998. "Thomas F. O'Dea." In *Encyclopedia of Religion and Society,* ed. William H. Swatos. Walnut Creek, Calif.: AltaMira Press.

Lynd, Robert S., and Helen M. Lynd. 1929. *Middletown: A Study in Modern American Culture.* New York: Harcourt, Brace.

————. 1937. *Middletown in Transition.* New York: Harcourt, Brace.

Mauss, Armand L. 2004. "Casting Off the 'Curse of Cain': The Extent and Limits of Progress since 1978." In *Black and Mormon,* ed. Newell G. Bringhurst and Darron T. Smith, 82–115. Urbana: University of Illinois Press.

Nelson, Lowry. 1952. *The Mormon Village: A Pattern and Technique of Land Settlement.* Salt Lake City: University of Utah Press.

O'Dea, Thomas F. 1957. *The Mormons.* Chicago: University of Chicago Press.

Vogt, Evon Z., and Ethel M. Albert, eds. 1966. *People of Rimrock: A Study of Values in Five Cultures.* Cambridge: Harvard University Press.

Walker, Ronald W., David J. Whittaker, and James B. Allen. 2001. *Mormon History.* Urbana: University of Illinois Press.

Young, Kimball. 1954. *Isn't One Wife Enough? The Story of Mormon Polygamy.* New York: Henry Holt.

REVISITING THOMAS F. O'DEA'S *THE MORMONS*

PART I

Engaging O'Dea

Thomas F. O'Dea

The New Spirit and Science of Mormon Studies

~ Lynn England ~

In O'Dea's *The Mormons* we see the formulation of a social scientific dogma or orthodoxy about Mormonism. The orthodoxy had been in development since the beginning of the twentieth century and reached its highest form in this work. *The Mormons* is a skilled synthesis of a collection of social scientific studies of Mormon communities, the research by several historians of Mormonism, a summary of an intellectual theological perspective commonly accepted in Mormonism of the first half of the twentieth century, and O'Dea's own sociological research on a Mormon community. It is an orthodoxy that builds on the work of academic Mormon sociologists who were committed to the scientific nature of their discipline and found that the study of Mormonism provided the material to be used in their scholarship. Most of them plied their skills by completing studies of rural, agricultural Mormon communities that were viewed as the defining sociological feature of Mormonism. The key figures in this effort were Lowry Nelson, Nels Anderson, Joseph Geddes, Ephraim E. Ericksen, and Hamilton Gardner. O'Dea used a Mormon historical view that was based in original sources such as Joseph Smith's *History* and his mother's account of her son's prophetic calling, Brigham H. Roberts's historical work when he was historian of the Mormon Church, and historians, contemporary with O'Dea, whose work was focused on providing a history that met the standards of professional and academic historical method. They were typically committed Mormons writing professional history from the "inside" (Arrington 1953, xii) and included scholars such as Leonard Arrington and Levi Edgar Young. Interestingly, he also relied heavily on the writings of Fawn M. Brodie, whose work was a landmark scholarly attack on the official history of Joseph Smith. The theological basis of the work is largely a collection of references from the Book of Mormon and the writings of Brigham H.

Roberts, a theologian and General Authority in the Mormon Church from 1888 to 1933. It was supplemented by the writing of John A. Widtsoe (*A Rational Theology* [1915]) and James Talmage (*The Articles of Faith* [1951] and *Jesus the Christ* [1973]), both of whom were scientifically trained and prominent in the Mormon Church as apostles and in academic circles as scholars and university administrators. Roberts, Talmage, and Widtsoe, as well as Parley P. Pratt and Orson Pratt, all wrote texts that were used as manuals for teaching theology in Mormon religious classes for all members. Their theology was treated by O'Dea and many Mormons as the orthodoxy, though some of the ideas were not given overt approval as church dogma. In addition, they were often in conflict with more conservative, less academic Mormon theologians and General Authorities. The theology was rational, liberal, and scholarly. Finally, this orthodoxy about Mormonism is provided with depth by O'Dea's own participation as a social scientist in a respected study of communities in the American Southwest under the direction of a team of Harvard social scientists, including Talcott Parsons, Evon Vogt, and Clyde and Florence Kluckhohn. The communities included a Mormon community, pseudonym Rimrock, which was O'Dea's focal interest and responsibility in the study. So, O'Dea, the Harvard sociologist, brought academic and scientific legitimacy and synthesis to the body of knowledge that had been developed by the others, most of whom were Mormon insiders. O'Dea synthesized the diverse evidence gathered by his social scientific predecessors whose research contained the Mormon insiders' depth of understanding and sensitivity to Mormon issues along with their social scientific research skills and interests. The others provided the material evidence, and O'Dea was the systematizer of their contributions. He did not "discover" the evidence, but he provided the system.

The basic purpose of this chapter is to situate O'Dea's work, especially *The Mormons,* in the context of the sociological and philosophical analysis of Mormonism. The argument will be developed that O'Dea's work focused on Mormonism as the object of a detached, scientific analysis and developed an orthodox interpretation of Mormon culture and society. It skillfully avoided the pitfalls encountered by many other efforts that either ended up being anti-Mormon polemics or pro-Mormon apologetics. It represents a tradition where the scholarship and demands of science and rationality take precedence over the apologetics and scholasticism of religious defense, but the polemics and apologetics served him well as data. The outcome was a social scientific orthodoxy well suited to the Mormonism of the 1900–1950 period of Mormon history. This chapter seeks to accomplish two tasks. First, I will examine the four bases listed above. Second, I will discuss their adequacy as a description of Mormonism since 1960 and the need for a sequel to *The Mormons.*

THE SOCIOLOGICAL FOUNDATIONS

During the first half of the twentieth century a growing collection of scholars trained as social scientists were writing about some of the central aspects of Mormonism. These scholars included Hamilton Gardner (1917, 1922), Ephraim Ericksen (1922), Lowry Nelson (1925, 1930, 1952), Nels Anderson (1942), and Joseph Geddes (1949). Four of the five were Ph.D. social scientists or philosophers, while the other was a hobby sociologist whose work appeared in the Harvard-published *Quarterly Journal of Economics.* The five shared some important characteristics that influenced their work and carried over into O'Dea's analysis. They were self-described adherents to the Church of Jesus Christ of Latter-day Saints (LDS). Each had his earliest experience with Mormonism in rural Mormon communities. They continued to claim allegiance to the church throughout most of their lives, especially during the time of their research cited by O'Dea. Their experience and the church identity of the time centered on rural communities characterized by agricultural roots and close cooperation in villagelike settings. The communities were founded under church direction and governed by church principles and principals. All five were part of a fourth generation of Mormons who were described in Ericksen's own research in which he compares his generation of scholars to the three preceding generations:

> On a psychological basis we may distinguish four Mormon generations. The first generation lived in a period of activity and excitement, of strife and stress. It experienced strong emotions and spiritual manifestations. The second generation lived on the sentiments and traditions created by the first. It too experienced strong group feelings which grew out of the thoughts and influence of the past. Like the first, this class was unreflective, but lived in a world of sentiment. Then comes, thirdly, a generation of philosophers or theologians who take an intellectual attitude toward Mormonism but whose group sentiments are still strong enough to determine their thinking. They have a feeling that Mormonism must be right and they set themselves the task to prove it. Theirs is a sort of rationalism similar to that of the Middle Ages. And finally we have a generation of critics and scientists who seem to sense very little feeling of obligation toward the group but are placing the institutions of their fathers on the dissecting tables for analysis. This class is making a demand for greater freedom of thought and discussion and it is this demand which is

bringing about a third Mormon crisis. Nearly all of the Mormons of the first generation have passed away but the second and third generations are still strong and it is these two classes on the one hand and the critics on the other that are bringing about the present day conflict, the maladjustment to which we shall now turn our attention. (1922, 59)

The five scholars were all deeply ingrained in and formulators of the perspective of the fourth generation. Ericksen notes their commitment to science and the critical attitude. Each of these scholars completed his research with sociological and social scientific audiences in mind. Their work was first and foremost social science written for the scholar. It was produced with an eye neither to promoting or rationalizing the faith nor to promoting its demise. When their faith conflicted with their science, the science took precedence. The science was in the foreground, the faith in the background. The studies were published in scholarly settings for the social scientist, not merely for those who were interested in Mormonism. They sought to understand the Mormon-community phenomenon, but in order to contribute to the science. For example, Nelson's research was part of a series of studies of small towns. His work fitted well into the research of his time and was an extension of sociological work on rural communities. His view was developed during his Ph.D. training at the University of Wisconsin. The research tradition was started by Charles Josiah Galpin (1915) when he did the pioneering study of a rural community. Galpin was then responsible, due to his position with the U.S. Department of Agriculture, for the funding of a series of studies of communities in Wisconsin, New York, and Missouri as well as Nelson's research (1925, 1930, 1952) on the Utah Mormon villages. Nelson's work was overtly patterned after Galpin and intended to be sociological with a sociological audience. The collection of scholars involved in the community studies were all major figures in sociology. Nelson and these others were among the most prominent of the founders of the Rural Sociological Society and its journal. He was its president in 1944.

Nelson's work selected three Utah agricultural communities for study. Part of the work formed his doctoral dissertation. He completed a follow-up study of the same communities in the late 1940s. Nelson's research continues to draw the interest of rural sociologists, and recent replications of his work have been completed and published (Goodsell 2000). Nelson's work emphasized the solidarity and cooperation of Mormon villages. They were established as part of an effort to preserve Mormon religious principles and to bring the sacred and spiritual into reality while caring for the temporal well-being of the people. Nelson's view of his work and its emphasis is found in his presidential address before the Rural Sociological Society: "The development of a science of human society is the goal. It may never be attained; but from what we know at present concerning the evolution of the older science of physics, it appears it will be reached—if at all—as a result of scholars' digging ever deeper in their various spade holes, until these individual efforts coalesce in an ultimate unity" (1945, 135).

A second sociologist, Nels Anderson, was a convert to Mormonism who claimed allegiance to the church until the end of his life. O'Dea not only cited his work but also wrote the foreword to the 1968 edition of Anderson's book, *Desert Saints,* originally published in 1942. It "was a pioneer effort in the study of Mormonism. It was also an important beginning in the application of social science and historical method to the study of a subject." He concluded that "Anderson's work ranks today among the best of social science scholarship" (x). Anderson's *Desert Saints* was a comparative study of a Mormon community, rural and agricultural, with a nearby mining community. He noted that "Silver Reef was worldly—a treeless, grassless, red-sand location.... St. George was *otherworldly*—a community of fields, gardens, and flowers" (428–29). However, he also concluded that the Saints often found the life of the miners enticing, especially the consumption of alcoholic beverages and miners' language. The Mormon men had trouble keeping the Mormon boys and girls in line.

The spirit of Anderson's work is captured in the foreword to the 1968 edition of *Desert Saints:* "One of the Twelve Apostles, who reviewed it for a Mormon periodical, said to me personally, 'The book might have been great; if you had written more with the Spirit of the Lord, you would not have included some of the passages which to me seem negative'" (xxii). The point for Anderson is not to attack the Mormon community but to provide an honest description. Neutral social scientific scholarship demanded that the "negative" be included.

Joseph Geddes was a sociologist who was on the faculty of Utah State University for many years and wrote on the United Order and Mormon institutions in the communities. His work also illustrates the focus on the social science. His analysis of Mormon institutions (1949) draws its form from the then popular sociological theory of structural functionalism. Geddes focused on the Mormon community with emphasis on the United Order, an enduring aspect of early Mormonism with great social scientific appeal. He also noted, "Another significant matter is the foundational framework on which Utah's institutions rest. This framework is a village or community economy. Each village is made up of a complex institutional cluster in which purely local public and private agencies compete and/or cooperate with state and national agencies with varying degrees of balance, order, and effectiveness" (i). His work has received much less notice within sociology than the others', but he continued to emphasize the centrality of sociological issues, not the theological and believers' issues, and he used Mormonism as the content of his research.

· Ephraim Ericksen was, by profession, a philosopher who spent most of his professional career at the University of Utah, where he was the first chair of the Philosophy Department. He was among a group of young Mormons who went "east" to pursue higher education and to bring the wisdom of the outside world to the Mormon setting. Ericksen's direct influence on scholarship has often been overlooked, but he was one to set the tone for much of the social scientific research and influenced many subsequent scholars of Mormonism. He went to the University of Chicago and studied under the direction of philosopher and social scientist George Herbert Mead, whose work is noted for the analysis of identity, language, and community. Ericksen was one of the first to attempt the social scientific and philosophical analysis of Mormonism from the perspective of academe. He based his analysis on pragmatism, whose major formulators, such as William James, John Dewey, and Mead, had seen much in Mormon theology and group life that illustrated the basic principles of their philosophy. Ericksen's research reflects Mead's understanding of identity, community, language, and their significance. Ericksen built from Mead's analysis of community in the abstract to his study of Mormonism in the concrete, which is centered on the development of Mormon group life and identity. He is important for his Meadian analysis of Mormon community and for the attitude he conveyed while a professor at the University of Utah and still represents.

For Ericksen, the trademark of Mormon life was the cooperation brought on by the persecutions of the eastern period and the challenges of arid-country agriculture and self-sufficiency. Cooperation resulted from the need to survive through irrigation, which was collective and communal. It was egalitarian. The theology that emerged early in Mormon history was one that stressed the involvement of the church in both the spiritual and the practical lives of the people. It came to be reflected in the unique forms of cooperation found in the United Orders and other communities. The early history founded a set of institutions that were characteristically Mormon, such as the family and the Mormon community. However, Ericksen noted two trends emerging to challenge the tradition. One was the growth of a capitalistic mentality among the leadership, and the other was the emergence of a group of scholars much like Ericksen who brought a new set of values and ideals to the study and analysis of Mormonism. His conclusions and ideas in general had a powerful influence on his students and colleagues such as Sterling McMurrin and W. P. Read, who were important informal sources for O'Dea.

Ericksen's commitment to social science and academic scholarship is clearly expressed in his biography and his life. In a biography, Scott Kinney characterizes Ericksen's view: *"Mormon Group Life* simply was not the historical interpretation most Mormons were accustomed to. It viewed the development of Mormonism not as the result of divine revelation, but as the product of adjustments occasioned by social and economic crises" (1978, 19).

The final figure in this group of scholars synthesized by O'Dea was Hamilton Gardner, an attorney, army officer, and historian. He is included here because of the content of his work and its placement in the *Quarterly Journal of Economics*. Gardner was not a trained social scientist but an attorney who shared in the interest in providing a careful, scholarly analysis of Mormonism. O'Dea drew from his analyses of cooperation and communalism in Mormon communities.

Gardner wrote that Mormon cooperation had taken three forms or phases: an initial informal phase, the period of the growth of cooperative stores, and the period of the growth of cooperative industries. Irrigation was a central feature of the informal communal effort, an observation common to studies of the early years in Utah. Water was allocated according to the effort the people put into canal and ditch construction under the direction of ecclesiastical and communal principles. Land- and water ownership both tended to egalitarian ideals. Mercantile cooperatives were an extension of cooperation to keep money and profits away from the Gentiles who were coming into Utah. The final period extended cooperation to industry such as woolen mills, life insurance, and the Hotel Utah. In this period many enterprises lost their cooperative foundation as they became stockholder enterprises.

An indication of the perspective used by Gardner is found in his 1917 publication: "But in all the voluminous mass of labored explanation, partisan propaganda, sincere criticism, zealous defense, confessed antagonism, and dishonest vilification which constitute the literature of that subject, the meagerness of scholarly effort to understand the economic life of the founders of Utah is astonishing" (462). The problem for Gardner is the "meagerness of scholarly effort." His writing is set in juxtaposition to that of the partisan and the zealot.

Hence, all five of these social scientists provided major ideas for O'Dea's work and were critical adherents to Mormonism. They placed their scholarship above questions of religious belief and were committed to the science before the theology. Questions of truth and testimony were external to their work though present in their lives. Their sociological analyses included many aspects of Mormon theology as central parts of their social scientific descriptions of the religion. The theological content was presented from the perspective of a well-informed, understanding integrator, but not that of an advocate. They may have been influenced, undoubtedly were, by their religious beliefs, but their writings and audiences were within the social sciences. This group was trained in methods of sociological inquiry and represented an effort to examine Mormonism, especially the Mormon community, in a way that would lead to careful comparisons between Mormon-community studies and those of other types of communities. There is some evidence that their devotion to Mormonism may have led them to find positive characteristics of Mormonism that were not supported by the evidence, but it seems to have been inadvertent. For example, Nelson discusses the cohesive nature of Mormon communities, but an examination of his notes and interview schedules provides little or no empirical support for his conclusions. The biases, where present, were those of perspective, not advocacy.

THE HISTORICAL BASES

The historical account of the emergence and development of Mormonism, as well as its historical and social context, is central to O'Dea's discussion. Obviously, he was limited to the historical materials that were available to him at the time of his writing. Although it is now out of date, the amount of material available was substantial. O'Dea was highly selective in the choice of historical writings: the choice of whom to include and whom to omit is informative in understanding *The Mormons.* He drew from the official and original accounts of Mormon origins, using Joseph Smith's own accounts and those of Lucy Mack Smith placed in the social context of professional histories of the region where the church developed. He drew extensively from the writings of three highly significant writers, each representing a different perspective on Mormon history and Mormonism. He drew on the historical writings of Brigham H. Roberts, who was a prolific writer of official and unofficial Mormon history. He was recognized for his careful scholarship and his position as a spokesperson for the Mormon Church. O'Dea also made extensive use of the work of Leonard Arrington, who was a "believing and practicing member of the Church of Jesus Christ of Latter-day Saints" and committed to academic historical research (Arrington and Bitton 1979, xiii). Finally, O'Dea worked liberally from the research of Fawn M. Brodie (1945). She wrote a view of Joseph Smith and the origins of Mormonism that was intentionally critical but also noted for its historical scholarship. O'Dea did not draw from the popular histories that took a stance, whether of the believer or nonbeliever. He avoided those with an overt polemical bias, except for Brodie. O'Dea's use of historical accounts that are scholarly in style and vary in their underlying theory of historical scholarship on Mormonism provides an important model for the historical content of social science of the sort O'Dea was engaged in.

It is helpful to see the structure of the writing of the history of Mormonism to better understand the historical content of O'Dea's work. It has been much more contested and controversial than the social science discussed above. In addition, the audiences have been more diverse, with historians writing both for the Mormon or non-Mormon popular audience and for professional historians. It seems that from the very beginning of the Mormon movement, its history has been a vehicle for the faithful to justify their faith and the opponents to discredit the church. For example, the historical accuracy of Joseph Smith's first vision and the production of the Book of Mormon have serious consequences for belief. Each has received extensive attention by advocates and enemies. Reflecting this role of history, Arrington notes the divisions within histories of Mormonism:

> Writings about the Mormons during the first seventy-five years after the Church was organized in 1830 consisted essentially of three kinds of works: (1) pietistic, missionary, and apologetic literature by church authorities, devout writers, and missionaries of the Church; (2) scathing attacks on the Church and its leaders by schematic, disaffected, or excommunicated Mormons, and by wrathful Gentile opponents; and (3) the "curiosa" literature of writers who were impressed with the peculiar characteristics of the Mormons and their religion and who wrote about the Mormons and their settlements as other journalists and travelers wrote about the Hottentots, the hairy Ainu, and the wild men of Borneo. (1966, 16)

Arrington claims that the histories began to change during the early part of the twentieth century as a reflection of the development of a generation with attitudes similar to the social scientists. He argues that this is reflected in the dissertations written about Mormonism, which include, in his list, the work of both Ericksen and Nelson. However, the disagreement about the role of belief and theological advocacy in the writing of histories of Mormonism continues to the present. Even the writers who argue for a new Mormon history, which emerged about 1945, still debate the place of "faithful" history in Mormon history (Bushman 2005; Quinn 1997).

Robert Flanders, an official historian for the Reorganized LDS Church, wrote of the divisions and changes in Mormon history in characterizing the situation in Mormon history:

> The practitioners of the Old Mormon History usually had a clear-cut position on Mormonism, either for or against, and tended to divide into two types: Defenders of the Faith (whatever that might be) and yellow journalists. With few exceptions, non-Mormon practitioners were anti-Mormon, and, likewise, with few exceptions, Mormons were pro-Mormon. Ex-Mormons often became anti-Mormon. The New Mormon History, on the other hand, exhibits different characteristics in both practice and practitioners. Most of the new historians are professionals whose work exhibits critical-analytical techniques. Many are Latter-day Saints in background or persuasion, but their work seems influenced by their literary or their historical training as much as or perhaps more than by their religious training. Their point of view might be described generally as interested, sympathetic detachment. One senses a shift in mood, too, from Victorian romantic sentimentality to a more realistic and tragic sense of the past.... In sum, the New Mormon History is a modern history, informed by modern trends of thought, not only in history, but in other humanistic and scientific disciplines as well, including philosophy, social psychology, economics, and religious studies. (1975, 35)

Whereas Flanders writes of the new history in somewhat glowing terms, others continue to see some of the old problems still present. Brodie's work is seen as the launching pad for the new history, but writers such as Roger Launius argue that much of recent history is still dominated by the issues raised by Brodie and that the writing of Mormon history is "ghettoized" to Mormon historians and Mormon audiences instead of becoming integrated into professional history. Launius identifies five issues raised by Brodie: "the first vision ... treasure seeking ... origins and content of the Book of Mormon ... the origins of plural marriage ... Smith as a would-be tyrant" (1996, 198–99). He points out that she attacks the vision, the Book of Mormon origins account, origins of plural marriage with a critical interpretation of what it meant for Joseph Smith, and Joseph Smith's political intentions. Launius argues these are issues the committed Mormon historian has felt he or she must respond to, focusing on issues of theological truth as well as the historical issues. He claims, "It crippled historical inquiry for more than forty years by forcing the answering of questions that are inappropriate for history to begin with and distorted beyond validity" (201).

In conclusion, Launius contends that both Brodie and Arrington drive Mormon studies toward a ghetto. Charles S. Peterson (1991) takes a similar position and charges that the new history promotes exceptionalist or insular accounts of Mormon history guided by issues and techniques that are unique to Mormon history and alienate it from history.

O'Dea succeeded in taking Arrington's history of such things as Mormon cooperation and economy, Roberts's histories of Mormon origins and development, and Brodie's concerns about Joseph Smith as a person and the historical veracity of his stories for their useful social science, without ever needing to comment on the issues of personal commitment or theological veracity. O'Dea brings the social scientific priorities of Nelson, Anderson, and Ericksen to his approach to the Mormon histories. It is engaged as part of the social scientific family and excludes the questions of theological veracity that have been so divisive to historians.

The Theological Bases

Arrington and Bitton fault O'Dea for his limited view of history—limited by the time he wrote—but they also see virtue in *The Mormons:* "A Roman Catholic sociologist of religion, Thomas F. O'Dea, produced *The Mormons* (1957), a one-volume study that contains valuable insights, but his references to Mormon history were limited to available published accounts. His analysis of values and internal tensions is nevertheless a real contribution" (1979, xii). O'Dea's discussion of Mormon values grew out of his analysis of Mormon theology. He selected a version of Mormon theology that was widely accepted in the 1950s by Mormon intellectuals such as Lowell Bennion, whom O'Dea cites, and Sterling McMurrin, whom he does not cite.

The theological orthodoxy being described by O'Dea integrates a theology based first on a reading and selection of Book of Mormon themes (righteousness leads to prosperity, repentance, free will, judgment based on works, mercy and grace for all through the atonement of Christ, prophecy, obedience to commandments, mortal life is a probationary state, perseverance, knowledge precedes culpability, America is the promised land, democracy is desired and monarchy opposed, and opposition to the "abominable" church) (1957, 26–37). This is supplemented by use of Joseph Smith's writings, as available at the time O'Dea was writing, and Brigham Young's (53–68, 121–54). It is interesting that two of Young's contemporaries and advocates of a particular version of Mormonism, Orson Pratt and Parley P. Pratt, are frequently cited in *The Mormons* (121–54). These brothers were not reluctant to disagree with each other or with other General Authorities, including Joseph Smith and Brigham Young. O'Dea discusses Orson's opposition to Brigham Young's identification of Adam with God that resulted in Brigham Young placing the teaching in abeyance (123). The Pratts were innovative and creative theologians who lacked formal education but who skillfully picked up on major theological and scientific issues. They developed unique ideas in Mormon thought about the nature of the universe and human nature based on Joseph Smith's nonscriptural discourses that placed human beings in an evolutionary process beginning with their uncreated foundation and ending with their potential ascension to godhood (for example, see O. Pratt 1879, 1990; and P. Pratt 1952, 1978).

B. H. Roberts's historical and theological writings are also significant to O'Dea's analysis of Mormon theology. Roberts takes on many of the same issues as the Pratts and offers a similar theological position, though he is able to place these ideas more directly in contrast to traditional Christian beliefs in a way that clearly shows the Mormon solution to many of the classical Christian dilemmas, but he does so in a way that also clearly shows the Mormon heresies on God's nature and that of man. Roberts is noted for theological treatises such as *The Gospel* (1966), *The Mormon Doctrine of Deity* (1903), and *The Truth, the Way, the Life* (1994). These writings engage theological problems in traditional Christianity and demonstrate the uniqueness and innovativeness of Mormon thought in avoiding traditional Christian dilemmas such as the problem of evil in the face of God's omnipotence. He also confronts contemporary challenges to Mormon orthodoxy such as biblical criticism and evolution. He does so with the faith of a believer but the skepticism and style of a scholar.

O'Dea also draws his description of Mormon theology from the writings of Roberts's younger contemporaries John Widtsoe and James Talmage. In the debates between Mormon leaders about theology, these two men along with Roberts usually sided with those taking positions that coincided with more modern ideas and took Mormonism to a rational, intellectual expression. For example, the structure of Widtsoe's *Rational Theology* (1915) reads like a geometry of religion when he begins the "basic realities" on which the theology rests. "These fundamental givens appear in [Widtsoe's] writings on science and other topics. He depicts man in the midst of a bewilderingly complex and seemingly mysterious universe, which man must come to understand, if only in part, in order to 'know if possible his own place in the system of existing things.'... [K]nowledge from which man develops his religion is learned through his physical and spiritual senses and the accumulated learning of other men" (LeCheminant 1997, vii).

Sterling McMurrin and L. Jackson Newell locate this theological style in opposition to that of many other Mormon writers on theology: "Today, much of that strength is gone as Mormonism suffers the impact of religious and social conservatism, as the Mormon mind, in the general pattern of contemporary religion, yields to the seductions of irrationalism, and as the energies of the Church are increasingly drained by practical interests" (McMurrin and Newell 1995, vi–vii).

The theologians used by O'Dea led him to see Mormons as a peculiar people set apart from non-Mormon society by their social practice and by their heretical theology:

> As separateness encouraged innovation, innovation in return increased separateness by providing a creedal basis for evolving peculiarity. The dynamic decade that lay behind them was one that saw three main kinds of theological development. New definitions of God and new understanding of man developed. In addition, new rituals were invented in terms of the temple and its place in Mormon life. And, most important of all, perhaps, new family relations were proposed and made the basis of polygamous family life among certain Mormon leaders. (1953, 654)

Mormonism developed a radical view of a temporal, finite God who was part of a pantheon of gods, with man capable of progressing to godhood instead of being mired in sin. This was supplemented by a form of group life that emerged soon after the removal to Utah, which Widtsoe integrated into his account of Mormon theology. O'Dea characterizes it as follows: "The fact is that Mormon group life had set up a civil government in all its attempts to build the kingdom. It had always been subordinate to church organization, which was the basic mechanism of social direction and control.... The experiences since Nauvoo had only strengthened authoritarian tendencies and made Brigham Young in a certain sense the embodiment of both church and state" (1957, 99).

The theology of deity, human progress, and social organization, combined with the development of community and authoritarianism of such interest to the social scientists, led to "a common homeland, a common culture, a common religion, common social institutions, a deeply felt common tradition, and the self-image of a separate and divinely chosen group with its own peculiar destiny—of such stuff is nationality born" (116). O'Dea eloquently summarizes the nature of Mormon theology: "Life is more than a vocation, more than a calling; it is an opportunity for deification through conquest, which is to be won through rational mastery of the environment and obedience to the ordinances of the church" (143).

O'Dea then points to a serious challenge to Mormon thought in the form of secularism, not theological refutation. He uses Ericksen as his major reference and points out the significance of Ericksen's crisis of the challenge of secular ideas about evolution, higher biblical criticism, and other secular issues that have led to "pologetics" and a "Mormon scholasticism" (149).

The trends O'Dea sees show a shifting orthodoxy in which the innovative and unique Mormonism depicted in Roberts's and Widtsoe's theology is being replaced by a scholastic rationalization of a Mormon version of neoorthodoxy of modern Protestantism and Mormon authoritarianism, an orthodoxy about which McMurrin commented, "A few years ago ... I talked about some of these things—a limited god and free will—and Daniel Rector said, 'You know, you are a Talmage-Roberts-Widtsoe Mormon.' He said, 'The Church doesn't believe that sort of thing anymore. They don't go in for that kind of theology anymore'" (McMurrin and Newell 1995, 58).

THE HARVARD STUDIES

O'Dea's own original research on Mormonism was initiated while he was at Harvard. O'Dea was a star undergraduate student, and when he began his graduate work, he was invited to join the team involved in the Comparative Study of Values in Five Cultures under the framework provided by Clyde Kluckhohn and Florence Kluckhohn (Vogt 1955; Vogt and Albert 1966). The design was to provide a comparative study of five cultures using a scientific framework that would involve sustained empirical research. O'Dea described the project as "testing the hypothesis that value-orientations play an important part in the shaping of social institutions and in influencing the forms of observed social action" (1953, 645). His major responsibility was the study of the Mormon community. He relied heavily on the work of Lowry Nelson, and took the stance of a scientist as much on the outside of Mormonism as he was on the outside of the Texas-Oklahoma immigrant study, the Zuni community, and the Navajo community that were all part of the design. He described a religious community using the Kluckhohns' framework for the study of values. His commitment was to the positivist values of detachment and objectivity and the intellectual tradition of the sociology of religion. Although much is made of O'Dea's Catholicism in commentaries of his work, his own religious beliefs remained external to the writing. He reports, "The stress on community cooperation in Rimrock [the Mormon community] contrasts markedly with the stress upon individual independence found in Homestead [the Texas-Oklahoma community]" (648).

In his concluding remarks, O'Dea refers to Lowry Nelson: "Nelson has recently shown that the general pattern of the Mormon village is neither a direct function ... of the requirements of irrigation agriculture, nor of the need for protection against Indians on the frontier. Rather, the basic pattern was a social invention of the Mormons" (652). O'Dea concludes that the major contributor to the Mormon village was the Mormon value orientation.

The five-cultures study laid the foundation and set the tone for *The Mormons*. It was based in the social scientific tradition of research on cultures by Evon Vogt, Talcott Parsons, and the Kluckhohns. It was to center on the neutrality of the social scientist, whether this was realistic or not, and to be prepared for consumption by the sociologist. It contained many of the basic ideas that O'Dea then elaborated and refined in the larger writing.

O'DEA, THE SEQUEL

The Mormons stands as an important synthesis of social scientific research, historical scholarship, and theological self-description. It avoids partisanship and advocacy where the truth or falsity of basic Mormon claims is not the issue. It is not a tradition inaugurated by O'Dea, but his work is a mature version of a style developed by Max Weber and elaborated by the Kluckhohns. It builds on the key sociological and historical literature that preceded his effort. *The Mormons* represents O'Dea's mature scholarship in which he goes beyond the five-cultures study and is developing his own ideas with greater independence. He remains the sociologist of religion who is synthesizing and systematizing the scholarship of others. He avoids the apologetic or destructive analysis often encountered in studies of Mormonism, especially in the historical studies. His work represents the influence of several Mormon intellectuals, mainly at the University of Utah, whose commitment was to the ideals of the intellect rather than to Mormon apologetics. They guided O'Dea to many of his sources and provided interpretive depth to the work. Several of these scholars called themselves the "Swearing Elders" and included Sterling McMurrin, who was working on analyses of the philosophical and theological bases of Mormonism at the time O'Dea was preparing his effort. Their view of Mormonism was an interesting blend of interpretation and criticism that was not always consistent with the contemporary theological orthodoxy, but became the basis of O'Dea's orthodoxy. A major component of O'Dea's significance to Mormon studies is the way in which he blended his original research with theirs to break with the earlier polemics and found a distinct intellectual approach to Mormon studies. One major value of his work is that he presented Mormonism before it became captured by the pessimistic Protestantism of neo-orthodoxy and anti-intellectualism.

Although O'Dea's work stands as a model of social scientific synthesis, it is now seriously out of date. It can be seen as an analysis of Mormonism at the end of a major era in Mormon history. It was the era described by Ericksen in which dissident scholars faced criticism and challenges to their membership in the LDS Church but one in which the prophet could call on the same scholars for advice and even position papers on issues such as civil rights and politics. It was succeeded by a new era when the exceptionalism, innovation, and "peculiarity" of Mormonism were beginning to decline as the leadership sought acceptance and integration into the cultural mainstream. It was a description of the Mormon era when the church was characterized by small towns that were cohesive, agrarian, and western. The new era was a time of dramatic expansion of the church outside of the intermountain region and outside the United States into Latin America and Africa. It was a new era of urban Mormonism, an era when the new membership was distinct culturally and historically from the members of the era described by O'Dea.

The new era calls for a new synthesis of the same elements relied on by O'Dea. Mormon studies is characterized by research undertaken by social scientists with a neomodern perspective on a social science, exploding historical material that broadens the view of the same history covered by O'Dea and examines the half century since, and a shifting theology in which there are no theologians but many apologists for Mormon neoorthodoxy. McMurrin describes the situation:

> Today it is difficult to determine what the official church doctrine is. Back when I was a college student and learning things about Mormonism, James Talmage, B. H. Roberts, and John Widtsoe were living-people of intellectual strength.... In those days you could tell what the Church believed and what it didn't.... [E]very Tom, Dick, and Harry of the general authorities wasn't turning out books all the time. Nowdays [*sic*] everyone turns out these books. (McMurrin and Newell 1995, 58)

It is a new time when Douglas Alder (1978) and Stan Albrecht (1990) reflect on the shift from the village as the basic unit of Mormonism to the ward, but there is a need for a synthesis of the move from community to wards, stakes, and an ever expanding layer of "General Authority" hierarchy with its focus on seniority and priority of pronouncement (Quinn 1997). The sequel needs to examine Mormonism in light of new scholarship on postmodernity, subalternity, and feminism to examine omissions, changed nuances, and women's place in the church. What is hidden in O'Dea that we are now able to reveal? What is ignored? Where are the women?

REFERENCES

Albrecht, Stan. 1990. "The Mormon Village and Its Contribution to Rural Community Studies." In *Rural Villages in the Twenty-first Century: A Symposium in Honor of Lowry Nelson,* ed. Richard Krannich, 26–50. Logan, Utah: Mountain West Center for Regional Studies.

Alder, Douglas. 1978. "The Mormon Ward: Congregation or Community?" *Journal of Mormon History* 5: 61–78.

Anderson, Nels. 1942. *Desert Saints: The Mormon Frontier in Utah.* Reprint, Chicago: University of Chicago Press, 1966.

Arrington, Leonard. 1953. "Early Mormon Communitarians." *Western Humanities Review* 7, no. 4: 352–69.

———. 1966. "Scholarly Studies of Mormonism in the Twentieth Century." *Dialogue: A Journal of Mormon Thought* 1, no. 1: 15–32.

Arrington, Leonard, and Davis Bitton. 1979. *The Mormon Experience: A History of the Latter-day Saints.* New York: Alfred A. Knopf.

Brodie, Fawn M. 1945. *No Man Knows My History: The Life of Joseph Smith, the Mormon Prophet.* New York: Alfred A. Knopf.

Bushman, Richard. 2005. *Joseph Smith: Rough Stone Rolling.* New York: Alfred A. Knopf.

Ericksen, Ephraim E. 1922. *The Psychological and Ethical Aspects of Mormon Group Life.* Salt Lake City: University of Utah Press, 1975.

Flanders, Robert. 1975. "Some Reflections on the New Mormon History." *Dialogue: A Journal of Mormon Thought* 9, no. 1: 34–41.

Galpin, Charles Josiah. 1915. *The Social Anatomy of an Agricultural Community.* Research Bulletin no. 14. Madison: University of Wisconsin Agricultural Experiment Station.

Gardner, Hamilton. 1917. "Cooperation among the Mormons." *Quarterly Journal of Economics* 31, no. 3: 461–99.

———. 1922. "Communism among the Mormons." *Quarterly Journal of Economics* 37, no. 1: 134–74.

Geddes, Joseph. 1949. *Institution Building in Utah.* Logan: Utah State Agricultural College.

Goodsell, Todd. 2000. "A Look Back at the Mormon Village." *Rural Sociology* 65, no. 3: 357–75.

Kinney, Scott. 1978. "E. E. Ericksen: Loyal Heretic." *Sunstone* 3, no. 5: 16–27.

Launius, Roger. 1996. "From Old to New Mormon History: Fawn Brodie and the Legacy of Scholarly Analysis of Mormonism." In *Reconsidering "No Man Knows My History,"* ed. Newell Bringhurst, 195–226. Logan: Utah State University Press.

LeCheminant, Dale. [1915] 1997. Foreword to *Rational Theology: As Taught by the Church of Jesus Christ of Latter-day Saints,* by John Widtsoe. Salt Lake City: Signature Books.

McMurrin, Sterling, and L. Jackson Newell. 1995. "McMurrin's Heresies, History, and Humor." *Sunstone* 18, no. 1: 55–62.

Nelson, Lowry. 1925. "A Social Survey of Escalante, Utah." *Brigham Young University Studies,* no. 1.

———. 1930. "The Mormon Village: A Study in Social Origins." *Brigham Young University Studies,* no. 3.

———. 1945. "Rural Sociology: Dimensions and Horizons." *Rural Sociology* 10: 131–35.

———. 1952. *The Mormon Village: A Pattern and Technique of Land Settlement.* Salt Lake City: University of Utah Press.

O'Dea, Thomas F. 1953. "A Comparative Study of the Role of Values in Social Action in Two Southwestern Communities." *American Sociological Review* 18: 645–54.

———. 1957. *The Mormons.* Chicago: University of Chicago Press.

Peterson, Charles S. 1991. "Beyond the Problems of Exceptionalist History." In *Great Basin Kingdom Revisited: Contemporary Perspectives,* ed. Thomas G. Alexander, 133–51. Logan: Utah State University Press.

Pratt, Orson. 1879. *Key to the Universe.* Salt Lake City: published by the author.

———. 1990. *Orson Pratt's Works.* Orem, Utah: Grandin.

Pratt, Parley P. 1952. *Writings of Parley Parker Pratt.* Salt Lake City: Deseret Book.

———. 1978. *Key to the Science of Theology.* Salt Lake City: Deseret Book.

Quinn, Michael. 1997. *The Mormon Hierarchy: Extensions of Power.* Salt Lake City: Signature Books.

Roberts, Brigham H. 1903. *The Mormon Doctrine of Deity.* Salt Lake City: Deseret News.

———. 1966. *The Gospel.* Salt Lake City: Deseret Book.

———. 1994. *The Truth, the Way, the Life.* San Francisco: Smith Research Associates.

Talmage, James. 1951. *The Articles of Faith.* Salt Lake City: Church of Jesus Christ of Latter-day Saints.

———. 1973. *Jesus the Christ.* Salt Lake City: Church of Jesus Christ of Latter-day Saints.

Vogt, Evon. 1955. *Modern Homesteaders: The Life of a Twentieth-Century Frontier Community.* Cambridge: Harvard University Press.

Vogt, Evon Z., and Ethel M. Albert, eds. 1966. *People of Rimrock: A Study of Values in Five Cultures.* Cambridge: Harvard University Press.

Widtsoe, John. 1915. *A Rational Theology: As Taught by the Church of Jesus Christ of Latter-day Saints.* Reprint, Salt Lake City: Signature Books, 1997.

2

Thomas F. O'Dea and
Mormon Intellectual Life

A Reassessment Fifty Years Later

~ O. Kendall White Jr. ~

My curiosity regarding Mormon intellectuals emerged during undergraduate and early graduate years at the University of Utah. Under the tutelage of Thomas O'Dea, Sterling McMurrin, Lowell Bennion, Waldamer Read, Max Rogers, and Ray Canning, I formally proposed a master's thesis on "the Mormon intellectual and the church." O'Dea's *American Catholic Dilemma* (1957), a poignant analysis of Catholic intellectual life, provided the model. Though the thesis did not survive, a lingering personal and scholarly interest in religion and the intellect did.[1] Some of my own work (1987, 1995), as well as my collaboration with Daryl White (D. White and White 1996; O. White and White 1999, 2004a, 2004b), addresses historical and contemporary aspects of Mormon intellectual life and the interplay between religion, the intellect, and identity. The influence of O'Dea in this as well as my other scholarship and teaching in the sociology of religion may be apparent to readers and students alike, especially those familiar with his theoretical writings.

Intellectually, nothing concerned O'Dea more than the challenge modernity posed for religious belief and practice. If a too complete embrace of modernity diluted religious insight and value as religion succumbed to secular thought and institutions (the fate of liberal Protestantism), rejection of modern scientific and philosophical thought doomed religion to a naive, unreflective position resulting in emotional excesses, rigid beliefs, and strict practices (fundamentalism). Something in between the two extremes, where authentic religious experience informs a coherent worldview and moral life, is what O'Dea thought modern human beings should require of their institutionalized religions. If Mormonism's past had "augured well for its future," as O'Dea concluded in *The Mormons* (1957b, 263), the predicament of intellectuals and the development of theology remained problematic. Here, he expressed less confidence in the future. His subsequent reflections (1966, xviii–xx; 1972) regarding institutional intransigence on blacks and the priesthood, which to O'Dea had come to symbolize reactionary responses to modernity, made him even less hopeful. Perhaps he would have embraced his earlier optimism had he lived to see the 1978 decision admitting blacks to the priesthood. However, there is little evidence to suggest that at the time of his death, in 1974, he had become more optimistic about prospects for intellectual vitality within the church in spite of significant growth in membership.

My purpose in this essay is to examine O'Dea's assessment of Mormon intellectual life and to address his claims regarding theological naïveté. I will concentrate primarily on developments during the fifty years following publication of *The Mormons,* which itself became an important impetus to the burgeoning scholarship on Mormonism and to more sophisticated theological efforts, primarily among professionally educated lay members.[2] Nothing comparable to the work of elder B. H. Roberts and apostles James E. Talmage and John A. Widtsoe has been produced by ecclesiastical officials during the past fifty years. What follows is organized in terms of O'Dea's evaluation of Mormon intellectual life, including his inclination to see intellectuals as either apologists or apostates, identification of limitations on theological development, my and Daryl White's use of a continuum rather than a dichotomy to understand Mormon intellectuals, and a concluding discussion of two major developments in Mormon theology since O'Dea published *The Mormons.*

O'Dea's Assessment of Mormon Intellectual Life

Defining intellectuals as people primarily involved in the creation, transmission, and preservation of culture, O'Dea identified an inherent dilemma with apparent contradictions in the critical and conservative functions of intellectuals in society. On the one hand, intellectuals are largely responsible for acquiring and interpreting the knowledge and traditions accumulated by society and then passing them on to new generations. In this sense, they are guardians of culture and responsible for preserving tradition and society. Their function is conservative, and they are revered for their knowledge and wisdom. On the other hand, their knowledge and analytical skills may turn some into social critics who challenge tradition and, at least potentially, create dissent and contribute to social conflict. Although dissent and conflict may lead to creative change, they are typically unsettling, and the resultant dismay encourages portrayals of intellectuals as a threat to society. Other intellectuals provide conceptual bridges enabling society to make smoother transitions into newer forms. These creative and conservative functions generate the ambivalence associated with the precarious position of intellectuals who may be perceived as indispensable yet threatening to society. "As creator and preserver, the intellectual is esteemed," wrote O'Dea, but "as critic and questioner, he is suspect" (1957b, 224). For O'Dea, this constitutes a universal dilemma in the relationship of the intellectual to society.

Beyond this general dilemma are those issues unique to specific societies or religious communities. Inherited from its environment and created through its development, Mormonism adds its own dilemmas to the universal tension between conservation and change. As a "stepchild" of "nineteenth-century American Protestantism" and a radical expression of the Restoration movement, Mormonism resolved the problem of religious authority with new sacred texts containing divine revelation. However, this created novel problems. If the Bible could be read liberally, accurate only insofar as it was "translated correctly," the Book of Mormon and the modern revelations provided much less flexibility. Indeed, many would argue that literal readings of these texts and accepted or official accounts of their origins are essential to the survival of Mormonism, and intellectuals inclined to more liberal and metaphorical interpretation can expect to be marginalized. Though we will return momentarily to the theological problems following from this dilemma, we must first consider that the problem of liberal versus literal readings of texts is exacerbated by elements of Mormon culture and social structure.

A very optimistic conception of human nature and cultural values emphasizing mastery of the environment combined to produce the activist nature of Mormon religion, and this activism is dependent on knowledge and education. Knowledge and effort were necessary to build the good society and prepare the world for the Kingdom of God and the arrival of Jesus. Thus, from the beginning, Mormons emphasized education with the study of Hebrew in Kirtland, Ohio, founding one of the first municipal universities in Nauvoo, Illinois, and establishing the University of Deseret, later to become the University of Utah, only three years upon their arrival in the Salt Lake Valley. To aid students in their encounter with secular education, the church has developed an elaborate institute (college-level) and seminary (secondary education–level) system to provide religious instruction (for an updated analysis, see Mauss 1994, 136–39). Obviously designed to keep Mormon youth in the church, the institutes of religion, seminaries, and church-owned colleges and universities attest to the integral connection of education to Mormonism and the "development of a native Mormon intelligentsia" that "would be particularly vulnerable to the secularization of Western thought and in the closest communication with the general intellectual life of the larger civilization." But, O'Dea wrote, "little did they realize that in placing their hopes in education they were at the same time creating the 'transmission belt' that would bring into Zion all the doubts and uncertainties that, in another century, were to beset the gentile world" (1957b, 225).

The cultural foundation for education is reflected in a typical exegesis of Mormon scriptures proclaiming that "the glory of God is intelligence" and "men are saved no faster than they gain knowledge," scriptures that have supported secular as well as religious education. Grounded in the Mormon notion of mastery of the environment, as noted above, both the value of mastery and the importance of knowledge underscored confidence in both reason and experience (empiricism) as authentic ways of knowing. An epistemology combining reason, empiricism, and revelation, though not without problems, was perfectly consistent with the metaphysics and theology articulated by Joseph Smith in the last few years of his life. Revelation had announced that the "elements are eternal" (uncreated), and in proclaiming his "doctrine of eternal progression," Smith had seen at least some implications of his new metaphysics in which matter, space, time, intelligence (human and divine essence), and moral law all exist necessarily, that is, are uncreated. He explicitly rejected the creation ex nihilo of classical Christianity in which nothing except God exists until God creates it. All created phenomena, which is everything other than God, exist contingently, that is, are dependent on God for their being, and, of course, can be destroyed at God's will. In contrast, to be uncreated and exist necessarily means that something cannot *not* exist. Smith (1938) appears to have recognized, in his famous 1844 "King Follett Discourse," that his doctrine of eternal progression required this metaphysics. God had advanced to his present status, and man might do the same. The famous aphorism "As man now is, God once was; as God now is, man may become" assumes the link between Smith's metaphysics and his doctrine of eternal progression and eloquently articulates the Mormon value of mastery that so impressed O'Dea. Only by obtaining knowledge, though not itself sufficient, could one attain exaltation and thereby realize his or her ultimate goal of godhood. Thus, Mormonism embedded knowledge and education in its very notion of exaltation as the ultimate purpose of the gospel.

Such is the context for the common claim that the gospel embraces all truth and that ultimately the knowledge derived from science will not conflict with that obtained through revelation. The task of sorting out and reconciling the various claims, a role for intellectuals, creates esteem for intellectual life and has encouraged the pursuit of science, philosophy, theology, and other educational endeavors among Mormons. Evidence suggests some success. Research of the distinguished psychologist E. L. Thorndike (1943) on "the origins of superior men" found Utah, when controlling for the size of the population, leading the nation in the production of scientists, and Kenneth R. Hardy (1974) argued that distinctive cultural values favoring education were responsible for the disproportionate success of undergraduates from universities in Utah in their subsequent careers as scientists and scholars. Many Mormon youth have gone to college in pursuit of education, believing it to be a religious obligation, only to find themselves in conflict with the church and its beliefs and practices. To O'Dea, this illustrates the dilemma of education versus apostasy. Although this conflict clearly occurs, evidence also suggests that higher educational levels are associated with higher levels of religious involvement among Latter-day Saints in contrast with other denominations (Albrecht and Heaton 1984; Merrill, Lyon, and Jensen 2003).

O'Dea identified "rationality versus charisma" as another dilemma affecting Mormon intellectual life (1957b, 241–42). Though there has long been a tendency for Mormons to accept uncritically claims of revelation at institutional levels and in private life, faith in the intellect, as noted above, and an orientation of commonsense rationality toward life and religious phenomena also obtain. An inclination "toward rationality from the start" has been "related to a certain utilitarianism in the general Mormon outlook," according to O'Dea, and this can be seen in intellectual emphases on Mormon scripture, the role of "argument rather than emotion" in proselyting, and development of "a kind of rationalistic apologetics to meet the problems raised by secular thought and science" (241). Without mentioning their names, O'Dea suggested that the generation of Widtsoe, Talmage, and Roberts "thought that this approach was successfully meeting the challenge" (241) while implying, as he wrote a generation or so later, that such was not the case. I would go further than O'Dea by arguing that even revelation, which he identified with charisma, is fundamentally rational in traditional Mormon thought. Its purpose is not to "baffle the intellect" or underscore the gulf between God and humanity—the wholly otherness of God—but rather to clarify. As I wrote in another context:

> God is neither incomprehensible nor the gospel paradoxical for traditional Mormonism. Nor is revelation antithetical to reason. In fact, Mormon revelation is rational; its purpose is to make matters more intelligible. It proposes to clarify, not to confuse, to solve problems and answer

questions, not to indicate that problems are illusory and questions illegitimate. Mormon revelation is explicit. When traditional Mormons tell of
God revealing himself to Joseph Smith, for example, God tries neither to
baffle the boy's intellect nor to demonstrate his paradoxical nature. God
was not something so large that he could fill the immensity of space and
yet so small that he could dwell within the heart of a man. God, for Joseph Smith, was a person, with a tangible body, with spatial and temporal
dimensions. He was comprehensible, not something beyond the logical
grasp or understanding of human beings. If differences between God and
humanity were evident, they were not so significant that Smith could not
intellectually apprehend the divine message. (1987, 161–62)

Two other dilemmas would profoundly affect Mormon intellectual life.
"Authority and obedience versus democracy and individualism" and "coercion versus consent" are interrelated, with significant consequences for intellectuals. A hierarchical structure in which the authority located at the apex
of the organization reinforced by a command for obedience often clashes
with a belief in free agency and the goal of exaltation through human effort. Some scholars, such as Mark P. Leone (1976, 1979) and Janet L. Dolgin
(1976), go so far as to claim that the hierarchical structure of the church
is largely a facade covering a pervasive individualism in doctrinal interpretation and experience, while critics argue that Leone and Dolgin ignore
the inordinate control and authoritarian behavior of ecclesiastical officials
(see O. White and White 1981; and Shepherd and Shepherd 1984, 10–12).
If the potential conflicts between authority and obedience and democracy
and individualism remain latent for many members of the church, they frequently become manifest for intellectuals. "Church government," according to O'Dea, "resulted in a democracy of participation within the context
of hierarchical organization and authoritarian operation" (1957b, 243), but
perhaps it is more accurate to identify the Church of Jesus Christ of Latter-
day Saints (LDS) as highly participatory but hardly democratic. All major
decisions, doctrinal and policy, are made by officials at the top of the hierarchy and simply "sustained"—through a perfunctory ratification ritual—by
church members at designated meetings. Ordinary members play no genuine role in the decision-making process. In contrast, the other major Mormon denomination—the Community of Christ (formerly known as the Reorganized Church of Jesus Christ of Latter Day Saints)—did develop and
extend the democratic propensities inherent within early Mormon polity.
It has an ecclesiastical structure with extensive democratic procedures (see
O. White and White 2004a for implications of these polity differences for

gay and lesbian members). The Community of Christ manifests the demo-cratic propensities and the LDS Church the authoritarian proclivities. Par-adoxical as it may seem, both tendencies, O'Dea believed, were inherent within Mormonism.

Governing generally reflects a clash between coercion and consent. After acknowledging that enemies and some critics of the LDS Church have as-sumed that coercion and exploitation were the foundations of the Mormon social order whereas followers and apologists have emphasized consensus, O'Dea sided largely with the latter, suggesting that consent has dominated, with occasional "use of coercion as a supplement" (1957b, 244). A "favorable balance between consensus and coercion" may have characterized Mormon experience historically, as O'Dea asserted, but even this consensus becomes problematic for intellectuals. Accepting the hierarchical structure as legiti-mate and the value of obedience as a religious imperative renders the Saints more susceptible to the use of coercive measures, both formal and informal, against intellectuals who are perceived as a threat to group cohesion. Indeed, there may be broad support for contemporary efforts to restrict dissenting views in the church educational system and to employ coercive disciplinary sanctions, including excommunication, against Mormon intellectuals and scholars (see Waterman and Kagel 1998; and O. White and White 2004b for the interplay of these forces at Brigham Young University [BYU]; and Mauss 1994, 182–85, regarding the intellectual subculture generally).

Beyond these general and particular dilemmas confronting Mormon in-tellectuals were constraints limiting theological development. The call for a liberalization of theology, which primarily meant abandonment of excessive literalism, was doomed to fail since it merely placed Mormons in the same predicament as secularists and many mainstream Protestants—that is, con-fronting an existential crisis of meaning, for, notwithstanding its technolog-ical and scientific advances, modernity, from O'Dea's perspective, failed to provide meaning for the most fundamental questions of human existence. Ironically, it was the antimodernity forces whose worldviews seemed to pro-tect them from the realities of modern life. However, these were inadequate, naive, escapist reactions that were both intellectually and religiously dis-honest. Failing to address the theological problems produced by modernity would simply leave Mormons with an antiquated belief system. Even so, O'Dea thought that a middle-ground position between liberalism and liter-alism was virtually impossible. "There is actually no room in Mormonism," he wrote, "for philosophy as distinct from theology." A "religiously oriented, though not divinely inspired, philosophy" could find "little place" in Mor-monism since "theology monopolizes the field philosophy would seek to

develop," potentially leaving Mormonism on shaky philosophical foundations (1957b, 233–34). Almost fifty years later, non-LDS theologian Douglas
Davies could write:

> Still, Mormonism has by no means developed as formal an academic tra-
> dition of theology as is present in many other major Christian denomi-
> nations. This is largely because it possesses prophetic revelation from the
> past and a living prophet in the present, both of which constrain the ex-
> ploratory tendencies of theologians in other churches. What Mormonism
> has come to possess is a relatively large group of historians who are some-
> times thought to substitute for theologians, but that is only partly true.
> (2003, 1–2)

Though prophetic revelation and a living prophet minimize the role a
theologian might play, the absence of a professional priesthood in which
theological training is necessary for ordination should not be underestimated as a constraint on Mormon theological development. Moving up
the ecclesiastical hierarchy has become sufficiently institutionalized to increasingly require missionary experience, a testimony of the truthfulness of
the gospel, commitment to a behavioral code, and evidence of some managerial skills, but it does not involve educational or theological training.
Consequently, even many of the top officials appear to have a rather naive
understanding of Mormon history and quite simplistic notions of theology.
Rarely have they professionally studied religion. On the other hand, many
Latter-day Saints are engaged in the professional study and teaching of religion, often at academic institutions, and others, with professional training
from elite universities, pursue Mormon history, textual analyses, philosophical issues, and theology as avocations. They often publish in major journals
devoted to Mormon scholarship, including *Dialogue,* the *Journal of Mormon
History, Sunstone,* and *Exponent II.* Though feared by ecclesiastical officials
and largely unknown among rank-and-file members, this increasingly sophisticated treatment of history, theology, philosophy, and textual analyses
is available to the Mormon intelligentsia, which now enjoys a viable subculture with identifiable networks and social structures. That these efforts
might inform theological development at an official level at some point in
the future is not inconceivable. In fact, in the case of the priesthood ban on
black members, the excellent research of Lester Bush (1973, 1999) apparently
influenced the decision to change Mormon racial policy.

A distinction between the LDS Church and the Mormon community
may clarify some changes in the constraints on Mormon intellectual life (see

O. White 1995; and D. White and White 1996). Whereas the institution and the community may have been coterminous during the nineteenth and the early part of the twentieth centuries, the increased assimilation into American culture and the emergence of divergent subgroups claiming a Mormon heritage have created a broader Mormon community. On the Right are the fundamentalists (polygamous subculture), who insist that when the church compromised on polygamy it lost its claim to be the authentic bearers of the Mormon tradition, and millennial survivalists whose version of Mormon apocalypticism posits a final war to protect the U.S. Constitution as a precondition for the return of Jesus. On the Left are most intellectuals, feminists, and gay and lesbian Latter-day Saints who also claim their place in the tradition, sometimes arguing that their views are more authentic expressions of the spirit of Mormonism than those embodied in the institutional church. Although the church remains the center of the community and represents the majority of the Latter-day Saints, it no longer enjoys the hegemony required to limit the community to the institution. The church obviously possesses sufficient power to impose disciplinary measures, including excommunication, against individuals from all of these groups. Indeed, its use of disciplinary procedures suggests that ecclesiastical officials are attempting to accomplish at least three things: define who may claim to be Mormon, that is, establish the appropriate boundaries for being Mormon; reaffirm their claim to be the exclusive bearers of the tradition; and reestablish control over the Mormon community. In fact, one of their rhetorical devices is to deny that their rivals are Mormon. Note, for example, President Gordon Hinckley's assertion that "there are no Mormon fundamentalists" (Stack 1998). Yet these subgroups, often with distinct subcultures, exist. It may be more useful to think of the Mormon community as this broad base of various subgroups all claiming their place within the Mormon tradition, with the institutional church at the center. The focus of this essay is on the intellectual subculture, which provides the social base for the Mormon intelligentsia, and the "plausibility structure," to use Peter Berger's term (1967), to reinforce Mormon identity for intellectuals. This subculture—with established journals, conferences, and now Internet groups—is far more developed than the small, informal discussion groups with which O'Dea was familiar, and it provides a means for intellectual activity that is independent of the church.[3]

In the meantime, as O'Dea argued, an uncritical and nonreflective orientation toward Mormon beliefs prevailed at both official and folk levels. This naïveté led him to frame the problem as a dichotomy between education and apostasy. Intellectuals were left with the choice between becoming apologists, defenders of the faith, or apostates who felt compelled to leave the church. As Daryl White and I have argued elsewhere, this dichotomy is too simplistic, and the relationship between the intellectual and the church is not only more complex but better conceptualized as a continuum, with ardent apologists at one end and apostates who have clearly abandoned the tradition at the other (O. White and White 1999).[4] In between are a variety of points where individuals construct their identities by negotiating their relationships with family, church, and community. Identity, in this context, refers to personal identity rather than collective or group identity—that is, to what and who people believe themselves to be and where Mormonism belongs in their construction of self. Both what Mormonism is to individuals and how their conceptions of it affect their identities determine their placement on the continuum.

THE CONTINUUM

At one extreme on the continuum are the apologists who are ardent defenders of the faith. Though they too may vary in their particular interpretations of Mormon doctrine, they share the position of perceiving ultimate and proximate reality, including social relationships, through the prism of Mormonism. If they sometimes differ in their interpretations of Mormon theology, all apologists at the extreme end of the continuum affirm the distinctiveness of Mormonism, asserting that it constitutes the fullest embodiment of truth. Indeed, in ideal-typical form, these apologists assert that Mormonism is "the only true religion" and view other religions, bodies of knowledge, or "avenues to truth"—including science and philosophy—as subordinate if not explicitly inferior to Mormonism. For apologists at the extreme end of the continuum, Mormonism provides the conceptual framework through which everything is understood. Rarely do these individuals experience conflict with the church, for Mormonism is the central element, the "master status," in their identities.[5] Mormonism defines who they are.

Apostates are at the other end of the continuum. In the most extreme form, apostates have left Mormonism, maintaining no relationship with either the church or the community. Mormonism disappears as a conscious element of their identities. It is simply an irrelevant aspect of their past. All current bases for self-definition include elements unrelated to Mormonism. Mormonism may be little more than a distant memory. In short, movement along the continuum is from intense identification with Mormonism, where Mormonism constitutes the principal basis for an individual's self-conception, to the other end, where it no longer plays any conscious role in the individual's identity. However, the same individual may be at various places on the continuum at different points in time. Conceivably, someone could move back and forth throughout his or her life. Whereas many apostates were once devoted apologists, some apostates become apologists, perhaps especially during the waning years of their lives.

However, as we move from the extreme ends of the continuum, we find the emergence of both internal and external conflict and the appearance of life on the boundaries of the church or community or both. Next to the "apostate" for whom Mormonism plays no conscious role in his or her life are a variety of individuals who may acknowledge a historical and cultural contribution of Mormonism to the formation of their personalities but who are not attached to the church or community in their everyday lives, nor do they maintain a Mormon worldview. These people perceive both proximate and ultimate realities, assuming that the latter even makes any sense, from a perspective other than Mormonism. Indeed, Mormonism itself is understood in terms of some other conceptual framework. The latter may derive from historical, philosophical, or social scientific perspectives, perhaps even a combination of the three, but it is likely to be naturalistic or secular. Mormonism, like other religious phenomena, is understood and explained through this conceptual framework. There is no reason to privilege Mormonism over other religions, and religion itself may be subordinated to science or philosophy or both when it comes to epistemological and ontological claims. Thus, Mormonism may be viewed as a social and cultural reality, but its truth claims are either denied explicitly or at least not taken seriously.

Some well-known Mormon scholars and intellectuals belong here on the continuum, but so also do scholars and other professionals who have limited connections to Mormonism. Because of the subordination of Mormonism to another conceptual framework, Mormonism often plays little role in the identities of these individuals. In fact, those who have very few or no ties to Mormons—for instance, community, family, friends, or acquaintances—are not likely to identify themselves as Mormon at all. They live beyond the boundaries of the church and community. On the other hand, some may regard themselves as "cultural Mormons" in their acknowledgment of socialization into Mormonism or current attachment to a Mormon community. Obviously, Mormonism is not irrelevant to the self-conception of a cultural Mormon, but typically it is far from the most salient feature of his or her identity. Yet even within the category of the cultural Mormon, we might expect considerable variation in the role Mormonism assumes in personal identity. For instance, a deceased Brigham Young University professor, who enjoyed some prominence among liberal Mormon intellectuals, rejected virtually all of Joseph Smith's claims to revelation and was confident that he had debunked many of the central tenets of Mormonism. Reluctant to publish his research for fear that he would be "cut off from the Church" and constantly warning Mormon scholars to be careful in what they say so as not to "spoil" matters for others, he informed O'Dea that he "'couldn't be anything else but a Mormon'" (n.d., box 5, file 7). Others, like philosopher Sterling McMurrin, U.S. commissioner of education during the Kennedy administration, might explicitly acknowledge their disbelief in Mormon theology, be highly critical of church policies and practices, and become the target of considerable hostility and anger. Yet McMurrin retained a fondness for Mormons as "my people" that spoke volumes about his personal identity. Anyone who knew him well could hardly miss an essential Mormon component to both his social and his personal identities. McMurrin would fall among the "sincere and troubled intellectuals" who "are still activated by many Mormon values" whom O'Dea met during his first visit to Utah in 1950. This initial experience led O'Dea to record in his notes that "there is, so to speak, a Mormon core to their character structures" (ibid., "Meeting...").

Whereas Daryl White and I would fall here on the continuum because of our general agnosticism and conceivable identification as "cultural Mormons," a number of people writing in *Dialogue* and *Sunstone* either are self-proclaimed cultural Mormons who no longer believe the theology but vary in the degree to which they participate in the church or community or, while eschewing labels, describe themselves in terms consistent with cultural Mormonism. Scientist David Tolman (2003b, 103–8), for instance, describes his experience as generally attempting to reconcile or compartmentalize Mormonism and science while holding offices in bishoprics and on high councils until the final point of disillusionment with the "September massacre," the excommunication and disfellowship of six Mormon intellectuals in September 1993. "I found no vantage point within the church upon which to stand," he writes, so "I resigned my church callings but continued to attend church though I soon realized that this was a futile attempt to hold on to what was no longer there." As things progressed, he became further disenchanted with "organized religion" and uncomfortable in the company of people who behaved like "cult members." He now identifies himself as an "ethical humanist" (104, 106). Responding to the comments of his friend and fellow scientist David Allred, he concludes that "on the evidence I am finally persuaded—though I have clearly failed to persuade my old friend—that there is life outside his religious community, and it is intelligent, moral, principled, and satisfying life" (2003a, 130). And David G.

Pace (1998), raised in an "ultra-neo-orthodox home," in the shadow of a popular, charismatic religion professor at BYU, has experienced family conflict, personal turmoil, disenchantment, resignation from the church, and a renewed identification as an "ethnic Mormon." Evoking an obvious parallel with ethnic rather than religious Jews, Pace finds new meaning and value in his Mormon tradition that enable him to claim his place within the broader Mormon community if not the church. How his ethnic Mormonism may differ from cultural Mormonism is less clear, but this obviously places him at the apostate end of the continuum, though not the most extreme end where there is a complete loss of conscious Mormon identity.

At the midpoint on the continuum between apologist and apostate are those who hold a Mormon worldview at the same time they utilize alternative conceptual frameworks from history, philosophy, science, social science, or literature. These individuals range from those who rigidly compartmentalize their Mormonism and alternative analytical frames of reference to those who more or less integrate the two. Rigid compartmentalizers maintain their "naive faith," as some theologians would say, without contamination from their scientific, philosophical, or historical framework. The more or less successful integrators modify their Mormonism, alternate conceptual framework, or both. Whereas the integrators are closer to the apostates, the compartmentalizers are nearer to the apologists. If the compartmentalizers often act as apologists, they differ from those at the extreme end of the continuum by their conscious use of another framework for understanding the world and perhaps limited aspects of Mormonism. Intellectuals who are rigid compartmentalizers cover the spectrum of academic disciplines. Among Mormon social scientists who fall into this category are those for whom sociological models are simply useful means of furthering a Mormon agenda and not primarily a way of understanding Mormon society and culture or their own beliefs and experience as Latter-day Saints.[6] An example is the use of social scientific models based on empirical research of conversion processes that are not employed to understand the phenomenon itself, or institutional processes, or one's own experience, but rather to enhance successful proselytizing for the church. For the truly rigid, the analytical framework is purely utilitarian. It is adopted to the extent that it supports the basic tenets of Mormonism as he or she understands them, and it is rejected if it poses any threat to established beliefs or institutional authority or is no longer useful for an apologetic agenda. Consider another example: the debate over archaeology in Book of Mormon studies. The selective use and unorthodox interpretation of archaeological findings thought to support Book of Mormon claims were prominent forms of apologetics in the

1950s and 1960s (see Coe 1973). A counterargument, which is also an apologetic argument, challenged the use of archaeology because of the inherent tentativeness of science. Since archaeological explanation and interpretation would surely change, grounding the authenticity of the Book of Mormon in archaeology was analogous to building one's house on a foundation of sand. As the sands of archaeological findings and interpretation shift, the edifice of the Book of Mormon collapses.

Historical examples of less rigid compartmentalization implying some integration of Mormonism and an alternative conceptual framework include prominent Mormon physical scientists. The limited integration appeared in their modification of a few Mormon beliefs or assumptions. However, their agenda was clearly apologetic, as ardent defenders of the faith, with minor conflicts over the age of the earth and biological evolution. Among the most celebrated was the internationally renowned chemist Henry Eyring, whom Sterling McMurrin described to Thomas O'Dea as a man "very accomplished in his field" but whose "religious beliefs were the same as they were in high school" (n.d., box 5, file 7). During the 1930s, one of Mormonism's more intellectually creative periods, a few church leaders initiated or at least embraced theological endeavors designed to reconcile Mormonism with developments in science. Elder B. H. Roberts and apostles John A. Widtsoe and James E. Talmage recognized implications of Mormonism's peculiar metaphysics for both a rapprochement with science and the necessity of education. The latter included knowledge of the laws governing nature as an essential element in an individual's religious development and as a requirement for ultimate salvation (exaltation). Though conservative antagonists eventually prevailed, Roberts, Talmage, and Widtsoe formulated the synthesis of "traditional Mormon theology" (O. White 1987, 57–87) and inspired a couple of generations of Mormon youth in their intellectual quests. The pursuit of science was a religious and not simply secular endeavor. That intellectuals inspired by these religious leaders would fall at different points on our continuum is not surprising since the church generally turned in a more conservative direction. Confronting institutional challenges and restraints, Roberts, Talmage, and Widtsoe were forced closer to the apologetic end of the continuum than their natural inclinations may have dictated (see Sherlock and Keller 1993; O. White and White 1998; and Mauss 1994, chap. 6).

A more integrated but still compartmentalized manifestation of Mormon and alternative conceptual frameworks appears among a number of contemporary Mormon scholars. In these instances, the weight accorded the alternative perspectives requires individuals to employ the highest standards of their discipline to their study of Mormonism. At the same time, the centrality of Mormonism to their own beliefs and personal identities results in religious affirmations that may be incomprehensible to outsiders. Included here are some of contemporary Mormonism's very best historians, sociologists, anthropologists, textual scholars, and literary critics. They range from those trained in biblical studies who apply textual and contextual analyses to scriptures without allowing the result to alter deeply cherished beliefs to sociologists and anthropologists whose analyses of Mormon belief, ritual, and behavior appear to have little impact on their own religious positions and historians who assemble their "facts" to tell stories of Mormon origins and history that are at odds with "official" accounts but who proclaim traditional beliefs in their own religious commitments. The reason Daryl White and I (1999) identified this with compartmentalization is because something approximating the official version of Mormonism is what the individual apparently believes, and the analysis utilizing the alternative conceptual framework is separated from his or her actual beliefs. These are not scholars inclined to redefine Mormonism to make it more consistent with what they know from using alternative frameworks. On the contrary, they retain a commitment to their traditional religious beliefs.

Based on public pronouncements and published records, Mormon historian D. Michael Quinn may belong at this point on the continuum. He is a prolific scholar whose work reflects a willingness not only to examine controversial topics but also to handle them with professional responsibility, with both detachment and objectivity. Consequently, his work on Mormon origins presents a picture of Joseph Smith that is very different from official accounts and current legends. From Smith's treasure hunting and obsession with magic to conflicting accounts of his own visions and revelations and his extensive entanglement with plural wives, some of whom were already married to other Mormon leaders, Quinn (1987, 1994) has documented profound changes in Mormon beliefs and practices. To his credit, Quinn has not hidden what he has found in his decades of research on Mormonism. Nor did he recant, avoid sensitive topics, or censure his work when university administrators threatened his employment and ecclesiastical officials challenged his worthiness to remain a member of the church. Eventually, he lost on both counts: he resigned from Brigham Young University in 1988 and was excommunicated from the church in 1993. Despite all of the controversy and his accounts of Mormon history, Quinn continually testifies to the truthfulness of the Book of Mormon, the prophetic status of Joseph

Smith, the authenticity of the church, and the accuracy of Mormonism's truth claims. Employing the language and form of typical Mormon testimonies, with a clear understanding of their meaning and ritualistic nature, Quinn (1995) implies that his testimony does not differ from that of other Latter-day Saints on these essentials. If he does mean something different from standard testimonies, then what this may be remains uncertain from his public pronouncements. Nor is it clear how Quinn's own research affects his deeper understanding of Mormonism.

As committed to the truth claims of Mormonism as Quinn may be, his profession of faith is not sufficient to shield him from the consequences of his scholarly career. Reporting on a growing propensity for religious studies departments to accept money from religious devotees for the establishment of endowed chairs, the *Wall Street Journal* recently described efforts to create endowed chairs on Mormonism at two public universities and the private Claremont Graduate University that are being funded by Mormon constituencies. When asked if Quinn might be considered at Claremont, an associate dean said "'probably not,'" while the prime mover at the University of Wyoming, a Spanish professor and LDS bishop, assured church leaders that it will not be "'a chair of anti-Mormon studies.'" (Note the following implications: This antiquated conceptualization of scholarship as "anti-Mormon" suggests its alternative of "pro-Mormon studies" with, at best, a category in the middle that is presumably more neutral since it cannot be subsumed under either of the existing categories. If Mormon studies is conceptualized in these terms, then it is easy to imagine to what the holder of such an endowed chair must assent.) Though it was still too early to discuss potential candidates, the chair of the History Department at Utah State University acknowledged that the university will be looking for someone "'who can get along with everybody'" since they "'know what the minefields are'" and will try "'to avoid them.'" No matter an individual's scholarly qualifications and professed belief in the truth claims of Mormonism, the deference to a Mormon audience reflected in each of these schools does not bode well for Quinn or for that matter any other scholar who may be out of favor with church officials or laity. Quinn was denied a position at the University of Utah in 2004 when referees and established members of the department praised his scholarship and teaching, one even claiming that he was the second best historian of Mormonism, but withheld their support and voted against his candidacy because of probable responses from the state legislature and the Mormon community. History repeated itself at Arizona State University, when the chair of religious studies was asked to review the "'risks and benefits'" of hiring Quinn for a visiting professorship, resulting in his rejection. The risks involved a potential affront to their Mormon constituency and a multimillion-dollar donor who referred to Quinn as "'a nothing person.'" "'We exercise sensitivity,'" said a university official, not "'censorship'" (Golden 2006).

The midpoint belongs to those who integrate Mormonism with their conceptual framework by reconceptualizing Mormonism. These people retain a Mormon identity, with perhaps varying degrees of participation in the church and community, but "being" Mormon to them differs significantly from what it may have meant in their youth or to more typical Latter-day Saints. Yet Mormonism is not something they are willing to relinquish as significant to who they are. Though some make this move privately without public presentation of their reconstructed Mormonism, others are quite vocal and provide much of the creative force for Mormon cultural development. Included here are writers and theologians who have attempted to reconcile Mormonism with modernity and the challenges posed by religious pluralism. Important figures among the past few generations include William H. Chamberlin, E. E. Ericksen, Lowry Nelson, Heber Snell, George T. Boyd, T. Edgar Lyon, and Lowell L. Bennion. If they varied in the extent to which they would reconceptualize Mormonism—what they would jettison, retain, or rework—they shared, at least at critical points in their lives, a commitment to making Mormonism more socially responsible and intellectually palatable. Though committed to values they identified with Mormonism, they explicitly rejected its racial policy, excessive textual literalism, anti-intellectual propensities, and authoritarianism.

A current generation of scholars utilizes its alternative conceptual frameworks, typically derived from specialized academic disciplines, to redefine Mormonism. Applying their skills in textual analyses, for instance, a few scholars trained in biblical studies have concluded that the Book of Mormon is not the ancient document it purports to be but rather a product of nineteenth-century America. In itself, this conclusion is not surprising, for it is the position typically held by cultural Mormons and others toward the apostate end of the continuum. What differentiates the two positions, however, is the special claim for the Book of Mormon as a sacred text, as scripture, that need not be dropped from the official canon. Instead of finding the Book of Mormon an embarrassment, this new generation of textual scholars continues to discover divine revelation within its covers (Metcalfe 1993). Rejecting more liberal readings of traditional Mormon theology, a few theologians have created a Mormon neoorthodoxy (as discussed in the next section) with conceptions of deity, human nature, and salvation that resemble Reformation Protestantism more than traditional Mormonism (O. White 1987). Among the more creative are Margaret Toscano and Paul Toscano (1990) who find in Mormonism's unique cosmology and rich symbolism, including the concept of a mother in heaven, fertile soil for a Jungian revitalization. Linda P. Wilcox (1980) and Janice Allred (1994) develop theological implications of a mother in heaven alongside a father in heaven. Other feminist scholars and activists identify oppressive structures in Mormon patriarchy while celebrating the agency of women throughout Mormon history (Hanks 1992). There is even a niche for addressing issues of gay and lesbian Latter-day Saints (D.White and White 1999; O. White and White, 2005.).

Some truly eminent scholars, whose reputations are based on work unrelated to Mormonism, have either returned to Mormon concerns or remained involved in the church or community or both. The independent journals, conferences, and symposia providing opportunities for addressing historical and theological matters have enabled some to reclaim or reaffirm their Mormon identities. A distinguished University of Chicago literary critic, the late Wayne Booth, is an example of someone reclaiming his religious roots. Having rejected most of Mormonism in his teens and been inactive in the church through most of his life, he became an active participant in the Mormon intellectual community during the 1990s, presenting papers at *Sunstone* symposia and publishing articles analyzing Mormon phenomena (see Booth 1998, 1999, 2006). In his posthumously published book, *My Many Selves* (2006), Booth tells his story. Although he has characterized himself as "actively inactive" in the church, in the later part of his life he became clearly engaged in the Mormon intellectual community and acknowledged that Mormonism constituted a salient feature of his identity.

Harvard University recently announced the appointment of Laurel Thatcher Ulrich, a "pre-eminent historian of early America," as its 300th Anniversary University Professor, making her one of nineteen holding current University Professorships (see Gewertz 2006; and Wilson 2006). Identified with an emergent Mormon feminism in the early 1970s and a founder of *Exponent II,* a Mormon feminist publication, Ulrich became famous with the publication of *Good Wives,* and her reputation was profoundly enhanced with her Pulitzer Prize–winning book, *A Midwife's Tale.* Her Mormon writings generally reflect a concern over women's issues in the LDS Church, but they do not suggest significant departure from rather orthodox Mormon beliefs or practice. They are published in periodicals she associates with the "'unsponsored sector' of contemporary Mormonism" (identified here as the intellectual subculture)—principally *Exponent II* and *Dialogue*—and reflect a strong commitment to fundamental Mormon values. Whereas Ulrich would probably fall toward the apologist end of the continuum because of an apparent commitment to rather orthodox beliefs, Booth would clearly belong more toward the apostate end. What both share, beyond preeminent status as scholars, is the significance of their Mormon experience as a fundamental component of their identities (see Ulrich 1993, 2002, for her own discussion of the relationship between her personal and professional identities).

The identities of contemporary Mormon intellectuals arguably are more varied than ever before. This variety is not simply a result of choice where individuals reconstruct Mormonism in meaningful ways. It is also a product of a hierarchy that is unwilling to incorporate diversity within the monolithic institution it controls. But this is not for want of trying. Ecclesiastical officials are not sympathetic to alternative versions of Mormonism. Consequently, some intellectuals have lost their jobs at Brigham Young University, and others have lost their membership in the church. Yet, as we have seen, many of these victims of autocratic ecclesiastical power remain remarkably Mormon, refusing to allow church officials to strip them of their claim to a Mormon identity. Nowhere is their position more eloquently expressed than in the words of Levi S. Peterson, a Mormon writer and former English professor who addressed dissidents at a 1993 *Sunstone* symposium:

> Finally, if your particular identity and indignation demand a course of action that seems fated to lead to excommunication, well, God bless you and give courage. Even here, I have some advice, which is that excommunication is no reason for withdrawing from Mormonism.
>
> I fancy that if I were excommunicated by a Church court on a weekday, I'd be back sleeping in sacrament meeting on the following Sunday. Presumably I'd be relieved of my duties as home teacher and occasional instructor of the high priest group. Presumably I'd not be called on to pray or preach. But those are petty losses. I'd continue to partake of the sacrament unless I were expressly forbidden to do so. In that case, I'd attend meetings from time to time in a ward where I wasn't known and would partake of the sacrament there....
>
> Though as a corporation the Church may be owned by its legally constituted officers, as a moral community Mormonism is beyond ownership. You and I belong if we choose to belong. I for one choose to belong. I'll not let another human being, however highly placed, drive me from Mormonism. (1994, 39)

Peterson's insistence that excommunication is not a sufficient reason to leave Mormonism underscores the distinction between the church and the community, suggesting that membership in the latter requires an active decision on the part of individuals and is not simply a function of social pressure and the control exercised by ecclesiastical officials. That this distinction has practical value is indicated by the response of Lavina Fielding Anderson, herself a victim of excommunication, who subsequently stated that she may no longer be a Latter-day Saint, but she *is* still a Mormon (Williams 2001).

Perhaps our most problematic case involves those apostates who have rejected Mormonism, conceiving themselves as "non-Mormon," but whose struggle against it is so intense as to leave them preoccupied with Mormonism. To them, Mormonism serves as a negative reference point. It is something that must be resisted. It is not unlike the "negative identity"— what one ought not be—that is crucial to the dialectical process of identity formation appearing in the psychoanalytical theory of Erik Erikson (1958, 1968). In the most extreme cases, these individuals are engaged in a holy crusade against Mormonism. Often embracing conspiratorial theories of Mormon domination and control, they attribute inordinate power and sinister motives to church officials while perceiving ordinary members to be "good people" who have been duped or "brainwashed." In fact, they often characterize their own experience as Mormons in these terms. They sound like many who have left new religious movements, popularly identified as "cults," with "atrocity tales" focusing on the inordinate control exercised by Mormon leaders and the complicity of unwitting followers.

Mormonism permeates the consciousness of the apostate who cannot let go, whether he or she chooses not to affiliate with another religious body or becomes an evangelical born-again Christian whose mission is to save the Mormons.[7] But why is this case problematic? Since the individual is an apostate, the level of identification should be minimal or nonexistent. However, identification is intense, though negative rather than positive. It is something against which the individual struggles rather than something that he or she is trying to affirm. Since Mormonism remains a preoccupation of the individual, it cannot be removed from his or her consciousness. Mormonism plays some role in this person's identity. But where this case fits on the continuum, with the rejection of Mormonism itself, is less clear. Yet it is a case that cannot be ignored.

Mormon Theological Developments

If O'Dea found a lack of philosophical rigor in Mormon theological efforts, he acknowledged, as fundamental to the development of Mormon belief and practice, the forces that Nathan O. Hatch subsequently identified in *The Democratization of American Christianity* (1989, 113–22, for specific analysis of Mormonism). The antinomian challenge to established authority, with greater confidence in the authenticity of the religious experience of common folk than the "book learning" of educated elites, the widening movement away from traditional Protestantism, and the creative integration of its secular milieu resulted in a "new religious doctrine" and a "new world view" (O'Dea 1957b, 120). Indeed, Mormonism

> combined materialism and visions, and the result was the conception of a God of flesh and bones, which later led to the doctrine of polytheism. It combined this-worldly hopes for a reformed society with the doctrine of the Second Coming of the Lord and produced the Mormon idea of building the kingdom of God on earth in preparation for the millennium. It combined secular progress and evangelical enthusiasm, and the result was eternal progression. It combined anthropomorphism and the universe of nineteenth-century science as common men were beginning to understand it, and the result was a finite God. These developments reconciled the contrarieties of the time and place in creative eclecticism which, although it failed to achieve logical consistency, nevertheless possessed a cohesiveness of tendency and congruity of fundamental principle that rendered it a unified point of view. (125–26)

As previously noted, this theological synthesis emerged early in the twentieth century through the work of Roberts, Talmage, and Widtsoe. I have referred to this synthesis as "traditional Mormon theology"—a "nineteenth-century heresy"—standing in sharp contrast to Joseph Smith's earliest theology and "Mormon neo-orthodoxy" as a post–World War II theological movement (see O. White 1969, 1970, 1987). The latter increasingly resembled Reformation Protestant doctrines of God, human nature, and salvation more than those of traditional Mormonism. At the heart of traditional Mormon theology are conceptions of a finite God, the fundamental goodness of human nature, and virtually universal salvation, with exaltation primarily through merit. Mormonism clearly rejected salvation by grace alone. Even influential traditional conservatives, such as Joseph Fielding Smith Jr., with their anti-intellectual inclinations, embraced a less expansive version of traditional Mormon theology given their commitment to the materialistic metaphysics, denial of original sin, and emphasis on salvation (exaltation) by merit or works. However, an inordinate textual literalism and failure to understand philosophical implications of Mormon metaphysics often led

to confusion. Though they attempted to affirm qualified versions of abso-
lutism—reflected in the use of classical Christian concepts of omniscient,
omnipotent, and omnipresent to describe the character of God—and to
deny creation ex nihilo, which they typically interpreted to be an absurd
claim that something could be created out of nothing, this conflicted with
their acceptance of the metaphysics asserting that the basic elements of reality are uncreated and eternal. What they failed to understand were implications of the ex nihilo creation for the distinction between necessity and contingency—necessary and contingent being—and the consequences of this
distinction for their conceptions of God and human beings. Nevertheless,
conservative literalists, because they accepted the materialistic metaphysics,
generally embraced the conceptions of God, human nature, and salvation
(exaltation) associated with traditional Mormonism as a nineteenth-century
Christian heresy.

Two years after publication of *The Mormons,* Sterling McMurrin, an esteemed philosopher at the University of Utah, published *The Philosophical
Foundations of Mormon Theology* (1959), examining the metaphysical foundations of Mormon belief. Ultimate questions about the very nature and
structure of reality—for instance, whether it is ultimately one (monistic)
or many (pluralistic) and unchanging (being) or in process (becoming)—
undergird and inform theological ideas and religious practice, even if the
latter was not logically or intentionally derived from the former. It is their
metaphysics that define the Mormon doctrines of God, human nature, and
salvation. "The most interesting thing about Mormon theology," McMurrin
later wrote, "is that it incorporates a liberal doctrine of man with a radically
unorthodox conception of God within the general framework of historic
Christian fundamentalism" (1965, foreword). In *The Theological Foundations of the Mormon Religion,* he set Mormon theology in the context of the
broader Christian tradition. Neither a defense nor a critique of Mormonism, McMurrin provided the most systematic statement of Mormon theology to date. He addressed a number of philosophical and theological issues,
including the problem of evil, arguing that Mormonism had more potential than traditional Christianity. Acknowledging that Mormon theology
is "young and unsophisticated" and "not overencumbered with creeds and
official pronouncements," McMurrin stated that it has been "virtually untouched by serious and competent effort to achieve internal consistency or
exact definition" (112). If reminiscent of O'Dea's judgment (1957b, 233–34)
that a "religiously oriented though not divinely inspired philosophy" could
find "little place" in Mormonism, making it difficult to resolve "inconsis-
tencies," it could be argued that whatever McMurrin's intent, no one moved

closer to providing coherence and consistency to Mormon theology than he. I suspect O'Dea would have recognized in McMurrin's work a significant challenge to his own judgment of philosophical paucity.

A number of scholars inspired by McMurrin have continued to explore these philosophical issues. A finite God, limited both in power and in knowledge, provides traditional Mormonism with "the best potential theodicy in the Western World," according to Community of Christ philosopher Paul M. Edwards (1980, 49; 1984), and the necessary (uncreated) existence of human intelligence leads to perhaps the most radical notion of human freedom in either religious or secular traditions. Why? Freedom inheres in human nature rather than some external source. Implications of Mormon metaphysics for its finite God and conception of freedom continue to be explored by competent philosophers, including Edwards (1980, 1984), Blake T. Ostler (1984, 2002), Kent Robson (1980, 1982, 1983), L. Rex Sears (1998, 2000), and R. Dennis Potter (2000). Mormon notions of eternal progression have been related to Alfred North Whitehead's process philosophy by Floyd M. Ross (1982) and Garland E. Tickemeyer (1984) and considered historically by scientist David H. Bailey (2000), who also has a good essay on problems with the "omnis" in contemporary Mormon theology (2004). As noted above, these philosophical and theological treatises are products of a professionally trained laity, a burgeoning intelligentsia who are participants in the Mormon community, and not ecclesiastical officials at the top of the hierarchy of the church. How much the philosophical and theological efforts of those working on implications of Mormon metaphysics for traditional Mormon theology may eventually percolate upward to influence more official presentations of Mormon belief remains to be seen. Since church officials appear to be swayed, perhaps some even enthralled, with another theological movement, it may never occur.

Partially reacting to the creative intellectual syntheses of traditional Mormonism—given its engagement with science, biblical scholarship, and a broader educational enterprise during the 1930s and early 1940s—and the potential of too much assimilation into American society, a conservative post–World War II theological movement emerged. Initially involving a few religion professors at BYU, it coalesced into a fairly coherent theology challenging the foundational tenets of traditional Mormonism. Because of parallels with Protestant neoorthodoxy, I referred to the phenomenon as "Mormon neo-orthodoxy" (1970, 1987). Though much less sympathetic to biblical scholarship and the acceptance of scientific claims than their Protestant counterparts, Mormon neoorthodox theologians attempted to minimize the implications of Mormon metaphysics for its conceptions of deity and human nature. In contrast to the finite God of traditional Mormonism, neoorthodox theologians proclaimed a sovereign God described by qualities of omniscience, omnipotence, and omnipresence, emphasizing a widening of the gulf between God and humanity. They also rejected the traditional conception of human nature as fundamentally good and emphasized contingency over necessity for human "intelligence," favoring a peculiarly Mormon notion of original sin. The depravity or corruptness of human nature—inherent sinfulness—required the transformation or regeneration of human nature rather than moral advancement toward increased perfection. If the traditional emphasis on exaltation, primarily via merit or works, reflected Mormonism's acceptance of universal salvation, with virtually all humanity enjoying some "degree of glory" in heaven, and meant that Mormon notions of grace clearly differed from those of classical Christianity, the neoorthodox saw helpless humans clearly incapable of doing anything to save themselves. Mormon neoorthodoxy moved much closer to classical Protestant notions of salvation by grace, even toward grace alone. As a result, the emphasis on the life and example of Jesus in traditional Mormon theology gave way to the cross of Christ in Mormon neoorthodoxy.

Although my original argument involved a rather limited group of academics, the neoorthodox movement enjoyed a resurgence during the early 1980s (O. White 1987, 139–52) and has become a vigorous movement today. Though contemporary advocates are not fond of the neoorthodox label and prefer to characterize their position as "redemptive theology" (Millet 1989, 1998, 2005), their focus on the role of grace and redemption has pushed them even further toward doctrines of divine sovereignty, human depravity, and salvation by grace alone. When a leading evangelical theologian, Richard J. Mouw, president of Fuller Theological Seminary, reviewed *Mormon Neo-orthodoxy: A Crisis Theology* (O. White 1987) in *Christianity Today* (1991), he raised the question of whether Mormons might be considered Christians in an evangelical sense of accepting Jesus Christ as their "personal savior"—that is, being "born again" or "saved." Since contemporary Christian fundamentalists and neoevangelicals often regard Mormonism as an anti-Christian cult, Mouw offended some evangelicals with his encouragement of dialogue with neoorthodox Mormons. An amicable evangelical-Mormon exchange was published by Craig L. Blomberg and Stephen E. Robinson in 1997, *How Wide the Divide? A Mormon and an Evangelical in Conversation,* and Mouw joined Millet and others in "closed-door discussions" that convinced him that some elements of Mormon thought could be de-emphasized, while others could be highlighted to "constitute a message within Mormonism of salvation by grace alone through the blood of

Jesus Christ." He pledged to fellow evangelicals, "I will work to promote that cause" (2004b, n.p.). In response to further criticism, he said that "our Mormon friends" are "determined to influence things in the direction of salvation by grace alone." Indeed, he wrote, "I am also convinced that things are moving—on the leadership level—in a direction in which we can hope that in the not too distant future Mormons will regularly hear from their own leaders that salvation cannot be earned—not even in part—by good works, but only by accepting the gift of sovereign grace that has been made possible through the shed blood of Christ on Calvary" (2004c, n.p.).

Mouw's confidence, and the responses identified above, was at least partially the result of an extraordinary event. On a Sunday evening, November 14, 2004, LDS officials opened the Salt Lake Tabernacle on Temple Square to evangelicals and neoorthodox theologians for an event called "An Evening of Friendship." Apparently not since Dwight L. Moody, the famous revivalist who spoke in the tabernacle in 1871, had an evangelical been at that podium. The main sermon, delivered by Ravi Zacharias, a highly respected evangelical, received a standing ovation from the Mormon and evangelical audience. Richard Mouw offered the opening remarks, and he apologized to the Latter-day Saints. "We have sinned against you," he said, by "bearing false witness" when we failed to listen and told you what you believed. We have "even on occasion demonized you, weaving conspiracy theories about what the LDS community is 'really' trying to accomplish in the world" (2004a, n.p.). He was joined by his Mormon friend Robert Millet. Although a sustained discussion between neoorthodox Mormons and evangelicals has enjoyed the legitimization provided by Mouw, the conflict among evangelicals prior to the event in the tabernacle is briefly described by Richard N. Ostling and Joan K. Ostling (1999, 315–25).

There are other indications that the neoorthodox phenomenon is gaining strength within the church. Whereas Kent Robson (1980, 1983) and Keith E. Norman (1985) have identified neoorthodox themes in the discourse of apostles Neal Maxwell and Bruce McConkie, Armand L. Mauss has carefully assessed the evidence supporting a growing emphasis on fundamentalist (in the Protestant sense) ideas and behaviors among Mormons. Two excellent chapters in *The Angel and the Beehive: The Mormon Struggle with Assimilation,* "Mormon Fundamentalism: The Institutional Matrix" and "Expressions of Folk Fundamentalism," provide evidence supporting a broader trend. Various institutional factors—including a lay clergy, increased bureaucratization (correlation), instability in the Mormon presidency, reactions to intellectuals, and selective conversion (recruitment)—have had "the unintended effect of fostering the spread of fundamentalism"

(1994, 174). Though available survey data are limited, research on BYU students in 1935 and 1973 and Mormon scientists in 1955 and 1992 shows significant shifts toward greater acceptance of fundamentalist ideas among both groups (178–81), and survey research documents conservative positions on social issues among Mormons paralleling those of Protestant fundamentalists (189–91).

Since Mauss published *The Angel and the Beehive,* other scholars have documented this trend. In a content analysis of the songbooks of the Primary Children's Association from 1880 to 1989, Kristine Haglund Harris found significant changes in the Christology presented to children. From 1905 to 1945 the songbooks portrayed Christ as "a gentle friend of little children, who is aware of their daily activities and who wishes them to follow His example by being kind to their families and their neighbors" (2004, 121). From midcentury onward a trend obtained toward a Christ who "is not only distanced from the daily affairs of Mormons but is no longer understood in distinctively Mormon terms." Indeed, the "Jesus presented in the Primary songbooks is becoming more ... assimilated with the Protestant Jesus" as children "sing more about 'the Savior' than about 'Jesus.'" Harris suspects that this "new emphasis on Christ," along with other elements of neoorthodoxy, "was already finding a place in materials published by the Church Educational System ... or by quasi-official presses like Deseret Book by the late 1970s, and thus filtering into grassroots consciousness" (123–27). John-Charles Duffy's analysis of missionary manuals found recent decades giving "increasing prominence" to "an evangelical Mormon discourse" that not only emphasizes that "Mormons are Christians" but, more important, "deploys a Protestant vocabulary about salvation by grace, the natural man, second birth, sanctification, and so on" (2005, 34). Acknowledging that Gordon Shepherd and Gary Shepherd's content analysis of general conference speeches, *A Kingdom Transformed: Themes in the Development of Mormonism* (1984), found that the "'single most salient subject at general conference'" between 1950 and 1980 was the "'life and ministry of Jesus Christ,'" Duffy also reports Jan Shipps's observation that in all venues, even private conversations, she encounters "'an escalating emphasis on the suffering of the Savior, the atonement of Christ, personal salvation, and so on'" (44n30). He rejects her inclination to attribute this move toward typical Christian rhetoric and themes to the LDS Church becoming more comfortable with other religions and consequently less sectarian in favor of a position that the Mormon move toward Protestant Christianity is a reaction to the threat posed by evangelical Protestants who often believe Mormons to be an anti-Christian cult (34).

I agree with Duffy, but I suspect that the ambiguity generated by growth and identification of Mormonism as potentially a "new world religion" contributes to anxiety over Mormonism's status within the broader Christian community. Mormons, including church officials, embraced Rodney Stark's demographic argument (1984) projecting 265 million Mormons by 2080, but they were more ambivalent about Jan Shipps's claim (1984) that Mormonism should be seen as a "new religious tradition" separating itself from Christianity as Christianity had separated from Judaism to become a new religion. When distinguished literary critic Harold Bloom (1992, 110) combined the demographic argument with the claim of a new religious tradition to conclude that Mormonism was "as much a separate revelation as ever Judaism, Christianity, and Islam were," he also praised Joseph Smith for exceptional "religious genius" that "surpassed all Americans, before or since" (1992, 96–97). Latter-day Saints clearly liked Bloom's assessment of Joseph Smith, and he frequently appeared in friendly documentaries and promotional films as a non-LDS expert. However, Bloom's and Shipps's arguments for a new religious tradition ran the risk of defining Mormonism outside Christianity, and given the competition with evangelical Christianity, the Mormons moved ever closer to Christian fundamentalism. Several years later, Shipps could write about a "renewed emphasis on Christianity"—with the addition of "Another Witness for Jesus Christ" to the title of the Book of Mormon, change in the church logo with greater emphasis on Jesus Christ, and a call from officials for members to identify the church by its full title or as the Church of Jesus Christ but not as the "Mormon Church." Shipps then began referring to Latter-day Saints as "Mormon Christians" (2000, 40).

She anticipates more significant shifts in Mormon symbols. Increasing emphasis on atonement may lead to "greater use of a cross as a symbol of Christ's suffering," including the possibility that "Mormon chapels will someday display crosses on their steeples" (2005, 270n33; see Norman 2001 for a theological defense). Ironically, when *Mormon Neo-orthodoxy* was published in 1987, my brother Daryl designed three possible covers that the publisher chose not to use. They varied from realistic to quite abstract, but all involved the Salt Lake Temple, perhaps the most recognizable symbol of Mormonism, with a cross replacing the angel Moroni. Intended to symbolize the "Protestantization" of Mormonism, the image was perceived as too blasphemous for the Mormon portion of the audience. It still may be too early to suggest a future with the cross on the temple as well as a chapel steeple. However, if Richard Mouw is correct, this may occur a lot sooner than we think.

CONCLUSION

Conceptualizing the role of Mormon intellectuals in terms of fundamental dilemmas, some generic to the intellectual life and others specific to Mormonism, enabled O'Dea to provide a truly insightful analysis of Mormon intellectual life. The institutional constraints, emphasis on education, conception of revelation, basic commitment to reason and empiricism, and interplay of coercion and consensus all affect the quality of Mormon intellectual experience. O'Dea's framing of the major dilemma as a dichotomy of apologetics versus apostasy identified a significant tension for Mormon intellectuals and reminds one of the tendency of many Latter-day Saints to think in either-or categories. Something is either pro-Mormon or anti-Mormon. Joseph Smith is either a prophet or a charlatan. The choice between apologists or apostates is a similar oversimplification that misses important nuances in the experience of many Mormon intellectuals. For this reason, I drew on my and Daryl's use of a continuum rather than a dichotomy to underscore the complexities confronting intellectuals as they negotiate their personal identities in relation to Mormonism—a Mormonism they have embraced or constructed. I suspect that today O'Dea would acknowledge a maturation of Mormonism, which he in fact anticipated, that would lead him to expect the more nuanced positions of contemporary Mormon intellectuals. Furthermore, this is consistent with his fundamental point that Mormonism, at the time he wrote, had succeeded because of its capacity to adapt creatively to its natural and social environment.

And his emphasis on adaptation may be the basis for explaining theological developments that he would find inimical to the "traditional" Mormonism he had described. Though not logically consistent, it was loosely coherent. This was the theology that he suspected left no room for a philosophy that might render it more consistent. As stated above, he may well have reconsidered his judgment following the subsequent work of Sterling McMurrin and his successors. But this is speculation on my part. Though O'Dea's adaptation hypothesis could explain the spread, if not the origin, of the neoorthodox movement, the shift toward a Calvinist version of salvation by grace alone envisioned by Mouw and Millet would surprise O'Dea, who saw Mormonism at its core to be rebellion against Calvinism. Should the neoorthodox movement continue with the momentum it now enjoys, the real question, which is also at the heart of Armand L. Mauss's retrenchment hypothesis (1994), becomes what remains to define Mormon distinctiveness. Will it be something significant or merely trivial?

Notes

1. My original thesis proposal was titled "The Mormon Intellectual and the Church," but the hearing, which lasted for more than two hours, did not get beyond the first paragraph. In fact, most of the time revolved around an apparent oxymoron in the title. Could one be an intellectual and a Mormon? Without clear approval, I moved on to a thesis examining a new theological movement that I called "Mormon neo-orthodoxy." For helpful comments I would like to thank Jonathan Eastwood, Harvey Markowitz, Kenneth Westhues, Brent White, and Daryl White.

2. No technical distinction between clergy and laity obtains for Mormons. There is no professional clergy with formal education required for ordination, salary for ecclesiastical office, or a distinct way of life. Latter-day Saints do have an extensive lay priesthood that worthy males enter at age twelve, and ecclesiastical offices are held by individuals chosen from the lay priesthood. Even top officials, known as General Authorities (First Presidency, Council of the Twelve Apostles, and so on) who are salaried, full-time employees, have no professional theological training.

3. Informal discussion groups where people meet to talk about various matters are quite pervasive among Latter-day Saints. During the summer of 1950, O'Dea was invited to participate in a group of graduate students and faculty, primarily from the University of Utah, though including Wilford Poulsen and Parley Christiansen from BYU, where papers were presented and various issues discussed. After several sessions, O'Dea learned that the group was known as the "Swearing Elders," apparently so dubbed by Lowry Nelson.

4. There have been a few attempts to distinguish among various types of Mormon intellectuals. E. E. Ericksen, for instance, spoke primarily of three types: "apologists," who were aggressive defenders of the faith, at least in terms of Mormon values; the "sophisticated, who call attention to the mythology"; and "evasive intellectuals," who were unwilling to acknowledge their real positions. "To paraphrase the apostle Paul," he said, "we have these three, and the worst of these is the evader." Presumably, they also were the most pervasive (O'Dea n.d., "Private Seminar...," box 5, file 7). A very popular dichotomy appears in Richard Poll's use of "Iron Rod" and "Liahona" orientations toward religious text and practice (1967). Using metaphors borrowed from the Book of Mormon, Poll's distinction is primarily between literal (Iron Rod) and nonliteral (Liahona) orientations toward texts and strict versus liberal forms of religious practice. It is not unusual for Mormons communicating with one another to use these categories.

Recently, Kevin L. Barney (2000), in a classification of Mormon scholars in terms of their orientation toward authorship of the Pentateuch—specifically, acceptance of the "Documentary Hypothesis" assuming multiple authorship—offered a classificatory scheme that could easily be broadened to include more general intellectual orientations. As is, he extends Philip L. Barlow's categories (1991, chap. 4) regarding positions toward higher criticism from liberal, centrist, and conservative to include a distinction between secularist and supernaturalist and finally, beyond that, scholarly and traditional. Within these categories, he introduces two subcategories, generating a possibility of six different positions. One and two fall within liberal, secularist, and scholarly; three and four within centrist, secularist, and scholarly; and five and six within conservative, supernaturalist, and traditional. Whereas Joseph Fielding Smith is placed in category six, Barney correctly locates me in category one. Category one is at the apostate end of our continuum, and six is clearly at the apologetic end. Not necessarily referring to intellectuals, though many would be included because of their marginal status, Armand L. Mauss (1998) has identified whistle-blowers, defectors, and apostates as three forms of disaffiliation from Mormonism.

    5. There are some apologists who come into conflict with institutional authority and the broader Mormon community, but they do not fall at the farthest end of the continuum. Some neoorthodox theologians, whose conflicts apparently have more to do with authority than doctrine, have experienced censure and even excommunication. Since they tend to introduce novel interpretations of doctrine rather than defending the faith in ways church officials and many Latter-day Saints would recognize as orthodox Mormonism, they would not fall at the far end of the apologist side of the continuum. However, they insist on their representation as the authentic Mormon position.

    6. This position is easy to adopt because of certain conceptions of social science. For instance, the sharp separation of the functions of religious beliefs and practices in the sociology of religion from their implications for truth claims enables many people to avoid serious reflection on the latter. The idea that science, including social science, cannot answer questions of ultimate reality functions itself as a belief, shielding many from serious consideration of implications following from social science research for ontological and epistemological questions. Social science becomes a way of understanding group relations, socialization processes, acculturation, and so on that is useful for more effective recruitment, retention, and control, without raising questions about the institution or theology.

    7. Jack White, a social psychologist who worked on the classic Robber's Cave experiment with Muzafer Sherif, was on the psychology faculty at the University of Utah for a number of years. He would occasionally observe that two types of people could not leave Utah. The first were Mormons who could not live in a pluralist environment where Mormonism was not dominant, and the second were the anti-Mormons whose hostility was so intense that they required an audience preoccupied with Mormonism for their lives to be meaningful. For stories of "career apostates," see Mauss (1998, 62–64) on Ex-Mormons for Jesus and Foster (1984, 1994) on the Lighthouse Ministry of Jerald and Sandra Tanner.

REFERENCES

Albrecht, Stan L., and Tim B. Heaton. 1984. "Secularization, Higher Education, and
    Religiosity." *Review of Religious Research* 26, no. 1 (September): 43–58.
Allred, Janice. 1994. "Toward a Mormon Theology of God the Mother." *Dialogue: A Journal
    of Mormon Thought* 27, no. 1 (Spring): 15–39.

Bailey, David H. 2000. "Mormonism and the Idea of Progress." *Dialogue: A Journal of Mormon Thought* 33, no. 4 (Winter): 69–82.

———. 2004. "Mormons and the Omnis: The Dangers of Theological Speculation." *Dialogue: A Journal of Mormon Thought* 37, no. 3 (Fall): 29–48.

Barlow, Philip L. 1991. *Mormons and the Bible: The Place of the Latter-day Saints in American Religion.* New York: Oxford University Press.

Barney, Kevin L. 2000. "Reflections on the Documentary Hypothesis." *Dialogue: A Journal of Mormon Thought* 33, no. 1 (Spring): 57–99.

Berger, Peter L. 1967. *The Sacred Canopy: Elements of a Sociological Theory of Religion.* Garden City, N.Y.: Doubleday.

Blomberg, Craig L., and Stephen E. Robinson. 1997. *How Wide the Divide? A Mormon and an Evangelical in Conversation.* Downers Grove, Ill.: InterVarsity Press.

Bloom, Harold. 1992. *The American Religion: The Emergence of a Post-Christian Nation.* New York: Simon and Schuster.

Booth, Wayne C. 1998. "Confessions of an Aging, Hypocritical Ex-missionary." *Sunstone* 21, no. 1 (March): 25–36.

———. 1999. "Do What Is Right, Let the Consequences Follow: Contrasting Messages in Mormon Hymns." *Sunstone* 22, no. 1 (March–April): 50–63.

———. 2006. *My Many Selves: The Quest for a Plausible Harmony.* Logan: Utah State University Press.

Bush, Lester. 1973. "Mormonism's Negro Doctrine: An Historical Overview." *Dialogue: A Journal of Mormon Thought* 8, no. 1 (Spring): 11–66.

———. 1999. "Writing 'Mormonism's Negro Doctrine: An Historical Overview (1973)': Context and Reflections, 1998." *Journal of Mormon History* 25, no. 1: 229–71.

Coe, Michael. 1973. "Mormons and Archaeology: An Outside View." *Dialogue: A Journal of Mormon Thought* 8, no. 2 (Summer): 107–17.

Davies, Douglas. 2003. *An Introduction to Mormonism.* Cambridge: Cambridge University Press.

Dolgin, Janet L. 1976. "Latter-day Sense and Substance." In *Religious Movements in Contemporary America,* ed. Irving Zaretsky and Mark P. Leone, 519–46. Princeton: Princeton University Press.

Duffy, John-Charles. 2005. "The New Missionary Discussions and the Future of Correlation." *Sunstone,* no. 138 (September): 28–45.

Edwards, Paul M. 1980. "Persistences That Differ: Comments on the Doctrine of Man." *Sunstone* (September–October): 44–49.

———. 1984. *Preface to Faith: A Philosophical Inquiry into RLDS Beliefs.* Salt Lake City: Signature Books.

Erikson, Erik. 1958. *Young Man Luther: A Study in Psychoanalysis and History.* New York: W. W. Norton.

———. 1968. *Identity: Youth and Crisis.* New York: W. W. Norton.

Foster, Larry. 1984. "Career Apostates: Reflections on the Works of Jerald and Sandra Tanner." *Dialogue: A Journal of Mormon Thought* 17, no. 2 (Summer): 35–60.

———. 1994. "'Apostate Believers': Jerald and Sandra Tanner's Encounter with Mormon History." In *Differing Visions: Dissenters in Mormon History*, ed. Roger D. Launius and Linda Thatcher, 343–65. Urbana: University of Illinois Press.

Gewertz, Ken. 2006. "Two University Professors Appointed: Laurel Ulrich and Peter Galison Recognized as 'Individuals of Distinction.'" *Harvard University Gazette*, January 24.

Golden, Daniel. 2006. "In Religion Studies, Universities Bend to Views of Faithful." *Wall Street Journal*, April 6, A1.

Hanks, Maxine, ed. 1992. *Women and Authority: Re-emerging Mormon Feminism*. Salt Lake City: Signature Books.

Hardy, Kenneth R. 1974. "Social Origins of American Scientists and Scholars." *Science* 185: 497–506.

Harris, Kristine Haglund. 2004. "'Who Shall Sing If Not the Children?': Primary Songbooks, 1880–1989." *Dialogue: A Journal of Mormon Thought* 37, no. 4 (Winter): 90–127.

Hatch, Nathan O. 1989. *The Democratization of American Christianity*. New Haven: Yale University Press.

Leone, Mark P. 1976. "The Economic Basis for the Evolution of the Mormon Religion." In *Religious Movements in Contemporary America*, ed. Irving Zaretsky and Mark P. Leone, 722–66. Princeton: Princeton University Press.

———. 1979. *The Roots of Modern Mormonism*. Cambridge: Harvard University Press.

Mauss, Armand L. 1994. *The Angel and the Beehive: The Mormon Struggle with Assimilation*. Urbana: University of Illinois Press.

———. 1998. "Apostasy and the Management of Spoiled Identity." In *The Politics of Religious Apostasy: The Role of Apostates in the Transformation of Religious Movements*, ed. David G. Bromley, 51–73. Westport, Conn.: Praeger.

McMurrin, Sterling M. 1959. *The Philosophical Foundations of Mormon Theology*. Salt Lake City: University of Utah Press.

———. 1965. *The Theological Foundations of the Mormon Religion*. Salt Lake City: University of Utah Press.

Merrill, Ray M., Joseph L. Lyon, and William J. Jensen. 2003. "Lack of a Secularizing Influence of Education on Religious Activity and Parity among Mormons." *Journal for the Scientific Study of Religion* 4, no. 1 (March): 113–24.

Metcalfe, Bruce L., ed. 1993. *New Approaches to the Book of Mormon: Explorations in Critical Methodology*. Salt Lake City: Signature Books.

Millet, Robert L. 1989. "Joseph Smith and Modern Mormonism: Orthodoxy, Neo-orthodoxy, Tension, and Tradition." *BYU Studies* 29, no. 3: 49–68.

———. 1998. *The Mormon Faith: A New Look at Christianity*. Salt Lake City: Deseret Book.

———. 2005. *A Different Jesus? The Christ of the Latter-day Saints.* Grand Rapids, Mich.: Eerdmans Publishing.

Mouw, Richard J. 1991. "Evangelical Mormonism?" *Christianity Today* 35, no. 13 (November 11): 30.

———. 2004a. "Opening Remarks, Mormon Tabernacle, Salt Lake City, UT, November 14." http://en.wikipedia.org/wiki/Richard_Mouw.

———. 2004b. "Response to Criticism of Richard Mouw." http://en.wikipedia.org/wiki/Richard_Mouw.

———. 2004c. "Response to Criticism of Richard Mouw, Dear Greg." http://en.wikipedia.org/wiki/Richard_Mouw.

Norman, Keith E. 1985. "Toward a Mormon Christology." *Sunstone* 10 (April): 19–25.

———. 2001. "Taking Up the Cross." *Dialogue: A Journal of Mormon Thought* 34, nos. 3–4 (Fall–Winter): 188–92.

O'Dea, Thomas F. 1957a. *American Catholic Dilemma: An Inquiry into the Intellectual Life.* Reprint, New York: Mentor, 1962.

———. 1957b. *The Mormons.* Chicago: University of Chicago Press.

———. 1966. Foreword to *Desert Saints: The Mormon Frontier in Utah,* by Nels Anderson, ix–xx. Chicago: University of Chicago Press.

———. 1972. "Sources of Strain in Mormon History Reconsidered." In *Mormonism and American History,* ed. Marvin S. Hill and James B. Allen, 147–67. New York: Harper and Row.

———. n.d. Papers. Mss. 1417. Special Collections, Harold B. Lee Library, Brigham Young University, Provo.

Ostler, Blake T. 1984. "The Mormon Concept of God." *Dialogue: A Journal of Mormon Thought* 17, no. 2 (Summer): 65–93.

———. 2002. *Exploring Mormon Thought.* Vol. 1, *The Attributes of God.* Salt Lake City: Gregg Kofford Books.

Ostling, Richard N., and Joan K. Ostling. 1999. *Mormon America: The Power and the Promise.* New York: HarperCollins.

Pace, David G. 1998. "After the Second Fall: A Personal Journey toward Ethnic Mormonism." *Dialogue: A Journal of Mormon Thought* 31, no. 1 (Spring): 85–95.

Peterson, Levi S. 1994. "The Art of Dissent among the Mormons." *Sunstone* 16, no. 8: 33–39.

Poll, Richard D. 1967. "What the Church Means to People Like Me." *Dialogue: A Journal of Mormon Thought* 2, no. 4 (Winter): 107–17.

Potter, R. Dennis. 2000. "Finitism and the Problem of Evil." *Dialogue: A Journal of Mormon Thought* 33, no. 4 (Winter): 83–95.

Quinn, D. Michael. 1987. *Early Mormonism and the Magic World View.* Salt Lake City: Signature Books.

———. 1994. *The Mormon Hierarchy: Origins of Power.* Salt Lake City: Signature Books.

———. 1995. "The Rest Is History." *Sunstone* 18, no. 3: 50–57.

Robson, Kent. 1980. "Time and Omniscience in Mormon Theology." *Sunstone* 5 (May–June): 17–23.

———. 1982. "The Foundations of Freedom in Mormon Thought." *Sunstone* 7 (September–October): 51–54.

———. 1983. "Omnis on the Horizon." *Sunstone* 8 (July–August): 21–23.

Ross, Floyd M. 1982. "Process Philosophy and Mormon Theology." *Sunstone* 7 (January–February): 16–27.

Sears, L. Rex. 1998. "Determinist Mansions in the Mormon House." *Dialogue: A Journal of Mormon Thought* 31, no. 4 (Winter): 115–41.

———. 2000. "Philosophical Christian Apology Meets 'Rational' Mormon Theology." *Dialogue: A Journal of Mormon Thought* 33, no. 3 (Fall): 67–95.

Shepherd, Gordon, and Gary Shepherd. 1984. *A Kingdom Transformed: Themes in the Development of Mormonism.* Salt Lake City: University of Utah Press.

Sherlock, Richard, and Jeffery E. Keller. 1993. "The B. H. Roberts/Joseph Fielding Smith/James E. Talmage Affair." In *The Search for Harmony: Essays on Science and Mormonism,* ed. Gene A. Sessions and Craig J. Oberg, 93–115. Salt Lake City: Signature Books.

Shipps, Jan. 1984. *Mormonism: The Story of a New Religious Tradition.* Urbana: University of Illinois Press.

———. 2000. *Sojourner in the Promised Land: Forty Years among the Mormons.* Urbana: University of Illinois Press.

———. 2005. "Signifying Sainthood, 1830–2001." In *The Collected Leonard J. Arrington Mormon History Lectures,* 155–81, 267–70. Logan: Special Collections and Archives, Utah State University.

Smith, Joseph. 1938. "King Follett Discourse." In *Teachings of the Prophet Joseph Smith,* ed. Joseph Fielding Smith Jr., 342–62. Salt Lake City: Deseret News Press.

Stack, Peggy Fletcher. 1998. "Hinckley on Polygamy: 'I Condemn It.'" *Salt Lake Tribune,* September 9, A1+.

Stark, Rodney. 1984. "The Rise of a New World Faith." *Review of Religious Research* 26: 18–27.

Thorndike, E. L. 1943. "The Origins of Superior Men." *Scientific Monthly* 56 (May): 424–32.

Tickemeyer, Garland E. 1984. "Joseph Smith and Process Theology." *Dialogue: A Journal of Mormon Thought* 17, no. 3 (Autumn): 75–85.

Tolman, David O. 2003a. "Response." *Dialogue: A Journal of Mormon Thought* 36, no. 1 (Spring): 126–30.

———. 2003b. "Search for an Epistemology: Three Views of Science and Religion." *Dialogue: A Journal of Mormon Thought* 36, no. 1 (Spring): 89–108.

Toscano, Margaret, and Paul Toscano. 1990. *Strangers in Paradox: Explorations in Mormon Theology.* Salt Lake City: Signature Books.

Ulrich, Laurel Thatcher. 1993. "An Epiphany in a Broom Closet." *Weber Studies* 10, no. 3 (Winter): 26–42.

———. 2002. "A Pail of Cream." *Journal of American History* 89, no. 1 (June): 43–47.

Waterman, Bryan, and Brian Kagel. 1998. *The Lord's University: Freedom and Authority at BYU.* Salt Lake City: Signature Books.

White, Daryl, and O. Kendall White Jr. 1996. "Charisma, Structure, and Contested Authority: The Social Construction of Authenticity in Mormonism." In *Religion and the Social Order: The Issue of Authenticity in the Study of Religions,* ed. David G. Bromley and Lewis F. Carter, 6:93–112. Greenwich, Conn.: JAI Press.

———. 1999. "Mormonism and Homosexuality: A Historical Overview." In *Anticipating the End: The Experiences of the Nineties; Proceedings of the 1999 Virginia Humanities Conference,* ed. Susan Blair Green, 109–20. Staunton, Va.: Mary Baldwin College.

White, O. Kendall, Jr. 1969. "Mormonism: A Nineteenth-Century Heresy." *Journal of Religious Thought* 26 (Spring–Summer): 44–55.

———. 1970. "The Transformation of Mormon Theology." *Dialogue: A Journal of Mormon Thought* 5, no. 2 (Summer): 9–27.

———. 1987. *Mormon Neo-orthodoxy: A Crisis Theology.* Salt Lake City: Signature Books.

———. 1995. "The Church and the Community: Personal Reflections on Mormon Intellectual Life." *Dialogue: A Journal of Mormon Thought* 28, no. 2 (Summer): 83–91.

White, O. Kendall, Jr., and Daryl White. 1981. "A Critique of Leone and Dolgin's Application of Bellah's Evolutionary Model to Mormonism." *Review of Religious Research* 23 (September): 39–53.

———. 1998. "Metaphysics, Epistemology, and the Pursuit of Truth in Traditional Mormon Theology." *Virginia Social Science Journal* 33 (Winter): 1–14.

———. 1999. "A Conceptual Framework for Understanding the Identities of Mormon Intellectuals." Paper presented at the British Sociological Association, Sociology of Religion Study Group, University of Durham, Durham, England, April 7–10.

———. 2004a. "Ecclesiastical Polity and the Challenge of Homosexuality: Two Cases of Divergence within the Mormon Tradition." *Dialogue: A Journal of Mormon Thought* 37, no. 4 (Winter): 67–89.

———. 2004b. "Ecclesiastical Power and the Elimination of Professors at Brigham Young University." In *Workplace Mobbing in Academe: Reports from Twenty Universities,* ed. Kenneth Westhues, 75–97. Lewiston, N.Y.: Edwin Mellen Press.

———. 2005. "Polygamy and Mormon Identity." *Journal of American Culture* 28, no. 2 (June): 165–77.

Wilcox, Linda P. 1980. "The Concept of a Mother in Heaven." *Sunstone* 5 (September–October): 9–15.

Williams, Troy. 2001. "Faith in Exile: Mormon Identity and the Excommunicated." *Salt Lake City Event Weekly,* August 16.

Wilson, Robin. 2006. "A Well-Behaved Scholar Makes History: How a Quiet Professor Became an Unlikely Hero for Feminists." *Chronicle of Higher Education* 24 (January): A12+.

3

Mastery and Mystery

~ Douglas J. Davies ~

Mastery and mystery are, as this chapter argues, the most significant of several coupled concepts employed by O'Dea in *The Mormons* to analyze this new movement—with all its "curious combination of typicality and peculiarity"—as an essentially American phenomenon (1957, 21). This reconsideration of O'Dea's book needs to be prefaced by the fact that my battered copy, purchased in 1969, already twelve years after its publication, was a particularly important personal acquisition because its very first sentence described my own situation: it was a study of Mormons by a non-Mormon, and I was at the very beginning of my first postgraduate research on Latter-day Saints. In this perspective it offered a rare commodity and was all the more telling for it. Returning to O'Dea with the rather unsettling wisdom of more than thirty years of hindsight, I would thank the editors "for the opportunity"—as the Saints might say—to explore once more some of O'Dea's far-reaching observations to see how they have stood the test of time.

My basic concern is with "mastery and mystery" as a highly influential pair of dominant motifs within O'Dea's descriptive-interpretative configuration of motifs by which he sought to explain the worldview of a group into which one enters as a stranger. Although, as a stand-alone volume,[1] the book says very little indeed about the methods informing that entry, its chapters on "values and social institutions" demonstrate a sociological intent, whereas others, including "The Gathering" and "Zion in the Mountains," add a historical complement. In the present chapter I reverse O'Dea's order by placing first the sharply explicit treatment of mastery-mystery that he dealt with in later chapters of his book to enable us, then, to appreciate their more implicit force in its earlier chapters. We begin with O'Dea's approach to individual and corporate values because they underlie his basic understanding of Mormonism as a developing social group. He accesses them through a sociological analysis of the social institutions of Mormonism in chapters 7–9 that effectively constitute the second half of his book where his engagement with the physical environment as an influence on

Mormon social organization becomes quite clear and enables us, in retrospect, to see why it pervades the entire volume. This is not to say that the history of American culture with all the depth of its religious, political, philosophical, and economic background is unimportant to O'Dea, far from it, for that occupies most of the earlier chapters, but it is to highlight the strong emphasis on material culture underlying and interplaying with those elements. In the present chapter I take O'Dea's mastery-mystery configuration and use it to explore a set of themes that seem central to some of his primary interests posed by Mormonism as an emergent American social phenomenon.

SELF-MASTERY

A key feature of O'Dea's interest in the emergent world of Mormonism lies in the way he deals with the longest standing of all sociological issues, namely, the relationship between the individual and society. Coming to sharpest focus in his chapter 8's prime theme of "co-operation and mastery," we might typify it as the mastery of self for others. He sees Joseph Smith as having combined two broad tendencies of western America—"hardy, self-reliant individualism" and a "friendly urge towards helpfulness"—a general combination that, later, becomes more specific in welding together a New England Protestantism and a commitment to hierarchical organization (187, 242).

For O'Dea, a major application of the combined individualism and friendly helpfulness lay in the desire to create a community-focused and -motivated economic organization broadly identifiable in the Church of Jesus Christ of Latter-day Saints' notion of a United Order. This, in turn, would respond to the Law of Consecration of 1831 and would continue to echo in Mormonism's future, even though it proved very difficult to implement and, at one point, moved Joseph to advocate "a balance or equilibrium" needed to frame decisions arrived at jointly by the bishop and the individual whose money or lands were under consideration (93). This notion of balance was a deeply held notion of the prophet and applied to many aspects of his thinking.[2] In terms of the United Order rationale it would necessitate a mastering of self for others through a curbing of selfish desire and by encouraging contributions to the well-being of other church members. Despite all, however, these particular economic ideals largely failed, meaning that this kind of self-mastery for the sake of the corporate "others," that is, for the church, failed. Though O'Dea follows others in seeing this failure as due to the Law of Consecration being enforced on people unready or ill-prepared for it, he does see in it a "creative proposal" (196), and that is highly germane because it helps highlight both the underlying significance of the idea for Joseph Smith and its role as an ideal retained by Mormonism long into the future when it was, in part, realized through the 1841 introduction of tithing, a factor of real importance within church growth and serving as its own example of self-mastery for the common good.

O'Dea's interest in mastery also appears in his treatment of Joseph's successor, Brigham Young, albeit in an indirect fashion and with some potentially negative outcomes. Indeed, to raise any theme of mastery within an essentially sociological study is, at some point, inevitably to engage with issues of power and control, and with the potentially negative employment of force, and O'Dea is, of course, keenly alert to this, as the following three examples of mastery will illustrate, one concerning polygamy, another "blood atonement," and the third an event that came to be known as the Mountain Meadows massacre.

The first expression of a negative mastery comes in O'Dea's description of when Joseph Smith came into serious disagreement over polygamy and financial issues with his associate William Law, himself a member of Joseph's First Presidency. Law's concerns, not least with polygamy, were expressed in the *Nauvoo Expositor* and caused Joseph to act with what O'Dea described as "supremely poor judgment" when he set about the destruction of the relevant printing press (66). This led to Smith's arrest, imprisonment, and, as it turned out, his murder through mob violence. O'Dea alludes to the case made by some, including the *Expositor* article, that Joseph had previously set up a Council of Fifty over which he "reigned as king." That act, or the rumor of it, would perhaps express a potentially negative expression of mastery, and one that would ill fit with the emergent LDS notion of mastery inherent in every person's agency. Certainly, Joseph's killing and the ensuing opposition that witnessed the exodus from Nauvoo in 1846 had called Mormon mastery into question. Nevertheless, O'Dea's description of that departure is of a theologically distinctive and powerfully united group whose "bitter conflict with men" would now turn to "an equally harsh struggle with elemental nature" (75). But, as I argue later, both of those endeavors were underpinned by a cosmic conquest that was, perhaps, slightly undervalued by O'Dea.

The second example of mastery that we might frame with some negative features O'Dea directly connects with Brigham Young, as one who "preached the doctrine of 'blood atonement'" (101). The essence of this teaching was that there are some sins for which divine forgiveness is not available unless the perpetrator's own blood is shed as a sin offering. Whether in terms of employing shooting as a form of capital punishment or as a general principle pertaining to a period in Utah's Mormon history, this view clearly expresses the notion of mastery over selves in ethical terms and in relation to ideas of atonement and salvation. Though blood atonement would, today, be an unusual topic of general Mormon discussion, there does exist some strong church support for "capital punishment...as an appropriate penalty for murder...but only after...lawful public trial by constitutionally authorized civil authorities" (Hinckley 1992, 255). Certainly, O'Dea regarded what came to be called the Mormon Reformation, a period in 1856–1857 when church leaders sought increased religious discipline among individual church members in Utah, as deeply engaged in issues of violence in relation to non-Mormon groups, but, more important, during which "obedience to authority became a most important mark of religious fervor" (1957, 101). Taking a cue from O'Dea, one might say that, for the future, a detailed history of "obedience" as a Mormon virtue and as part of a growing bureaucratic institution would be a valuable contribution to the sociology of Mormonism. In the 1850s context, mastery of self comes to be, more expressly than ever, aligned with the mastery of leadership, ensuring that previous ideas of the relationship between member and church would be embedded in individual agency responding to leadership directions or appeals. Here "discipline" appears as a form of mastery, more particularly the mastery of religious leaders over their membership and a desire for mastery over their enemies. The latter emerges when O'Dea includes reference to accusations of "terrorism" leveled against certain LDS individuals and groups that sought to control the seriously dissident.

This brings us to the third example of mastery that O'Dea does not directly relate to Brigham Young, though he sees both Young and other senior leaders as setting "the general atmosphere that made it possible" (103). It is that of the 1857 Mountain Meadows massacre. O'Dea is forthright in his description of "this frightful and treacherous assault" in which a company of non-Mormon and rather anti-Mormon immigrants to California passing through Mormon territory were turned on by Mormons and Native Americans and slaughtered. These were days of tense relations with federal authorities, but the mark on Mormon history had been made. O'Dea tells how one of those involved, John D. Lee, was some twenty years later brought to civil justice for this act and was "made to bear the whole guilt." O'Dea rehearses John Taylor's words that describe the event as a sacrifice brought about in "a cowardly and dastardly manner" (104). Lee's execution, on March 25, 1877, was not only exacted at the scene of the original crime but also accomplished by firing squad. Though O'Dea makes no connection between this event and Brigham's notion of blood atonement, it is not difficult to draw. Certainly, he drew attention to the long years of silence over this episode in Mormon history. One wonders how O'Dea would have responded to the fact that the *Encyclopedia of Mormonism,* itself not an official publication of the church but as much a semiofficial document as it is probably possible to be, contains not only an article on the Mountain Meadows massacre but also a photograph of John D. Lee sitting next to the coffin that would soon hold him after his execution.

One feature of that article merits attention here because it prepares the way for our later discussion of yet another kind of mastery that may be regarded as typifying Mormonism: the mastery of history. The encyclopedia entry begins not with the massacre of the 1850s, nor the execution of the 1870s, but 120 years later in September 1990 when an act of reconciliation took place at the Meadows site between descendants of some of those massacred and current LDS leaders. On that occasion, a memorial monument was unveiled by Gordon B. Hinckley, who later became president of the church. He spoke of reconciliation and the need for love and understanding "across a chasm of cankering bitterness" (Ludlow 1992, 966–68). This event demonstrates something of the way in which developing Mormon notions of history become aligned with a mastery of history but also with an awareness that negative moral features are sometimes netted in the process and require appropriate response. This kind of mastery of history also discloses a process in which Latter-day Saints engage with history in and through ritualized events. History does not remain simply textual or documentary but is enacted. In this particular case of a memorial event, late-twentieth-century Mormonism showed itself as an early example of a church seeking some form of reconciliation with an apology for relatively long-past events. Other churches have subsequently engaged in analogous acts, as with Catholicism over its persecution of some early modern scientists and Anglicanism over the slave trade.

Nature Mastery

Although such events exhibit the complexity of social life and forms of its attempted mastery, the case to which we now turn, water management, is grounded much more in the conquest of nature motivated by the need to survive. This utterly pragmatic issue of irrigation in the Utah desert influenced a great deal of O'Dea's reflection on LDS life and is expressed in his assertion that "Mormon efforts conquered hostile nature" (1957, 90). One example of its formal place in his thinking is manifest when he aligns the necessary "tightly knit social organization" developed by the Saints to achieve communal control of water with the historical examples of "the ancient empires of Egypt and Mesopotamia" (88). For him, irrigation becomes an example of that communitarian or "United Order" ethic mentioned earlier as when, for example, he notes the "hardly distinguishable" nature of early LDS water associations and emergent ward organization (201). O'Dea tells how, in 1853, the "water masters" took over from the bishops as managers of the vital water systems in Salt Lake City. The very name "water master" should not be passed over too rapidly on the assumption that it was only water that was being mastered through "disciplined co-operation." It is obvious that the notion of mastery is likely to have revealed itself at more than one level of significance, extending from pragmatic irrigation to aspects of moral, self-, and communal reflection. As O'Dea expressed it, "The conquest of the desert increased an already strong emphasis upon mastery in Mormon theology and popular awareness" (205). So basic is this that, were we to pursue this mastery theme under a different form of sociological emphasis, we might decide to speak of it in terms of the Mormon *habitus*—the embodiment of prime values expressed in distinctive cultural practices.[3] The original agrarian environment was vital for his view of an emergent LDS ethic, understood in the Weberian sense of an interplay between ideology and action and action and ideology. In what is strongly expressive of Weberian sociology O'Dea constructs a description of an orientation to the world with just that double relatedness of ideology to action and action to ideology, each in mutual reinforcement. O'Dea's acknowledgment of the Weberian scheme is firmly marked in background notes to his general account of Calvinism in chapter 1 (265n6), though it is, perhaps, the more general nature of the book that precludes its treatment in the main text when he gives a brief account of the "doctrine of evidences," the desire for signs of divine favor and thus of election among those committed to notions of predestination. In all this, as he makes clear at the close of the eighth chapter—which itself focuses so much on utilitarian aspects of irrigation and other welfare programs—the cooperative spirit of Mormons that fostered group solidarity actually constituted an "ethic of mastery for the individual" (221). And that ethic embraced not only agrarian and social pragmatics but also "the path of eternal progression."

URBAN MASTERY

Before considering that eternal path there is one aspect of O'Dea's descriptive history that merits attention given that he seems to vest no real significance in it despite its potential in relation to the notion of mastery, namely, town planning and building. It is as though the agrarian model of Utahan development takes such a priority that the ventures, contexts, and ethics that might be related to those contexts of the earlier Saints, though described in a substantial chapter called "The Gathering," are not deemed of long-term significance. O'Dea does make it clear that, in 1833, Joseph was making Kirtland "the real center of the church," and prepared a plan "for a city of twelve temples, with squared blocks, intended for a population of fifteen to twenty thousand" (43). The potential implications for a future urban Mormonism would be enormous, but O'Dea raises no such issue, perhaps because Kirtland failed, but perhaps not. What, then, of the politically enforced move to Illinois and the planning and development of Nauvoo in the period 1839–1846? This, too, might have served as a concrete expression of Mormon community building and an ideal type of urban religion, with its triple expression of civic identity and power in temple, army, and university. However, the military, in the fully legal Nauvoo Legion of which Joseph Smith was lieutenant general, more fully realized its strength than did the much more germinal "University of the City of Nauvoo" (53). The Mormon "ambition" in seeking the distinctive charter for the city along with the degree of independence gained is not difficult to interpret in terms of mastery, but, it would seem, anything like the notion of "urban mastery" did not come easily to O'Dea. This is particularly interesting given O'Dea's full accounting for the Mormon self-recognition as a people of God engaged in the "constructive activity" of building a "city of God," including his interpretation that they had taken the old Puritan values of virtue and prosperity and channeled them in "their efforts to build a city" (56). He notes this for Kirtland and for Nauvoo, emphasizing elsewhere that "for sixteen years they were driven about, attempting four times to build their holy city" (115). So it is that the notion of a "divinely appointed holy city" is rehearsed but taken very little further in terms of analysis (112). Why did he not analyze that drive for city building or the consequences of its failure more fully? What he does do is clearly identify the Nauvoo Charter as the legal expression and fulfillment of the LDS "aspiration" to "combine secession from the secular community with citizenship in the American commonwealth" (113). His agrarian focus and the mastery of nature seemed to be the story he was pressing on to tell, leaving him with as little desire to dwell on those lost cities as the Saints had time to live in them.

This fact of city making might, however, give pause for further theoretical thought, raising the wider sociological question, one also germane within the history of religions, as to the status of Mormonism as an essentially rural or urban manifestation of religion. Not least significant is the question of the context of temples. Was a temple essentially an urban phenomenon in Joseph Smith's thought? What are the implications of the notion of the potential Kirtland town plan possessing twelve temples? Would such town-block temples be, essentially, meetinghouses in the conventional sense rather than the sacred arenas for more esoteric ritual that they later came to be? This important issue cannot be investigated here and can serve only to highlight O'Dea's developing preference for the dominant agrarian model of Mormon mastery. Although it is understandable that O'Dea's thought should be marked by the dominant century of agrarianism, and that he should see mastery as typically played out in the control of water and desert, it is curious that the potential of Mormonism as an essentially urban religion was not raised or explored more fully. This is particularly so given his consideration of Mormonism's eclectic religious values, especially its appropriated sense of identity derived from biblical Israel whose promised land centered on a holy city that itself was focused on a holy temple. Indeed, his chapter "Zion in the Mountains" is entirely evocative of that association.

SOCIAL MASTERY

Still, one feature that is important for O'Dea, which underlies civic ideals and can be identified as a form of mastery, concerns the emergent Mormon community "with its own peculiar culture" (113). It would be easy to ignore this tremendously important feature of historical Mormonism precisely because it is so obvious, but it is no easy thing to attract large numbers of people together and then generate among them a sense of identity that allows ideology and practice to cohere throughout broad reaches of individual and communal life and to extend over time and place. By framing this social emergence with the idea of mastery, we are able not only to emphasize the fact of its achievement but also to see how the "mastery" theme is as dominant a feature within it as within the domains of "self," "nature," and "urban" mastery.

Although it might appear circular in argument to talk about a "community" mastering a "society," there is a difficult yet important reflexive point to be made about emergent communal dynamics and their consequence. The theoretical oddity involved in such a discussion readily leads scholars to focus more on the external factors in response to which an integrated social group is formed rather than ponder how a "society" may emerge from a collection of individuals. For O'Dea, it was the conquest of a landscape that was of paramount importance in the process of LDS social development, with the image of pioneer and settler occupying pride of place in it (1). The mastery image is crisply clear when he contrasts the Midwest, where the Mormons "were always newcomers," with the West, where they were the "first settlers and pioneers" (114).

For O'Dea, the LDS identity of settlers and pioneers is framed by their organizational rigor. His sociological perspective on Mormonism seems to find a distinctive affinity not only with the whole episode of the settlement of the Salt Lake basin symbolized in water control but also, for example, in his characterization of Brigham Young as the manager of that venture. Indeed, Young typifies that attitude to mastery that is embedded in rational control, and O'Dea certainly sees "this superb organizer" as decisively important for the survival and success of Mormonism (77). Brigham's religious nature is, similarly, accounted for in a largely rational fashion, not only in his relatively staged conversion that "rescued him from oblivion as an itinerant painter, carpenter and glazier" but also through the "clever and quiet manner" through which he achieved full status as prophet, seer, and revelator (79). Though O'Dea does, in five lines, mention what came to be called the "Day of the Prophet's Mantle," when Young gained public acclaim over Sidney Rigdon for the effective leadership of the Saints following Joseph's death, there is no emphasis on its mystical potential, a factor that has occupied numerous LDS commentators over the years (70; see, for example, Harrington 1986, 114). Here, then, Brigham Young, as a major architect and builder of agrarian Mormonism, is typified by O'Dea largely within the mastery motif and not that of mystery.

Mastery to Mystery

As indicated at the beginning of this chapter, the theme of mystery is also one of real importance to O'Dea's overall view of Mormonism. In developing this theme we are alert to the way in which the mystery motif relates to that of mastery, albeit a less dominant force in O'Dea's thought. This is reflected, for example, in the case of Brigham Young, for O'Dea is familiar with the popular tradition that ascribed at least moments of more mysterious "power" to Brigham Young, including the "heights of ecstasy" reached by some at the dedication of Kirtland's temple, though O'Dea does not dwell on it (44). Any fuller treatment would inevitably need to interpret the interplay of these features within an evaluation of how the Saints at large portrayed religious power in Young, who is often characterized as distinctively pragmatic.

PROPHETIC MASTERY-MYSTERY

This pragmatic aspect of Mormon thought is, however, often deeply aligned with the practice of religious ritual and the expression of prime religious values and cannot be easily subjected to a sharp holy-common dichotomy. With Joseph Smith's "radical repudiation of creationism" (122) and the development of his theory of matter and spirit as but differentially refined, all such sacred-profane or religious-secular dichotomies are rendered relatively redundant.

Perhaps the single most important assertion in *The Mormons* comes early in chapter 1, as O'Dea sets the religious and cultural scene out of which Mormonism grew. In approaching it we find him appreciating the four major tendencies of "sectarianism, ecumenism,[4] communitarianism and the recognition of human freedom and striving" (18) that would mark LDS life, and see him emphasizing the importance of the Book of Mormon as an influential possession for a new church. He has already described Joseph Smith's previous engagement in the "innocent occultism" of gold digging and the use of a seer stone (6) and now tells how, in the process of "miraculously" translating the text of the Book of Mormon, the first 116 pages are destroyed "in a fit of spite" by the wife of Martin Harris, Joseph's scribe. What should Joseph do in the face of such a calamity? O'Dea tells of Joseph seeking divine advice, "a solution as pregnant with possibilities as the *Book of Mormon* itself" (20), and sees a "weighty precedent" set by the resulting two revelations concerning transgression and the need to translate "other plates." And it is here that his important assertion comes: "Before latter-day scripture was quite born, latter-day revelation through the agency of a modern prophet had sprung full grown from the head of Joseph Smith" (20). Here, it seems to me, we see O'Dea begin to apply his notion of mastery to the life and endeavor of the prophet himself, for, as he puts it, "Joseph used revelation to solve problems as they arose." The solving of problems by prophecy resulted in the masterful status of being a prophet, or, to elaborate this situation, we might say that the status of prophet combined the mastery of events with the mystery of prophetic knowledge. Mastery and mystery are embodied in the prophet-founder.

CELESTIAL MASTERY-MYSTERY

Mastery continues within O'Dea's very accurate account of the content of the Book of Mormon when he identifies Arminianism as "wholeheartedly and completely" typifying the book's cyclical model of "virtue and prosperity" leading to pride, social divisiveness, divine chastisement, and repentance (27). Pressing the point, Arminianism, with its notion of freedom of religious agency, underlies the possibility of mastery in a way opposed by Calvinism, where mastery is God's alone. The religious picture of mastery that O'Dea also makes available is reinforced by his stress on the fact that Mormon enthusiasm did not take the form of overwhelming experience. Engagement with the Holy Spirit was very largely a mutual venture that left the human agent fully responsible, not least to gain as much knowledge as possible; even Mormonism's millenarianism "is calm in its hopes" (35). But mastery comes into its own when, as O'Dea expresses it, Mormonism finally "brought into existence a new American religion" (56). This took place not in the 1820s–1830s Book of Mormon and early church phase of its life but in the early 1840s with the new revelations on the spiritual nature of matter, the related notion of the physical nature of deity, and the vocation of men to become gods themselves, along with the new ceremonies that ritualized these material spiritualisms.

At the core of this new tradition, as O'Dea clearly observes, lies baptism for the dead and endowments for the dead and for the living. It is precisely within these rites that the theme of mastery becomes most clear, in relation to the topic of mystery. The way in which O'Dea deals with these rites and their import is significant. He speaks of their secrecy in terms of enhanced commitment and loyalty on the part of core members, and also of the relation of the rites to plural marriage and ideals of heavenly goals of celestial glory. What is entirely absent, however, is the issue of death itself. It is as though death was of no particular life concern to converts or, indeed, for Joseph and his own life experience. Though sensitive in my criticism of O'Dea on this feature, given that I have argued elsewhere for the deep import of death and grief in Joseph's life for his beliefs and practices on behalf of the dead (2000b, 86–104), it is curious that Mormonism's varied and intense play on issues of death and its conquest both in doctrine and in ritual practice attracted so little of O'Dea's critical analysis. Not least, perhaps, in relation to the idea that plural marriage, for example, was "for time and eternity," this very phrase providing an opportunity for pondering the theme of mastery. The mastery of death is one thing for a religion, but to set it within a mastery of time and eternity is something else. In other words, Joseph Smith and the emergent ritual Mormonism of Nauvoo take mastery into realms that wider Christian traditions had left untouched, or at least had assumed lay in the sole domain of God.

MASTERY-MYSTERY AND METAMORPHOSIS

This is where Mormonism comes to speak of eternal intelligence and its development, of self-made gods, of free will and effort, of revelation and problem solving. Here O'Dea's basic description of Mormon theology— rooted as it is in the notion of mastery and embracing mystery as it reveals the truth of the way things are—extends to issues of anthropomorphism and projection. Chapter 6, "The Values of Mormonism," begins with the ideal of the self-improvement of the common man and rapidly passes to the notion of God as a "self-made deity, who through activism and effort has achieved a relative mastery over the world": O'Dea readily employs the language of "conquest" to describe God's achievements in attaining his current status. And this is a "projection of the relation of American man to the American continent" (1957, 124). Salvation beliefs, too, depend on self-mastery, "progressive mastery" in the terms of John Widtsoe as cited by O'Dea, with the "gaining of knowledge" being essential to advanced forms of heavenly life (129). Everything that exists does so as some form of density of matter. The human venture lies in harnessing knowledge and will "in advancing man in his mastery of matter": "mastery and power are prizes to be gained"; the "challenge to active mastery" comes to lie at the heart of the Latter-day vision (132–33).

O'Dea takes this image of mastery as his basic approach to understanding the Mormon God who, like man, "is concerned with mastering" the universe. It comes into sharpest focus when he talks of how "in some way this process of external mastery either causes or parallels a continual internal metamorphosis" within God (152). O'Dea makes the point that, for him, it is "not clear why mastery and conquest should bring deification." What he does see clearly is that both God and people are engaged in a manipulative kind of mastery, an engagement of "utility" with an eternal universe that provides an ongoing opportunity for mastery and therefore for progressive development. It is in connection with both his discussion of the transcendentalism of achievement and his question of how ethics relates to its inherent "dynamic voluntarism" that we need to draw attention to an interesting absence in O'Dea's book, one that was important within Mormonism at the time when *The Mormons* was being researched and written, namely, the place of the Gethsemane event within the story of Christ's life and Mormon theology (Davies 2000a, 19–31). This needs brief consideration alongside the place of the death of Jesus within Mormon attitudes toward active life, achievement, and times of failure.

CHRIST'S MASTERY-MYSTERY

Gethsemane represents an absence of what might have been clearly expected in a study concerned with how mastery relates to salvation, for it concerns the act of atonement through Jesus as the Christ. O'Dea frequently stresses the Arminian theological tendency of Mormonism, with its powerful advocacy of human choice and endeavor. He does so with some emphasis when framing his brief account of atonement with the "extreme Arminianism" of Mormonism's roots in the "freedom of the human will" (1957, 129). In fact, the brevity of this section makes it potentially misleading. He draws primarily from John Widtsoe and simply refers to "individual salvation or rescue from the effects of personal sins [that] is to be acquired by each for himself, by faith and good works through the redemption wrought by Jesus Christ" (130). O'Dea takes this to be Mormonism both preserving and reinterpreting traditional doctrines of the Fall and Redemption. The critical distinction not explicitly made by O'Dea is that although atonement does deal with personal sins and guarantees a resurrection to all, the quality and precise heavenly location of that life will depend on the moral life lived and the nature of obedience to divine and church commandments and covenants. More significant than that even is the easy assumption that any general non-Mormon reader may make over words such as *atonement* and *redemption*. The real omission from O'Dea's account lies in the LDS stress on the encounter between Jesus and the sins of all time that took place within the garden of Gethsemane. At the time of O'Dea's writing the LDS emphasis on "the garden experience" was strong, with a corresponding underemphasis on Christ's death on the cross. The LDS rationale for that is also the reason it is odd not to find O'Dea dwelling on the issue, namely, the mastery of Christ over sins and over any self-will not to pursue the Great Plan previously agreed upon in preexistence. Arminianism, free agency, and the emphasis on human endeavor all point to and partly explain the LDS affinity with Christ's garden experience. There, it is believed, Christ so deeply and inwardly experienced the suffering caused by the sins of the world that he sweated, as it were, great drops of blood. This, we could suggest, is the archetypal moment and example of "active mastery": I have, elsewhere, described this in terms of a "pro-active Christ" (2000b, 46–52). Unlike the cross, which can be interpreted as a passive experience in which things are done to Christ, in the garden Jesus brings things upon himself. Thus is the Great Plan enacted through active obedience and self-mastery and also, it might be said, through the mystery of being able to encounter the sins of all time in and through one person's being. If, as O'Dea postulates in his tellingly subheaded section, "The Transcendentalism of Achievement," "the central implication of Mormon theology is a definition of human life as a period of advancement through mastery," then we might add that the garden experience could have served as its prototype (1957, 150). But O'Dea did not consider it.[5]

MASTERY, ETHICS, AND FAILURE

This brings us to the allied issue of O'Dea's preoccupation with LDS life and prospective deification through the human "mastery of matter," and to the "high degree of activism" enjoined upon the Saints. He takes this for granted and, though he is unsure of whatever the ultimate principle might be that ensures that activism produces divine status in the progressive development of believers, simply notes that this is what the Saints believe and how they live. The question that now arises with the wisdom of hindsight concerns the outcome of such activism. Though he does not dwell on the Weberian sociological background to his theoretical point, O'Dea makes it clear that practical activism for the Mormon means that life is "more than a vocation, more than a calling" (143), and he explores the nature of activism in work, health, education, and play. Though noting the retention of older Protestant notions of obligation to moral codes and the fact that people sin, O'Dea never raises the issue of failure. So emphatic is his stress on mastery that the state of those who fail is ignored. The nearest he comes to the topic, in no more that a few sentences, is when he observes that not all church members are active, which results in active members being overburdened with organizational duties (184). Still, this inactive-overactive dichotomy does not deal with any sense of failure.

Indeed, it is interesting to see what occupies his mind in the place where one might have expected him to treat failure, those who sense that they "have not done what we ought to have done," as the Church of England's Book of Common Prayer expresses it. At that point he moves to a brief note on a felt "need for ceremony and mystery" and mentions the emergence of temple rites, though here too he is keen to stress the Mormon classification of such rites as "work," thus maintaining the activist-mastery perspective. This is an interesting move on his part and leads him to assert that this "work" is framed by a lack of "symbolic richness" in Mormonism and, even more telling, by the assertion that "a receptive, contemplative relationship to God is not found as part of Mormon prayer and worship" (154).

To reiterate, O'Dea had not sought to discuss those Saints who may have failed in their duty or did not meet church expectations. Given the extreme stress laid on mastery, one might have anticipated some sociological attention being paid to failure in the system. How, for example, would such an ideal of mastery rebound on those who made mistakes? How might leaders respond to failure? How might they engage in pastoral care? These, perhaps, would be questions more for the future, as the church grew in numbers and asked even more of its members in maintaining and extending that organization, for they certainly became organizational issues half a century after O'Dea's work (Robinson 1992; Millet 2003). The theological ideas invoked to deal with such problems have come to include the nature of grace and religious experiences of a "conversionist" kind (Millet 1995, 33). They seem to be demanding a reframing of mastery within a more devotional and receptive attitude to God, and this may also involve a change in LDS approaches to the notion of mystery. Any serious account of such developments would have to reconsider how a Mormon "need for ceremony and mystery" might relate to a developing sense of "receptive" spirituality, and would certainly show how changing times, structures, and organization affect worldviews. And it might be that such considerations would need to ponder again the agrarian-conquest model in relation to subsequent urban-interpersonal models of life experience. Only in the later years of the twentieth century and the beginning of the twenty-first are Mormon thinkers drawing LDS theology and devotionalism back to the cross as a medium that enhances such pastorally inclined considerations.

MASTERY OF MYSTERY

Mormon thinkers are fostering a kind of reflective religion that advocates a more extensive consideration of LDS sacred texts and, along with that, a potentially more meditative form of piety. This touches directly on O'Dea, both where he talks of the absence of a "receptive, contemplative relationship to God in Mormon 'prayer and worship'" (1957, 154) and where he suggests that perhaps "the basic need of Mormonism" lies in a "search for a more contemplative understanding of the problem of God and man" (262). The latter he aligns with the development of temples in Mormonism's emergent diaspora. Since then, of course, Mormonism has grown such that more Saints now live outside North America than within its domains, and temple activity has come, increasingly, to distinguish Mormonism's core belief and inner practice, just as temple work distinguishes core members from a more peripheral membership. Genealogical research combined with temple work for the dead, for example, might now be described as integrating aspects of what we have discussed above as the mastery of history framed by mystery. The way many Mormons speak of engaging in these complementary practices exemplifies a developing sense of mystery alongside practical activities.

RATIONALITY AND MIRACLE

One of the unfortunate moves O'Dea made, in chapter 9, was to set "rationality versus charisma" as a key feature in accounting for Mormonism's encounter with modern secular thought (223). It was unfortunate because his real concern lay in the opposition between a commitment to rationality, on the one hand, and to "the miraculous," on the other. To align the miraculous with charisma was problematic because it conflated the difference between principles and persons. It would have been wiser to maintain a sharp distinction between reason and the miraculous as abstract notions and retain the idea of charisma for use with actual persons engaged in leadership and the kinds of issues he considers in chapter 7.

However, remaining with O'Dea's scheme, the theme of mastery arises within his discussion of rationality versus charisma as he describes Mormonism's "supreme confidence in man's ability to master his environment and build a good society through knowledge and effort" (225). Here we encounter O'Dea's underlying sociological grammar employed to describe how this commitment to the masterful power of education involved the "latent" and "unintended consequences" of bringing elements of secular, rational, criticism to bear on the original and, indeed, miraculous origins of the faith. As to the future of such secular influence, O'Dea is both unsure and uneasy. Would there be a "subtle secularization" or an ongoing "normalized state of crisis" and "festering discontent" for certain individuals? (232). He notes the scant evidence of his day. His ambiguity is strong, yet he ponders the view that increased higher education would be likely to bring about an infiltrated compromise between a literalist background and an intellectual appreciation of beliefs and their origins. Indeed, one is struck by O'Dea's extensive preoccupation with the issue of liberal and conservative thought within Mormonism, with his stress on education and its encounter with the problem of the group's miraculous origin. His own intellectualism and theological outlook must, it seems, have made him particularly sensitive to this issue. As to the likely trajectory of particular academic traditions within Mormonism, it would seem that he was, in many respects, wrong over his sense that philosophy was likely to be a misplaced discipline in future Mormon developments, with theology having a better chance of success within the creative thinking of appropriate intellectuals. Both have been relatively slow to develop as media in and through which to pursue Mormon thought. As has often been observed, that academic place was more often allocated to history as a medium of reflection. The nature and role of history within Mormonism are, indeed, so significant in pondering the very nature of Mormonism's self-appraisal that it is important to give them some explicit attention in and through O'Dea's motif of mastery.

MASTERY OF HISTORY

O'Dea's concern over literalism and liberalism and his notion of mastery have an obvious place in this present chapter, not least as a commentary on the place of "faithful" versus critical history within Mormon circles. Although a great deal has been written on history in Mormon culture, it is worth asking whether one reason for its dominance lies in a factor much mentioned by O'Dea, namely, the community rootedness of many Mormon historians. He often emphasizes the way in which some LDS intellectuals "testify to a strong loyalty to their own people and their own traditions" (239). Basic to those traditions is, of course, a community interest in "history." Whatever else is the case, a young Mormon emerging as an academic historian must inevitably be aware of the engagement with "history," or at least the powerful significance of the past, by his social group. For the young LDS scholar in the middle and later decades of the twentieth century, becoming a "historian" was not as strange or unacceptable an endeavor as becoming a "philosopher" or, more particularly, a "theologian." Both latter categories had, for some time, been aligned with the kind of worldly wisdom much evident and often prized in those other Christian churches that confused the teenage Joseph Smith: the substance and rationale of both philosophy and theology were to be contradicted by the divine restoration of truth and rite to the prophet. History was to be different, its authenticity accepted as and with the acceptance of Joseph as a prophet in receipt of divine revelation. But, of course, this was a very particular idea of history, one that was grounded in a faith perspective and one that differed from the value assumptions upon which canons of critical notions of history would develop. It is here that O'Dea's interest in community loyalty among scholars becomes significant because that shared sense of belonging includes a shared commitment to the faith-grounded category of "history." The obvious problem that can now so easily emerge is grounded in this diversity of meaning of the very word *history*. Within this complex field, the community meaning and the academic meaning of the word *history* differ because the purpose of the concept and the purpose of relating to that concept differ. In this context, then, it becomes appropriate to ask what it might mean to possess a mastery of history within Mormonism.

If a notion such as that of mastery is perceived to underlie a particular group's worldview, as it does in O'Dea, one expects it to be manifested throughout a group's organization and operation. That kind of assumption—of an underlying pattern of values dominant in a culture—is basic to the kind of functionalist sociology evident in O'Dea, as it is, for example, in various forms of symbolic anthropology and sociology that have, subsequently, proved useful when studying groups like the Latter-day Saints. And this includes the notion of *habitus*. What, then, of mastery and Mormon history? Certainly, in terms of the academic discipline of history it would seem that a degree of mastery has been evident over the past half century. But it is neither a simple nor a single mastery but a double and competing desire for mastery.

The first mastery relates to a folk view of history and the fact that Mormonism was born into and with a self-awareness of history. Its early message was millenarian, with an expectation of the advent of Christ to America: time and place fused in a sense of imminent significance. Then the Book of Mormon showed itself to be preoccupied with presenting records and accounts of past events and of bringing them into the present through the miraculous union of the young seer with a hidden text. It continued to be absorbed by time and event, noting the dates of revelations in its Doctrine and Covenants, and even formally appointing a church historian. The church's identity came to cohere with its history. In terms of wider Christian theology, one might even say that the emergence of the text and its translation into a concrete volume symbolized and materialized the idea of the Restoration in a way that paralleled the function of the Incarnation as a doctrine in broad Catholic traditions. And here I would, very clearly, emphasize the notion of the *function* of a doctrine within a theological scheme so as not to invite the criticism of equating the content of those rather different phenomena. In other words, the Book of Mormon's "coming forth" (in LDS terminology) and the "word being made flesh" (in wider Christian theology) serve the similar function of marking a key feature of theophany. In saying this, I am aware that it is a moot point, for many LDS scholars would, I imagine, prefer to identify the first vision of Joseph as the crucial event, and it certainly is dynamically vital, but it does not result in a materialized entity available to all subsequent Saints. It exists as a story told in texts, and the Book of Mormon is a text in such a way that it manifests a mastery of history. Together, then, the first vision, Mormonism's initial Adventist spirit, and the concrete text of the Book of Mormon with its internal "history" of the past expressed a mastery of history. This would extend further to other "standard works" of the church, including the Doctrine and Covenants and, significantly, the Pearl of Great Price and the Book of Abraham.

This brings us to the second subtlety of history and mastery; it, too, is complex. At the outset it continues the previous sense of the mastery of history as the ongoing history of the church and LDS communities are written and has resulted in an immense corpus of records. This embraces the dynamic growth of genealogical records, which is its own dedicated example of "mastering" the past, but it then moves into the domain of the academic tradition of history. Indeed, the church has fostered historians who are born into and grow up in a historical medium in the way that young Catholics grow up in a strong liturgical medium, or a Protestant in a commitment to the "Word." And this is where O'Dea's concerns become evident, for critical academic history cannot be guaranteed to produce studies of the church's cultural past that are entirely in accord with official views of that past. What the church has developed, as have all churches, is a folk history. It is not the same phenomenon as a critical history. At this point the issue of "mastery" becomes highly problematic, for, as indicated, there are, as it were, two masters. The academic historian wants mastery over his data, and the church leader wants mastery over what the academic says about church "history."

This potential conflict is not unique to Mormonism, for, as O'Dea was keen to make clear, any church that fosters scholarship and praises knowledge is likely to breed intellectuals who may disagree with received traditions. In other churches it is not so much history as philosophy, theology, or textual studies that face this problem. In England, for example, theology is taught both in state universities, and therefore academically nonreligious institutions, and also in confessional theological colleges run by denominational churches. This leads to periodic discussions, debates, and even discord over just what it is that "academic theology" might be. Some favor the teaching of "religion" in state universities rather than "theology," for which a sense of commitment and church rootedness of belief are involved. In many European countries there are, by partial contrast, distinct Protestant and Catholic faculties of theology, marking the ecclesiastical differences lying behind intellectual perspectives. In the United States, too, distinctions also exist between "religion" and "theology," with the latter often restricted to confessional institutions.

This brings me to an important issue as far as history and the mastery of history in its two forms are concerned, what we might call the practice of history. This is germane in that it is absent in O'Dea's overall discussion of LDS intellectualism in relation to scholarship and church engagement. History in what an outsider non-Mormon academic might call its folk-mythological form is a "practiced" history. Here I specifically refer to LDS temple ceremonies that ritualize ideas of the past as they are presented in the Plan of Salvation. For LDS scholars who engage in these pivotal rites of salvation, it is quite understandable that their ritual experience will pervade their wider patterns of thought and appreciation of life in a way that one could not expect of a nonpractitioner. By sharp contrast, for the non-LDS scholar committed to historical scholarship, the major experiential dimension lies in research, seminars, and the like. The former conduces to a more receptive and the latter a more critical attitude of mind. What is more, the differences of experience affect the desired nature of mastery of a subject. A similar case could be made for other churches and their members whose engagement with theology as an academic discipline is also much influenced by their practice of liturgy. And that liturgical practice is very likely to be under the authoritative control of church leaders, some of whom are charismatic and whose charisma can help frame or catalyze the mysterious nature of liturgy, worship, and devotion that almost always involves degrees of self-transcendence not readily subsumed into rational categories and has its own effect on scholar-believers.

Not all church leaders will appreciate the complex constraints inherent in the conflict of interpretations that Mormon academic historians suffer, for they are most often men whose sense of self-mastery has been formed within a church advocating self-mastery under obedience to the overall mastery of the prophet and central leadership. Here O'Dea's uniting of charisma and mastery does apply with force. Their attitude is also likely to have been forged through self-mastery that has produced successful and fruitful lives. And this is where one of the most widely transferable of O'Dea's assertions merits attention. It concerns mastery and spheres of knowledge, for O'Dea observes that Mormonism found it relatively easy to bring its sense of "rational control over nature" to bear on the domain of natural science. Extending his case, he makes a further observation: "It is a curious fact that, despite the importance of the conflict between science and religion in earlier years, today it is not physical science so much as the humanities and social sciences that seem to offer a threat to religion" (239). This is a profoundly accurate observation for most contemporary religions. Many churches often point to distinguished scientists or engineers in their midst and see in such people a kind of intellectual capital that adds to the credibility of the religion as such. Many such scientists, though sophisticated in their science, are relatively naive in terms of theology and shift easily from large scientific pictures to focused sentiments of personal piety. In more fundamentalist churches, for example, such a stance is adopted toward ideas of creation versus evolution. What are often entirely ignored in those debates are not the scientific issues of genetics and the fossil profile of change—they certainly receive a great deal of detailed treatment—but the far more sub-stantial issues of, for example, the nature of the book of Genesis and other biblical texts as literary and religious material, most especially as myth set amid other ancient Near Eastern myth and the very nature of the develop-ment of theological ideas. Very few scientists have the detailed knowledge, or sometimes the personal desire, to devote to the history of interpretation of scripture and the theological traditions framing that interpretation to make sense of it all. It is just such issues that underpin O'Dea's rather heavy emphasis on the paradoxical and strained position of intellectuals within the Mormon Church. I hope that by rehearsing these well-known issues in relation to O'Dea's notion of mastery, some further point may be seen in it.

PROBLEMATIC CONSEQUENCES

I noted when beginning this chapter that O'Dea regularly employs paired opposites as categories within various arguments, and this becomes ex-tremely forceful in chapter 9 when he sets "authority and obedience versus democracy and individualism" (242). His explicit reason for doing so was that he thought Mormonism had acquired a variety of essentially contradic-tory values from its environment, as with a basic New England Protestant-ism favoring a strongly motivated individualism that, in relation to a strong hierarchical organization, would become a source of "strain" (242). This strain can, however, be approached in another way, through the notion of mastery, for individualism demands mastery of self, whereas authoritarian control of an organization demands mastery of a group. If such an underly-ing commitment to mastery is, essentially, the driving factor, that might help explain why a degree of accommodation between "these two tenden-cies has worked well enough" (243). O'Dea finds it necessary to employ an-other opposition, that of "consent versus coercion," when discussing polit-ical forces employed by Mormons, and he brings into that discussion the notion of "obedience." This is perfectly acceptable as far as it goes, but, per-haps, he does not take it far enough.

One way of going further is to suggest that obedience is, in effect, but another facet of mastery. Though this may, at first sight, appear paradoxi-cal, it may not be. O'Dea's preference for organizing his material through dichotomies leads to issues that need not arise if one ponders the opposed factors as expressions of an underlying phenomenon. And here I think mas-tery might constitute just such a fundament: mastery of self may readily involve the desire for a group within which the self is structured for mastery. If that is accepted, one no longer needs to structure an argument in terms of loyalty to a leader, necessitating a denial of individualism. O'Dea finds that he has to speak of "passive loyalty" (244), in so doing acknowledging that Mormon polity resembles "all leadership and government." I am not sure that this is necessary or even consistent with the image of the Mormon self and society that he otherwise details and explicitly describes as largely existing in a "favorable balance" (245). If we accept that the model of mastery that O'Dea goes so far to establish may be pressed further than he himself does, then we are better able to interpret the emergent Mormon self as self-consistent whether in its implementation of personal discipline or when it acts collaboratively and in response to prophetic leadership. If this is the case, it will require a rethinking of the many contexts in which "obedience" in a Mormon context is understood in the ordinary sense of that term as the act of an inferior before a superior.

But did Mormons conceive of themselves as such masters and servants? I think not. If one thinks of "obedience" as self-mastery, then individuals express themselves as authentically when acting in response to prophetic leadership as when ruling their personal or family life. And that self-directedness is precisely what underlay the strongly emphasized LDS notion of agency. This perspective then changes the inherent notion of concepts such as "loyalty." What is more, if one were to accept this obedience-mastery view, then the nature of the relationship between mastery and mystery will take on a new significance and allow the notion of obedience to be pervaded by the force of Mormonism's developing secret rites. Mormon mastery has, ultimately, to do with the eternal future of Saints as emergent deities, and that certainly includes a sense of mystery, not least engendered through temple rites that, perhaps, became more reflective in the half century after O'Dea wrote. The nature of a "god in embryo" is more consonant with mastery than slavish obedience and with mystery than any sense of pure pragmatic ritual might imply. Such a perspective is also of real value when interpreting male-female equality than is any subservient model of "obedience."

With that in mind, it is interesting that, as one might expect, O'Dea deals with this equality more descriptively than interpretively. I may be pressing the point too far, but it is worth suggesting because it raises the theoretical issue of the way in which sociological analysis should or should not employ the values of a group when seeking to interpret that group's thought and practice.[6] It also shows that O'Dea's view of the Mormons at large combined description and interpretation in such a way that, fifty years on, it still provides material for reanalysis and issues for theoretical reconsideration.

NOTES

1. Here I treat *The Mormons* as a discrete volume without contextualizing it amid his other works.

2. Such "balance" expresses the importance of what I have described elsewhere as the "relations and principles" that underlay much of Joseph Smith's thought (Davies 2003).

3. *Habitus* is a notion that runs sociologically from Max Weber. Though intrinsically aligned with "character formation and the moral life" (O'Dea 1957, 261), it also embraces the cultural expression of values embodied in stylized schemes (cf. Davies 2000b, 108–38).

4. *Ecumenism* seems an even more oddly anachronistic term to use of early-nineteenth-century Mormonism than it would of Christianity at large.

5. For future research it will be important, for example, to explore the Gethsemane episode in relation to the LDS notion of a premortal heavenly council in which Jesus emerges as the Savior figure, for structurally and symbolically these may be found to correspond to each other.

6. As in the long established notion of emic and etic categories of analysis.

REFERENCES

Arrington, Leonard J. 1986. *Brigham Young, American Moses.* Urbana: University of Illinois Press.

Davies, Douglas J. 2000a. "Gethsemane and Calvary in LDS Soteriology." *Dialogue: A Journal of Mormon Thought* 34, nos. 2–3: 19–29.

———. 2000b. *The Mormon Culture of Salvation.* Burlington, Vt.: Ashgate Publishing.

———. 2003. *An Introduction to Mormonism.* Cambridge: Cambridge University Press.

Hinckley, Stuart W. 1992. "Capital Punishment." In *Encyclopedia of Mormonism,* ed. Daniel H. Ludlow, 255. New York: Macmillan.

Ludlow, Daniel H., ed. 1992. *Encyclopedia of Mormonism.* 4 vols. New York: Macmillan.

Millet, Robert L. 1995. *Within Reach.* Salt Lake City: Deseret Book.

———. 2003. *Grace Works.* Salt Lake City: Deseret Book.

O'Dea, Thomas F. 1957. *The Mormons.* Chicago: University of Chicago Press.

Robinson, Stephen E. 1992. *Believing Christ: The Parable of the Bicycle and Other Good News.* Salt Lake City: Deseret Book.

4

"Common Sense"
Meets the Book of Mormon

Source, Substance, and Prophetic Disruption

~ Terryl L. Givens ~

Thomas O'Dea's opinion of the Book of Mormon's importance in Mormonism is evident in his choice to make it the first chapter following his introduction. He spends little more than a page summarizing the Book of Mormon before he immediately turns to the question that seems inevitably to impose itself at the forefront of so many Book of Mormon discussions: how do we explain its origin? Such a preoccupation does not self-evidently present itself; one would not expect to find, and in fact does not find, that accounts of the Qur'an, for instance, typically exhibit the felt burden of "explaining" the revelations that constitute that book of scripture. That the question arises so starkly in the case of the Book of Mormon may have to do with the striking nearness in our past of such claims to supernaturalism—"seeing visions in the age of railways!" as Charles Dickens marveled.

Even though O'Dea, like virtually all non-Mormon scholars who have tackled the subject before and since, could not bracket the problem of the book's origin, the respect and seriousness of intent he accorded Mormons and their book of scripture were certainly historic milestones. O'Dea was able to take the Book of Mormon seriously precisely because he did *not* take seriously Mormon claims of its origin. By matter-of-factly naturalizing the supernatural story of its coming forth, he could consider the problem one of simple environmental influence—a "common-sense" explanation, as he put it.

He quickly dismisses the Spaulding theory of authorship as an anti-Mormon ploy, before rejecting I. Woodbridge Riley's 1902 theory that made "bad ancestry and epilepsy" the catalysts to Smith's visions, on the charge that medical evidence is lacking for the epilepsy. Apparently, he believed dubious progenitors alone cannot account for spontaneous revelations. Instead, O'Dea follows in the track laid down by Alexander Campbell in 1831. In his rather vehement assault on the Book of Mormon, Campbell characterized the work as a mishmash of

> every error and almost every truth discussed in New York for the last ten years. He decided all the great controversies:—infant baptism, ordination, the trinity, regeneration, repentance, justification, the fall of man, the atonement, transubstantiation, fasting, penance, church government, religious experience, the call to the ministry, the general resurrection, eternal punishment, who may baptize, and even the question of free masonry, republican government and the rights of man. (1832, 85)

With heftier scholarly credentials but a like hostility to Mormonism's founder, Fawn M. Brodie employed the same approach in her influential 1945 biography.[1] She cites the above passage from Campbell approvingly, arguing that "the book can best be explained, not by Joseph's ignorance nor by his delusions, but by his responsiveness to the provincial opinions of his time." The book, she writes in terms that parallel Campbell's, is "absolutely American, . . . an obscure compound of folklore, moral platitude, mysticism, and millennialism" (69, 67). So it is that O'Dea also opts for this "simple common-sense explanation," which he attributes to Fawn M. Brodie rather than its original expositor, Campbell. His characterization of Smith's motives, however, was less hostile than either. True enough, he thinks Smith a deceiver (after slipping into the wrong tense at one point in the "translation," O'Dea writes, Smith had to scramble "to keep from exposing himself before his scribe" [1957, 40]). So it is far from clear, having stripped Smith's modus operandi of a supernatural character, exactly what O'Dea might mean by his conclusion that "an atmosphere of religious excitement led [Smith] from necromancy into revelation, from revelation to prophecy, and from prophecy to leadership of an important religious movement" (24).

It is perhaps inevitable that, bidden or unbidden, preconceptions about the origins of a book so thoroughly immersed in supernaturalism and controversy will condition the reading of the text. But by raising the question of origins at the outset, stipulating a naturalistic origin, and then defining it summatively as "an American document" "in content as well as origin" (26), O'Dea (like Brodie) has transformed his whole enterprise in this chapter into an elaboration of, and only of, those Book of Mormon themes that correspond to religious and political concerns of early-nineteenth-century New York. This is lamentable. Not because supernatural origins are precluded, but because such reductionism impoverishes the text and one's openness to any mystery or surprises it may have yielded under a less constraining paradigm. This is apparent when one considers how robbed one would feel if an otherwise perceptive and astute critic were to apply the same method to *Hamlet*. What would be lost in proving its "origins and content" are comprehended through the "simple common-sense explanation" of its being an Elizabethan document that in a straightforward, unproblematic manner reflects religious and political ideas swirling about in early-seventeenth-century England?

So also is it too simple to call the Book of Mormon "obviously an American work growing in the soil of American concerns" in terms of its "plot" and "patriotism" and "conception of government" (32, 34). Richard Bushman, writing in 1976, argues convincingly that any alleged correspondence between the Book of Mormon themes and nineteenth-century American political culture, though superficially appealing, collapses upon inspection. He locates in political literature of the 1820s three "of the most obvious contemporaneous ideas about government and the American Revolution": revolution as heroic resistance to tyranny, the stimulus of enlightened ideas about human rights, and the merits of (largely Lockean) constitutional principles. The Book of Mormon text, he demonstrates,

> was an anomaly on the political scene of 1830. Instead of heroically resisting despots, the people of God fled their oppressors and credited God alone with deliverance. Instead of enlightened people overthrowing their kings in defense of their natural rights, the common people repeatedly raised up kings, and the prophets and the kings themselves had to persuade the people of the inexpediency of monarchy. Despite Mosiah's reforms, Nephite government persisted in monarchical practices, with life tenure for the chief Judges, hereditary succession, and the combination of all functions in one official.

"In view of all this," he concludes, "the Book of Mormon could be pictured as a bizarre creation, a book strangely distant from the time and place of its publication" (17–18).

Even among non-Mormon readers of the text, no consensus has emerged on the question of the Book of Mormon's relationship to Smith's environment. Some critics have continued to ferret out connections to contemporary issues—but they at times see diametrically opposed influences. Like Campbell and Brodie, more recent scholars have drawn attention to the book's engagement with theological issues of contemporary relevance.

Ironically, O'Dea thought it patently obvious that "the doctrine of the book is wholeheartedly and completely Arminian" (1957, 28), whereas Marvin S. Hill follows Brodie in writing, "Theologically the Book of Mormon was a mediating text standing between orthodox Calvinists and emerging Arminians," and he points to "passages which are strongly anti-Universalist" as evidence of "the Calvinistic inclinations in the text" (1989, 21). Even Mormon scholar Thomas G. Alexander agrees in an influential 1980 essay that the Book of Mormon betrays a "pessimistic" assessment of human nature that Smith only gradually moved beyond (24–33). Echoing this appraisal of the Book of Mormon's purported Calvinism, one scholar contrasts it with the radical humanism of Smith's later preaching and asks, referring to a sermon expounding the doctrine of theosis, "Was the Book of Mormon Buried with King Follett?" The same scholar insists that "while human beings are, as some Mormons are fond of repeating, 'gods in embryo' in the sense that they are the spirit offspring of a divine being, the Book of Mormon teaches that humans are also devils in embryo in the sense that, without a savior, they would naturally devolve into diabolical, not divine, beings" (Voros 1987, 15–18). Community of Christ scholar A. Bruce Lindgren cites Helaman 12:4–7, referring to human foolishness, vanity, evil, and "nothingness," as further proof that the book is "pessimistic about human nature" (1986; see also 1983).

Jon Butler, in a different vein, explores frontier cultural continuities with Alma 36. In this conversion narrative, Alma the Younger lapses into three days of unconsciousness, only to be restored three days later, spiritually reborn of God through the mercy of Jesus Christ. Butler writes that "during Methodist 'love-feasts,' some participants fainted." In one recorded case, a man "'continued so long, that his flesh grew cold.'…But the man did not die and, like others, was physically revived and spiritually reborn. 'He began to praise God for what he had done for his soul'" (1992, 240). O'Dea likewise notes similarities to the "dignified revivalism of New England" (1957, 28, 40). Other parallels that continue to emerge in environmental discussions include nineteenth-century antimasonry and anti-Catholicism.

The author's view of human nature is not the only point of controversy among theorists of the Book of Mormon's origins. Alexander Campbell was absolutely confident in asserting that "there never was a book more evidently written by one set of fingers" (1831, 93).[2] Philastus Hurlbut and Eber D. Howe propounded in 1833 that the real author was Solomon Spaulding, whose manuscript Sidney Rigdon reworked with Joseph Smith.[3] "The book of Mormon is a bungling and stupid production" ("The Mormons" 1840, 1), wrote one journalist, a "farrago of balderdash," decreed Edmund Wilson

(De Voto 1930, 5; Wilson 1985, 275). Critics have "failed to note the intellectuality of the Book of Mormon," and "there are places where the Book of Mormon rises to impressive heights," complains O'Dea, again following Brodie (1957, 30, 37).[4] Clearly, O'Dea's treatment, although it represented progress in its tone, enhanced our understanding of the Book of Mormon very little, by remaining within the narrow constraints of a facile environmentalism.

Recognizing the ultimate insufficiency of cultural influences to account for the Book of Mormon taken as a whole, an intrigued observer such as Harold Bloom, perhaps the most famous contemporary (non-Mormon) admirer of Joseph Smith, refers to the prophet as an "authentic religious genius" (1992, 80). Many Mormons would be happy for the compliment. Such a tribute, however, as foremost historian of Mormonism Richard Bushman realizes, is still just another kind of intellectual failure to come to terms with the golden bible. "Genius, by common admission, carries human achievement beyond the limits of simple historical explanation, just as revelation does. To say that the Book of Mormon could only be written by a genius is logically not much different from saying God revealed it. In both cases, we admit that historical analysis fails us" (1996, 69).[5]

At the same time, Bloom does move us beyond the confines of environmentalism, by at least acknowledging there is more here than can be dispatched of by a glance at the Manchester Library holdings. Although he seems more intrigued by the writing Smith later produced purporting to be the "Book of Abraham" than in the Book of Mormon, Bloom (1992) was himself impressed by Smith's uncanny ability to tie into occult and kabbalistic traditions, with no vehicle of transmission apparent—or even plausible—in the immediate cultural context. Other scholars have also, moving beyond Bushman, argued for connections to sources and ideas that are "strangely distant" from, rather than contiguous with, New York folk culture and proximate religious currents. Expanding the search from Smith's neighborhood to the entire Western occult tradition, John Brooke has gone further afield than most in his search for influences and sources. As one review fairly characterizes his study,

> Brooke attempts to find hermeticism, Freemasonry, and alchemy in the translation process and text of the Book of Mormon. Brooke searches for any and every thought or act of Joseph Smith and other early Mormons that he can see as related—however vaguely—to hermetic, Masonic, alchemical, or other occultic ideas. He first focuses on ideas of priesthood, mysteries, temples, cosmology, and preexistence.... Joseph's marriage, sex

life, and plural marriages are seen as "replicat[ing] the hermetic concept of conjunctio, the alchemical marriage." (Hamblin, Peterson, and Mitton 1994, 8)

Brooks concedes that the question of how these elements might have been conveyed from "late-sixteenth-century Europe to the New York country-side" in the early nineteenth century is "problematic" (1994, 19).

It is, of course, possible that a genuinely ancient record could appear, shrouded in spurious stories about its recovery. For most readers, how-ever, ancient Israelites in America who kept records on plates of gold are just as incredible as angel messengers and miraculous "interpreters." O'Dea does not explicitly state why the Book of Mormon does not deserve con-sideration as ancient history or ancient scripture, but implies that it is the modern resonance of the content—nowhere more baldly in evidence than in its explicit messianism. "The expectations of the Nephites are those of nineteenth-century American Protestants rather than of biblical Hebrews," he writes, and says there is but little "difference between what a Nephite prophet and a New York revivalist says" (1957, 39). Indeed, Latter-day Saints are even more unabashed about proclaiming the text a pre-Christian testa-ment to Christ today than they were in 1957. Since 1982, the scripture has borne the subtitle "Another Testament of Jesus Christ."

Perhaps the most that can be offered in this regard is that Book of Mormon writers seem themselves aware of the anomalous nature of their prophecies, always couching them in the context of extraordinary revela-tion. Lehi preaches the time of the Messiah's coming apparently based on an inspired dream (1 Nephi 10:2–4). Nephi refers to the coming Messiah as Jesus Christ, "according to . . . the word of the angel of God" (2 Nephi 25:21). His mother's name, Mary, was likewise made known to King Benja-min "by an angel from God" (Mosiah 3:2–8). Alma knows the Savior shall be born of Mary in Jerusalem, because "the spirit hath said this much unto me" (Alma 7:9), and so on. Still, the Book of Mormon's Christocentrism is radically pervasive and explicit and detailed, vastly more so than the vague Messianic prophecies of an Isaiah or Psalmist. If the extensive supernatural-ism surrounding Joseph's production of the Book of Mormon is not imme-diately dissuasive, the pre-Christian Christianity of the Nephites frequently is. Perhaps, since both ultimately rely on an embrace or rejection of highly personalized, extracanonical revelation, one to modern prophets like Joseph Smith and the other to ancient dispersed Israelites, Latter-day Saint apolo-gists have concerned themselves but little with the scripture's most prima facie anachronicity.

As for the other elements of the record amenable to historical investigation, Mormons had before 1957 produced little evidence to lend them particular plausibility. O'Dea wrote at a moment when Mormons were just beginning to apply the tools of archaeology to buttress their belief in the Book of Mormon as an authentic, ancient text. Brigham Young University had created a chair in that discipline in 1945, and a few years later fieldwork began in southeastern Mexico—deemed the heart of Book of Mormon lands by Church of Jesus Christ of Latter-day Saints (LDS) scholars. Thomas Ferguson, an amateur scholar, became a fund-raiser, proponent, and organizer behind the effort to solve "the paramount problem of origins of the great civilizations of Middle America" (Kidder and Ferguson 1996, 43). The solution, he clearly believed, was to be found by corroborating archaeologically the account given in the Book of Mormon. Mormons devoured the products of the effort, such as the 1950 publication by Ferguson and Milton R. Hunter, *Ancient America and the Book of Mormon.* Similar titles quickly followed, but non-Mormon scholars paid no attention, and serious scholars within the church criticized such efforts for doing more harm than good to the cause of Book of Mormon apologetics. O'Dea apparently was oblivious to their efforts, or felt the evidence mustered in such volumes beneath notice.

More serious—and durable work—was being done at this time by Hugh Nibley, whose publications on the Book of Mormon remain the standard for apologetic research. A recent outline of his contributions surveys forty-five topics in which he finds historical corroboration for Book of Mormon themes, practices, and textual elements (McKinlay 2002). From Egyptian etymologies for personal names and the word for "honeybee" *(deseret)* to the motifs of luminous stones and dancing princesses in the Book of Ether and the practice of Olive culture and naming of geographical features, Nibley excavates a host of ancient cultural information to make the Book of Mormon appear naturally congruent with a Middle Eastern setting. His analysis includes comparing Lehi's rhetoric with the *qasida,* or desert poetry, and examining Book of Mormon assemblies in light of new-year rites described in Old World texts. He finds ancient precedents for unusual phraseology (such as "the cold and silent grave, from whence no traveler can return," and the often mentioned "land of Jerusalem") and for the book's introductory and concluding style of colophons. He verifies the historical correctness of Nephi's hunting weapons (bows and slings) and finds a striking etymology for the peculiar word *Hermounts,* a Book of Mormon wilderness infested with wild beasts. In Egypt he locates a district called Hermonthis, named after Month, the Egyptian god "of wild places and things." Ritual games in which life and limb are forfeit, peculiar rites of execution, and hiding up treasures

unto the Lord are all Book of Mormon elements that find Old World ante-
cedents under Nibley's expansive scholarship.

For all his efforts, Nibley found few to pay attention to his work outside Mormon circles. One prominent scholar of Near Eastern studies, though
completely unpersuaded by Smith's angel stories, nonetheless agreed with
Nibley that one cannot explain away the presence in the Book of Mormon
of genuinely Egyptian names, such as Paanchi and Pahoran, in close connection with a reference to the text as written in "reformed Egyptian" (communication of William F. Albright to Grant S. Heward, July 25, 1966, in
Tvedtnes, Gee, and Roper 2000, 45). Otherwise, Nibley registered little
outside impact.

A few decades after O'Dea wrote, Book of Mormon scholarship gathered new life with the formation of the Foundation for Ancient Research
and Mormon Studies (FARMS) in 1979. In the years since, scholars associated with that institute are growing in confidence that "there is mounting
up a considerable body of analysis demonstrating that at least something of
the strangeness of the Book of Mormon is due to the presence in it of other
ancient and complex literary forms which Joseph Smith is highly unlikely
to have discovered on his own, and showing as well that its contents are
rich and subtle beyond the suspicions of even the vast majority of its most
devout readers" (Peterson 1990, xxiii). As even a determined skeptic admits,
it is hard to ignore the "striking coincidences between elements in the Book
of Mormon and the ancient world, and some notable matters of Book of
Mormon style" (Wright 1993, 165n). In a much heralded 1998 paper, two
evangelicals, Paul Owen and Carl Mosser, acknowledge that "in recent years
the sophistication and erudition of LDS apologetics has risen considerably... [and] is clearly seen in their approach to the Book of Mormon" (181,
185). As difficult as it may be to accept, "LDS academicians are producing
serious research which desperately needs to be critically examined," they insist (189).[6]

John W. Welch (1969) first noted how chiasmus, or inverted parallelism,
a poetic structure common in antiquity, turns out to be pervasive in the Book
of Mormon. Though it is common, in small doses, to many poets across
time, the examples in the Book of Mormon are at times remarkably intricate
and prolonged. Donald Parry (1992) and others have focused on many other
examples of Hebraic structures in the Book of Mormon. And John L. Sorenson (1996) has made an impressive case, based on both geographical and anthropological approaches, for an ancient American setting for the Book of
Mormon, working with some seven hundred geographical references in the

text. Other scholars have followed Nibley in arguing for compelling parallels involving coronation festivals and other cultural practices.[7]

More recent work has involved mapping the possible route of Lehi's family through the Arabian wilderness, and finding a number of striking fits. Candidates for the River of Lemuel have been argued, a general route along the Incense Trail agreed upon, and consensus reached that the point of departure in the verdant land Bountiful "must have been located along the southern coast of Oman" (Kent et al. 1998, 12).[8] One of the most vocal critics of Book of Mormon historicity has scoffed that archaeologists have no more chance of finding evidence of Book of Mormon place-names "than of discovering the ruins of the bottomless pit described in the book of Revelations [*sic*]." Yet in the 1990s, archaeologists found altars near Sanaa, Yemen, that confirm unequivocally the historicity of a place-name mentioned early in the Book of Mormon ("Nahom"), at the very locale where it should be if the record is authentic.[9] In this instance, at least, hard archaeological evidence sustains in very focused, dramatic fashion a specific claim made by the Book of Mormon a century and three-quarters ago. As of 2005, researchers at FARMS felt confident enough of the accumulated evidence to produce a film, *Journey of Faith,* that recapitulates the journey of Lehi from Jerusalem to the Arabian Sea.

Others have worked assiduously to establish the plausibility of Israelite settlement of the New World, either directly, by establishing linguistic parallels (such as Brian Stubbs, a published expert on the Uto-Aztecan languages, who claims a high percentage of Semitic connections in both grammar and morphology [Sorenson 2000]), or indirectly, by compiling massive bibliographies of diffusionist evidence (such as John Sorenson and Martin Raish, who published *Pre-Columbian Contact with the Americas across the Oceans* [1996]). More recently, Sorenson (2006) has collated an impressive array of biological evidence to the same ends.

None of these items, of course, taken singly, constitutes decisive proof that the Book of Mormon is an ancient text. Even their cumulative weight is counterbalanced by what appear to be striking intrusions into the Book of Mormon text of anachronisms, nineteenth-century parallels, and elements that appear to many scholars to be historically implausible and inconsistent with what is known about ancient American cultures. In addition to the echoes of nineteenth-century folk magic, anti-Catholicism, and religious debates, the Book of Mormon entails an array of dilemmas for the believer. Critics have given over, latching onto a number of purported gaffes that turn out to be bull's-eyes: Alma is not a Latin feminine, for example, but an ancient Hebrew name attested by the Dead Sea Scrolls. The purported "Reformed Egyptian" of the plates does in fact turn out to reflect a genuine mingling of Egyptian and Hebrew cultural traditions in the exilic era, and referring to the "land of Jerusalem" has ancient precedents. The barley mentioned in the Book of Mormon was roundly mocked by critics as recently as 1980 (Scott 1980, 82). By the next decade, a best-selling book referred to a variety of barley as a Native American staple (Diamond 1997, 150).

The most recent development in the Book of Mormon wars has been a flurry of claims that DNA evidence proves the absence of any genetic link between Native American populations and an Israelite heritage. Unfortunately, inflated claims by disaffected Mormons and extensive media exposure have granted a degree of gravity to these allegations far in excess of their potential for scientific merit. Quite simply, DNA would be a relevant tool in the debate only if a number of extraordinary conditions were present. The science can get quite complicated, but the assumptions on which it is based are not. As Michael Whiting (2003), a molecular biologist and member of a scientific review panel for the National Science Foundation, points out, at least ten factors make the hypothesis of American Indian–Israelite connections untestable. Among these are the unlikelihood of the Book of Mormon peoples remaining genetically uncontaminated by any other peoples during their thousand-year presence in this hemisphere. One would also have to ignore the effects of genetic contamination among indigenous populations that doubtless occurred in the fifteen centuries after Book of Mormon history ends. One would also have to know precisely who, among the vast American Indian populations of today, are the descendants of what the Book of Mormon calls "Lamanites." The very small size of the founding genetic pools and the shifting genetic identity of the Middle Eastern host population also present challenges to experimental validation.

Rebutting such objections, critics point out that the Book of Mormon's (noncanonical) introduction refers to the American Indians in toto as "the principal descendants of the Lamanites," and that generations of church leaders and members have asserted the monopoly of Book of Mormon peoples in this hemisphere. At this stage of the debate, it is clear that church teachings, rather than the Book of Mormon itself, are the vulnerable target. As Book of Mormon scholars have been pointing out for generations, the scripture itself nowhere claims that the Jaredites or Lehites established or sustained a presence in the utter absence of other indigenous or subsequently arrived groups. Similarly, the record nowhere imputes to them a hemispheric dominion. In fact, as John L. Sorenson and others argued long before *DNA* was a buzzword, the actual dominions intimated in the geographical references more nearly approximate the modest size of Palestine than half the globe. As long ago as 1927, Janne M. Sjodahl wrote that "students should be cautioned against the error of supposing that all the American Indians are the descendants of Lehi, Mulek, and their companions" (28), and in 1938 a Church Department of Education study guide for the Book of Mormon told students that "the Book of Mormon deals only with the history and expansion of three small colonies which came to America and it does not deny or disprove the possibility of other immigrations, which probably would be unknown to its writers" (Berrett and Hunter 1938, 48).[10] Finally, the Book of Mormon explicitly makes Lamanite a political and religious, rather than ethnic, designation by the record's conclusion.

This leaves unaddressed, of course, the very real—and problematic—doctrinal and cultural interpretations of the Book of Mormon that still infuse LDS rhetoric and writings. In Mormon popular idiom, *Lamanite* has long meant and continues to mean Native American. In that regard, it may well be that even Book of Mormon devotees can find the DNA debates salutary for necessitating a more careful scrutiny of the textual foundations that support traditional interpretations.

Just as the DNA controversy has focused attention on the parameters of the designation "Lamanite" in ways that make its broad application difficult to sustain, other pressures on conventional Book of Mormon geography (the "hemispheric model") have similarly been followed by a shrinking Book of Mormon stage. Since shortly after O'Dea wrote, scholars at Brigham Young University (BYU) have zeroed in on Mesoamerica as the theater of operations for Book of Mormon history, but it was only with the work of John Sorenson in the 1980s that that model gained general currency.

Narrowing the target solves many problems, but incurs others. At least one objection that so stymied formidable Book of Mormon scholar B. H. Roberts would have been largely obviated by claiming a limited model of Book of Mormon settlement. "How to explain the immense diversity of Indian languages, if all are supposed to be relatively recent descendants of Lamanite origin?" asked a correspondent.[11] If the clan of Lehi is not the source of an entire hemispheric civilization, and the Book of Mormon not the record of half the globe's history for a thousand years, then a great many objections are indeed seen to be straw men. Similarly, the daunting population problems are potentially resolved if Book of Mormon peoples are seen as coexisting with and occasionally assimilating other contemporaneous groups. On the other hand, by locating with geographical precision the alleged locale for the book's millennium-long history, there is no place to hide.

John E. Clark is one anthropologist who believes the fifty years since O'Dea have brought more than a redefinition of the Book of Mormon's scope. "Only during the last fifty" years, he writes, "has American archaeology been capable of addressing issues of history and generating reliable facts" (2005, 87). Most impressive, he believes, is the congruence of time lines for the major population groups in the Book of Mormon and in Mesoamerica. The Olmec civilization, not dated until a decade after O'Dea wrote, is now considered to have flourished until the fifth century B.C., just when the Jaredite people were annihilated. The largest upland and lowland Mayan cities were similarly destroyed or abandoned at the same time the Nephite civilization came to its catastrophic end in the fifth century A.D. Clark frankly acknowledges that many problems remain unsolved, but insists the trend is toward fewer, not more, discrepancies between the record and historical knowledge. Evaluating sixty criticisms of three nineteenth-century works, for instance, Clark finds that 60 percent of them have been resolved in favor of the Book of Mormon. He mentions as examples Old World steel swords and metal plates and New World cement, barley, and writing systems.

Clearly, many anachronisms and improbabilities remain. "The most frequently mentioned deficiencies of the book," Clark continues, "concern the lack of hard evidence in the New World for the right time periods of precious metals, Old World animals and plants and Book of Mormon place names and personal names.... Other probable items await full confirmation, including horses, Solomon-like temples, scimitars, large armies, a script that may qualify as reformed Egyptian, and the two hundred years of Nephite peace" (95).

Smith was himself confident that time would vindicate his claims regarding the Book of Mormon. "We can not but think the Lord has a hand in bringing to pass his strange act, and proving the Book of Mormon true in the eyes of all the people," he wrote (*Times and Seasons* 1842, 921). "Surely 'facts are stubborn things.' It will be as it ever has been, the world will prove Joseph Smith a true prophet by circumstantial evidence" (923). So far, however, it may be that historical approaches are more effective tools in the hands of critics than believers. This is not necessarily because the balance of evidence weighs more heavily in the former's favor. Rather, it is because supporting historical research can do little to ground or establish religious faith that is not already present, whereas contrary historical evidence can do much to disable interest and serious investigation on the part of the uncommitted. History as theology is indeed perilous, as Grant McMurray, past president of the Community of Christ, has warned[12]—and his denomination has found a more comfortable and uncontroversial niche in Protestantism by retreating from foundational historical narratives about Joseph Smith and the Book of Mormon. The same impulse led him to say, upon his succession, that his members needed to move from being "a people with a prophet" to being a "prophetic people" (Stack 1996, D1).

The Latter-day Saints, however, have opted to make the prophet Joseph Smith—and the particular history he related—not just an essential part of Mormon theology, but *the* foundation of Mormonism's theology. Retreat from that commitment is not a possibility in a church and tradition that has erected its entire doctrinal edifice as a logically interconnected series of historical propositions, running from Smith's visitation by embodied deities in the Sacred Grove through his translation of actual gold plates to the receipt of priesthood keys by a whole series of resurrected beings.

The Book of Mormon's place as LDS scripture is constituted in part by the role it has consistently played as both the evidence and the very ground of Joseph Smith's prophetic calling, a divine sign of the opening of a new dispensation that he and he alone was authorized to initiate, the ground and evidence and physical embodiment of a rift in heaven through which angels and authority and revelations poured forth in torrents. It is not what the Book of Mormon contains, which Mormons value, but what it enacts. And that miraculous enactment *is* its history. This history began with prophets inscribing their words on gold plates two and a half millennia ago; becomes a long history of providential preservation; includes divine assurances and prophecies of the manner, timing, and agency by which it would be committed to a future generation; and culminates as a marvelous work and a wonder, whispering out of the dust, in Isaiah's words, delivered up to Joseph Smith by a messenger from the presence of God, and translated by means of priestly oracles that attest to his role as seer and revelator, the record itself testifying of, and embodying, and provoking millions to experience personally the principle of dialogic revelation—all this is what the Book of Mormon means to a Latter-day Saint.

"Christianity," Arthur Schopenhauer notes, "has this peculiar disadvantage of not being, like other religions, a pure *doctrine,* but is essentially and mainly a *narrative or history,* a series of events...; and this very history constitutes the dogma, belief in which leads to salvation" (1974, 369). If this is true of Christianity in general, it is doubly true of Mormonism in particular. It is therefore hard to bracket the book's claims to historical facticity when those claims are both integral to the religious faith of Mormons and the warp and woof of the record. In this latter regard, the Book of Mormon is much more like the book of Exodus or Acts than the Psalms or Sermon on the Mount.

What can and should be done is to reshift the focus from what the book is to what it enacts. To reframe the question, "is the Book of Mormon true scripture?" to become, "how does new scripture come to be constituted?" Ask not what truth it contains, but what truths it reveals. The irony of the search for a common ground where believers and skeptics, the devout and the curious, and academics of any persuasion can find agreement is that the common ground has always been quite obvious. From the fulminations of the Baptist *Religious Herald* editorialist who confessed in 1840, "We have never seen a copy of the book of Mormon," and then proceeded to damn it unreservedly as a "bungling and stupid production" ("The Mormons" 1840, 1) to the generations of Mormon converts who have testified to its truthfulness, the key truth and point of consensus about the Book of Mormon have been the same and are revealed in O'Dea's own comic but potent insight. "The Book of Mormon," he writes, "has not been universally considered by its critics [or its followers!] as one of those books that must be read in order to have an opinion of it" (1957, 26).

Whether by guile or by inspiration, Smith unarguably produced something more momentous than a pastiche of biblical verses and nineteenth-century cultural flotsam and jetsam. O'Dea rightly appreciated that the Mormons were effectively reenacting in the "conditions of nineteenth-century America the experience of the biblical Hebrews" (O'Dea and Aviad 1983, 86). But he failed—and this was a major failing—to comprehend the significance of the Book of Mormon as a reenactment, and hence demystification and radical reconceptualization, of the very notion of sacred scripture. To reduce the Book of Mormon to the uncomplicated reworking (by "a normal person living in an atmosphere of religious excitement") of a few "basic themes," as O'Dea denominates them (1957, 24), Arminian ideas from here, a little anticlericalism there, with some dashes of New England revivalism, is entirely to miss the essence of the book's phenomenal power to instill discipleship and to incite hatred, to found a major religious tradition and to incite hostility, opposition, and displacement. The Book of Mormon embodies the principle laid down by William Cantwell Smith and William A. Graham, and endorsed by Shlomo Biderman: "The element of content is not the major factor in establishing scripture.... Because of the enormous diversity of what is said in scripture, it cannot be defined or characterized by its content" (1995, 12–13). Rather, he writes, "to understand scripture is to understand the conditions under which a group of texts has gained authority over the lives of people and has been incorporated into human activities of various important kinds" (50). Joseph Smith understood, as did his disciples and detractors, that scripture is what is written by prophets and that what prophets produce is scripture. The Book of Mormon was a sign of Smith's claim to prophet status, even more emphatically and concretely than was his claim to holy visitations from God and Christ and receipt of priesthood keys from John the Baptist and Peter, James, and John. The latter were portents and indications of his call; the former was the very execution and evidence of the office.

What Joseph produced was, of course, of "enormous diversity": migrations and genealogies and sermons and wars and prophecies and midrash and allegories and details on coinage, horticulture, and military tactics. Ultimately, however, the diversity was daunting, but a distraction. It was the book's transgression of boundaries and limits through a series of paradoxical displacements that constituted his real work of prophetic disruption. The Book of Mormon affirmed the Bible's status as scripture, even as it undermined it. "These last records," the book prophesied of itself, "shall establish the truth of the first, which are of the twelve apostles of the Lamb." But as Nephi reveals in his next sentence, to "establish" the truth of the Bible actually entails establishing its insufficiency. "[These records] shall make known the plain and precious things which have been taken away from them" (1 Nephi 13:39–40). Even as it affirms "the gospel of Jesus Christ" and guarantees its restoration in purity, the Book of Mormon demolishes the Bible's monopoly on its articulation: "I shall speak unto the Jews and they shall write it; and I shall also speak unto the Nephites and they shall write it; and I shall also speak unto the other tribes of the house of Israel, which I have led away, and they shall write it; and I shall also speak unto all nations of the earth and they shall write it" (2 Nephi 29:12).

It testifies to Christ's incarnation, crucifixion, and resurrection, then explodes their sublime historical uniqueness by reenacting Christ's ministry and ascension in a New World setting. Similarly, the book affirms Jehovah's covenants with Israel, even as it specifies America as a separate "land of promise" and then chronicles a whole series of portable Zions founded and abandoned in successive waves.

Such multiple disruptions galvanized or offended those who knew the Book of Mormon or its message, but they were the unmistakable focus of proselytizing and criticism alike. As such, the Book of Mormon revealed a great deal—and still does—about the boisterous interplay of democratic yearnings and covenantal elitism; of visionary utterance with its promise and danger; of the longing for religious tradition, stability, and boundaries; and of the appeal of religious dynamism and exceptionalism. The Book of

Mormon, in terms of origin and production, may still be a conundrum for the majority who approach it. But it may serve much more effectively than it has as a lens to better understand the conceptual universe it both engaged and provoked, and to affect the hearts and minds of those who cannot read it with indifference. ·

NOTES

1. Brodie's was by no measure an attempt at objective history. In her own words, though raised a Latter-day Saint, she had become "convinced before I ever began writing that Joseph Smith was not a true Prophet." Confessing afterward to resentment at having been "conned" by the church, she set out to account for "the whole problem of [Joseph's] credibility" (1975, 79).

2. A useful overview of Book of Mormon critics, with a lively rebuttal, is the nine-part series by Hugh Nibley, "'Mixed Voices': A Study on Book of Mormon Criticism," first published in the *Improvement Era* (May–June 1959) and reprinted in *The Collected Works of Hugh Nibley* (1989).

3. Hurlbut first proposed the connection, which Howe then elaborated in print as *Mormonism Unvailed* (1834).

4. Though considering the Book of Mormon an imposture from first to last, Brodie also acknowledged its "elaborate design" and "coherently spun narrative" revealing "a measure of learning and a fecund imagination" (1945, 68–69.)

5. Compare Rodney Stark's criticism of Max Weber: "When Weber wrote that 'We shall understand "prophet" to mean a purely individual bearer of charisma,' he said nothing more than that charismatics have charisma" (1999, 304).

6. James White is an evangelical who does not share Owen and Mosser's respect for the work at FARMS. An author himself of anti-Mormon works, White (1996) provides some anecdotal evidence to support his claim that FARMS scholarship is at times smug, ad hominem, and misapplied. Of this article, Mosser and Owen say it is "nothing more than straw man argumentation" (1998, 202). The only other example of an attempt to refute Mormon scholarship they can identify is *Behind the Mask of Mormonism: From Its Early Schemes to Its Modern Deceptions* by John Ankerberg and John Weldon (1992), which they dismiss as "ugly, unchristian, and misleading" (203).

7. Nibley first cast the Benjamin speech as an ancient year-rite festival in 1957. See Nibley 1988.

8. An overview of Lehi's trail is given in Brown 2002.

9. The altar inscription is "NHM." Interpolating the correct vowels with certainty is not possible. However, it is certain that what Smith spelled as "Nahom" would have been rendered "NHM."

10. The limited geography model centered in Mesoamerica was originally put forth by a Reorganized Church of Jesus Christ of Latter Day Saints (now called Community of

Christ) researcher, Louis E. Hill, in two books: *Geography of Mexico and Central America from 2234 B.C. to 421 A.D.* (1917) and *Historical Data from Ancient Records and Ruins of Mexico and Central America* (1919). It was widely introduced to Latter-day Saints by Jesse A. and Jesse N. Washburn beginning in the 1930s.

11. The question, posed by one "Mr. Couch," was passed on by W. E. Riter to James E. Talmage, August 22, 1921, in Roberts 1992, 35.

12. Grant McMurray made this statement in his keynote address at the Mormon History Association annual meeting, Kirtland, Ohio, May 22, 2003.

REFERENCES

Alexander, Thomas G. 1980. "The Reconstruction of Mormon Doctrine: From Joseph Smith to Progressive Theology." *Sunstone* 5: 24–33.

Ankerberg, John, and John Weldon. 1992. *Behind the Mask of Mormonism: From Its Early Schemes to Its Modern Deceptions.* Eugene, Ore.: Harvest House.

Berrett, William E., and Milton R. Hunter. 1938. *A Guide to the Study of the Book of Mormon.* Salt Lake City: Department of Education of the Church of Jesus Christ of Latter-day Saints.

Biderman, Shlomo. 1995. *Scripture and Knowledge: An Essay on Religious Epistemology.* New York: Brill.

Bloom, Harold. 1992. *The American Religion: The Emergence of the Post-Christian Nation.* New York: Simon and Schuster.

Brodie, Fawn M. 1945. *No Man Knows My History: The Life of Joseph Smith, the Mormon Prophet.* New York: Alfred A. Knopf.

———. 1975. "Biography of Fawn McKay Brodie." Interview by Shirley E. Stephenson. Oral History Collection, Fullerton State University, Fullerton, Calif., November 30. Cited in Newell G. Bringhurst, "Fawn Brodie and Her Quest for Independence." *Dialogue: A Journal of Mormon Thought* 22, no. 2: 79.

Brooks, John L. 1994. *The Refiner's Fire: The Making of Mormon Cosmology, 1644–1844.* New York: Cambridge University Press.

Brown, S. Kent. 2002. "New Light from Arabia on Lehi's Trail." In *Echoes and Evidences from the Book of Mormon,* ed. Donald W. Parry, Daniel C. Peterson, and John W. Welch, 55–125. Provo: FARMS Research Press.

Brown, S. Kent, Terry B. Ball, Arnold H. Green, David J. Johnson, and W. Revell Phillips. 1998. "Planning Research on Oman: The End of Lehi's Trail." *Journal of Book of Mormon Studies* 7, no. 1: 12.

Bushman, Richard L. 1976. "The Book of Mormon and the American Revolution." *BYU Studies* 17, no. 1: 17–18.

———. 1996. "The Secret History of Mormonism." *Sunstone* (March): 66–70.

Butler, Jon. 1992. *Awash in a Sea of Faith.* Cambridge: Harvard University Press.

Campbell, Alexander. 1831. "Delusions: An Analysis of the Book of Mormon." *Millennial Harbinger* 11 (February 7): 85–96.

———. 1832. *Delusions: An Analysis of the Book of Mormon, with an Examination of Its Internal and External Evidences, and a Refutation of Its Pretenses to Divine Authority.* Boston: Benjamin H. Greene.

Clark, John E. 2005. "Archaeological Trends and Book of Mormon Origins." In *The Worlds of Joseph Smith: A Bicentennial Conference at the Library of Congress,* ed. John W. Welch, 83–104. Provo: Brigham Young University Press.

De Voto, Bernard. 1930. "The Centennial of Mormonism." *American Mercury* 19: 5.

Diamond, Jared. 1997. *Guns, Germs, and Steel: The Fate of Human Societies.* New York: W. W. Norton.

Hamblin, William J., Daniel C. Peterson, and George L. Mitton. 1994. "Mormon in the Fiery Furnace; or, Loftes Tryk Goes to Cambridge." Review of *The Refiner's Fire: The Making of Mormon Cosmology, 1644–1844,* by John L. Brooke. *FARMS Review of Books on the Book of Mormon* 6, no. 2: 8.

Hill, Louis E. 1917. *Geography of Mexico and Central America from 2234 B.C. to 421 A.D.* Independence, Mo.: n.p.

———. 1919. *Historical Data from Ancient Records and Ruins of Mexico and Central America.* Independence, Mo.: L. E. Hills.

Hill, Marvin S. 1989. *Quest for Refuge: The Mormon Flight from American Pluralism.* Salt Lake City: Signature Books.

Howe, Eber D. 1834. *Mormonism Unvailed.* Painesville, Ohio: printed and published by the author.

Kidder, Alfred V., and Thomas Stuart Ferguson. 1996. "Plan for Archaeological Work in an Important Zone in Middle America." In *Quest for the Gold Plates: Thomas Stuart Ferguson's Archaeological Search for the Book of Mormon,* by Stan Larson. Salt Lake City: Freethinker Press, Smith Research Associates.

Lindgren, A. Bruce. 1983. "Sin and Redemption in the Book of Mormon." In *Restoration Studies II,* 201–6. Independence, Mo.: Herald House.

———. 1986. "Sign or Scripture: Approaches to the Book of Mormon." *Dialogue: A Journal of Mormon Thought* 19, no. 1: 69–75.

McKinlay, Daniel. 2002. "Appendix: Echoes and Evidences from the Writings of Hugh Nibley." In *Echoes and Evidences from the Book of Mormon,* by Donald W. Parry, Daniel C. Peterson, and John W. Welch, 453–88. Provo: Foundation for Ancient Research and Mormon Studies, Brigham Young University.

"The Mormons." 1840. *Religious Herald* 59, no. 1 (April 9): 1.

Mosser, Carl, and Paul Owen. 1998. "Mormon Apologetic, Scholarship and Evangelical Neglect: Losing the Battle and Not Knowing It?" *Trinity Journal* (Fall): 179–205.

Nibley, Hugh. 1988. *An Approach to the Book of Mormon.* 3d ed. Vol. 6 of *The Collected Works of Hugh Nibley.* Salt Lake City and Provo: Deseret Book and FARMS Research Press.

————. 1989. "Mixed Voices: A Study on Book of Mormon Criticism." In *The Prophetic Book of Mormon,* ed. John W. Welch, 148–206. Vol. 8 of *The Collected Works of Hugh Nibley.* Salt Lake City and Provo: Deseret Book and FARMS Research Press. First published in the *Improvement Era* (May–June 1959).

O'Dea, Thomas F. 1957. *The Mormons.* Chicago: University of Chicago Press.

O'Dea, Thomas F., and Janet O'Dea Aviad. 1983. *The Sociology of Religion.* 2d ed. Englewood Cliffs, N.J.: Prentice-Hall.

Parry, Donald W. 1992. *The Book of Mormon Text Reformatted according to Parallelistic Patterns.* Provo: FARMS Research Press.

Peterson, Daniel C. 1990. "Editor's Introduction: By What Measure Shall We Mete?" *FARMS Review of Books* 2: xxiii.

Roberts, B. H. 1992. *Studies of the Book of Mormon.* Ed. Brigham D. Madsen. 2d ed. Salt Lake City: Signature Books.

Schopenhauer, Arthur. 1974. *Parerga and Paralipomena: Short Philosophical Essays.* Vol. 2. Trans. E. F. J. Payne. Oxford: Clarendon.

Scott, Latayne Colvett. 1980. *The Mormon Mirage.* Grand Rapids, Mich.: Zondervan.

Sjodahl, Janne M. 1927. *An Introduction to the Study of the Book of Mormon.* Salt Lake City: Deseret News Press.

Sorenson, John L. 1996. *An Ancient American Setting for the Book of Mormon.* Salt Lake City and Provo: Deseret Book and FARMS Research Press.

————. 2000. "Was There Hebrew Language in Ancient America? An Interview with Brian Stubbs." *Journal of Book of Mormon Studies* 9, no. 2: 54–63.

————. 2006. "Biological Evidence for Pre-Columbian Transoceanic Voyages." In *Contact and Exchange in the Ancient World,* ed. Victor H. Mair, 238–97. Honolulu: University of Hawaii Press.

Sorenson, John L., and Martin Raish. 1996. *Pre-Columbian Contact with the Americas across the Oceans.* Provo: FARMS Research Press.

Stack, Peggy F. 1996. "RLDS Head Downplays His Role as a Prophet." *Salt Lake Tribune,* June 29, D1.

Stark, Rodney. 1999. "A Theory of Revelations." *Journal for the Scientific Study of Religion* 38, no. 2: 304.

Times and Seasons. 1842. 3: 921–23. (Newspaper published for a short time in Nauvoo, Ill.)

Tvedtnes, John A., John Gee, and Matthew Roper. 2000. "Book of Mormon Names Attested in Ancient Hebrew Inscriptions." *Journal of Book of Mormon Studies* 9, no. 1: 42–51.

Voros, J. Frederic, Jr. 1987. "Was the Book of Mormon Buried with King Follett?" *Sunstone* 11, no. 2 (March): 15–18.

Welch, John W. 1969. "Chiasmus in the Book of Mormon." *BYU Studies* 10, no. 1: 69–84.

White, James. 1996. "Of Cities and Swords: The Impossible Task of Mormon Apologetics." *Christian Research Journal* 19, no. 1: 28–35.

Whiting, Michael. 2003. "DNA and the Book of Mormon: A Phylogenetic Perspective."
    Journal of Book of Mormon Studies 12, no. 1: 24–35.
Wilson, Edmund. 1985. *The Dead Sea Scrolls, 1947–1969*. Glasgow: William Collins and Sons.
Wright, David P. 1993. "'In Plain Terms That We May Understand': Joseph Smith's
    Transformation of Hebrew in Alma 12–13." In *New Approaches to the Book of Mormon,*
    ed. Brent Lee Metcalfe. Salt Lake City: Signature Books.

Part II

*Contemporary
Social Issues*

5

LDS Family Ideals versus the Equality of Women

Navigating the Changes since 1957

~ Carrie A. Miles ~

Here, you see, it takes all the running you can do, to keep in the same place.

—The Red Queen, *Through the Looking Glass,* by Lewis Carroll

In his chapter "Sources of Strain and Conflict," Thomas O'Dea wrote that many of the stresses experienced within the Church of Jesus Christ of Latter-day Saints (LDS) were the result of "its own structure. These sources of conflict have created grave problems for the Mormon movement, and some of them are even now capable of severe threats to its welfare" (1957, 222). One such contradiction was found between Mormonism's acceptance of "the equality of women with men" and its simultaneous belief in a patriarchal family structure. "Women as well as men are eternal intelligences in Mormon doctrine," O'Dea wrote, "but women are dependent upon men and upon marriage for exaltation in the afterlife and are subordinate to men on this earth within the family. Yet there is a genuine equality in many respects between the sexes." He concluded that although this inconsistency indeed posed a problem when the Saints practiced polygamy, "Today, practically no difficulty arises from this problem" (250).

Of course, within a decade of the publication of *The Mormons,* patriarchy versus gender equality became one of the more pressing issues facing the church. Indeed, in retrospect it is clear that in the latter half of the twentieth century, marriage, family, and gender relations underwent their most significant changes in human history, causing problems not just for the LDS Church but for the entire developed world. This chapter explains the source of these social changes, the difficulties they pose for religious institutions in general, why they caused particular difficulties for Mormonism, and how the church has responded to this crisis. It also suggests how the church may now be using the problem to its advantage.

THE RISE AND FALL OF PATRIARCHY

The Historic Family

To understand the stresses the LDS Church experienced in conflict over gender equality versus patriarchy, I will start with the forces behind women's inequality. The social system called patriarchy, or, less pejoratively, the historic sexual division of labor, was the natural outgrowth of the economic conditions that prevailed prior to the Industrial Revolution (dated to about 1800). In his foundational work *A Treatise on the Family* (1991), economist Gary S. Becker traces the pattern of men and women performing different tasks to the demands of preindustrial household production. Prior to the Industrial Revolution, households produced for themselves much of what they consumed. Well into the nineteenth century, for instance, American households purchased metal tools and salt, which generally could not be produced at home, but grew or made everything else (Cowan 1983, 32).[1] Achieving subsistence in such economies usually required the unified efforts of many people. A newly married couple might start off alone, but they strove to acquire some kind of help—servants, apprentices, or slaves—as soon as possible. A better source of labor than servants, however, was children. Children were much more likely to be devoted to their family's welfare, if for no other reason than that their family's welfare was also their own. Moreover, children could be produced at home. Children were also the principal form of "insurance" against illness, widowhood, disability, and old age (Becker 1991, 38, chap. 2).

Given the need for large families and the high rates of child mortality in preindustrial economies, married women spent much of their adult lives either pregnant, trying to get pregnant, or nursing infants. This meant that women had little choice but to specialize in work that they could do while also bearing and caring for babies. Strenuous labor can lead to miscarriages; nursing mothers cannot go far from their infants; mothers accompanied by small children must not engage in dangerous activities. Societies quickly learn to divide work so that mothers do the tasks that are most compatible with these physical limitations. Thus, "women's work" came to mean spinning, weaving, sewing, cooking, vegetable gardening and horticulture, nursing the sick and the aged, processing herbs for medicine, and supervising family hygiene (Bleier 1984; Becker 1991).

The need for women to contribute to household production while continuing to bear children resulted in what economists call their "domestic specialization." This specialization in effect made a woman's husband and household her employer. Changes in her employment could be made only at the price of a major and risky disruption in her life. In contrast, the husband's more flexible skills allowed him to be less tied to any particular household. As a result, although a man depended on what his wife produced, he could replace her more easily than she could replace him. Becker suggests that virtually every society has developed some form of the marriage contract in order to protect women in this domestically specialized role (1991, 30–31).

Though a housewife might nonetheless hold considerable power within her domestic areas of concern, her home-centered role limited her power in other ways. Many of the political, military, religious, and business concerns that gave men power in the larger community made little difference to the work that kept a housewife fully occupied—how could she justify taking time with them? In consequence, most women had little decision-making authority or ability outside the household. Thus, the strong economic need for children resulted in the economic realities of separate spheres for men and women and in women's subordination to men in family, government, and church.

The LDS Twist on Family Values

As predominately agrarian members of American society, the early Saints were subject to the same forces shaping the family as their more conventional neighbors. Early in LDS history, however, Joseph Smith introduced Mormonism's "peculiar institution," the practice of plural marriage, or polygamy, which set LDS attitudes toward marriage and family on a decisively different level. This anomalous practice was itself tightly tied to the LDS expansion of the traditional Christian concept of heaven and hell. In Mormon thought, the eternal state of those who go to heaven differs depending on their conformity to church teachings and participation in its various rituals. The highest reward is "exaltation" or "eternal salvation" in the "celestial kingdom" of God bestowed on those who participate in all the rituals and prove their allegiance to church teachings. Those who are exalted, Joseph Smith taught in the last years of his life, will progress eternally, ultimately becoming gods themselves (Smith 193?; Doctrine and Covenants 132). As Smith's teachings evolved, they revealed God as a corporeal being who had followed just this course of progression. It is difficult to know exactly all that Smith taught in this regard, as he wrote down little of it. Eventually, however, it was systematized as the "Plan of Salvation," "Plan of Progression," or "Great Plan of Happiness." This plan holds that every human being existed prior to birth as a spirit child of God the Father and a heavenly mother. These spirit children are sent into mortality in order to acquire the physical body needed for further progression. Faithful Saints were therefore urged to bear as many children as possible, in order to provide these waiting spirits with both bodies and righteous homes that put them on the path to achieving their own exaltation.

As the focal point of the restoration of the true gospel to the earth, Joseph Smith himself was the conduit through which the authority to conduct these critical rituals was dispensed. This meant, essentially, that the eternal salvation of anyone living in the "latter days" would have to come directly or indirectly through Smith. Moreover, Joseph had a unique assurance that he himself would be exalted, and could exalt anyone "sealed" to him (Lightner 1905).

Joseph Smith was not the only one who held priesthood authority: all conforming LDS men did, but to differing degrees and with less assurance of exaltation. To a secret cohort of those closest to him, Joseph taught that participation in "celestial marriage"—one of the many terms by which the LDS practice of polygamy was called—was one way of gaining an assurance of exaltation. A man could build his priesthood power by acquiring a large number of wives and children, who were sealed to him for all eternity. Most women taught the "principle" resisted at first, but many were eventually converted, persuaded that they would be better off as a plural wife of the prophet or another high-ranking priesthood bearer than as the sole wife of a man who could not promise them eternal salvation (Miles 1998).

After a substantial struggle with the U.S. government in the late 1800s, the Saints were forced to abandon the polygamous aspect of eternal marriage. The Church of Jesus Christ of Latter-day Saints today disavows polygamy in the strongest terms. Nonetheless, doctrines related to plural marriage underlie many of the uniquely LDS doctrines that survive today, including the Plan of Salvation and all its components: teachings about the physical nature of God, the requirement that everyone marry for "eternity," the sanctity of motherhood and the importance of having many children, and the universal-male priesthood.

As the impact of polygamist practice faded from daily life, the strongly profamily values of the LDS Church appeared to merge with those of mainstream America in the first half of the twentieth century. Both cultures valued large and emotionally close families, premarital chastity, marital fidelity, and marriage at relatively young ages. Both discouraged divorce. These similarities, however, masked a deep difference between the two cultures, a difference that would leave Mormonism particularly unwilling to accept the changes that were coming in the second half of the century. Whereas other Americans *think* of God as male and view marriage, childbearing, and gendered family life as the standard for good Christians, in the final analysis neither Protestant nor Catholic teachings admit these beliefs as actual doctrines. As O'Dea observed, Mormonism had absorbed patriarchy into its most basic ontology, teaching that God is a physical being who is literally male (or as an anecdote he quotes crudely puts it, "God has hair on his back") (1957, 124, 237). Mormon doctrine holds that "sex [and gender] has always existed and will continue forever" (Bennion 1917, 169). Thus, conflicts between gender equality and the church's doctrinal legacy would re-emerge in the mid-twentieth century as economic support for the sexual division of labor collapsed.

The Industrial Revolution and the Transformation of the Family

The technological and economic developments that radically altered the sexual division of labor and created the postindustrial family began to take shape in the United States and western Europe around the turn of the eighteenth century. Shortly after 1780, a man named Oliver Evans designed the world's first partially automated flour mill. Prior to this development, the staple of most American farm households was maize, which individual households grew, ground, and baked at home as cornbread. With Evans's invention, however, it soon became more efficient for families to buy wheat flour (and, eventually, ready-made white bread) than to grow their own corn (Cowan 1983, 48).

Historian Ruth Schwartz Cowan shows how this and other technological developments "industrialized the home," as more and more of the necessities of life—food, clothing, shelter, education—could be purchased more economically than they could be produced at home (49). She summarizes:

> Butchering, milling, textile making, and leatherwork had departed from many [U.S.] homes by 1860. Sewing of men's clothing was gone, roughly speaking, by 1880, of women's and children's outerwear by 1900 … almost all items of clothing for all members of the family by 1920. Preservation of some foodstuffs … had been industrialized by 1900; the preparation of dairy products … by about the same date. Factory-made biscuits and

quick cereals were appearing on many American kitchen tables by 1910, and factory-made bread had become commonplace by 1930. The preparation of drugs and medications had been turned over to factories or to professional pharmacists by 1900, and a good many other aspects of long-term medical care had been institutionalized in hospitals and sanitariums thirty years later. (78)

One of the first things that advancing technology changed was the daytime composition of the home. Cowan writes, "Virtually all of the stereotypically male household occupations [such as growing and grinding corn] were eliminated by technological and economic innovations during the nineteenth century, and many of those that had previously been allotted to children [such as carrying water, gathering firewood, and herding cattle] were gone as well" (64). No longer required at home, but needing cash to pay for newly available products, men increasingly spent most of their waking hours away from the household. Most significantly for the structure of the historic family, the Industrial Revolution required that children have a different set of skills than they had been getting at home. By the 1930s even poor American children were in school and for the most part out of the productive labor market (Zelizer 1985, 6).

Whereas children who help with the farmwork or bring home pay offer an economic benefit to the family, children who contribute nothing financially and have to be educated pose significant costs. In response, the movement of production out of the household triggered a dramatic decline in the birthrate in the United States and Europe. Census data show that the average number of children borne by an American woman dropped exponentially from 7.04 in 1800 to 3.56 in 1900 and to slightly less than 2 in 2000 (Cowan 1983, 43; U.S. Bureau of the Census 2000).

By the mid-twentieth century the housewife was home alone for much of the day, with no need for the labor of men, children, or servants. Soon, technological change in the United States eliminated much of the need for her presence there as well. Advances made houses cleaner and ever more comfortable, maintained living spaces at just the right temperature with virtually no effort, offered preprocessed and ready-to-cook food, and presented relatively inexpensive clothing and vastly improved methods of cleaning it. Except for a very small number of households, home production of items for sale had ceased (Cowan 1983, 100). Although housework still requires a nontrivial amount of time a week, most of it is no longer a matter of survival or even basic comfort, the way that chopping wood used to be. As a result, it became more economically efficient for *women* to join men in purchasing rather than producing their traditional items and services. In consequence, women began to experience what writer and mother of the modern women's movement Betty Friedan (1963) called the "problem that has no name": a sense of restlessness and lack of fulfillment, the perception that traditional women's work was no longer valued and that women needed to find something else to do. The second wave of the women's movement began in earnest.[2]

I show in detail elsewhere how the decline in the economic need for home production, especially the need for children, quickly resulted in challenges to family forms themselves (2006, chap. 5). As children lost their economic value, so did marriage, the institution designed to protect women in their childbearing capacities. In turn, norms of female chastity before marriage, a critical part of the marriage contract, have also proved difficult to sustain (126). In response, American birthrates have dropped, sex before marriage has become the norm rather than the exception, age at marriage has risen, growing portions of the population have not married at all, and the number and social acceptance of nonmarital births and cohabitation have risen sharply.[3]

THE PROBLEM OF CHANGE

In earlier work I point out that social change poses a profound difficulty for religious institutions (1982; Iannaccone and Miles 1990). When a church and its surrounding culture share a system of belief, the norms and behavior surrounding it are taken for granted. As economic forces move societal norms out from under that belief, however, both individual adherents and the organizations find themselves in a dilemma. Religious adherents are not asked to conduct themselves any differently than they had in the past—in fact, they are asked to behave exactly as they always have—but in the face of new economic possibilities, continuing to behave as they had before takes on significant new costs. The more general principle is that technological development and its resultant social change shift the meaning of the previously shared beliefs to the point that simply standing still becomes deviate behavior. Similarly, practices and attitudes that were regarded benignly may suddenly take on a more sinister meaning. Insisting on the continuing correctness of what has become a socially deviate role puts a church at odds with the culture in which it is embedded and risks alienating both current members and potential converts. The culture, individual members, and the institution must all renegotiate both their beliefs and their relationships with each other.

Resistance to Change

One of the most salient conflicts induced by postindustrial change had to do with women leaving home for paid employment. As production of physical items moved out of the home, a good many less tangible tasks moved out as well. Some of these functions, such as insurance against disaster, occupational training, nursing the sick, and care of the aged, left the household so long ago that people today do not have a clear sense of them as family concerns. In contrast, functions such as the care and socialization of children have moved out only partially, not because it is impossible to perform this function outside of the home but because such a move would conflict with many people's motives for having children in the first place. Further, religiously oriented individuals resist relinquishing their children's upbringing to other institutions that advocate contradictory values. In consequence, even those religious systems that assign no spiritual value to childbearing itself nevertheless require their adherents to raise the children they have in a different manner than a nonreligious parent might. The more conservative or sectarian the religion, the more it will require parents to provide specialized training and socialization for their children. As a result, even otherwise "liberated" couples may end up adhering to a fairly traditional division of labor. That is, if proper spiritual upbringing requires extensive parent-child interactions but economic necessity requires that at least one adult be employed outside of the household, the relative advantage that women have as child bearers over men tips the balance in favor of the mother as the at-home parent.[4] In these circumstances, for the same reasons that women became domestically specialized historically, at-home mothers will end up doing most of the other household tasks—cooking, cleaning, laundry, child transportation, nursing sick children—since they are compatible with child care.

Previous Work

To understand how the church dealt with twentieth-century changes in the status of women, I analyzed the contents of the official church periodicals, the *Improvement Era,* from 1940 to 1970, and its successor, the *Ensign,* from 1971 to early 2006. As the church Web site, http://www.lds.org, became available, I used material from it as well. These sources contain church news, announcements, directions, advice, and, most important, the talks given by the leadership to the church (presidents, counselors to the president, apostles, and Relief Society presidents and counselors) at twice-yearly general conferences. The authorities of the church require that anything published in the *Ensign* be approved prior to publication, and members are encouraged to view the magazine as a form of scripture, making the articles and speeches published therein a reliable source of information on church opinion.

Although there are several topics relating to family values that could be considered, I focus here on the church statements about the activities of women in the home versus the paid workforce. The progression of such statements provides insights into how the church experienced challenges to behaviors and attitudes that were once taken for granted and how these challenges have required the church to clarify, elaborate, and defend a new theology to protect its old teachings.

LDS Response to Changing Family Norms

Official church interest in women's roles does not appear to have been very strong prior to World War II. Sociologist Laura Vance, who included pronouncements before 1940 in her analysis of Mormon ideals for women, writes that women's roles were not attended to with any regularity in the early part of the twentieth century. Conference talks rarely addressed women's issues, and there were only eighteen articles indexed under *women* in the *Improvement Era* in the first fifty years of its publication (1891 to 1940). Vance observes that "Mormon women were, for the first time, told in the pages of the *Era* to restrict their activities to homemaking" in the 1940s, as women began moving into the paid workforce to replace the men fighting in World War II (2002, 104). The first such article was by LDS apostle John A. Widtsoe (1942), in which he argued that women should devote themselves chiefly to the home. However, Widtsoe also encouraged women to learn marketable skills "should circumstances require" that they earn a living.

An article from the same year by the First Presidency (the president of the church and his two counselors) also directed that mothers should not work. These authors argued that the "divine service of motherhood can be rendered only by mothers. It may not be passed to others. Nurses cannot do it; public nurseries cannot do it; hired help cannot do it.... The mother who entrusts her child to the care of others, that she may do non-motherly work, whether for gold, for fame, or for civic service, should remember that 'a child left to himself bringeth his mother to shame'" (Grant, Clark, and McKay 1942, 608, citing Prov. 29:15). This 1942 article may also be the first time motherhood is referred to as "divine" in LDS literature—a reference that would become increasingly salient as time went on.

On the other hand, other articles from the same period actually encouraged women to work outside the home. M. C. Josephson observes that there were women "whose abilities have made it possible for them to rear their own children well and still have enough energy and capability to turn their minds to other activities outside the...home" (1947, 453). Richard L. Evans applauded women's access to equal "professional rights" with men (1943), and H. S. Neal encouraged women to develop careers "when the children are grown" (1948). For all of these authors, however, careers were to be secondary to homemaking.

The postwar years and the sudden surge of marriage and childbearing that produced the baby boom resulted in a return of women to the household on a nationwide level. In consequence, in the whole decade of the 1950s only seven articles addressed the subject of women and paid work. Articles attributed women's motives for working to the desire for financial security and for being able to afford hairdressers and nice clothes (Robinson 1956). They also depicted working women as being always tired and not "living for today."

Other articles, such as one by Belle S. Spafford, then president of the women's auxiliary, the LDS Relief Society, quoted approvingly the data on the number of women currently employed. However, she warned, "while women generally point with pride to their accomplishments in industry, in professions, and other fields of human endeavor, some are beginning to wonder if the spirit of our day and the acceptance of woman in the work of the world are not becoming subtle and artful enemies of the family" (1958, 354). In this and other articles, discrimination against women in the world of work is criticized, and women's ability to enter into careers successfully is affirmed. Nonetheless, women are admonished to stay out of the workplace for the sake of raising children.

Women's Liberation Strikes

The rise of second-wave feminism is often traced to 1963, when Betty Friedan, responding to American women's growing ennui, published *The Feminine Mystique.* U.S. Census data show that the labor-force participation of American women, already climbing steadily, in fact experienced a sharp acceleration within a few years of this publication (fig. 5.1). In 1940, 14 percent of married women were employed outside the home; by the late 1960s, more than 40 percent of them were. In response, the number of articles in the *Ensign* addressing women and work outside of the home rose precipitously, from fifteen in 1960–1969 to fifty-three in 1970–1979 (fig. 5.2).

The initial response to the movement of women out of the home was strongly corrective. In 1963 apostle Spencer W. Kimball wrote about increases in juvenile delinquency and suggested that working mothers might be part of the problem. Asking, "How can mothers justify their abandonment of home when they are needed so much by their offspring?" he quoted

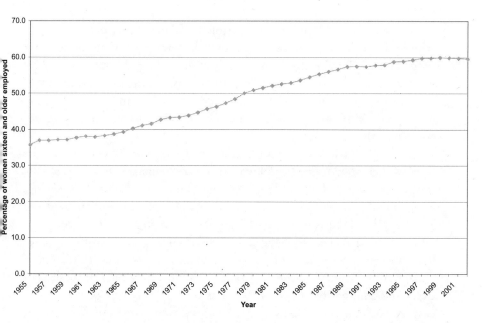

FIGURE 5.1. Labor-force participation rates of U.S. women sixteen and older.

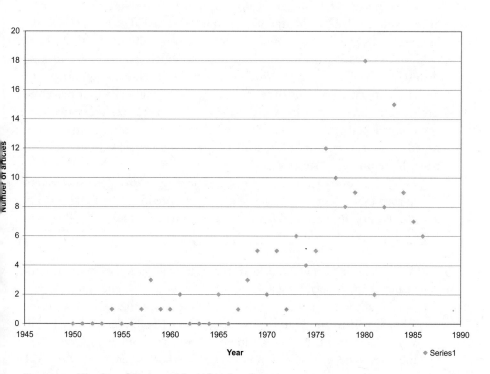

FIGURE 5.2. Number of *Ensign* articles indexed under *women*.

a judge, who urged, "Get women out of the factories and put them back into the home where they belong … cooking, sewing, cleaning house, and doing the traditional woman's work. It would do both for them and their neglected youngsters a world of good" (1073). As we will see below, in 1977, as president of the church, Kimball would repeat this theme of "Mother, come home," a phrase that would be echoed with varying and telling response over the next forty years.

Similarly, David O. McKay, president of the church, voiced concern about women seeking paid employment out of financial need: "It is a matter of deep concern that social and economic conditions today are enticing, if not forcing women out of the sphere in which she herself can find the most happiness and can render the greatest good to mankind" (1969, 2). Apostle Harold B. Lee (1972) urged mothers who "had to" work to nonetheless maintain the welfare of their children as their first priority.

But as the women's movement came into full and vocal swing, the welfare of the children of employed mothers became only one of many concerns. A Brigham Young University (BYU) professor expressed alarm about these ancillary issues when he warned that working outside the home gave a wife too much power in her relationship with her husband (Barlow 1973). Such a wife challenged the divinely ordained patriarchal order in which the husband is to "preside" and must inevitably disrupt the home. C. L. Hurtado also warned "against women who take too much responsibility, making themselves the focal point in the home instead of lending support to the husband" (1973, 50). Similarly, apostle Boyd K. Packer called on perceived gender differences when he wrote, "A man … needs to feel protective, and yes, dominant, if you will, in leading his family. A woman needs to feel protected.… What would it be like if they both naturally needed to feel dominant all the time …?" (1977, 8).

Discussion in terms of dominance and power was dropped, however, to be replaced by assurances that husbands were to preside in love and equality and should not attempt to dominate their families. For example, President Howard W. Hunter wrote,

> A man who holds the priesthood accepts his wife as a partner in the leadership of the home and family with full knowledge of and full participation in all decisions relating thereto. Of necessity there must be in the Church and in the home a presiding officer (see D&C 107:21). By divine appointment, the responsibility to preside in the home rests upon the priesthood holder (See Moses 4:22). The Lord intended that the wife be … a companion equal and necessary in full partnership. Presiding

in righteousness necessitates a shared responsibility.... [T]ogether you act ... in all family matters. For a man to operate independent of or without regard to the feelings and counsel of his wife in governing the family is to exercise unrighteous dominion. (1994, 49)

Another feminist issue that went beyond financial necessity was women's desire for meaningful work and self-fulfillment. Bishop H. Burke Peterson wrote, "Earning a few dollars more for luxuries cloaked in the masquerade of necessity—*or a so-called opportunity for self-development of talents* in the business world, a chance to get away from the mundane responsibilities of the home—these are all satanic substitutes for clear thinking" (emphasis added). Peterson noted that some mothers are the family's sole earners and so must work, but they were to be considered exceptions only. He advised that before parents decide they must have a second income, they should go to God in prayer and make sure he approves. Further, he stated, "No babysitter, no grandmother, no neighbor, no friend, no Relief Society sister, older brother or sister, or even a loving dad can take your place" (1974, 31). Although the First Presidency's 1942 statement warned that neither nurses, public nurseries, nor hired help could replace mother's divine service, Peterson's exclusion of other church and family members, even a "loving dad," from child care is significant.

Apostle Neal A. Maxwell also criticized feminist rhetoric: "Women, more quickly than others, will understand the possible dangers when the word *self* is militantly placed before other words like *fulfillment.* You rock a sobbing child without wondering if today's world is passing you by, because you know you hold tomorrow tightly in your arms." He added, "The act of deserting home in order to shape society is like thoughtlessly removing crucial fingers from an imperiled dike in order to teach people to swim" (1978, 10–11).

I have presented only a few examples here, but all together, more high-level church officials addressed the single issue of self-fulfillment in the 1970s than had spoken to all women's issues in the 1950s.

Pressures toward Accommodation

The salience of women's issues for the church rose dramatically in the 1970s (see fig. 5.2). In the late seventies, a proposed amendment to the U.S. Constitution prohibiting any abridgement of rights based on gender, the Equal Rights Amendment (ERA), neared ratification. Although initially supportive of the ERA, around 1977 the church began a more or less covert campaign to stop it. These activities, including LDS feminist Sonia Johnson's very public excommunication in 1979, exposed the church to much un-wanted attention (Johnson 1989). One manifestation of public interest in LDS family practices was the 1978 publication of a book critical of the church, *Patriarchs and Politics: The Plight of the Mormon Woman* (Warenski 1978). The title captures some of the growing disconnect between church teachings and the broader American culture: much of LDS doctrine was built around a word (*patriarchal* priesthood, *patriarchal* marriage, *patriarchal* family, *patriarchal* blessing) that was fast becoming a pejorative.

But the sources of pressure were not all external. Quantitative data from an earlier study found that although the church's affirmation of traditional roles strengthened the commitment of more experienced members, it weak-ened that of younger, less experienced members and potential converts (Ian-naccone and Miles 1990). This weakened commitment could also be seen in falling participation rates of young women (Hinckley 1988; Goaslind 1992). Female members of the church were following the same trends in employ-ment and decreased family size as other American women. Though LDS women have always had more children on average than other American women, their birthrate followed the same trend downward (Heaton 1968),[5] and married LDS women in general were participating in the paid work-force at about the same rate as their non-Mormon counterparts (although more were working part- rather than full-time) (Heaton 1994).[6]

Furthermore, LDS women were not working just for self-fulfillment or unnecessary consumer items: unpublished surveys of the membership under-taken by the church in the 1980s and '90s reportedly indicated that a signifi-cant number of LDS families would have relatively low incomes were it not for the mothers' earnings. Ironically, the church's simultaneous emphasis on large families, college education, and family-financed missionary service for young adults provided additional reasons to seek a supplement to fathers' in-comes (Hafen 1992). All together, these social forces probably explain church leaders' increasingly sympathetic treatment of working mothers.

Accommodations for Working Mothers

Although Peterson and others decried selfish motives for women's employ-ment outside the home, they nonetheless recognized that some women were their families' sole earners and must work. Such women, Peterson said, were exceptions. Nonetheless, these exceptions appeared to be common enough that writers began to spell out the conditions under which a mother might go to work. One of the earliest, Relief Society president Barbara Smith, was nearly as cautious as Peterson but concluded that a woman "should evaluate the needs and/or reasons for gainful employment and be sure that her children are not neglected before she and her husband decide if she should enter or reenter the labor force" (1979, 22).

Ensign staff member Lavina Fielding also noted, "Even though a woman's most important contribution is ... to her family, it need not be her only contribution—if she has the active support of her husband and family in her choice and *if* that choice receives the approbation of the Lord. I would imagine that the Lord would not give his approval with any great frequency, but there will be situations and times when he does and will approve of a woman working outside the home" (1976, 20). Perhaps not entirely comfortable with this solution, Fielding warned that Satan and individuals can subvert the system of receiving God's approval. She urged anyone receiving an answer that takes them away from what most Latter-day Saints are doing should check their answer very carefully. Falling back onto patriarchal authority, she also counseled that husbands and priesthood leaders have the right to receive corroborating revelations for women.

But since God *might* give approval to mothers working outside the home, Fielding appealed, "It is especially distressing to see the divisions that can separate sisters when they judge each other ... where it is so very hard ... to know *all* the facts" (ibid). This article, though advising that mothers in general should not work, also taught that they might if God specifically approved, and that these women should not be condemned by other church members.

These articles and others stated that although a mother's employment was not ideal, if she has a true financial need (not just a desire for "luxuries") and her husband's approval, has ascertained that her children will be well cared for, and has prayed for and received the Lord's approval, then she is justified in going to work. Furthermore, other members should refrain from judging a working mother, as they have no way of knowing that she has not met these criteria.

Though recognizing financial hardship as a valid reason for a mother to pursue a career, a number of testimonials from former working mothers gently suggested that perhaps, if one were faithful, the financial need would be met in other ways. Later speeches stressed that providing materially is the husband's responsibility, not the wife's. Apostle Ezra Taft Benson, for example, believed that wives should not be concerned with providing financially: "It is a misguided idea that a woman should leave the home, where there is a husband and children present, to prepare educationally and financially for an unforeseen eventuality. Too often, I fear, even women in the Church use the world as their standard for success and basis for self-worth" (1981, 105). This theme would be repeated in later years. But strong objections to women's employment were becoming a minority, as seen in a 1990 article, "When Mom Can't Be Home: Making the Best of Second Choice." This article laid out child-care options for women who must work. The authors clearly regarded nonparental child care as dangerous, but the presence of this article in the church magazine stands in surprising contrast to the First Presidency's 1942 and Peterson's 1974 insistence that no one besides a child's own mother can adequately care for him or her. The writers acknowledged,

> For many mothers, day care is not a choice—it's a necessity. Due to divorce, death of a spouse, or economic hardship, mothers sometimes find it necessary to work outside the home. Who should care for their children? When first choice for day care—Mother—isn't possible, who's second? Can anyone adequately replace her? The answers aren't simple. *It is a matter requiring inspired guidance.*
>
> ... Latter-day Saints who, of necessity, must leave their children for a period of time should plan carefully in order to lessen the negative effects of nonparental child care. (Winder, Evans, and Doxey 1990, 16; emphasis added)

The authors suggested that local congregations hold seminars to help parents with these choices and asked that leaders and members be more sensitive to the needs—and less judgmental—of parents who require day care.

The extent of accommodation to working mothers can be seen in members' reactions to the same pronouncement made at different points in time. In 1977, then church president Spencer W. Kimball gave a talk in which he repeated his 1963 call for mothers to "come home":

> I beg of you, you who could and should be bearing and rearing a family: wives, come home from the typewriter, the laundry, the nursing, come home from the factory, the café. No career approaches in importance that of wife, homemaker, mother—cooking meals, washing dishes, making beds for one's precious husband and children. Come home, wives, to your husbands. Make home a heaven for them. Come home, wives, to your children, born and unborn. Wrap the motherly cloak about you and, unembarrassed, help in a major role to create bodies for the immortal souls who anxiously await. (8)

When they were given, Kimball's remarks fitted neatly with other admonitions from this period. However, when Kimball's successor, Ezra Taft Benson, quoted extensively from this talk in a 1987 special fireside address (which was afterward published as a widely distributed pamphlet titled *To the Mothers in Zion*), his repetition of Kimball's call for mothers to "come home" was quite out of keeping with the accommodations that had been made in the intervening years. *Salt Lake Tribune* religion writer Peggy Fletcher Stack reported the quiet uproar it caused, as "dozens if not hundreds of Mormon women quit their jobs... while others felt guilty for ignoring that mandate" (2003, C1).[7] An *Ensign* article published in 1988 also recounted the guilt and consternation that resulted from Benson's reminder that

> the Lord's way to rear our children is different from the world's way.... In the beginning, Adam—not Eve—was instructed to earn the bread by the sweat of his brow. Contrary to conventional wisdom, a mother's calling is in the home, not in the marketplace. One woman interviewed said, "Before, I would cry every time I'd hear a Church leader say I should be home with my children.... [W]hen President Ezra Taft Benson... told mothers to stay home, I felt so guilty and miserable that all I could do was cry." (Rodriguez 1988, 13)

Other leaders voiced strong sympathy for working mothers, sometimes suggesting that their situation was nearly impossible (Pinborough 1986, quoting Kimball 1978). In a continuation of the Benson's-citation-of-Kimball saga, later church president Gordon B. Hinckley referred to Benson's 1987 speech:

> Some years ago President Benson delivered a message to the women of the Church. He encouraged them to leave their employment and give their individual time to their children. I sustain the position which he took.
> Nevertheless, I recognize, as he recognized, that there are some women (it has become very many in fact) who have to work to provide for the needs of their families. To you I say, do the very best you can. I hope that if you are employed full-time you are doing it to ensure that basic needs are met and not simply to indulge a taste for an elaborate home, fancy cars, and other luxuries. The greatest job that any mother will ever do will be in nurturing, teaching, lifting, encouraging, and rearing her children in righteousness and truth. None other can adequately take her place.

It is well-nigh impossible to be a full-time homemaker and a full-time employee. I know how some of you struggle with decisions concerning this matter. I repeat, do the very best you can. You know your circumstances, and I know that you are deeply concerned for the welfare of your children. (1996, 67)

Later, President Hinckley went beyond sympathy for working mothers to providing role models for them. As Stack has noted, in a talk to teenage girls, Hinckley spoke about meeting an LDS nurse who was raising three children while working:

There is such a demand for people with her skills that she can do almost anything she pleases," the 93-year-old leader said. "She is the kind of woman of whom you might dream as you look to the future."

The work of raising a family should be tantamount to a woman's life, he says, but it is up to individual women (with their spouses) to decide when and how best to accomplish it. Education is important for women and so is self-respect. Simple ideas, maybe, but in a Mormon context almost revolutionary. (2003, C1)

In 2004 Hinckley told the church's twelve- to eighteen-year-old girls to "study your options. Pray to the Lord earnestly for direction. Then pursue your course with resolution. The whole gamut of human endeavor is now open to women" (82). According to Hinckley, then, women who study their options and pray for direction can "pursue [their] course with resolution."

Self-fulfillment and Sequential Careers

In articles published prior to the midsixties, women who chose careers over having children, or who insisted on working when their children were young, were condemned for craving material possessions over the welfare of their children. Later articles attributed women's desire for careers to personal needs, such as a desire for attention, acclaim, or self-fulfillment. They insisted that these were unworthy motives and that homemaking should be challenging enough for any woman. By the middle of the 1970s, however, the literature began to make allowances for a woman's need for self-expression outside of the family. Particularly notable in this regard were articles from about 1974 to 1980 that, while urging women to put their families' needs before their own, also encouraged a "sequential" arrangement in which women first raise families and then seek careers or other extrahousehold activities.

Although as early as the 1940s church leaders allowed that women could pursue extrafamilial interests after the children were grown (Neal 1948), one of the first attempts to flesh out this possibility can be found in a talk given by President Kimball's wife, Camilla Kimball, in 1977. She hoped that "every girl and woman ... had the desire and ambition to qualify for two vocations—that of homemaking, and that of preparing to earn a living outside the home." She recognized the importance of being able to earn a living, but earnings aside,

> another valid reason for a woman to prepare herself to fulfill a vocation is that not all of her lifetime could possibly be completely filled with demands of a family, home, and children. The later years of a woman's life should be viewed as a time that can be socially and professionally productive. When a mother's children are reared, or if she is childless, the years after forty or fifty may begin to look bleak.... Let her study a profession or adopt a trade, or find some absorbing subject for study and research. (58–59)

Relief Society president Barbara Smith, who joined H. Burke Peterson and others in warning against the pursuit of "personal gratification at the expense of ... one's children, husband, or other close associates," also advised that women need not abandon all hope of fulfilling personal or career goals. "The years before and after child rearing," she wrote, "should be productive" (1976, 23).

The sequential-careers solution became even more prominent in the 1980s and '90s. In an address given at Brigham Young University and later published in the *Ensign,* apostle James E. Faust said:

> The struggle to improve the place of women in society has been a noble cause and I sincerely hope the day will come when women with equal skills will be fully equal with men in the marketplace.
>
> But ... you cannot do everything well at the same time.... Says [one young mother]: "The only answer I come up with is that you can have it sequentially. At one stage you may emphasize career, and at another marriage and nurturing young children, and at any point you will be aware of what is missing. If you are lucky, you will be able to fit everything in." (1988, 36; repeated to a great extent in Faust 1998)

Broadening Role Definitions

Another way in which the LDS Church accomodates extradomestic activities for women has been by broadening the definition of "strengthening the home." In an interview, Relief Society president Barbara W. Winder did just this:

> President Spencer W. Kimball told us that our prime priority in life ought to be to enrich, to protect, and to guard the home. There are many ways we can do this. Many women are at the hearth, teaching their children by their side. Some women are in the classroom. Some are in the courtroom, guarding and defending the home. Some are in medicine, helping to protect us against the ills and dangers of life.
>
> We watched a group of women in Tallahassee, Florida, leave their homes for a period of time to lobby for some important legislation for their community. To me, that is guarding and defending the home. (1986, 19)

In 1984 another leader, though still affirming motherhood's special status and responsibilities, widened Kimball's injunction of "Mother, come home" to include fathers too, writing, "Parents come home" (Cook 1984, 30). Playing on this theme, Faust gave a talk titled "Father, Come Home" (1993). More recent articles also urge fathers to take a greater role in caring for children and helping their wives with household chores (Hafen 1992; Faust 1988, 1993; Matheson 1989; Hinckley 1993; Pinborough 1986; Nelson 1999).

Accommodating Change without Changing

Although the first writers note that the option of a career after the children are grown is permissible, later articles endorse it so strongly as to make it virtually a new part of the "ideal" woman's life. By asking that women postpone gratification of these interests until later in life, the literature assures women that they can have both a family and a career—and put their educations to good use—while still maintaining the divinely approved family structure of "father-provider" and "mother-homemaker."

The concessions allowing employment for mothers with children still at home make it possible for the member who needs to work to do so without being in open conflict with church teachings. However, even though the literature allows for the employment of mothers, it continues to hold up the ideal of the nonworking mother caring full-time for her family. Even the exceptions to this ideal are justified in terms of it. The requirement that women seek divine approval for employment, for example, acknowledges that this is a rule so steadfast that only God can grant dispensation from it. Having decreed woman's eternal role, only God (and her husband) can (temporarily) release her from it. When mothers talk about their employment in deprecating terms—"I wish I didn't have to work, but I need a paycheck to sustain my family"—leaders can respond, "Your situation is not the ideal, and we feel sorry for you, but it is okay. Do the best you can" (Jack 1990, 88).

These examples illustrate how an organization can exercise flexibility in practice while maintaining purity of doctrine (Tawney 1926). Continuing to express a traditional value protects organizational integrity; allowing deviations from the ideal gives the individual member a means of reconciling the conflict between the religious ideals and the behaviors rewarded by society and the economy. Although on a symbolic level the conflict between church and society persists, on a practical level members may do what they have to do without becoming alienated from the church.

Unexpected Change versus Negotiated Difference

Social and economic changes that take individuals in directions opposed by the moral institution of which they are a part cause problems because they create a new boundary between society and the organization, one that was not considered when the adherents committed to the organization. The economic and social shifts of the sixties took many women, families, and churches by surprise, and required those straddling the boundary to renegotiate their commitment to the church. But although social change can cause severe crises for organizations and individuals, *differences* with the culture in which they are embedded per se are not necessarily a problem. In fact, work by Laurence R. Iannaccone and others suggests that difference—an "optimal gap," or tension—with the surrounding culture is a critical characteristic of a strong church (Iannaccone and Miles 1990; Iannaccone 1994). A well-calibrated gap works to the organization's advantage, setting members apart from the rest of society and discouraging "free-riders" (Iannaccone 1992). Leaders of strict religious organizations are often aware of the need for difference with secular culture. Gordon B. Hinckley, for example, has stated, "If we were entirely without criticism, we would be concerned. Our responsibility is not to please the world but, rather, to do the will of the Lord, and from the beginning the divine will so often has been contrary to the ways of the world" (1993, 54; see also Ballard 1993).

Although the conflict between LDS family values and the equality of women as a secular feminist would define it still exists, I suggest that the conflict is no longer that of unexpected *change* but of a negotiated *difference*.

After all, the greatest change in women's roles occurred in the late sixties and early seventies. In a 2003 article for the *Salt Lake Tribune,* Peggy Fletcher Stack asked, "Where have all the Mormon feminists gone?" The answer, according to LDS historian Claudia Bushman, is that Mormon feminism died with the generation that conceived it. According to Jill Derr, managing director of BYU's Smith Institute of Latter-day Saint History, young scholars today—those most likely to be affected by the new boundary between church and society—"take equality between men and women on a personal and professional level as a given. They did not live through the polarizing era that was such a marked part of our lives" (Stack 2003, C1).

Clarifying and maintaining a difference, however, require a certain amount of doctrinal tidiness, and a not inconsiderable amount of energy to maintain the difference as a boundary. Though it is difficult to name the date on which the situation switched from fighting change to maintaining a boundary, below I present evidence that just such a working out of doctrine has taken place, culminating in the 1995 "Proclamation on the Family."

Elaboration of the Doctrine of the Family

As I suggested earlier, before a social or economic change emerges, religious and social norms may be identical and taken for granted. When secular practices move out from under old societal patterns, however, resistant institutions have to find a way to justify and support practices and teachings that are no longer so obviously correct.

As the twentieth century and the women's movement out of the household progressed, LDS leaders' talks betrayed an interest in finding a firmer doctrinal foundation to support their resistance to change. Though as Dallin H. Oaks said in 2005, "The theology of The Church of Jesus Christ of Latter-day Saints centers on the family" (24), I suggest that church leadership found it is difficult to support either this high view of family or the historic sexual division of labor from its scriptures. No biblical passage demands marriage and family as essential for salvation or requires the sexual division of labor—Jesus in fact says that following him will set family members at war with each other. Nor can support for these views be found in uniquely LDS scriptures; Joseph Smith never systematized or widely taught his doctrines about the nature of God and humankind's potential as gods in embryo. The only public forum in which he discussed them was in a funeral sermon given in the last year of his own life (Smith 193?).

This lack of scriptural support for LDS teachings on family is evident in less than successful attempts by church leaders to provide it in talks from about 1990 on. The article by the Relief Society General Presidency (1990) on child care cites a number of Book of Mormon references to provide scriptural support for their argument that parents' first priority should be the spiritual needs of their children. Similarly, Faust (1988, 1993), Hinckley (1993), and others have cited Doctrine and Covenants 83:2: "Women have claim on their husbands for their maintenance, until their husbands are taken." Hinckley (1993) quoted a similar passage in the New Testament: "But if any provide not for his own, and especially for those of his own house, he hath denied the faith, and is worse than an infidel" (1 Tim. 5:8). None of these verses are particularly apt for the problem at hand, however. To state that women have a financial claim on their husbands does nothing to address women's desire for a career outside the family, nor situations in which the husband cannot provide that maintenance despite being told of his obligation to do so.

Others have quoted a revelation on celestial or eternal marriage in Doctrine and Covenants 132 (Black 2002; Howard 2003; Kofford 1998). This revelation certainly lays out the religious significance of motherhood and the need for an eternally sealed marriage and for humankind's future as gods. But referring members to Doctrine and Covenants 132 may raise more questions than it answers, as it was given as a revelation defending celestial marriage in its original sense, that is, polygamy. It justifies polygamy in terms of women's need to "bear the souls of men" and assures the reader that the giving of many virgins to one man is fine, as long as the women are virgins. Neither of these explanations, however, is likely to play well in the postfeminist, monogamous culture to which Jill Derr referred.

Nor are these verses strong enough to support the church's lofty and romantic view of motherhood, marriage, and family relationships. One verse that does capture some of this high view, used several times to back up claims that the Plan of Salvation requires marriage of everyone, is 1 Corinthians 11:11: "Neither is the man without the woman, neither woman without the man, in the Lord." Using this verse to make this point proves dangerous, however, as just a few pages earlier its author, the apostle Paul, stated that he preferred Christians not to marry (1 Cor. 7).

The Proclamation on the Family

The problem of supporting the LDS family doctrine from scriptures was explicitly acknowledged by Boyd K. Packer at a Church Educational System symposium: "Individual doctrines of the gospel are not fully explained in one place in the scriptures, nor presented in order or sequence. They must be assembled from pieces here and there. They are sometimes found in large segments, but mostly they are in small bits scattered through the chapters and verses" (1993, 1).[8]

The church solved this problem in 1995 with the publication of "The Family: A Proclamation to the World." Neither sermon, revelation, nor manifesto, the proclamation was issued in the name of the First Presidency and Quorum of the Twelve Apostles and appeared as a new and unique form of communicating God's will to church members. As another chapter in this volume addresses the proclamation, I will not give much detail here, except to say that it covers all of the issues with which church leadership had been struggling since the 1960s: the centrality of marriage and family in the "Creator's plan," that this "divine plan of happiness enables family relationships to be perpetuated beyond the grave" through participation in LDS rituals, the essential and eternal nature of gender, the ongoing importance of obeying God's command to "multiply and replenish the earth" (but only within lawful marriage), and parental accountability to rear their children well. Most significantly for the present discussion, "The Family: A Proclamation to the World" provides, finally, a scriptural basis for the sexual division of labor: "By divine design, fathers are to preside over the families in love and righteousness and are responsible to provide the necessities of life and protection of their families. Mothers are primarily responsible for the nurture of their children." But though defining gender roles as absolute, the proclamation still gives a nod to modern economic forces: "In these sacred responsibilities, fathers and mothers are obligated to help one another as equal partners. Disability, death, or other circumstances may necessitate individual adaptation. Extended families should lend support when needed" (102).

Although the proclamation has not been officially canonized, it serves the function of scripture in offering an authoritative reference for Mormons concerned with family issues. Issued and publicized with a great deal of fanfare, members are encouraged to have a copy and to read and reread it "carefully and prayerfully," sentence by sentence (Hinckley 1998, 97). Frequent references are made to it in church settings, and testimonies bear out its truthfulness and effectiveness.[9] General Authority L. Aldin Porter even warned "those who are not yet married [that if] your proposed marriage partner is not in agreement with the doctrines taught therein, know there is danger in your committing your life to him or her" (2001, n.p.). Members frame the proclamation and hang it on the wall next to pictures of the temples, Jesus, or the leaders of the church.

Getting a Testimony of Motherhood

When an organization makes the decision, consciously or not, to enforce a boundary between itself and its social environment, it has to persuade its adherents to accept that boundary. Although since the 1950s *Improvement Era/Ensign* articles have occasionally included "testimonies" given by women who made the decision to stay at home rather than work, the number of them as well as the number of short pieces on the general topic of motherhood have increased dramatically since the publication of Benson's pamphlet *To the Mothers in Zion* in 1987. An article published shortly after this publication, for example, paid explicit testimony to Benson's teachings. After giving passing recognition to mothers who "must work outside the home as a matter of necessity," the article provided "several accounts of mothers who did have a choice to be at home—and how they made the decision to be with their children." These women all told of their resistance to the idea of staying at home, of how painful they found actually being there (crying every day when the husbands left for work), of the financial sacrifices they had to make, or of how turning down a job offer was one of the hardest things they ever did. Then all spoke of the good things that came their way as a result of their decision to obey the prophet: "As [the husband and wife] prayed together, the peace that engulfed them testified that they had made the right decision" (Rodriguez 1989, 13).

Many other articles followed this pattern, telling of women struggling with stay-at-home motherhood until some key turning point or insight that gave them a new appreciation of the religious importance of their role, often brought about by prayer (Nunes 1996; Gaines 1992; Horeth 1996; Bramwell 1998; Dalley 1999; Dalton 1995; Burr 2001). One frustrated mother wrote explicitly of how she "needed"—and received—"a personal testimony of the divine calling of motherhood" (Lanoy 1999, 53). In conference talks, leaders often bear witness to the "divine nature" of motherhood, some using the standard LDS formula for testimony bearing (Hinckley 1996; Scott 2000). Consider for example Relief Society counselor Sheri L. Dew's 2001 statements that the "doctrine of motherhood" "*is* a doctrine" and that "I know, I absolutely know, that these doctrines about our divine role are true" (96). Others bear testimony to the Proclamation on the Family (Relief Society General Presidency 2000), calling the proclamation a product of "most certainly the inspiration of heaven" (Porter 2001, n.p.).

One mother's statement about motherhood provides a classic example of the LDS testimony-bearing formula. First writing of how prayer and inspiration helped her make the decision to stay at home, she said,

I am grateful to be a mother. I bear testimony that mothering is, in the words of my patriarchal blessing, "a great and important work given to women of the Church." I thank Heavenly Father for this privilege to assist in his work—"to bring to pass the immortality and eternal life of man" (Moses 1:39).

I bear testimony of his love and interest in helping us, of the accessibility of his guidance through prophets and prayer, and of his kindness and forgiveness for the errors we may make. As mothers in Zion and as sisters in the gospel of Jesus Christ, we are on the Lord's errand. (Inouye 1993, 96)

A 2000 piece by convert Marian Pond provides perhaps the most enlightening example of how a religious organization's difference with its social environment requires explicit acceptance of its boundaries. In 1977, Pond was a graduate student planning a career in biochemistry, a male-dominated field. She wrote, "I certainly did not plan to be a mother." When she became interested in joining the church, she "struggled to reconcile [her] career goals with teachings about the importance of motherhood," writing in her journal, "My heart really wants to know if, in truth, the role of wife and mother *is* my place. And if I find it is, I hope God will grant me the grace to accept and grow in that role." As she studied, prayed, and attended church, she experienced "a growing assurance in my heart of the direction I should take, and with that I abandoned the familiar women's rights compass and the goals that came with it" (59). To join the church today, the potential member, especially a woman, not only has to obtain a testimony of the truthfulness of the church but must also develop a testimony of the eternal and earthly importance of motherhood.[10]

Using Difference

In that earlier article, Laurence R. Iannaccone and I suggest that the church uses this emergent boundary as a marketing device. The contemporary church now offers not just a Golden Bible, living prophets, and the Word of Wisdom but also a means of saving each individual family and family member. Moreover, it offers a refuge for potential members who are also disturbed over the decline of the family in the modern world. From a marketing perspective, the church's emphasis on family life is probably an effective tool. A recent survey found that most American women are less concerned about their careers than they are about spiritual values and the welfare of their families, and another reported that 41 percent of Americans answered "better" to the question, "Considering everything, do you think it would be better or worse for the country if men and women went back to the traditional roles they had in the fifties...?" (Patterson 1998, 113). The movement of women into the workplace has leveled out since the 1990s (see fig. 5.1). Finally, from a proselytizing point of view, there is the simple fact that women who are greatly concerned about high-powered careers and women's rights are not the sort of people who join any church at all. Why bother reforming a belief system in order to appease a category of people who would not be interested under any circumstances?

Running Up the Value of Motherhood

One other trend in the LDS literature suggests that it may be easier to attract and retain members with a positive difference rather than a negative one. In my original study of LDS literature, I coded articles on what they said or implied about equality between the sexes. As it turned out, there was no variation on this factor. Although LDS leaders insist that men and women are given different assignments or roles to play in this life, as Thomas O'Dea notes, they consistently affirm women's inherent ability to perform other roles or to perform well in the workplace (1957, 249).

With the new doctrine of motherhood, however, the church goes far beyond affirming equality. More recent talks and articles offer literal paeans to female virtue and the critical importance of the feminine role. In a 1994 conference talk, President Howard W. Hunter quoted the First Presidency in saying, "Motherhood is near to divinity. It is the highest, holiest service to be assumed by mankind" (49). Similarly, James E. Faust wrote, "In recent years a debate has raged about the equality of the sexes. Women are not in any sense lesser creations than men. In fact, they lose something when they are compared to men.... [A] 'beautiful, modest, gracious woman is creation's masterpiece'" (1988, 36; citation from David O. McKay). President Hinckley (1991, 2004), asked in a letter from a fourteen-year-old girl why Adam was created first, replied that Eve was made last because she was God's masterpiece. Leaders have also stressed that whereas "women are dependent upon men and upon marriage for exaltation," men are equally dependent on women (O'Dea 1957, 250).[11]

The 1942 message from the First Presidency of the Church included perhaps the first mention of the "divine nature of motherhood" (Grant, Clark, and McKay).[12] This "divine nature" and mothers' partnership with God in creating life became very common themes in the decades that followed. Comments by late president Kimball give a good example of such teachings. Noting that God held motherhood sacred and in the highest esteem,

Kimball continued, "He has entrusted to his daughters the great responsibility of bearing and nurturing children. This is a great, irreplaceable work of women. Life cannot go on if women cease to bear children. Mortal life is ... a necessary step in eternal progression" (1978, 106).

Other writers call women and mothers beings of "infinite worth" (Nelson 1989, 20); "a partner with God" (Dalton 1995, 19; Kimball 1978); "a sacred role" (Kimball 1978, 106); a "regenerating force," "something divine," an "unparalleled role" (Dew 2001, 96); the "real builders of the nation" (Hinckley 1996, 67); "an instrument in the hands of God" (Ballard 2002, 89); "a thing sacred and divine" (Hinckley 1988, n.p.). "Each mother has been given a sacred trust and ... no responsibility exceeds hers in importance" (J. Evans 1999, 56). Motherhood is so important that Satan himself opposes this role (Nelson 1989, 20).

CONCLUSION

Many other conservative religious institutions, Christian and otherwise, reacted strongly to mid-twentieth-century threats to conventional morality and family life. Whether these changes proved *more* difficult for the Church of Jesus Christ of Latter-day Saints than for these other institutions is an empirical question that I have not attempted to answer here. But these changes posed difficulties enough, and as O'Dea observed, the source of these problems lay in the church's own structure, particularly in belief in the patriarchal family structure that was a residual of its practice of polygamy (1957, 222). Teaching that marriage, childbearing, gender, and sexuality are eternal attributes not just of humankind but of God, the LDS Church had to tread carefully in renegotiating its boundaries in the face of technological change that undermined social support for historic family forms.

A parallel to the church's ultimate tactic of enforcing family ideals in a positive, noncoercive manner can be found in its treatment of the use of birth control. In the early twentieth century, the LDS Church, like nearly all other Christian churches, came down strongly against "tampering with the fountains of life." But the Mormon emphasis shifted from the prohibition of birth control to stressing the glories of having a large family.[13] This was probably an effective strategy, especially when contrasted with the approach taken by the Roman Catholic Church. Catholicism prohibits the use of contraceptives and has gone so far as to make its teachings against it doctrinal. Sociologist Andrew Greeley (1976) argues that the Catholic Church has lost authority as a result. The LDS Church's positive emphasis on having large families has the advantage of, if producing only slightly more children than those born to their non-Mormon counterparts, at least not alienating members who are unwilling or unable to have a large family.

Similarly, in the case of the employment of mothers, outright prohibition puts too many members in the position of having to choose between "following the prophet" and meeting the economic needs of their family. By instead stressing the importance of parenting, family, and devoted motherhood and by praising women and their innate virtues and strengths, the church has found a way to turn its difference with society into an appealing feature rather than a repellant bug.[14] Consider the difference between being known as the church that can help members build family health and harmony in the midst of destructive forces versus being known as the patriarchal institution that defeated the Equal Rights Amendment.

Having tidied up its teachings on the eternal nature and import of family life in a manner independent of its polygamous past, the church may have resolved the contradictory forces that O'Dea warned about. The Proclamation on the Family also addresses many of the trends that few people writing fifty years ago could have anticipated: the rising age of first marriage, increases in the percentage of the adult population in the United States and Europe that have never married at all, increasing nonmarital births, continued decline in belief in chastity before marriage, birthrates that are dropping below replacement levels in many developed countries, and demands for same-sex marriage. Whether the proclamation is effective in addressing the conflicts it is currently facing on these issues will perhaps be a subject for a one hundred–year retrospective on *The Mormons*.

NOTES

1. Although this system has virtually disappeared in the United States and Europe today, these conditions persist in most of the rest of the world.

2. The social and moral upheavals of the 1960s should not be considered as discrete events but rather as a continuation of trends in family life and sexuality under way for decades but interrupted by the Great Depression, world wars, and the reactive but temporary return to domesticity that characterized their ends.

3. Another consequence of the shift of production from the home and the fading need for sexual complementarity is the increasing demand for acceptance of homosexual practice, including same-sex marriage.

4. Or conversely, the disadvantage that mothers have relative to fathers in the workplace—the physical demands and disability of pregnancy, childbirth, and breast-feeding, including lost sleep. The career advancement lost to childbearing will be especially significant if a woman bears several children.

5. In a 2005 speech, LDS apostle Dallin Oaks noted this trend at work among the Mormons as well, with a rising age of marriage for young Saints and decline in the LDS birthrate (Lee–St. John 2005).

6. For the impact of varying levels of religious commitment on women's employment, see Chadwick and Garrett 1995.

7. Benson also urged couples to have more children. However, although his call for mothers to quit their jobs struck a responsive chord, I found no later allusions to this aspect of his talk.

8. This conclusion sets the family-oriented Plan of Salvation in sharp contrast to the well-developed doctrines of the early Latter-day Restoration. O'Dea (1957), for example, observed that the Book of Mormon provided definitive answers to every religious controversy of Joseph Smith's day.

9. For example, Relief Society general president Mary Ellen Smoot told of a congregation in Brazil that decided "to not let even one week pass without each newly baptized sister receiving . . . a copy of 'The Family: A Proclamation to the World.' . . . [S]o far they haven't lost any sisters to inactivity" (2000, 89).

10. The flip side of testimony bearing on the rightness of staying home is the numerous articles that counsel women who had prayerfully made the decision to work outside the home to also turn to the Lord for "the sense of peace we need in order to follow our personal decisions. Knowing that the Spirit has confirmed our course brings comfort and assurance" (Pinborough 1986). These statements are made hand in hand with those urging members to refrain from judging employed mothers. Although the answer that outside work is permissible may be received with surprise (or disbelief on the part of judgmental observers), the fact that it is received according to the "rules" contributes to its credibility.

11. Doctrine and practices that implied that women were spiritually dependent on their husbands' discretion for their exaltation have been eliminated.

12. Gordon Shepherd and Gary Shepherd's massive content analysis of church publications revealed no use of this term prior to 1942 (1984).

13. The 1999 *Handbook of Instruction* is reputed to have directed bishops to avoid discussing the topic of family size at all.

14. Increasing references to the "Plan of Salvation" as the "Great Plan of Happiness" also look like a calculated attempt to make religious requirements look more attractive.

REFERENCES

Ballard, M. Russell. 1993. "Equality through Diversity." *Ensign*, November, 89.

———. 2002. "Women of Righteousness." Devotional address given at Brigham Young University. *Ensign*, April, 66–73.

Barlow, Brent A. 1973. "Strengthening the Patriarchal Order in the Home." *Ensign*, February, 28–33.

Becker, Gary S. 1991. *A Treatise on the Family.* Cambridge: Harvard University Press.

Bennion, Adam S. 1917. *What It Means to Be Mormon.* Salt Lake City: Deseret Sunday School Union.

Benson, Ezra Taft. 1981. "The Honored Place of Woman." *Ensign,* November, 104–7.

———. 1987. *To the Mothers in Zion.* Fireside address, February 22. Printed 1987. Salt Lake City: Church of Jesus Christ of Latter-day Saints.

Black, Susan Easton. 2002. "Happiness in Womanhood." *Ensign,* March, 12.

Bleier, Ruth. 1984. *Science and Gender: A Critique of Biology and Its Theories on Women.* New York: Pergamon Press.

Bramwell, Mary Ellen. 1998. "Was I Meant to Be a Mother Today?" *Ensign,* June, 53.

Burr, Cheryl Cole. 2001. "A Better Mother, with the Lord's Help." *Ensign,* July, 72.

Chadwick, B. A., and H. D. Garrett. 1995. "Women's Religiosity and Employment: The LDS Experience." *Review of Religious Research* 36, no. 3: 277–93.

Cook, Gene R. 1984. "Home and Family: A Divine Eternal Pattern." *Ensign,* May, 30.

Cowan, Ruth Schwartz. 1983. *More Work for Mother: The Ironies of Household Technology from the Open Hearth to the Microwave.* New York: Basic Books.

Dalley, Winnie. 1999. "Seize the Joy!" *Ensign,* March, 58.

Dalton, Davida (as told to JoEllen Johnson). 1995. "In His Mother's Footsteps." *Liahona,* November, 19.

Dew, Sheri L. 2001. "Are We Not All Mothers?" *Ensign,* November, 96.

Evans, Joy F. 1999. "Meditations on Motherhood." *Ensign,* February, 56.

Evans, Richard L. 1943. "To the Mothers of the Race." *Improvement Era,* 288.

"The Family: A Proclamation to the World." 1995. *Ensign,* November, 102.

Faust, James E. 1988. "The Highest Place of Honor." *Ensign,* May, 36.

———. 1993. "Father, Come Home." *Ensign,* May, 95.

———. 1998. "How Near to the Angels." *Ensign,* May, 95.

Fielding, Lavina. 1976. "Problems, Solutions: Being a Latter-day Saint Woman Today." *Ensign,* March, 16–22.

Friedan, Betty. 1963. *The Feminine Mystique.* London: Penguin Books.

Gaines, Karla. 1992. "Motherhood: Expectations and Lessons." *Ensign,* March, 28.

Goaslind, Jack H. 1992. *BYU Daily Universe,* August 31.

Grant, Heber J., R. L. Clark, and David O. McKay. 1942. "Message from the First Presidency." *Improvement Era,* 601–12.

Greeley, Andrew. 1976. "Council or Encyclical?" *Review of Religious Research* 18: 3–24.

Hafen, Marie K. 1992. "Celebrating Womanhood." *Ensign,* June, 50.

Heaton, Tim B. 1968. "How Does Religion Influence Fertility? The Case of Mormons." *Journal for the Scientific Study of Religion* 25, no. 2: 248–58.

———. 1994. "Familial, Socio-economic, and Religious Behavior: A Comparison of LDS and Non-LDS Women." *Dialogue* 27, no. 2: 169–83.

Hinckley, Gordon B. 1988. "Our Responsibility to Our Young Women." Regional Representatives Seminar, April 1.

———. 1991. "Daughters of God." *Ensign,* November, 97.

———. 1993. "Bring Up a Child in the Way He Should Go." *Ensign,* November, 54.

———. 1996. "Women of the Church." *Ensign,* November, 67.

———. 1998. "Walking in the Light of the Lord." *Ensign,* November, 97.

———. 2004. "The Women in Our Lives." *Ensign,* November, 82.

Horeth, Karen. 1996. "Only Three Dollars in the Bank." *Ensign,* October, 53.

Howard, F. Burton. 2003. "Eternal Marriage." *Ensign,* May, 92.

Hunter, Howard W. 1994. "Being a Righteous Husband and Father." *Ensign,* November, 49.

Hurtado, C. L. 1973. "Much More than Housewives: The American Mothers of the Year." *Ensign,* November, 49–53.

Iannaccone, Laurence R. 1992. "Sacrifice and Stigma: Reducing Free-Riding in Cults, Communes, and Other Collectives." *Journal of Political Economy* 100, no. 2: 271–92.

———. 1994. "Why Strict Churches Are Strong." *American Journal of Sociology* 99, no. 5: 1180–1211.

Iannaccone, Laurence R., and Carrie A. Miles. 1990. "Dealing with Social Change: The Mormon Church's Response to Change in Women's Roles." *Social Forces* 68, no. 4: 1231–50. Reprinted in *Contemporary Mormonism: Social Science Perspectives,* ed. Marie Cornwall, Tim B. Heaton, and Lawrence A. Young, 265–86. Urbana: University of Illinois Press.

Inouye, Jeanne. 1993. "Be of Good Cheer." *Ensign,* November, 96.

Jack, Elaine L. 1990. "These Things Are Manifested unto Us Plainly." *Ensign,* November, 88.

Johnson, Sonia. 1989. *From Housewife to Heretic.* New Haven, Conn.: Wildfire Books.

Josephson, M. C. 1947. "Woman's Place in the Forward March of the Church." *Improvement Era,* July, 452–55.

Kimball, Camille. 1977. "A Woman's Preparation." *Ensign,* March, 58–59.

Kimball, Spencer W. 1963. "Keep Mothers in the Home." *Improvement Era,* December, 1071–74.

———. 1977. Fireside address, San Antonio, Texas, December 3. Cited in *To the Mothers in Zion,* by Ezra Taft Benson. Fireside address, February 22. Printed 1987, Salt Lake City: Church of Jesus Christ of Latter-day Saints.

———. 1978. "Privileges and Responsibilities of Sisters." *Ensign,* November, 102–6.

Kofford, Cree-L. 1998. "Marriage in the Lord's Way." *Ensign,* July, 15.

Lanoy, Janet Drake. 1999. "Discovering Me in Motherhood." *Ensign,* March, 53.

Lee, Harold B. 1972. "Maintain Your Place as Women." *Ensign,* February, 48–56.

Lee–St. John, Jeninne. 2005. "Alone in the Pews." *Time,* December 12, 53.

Lightner, Mary Elizabeth Rollins. 1905. *The Testimony of Mary Elizabeth Rollins Lightner.* Address at Brigham Young University, April 14. BYU Archives and Manuscripts, Provo.

Matheson, Kenneth W. 1989. "But I Thought Husbands Took Out the Garbage!" *Ensign,* October, 29.

Maxwell, Neal A. 1978. "The Women of God." *Ensign,* May, 10–11.

McKay, David O. 1969. "These Two Together." *Improvement Era,* May, 2–3.

Miles, Carrie A. 1982. "Saints and Society: The Effect of Social Change on the Mormon Church." Ph.D. diss., University of Chicago.

———. 1998. "Polygamy and the Economics of Salvation." *Sunstone* (August): 34–45.

———. 2006. *The Redemption of Love: Rescuing Marriage and Sexuality from the Economics of a Fallen World.* Grand Rapids, Mich.: Brazos Press.

Neal, H. S. 1948. "Homing: Pattern for a Day." *Improvement Era,* July, 450–52.

Nelson, Russell M. 1989. "Woman—of Infinite Worth." *Ensign,* November, 20.

———. 1999. "Our Sacred Duty to Honor Women." *Ensign,* April, 3.

Nunes, Rachel Ann. 1996. "The Ruined Dress." *Ensign,* August, 8.

Oaks, Dallin H. 2005. "Priesthood Authority in the Family and the Church." *Ensign,* November, 24.

O'Dea, Thomas F. 1957. *The Mormons.* Chicago: University of Chicago Press.

Packer, Boyd K. 1977. "The Equal Rights Amendment." *Ensign,* March, 6–9.

———. 1993. "The Great Plan of Happiness." Address to the Church Educational System Symposium.

Patterson, Orlando. 1998. *Rituals of Blood: Consequences of Slavery in Two American Centuries.* Washington, D.C.: Civitas.

Peterson, H. Burke. 1974. "Mother, Catch the Vision of Your Call." *Ensign,* May, 31.

Pinborough, Jan Underwood. 1986. "Working Double-Time: The Working Mother's Dilemma." *Ensign,* March, 22.

Pond, Marian. 2000. "Loving the Role I Once Shunned." *Ensign,* October, 59.

Porter, L. Aldin. 2001. "Search the Prophets." Fireside address, Church Educational System, Brigham Young University, February 4.

Relief Society General Presidency. 2000. "Who We Are." *Ensign,* March, 72.

Robinson, M. H. 1956. "Marriage Is Now My Career." *Improvement Era,* March, 148–49, 204.

Rodriguez, Derin Head. 1989. "Mom—at Home." *Ensign,* October, 13.

Scott, Richard G. 2000. "The Sanctity of Womanhood." *Ensign,* May, 36.

Shepherd, Gordon, and Gary Shepherd. 1984. *A Kingdom Transformed: Themes in the Development of Mormonism.* Salt Lake City: University of Utah Press.

Smith, Barbara B. 1976. "New Lamps for Old." *Ensign,* April, 67–69.

———. 1979. "Makers of Homes." *Ensign,* March, 22–24.

Smith, Joseph. 193? [*sic*]. *The King Follett Discourse,* ed. B. H. Roberts. Salt Lake City. Cited in Thomas F. O'Dea, *The Mormons* (Chicago: University of Chicago Press, 1957), 122.

Smoot, Mary Ellen. 2000. "We Are Instruments in the Hands of God." *Ensign,* November, 89.

Spafford, Belle S. 1958. "The Place of the Latter-day Saint Woman." *Improvement Era,* May, 335, 354.

Stack, Peggy Fletcher. 2003. "Where Have All the Mormon Feminists Gone?" *Salt Lake Tribune,* October 4, C1.

Tawney, R. H. 1926. *Religion and the Rise of Capitalism: A Historic Study.* London: J. Murray.

U.S. Bureau of the Census. 2000. *Population Profile of the United States, 2000.* http://www.census.gov/population/pop-profile/2000/chap04.pdf.

Vance, Laura. 2002. "Evolution of Ideals for Women in Mormon Periodicals, 1897–1999." *Sociology of Religion* 63, no. 1: 91–112.

Warenski, Marilyn. 1978. *Patriarch and Politics: The Plight of the Mormon Women.* New York: McGraw-Hill.

Widtsoe, John A. 1942. "What Is the Place of Woman in the Church?" *Improvement Era,* March, 161, 188.

Winder, Barbara W. 1986. "Enriching and Protecting the Home: A Conversation with Barbara W. Winder, Relief Society General President." *Ensign,* March, 19.

Winder, Barbara W., Joy F. Evans, and Joanne B. Doxey. 1990. "When Mom Can't Be Home: Making the Best of a Second Choice." *Ensign,* February, 16–18.

Zelizer, Vivana A. 1985. *Pricing the Priceless Child.* Princeton: Princeton University Press.

6

Mormon Women's Issues in the Twenty-first Century

~ Janet Bennion ~

The Trouble with O'Dea

O'Dea is a master at portraying Mormon history, culture, and social structure from the prevalent 1950s male perspective (1957).[1] To his credit, he recognizes the essential dichotomy inherent in Mormon life: self-actualized individualism versus patriarchal totalitarianism. Yet he fails to apply this dialectic to the experience of women.

It is not his fault, entirely. He, like many scholars of the era, was more keenly aware of the male world and the influence on culture that came from male efforts and vision. Certainly, most American religious movements were strongly patriarchal in the 1950s, as they still are today. O'Dea was simply painting a true depiction of what was served up to his own eyes: a system in which men were in the public forefront as political and religious actors, and women remained in the background as dutifully supportive "auxili-aries" of the larger patriarchal structure. Paradoxically, O'Dea genuinely felt women in Mormon society *were* equal to men, while in the same breath he underscored the basic inequities that women faced within that society: "The father is the head...the legislator, the judge, the governor" of the family, and "women are dependent upon men and marriage for exaltation and are subordinate to men on this earth" (1957, 249–50). O'Dea, like many scholars of the '50s, was blinded to the diversity of female experience and the chang-ing nature of women's roles in the contemporary world.[2]

Surely, as a sociologist and contemporary of Margaret Mead, O'Dea should have incorporated the often hidden half of the Church of Jesus Christ of Latter-day Saints (LDS) cultural life—women's daily regimen, their work in the public realm, their spiritual and emotional needs, and their unique perspectives as Mormon women—rather than house the entire female experience in one paragraph, which he does on page 182. Equally unsettling is O'Dea's attempt to discard any gender-based contradictions or tensions within Mormonism as epiphenomenal or "unimportant," suggesting that in the area of equity, "no difficulties arise" (249). This mirrors the recent sentiment of current LDS prophet Gordon B. Hinckley in the *Boston Globe:* "I haven't found any complaint among our women. I'm sure there are a few, a handful somewhere who may be disaffected for one reason or another, but I've never seen any evidence of it" (Radke 2005, 3).

As one of those few "disaffected" Mormon women, and a product of several generations of "native Mormon intelligentsia" (225),[3] I challenge the efficacy of applying the 1950 "homogeneous" O'Dea depiction of Mormon life, which is still used as a blueprint for social organization and an ecumenical standard, to the vastly heterogeneous and culturally diverse church body. Such an archaic depiction serves to further marginalize and trivialize the lives of Mormons whose experiences do *not* mirror the goals of the 1950s behavioral charter.

For example, there are many Mormon women—and some men—who are underrepresented in both O'Dea's volume and in the church's policies and programs: single women, unmarriageable women, single mothers, lesbian women, feminists, women of color, working or career women, female academics, "Jill" Mormons,[4] barren women, female environmentalists, single fathers, female heads of households, gay men, and polygamous women. These individuals on the fringe are seen as problematic since they do not express the Mormon ideal of eternal marriage and kingdom building, as described in O'Dea's work and in "The Family: A Proclamation to the World" (First Presidency and Council of the Twelve Apostles 1995), used by orthodox Saints as a guide to obtaining the perfect family life. Yet, ironically, as I shall illustrate later in this chapter, the heterogeneous, often marginalized women actually represent the *majority* of female experiences in the church. For example, among the world's approximately six million Mormon women,[5] most are not actually living within a traditional family unit.[6] Mormon divorce rates are only *slightly* lower than the national average for both temple and nontemple, active and inactive, individuals (Judd 2000). Further, more Mormon women than men opt for divorce, indicating that women are not as satisfied in the marriage.[7] Additional studies on Mormon women show that they, more than any other category, are prone to seek therapy and take antidepressants (Ponder 2003). And, finally, there is a growing ennui and dissatisfaction among Mormons, especially young women, as seen in the negative retention rates within Utah (Canham 2005) and the falling participation rates among females (Hinckley 1988).

Although the emphasis that the modern-day church has on the traditional family, as embodied in the proclamation, mirrors the same values and gender roles of the 1950s, it is no longer a true representation of the majority of women's experiences, nor does it reflect a true composition of the contemporary family. Yet O'Dea in the 1950s and the First Presidency of the church in the '90s both depict a relatively idealistic view of men and women and the nature of the Mormon family. According to the proclamation, a man and a woman will be married in the temple and provide a home for the children that are waiting to join them. Men and women are created in the image of God and are expected to follow in his footsteps, marrying as he did, raising his children in a monogamous, loving home, and so on. Gender, in this regard, is seen as a biological given—if you are born with a penis, you are male; if you have a vagina, you are female. Your roles in life follow this biological propensity, defining your purpose and your identity. Further, a child that is born into the union is divinely appointed by God and is sacred, playing out his role in the eternal plan of life. That child shall be loved and cared for; all his or her economic, physical, and spiritual needs shall be provided by the two loving parents.

In this ideal, as depicted by O'Dea on numerous occasions (1957, 249–50), the man of the family is the one to hold the priesthood of God and become the head of the family in all economic, social, and religious decisions. A mother's role is to stay in the home and nurture the children. Finally, the goals of the proclamation will be promoted by citizens and officers of the government in order to strengthen the family unit. Only in one area of the document do the brethren allow for individual variation on this ideal: "disability, death or other circumstances [that] may necessitate individual adaptation." It is the ambiguous arena of "other circumstance" that I emphasize in this paper as, I argue, it represents *most* women's lives and experiences.

A further critique of O'Dea's work is his lack of explanation of the contradiction between early feminism and present-day totalitarian patriarchy. On the one hand, Saints were encouraged by Joseph Smith to access personal revelation from God, provide a self-actualizing critique of their own unique path to God, and embrace their liberal birthright given to them by Jesus of "absolute freedom of choice" (O'Dea 1957, 128). According to early apostle John A. Widtsoe, "The place of woman in the Church is to walk beside the man, not in front of him nor behind him. In the Church there is full equality between man and woman" (1939, 90–91). Mormon women, in particular, were among the first in the nation to experience the vote, co-education, autonomy, and leadership and to participate, at least in the early church, in healing and religious ceremonies.[8] Yet, on the other hand, they currently must submit to a patriarchal head or heads who constitute the geriatric, predominantly conservative, leadership of the church or face losing their membership through excommunication or disfellowship. Such were the cases of contemporary feminist authors and theologians Lavina Fielding Anderson, Sonia Johnson, Maxine Hanks, and Lynne Whitesides (Stack 2003, Anderson 1993, 1998).

O'Dea's writings suggest, in agreement with Mormon feminist historians (Bushman 1997; Newell and Avery 1994; Hanks 1992), that the early church made a greater attempt to preserve autonomy and liberal Protestantism than it does today. In the days of the early Saints, women held the priesthood and were active in social production, temple work, and worship.[9] This is unsurprising, as Joseph Smith was surrounded by individualistic feminist leaders during his imprinting years: in his own home through his grandmother Lucy Mack, who organized religious communes for the poor (Anderson 2001), and in his western New York community through the examples of Anna Lee, a self-proclaimed incarnation of the godhead who established a Shaker colony only thirty miles from Palmyra, and former Quaker Jemima Wilkinson, who founded the Publick Universal Friend Church (O'Dea 1957, 15). Joseph's enigmatic first wife, Emma, was a scribe of the Book of Mormon and was president of the Relief Society, and his second wife, Eliza R. Snow, was author of early Mormon doctrine,[10] a poet, and a Relief Society administrator.

Today, by contrast, twenty-first-century women's roles are often heavily shadowed by the work and policies of men who do not always represent women's experiences and needs. Women cannot hold the priesthood and are not allowed to pray to their heavenly mother, nor are they allowed to administer healing blessings to their children, as they had done in the past.[11] Further, feminists, female intellectuals and academics, homosexuals, and women who practice or are sympathetic to polygamy may face disfellowship or excommunication. In the 1990s, there were several purges of these categories, most of whom comprised women.[12]

Because of the disjunction between the more liberating early church teachings and the modern patriarchal dogma, the true role of LDS women is difficult to assess (Beck 1994). On the one hand, women are depicted in the national media as depressed, subordinated housewives, subjected to the authority of their patriarchal husbands and male geriatric leaders. On the other hand, women within the church are often depicted in *Ensign* magazine, the "Visiting Teaching Message," and various other forums (http://www.fairlds.org) as empowered, contented wives and mothers who have jurisdiction over their families and experience joy and autonomy. The latter category, according to Andrea Radke (2005), contains women who embrace their roles as mothers and daughters of God who have rare opportunities to advance spiritually, intellectually, and socially. As Brigham Young University (BYU) law professor Cheryl Preston put it, "Am I less of a feminist because I am deeply religious and devoted to this traditional, conservative organized religion?" (2004, 12).

Yet even Mormon women who consider themselves feminists, academics, and orthodox often speak of the contradictory messages presented to them in Mormonism: "How do Mormon women maintain their autonomy and agency in the context of institutionalized patriarchy and then how do they make sense of church prescriptions on male authority both within the family and in the church hierarchy?" (Beaman 2001, 65), and "Why do women disproportionately invest in an institution that systematically devalues them?" (Ozorak 1996, 17). Further, Marie Cornwall asks, "How are women simultaneously 'present and silent' in religious traditions, and what social processes maintain their presence and silence?" (1994, 240).

In short, O'Dea did not anticipate current issues of feminism, equal rights, autonomy, and self-actualization for women in his nearly three hundred–page volume on the Mormon experience. In seeking a more contemporary, and accurate, portrayal of women in the Mormon culture, I will be underscoring the experiences and needs of four categories of marginalized women: polygamous women, lesbians, career women, and single mothers.

Polygamous Women in Fundamentalist Movements

Polygamous Mormon women's lives are now paraded on prime-time television and in the pages of the *New York Times.* The Home Box Office television show *Big Love,* which debuted in 2006, provides the first television series of the contemporary Mormon fundamentalist, polygamous family lifestyle. In spite of its overemphasis on sex, which often confounds the real issues for women in these movements, the series has the potential to awaken the mainstream to the realities of Mormon polygamous women's lives. Not surprisingly, many prominent Mormons, such as Governor Mitt Romney (who is currently running for U.S. president), are worried about the negative publicity it can bring to mainstream Mormonism. My purpose here is to dispel some of these myths and tap into the real experiences of polygamous women who are often marginalized by the larger mainstream.

My remarks are drawn from fifteen years of anthropological fieldwork conducted in three environments: the Allreds of the Bitterroot Mountains of Montana, the Allreds and surrounding independent polygamists of the Salt Lake Valley of Utah, and the LeBaron group of Galeana, Chihuahua, Mexico. I have lived and worked with fifteen extended polygamous families and interviewed more than 355 individuals about their conversion to the movement, their living arrangements, and their lifestyles. In 1995, I documented the conversion patterns of 150 women from the mainstream Mormon Church into fundamentalism, finding that most women were drawn to socioeconomic stability (Bennion 1996, 1997, 1998). In 1998, I published the first ethnography of contemporary Mormon polygamists, focusing on the Allred Group in Pinesdale, Montana. And finally, in 2004, after conducting fieldwork in the Chihuahua Desert, I published *Desert Patriarchy*, which highlights the lifestyle of one LeBaron polygamous man and his three wives.

Mormon polygamy is practiced by as few as 38,000 or as many as 60,000 individuals in the Intermountain West, depending on which monograph you read (Quinn 1998; Van Wagoner 1986; Bennion 1998). Although many Mormons seek to distance themselves from contemporary expressions of their own ancestors' history, polygamy is a part of the Mormon culture and will remain so for many years to come. Polygamous Mormon fundamentalists are offshoot sects that are dedicated to the principle of plural marriage and economic communalism as was practiced by Mormons in the early to mid-nineteenth century. Men marry many women in order to fulfill their kingdom-building paradigm, taking after their esteemed paragon, Joseph Smith, who married as many as 30 women (originally published as Doctrine and Covenants 132). Some groups, such as the Kingston and Colorado City (Fundamentalist LDS) sects, sanction the marriage of girls as young as thirteen. Other groups, such as the Apostolic United Brethren, commonly called the Allred Group, prohibit marriages of young women under eighteen. Under the direction of Owen Allred, the Allred Group is considered one of the more liberal sects and will often provide women with easy releases from unsuitable marriages. Because of this, their 35 percent divorce rate is much higher than what you would find in other groups (Bennion 1996, 1997, 1998). There are also many unaccounted-for independent polygamists living in and around Utah. These families do not want to defer to any prophet or priesthood leadership. They seek to build their autonomous family kingdoms and live freely, sometimes directly within the Mormon orthodox community. Although the mainstream LDS Church now excommunicates polygamists, it actually houses a very large population of independent polygamists within its wards and stakes. Women cloak their identity by posing as single mothers, keeping their maiden names and accepting church welfare and assistance whenever necessary.

In 2000, I was invited to speak at an American Civil Liberties Union–sponsored panel with two polygamous women and two lesbians to help clarify the reasons that certain Mormon women are attracted to alternative sexual lifestyles. I argued that the debate for women's rights must include discourse about lesbians and polygamous women. Polygamy is especially misunderstood. Many Mormon women experience more individual satisfaction within the dynamics of a polygamous family than they could in any other marital form, which may account for the extremely high rate of female conversion (Bennion 1996, 1998). Likewise, for some women, polygamy can be a living hell. I have recorded many horror stories of the abusive conditions of some fundamentalist families, especially those who live in poverty, where there is overcrowding, male supremacy, father absence, and circumscription (Bennion 2006).

The important issue here is to acknowledge the widespread presence of polygamy and women's active roles within it. In my research among the Allred Group, I met hundreds of women who were, for various reasons, attracted to Mormon fundamentalism. All of the female converts to the Allred Group in my study came directly from the orthodox Mormon Church. Most of the conversion stories (68 percent) spoke of being stigmatized in the mainstream because they were unmarriageable, divorced, widowed, single mothers, or in some way not able to fulfill their roles as described in the proclamation. They were drawn to plural marriage, often as a last measure, because their socioeconomic conditions did not match the mainstream reality of monogamy. Once within the group, they were often instantly incorporated into a family as a third or fourth wife, with access to their husband's sperm, his priesthood powers, and the valuable economic and emotional network established by his wives. Their children, if they have any, are promised a home in an already established family kingdom, with several "aunts" to help meet their needs.

One woman described her conversion as a way to be tied to her BYU girlfriend for eternity. She said, "Jill and I were roommates at college, and then I joined the group. When she wrote me about the lack of good men down in Provo, I told her to come on up to Montana and I'd hook her up to my husband." Another woman, who was trained as an accountant, described her marriage to a man who worked in an auto shop for minimum wage. He had three wives who were having trouble meeting their financial needs. When she married into the family, the accountant brought in thirty thousand dollars to be divided among the other wives.

Within the Allred Group, many women described their ability to access healing powers and feminist ideologies that the mainstream church long ago abandoned, such as using the priesthood to bless one's child and praying to the heavenly mother (Bennion 1992, 1998). Further, through an emphasis on communalism, many women are able to tap into a very large economic and emotional network to take care of the needs of their growing families. Women also explained that they had control of the reproductive schedule (that is, the sleeping arrangements of their husband) and the financial budgeting of their families. They would often say to me that they felt sorry for monogamous women who were continually under the thumb of their husbands "24/7." Within polygamy, and with the help of cowives, they argued, one could gain respite from their husband and engage in individual pursuits in education or careers.

Of course, not all stories of converts are happy ones. In another case, as I describe elsewhere, a woman named "Beth" was physically abused by her husband and feared for her children's welfare. She sought to leave the group but was told that if she tried to do so, her husband's "pureblood" family would kidnap her children, confiscate her possessions, and jeopardize her salvation. She decided to stay in the group until her youngest child graduated from high school. In a similar case, a woman who was seeking asylum from a bad marriage in the mainstream Mormon Church (her husband announced, after four children, that he was gay) fell in love with a man who had two other wives. They all got along famously until her husband showed favoritism toward the senior wives' children, neglecting to provide resources and attention to the other wives' sons and daughters. One of the older sons of this same senior wife also began sexually abusing the latest wife's young daughter. This woman soon left the group and went back to the mainstream church.

The experiences of polygamous women are rich and varied, and most are ignored by the larger Mormon culture as peripheral. Yet they are hardly outside the Mormon experience. Most converts come directly from the Mormon Church, and many of the polygamous wives continue to raise their children using Mormon doctrine, incorporating policies and practices from the Relief Society into their fundamentalist organizations. They feel they are living the pure form of Mormonism and that they will inherit a prized place in heaven for their efforts in living the "eternal round": the perfect Mormon family. They further feel that by living the principle of plural marriage, they are being polished like diamonds, worthy of the greatest glories in the kingdom.

As an anthropologist who has studied Mormon fundamentalism since 1989, I find it ironic that these unique, fully Mormon, women are often ignored in studies about LDS women. They, perhaps like lesbians, single mothers, divorced women, and working mothers, do not easily fit within the descriptions of the proclamation, yet their experiences as Mormon women are just as vibrant.

THE LESBIAN QUAGMIRE

In the proclamation there is no room in heaven for lesbians. Likewise, in O'Dea's account of Mormon culture, there is no mention of the existence of emotional and sexual bonds between women, in spite of the fact that these bonds were written about in early church magazines, discussed in public, and often encouraged by nineteenth- and early-twentieth-century church officials (Quinn 1996). In the contemporary Mormon world, lesbians attend church, take their children to primary, and pose as single mothers and single women who seek to be part of the church community while maintaining a secret life with a female partner.[13] Lesbians are more able to live this dual existence than their gay counterparts, as the stigma on male homosexuality is quite severe in the church, associated with the sin of sodomy, which is considered second only to murder, and is associated more directly by church members (and within fundamentalist circles) with the taint of HIV. For these reasons, bisexual and lesbian women can more easily float among the membership. Their activities are less institutionalized and visible than those of males—that is, until they express their sexuality so vocally and overtly that bishops and stake presidents are compelled to excommunicate them.

Being lesbian in the modern-day church means that one is going against nature and God. The proclamation clearly states that Saints should obey a single standard of gender, that of heterosexual male and female, which was constructed in the preexistence and shall follow individuals throughout their eternal destinies. From a biological viewpoint, however, gender is actually on a vast continuum, and cannot always easily be separated into two distinct arenas of "male" and "female" (Kinsey, Pomeroy, and Martin 1948). Furthermore, homosexuality has been linked to differential cell size in the hypothalamus (LeVay 1991). There is also abundant cross-cultural data that suggests lesbianism is often adopted as a natural progression toward a stronger heterosexual marriage (Blackwood 1993; Gay 1986).

The official LDS position on lesbianism is that it is an express category of sin; those who are guilty must confess their homoeroticism, but they also must confess engaging in sex before marriage, a separate offense. In other words, if homosexuals can abstain from sex, their membership will remain intact. Otherwise, they must go through a repentance process. To aid in this process, the brethren provide Mormon counseling services with the proper protocol of treatment for the pathology. Often, even LDS psychologists themselves see it as an illness, or as "immoral," seeking to alter sexual behaviors by adopting "reparative therapy" (Bingham and Potts 1993). Rarely are empirical biological data employed in the analysis and treatment of clients in the LDS Social Services.

The Mormon discourse on lesbianism is often guided by ecclesiastical generalizations of promiscuity and Western notions of dysfunction and mental illness (Carrier 1980), with little regard to the actual lives of women. According to R. D. Bingham and R. W. Potts, the information provided about homosexuality is founded on stereotypes distancing lesbian Mormons from the rest of the fold. The unstated assumption is that all humans are created as heterosexual, and therefore "anyone who is lesbian, *chooses* to be lesbian of their own capricious volition, going against the grain of nature. They must be confused or deceived by other lesbians, then, for them to stray off of the heterosexual path so easily, being recruited or cajoled by the dark side. Some are counseled to [pursue] men to curtail their lesbian urges" (1993, 4). Furthermore, since there are no biblical accounts of lesbianism, it is considered to be unnatural, especially given the emphasis on God's commandment to reproduce offspring (Oaks 1995). Under this later prerogative, however, many heterosexual individuals would also be excluded from the fold, as many cannot reproduce (Michael et al. 1994) and many, through the use of birth control, choose not to reproduce.

Although doctrine on the subject is important, even more vital to this chapter is recognition of the growing number of lesbians within church membership who are alienated by such doctrine. Whereas the most obvious heterosexual perspective of gays and lesbians suggests that you will be able to quickly spot and then ostracize the homosexual, the majority of gays and lesbians have "no identifiable evidence of their sexual orientation by their gender role, appearance, mannerisms, or language" (McWhirter 1993, 42). Although somewhat misinformed, the LDS Social Services document *Understanding and Helping Individuals with Homosexual Problems* (1995) suggests that lesbian behavior results from the mother's dependency on her daughter in the absence of her husband, rendering her daughter "masculine." The LDS document suggests that lesbian women are seen as extremely dependent on other women for love and affection. To be normal, a woman should transfer that dependence to a man. By extension of this theory, any woman who is independent of a man may also be perceived as having lesbian tendencies.

D. Michael Quinn sheds refreshing light on the subject of Mormon lesbianism in his study of nineteenth- and twentieth-century women. He explains that same-sex sexual relationships were not uncommon in the early history of the church. For example, he writes, in 1837 Mary Fielding Smith commented that "some of the Sisters were engaged in conversing in tongues their countenances beaming with joy, clasped each other's hands and kissed in the most affectionate manner," which indicates advanced stages of physical intimacy (1996, 91). The nature of women's relationships was often obscured. For example, in the 1830s, a Mormon girl in her twenties, enrolled at Amherst, wrote, "If I could sleep with you one night, [I] think we should not be very sleepy … at least I could converse all night and have nothing but a comma between the sentences, now and then" (Beecher 1992, 155).

Quinn refers to this intimacy between Mormon women as "female homoeroticism," taking it from an 1856 reference about an LDS woman who was recorded as "trying to seduce a young girl." The word *lesbian* was recorded in an 1870 Mormon diary, and the phrase *women lovers* appeared in the magazine *Women's Exponent* in 1873. In his study he discovered that Mormon women have expressed their love for each other since the days of the early pioneers and continued to do so in the form of a lesbian and gay club in 1891, organized by Katherine Young Schweitzer, granddaughter of Brigham Young.

He further writes that near the turn of the century, relationships between women within the LDS community were often celebrated or encouraged. For example, "Mormon suffragist Emmeline Wells publicly praised the same-sex relationship of Francis Willard, President of the national Women's Christian Temperance Union" (1996, 424–25). Then, in 1912, an LDS magazine referred to "lesbianism" in a tribute to "Sappho of Lesbos." The magazine also published a poem by devout Mormon Kate Thomas about her female lover.

After recognizing the increase in the expression of female homoeroticism in Mormonism, scholars should turn their view to the various contexts within which female-female love is exhibited. In my studies of polygamous women in the Allred Group (1992, 1998), for example, there were cases where women were abandoned by their husbands during the cold winter months in the isolated Bitterroot Valley of Montana. In order to survive and provide for their children, they would share economically and emotionally. They often described with fondness the many nights they "comforted each other," referring to sexual sharing that occurred in the form of a clandestine women's association known as the "sisterhood." This sisterhood was separate from the larger Relief Society organization in its purpose and modus operandi; it was designed to orchestrate love trysts for women without their husbands' knowledge. When asked if they thought the sisterhood sinful, they said that they did not see it as such; their love for each other was real and sanctioned by God. After all, they told me, they had been married to each other in the Law of Sarah, which sealed them as much to each other as to their husband.[14]

Further research on Mormon lesbians should include investigations within the missionary community and among young women and girls in their marriage-fantasy play. The construction of Mormon lesbian lifestyles is going to shake the basic assumptions about girls and women perpetuated by a male-dominant model of sexuality. Lesbianism both rejects conventional heterosexual relationships and the necessity of incorporating male priesthood authority within the dyad. One hopes that the research will provide a guide to approaching this alternative sexual construct in Mormon society.

MORMON WOMEN AND WORK

Also ignored in O'Dea's volume is any mention of female work experience, yet church magazines from the 1930s have contained ample evidence of women's work, from child care and gardening to community service. Virtually no mention of women's economic contributions are included in O'Dea's description of pioneer life, except for the brief mention of a clever woman who discovered that the rocking motion of the covered wagon could churn butter. In the contemporary church, discourse on Mormon women's work is sketchy, and somewhat contradictory. President Spencer W. Kimball (1963), for example, advised women to prepare themselves to be ready to earn their own living and get the best education they could, while at the same time he told them to stay at home, blaming career women for juvenile delinquency. Likewise, prophet David O. McKay (1953) said that women are the happiest in the home and should not be "forced" to work outside that blessed sphere. In prophet Ezra Taft Benson's time, women were encouraged to get a college degree in a field of their choice, but were also told that they should not pursue a career outside the home. "It is a misguided idea that a woman should leave the home, where there is a husband and children present, to prepare educationally and financially for an unforeseen eventuality. Too often, I fear, even women in the Church use the world as their standard for success and basis for self-worth" (1981, 104). Paradoxically, at the end of the 1980s, when Mormon women were matching their non-Mormon counterparts in working outside the home (Heaton, Goodman, and Holman 1994), Benson (1987), in a direct commandment, told women to quit their jobs and return home.

The decision to enter the paid labor force is especially complicated for LDS women, who are taught to be self-sufficient, even though they are expected to marry, have children, and stay at home. The desire to pursue one's career "calling" is laced with heavy guilt. Careers require dedicated study and concentration outside the home. How can a woman both pursue a career and be a full-time homemaker and mother? This dilemma has given rise to several generations of supermoms within the Mormon culture.

In short, although employment participation rates for LDS women match (and sometimes exceed) the national average (Chadwick and Garrett 1995; Heaton, Goodman, and Holman 1994),[15] the brethren continue to reaffirm the following 1950s sex roles: the role of the man as natural leader and provider and the role of woman as natural nurturer and teacher, as confirmed by official doctrine: "Woman's primary place is in the home, where she is to rear children and abide by the righteous counsel of her husband" (McConkie 1991, 844).

Mormon women may never completely bridge this paradoxical gap between work and religious duty. Lawrence Foster points to the interesting contrast between rhetoric and reality here: "While approximately half of married Mormon women work at least part time outside the home to help make ends meet, the church criticizes women who work and thereby neglect their families" (1991, 209).

A further O'Dea omission and contradiction is found in the admonition for Saints to attain the best education they can afford, as depicted by the Mormon aphorism "The glory of God is intelligence," yet women are not often given academic freedom, nor are they encouraged to advance to a career that might jeopardize their duty to the domestic sphere. According to Merlin B. Brinkerhoff and Marlene Mackie (1985), Mormon women are more likely to graduate with their bachelor's degree and pursue graduate work than Catholic or other Protestant women. Yet once women become educated and seek work at the church-owned institution Brigham Young University, their scholarship is often suppressed and their personal life scrutinized. According to the BYU chapter of the American Association of University Professors (1996), in the university's entire seventy-five-year history, a woman faculty member has never been chosen to present BYU's distinguished faculty lecture. Further, in 1992, BYU leadership would not hire a female candidate to the English Department, even though the majority of the faculty voted *for* her. In that same year, the head of the BYU Women's Research Institute, Marie Cornwall, was reprimanded and censured for allowing an open discussion about the Relief Society, and Pulitzer Prize–winning author of the acclaimed *A Midwife's Tale,* Laurel Thatcher Ulrich, was not allowed to speak at the women's conference. In 1993, BYU fired the chair of the women's conference, Carol Lee Hawkins, and kept Claudia Bushman from speaking in a weeklong faculty seminar sponsored by the dean of honors and general education, although her husband, Richard Bushman, was approved to speak. They had *both* been invited as speakers. That same year Cecilia Konchar Farr, a feminist activist who worked to educate people about violence against women, was fired, and Holocaust scholar Marian Bishop Mumford was selected for hire only if she would agree to discontinue her current scholarship. Further, female scholars are often asked by BYU administrators and church officials to avoid publishing their research findings. In 1995 Professors Karen E. Gerdes and Martha N. Beck were forbidden from publishing the results of their study of the experiences of Mormon women survivors of childhood sexual abuse who asked for help from their Mormon ecclesiastical leaders.

DISILLUSIONMENT, DIVORCE, AND SINGLE MOTHERHOOD

Because Mormon women are trained to desire above all else to please ... we spend enormous amounts of energy trying to make the very real, but—for most of us—limited satisfactions of mother- and wife-hood substitute satisfactorily for all other life experiences. What spills over into those vacant lots of our hearts where our intellectual and talented selves should be vigorously alive and thriving are, instead, frustration, anger, and the despair which comes from suppressing anger and feeling guilty for having felt it in the first place.

—LINDA SILLITOE, "Church Politics and Sonia Johnson:
The Central Conundrum"

In the heavens are parents single?

—ELIZA R. SNOW, "O My Father"

According to "The Family: A Proclamation to the World," men and women must be united in a traditional family unit (First Presidency and Council of the Twelve Apostles 1995). However, as church membership becomes increasingly multicultural and multifaceted, people are turning to alternative strategies for designing family structure. For example, statistics show that the model LDS family that is sealed in the temple describes only 20 percent of Mormons in the United States and 19 percent in Mexico (Heaton 1992). So, if one in five women is in a traditional family, where are the other 80 percent?[16] When one looks closely at the nature of the female congregation, one can see a growing number of divorced women, single women who wish to delay marriage until later, unmarriageable women, and career women, all of which increase the number of women who are single in the church.

Divorce

The O'Dea 1950s model of Mormon life does not take into account the large, and ever growing, percentage of divorced couples in the church. Recent statistics illustrate that Mormons are close behind the national average of divorce (Judd 2000). Further, marital instability is higher in Mormonism than most other religious groups (Heaton 1992).

Who seeks the divorce in a Mormon marriage? According to George K. Jarvis, more women want to dissolve the relationship than men. For example, the percentage of Canadian LDS men who are divorced is lower than the national average, whereas the percentage of women is higher (1990, 242). Similarly, Tim Heaton found that 14 percent of Mormon men and 19 percent of Mormon women had divorced (Heaton and Goodman 1985). In most cases, more women sought to end the marriage.[17]

Men also seek to remarry sooner after the divorce than women do. They marry with greater ease than females, as the stigma is less, primarily due to the fact that most single mothers are granted child custody in Utah. A similar study found that Mormon men, in general, are very interested in marriage, at an early age, even more so than their female counterparts (Heaton, Goodman, and Holman 1994). The national average shows the same trend, but it still begs the question, "Why is it that Mormon men remarry with more satisfaction than do Mormon women?"

The rationale for such high rates of dissatisfaction is often best understood in the context of extraordinarily high ideological and cultural expectations for happiness and perfection.[18] One of the most stringent expectations for women in the church is to bear many children. Latter-day Saints have been taught that "some of the most noble spirits are waiting with the Father to this day, to come forth through the right channel and the right kind of men and women," and that "there are thousands, and millions, of spirits waiting to obtain bodies upon this Earth" (H. Kimball 1860, 92). Mormon women are often, therefore, surrounded by children all day, typically between the ages of eleven months and twelve years of age, without many adults to speak to or share time with. There is also the added workload of diapers, laundry, meals, entertaining, and disciplining that falls on the shoulders of stay-at-home Mormon moms. The only reprieve for many women is the presence of a husband who helps with child care and housework. Yet most Mormon males do not help out at home; they are told it is women's work, as written in the proclamation: "Fathers are to preside over their families in love and righteousness and are responsible to provide the necessities of life and protection for their families. Mothers are primarily responsible for the nurture of their children." LDS males spend about the same amount of time performing household tasks as non-Mormon males, but Mormon females spend significantly *more* time at such tasks than non-Mormon females. Furthermore, LDS women spend more time performing not only traditional female tasks but also traditional male tasks (for example, outdoor work, paying bills, and auto maintenance) than do non-LDS women (Heaton and Junsay 1989).

Another trigger for divorce comes from the amount of violence, neglect, and sexual abuse in the home. According to the Utah Division of Family Services' Web site (http://www.dcfs.utah.gov), there are more than 37,218 complaints of child abuse in Utah each year. In a *Sunstone* article in 1991, it was reported that sex-abuse rings were popping up around the Salt Lake area, due primarily to an attitude of male supremacy, "where the priesthood holder's authority is not questioned allowing pedophiles a unique opportunity. Bishops often support the perpetrator because he is a priesthood holder" (Smith 1991).

In 1999 I conducted a study of sex-offender profiles provided by twenty-two licensed sex-abuse counselors in the state of Utah, focusing on father-daughter incest (Bennion 2006). I showed that the typical perpetrator profile was of a male, aged thirty to fifty, who had himself been victimized as a child. This man exerted formal control over a typically large, overcrowded household, and often traveled away from the home on business or to visit other families. The perpetrator was "religious," predominantly Mormon, with high expectations of righteousness for himself and his family. Yet in spite of religiosity, he had a history of using pornography and was described as having a sexual addiction. Furthermore, the perpetrator lived with his family in relative poverty in a rural, isolated region. In sum, these Utah cases revealed that the offender had a high level of eroticism and tended to take out his economic frustration on a submissive wife and vulnerable children in a confining, troubled household. He reinforced his dominion over his wife and children through physical and sexual abuse, as well as restricting their access to the larger mainstream world.

Another variable contributing to divorce is the delay in the age at which women marry. According to BYU scholar Tim Heaton, Mormon women are waiting longer to marry, and the number of couples choosing to cohabit is increasing (Estes 2001). Young women who get their degrees are then often compelled to enter the workforce, further delaying the age of marriage and further reducing the birthrate in the process. These women see themselves as singular, autonomous beings who are responsible for their own happiness and direction in life. In sum, Mormon women, in increasing numbers, are opting to delay the age at which they first marry, resort to divorce as an option when dissatisfied with their marriage, and delay entrance into or abstain entirely from future marital unions.

Single Motherhood

O'Dea would not have had access to data on single motherhood, as divorce rates were extremely low, and teen pregnancies, if they occurred, were hidden within the larger extended family network. Today, a growing number of single-parenting families, made up of mostly mothers, creates new challenges for members in their attempts to reach the goal of raising "a righteous seed" (Book of Mormon, Jacob 2:30). Without a supportive husband, many women are forced to go on church and government welfare, and fall well below the poverty line. This problem is exacerbated by the fact that few men in the Mormon culture desire to marry a women who has already had children or who has been sealed in the temple for "time and all eternity" to another man.

What caused the rise in single motherhood among Mormons? Although most single mothers are divorced women, some have never been married. In Utah nearly 17 percent of live births are born to unwed mothers, a figure that has quadrupled in the past twenty-nine years (Estes 2001). Further, similar to the rest of the nation, Mormon youth are having more premarital sex than they used to; in fact, the number of sexually transmitted diseases is on the incline (Toth 2006). Further, young Mormon women are finding creative venues for expression of eroticism within the LDS community, which has a direct bearing on increases in unmarried pregnancies, as many do not use birth control (Fillmore and Bennion 2000). If they agree to use birth control, it would be admitting to their sexual partners, and to themselves, that they are committing a sin.

Often single moms in the church are stigmatized because they do not easily fit into the paradigms preached about the eternal family over the pulpit. Women are designed to be cared for by their husbands, utilizing his priesthood to access the spiritual and economic resources necessary to return to the presence of God. A further stigma is generated by the paradoxical directive to find a new eternal mate, which requires being "on the prowl," yet also to remain virtuous, motherly, and attentive to church and family duties. There are very few acceptable venues of courtship for single moms, or, for that matter, women who delay marriage. According to twenty-nine-year-old Adia Waldburger of Salt Lake, career women and single moms feel that they are out of the dating loop because they are above the appropriate age for marriage, which among Mormons is twenty-two (Adams and Karras 2006).

Of greatest concern to single mothers in the church are their feelings of exclusion from the "normal" Mormon way of life, including access to love, resources, and priesthood "blessings." They deal with the O'Dea paradox of self-actualization and priesthood authority more keenly than any other category of marginalized women. They are pursuing the motherhood ideal yet are not treated by the church as equals, or as full-fledged members, until they have obtained a male priesthood-bearer. Such doctrine and cultural perceptions can often alienate single moms in spite of the fact that they are a significant proportion of church membership.

Conclusion: An Autoethnographic Perspective

As a test case, my own life presents an excellent critique of O'Dea's examination of Mormon women's experiences—or, should I say, it represents many of the elements missing from his volume: career women, divorced women, and single motherhood. I was raised in a small, tight-knit Mormon community in the West Desert of Utah. I married my college sweetheart in the Logan Temple and bore two children who attended LDS Primary and Sunday-school programs. I held leadership callings in the Primary, Young Women's Sunday School, and Relief Society. Then, during my doctoral program at the University of Utah, I began to experience a series of obstacles that changed my status from "traditional" to "marginalized" woman. First, I was reprimanded by Loren C. Dunn for my research interests in contemporary polygamous communities. I was asked if my husband was aware of my activities and told to drop the research project as a direct request from the brethren. Later, as an anthropology candidate in a BYU faculty search, the chair of the committee said they would hire me if I would agree to change my research from Mormon fundamentalist polygamy to African polygamy. That same year at BYU, I was given an introductory-level anthropology class and told to teach in my normal manner, as if I was teaching a course at my alma mater, the University of Utah. I was not renewed, and when I asked why, I was told that I spoke about sexual matters of native New Guinea tribesmen too graphically.

Yet I remained active in the church, although my husband disavowed the church one year after my marriage to him. In 1990, while living and studying in Portland, Oregon, I remember reading prophet Ezra Taft Benson's admonition to women to stay home and quit their jobs (1981). At the time, I had lived on my husband's earnings while raising our two daughters, but after our divorce, in Salt Lake City, I was often "compelled" to work outside the home to pay the bills, working as an adjunct throughout Salt Lake and Utah Valleys. Currently, even as a remarried career mother, we would not survive economically without my additional salary. Like other women I knew in my ward, I was forced to work for survival, yet was often in direct disobedience to the prophet's counsel. In the end, I waited until my girls were of school age and then began to work full-time, sensing that this compromise would provide me with less "cognitive dissonance."[19]

It is not possible to go back to the 1950s and ask O'Dea to rewrite his section on Mormon women, but we can encourage future scholars to examine more thoroughly women's experiences at all age levels, in all social classes, in all orientations, occupations, political parties, and geographic regions. We can generate a more thoughtful discussion of the richness and diversity of what it is to be female in the church. In conclusion, O'Dea and the contemporary Mormon Church have both omitted vital elements of the female experience as indicated in the proclamation and O'Dea's classic volume on Mormon culture. LDS policies and doctrines—and sociological texts—that continue to exclude and misrepresent Mormon women are going to alienate a vast, diverse group of females who will certainly go on to something better for themselves and their daughters, unless change can be made to accommodate their differential needs and experiences. Although church directives regarding the use of birth control have softened and so has the Benson command for women to stay home, there are still constraints for women in pursuing careers beyond the household. There are also tremendous barriers to freedoms in women's sexuality, intellectual expression, and ability to access politico-religious resources in the church. The secret to satisfying, converting, and retaining the female membership will come from, as Andrea Radke notes, "a greater gendered and social awareness that result[s] from modernization, scientific studies and even feminist awareness, to the priesthood-led decisions and policies of the institutional Church" (2005, 14). It will come from an acknowledgment of the diversity of female genres, lifestyles, and attitudes, and from the recognition of several marginalized segments of society that are at great risk for apostasy: single mothers, lesbians, polygamous women, and career women.

NOTES

1. As in my recent book *Desert Patriarchy* (2004), I use participant observation as a primary methodology, coupled with a postmodernist ethnographic style that introduces the scholar's own voice and interpretations of culture, as a native.

2. Incidentally, he also neglected to acknowledge the enormous pressures on twenty-first-century males to conform to extraordinary expectations of living a righteous priesthood-oriented life.

3. I take after my esteemed cousin, author and teacher Lowell Bennion, when he admonished Mormons to continually reevaluate their beliefs, question authority, and update their spiritual connections to the gospel (L. Bennion 1983).

4. In 2002, at the Society for the Scientific Study of Religion conference in Salt Lake City, I introduced a category of Mormon experience titled "the Jill Mormons." These are women who are unable, for whatever reason, to match the Mormon ideal of the traditional family with their socioeconomic and psychological realities. In Robert Merton's terms, these women are innovative creators of new cultural means by which they can attain age-old cultural goals. In other words, these Jill Mormons are redesigning codes within the Mormon doctrine to account for their need to adopt careers, explore alternative relationships, or incorporate a more feminist approach to the Plan of Salvation.

5. The 2004 data suggest that there are approximately 12 million Mormons in the world. Armand Mauss (2004) predicts there will be nearly 240 million in the year 2080, but this seems to be a fantastical figure given current demographic information on fertility. We are actually seeing a decrease in the number of children born each year.

6. In Utah, which is 70 percent Mormon, 37 percent of couples are not living within a traditional heterosexual, monogamous family unit (Utah Census 2000). Further, according to Tim Heaton (1992), only 20 percent of LDS families are actually members of a traditional temple-sealed family structure.

7. Temple goers are far less likely to divorce: only 6 percent were found to dissolve their temple vows. This indicates the incredible diversity within the Mormon population between conservative temple goers and inactive members. Further, only 13 percent of LDS couples have divorced after five years of marriage, compared with 20 percent for religiously homogamous unions among Catholics and Protestants and 27 percent among Jews (Judd 2000).

8. O'Dea does not recognize notable Mormon feminists such as Emma Smith, Joseph's first wife, who wrote about the active role of women in the priesthood in the early days of Nauvoo (Newell and Avery 1994), or note the words and accomplishments of Dr. Martha Hughes Cannon, the first female senator in the United States (Lieber and Sillitoe 1993).

9. D. Michael Quinn states that Joseph Smith issued the right of the priesthood to women, giving them endowment rights to become priestesses and queens in the church (1992). Other scholars have argued that women have always held the priesthood, by virtue of the Relief Society organization, which they claim Joseph Smith intended as a "kingdom of priestesses," with women receiving ordinations and performing temple rites. Further,

historians hark back to nineteenth-century Mormon women being ordained as healers with the power to anoint and lay on hands for healing the sick (Radke 2005).

10. Again, it was Eliza who introduced the concept of a heavenly mother, in the famous hymn "O My Father" (1845). Later, Bruce R. McConkie, in compiling *Mormon Doctrine,* validated this belief: "Implicit in the Christian verity that all men are the spirit children of an Eternal Father is the usually unspoken truth that they are also the offspring of an Eternal Mother" (1991, 467).

11. In my study (1998) of Allred fundamentalist Mormon women, women are described as performing the "mother's blessing" of healing on their sick children, which is extended to other occasions of need for sister wives and friends without the presence of a priesthood bearer, as it was done in the "old days."

12. In 1993, six Mormon intellectuals were ostracized, and one, Lynne Whitesides, a feminist noted for emphasizing "Mother in Heaven" in public, was disfellowshipped. Two of the six excommunicated Mormons were women: feminist author Lavina Fielding Anderson and feminist theologian Maxine Hanks. One, Mormon historian D. Michael Quinn, wrote about same-sex dynamics among nineteenth-century Mormons. The excommunicated feminists challenged assumptions of a male-only priesthood in the church and the right for women to pray to their "Mother in Heaven." Quinn challenged official church positions. The brethren were instructed to discipline those who were considered too liberal, feminist, or intellectual ("Six Intellectuals" 1993).

13. Although it is virtually impossible to guess how many lesbian Mormons exist, there are about one thousand people who are associated with Affirmation, an organization for gay and lesbian Mormons, founded in the 1970s.

14. The Law of Sarah is used by fundamentalist Mormons to join the previous wife to the newly obtained wife, where their hands are blended with their husband's in an eternal, sacred grip, married to each other as much as to their husband.

15. Yet because of the emphasis in the church on motherhood and the evils of being drawn into careers that jeopardize the relationship between a mother and child, Bruce A. Chadwick and H. Dean Garrett also found a relationship between religiosity and lowered employment. The authors admit that many Mormon women are able to "maintain their religiosity in spite of the time demands of full-time employment" (1995, 291).

16. Although only 19–20 percent of LDS families would fit under the category of the "traditional ideal family," many others could be described that way, such as those who have no children left at home and single college students. Others are married but do not yet have children. And still others are married, but not in the temple. Heaton's 19 percent figure represents only a subset of those that would be called traditional-idea families.

17. Granted, Latter-day Saints married in a temple ceremony are considerably less likely to divorce than those married outside the temple (Thomas 1983). Among men and women who were married in the temple, 6 percent of the men and 7 percent of the women have been divorced, whereas among men and women not married in the temple, the figures were 28 percent and 33 percent, respectively (Heaton and Goodman 1985).

18. Granted, some of the quotes about bearing as many children as possible are from the nineteenth century. This emphasis has diminished considerably as the church has increasingly become an international church.

19. See both L. Festinger (1957) and Lori G. Beaman (2001) who speak of the necessity for religious women to make cognitive bridges in the gap between their ideological values and their socioeconomic realities.

References

Adams, Brooke, and Christy Karras. 2006. "Utah Singles Complain of Social Stigma." *Salt Lake Tribune,* July 2.

American Association of University Professors. 1996. "Limitations of the Academic Freedom of Women at Brigham Young University." http://www.ldsmormon.com/aaupwomn.shtml.

Anderson, Lavina Fielding. 1993. "The LDS Intellectual Community and Church Leadership: A Contemporary Chronology." *Dialogue: A Journal of Mormon Thought* 26, no. 1: 7–64.

———. 1998. "Six Intellectuals Disciplined for Apostasy." *Sunstone* (November): 65–73.

———. 2001. *Lucy's Book: A Critical Edition of Lucy Mack Smith's Family Memoirs.* Salt Lake City: Signature Books.

Beaman, Lori G. 2001. "Molly Mormons, Mormon Feminists, and Moderates: Religious Diversity and the Latter Day Saints Church." *Sociology of Religion* 62, no. 1: 65–86.

Beck, Martha N. 1994. "Flight from the Iron Cage: LDS Women's Responses to the Paradox of Modernization." Ph.D. diss., Harvard University.

Beecher, Maureen U. 1992. *Sisters in Spirit: Mormon Women's Historical and Cultural Perspective.* Urbana: University of Illinois Press.

Bennion, Janet. 1992. "My Sister, My Wife: An Examination of Sororal Polygyny in a Contemporary Mormon Fundamentalist Commune." *Syzygy: Journal of Alternative Religion and Culture* 1, no. 4: 315–22.

———. 1996. "Kings, Queens, and Covenants: An Analysis of Male and Female Conversion and Integration in a Mormon Fundamentalist Community." Ph.D. diss., University of Utah.

———. 1997. "A Separate Unity: Female Networking and Status in a Contemporary Mormon Polygynous Commune." In *Mixed Blessings: Gender and Religious Fundamentalism Cross Culturally,* ed. Judy Brink and Joan Mencher, 73–89. New York: Routledge.

———. 1998. *Women of Principle: Female Networking in Contemporary Mormon Polygyny.* New York: Oxford University Press.

———. 2004. *Desert Patriarchy: Mormon and Mennonite Communities in the Chihuahua Valley.* Tucson: University of Arizona Press.

———. 2006. "Female Abuse in Fundamentalism." Paper presented at the Oxford Round Table, Oxford University, March 23.

Bennion, Lowell. 1983. *I Believe.* Salt Lake City: Deseret Book.

Benson, Ezra Taft. 1981. "The Honored Place of Woman." *Ensign,* November, 104.

———. 1987. *To the Mothers in Zion.* Fireside address, February 22. Printed 1987. Salt Lake City: Church of Jesus Christ of Latter-day Saints.

Bingham, R. D., and R. W. Potts. 1993. "Homosexuality: An LDS Perspective." *AMCAP* 19, no. 1: 1–16.

Black, Courtney, and Maxine Hanks. 2000. "Mormon Women Must Be Heard." *Boston Globe,* October 7.

Blackwood, Evelyn. 1993. "Breaking the Mirror: The Construction of Lesbianism and the Anthropological Discourse on Homosexuality." In *Culture and Human Sexuality,* ed. David N. Suggs and Andrew W. Miracle, 328–40. Pacific Grove, Calif.: Brooks/Cole.

Brinkerhoff, Merlin B., and Marlene Mackie. 1985. "Religion and Gender: A Comparison of Canadian and American Student Attitudes." *Journal of Marriage and the Family* 47: 415–29.

Bushman, Claudia L. 1997. *Mormon Sisters: Women in Early Utah.* Logan: Utah State University Press.

Canham, Matt. 2005. "Mormonism/Mormon Church: Retention of New Members Challenge for LDS Church." *Salt Lake Tribune,* October 17.

Carrier, Joseph M. 1980. "Homosexual Behavior in Cross-cultural Perspective." In *Homosexual Behavior: A Modern Reappraisal,* ed. Judd Marmor, 100–122. New York: Basic Books.

Chadwick, Bruce A., and H. Dean Garrett. 1995. "Women's Religiosity and Employment: The LDS Experience." *Review of Religious Research* 36, no. 3: 277–93.

Cornwall, Marie. 1994. "The Institutional Role of Mormon Women." In *Contemporary Mormonism: Social Science Perspectives,* ed. Marie Cornwall, Tim B. Heaton, and Lawrence A. Young, 239–64. Urbana: University of Illinois Press.

Estes, Ashley. 2001. "Births to Unwed Mothers." *Salt Lake Tribune,* April 4.

Festinger, L. 1957. *A Theory of Cognitive Dissonance.* Palo Alto: Stanford University Press.

Fillmore, Jane, and Janet Bennion. 2000. "Female Eroticism in Conservative Environments." Paper presented at the convention of the Society for the Scientific Study of Sexuality, Orlando, Florida.

First Presidency and Quorum of the Twelve Apostles of the Church of Jesus Christ of Latter-day Saints. 1995. "The Family: A Proclamation to the World." *Ensign,* November, 102.

Foster, Lawrence. 1991. *Women, Family, and Utopia: Communal Experiments of the Shakers, the Oneida Community, and the Mormons.* New York: Syracuse University Press.

Gay, Judith. 1986. "Mummies and Babies." In *The Many Faces of Homosexuality,* ed. Evelyn Blackwood. New York: Harrington Park Press.

Hanks, Maxine, ed. 1992. *Women and Authority: Re-emerging Mormon Feminism.* Salt Lake City: Signature Books.

Heaton, Tim. 1992. "Demographics of the Contemporary Mormon Family." *Dialogue: A Journal of Mormon Thought* 25, no. 3: 19–34.

Heaton, Tim, and Kristen Goodman. 1985. "Religions and Family Formation." *Review of Religious Research* 26, no. 4: 343–59.

Heaton, Tim, Kristen L. Goodman, and Thomas B. Holman. 1994. "In Search of a Peculiar People: Are Mormon Families Really Different?" In *Contemporary Mormonism: Social Science Perspectives,* ed. Marie Cornwall, Tim B. Heaton, and Lawrence A. Young, 87–117. Urbana: University of Illinois Press.

Heaton, Tim, and Alma Junsay. 1989. *Working Women: Comparative Perspectives in Developing Areas.* New York: Greenwood Press.

Hinckley, Gordon B. 1988. "Our Responsibility to Our Young Women." Regional Representatives Seminar, April 1.

Jarvis, George K. 1990. "Demographic Characteristics of the Mormon Family." In *The Mormon Presence in Canada,* ed. Brigham Young Card, Herbert C. Northcott, and John Foster, 281–301. Edmonton: University of Alberta Press.

Judd, Daniel K. 2000. *Religion, Mental Health, and the Latter-day Saints.* Provo: FARMS Research Press.

Kimball, Heber C. 1860. "Oneness of the Priesthood—Impossibility of Obliterating Mormonism—Gospel Ordinances—Depopulation of the Human Species—The Coming Famine, etc." *Journal of Discourses* 5 (1852–1885): 86–95.

Kimball, Spencer W. 1963. *The Teachings of Spencer W. Kimball.* Ed. Edward L. Kimball. Salt Lake City: Bookcraft, 1982.

Kinsey, Alfred C., Wardell B. Pomeroy, and Clyde E. Martin. 1948. *Sexual Behavior in the Human Male.* Reprint, Bloomington: Indiana University Press, 1998.

LDS Social Services. 1995. *Understanding and Helping Individuals with Homosexual Problems.* Salt Lake City: Church of Jesus Christ of Latter-day Saints.

LeVay, Simon. 1991. "A Difference in Hypothalamic Structure between Heterosexual and Homosexual Men." *Science* 253: 1034–37.

Lieber, Constance L., and John Sillito, eds. 1993. *Letters from Exile: The Correspondence of Martha Hughes Cannon and Angus M. Cannon, 1886–1888.* Salt Lake City: Signature Books.

Mauss, Armand L. 2004. *All Abraham's Children: Changing Mormon Conceptions of Race and Lineage.* Urbana: University of Illinois Press.

McConkie, Bruce R. 1991. *Mormon Doctrine.* Salt Lake City: Bookcraft.

McKay, David O. 1953. *Gospel Ideals: Selections from the Discourses of David O. McKay.* Salt Lake City: Improvement Era.

McWhirter, D. P. 1993. "Biological Theories of Sexual Orientation." In *Review of Psychiatry,* ed. J. Oldham, M. Riba, and A. Tasman, 12:41–57. Washington, D.C.: American Psychiatric Press.

Michael, Robert T., John H. Gagnon, Edward O. Laumann, and Gina Kolata. 1994. *Sex in America: A Definitive Survey.* New York: Little, Brown.

Newell, Linda, and Val Avery. 1994. *Mormon Enigma: Emma Hale Smith.* 2d ed. Urbana: University of Illinois Press.

Oaks, Dallin H. 1995. "Same-Gender Attraction." *Ensign,* October, 1–14.

O'Dea, Thomas F. 1957. *The Mormons.* Chicago: University of Chicago Press.

Ozorak, Elizabeth Weiss. 1996. "The Power but Not the Glory: How Women Empower Themselves through Religion." *Journal for the Scientific Study of Religion* 35, no. 1: 17–29.

Ponder, Kent. 2003. "Mormon Women, Prozac and Therapy." http://home.teleport. com/~packham/prozac.htm.

Preston, Cheryl. 2004. "Women in Traditional Religions: Refusing to Let Patriarchy Separate Us from the Source of Our Liberation." Paper presented at "Perspectives: LDS Women in the Twentieth Century," Joseph Fielding Smith Institute for Church History, March 20, Provo.

Quinn, D. Michael. 1996. *Same-Sex Dynamics among Nineteenth-Century Americans: A Mormon Example.* Urbana: University of Illinois Press.

———. 1998. "Plural Marriage and Mormon Fundamentalism." *Dialogue: A Journal of Mormon Thought* (Summer): 1–68.

Radke, Andrea. 2005. "The Place of Mormon Women: Perceptions, Prozac, Polygamy, Priesthood, Patriarchy, and Peace." Paper presented at the FAIR conference, Mesa, Arizona, August.

Sillitoe, Linda. 1980. "Church Politics and Sonia Johnson: The Central Conundrum." *Sunstone,* no. 19 (January–February): 35.

"Six Intellectuals Disciplined for Apostasy." 1993. *Sunstone* (November): 65–73.

Smith, Marion B. 1991. Letter. *Sunstone* (December): 4–6.

Stack, Peggy Fletcher. 2003. "Exiles in Zion." *Salt Lake Tribune,* August 16, C1.

Thomas, Darwin. 1988. "Future Prospects for Religion and Family Studies: The Mormon Case." In *The Religion and Family Connection: Social Science Perspectives,* ed. Darwin Thomas, 357–82. Provo: Religious Studies Center, Brigham Young University.

Toth, H. 2006. "STDs in the County Are on the Rise." *Central Utah Daily Herald,* August 17.

Utah Census. 2000. http://www.utah.gov.

Van Wagoner, Richard. 1986. *Mormon Polygamy: A History.* Salt Lake City: Signature Books.

Widtsoe, John A. 1939. *Priesthood and Church Government.* Salt Lake City: Deseret Book.

7

The Peril and Promise of Social Prognosis

O'Dea and the Race Issue

~ Armand L. Mauss ~

[The race issue in 1957] did not possess sufficient prominence to warrant consideration.

[The race issue in 1972] is ... diagnostic of the church's most profound problem ... [namely, its] adequacy to handle the problems of its encounter with modernity.

—Thomas F. O'Dea, "Sources of Strain in Mormon History Reconsidered"

In the final chapter of *The Mormons* (1957), and further in the epilogue that follows it, O'Dea considered "the sources of strain and conflict" likely to create a bumpy future for a religious community that the rest of the book had generally treated as vital, viable, and flexible in responding to crisis. In the retrospect of a half century, O'Dea's perceptive assessment seems quite prescient in some ways but not in others. The encounter of the church with modern secular thought has brought no less conflict since midcentury than before. Traditional beliefs and truth claims have indeed proved harder for diaspora Mormons to retain when confronted with an outside environment that is not only secular but actually hostile to many of those beliefs. The countervailing values of obedience versus agency have recurrently clashed, not only in challenges from unruly intellectuals but also in a more passive resistance at the Mormon grassroots to traditional norms and obligations. The patriarchal family model, at least in its rhetoric, continues to constrain the aspirations of many Mormon women for fuller equality in both domestic and ecclesiastical governance, although it seems almost as true today as when O'Dea wrote in 1957 that "practically no difficulty arises from this problem" at the grassroots (250).

Most of the other strains anticipated by O'Dea seem to have been well enough managed, or else to have diminished with the changes time has wrought, both in the nation and in the church—at least for American Mormons. O'Dea completely overlooked, however, one serious source of strain for the Church of Jesus Christ of Latter-day Saints (LDS) that was to become more severe than any of the others he considered—and certainly a lot more public. I refer, of course, to the traditional ban against priesthood ordination and temple privileges for black members, which remained until 1978, and thus was very much in force when O'Dea was writing his 1957 book. Fifty years later, it seems almost incomprehensible that he would not have noticed such a storm cloud on the horizon. By the time he addressed the LDS sources of strain and conflict again fifteen years later (1972), he had become so preoccupied with the race issue (perhaps with some retrospective embarrassment) that he had come to consider it a "diagnostic issue"—the resolution of which, that is, would be the chief indicator of the future prospects for Mormonism in the modern world. In what follows, I will consider primarily three questions: Why would O'Dea have failed in 1957 to include the race issue among the sources of strain and conflict he envisioned in the future of the LDS Church? How appropriate and useful was it for him to consider it a "diagnostic issue" for the church in 1972? And how well does the church seem to have responded to the general predicament that O'Dea was trying to diagnose in 1972?

O'Dea's Field of Vision in the 1950s

With a somewhat superficial backward glance, one might be inclined to assume that the Mormon priesthood restriction for blacks should have been conspicuous early on, given a special feature of the Mormon priesthood, namely, that it is a lay priesthood, which is available in varying degrees to *all* males from age twelve onward. Unlike the case with other denominations, this Mormon priesthood is not professionalized and does not require seminary training. Up to at least midcentury, seminaries were the gatekeepers to the clergy profession in most denominations, just as medical schools and law schools were for their respective professions. Very few black candidates gained access to any of those professions in Jim Crow America, and accordingly no Christian denominations had appreciably more black clergy than the Mormons had (except, of course, for traditionally black denominations). However, a race-based restriction on entrance to seminary, common in other denominations, was not available to the LDS Church, which was thus obliged to make its discrimination obvious and de jure for all its black members, rather than de facto for only those few who applied to seminaries (and still fewer who were admitted, graduated, and ordained).[1] The priesthood restriction was therefore always potentially much more conspicuous among the Mormons than in most other denominations. Why wouldn't O'Dea (and many others) have taken notice of such a flagrant instance of racial discrimination in the 1950s?

One answer is that the LDS Church itself was not very conspicuous. With a little more than a million members, nearly all of whom were confined to the sparsely settled desert states of Utah, Idaho, Arizona, and Nevada, not much that transpired among the Mormons ever came to national attention (except, of course, for salacious periodic stories about the polygamy schismatics).[2] In that entire region, the proportion of black citizens was minuscule, including only some four thousand in Utah itself (0.5 percent), most of whom would not even have been members of the LDS Church.[3] So Mormons were not very visible nationally, and blacks were scarcely noticeable among the Mormons, as a practical reality. It is entirely possible that during his visits to Utah in the 1950s, O'Dea never even saw a black person.

Yet O'Dea was not limited to what he could observe from the outside. He had spent a summer in Utah visiting with a number of key informants who were anxious to help him get oriented, and most of them were academics of a fairly liberal stripe, who might (one would think) have made O'Dea acquainted with the looming race issue in the church (Bahr 2005). One of these informants, indeed, was Sterling M. McMurrin, who later discussed the race issue at some length with LDS president David O. McKay in 1954.[4] Even if O'Dea had availed himself of the national liberal press, such as the *Nation* magazine, he might have come across the stinging criticism of the LDS racial policy by Mormon sociologist Lowry Nelson in 1952 (488).[5] Why didn't O'Dea get any advance clues from such sources? The answer probably lies in the happenstance that underlay the timing of his comings and goings in Utah. For example, his summer visit to Utah was in 1950, well before McMurrin (or anyone else but Nelson) was importuning LDS leaders about the matter. O'Dea left Utah for fieldwork in New Mexico on the Kluckhohn project, from which he finished his doctoral dissertation in 1953. Clearly, he was outside Utah while the race issue was starting to get noticed there, and after his dissertation he turned immediately to his book manuscript. Eventually, he got back to Utah for a five-year stint on the faculty of the University of Utah (1959–1964), and by that time he had a front-row seat for the burgeoning racial controversy in both state and church; one suspects that he was also chiding himself by then for having overlooked that controversy among the "strains and conflicts" discussed in his celebrated 1957 book![6]

The simple historical reality is that racial discrimination during the 1950s was not much of an issue in Utah or in most of the rest of the nation. Up until about 1960, Mormons and other Americans living outside the South were able to enjoy the luxury of defining racial conflict as a southern problem. That was the part of the country that had always had "trouble with the Negroes." The rest of the country naturally deplored slavery, lynchings, the Ku Klux Klan, and certain of the harsher aspects of black treatment by the white establishment in the South. Most Americans were not inclined, however, to question Jim Crow laws, segregated schools and neighborhoods, or laws against racial intermarriage. Indeed, most of these same features were commonplace de facto, if not de jure, in the northern and western states as well. It was with some ambivalence, then, that most Americans read and heard about the federal campaign against school segregation exemplified in *Brown v. Board of Education* (1954) and in the desegregation of the high school in Little Rock (1957), as well as bus boycotts in Alabama (1955 and 1956), lunch-counter sit-ins in various southern states during the late 1950s and early 1960s, and so on. Most Americans elsewhere might have thought that what "Negroes" demanded seemed fair enough, on the one hand, but on the other hand, the protests were very disruptive, so a more gradual approach was generally preferred.

In the early twenty-first century, we tend to forget how conservative American public opinion was in the 1950s and '60s, whether Mormon or non-Mormon. As late as 1964, for instance, in a carefully drawn national sample, only 38 percent of white Americans favored the racial integration of schools, and that percentage did not increase much in the succeeding years. In the same survey, only 41 percent of white Americans nationwide were willing to grant blacks equal access to hotels and businesses, a bare majority (53 percent) favored open housing, and a mere 27 percent favored a general desegregation of the races. At the same time, 68 percent were convinced that civil rights advocates were "moving too fast," and 63 percent felt that blacks had damaged their cause by their exertions on behalf of equal rights—and this was *before* the major urban disorders in northern cities (Campbell 1971, esp. chap. 7). Another major survey of white Protestants and Catholics around the same time, in the relatively liberal San Francisco area, found half of the sample agreeing that blacks did not adequately take care of their property, which was why their neighborhoods were "run-down." Nearly half also believed that there would be no racial strife if "Communists and radicals" did not stir up trouble. One-fourth preferred segregated schools and churches and subscribed to the stereotype that "it's too bad Negroes are so immoral" (Glock and Stark 1966, 168). In such a general national climate of opinion even in the 1960s, it should not be hard to understand why Mormon racial ideas and practices would not have stood out in O'Dea's mind during the 1950s, even though he had made himself very well informed about Utah and Mormons in general.

Race as a "Diagnostic" Issue for the Mormons?

O'Dea took full advantage of an opportunity presented fifteen years later to revisit the race issue in the LDS Church. By this time, the issue had come to loom so large in his mind that he considered it a "diagnostic" harbinger of the future. He had concluded *The Mormons* in 1957 with a discussion of various "strains and conflicts" faced by the church at midcentury, the successful resolution of which, he predicted, would be necessary if the church were to continue to meet the moral and intellectual needs of the Mormon community in the modern world. The Mormon movement by midcentury had evolved, in the usual Weberian sect-to-church direction, from a persecuted charismatic sect to an established religious denomination, but it had not yet really become a church with all the societal accommodation implied by that term. It had, however, avoided the "sectarian stagnation" so common to those sects that do not continue to grow and prosper in the church-like direction. Indeed, in their kingdom-building program and relative geographic isolation, the Mormons had, in effect, almost become a separate ethnic group with its own nation-state.[7]

Now that the kingdom-building phase had been accomplished, and the LDS Church, as an American denomination, had been forced to seek a satisfactory accommodation with the surrounding secular society, would it continue to thrive? In its kingdom building, after all, Mormonism had "emphasized … this-worldly spheres of activity" (1972, 152). "For organized religion to offer competition in spheres of life in which non-religious organizations do better … is to be found wanting." To succeed in the future, the "basic need of Mormonism may well become a search for a more contemplative understanding of the problem of God and man" (1957, 262). Mormonism would have to become more theological, as it were, more focused on such ultimate questions as the meaning of life, on "what men ought to be doing on earth" (1972, 156). Yet, as O'Dea further explains, such a theology-driven agenda, it becomes clear, is scarcely less worldly than that of nineteenth-century Mormonism, for it amounts to a social-reform agenda that would address the national "spiritual crisis" of the 1960s epitomized especially in the issues of race and war (152, 155).

O'Dea's 1972 essay is clearly intended as an updating of the concluding observations in his 1957 book about the organizational predicaments of the

LDS Church at midcentury. Given the historical context of the 1960s that had intervened, it is not surprising that this new context would have shaped O'Dea's later treatment of the race issue in the church. Nor is it surprising that O'Dea would not have found the response of the church on that issue to be very encouraging by the time he wrote in the early 1970s. He had concluded his 1957 book with the optimistic prognosis that despite a certain "rigidity of structure and attitude," the church had proved "its viability under the most diverse conditions" and that there was "still too much vitality … remaining" for a pessimistic prognosis (262–63). By the time he was writing his 1972 essay, however, he had become rather pessimistic. He had come to see the race issue as "diagnostic of the church's most profound problem … [namely,] [h]ow to renew the original democratic and ethical spirit of Mormonism … and thereby provide the basis for a more contemporary and more vital understanding of Mormon values." The race issue was therefore "diagnostic" in the sense that the "church's adequacy to handle the problems of its encounter with modernity [more generally] will eventually be judged by … its response to the problem of racial justice" (162). O'Dea's verdict at that time was ominous: "The Mormon church in its defensive and stand pat position reveals itself as responding inadequately to [this] diagnostic issue" (165). Indeed, the church "stands before enlightened American opinion at worst as guilty of unchristian behavior, or at best as being tied up in obsolete provincial American and Mormon racist attitudes and unable to shed them" (164).

In this assessment of the racial situation in the LDS Church, O'Dea relied heavily on a few like-minded critics and seemed unaware of (or ignored) developments that might have given him evidence of the potential for a loosening of the traditional racial policy.[8] Of course, he would not have been privy to many developments that we now know were going on behind the scenes within the church hierarchy (Mauss 1981, 11–19; Prince and Wright 2005, chap. 4). However, he could certainly have learned something about them if he had once again sought out his earlier Utah informants, especially Sterling McMurrin. If he did resume his 1950s associations in Utah, it is not apparent from his 1972 essay. Had he consulted McMurrin, O'Dea would presumably have learned a lot about the *range* of opinion among the General Authorities over the race issue in the 1960s (for instance, the range between Ezra Taft Benson and Hugh B. Brown), about President McKay's own softening attitude toward the racial ban during the 1950s, about the background of President Brown's general conference statement on civil rights in 1963 (which McMurrin himself claimed to have instigated, and, indeed, drafted), as well as perhaps other signs that the racial policy was being reconsidered in the leading councils of the church (McMurrin 1979; Quinn 1993; Prince and Wright 2005). If O'Dea had been more inclusive in his purview of LDS developments just prior to publication of his 1972 essay, he might also have learned about the creation of the Genesis Group, organized by three apostles in 1971 to provide social and spiritual support for the few black Mormons in Utah (Mauss 1981, 23–24).[9]

Somewhat more surprisingly, O'Dea apparently did not avail himself of any of the articles that had been published by 1971 in *Dialogue: A Journal of Mormon Thought,* except for a reference to some 1968 treatments there of the Book of Abraham controversy—and that only in a passing mention. A glance through the issues of this journal during its founding years (starting in 1966) would have revealed some major articles and letters to the editor on the church's racial quandary, most of them by practicing Mormons. Not the least of these would have been the lengthy 1969 review by Lester E. Bush of the Stephen G. Taggart book, *Mormonism's Negro Doctrine: Social and Historical Origins* (1970), which O'Dea embraced in his 1972 essay but which Bush had rather severely criticized for advancing the so-called Missouri thesis to explain the origin of the Mormon racial policy.[10] Since O'Dea was on the faculty of the Religious Studies Department at the University of California–Santa Barbara (UCSB) during the period 1967–1974, he would have had access to *Dialogue* right there in the library of that university (Michaelsen 1978, 44).[11]

In short, it seems fair to say that O'Dea did not keep up very well on Mormon developments after publishing his 1957 book, even though he spent 1959–1964 at the University of Utah. When he finally turned to write his 1972 essay (presumably at the invitation of the editors), it would have seemed logical to return to the "strains and conflicts" theme with which he had concluded his book, given the new strains over the race issue in both the church and the nation. Yet he did not merely place his discussion of the LDS race issue within that *general strains-and-conflicts context;* rather, he invested the issue with a *special significance and priority* as a "diagnostic" test of the church's ability to respond to the "challenge of modern secular thought" (164). Having embraced that conceptualization of the issue, he then relied mainly on sources of information that shared his "modern secular" outlook, and he did not look very hard for evidence that LDS leaders were already grappling with the issue.

Accordingly, O'Dea's prognosis for the future of the church was pessimistic. His untimely death in 1974 prevented him from seeing several developments in the immediate future that would probably have neutralized much of his pessimism. Climactic among these, of course, was the 1978 revelation and policy change pertaining to black people, a development that would probably have taken O'Dea as much by surprise as did his discovery of the race problem itself after omitting it from his 1957 book. If the race issue was as "diagnostic" as O'Dea claimed, then the "patient" actually started down the road to recovery somewhat sooner than the "doctor" had expected. However, considering how quickly the race issue was replaced by strains and conflicts over feminism and pesky intellectuals, it is at least debatable how appropriate was O'Dea's use of race as a truly "diagnostic" issue.

THE RESPONSE OF THE LDS CHURCH

The church did not, of course, respond to O'Dea's analysis in any direct manner, either to his 1957 book or to his 1972 essay. Indeed, it is doubtful that many church leaders, if any, actually read these works when they appeared—or, for that matter, during the ensuing years. However, it is clear in retrospect that the church did attempt to deal in various ways with the "strains and conflicts" that O'Dea had identified in *The Mormons*, though not necessarily in the ways he might have advocated. By the time O'Dea finally addressed the race issue specifically as among those strains and conflicts, church leaders were already grappling with several of the others on his original list.

The General LDS Response to Modern Secular Thought

As O'Dea was concluding *The Mormons*, he declared that "Mormonism's greatest and most significant problem is its encounter with modern secular thought" (1957, 222). He dealt at some length with this general problem (222–40), and then went on to discuss briefly some specific contradictions that seemed to complicate that predicament in one way or another. He saw nine such contradictions that had developed in Mormon values across time, and he expected the future of the LDS Church and community to depend on the resolution of those contradictions as part of the Mormon struggle with modern secular thought. As already explained, O'Dea did not include among them the contradiction between the racist heritage and the egalitarian ethos in Mormonism until his later essay. When he wrote again in 1972, he could not see much progress in the church's management of its "encounter with modern secular thought" (161–65), and that "encounter" clearly framed O'Dea's analysis of the race predicament in the church. A general assessment of the encounter, and of the efforts of the church to resolve the various contradictions, as important and interesting as that might be, is far beyond the scope of this chapter, though I have addressed such matters elsewhere (1994).[12]

Suffice it to say at this point simply that during the second half of the twentieth century, the chief enemy to the Mormon religion, as O'Dea foresaw, did indeed become modern secular culture, with its relentless challenges to traditional institutions and religious truths of all kinds, and its seductive moral and cultural relativity (Mauss 1994, chaps. 5–6, also pp. 85–86, 126–30). To contend with these new challenges, LDS leaders continued to call for loyalty, obedience to authority, and the exercise of agency in support of the church both internally and externally. The resulting *retrenchment* has been accompanied by some apostasy, as O'Dea would have expected, having "creat[ed] enemies without [but] acted as a purgative within" (O'Dea 1957, 244; see also Mauss 1994, 81–88). In the United States, at least, the recurrent injunction to "follow the prophet" has brought a degree of compliance with moral and lifestyle strictures and a commitment of both time and money among most members that are unusual even for a relatively religious American population (Heaton, Bahr, and Jacobson 2004, chaps. 3, 5, 6; Stark 2005, chaps. 4–6).

To the consternation of many other Americans, furthermore, Mormon compliance with the *political* preferences of church leaders also remains conspicuous, at least in the United States. The generally conservative tendency dominant among Mormons in recent decades can be seen, for example, in Republican presidential and congressional preferences; a "patriotic," if somewhat ambivalent, view of militarism in foreign policy; conservative views on abortion; and a strong if losing rearguard resistance to liberalizing laws on alcohol and drug use (Mauss 1994, 112–22; Heaton, Bahr, and Jacobson 2004, chap. 7). In gender politics, the feminist agenda was overtly resisted, with church resources and political mobilization, during the International Women's Year campaign and the Equal Rights Amendment (ERA) struggle of the 1970s (Bradley 2005). More recently, too, in the statewide controversies and campaigns over legitimating same-sex marriages, the LDS Church has again asserted itself strongly against any such developments.[13] In its public opposition to the political aspirations of both feminists and gay-rights advocates, however principled that opposition might be, the church has paid some price in its public image but has been glad to do so, considering the values that it has seen to be at stake.

When O'Dea took up the race issue in his 1972 essay, it was against such a general background and context of Mormon loyalty to leadership in a time of crisis. Mormons and their leaders had seemingly dug in their heels against insistent secular pressure, both social and political, that had been building with the civil rights movement throughout the 1950s and '60s. What critics of the church, including (by then) O'Dea, could never fully understand was that for Mormons, racial discrimination, though important, was a secondary issue. The primary issue was whether church policy was to be determined by political pressure or by prophetic leadership.[14] Accordingly, the Mormons, both as a church and as individuals, endured pillory in the press to a degree not seen since polygamy days. Throughout the late 1950s and '60s, the otherwise favorable coverage given the Mormons by the mass media was largely overshadowed by a growing press preoccupation with the apparent Mormon refusal to join the burgeoning civil rights movement and drop all racial restrictions (Lythgoe 1968, 50–52, 57). Highly publicized snubs of the church were widely reported: the growing number of college athletic teams refusing to play BYU teams, cancellations of Tabernacle Choir bookings in some cities, and the aborting of a new mission to western Africa that had been requested by local Nigerians but denied entry by their government because of the racial policies of the church (Mauss 1981, 14–19).

Presumably, O'Dea had followed the news reports about all these developments, which would have added to the new pessimism apparent in his 1972 essay. Yet by then the mass media and the other major institutions of the nation had already seemingly given up on the obstinate Mormons and had started to move on to other national issues (especially the Vietnam War) that had come to seem more pressing than racial discrimination. An analysis of press coverage during the 1970s found that Mormons were already being portrayed more favorably than had been the case in the 1960s. The race issue, though still treated negatively by journalists, was nevertheless increasingly relegated to the background and replaced by coverage of certain notable and curious aspects of modern Mormon life, such as the several transitions in the presidency of the church between 1969 and 1974, the LDS welfare program, the ERA, Mormon genealogy and temples, Mormon health habits, and prominent Mormons such as the Marriotts and the Osmonds. Jan Shipps attributes much of this improvement in media coverage to the establishment of a new and highly professional public relations program in the church during those years (Stathis and Lythgoe 1977; Mauss 1981, 20–24; Shipps 2000, chap. 3).[15]

The Race Issue as a "Diagnostic Test"

Had O'Dea lived just a little longer, then, he would have seen the racial restriction on priesthood overturned in 1978 and might thus have concluded that the church had passed his "diagnostic test." Even before that, however, had he been more closely attuned to the Mormon scene, he might have noticed several instances of an LDS outreach to black people, including the establishment of the Genesis Group, as well as other hints of the impending fall of the racial restriction (outlined in Mauss 1981, 20–26). The year O'Dea died, 1974, was the very year that President Spencer W. Kimball and his colleagues decided to build a Mormon temple in Brazil. All of the rituals in Mormon temples require access to the priesthood by participants. The temple in Brazil was to be built largely through the labor and resources of the (then) forty-one thousand Brazilian Mormons, probably the most racially mixed Mormon population in all of South America. Although the actual revelation changing the racial policy was not finalized and announced until June 1978, it seems unlikely that the LDS leaders would have authorized a temple in such a location without full realization of the implications of that decision for the traditional racial policy (Deseret News 1974, A7).[16] Yet if they had seen that decision as an occasion for reconsidering the policy, it is not apparent from historical evidence that has emerged since then (even from the new Kimball biography cited below). Nor did most Mormons see the temple decision as a harbinger of change, though some might well have wondered. Most important for purposes of the present discussion, however, is the point that O'Dea was not in a very good position to see a policy change coming if but few Mormons could have seen it. Thus, O'Dea was constrained to underestimate greatly the LDS potential for drastic change even as late as his 1972 "diagnosis."

The evidence emerging since that time indicates that the "1978 revelation," as it is often called, was actually a rather long *revelatory process* that had its first stirrings at least as early as the administration of President David O. McKay in the 1960s. A biography of that president, based on primary sources, indicates that he grappled with the racial policy up to the very end of his life, and apparently gave serious consideration to reversing it on several occasions. Already in the 1950s he had softened the policy around the edges, as it were, with small administrative decisions making it easier for certain individuals and groups of possible (but not definite) African lineage to receive the priesthood (Prince and Wright 2005, 77–81, 95; Mauss 1981, 11–14). McKay's colleagues in the church leadership included both vigorous proponents and equally vigorous opponents of changing the policy outright. However, McKay himself sincerely believed that such a policy change would require a definite revelation directly to him, and he never felt that he had experienced such a divine encounter (Prince and Wright 2005, 103–5). His two successors in the presidency were short-termers who died in office after serving a total of only four years between them, and in any case they had both been firm opponents to changes in the racial policy throughout their lives. Thus, the quandary of the church's policy was inherited by Spencer W. Kimball, who took the office of church president at the very end of 1973.

Kimball had been sensitized to racial issues by a career devoted in large part to the plight of Native American peoples among whom he had been reared in Arizona, and as an apostle he had been chiefly responsible for a major allocation of church programs and resources to improving the physical and spiritual condition of American Indian church members and potential members. Although his public comments about Indians, and the church programs he created, reflected the patronizing attitude common to white Americans throughout history, he nevertheless showed a genuine love and concern for the well-being of the various tribal peoples, especially those in the Mountain West.[17] His visits to Latin America had acquainted him also with the various indigenous peoples there, as well as with the black LDS population particularly in Brazil, which was growing rapidly. The decision to build a temple in Brazil, whether because of or in spite of the racially mixed but faithful LDS membership, was made during his very first year as president. He would also have been well aware of the debacle that had occurred in 1963, when Mormon missionaries to West Africa had been denied visas because of the church's racial policy and were thus prevented from establishing an LDS Church presence among some hundreds of Nigerians who had, in effect, already converted themselves to Mormonism through reading its literature.[18]

Although Kimball and his colleagues had also had to endure a stormy decade of bad public relations over the discriminatory LDS racial policy in the United States itself, it seems likely that they were far more concerned about the impact of that policy on their missionizing efforts in other countries, where the potential for conversions of black people was much greater than that among black Americans of the period. In that sense, as I have argued elsewhere, the incentive for an eventual change in the racial policy came far more immediately from an *internal* imperative to increase church membership worldwide, rather than as a capitulation to *external* pressure from the American civil rights movement.[19] Indeed, had the policy changed in the 1960s when that pressure was greatest, the church leaders would have faced even more than the usual suspicion that political expediency played a bigger role than divine revelation in bringing the eventual change. In any case, it is apparent that Kimball moved early in his presidency to seek a resolution of this vexing issue.

Insofar as we can reconstruct that revelatory process from Kimball's latest biography and from the comments of his closest colleagues, it seems to have been a synergistic process involving not only his own deep and frequent prayers and meditations but also regular communications with his apostolic colleagues about developments in his own thinking, and eventually a periodic testing of their thinking as individuals (Kimball 2005, 195–214).[20] In that process, he seems to have been cultivating an increasing openness to change, not only in his own thinking but in theirs as well.[21] What finally emerged as the revelation of 1978 was what he called a "confirmation" that the time had come for the priesthood to be extended to all men without regard to race or color. Such language implies a prior, if tentative, decision that then calls for confirmation.[22] The decision to be confirmed seems to have resulted from a growing consensus among President Kimball and his brethren that developed without any overt pressure or "lobbying" on his part. When he finally announced to his two counselors in the First Presidency that he had received the requisite confirmation, he urged them to seek their own individual confirmatory encounters (215). Then, when the three of them testified to the twelve apostles of their collective individual spiritual confirmations, the twelve were presented with strong incentives to seek their own, which they successfully did. This whole process took some months, so it was not limited to a particular event or episode of the Pauline kind. Indeed, it followed the pattern that Terryl L. Givens has called "dialogic revelation," and it reflected the teachings in Mormon scriptures that place the burden on the petitioner for initiating the revelatory process.[23]

The highly truncated account of the revelatory process in the above paragraph probably does not do justice to the importance of Spencer Kimball's own individual efforts in initiating the process. It is clear from his biography that the racial policy had been weighing increasingly on his mind as he took the mantle of church president, though surprisingly he did not recall thinking much about how that policy might complicate the decision (made early in his presidency) to build a temple in Brazil (213–14). Even though his biographer makes clear enough that the revelatory process involved some historical research and wide consultation, it is equally clear that President Kimball's own initiative was crucial in raising and keeping the issue of the racial policy before his apostolic colleagues. An observation made to his son and biographer (some years after the revelation) epitomizes well the part played by human initiative in the Mormon understanding of the revelatory process: "Revelations will probably never come unless they are desired. I think few people receive revelations while lounging on a couch. . . . I believe most revelations would come when a man is on his tip toes, reaching as high as he can for something he knows he needs, and then there bursts upon him the answer to his problems" (216).[24]

Even before the revelation of 1978 had changed the policy, furthermore, the church undertook an impressive campaign of public relations and sincere outreach, as if trying to undo more than a century of discrimination against black people (Mauss 1981, 20–24). Then especially after the change, starting at first in small ways, this campaign gradually picked up steam to the point that by 2006 it was attracting considerable media attention.[25] The campaign began with a well-publicized effort to recognize and cultivate the shrinking pool of loyal black LDS members in Utah and a few other parts of the United States. Ordinations to the priesthood and access to the temples were immediate. The Genesis Group, which had started to languish, was gradually revivified and partly redefined as an outreach program for black LDS families and families of mixed race in Utah and elsewhere.[26] Other support groups and publications, started on the initiative of black LDS members themselves, were encouraged and nourished by church funding and sponsorship behind the scenes, especially during the first decade or so after the policy change (Mauss 2003, 241–59). By 1987, the church was also supporting commemorations by black Mormons and others of Martin Luther King Day each January and the annual national Black History Month each February. Special commemorations were also held under church auspices on the tenth and again on the twenty-fifth anniversaries of the 1978 revelation and priesthood policy change (Mauss 2003, 245; 2004a, 104–5 and n. 77). Church backing for special commemorations by black Mormons of Black History Month became increasingly noticeable during the 1990s, and by the turn of the new century the church had discovered a particularly appropriate way to join in on the commemorations itself, namely, through conferences promoting black history and genealogy.

Already in 1988, the tenth-anniversary commemoration of the revelation and policy change, held on the campus of Brigham Young University, featured as its concluding speaker James D. Walker, founding president of the Afro-American Historical and Genealogical Society of Washington, D.C. At around the same time as that event, or shortly afterward, a church genealogist working in the National Archives had happened upon the records of the Freedman's Bank, a Reconstruction-era institution that went defunct in 1874 but left behind the banking records of thousands of freed slaves. With the backing of the church and the volunteer labor of 550 family history "buffs" (who happened to be inmates of the Utah State Prison!), these banking records were electronically compiled from microfilms and collated into family groups. The resulting electronic disks made it possible to identify vital statistics and family connections for nearly a half-million freed slaves, ancestors to perhaps as many as ten million contemporary black Americans.

During Black History Month of 2001, the disks were released at a highly publicized news conference in Salt Lake City, a rather dramatic manifestation, both substantively and symbolically, of the new LDS recognition that black families and family trees also belong in the Mormon fold (Mauss 2003, 250–51).

Since then, the common interest in genealogy shared by the LDS Church and many black Americans (Mormon and non-Mormon) has proved to be a particularly effective vehicle for rapprochement between Mormons and African Americans (as well as Africans). Conferences and workshops on genealogy, with a particular focus on the special problems and techniques involved for researching African American families, have been held in various cities around the United States annually during Black History Month since 2002. These conferences have drawn increasing numbers of registrants and have featured prominent black spokespersons for African American genealogy (for example, Chris Haley and Frederick Douglas IV). Such conferences in Los Angeles and Washington, D.C., particularly, have received increasing attention in the national media (246–47, 251).[27]

They also have apparently helped to improve the image of the LDS Church among black Americans: although black membership growth in the church seems to have been relatively slow (even since 1978), there is evidence of a recent growth spurt, if we judge by the large new Mormon buildings erected last year in Harlem and in Philadelphia's inner city.[28] Recent growth in black American LDS membership is apparently occurring in other eastern cities, too, especially in the South (Driggs 2004). Though systematic data on new black converts cannot be obtained (since the church does not keep records by race), such data as are available indicate that these converts tend to be upwardly aspiring Americans across the broad middle-class spectrum from lower to upper middle (Jacobson 1991, 2004; Jacobson et al. 1994). The formalized LDS proselyting program, as well as the focus on genealogical research, might make for a selective appeal of the religion to black people in these social strata. In any case, such selective conversions suggest a homogeneity in social status between the general white American LDS membership and the incoming black converts, which should bode well for future interracial relationships within the church, despite occasional setbacks. Meanwhile, in their attitudes toward national civil rights in general, white Mormons have never differed much from other Americans, but since 1978 they have tended to express even more tolerance than other Americans in national surveys (see Mauss 2003, chap. 9, esp. 252–55; and Jacobson 2004, 118–21). All things considered, it seems fair to conclude that Mormons have passed O'Dea's "diagnostic test" convincingly, although the virus of racism has not yet been entirely overcome.

CONCLUSION

On balance, then, all things considered, how might we assess O'Dea's belated diagnosis and prognosis about the future of the LDS encounter with "modern secular thought," and particularly its resolution of the "race issue" as an institutional quandary? On the latter issue, it seems fair to say that the church eventually rose to the challenge posed by O'Dea's diagnosis, so that archaic racial conceptions no longer complicate the LDS relationship with the rest of the world, in either secular or religious terms. Had O'Dea lived just a few years longer, he would have seen the momentous 1978 change in the Mormon racial policies. Some white Mormons have continued to hold the old conceptions about race, but at a clearly diminishing rate.[29] Black populations in most of the world are joining the church in large numbers. Even in the United States, where the church has taken longer to live down its racist stigma among black Americans, there are signs that at least younger African Americans are willing to view the future of Mormonism as much more relevant to their lives than its past.[30]

What of the more *general* question that preoccupied O'Dea in 1957 and again in 1972? Would he now be more or less optimistic than then about the outcome of the Mormon encounter with modern secular thought? Clearly, O'Dea was justified in being concerned about this question, for conflicts between the LDS religion and the modern world have been recurrent from the beginning. More specifically, though, how about the period since the middle of the twentieth century, when O'Dea first began assessing the likely outcomes of the "strains and conflicts" within Mormonism that would complicate its encounter with modernity? If O'Dea were commenting today from the same theoretical perspective that he used in his lifetime, he would probably see a very mixed record in the Mormon encounter with modern secular thought. He would find evidence in modern Mormonism of both resistance and accommodation to modern social and intellectual developments. Like other intellectuals who discussed the future of religion in the middle of the century, O'Dea operated from the conventional wisdom that religion would inevitably have to accommodate itself to the enlightened social prescriptions of modern industrial and democratic societies. Science and secularism were the wave of the future. In its extreme form, this "secularization model" of the future anticipated the extinction of religion altogether, since modern people would not be able to endure indefinitely the intellectual and normative tension between science and the religious myths of the past. What O'Dea did not foresee was the emergence of a "new para-digm" in the sociology of religion with somewhat different predictions about the wave of the future, at least the future of religion (Stark and Finke 2000, 27–41).[31] In this new paradigm, which might be called the "tension-management model," the viability of religious movements and denomina-tions would depend not on their unilinear progress toward accommodation with the cultures of the world but rather on their success in maintaining an *optimum degree of tension* with their respective host cultures.[32] If the recent history of Mormonism is considered in light of this "tension-management model," then the record of the church's relationship with American culture could be read as flexible, or even nimble, rather than merely as a "mixture" of accommodation and resistance to secularization.[33] That is, whether by revelation, calculation, or serendipity, the church has moved to reduce ten-sion when it has become severe enough to hamper the conversion and re-tention of members, but then increased tension at other times when accom-modation has threatened to undermine internal discipline and solidarity.

We might, for example, understand the 1978 change in racial policy as a tension-reducing response to the national battering of the LDS public image during the 1960s and early 1970s. Yet during the 1970s and '80s, the church publicly resisted the agenda of national political feminism by inter-fering with the International Women's Year activities and by opposing the Equal Rights Amendment, mainly because of a belief by LDS leaders that secular feminist values threatened Mormon family values. Since the nation itself was divided over the feminist agenda, and Mormon women gener-ally supported the church's positions, the increased tension between church and society was dissipated more rapidly than had been the case with the race issue.[34] Even so, however, after helping to defeat the ERA, the church moved quickly to make certain concessions to its own women and to give more public attention to the accomplishments of women.[35]

Tension with the media and with other national institutions had thus been reduced by the change in the LDS racial policy, but then increased again somewhat as church leaders sought to reclaim their control over the teachings and policies of the LDS Church on women's roles. In sum, whether recent Mormon history is best understood through the "seculariza-tion model" or through the "tension-management model," that history at least justifies O'Dea's early optimism about the viability of the Latter-day Saints as a church and as a people. The Mormon accommodation with "mo-dernity" is unlikely ever to reach a stage that would reassure O'Dea or his like-minded intellectual descendants, but in eventually changing its racial policy the church at least seems to have passed the "diagnostic test" that was the most challenging in O'Dea's mind.

Notes

1. See, for example, Wood 1990, the final three chapters of which are devoted to the manifestations of racism in the various denominations from Civil War times all the way down to the present. Even as late as 1985, black bishops in the Roman Catholic Church, constituting only 3 percent of the total American bishops, complained about racial bias in the church (Chandler 1985).

2. The *Deseret News Church Almanac* (for any year) gives a figure of 1.5 million for the total membership of the church in 1957 (*Deseret News* 1984, 250).

3. U.S. Census figures show the black population of Utah as rising from about twenty-seven hundred in 1950 to some forty-one hundred in 1960, according to Newell G. Bringhurst (1981b, 228).

4. See the account of the McKay-McMurrin encounter in Prince and Wright 2005, 96–97.

5. This comment by Nelson was in part his response to a rebuke that he received from LDS leaders for criticizing the traditional church ban on priesthood for blacks, after they had sought his advice about extending missionary work to Cuba. See the brief account in Prince and Wright 2005 and Mauss 1981. The encounter with Nelson had, in fact, apparently necessitated the issuance in 1949 of the only official church statement on the racial policy ever issued up to that time. See the full text in Bush and Mauss 1984, 221 (app.).

6. See the collection of articles in the symposium on O'Dea's career in *Sociological Analysis* (later renamed *Sociology of Religion*) 38, no. 2 (Summer 1977): 126–66, from which I draw these details. See also the appreciative postmortem of Michaelsen 1978.

7. See a fuller treatment of this conceptualization in O'Dea 1954.

8. His main citations are to Turner 1966; Brodie 1960, 1970; Brewer 1968; and Taggart 1970.

9. See also "History of Genesis" on the Genesis Group Web site, http://www.ldsgenesisgroup.org. In fairness, it must be conceded that O'Dea's 1972 essay might have gone to press before he could have learned about the Genesis Group, which was organized in October 1971, although it had been under discussion between the apostles and the leaders of the black Mormon community for several months by that time. O'Dea did have time to include a reference in his article (167) to the appointment of Dallin Oaks as president of Brigham Young University (BYU), which occurred in August 1971, so it is not impossible that he could have included a reference to the Genesis Group emerging during that same period.

10. Though the publication date for this issue is late 1969, it probably did not actually appear until well into 1970, given the lagging publication schedule of the journal in those days. However, that still should have been in time for inclusion in O'Dea's 1972 essay. For a recent review and demurral on the "Missouri thesis," see Bringhurst 2004, 13–33.

11. The catalog at UCSB still includes *Dialogue* for those years, so presumably it was in this library's holdings from 1966, the first year of its publication.

12. See also my other essay in this collection (Chapter 11).

13. See the comprehensive (if indignant) account in Quinn 2000, followed by my reply, pp. 53–65.

14. This is not to deny that racism among Mormon leaders and members was an important factor in the LDS conflict with the nation during that period. However, considering how quickly Mormon public opinion on race "turned around" after the leaders changed the priesthood policy in 1978, it seems unduly simplistic to dismiss acquiescence in the pre-1978 race restrictions as sheer racism. See the changing public opinion data on LDS and others in Mauss 1994, 52, 153; and Mauss 2003, 252–54, chap. 9.

15. Shipps (2000, 100) offers the intriguing if ironic hypothesis that a growing national concern with the youthful counterculture of this period (which was also seen as a nemesis by the Mormons) had helped to sideline the media interest in the Mormon racial situation.

16. The *1980 Church Almanac* notes that the decision to build a temple in São Paulo was officially and publicly announced on March 1, 1975, during an area conference there (Deseret News 1979, 296). Obviously, the decision itself would have been discussed and formulated during the previous year.

17. This observation is readily inferred from various chapters in Kimball and Kimball 1977. See also Mauss 2003, 82–104.

18. See Prince and Wright 2005, 81–94, where it is noted, however, that the unrest and eventual war in Biafra that broke out in 1967 would have made it difficult to maintain a Mormon Church presence in Nigeria anyway during the 1960s.

19. On the public relations setbacks for the church over the race issue in the 1960s and '70s, see Prince and Wright 2005, 66–73; and Mauss 1981, 14–25. On political pressure and the timing of the policy change, see Mauss 1981, 30–31.

20. See also the description of the process in Mauss 1981, 24–31, which accords well in general with Edward Kimball's account.

21. Kimball 2005 (for example, 212, 216) indicates that Spencer Kimball was regularly posing questions to church leaders at both the local and the general levels to get their opinions on the policy and its potential change. With the help of his apostolic colleagues, he also sought historical evidence on the origin of the priesthood restriction in the first place (203, 216, 220).

22. The whole process is described in some detail in Kimball 2005, 215–24. The final announcement of the policy change explicitly referred to a "confirmation" of a revelation. No text was ever offered for the revelation itself (though an unknown forger made an attempt!) (227–30).

23. On Givens's conceptualization of "dialogic revelation," see Givens 2001, among other places. Relevant LDS scriptures would include Book of Mormon, Moroni 10:4–5, and Doctrine and Covenants 8:1–3, 9:7–8, and the official account of Joseph Smith's own first

encounter with Deity in the Pearl of Great Price (Joseph Smith 2:1–26). Rodney Stark offers a respectful but naturalistic or demystified explanation for the process of revelation in his "A Theory of Revelations" (1999).

24. See the similar characterization of the revelatory process in Mauss 1981, 30–31.

25. This campaign is described and illustrated extensively in chap. 9 of my book *All Abraham's Children: Changing Mormon Conceptions of Race and Lineage* (2003). A slightly updated version of this chapter will be found in my essay "Casting Off the 'Curse of Cain'" (2004). Somewhat ironically, the campaign to win over American blacks was partially eclipsed during the 1980s by a massive new missionary enterprise to West Africa, where self-identified black Mormons had been waiting for the church since 1963. For the 1963 West African story, see Prince and Wright 2005, 81–94; Kimball 2005, 239–45; Bush 1973, 45; Mauss 1981, 16 and n. 37; and Bringhurst 1981a, 17–18. The best overview of the West African story will be found in J. Allen 1991, 207–47.

26. On developments in the Genesis Group, see Mauss 1981, 23–24; 2004a, 101–4; plus the Genesis Web site, http://www.ldsgenesisgroup.org.

27. See also coverage of similar recent genealogy conferences on the Genesis Group Web site—for example, http://www.ldsgenesisgroup.org>Newsletter>AAHGSConference in Utah.

28. On the initially slow growth of LDS membership among African Americans (in contrast to growth among Africans), see Bringhurst 1992. On more recent growth in eastern inner cities such as Washington, D.C., Philadelphia, and New York's Harlem, see various syndicated news stories during December 2005 (for example, Hill 2005; and Banks 2005).

29. These setbacks result from different forms of insensitivity among white Mormons who generally have not experienced much contact with black people, especially in the Mountain West, but also, less often, from special sensitivities among black members surprised by the persistence of the old racist folklore among white Mormons. See, for example, Mauss 2003, 261–64, 274–75; 2004b. For a more critical view of the white Mormon posture, see Smith 2003, 2004.

30. In an apparent condemnation of the racist folklore still persisting at the Mormon grassroots, President Gordon B. Hinckley made some unusually pointed critical comments during the church's annual general conference in April 2006: "I am told that racial slurs and denigrating remarks are sometimes heard among us.... [N]o man who makes [such] disparaging remarks...can consider himself a true disciple of Christ. How can any man holding the Melchizedek Priesthood arrogantly assume that he is eligible for the priesthood whereas another who lives a righteous life, but whose skin is of a different color, is ineligible?" (58).

31. The "new paradigm" specifically was first labeled and described in Warner 1993.

32. I take the idea of a "tension-management system" from Moore 1963, in which it was used to characterize social systems in general (see Mauss 1994, 4–14). I have inferred the idea of "optimum tension" from my reading of the work of Rodney Stark and colleagues, originally from Stark and Bainbridge 1985, esp. 50–60, 149–67, 363–65.

33. In my other essay for this collection, I discuss at some length the significance of this paradigm shift for understanding developments in the LDS Church.

34. Indeed, by the 1990s, social scientists and commentators were finding data that raised considerable doubt about feminist assumptions that modern educated women were chafing under traditional gender roles. This is not the place to review all that literature, but see, for example, the recent article by Charlotte Allen, "The Return of the Happy Housewife" (2006), which cites research by University of Virginia sociologists W. Bradford Wilcox and Stephen L. Nock in the journal *Social Forces.*

35. See, for example, Iannaccone and Miles 1990, in which the concept "optimum tension" is implicit, if not explicit.

References

Allen, Charlotte. 2006. "The Return of the Happy Housewife." *Los Angeles Times,* March 5, M1.

Allen, James B. 1991. "Would-be Saints: West Africa before the 1978 Priesthood Revelation." *Journal of Mormon History* 17: 207–47.

Bahr, Howard. 2005. "Finding Oneself among the Saints: Thomas F. O'Dea and the Liberal Mormon." Unpublished manuscript, Department of Sociology, Brigham Young University, Provo.

Banks, Adelle M. 2005. "Racial Diversity Allows for More LDS Church Growth." *Salt Lake Tribune,* December 17.

Bradley, Martha Sonntag. 2005. *Pedestals and Podiums: Utah Women, Religious Authority, and Equal Rights.* Salt Lake City: Signature Books.

Brewer, David L. 1968. "The Mormons (with Commentary by Lowell L. Bennion)." In *The Religious Situation, 1968,* ed. Donald R. Cutler, 521–52. Boston: Beacon Press.

Bringhurst, Newell G. 1981a. "Mormonism in Black Africa: Changing Attitudes and Practices." *Sunstone* (May–June): 17–18.

———. 1981b. *Saints, Slaves, and Blacks: The Changing Place of Black People within Mormonism.* Westport, Conn.: Greenwood Press.

———. 1992. "The Image of Blacks within Mormonism as Presented in the *Church News,* 1978–1988." *American Periodicals* 2 (Fall): 113–23.

———. 2004. "The 'Missouri Thesis' Revisited: Early Mormonism, Slavery, and the Status of Black People." In *Black and Mormon,* ed. Newell G. Bringhurst and Darron T. Smith. Urbana: University of Illinois Press.

Brodie, Fawn M. 1960. *No Man Knows My History: The Life of Joseph Smith, the Mormon Prophet.* New York: Alfred A. Knopf.

———. 1970. "Can We Manipulate the Past?" Lecture, Center for the Study of the American West, Salt Lake City.

Bush, Lester E. 1969. "A Commentary on Stephen G. Taggart's *Mormonism's Negro Doctrine: Social and Historical Origins.*" *Dialogue: A Journal of Mormon Thought* 4, no. 4: 86–103.

———. 1973. "Mormonism's Negro Doctrine: An Historical Overview." *Dialogue: A Journal of Mormon Thought* 8, no. 1: 45.

Bush, Lester E., and Armand L.Mauss. 1984. *Neither White nor Black: Mormon Scholars Confront the Race Issue in a Universal Church.* Salt Lake City: Signature Books.

Campbell, Angus. 1971. *White Attitudes toward Black People.* Ann Arbor, Mich.: Institute for Social Research.

Chandler, Russell. 1985. "Bishops Urge Leadership Roles for Catholic Acceptance of Blacks." *Los Angeles Times,* November 14, 5.

Deseret News. 1974. *Deseret News 1975 Church Almanac.* Salt Lake City: Deseret News.

———. 1979. *Deseret News 1980 Church Almanac.* Salt Lake City: Deseret News.

———. 1984. *Deseret News 1985 Church Almanac.* Salt Lake City: Deseret News.

Driggs, Ken. 2004. "'How Do Things Look on the Ground?' The LDS African American Community in Atlanta, Georgia." In *Black and Mormon,* ed. Newell G. Bringhurst and Darron T. Smith, 132–47. Urbana: University of Illinois Press.

Givens, Terryl L. 2001. "The Book of Mormon and Religious Epistemology." *Dialogue: A Journal of Mormon Thought* 34, nos. 3–4: 31–54.

Glock, Charles Y., and Rodney Stark. 1966. *Christian Beliefs and Anti-semitism.* New York: Harper and Row.

Heaton, Tim B., Stephen J. Bahr, and Cardell K. Jacobson. 2004. *A Statistical Profile of Mormons: Health, Wealth, and Social Life.* Lewiston, N.Y.: Edwin Mellen Press.

Hill, Miriam. 2005. "Mormons Gain Diverse Members in Inner Cities." *Fort Wayne (Ind.) News Sentinel,* December 21.

Hinckley, Gordon B. 2006. "The Need for Greater Kindness." *Ensign,* May, 58.

Iannaccone, Laurence R., and Carrie Miles. 1990. "Dealing with Social Change: The Mormon Church's Response to Change in Women's Roles." *Social Forces* 68: 1231–50.

Jacobson, Cardell K. 1991. "Black Mormons in the 1980s: Pioneers in a White Church." *Review of Religious Research* 33 (December): 146–52.

———. 2004. "African American Latter-day Saints: A Sociological Perspective." In *Black and Mormon,* ed. Newell G. Bringhurst and Darron T. Smith, 116–31. Urbana: University of Illinois Press.

Jacobson, Cardell K., Tim B. Heaton, E. Dale LeBaron, and Trina Louise Hope. 1994. "Black Mormon Converts in the United States and Africa: Social Characteristics and Perceived Acceptance." In *Contemporary Mormonism: Social Science Perspectives,* ed. Marie Cornwall, Tim B. Heaton, and Lawrence A. Young, 326–47. Urbana: University of Illinois Press.

Kimball, Edward L. 2005. *Lengthen Your Stride: The Presidency of Spencer W. Kimball.* Salt Lake City: Deseret Book.

Kimball, Edward L., and Andrew E. Kimball Jr. 1977. *Spencer W. Kimball, Twelfth President of the Church of Jesus Christ of Latter-day Saints.* Salt Lake City: Bookcraft.

Lythgoe, Dennis L. 1968. "The Changing Image of Mormonism." *Dialogue* 3, no. 4: 45–58.

Mauss, Armand L. 1981. "The Fading of the Pharaohs' Curse: The Decline and Fall of the Priesthood Ban against Blacks in the Mormon Church." *Dialogue: A Journal of Mormon Thought* 14, no. 3: 10–45.

———. 1994. *The Angel and the Beehive: The Mormon Struggle with Assimilation.* Urbana: University of Illinois Press.

———. 2003. *All Abraham's Children: Changing Mormon Conceptions of Race and Lineage.* Urbana: University of Illinois Press.

———. 2004a. "Casting Off the 'Curse of Cain.'" In *Black and Mormon,* ed. Newell G. Bringhurst and Darron T. Smith, 82–115. Urbana: University of Illinois Press.

———. 2004b. "Dispelling the Curse of Cain." *Sunstone* (March): 31–33.

McMurrin, Sterling M. 1979. "A Note on the 1963 Civil Rights Statement." *Dialogue: A Journal of Mormon Thought* 12, no. 2: 60–63.

Michaelsen, Robert S. 1978. "Thomas F. O'Dea on the Mormons: Retrospect and Assessment." *Dialogue: A Journal of Mormon Thought* 11, no. 1: 44–57.

Moore, Wilbert E. 1963. *Social Change.* Englewood Cliffs, N.J.: Prentice-Hall.

Nelson, Lowry. 1952. "Mormons and the Negro." *Nation* 174 (May 24).

O'Dea, Thomas F. 1954. "Mormonism and the Avoidance of Sectarian Stagnation: A Study of Church, Sect, and Incipient Nationality." *American Journal of Sociology* 60 (November): 285–93.

———. 1957. *The Mormons.* Chicago: University of Chicago Press.

———. 1972. "Sources of Strain in Mormon History Reconsidered." In *Mormonism and American Culture,* ed. Marvin S. Hill and James B. Allen, 147–67. New York: Harper and Row.

Prince, Gregory A., and William Robert Wright. 2005. *David O. McKay and the Rise of Modern Mormonism.* Salt Lake City: University of Utah Press.

Quinn, D. Michael. 1993. "Ezra Taft Benson and the Mormon Political Conflicts." *Dialogue: A Journal of Mormon Thought* 26, no. 2: 1–87.

———. 2000. "Prelude to the National 'Defense of Marriage' Campaign: Civil Discrimination against Feared or Despised Minorities." *Dialogue: A Journal of Mormon Thought* 33, no. 3: 1–52.

Shipps, Jan. 2000. *Sojourner in the Promised Land: Forty Years among the Mormons.* Urbana: University of Illinois Press.

Smith, Darron T. 2003. "The Persistence of Racialized Discourse in Mormonism." *Sunstone* (March): 31–33.

———. 2004. "Unpacking Whiteness in Zion: Some Personal Reflections and General Observations." In *Black and Mormon,* ed. Newell G. Bringhurst and Darron T. Smith, 118–21. Urbana: University of Illinois Press.

Stark, Rodney. 1999. "A Theory of Revelations." *Journal for the Scientific Study of Religion* 38, no. 2: 287–307.

————. 2005. *The Rise of Mormonism,* ed. by Reid L. Neilson. New York: Columbia University Press.

Stark, Rodney, and William Sims Bainbridge. 1985. *The Future of Religion: Secularization, Revival, and Cult Formation.* Berkeley and Los Angeles: University of California Press.

Stark, Rodney, and Roger Finke. 2000. *Acts of Faith: Explaining the Human Side of Religion.* Berkeley and Los Angeles: University of California Press.

Stathis, Stephen W., and Dennis L. Lythgoe. 1977. "Mormonism in the Nineteen Seventies: The Popular Perception." *Dialogue: A Journal of Mormon Thought* 10, no. 3: 95–113.

Taggart, Stephen G. 1970. *Mormonism's Negro Policy: Social and Historical Origins.* Salt Lake City: University of Utah Press.

Turner, Wallace. 1966. *The Mormon Establishment.* Boston: Houghton-Mifflin.

Warner, R. Stephen. 1993. "Work in Progress towards a New Paradigm for the Sociological Study of Religion in the United States." *American Journal of Sociology* 98: 1047–93.

Wood, Forrest G. 1990. *The Arrogance of Faith: Christianity and Race in America.* Boston: Northeastern University Press.

8

The Current Crisis in the Formation and Regulation of Latter-day Saints' Sexual Identity

~ Melvyn Hammarberg ~

The current crisis in the formation and regulation of sexual identity within the Church of Jesus Christ of Latter-day Saints (LDS) provides a deep puzzle that may be stated as a question: why have LDS Church leaders and members been unable to accommodate homosexuality within the marriage and family system that otherwise is such a strikingly positive and powerful aspect of the church's personal and institutional life? In the spirit of Thomas F. O'Dea's sociological orientation to Mormon cultural values, *The Mormons* (1957), my purpose in asking this question is to explore LDS sexual ethics and sexual identity as sources of strain within Mormonism. Although O'Dea gave direct attention to plural marriage and family ideals, sexuality itself was not focal to his examination of stresses and strains in the church (see his chapter 9). But after he wrote, the sexual revolution of the 1960s changed the cultural context for understanding sexuality in marriage, the family, the LDS Church, and American society. For the church, among the most troubling issues in this new context have been homosexual identity. Exploring these issues in the LDS Church is the task of this article.

At the outset, I wish to acknowledge that I am a divorced and remarried father of an adult lesbian daughter and adult gay son among my three children. The issues of marital, sexual, and family ethics and practices are therefore part of my own non-LDS background. In addition, I claim my academic identity as an anthropologist and cognitive psychologist with a special interest in religion. These factors undoubtedly have a bearing on my efforts to examine the central question of this article: the perceived threats posed to LDS identity by homosexuality.

My working definition of identity is one proposed by Anthony F. C. Wallace originally in 1967. In Wallace's words,

> Identity is any image, or set of images, either conscious or unconscious, which an individual has of himself [or herself]. An image in this sense, may be recognized introspectively as an internal "visual" or "verbal" representation, but it is observed in others as an external assertion in words, deeds, or gesture which is assumed to reflect in some way an internal representation. The full set of images of self (or *total identity*) refers to many aspects of the person, on a number of levels of generality: his [or her] appetites,... strengths and capabilities,... fears,... vulnerabilities and weaknesses,... past experience,... moral qualities,... social status and role,... physical appearance, and so on. There is no requirement that the several images which compose this total identity be noncontradictory; thus identity may, in some of its domains, be ambiguous or inconsistent. (2003, 283)

LDS IDENTITY AND THE AUTHORITY STRUCTURE OF THE CHURCH

In the fullest sense, total identity today as a member of the Church of Jesus Christ of Latter-day Saints centers on kinship relations linking the generations, living and dead, through the ordinance of celestial marriage, creating what are popularly known as "forever families" (Church of Jesus Christ of Latter-day Saints [hereafter "Church"], Church Educational System, 2001, 100). As Lawrence Foster has noted, "Mormonism has gone farther than have most other religious movements in seeing the family not merely as the basis of social order in this life, but also as the foundation for all growth and development in the afterlife as well. In a very fundamental sense, Mormonism is not simply concerned *with* the family; it is [fundamentally] *about* the family. The church is conceived as the family writ large" (1994, 2).

The plural-wife system was central to O'Dea's view of strains within Utah Mormon families in the nineteenth century as well a source of conflict with the federal government, which finally led to the Manifesto of 1890 (1957, 245–49). That plural-marriage tradition continues today among the fundamentalist followers of LDS founding prophet Joseph Smith, who introduced plural marriage as part of "the new and everlasting covenant" (Doctrine and Covenants 132). Among the main body of Saints, however, the core image of Latter-day Saints' identity consists jointly of adult men holding the Melchizedek priesthood and adult women active as members of the Relief Society, who are endowed, sealed in a monogamous temple marriage, and the parents of children ranging from infancy to unmarried early adulthood. The total image is a two-gendered composite that also constitutes the prototype of an LDS nuclear family of parents and children, and is the culturally normative family image within the church. It consists of these individuals in family roles, even though many worthy families and members depart from these ideals as too young, single, disabled, widowed, part-member, step-person, unendowed, or not sealed—who also bring to their gendered self-understandings many rich experiences that add to the core images of male-female, husband-wife, parents-children. Additional aspects of gender include gay, lesbian, bisexual, and transgendered identity among Latter-day Saints as these have become increasingly public as part of the current homosexual identity crisis within the church.

Also as O'Dea noted, authority and obedience in the church come by way of revelation as "a divine commission or calling from God" (1957, 242). The structure of authority is organized in a hierarchy beginning with God as Heavenly Father who directs his son, Jesus Christ (Cameron 1992), whose divinity in turn is affirmed by the testimony of the Holy Ghost. In the church's view, it was under Christ's direction that Joseph Smith spoke and acted in the role of "prophet, seer, and revelator" as the presiding high priest of the church. As president he was authorized to choose two counselors. These three positions—the president and the first and second counselor—are now known as the First Presidency. Under Smith's direction the Quorum of the Twelve Apostles was also organized. Today, the men holding these fifteen positions are the preeminent General Authorities of the LDS Church. They provide the public voice of the church in their roles as prophets, seers, and revelators, and speak in the name of Jesus Christ and the Heavenly Father.

The centralized power of the church's lay priesthood extends from the First Presidency and the twelve through multiple quorums of seventies, and finally reaches into the homes of all members, including men, women, and children alike, through the high priests and elders of the Melchizedek priesthood, which includes all worthy adult men of the church. The standards of worthiness are controlled by the brethren and implemented through the priesthood, and set the criteria according to which members are expected to live, including their standards for sexual beliefs, values, attitudes, and behavior.

THE SEXUAL REVOLUTION OF THE 1960S

The post–World War II beginnings of the sexual revolution in America were first marked by Alfred Kinsey, an entomologist who built his early reputation as an empirical scientist on studies of the gall wasp, but then turned to the study of human sexuality. In two major books Kinsey held up a mirror to American sexual practices among both men (Kinsey, Pomeroy, and Martin 1948) and women (Kinsey et al. 1953), showing for both sexes that masturbation was much more common than anyone thought and that orgasm served many individuals as a personal measure of sexual pleasure. He also developed a rating scale across a continuum of seven categories that showed the behavioral gradations between exclusively heterosexual and exclusively homosexual categories, introducing complexities of gender identity that many people had not previously envisioned (McLaren 1999, chap. 8).

Further, the late 1950s also saw the publication of such novels as Grace Metalious's *Peyton Place* (1950) and Philip Roth's *Goodbye Columbus* (1959). And in 1957 the Supreme Court established new, less restrictive criteria for obscenity in *Roth v. United States* that opened the door to previously censored erotic fiction as well as the erotic work of contemporary authors and artists.

But the full sexual revolution, and its reaction, began when the birth control pill was approved by the U.S. Food and Drug Administration in 1960 (McLaren 1999, chap. 9). The pill, allowing for sexual intercourse without fear of pregnancy, created for both men and women an image of sexuality separated from pregnancy and reproduction while emphasizing sensual pleasure. This shift gave women new power and control over the consequences of intercourse. Then, in 1961, the State of Illinois adopted the first "consenting adult" law, decriminalizing sexual behavior between consenting adults. In turn, these changes empowered other entrepreneurs who exploited sex as pornography, depicting in graphic display many varieties of sexual activity. An American classic of a new marital genre was also published, Alex Comfort's *Joy of Sex: A Gourmet Guide to Love Making* (1972).

This same period from the mid-1950s through the mid-1970s saw the rise of a number of movements of social transformation. The key event was the Supreme Court decision *Brown v. Board of Education of Topeka, Kansas* in 1954, which concluded that "in the field of education the doctrine of 'separate but equal' has no place. Separate educational facilities are inherently unequal." Out of this decision the modern civil rights movements were born, not only in education but also in other spheres involving African American minority rights, women's rights, Native American rights, and gay rights. Each "status group" sought to bring forward its claims to recognition and equal standing before the law. Each movement had its turning point and subsequent trajectory in the march against perceived discrimination and injustice. Such a turning point for homosexual rights followed on the 1969 Stonewall Inn riot in Greenwich Village, New York City, when many of the homosexual patrons rebelled against police harassment and launched their own gay-rights and gay-pride movement (Carter 2004).

In addition to the beginnings of these social movements, film, then television, and later the computer and World Wide Web (Internet) provided powerful new technologies for the mass distribution of images and information. For all the good that these technologies promised for communication, in the area of sexuality they also provided images of sensual exploitation that posed a danger and threat to the sexual and family ethics of many Americans—indeed of many people around the world—as was perceived by Latter-day Saints' authorities, and equally by leaders of other religious and secular groups. These movements and the new information technologies affected leaders and members of the Church of Jesus Christ of Latter-day Saints in a number of ways, including their response to a newly visible homosexuality (Forrest and Bigler 1999).

The LDS Response to the Sexual Revolution

Changes in American sexuality since the end of World War II prompted a number of responses within the LDS community, among both church authorities and members, with an increasing focus on homosexuality (also referred to by Latter-day Saints as same-gender attraction). Among General Authorities, J. Reuben Clark first used the words *homosexual* and *homosexuality* in public during an address before the annual meeting of the General Relief Society Conference in 1952. Introducing this topic, President Clark said, "We now speak of homosexuality, which, it is tragic to say, is found among both sexes.... Not without foundation is the contention of some that the homosexuals are today exercising great influence in shaping our arts, literature, music, and drama" (quoted in O'Donovan 1994, 146). Rocky O'Donovan suggests that this statement reveals the LDS Church's viewpoint as very much in keeping with the general societal orientation during the McCarthy era, which he says bordered on homophobic hysteria.

In 1959 two apostles, Spencer W. Kimball and Mark E. Peterson, were assigned by church president David O. McKay to help lesbians and gays try to overcome their same-gender attraction. As church counseling of members expanded, Kimball estimated that about 75 percent of their work was devoted to issues of same-sex attraction. He began making notes and subsequently published three major works that helped shape the LDS approach to homosexuality. In 1969, the year of the Stonewall Inn riots, Kimball published his classic treatise on sin and repentance, *The Miracle of Forgiveness,* with a chapter titled "The Crime against Nature" that included his theory that masturbation causes homosexuality, which causes bestiality, and therefore is a threat to the family. He underscored his belief in its seriousness, indicating that "the sin of homosexuality is equal to or greater than that of fornication or adultery; and that *the Lord's Church will as readily take action to disfellowship or excommunicate the unrepentant practicing homosexual as it will the unrepentant fornicator or adulterer*" (81–82).

In addition, the First Presidency issued an official statement in 1973 declaring that "homosexuality in men and women runs counter to... divine objectives and, therefore, is to be avoided and forsaken" under "threat of prompt Church court action" (O'Donovan 1994, 149). And in an evening priesthood session during the semiannual fall general conference, apostle Boyd K. Packer (1976) addressed the "perversion" of homosexuality in a talk titled "To Young Men Only," proposing "selfishness" as the primary cause of same-sex attraction. This presentation was subsequently printed as a pamphlet by the church for use in counseling its members (O'Donovan 1994, 150).

Over the next two decades, several nonchurch publications tracked salient issues dealing with sexuality among the Latter-day Saints. The first was a 1976 special issue of *Dialogue: A Journal of Mormon Thought,* edited by Harold T. Christensen and Marvin B. Rytting, that sought to explore sexuality and Mormon culture. The second was a collection of essays edited by Ron Schow, Wayne Schow, and Marybeth Raynes, published by Signature Books under the title *Peculiar People: Mormons and Same-Sex Orientation* (1991). And the third was another collection, edited by Brent Corcoran, titled *Multiply and Replenish: Mormon Essays on Sex and Family* (1994). Together these three publications covered important aspects of sexuality among Latter-day Saints during the second half of the twentieth century.

Dialogue's Assessment of LDS Sexuality in the Mid-1970s

Dialogue is not an official publication of the LDS Church, but a private, moderately liberal undertaking by interested members and friends who desire to think through the commitments of the LDS faith. Clearly, this 1976 special issue was one response to what its editors perceived as the "permissiveness" of American society during the 1960s and 1970s. In their introduction, Christensen and Rytting noted two simultaneous movements on the sexual front that were emerging after the war; one increased the distance between Mormon culture and the host American culture, and the other involved stresses of sexuality *within* Mormon culture itself. With regard to the first, they noted that Mormons were less secluded, less concentrated in Utah, and more influenced by the mass media than before the war. "Thus we

feel—perhaps more keenly than ever before—the conflict between our values and those of 'the world.'" However, "the world" itself was divided in
ways that required Latter-day Saints to pick and choose their way along an
unknown path to the future. To this end, the editors believed that "a good
case can be made for being discriminating—that is, knowingly and intelli-
gently choosing to control sexual behavior within meaningful boundaries" (9).

The 1976 *Dialogue* essays examined four main areas of sexuality: birth
control, the LDS repression of sexuality, the LDS norm of premarital chastity, and homosexuality. A physician and historian, Lester E. Bush examined the issue of birth control. He noted that to a church leader of the early
post–World War II era such as J. Reuben Clark, "the primary purpose of
sex desire is to beget children. Sex gratification must be had at that hazard"
(1976, 25–26). Birth control seemed to undermine this primary purpose.
Nonetheless, by 1969, church leaders had adopted a compromise position:
"While the Church continued to encourage having a large family, and to
condemn family limitation for 'selfish' reasons, the actual decisions regarding family size and spacing and the means by which these were achieved had
in effect been placed above ecclesiastical review. In the popular phraseology,
these matters were strictly 'between husband, wife, and the Lord'" (29).

In regard to "repression" as a second issue, Klaus Hansen suggested
that "Mormon culture experienced a transformation from a traditional to
a modern society analogous to the one occurring in the larger American
culture but within a different time frame," and that "much of the friction
between Mormons and Gentiles [non-Mormons] was a result of the fact
that the two metamorphoses were out of phase" (1976, 45). In effect, the
modernization that American society underwent from the 1820s through
the 1890s was experienced by the Mormons from about 1880 to 1920. In this
context, "having been branded sexual outcasts [due to polygamy], the Saints
may well have felt that they had to 'out-Victorian' the Victorians in order to
become respectable members of American society" (53).

The third issue, chastity, is a central LDS norm regulating premarital
sexuality, which was examined by Harold T. Christensen, Wilford E. Smith,
and Armand L. Mauss, each focusing on college students' sexual attitudes
and behavior. Comparing European and American subgroups, Christensen
noted that "Mormons [tended] to be considerably more conservative than
non-Mormons: fewer of them accept open pornography, fewer of them like
the idea of marrying a non-virgin, fewer approve [of] either petting or coitus before marriage, fewer actually engage in premarital coitus or become
pregnant." Though a lower proportion than among non-Mormons, still about

one-fourth of LDS college students reported having premarital coital experience, including a small percentage who were premaritally pregnant. His data also "suggest that Mormons are somewhat more promiscuous when they *do* have premarital coitus, that they may be expected to step up the wedding day following coitus, and are more divorce-prone than others in cases involving premarital pregnancy" (1976, 71). He suggested that some of these results might be due to the effects of a "rigid sex code" that enjoins absolute chastity before marriage.

Smith's survey of several thousand college students over a twenty-year period in regard to their experiences of and attitudes toward heavy petting, coitus out of wedlock, masturbation, and homosexual activity showed similar patterns (though differing in relative levels). But Latter-day Saints' students who were frequent church attenders showed increasingly conservative responses from 1950 to 1961 to 1972 as compared to infrequent church attenders and non-Mormons, suggesting an effect that may have been induced by church leaders' increased attention to sexual matters during this period. Moreover, in these data the levels of abstinence were higher than the attitudes against these sexual practices. In the area of homosexuality, however, there was a strong trend toward more liberal attitudes among all students except the most active churchgoers. Thus, the level of *commitment* (measured by church attendance) was shown to be important for measuring attitudinal and behavioral effects (1976, 80).

Mauss compared age-cohort survey samples of Mormons from Salt Lake City and "Coastal City" in California in terms of attitudes toward premarital sex, extramarital sex, the use of contraceptives, and marrying outside the church. Across all age cohorts the taboo against extramarital sex was strongest, followed by premarital sex, then marrying outside the faith, with most flexibility shown in attitudes toward the use of contraceptives. There were some differences between the two cities that could be interpreted as involving less rigid norms among "Coastal City" Mormons. In neither place, however, could the youngest cohorts (twenty-five years old and under) be interpreted as standing apart from the other age groups. Mauss proclaimed: "No! The youth of Zion are not faltering" (1976, 83). He also made an important point in the subsequent discussion: "punitive responses won't serve [the church's] needs in the long run. We are going to have to get into the sex education business. The youth must be shown the positive outcomes of LDS values and standards" (88). Clearly, active Mormons were acquiring the church's norms for both attitudes and behavior. In that important sense, leaders' statements and discourses seemed to be having a real impact.

Perhaps the most important contribution to this 1976 assessment was the personal voice of "Solus," speaking as a Latter-day Saint who had suppressed his same-gender attraction well into middle adulthood, though it had first emerged as part of his earliest memories and self-awareness. Of his life in the church, he wrote:

> I have yet to hear a single word of compassion or understanding for homosexuals spoken from the pulpit. We are more than a family oriented church. Our auxiliaries and priesthood quorums presuppose marriage. A single [person], much less a homosexual [person], simply does not fit in. ... I doubt that my community is ready to accept a self-proclaimed homosexual teacher, and it is highly unlikely that the Church will accept a declared homosexual into fellowship.
>
> Still, I have a strong testimony of the gospel. I know the Church is true and I want to remain loyal and active. I can only hope that He who welcomed to His side sinners, publicans and harlots will grant the same grace to me—and that His church will also. (99)

Subsequent to this special issue of *Dialogue,* events related to homosexuality began to unfold at Brigham Young University (BYU). Students who confessed to same-gender attraction were being subjected to electrical shock treatments, and others were threatened with expulsion for violations of the school honor code. In the spring of 1977 an anonymous fifty-two-page letter was published, directed to psychology professor Reed Payne (the "Payne letter") in response to his lecture on homosexuality in an introductory psychology class. The letter's author asserted that homosexuality is not chosen but rather is a central part of a person's identity, that it is not a condition that can be cured, and that its causes are unknown (Jenkins et al. 1989). Shortly after excerpts of this letter were published, apostle Boyd K. Packer delivered a fireside address titled "To the One" (1978) that reemphasized the church's policy on homosexuality while using the word only once.

TRACKING THE EMERGENCE OF SAME-GENDER ATTRACTION AS AN LDS ISSUE

The second nonchurch LDS publication to track emerging issues of sexuality was the book *Peculiar People: Mormons and Same-Sex Orientation* (Schow, Schow, and Raynes 1991), which explored a variety of "voices" using first-person narratives representing different perspectives on homosexuality. The first section included initial essays by gays and lesbians that offered their personal perspectives on homosexual struggles in the church and in society.

The second section provided the viewpoints of partners who not infre-quently were spouses, which highlighted the emphasis on marriage and fam-ily within Mormonism. The third and longest section explored the voices of other family members and friends, including many from beyond the bound-aries of the LDS Church.

In the introduction, the editors laid to rest several misconceptions about homosexuality, including that it is an identity dealing primarily with sexual impulses, feelings, and behavior simply because *sexual* is part of the word *homosexual.* As they sought to make clear:

> Both gays and lesbians affirm that their sense of self is not rooted mainly in their sexual impulses. Rather this sense of self is tied to those with whom they are bonded, with whom they feel trust and delight, with whom they primarily want to spend their life. They assert that their sex-ual interest and response are tied to the basic feeling of deep connection with the same sex. Most homosexuals say that they felt a stronger friend-ship, interest, or bond with people of the same sex long before sexual in-terest emerged. We [the editors] do not want to discard the idea of sexu-ality; it simply needs to be placed in correct context. (xiv–xv)

In these essays, recollections of a dawning awareness of same-sex attrac-tion range across highly varied life situations and ages, but with a focus in childhood and adolescence. For instance, the anonymous writer quoted ear-lier who referred to himself as "Solus" traced his same-sex feelings to his early childhood: "I cannot remember how it felt not to be haunted by homosexu-ality. Not that I would ever have used the word! I was well into middle age before I would bring myself to say 'homosexual' even in private prayers—which always concluded with a plea for help in 'overcoming my problems'" (1976, 5–6). An adult woman calling herself "Anna Hurston" recalled writ-ing her first "love" letter to a girl when she was in third grade, "I was hon-estly expressing the true feelings of my heart and thought nothing of it. A few years later another girl showed a similar note from me to her friends, and I was ridiculed unmercifully. Already I was learning that life could be treacherous for one with a sensitive heart" (1991, 15). Gordon Johnston, a musician, looked back on himself as "a teenager [with] the requisite series of girlfriends and heartbreaks." He noted, "Although I enjoyed the company of my girlfriends, I had little problem keeping the church's standard of moral-ity, since I was never sexually attracted to women. From my earliest stirrings of sexual awareness, my feelings have always been homosexual. I learned at an early age that sexual feelings were private and homosexual feelings were especially private. I accepted the church's teaching that homosexuality was an unnatural and wicked temptation" (1991, 44).

No one story, or even several, could plumb the depth of identity conflict and confusion that surge through these personal accounts, but it may be useful to give an indication of their introspective quality. When Gerald told his wife, Carol Lynn Pearson, of his homosexuality and she asked, "Gerald, since you and I have been married, have there been any...men?" he answered, "Yes. Yes, there have been" (1991, 71). And from that point she begins the slow telling of her interior conversations while trying to carry on with her life. Among other inner reflections was this one: "If my house had been destroyed by fire, if my child had been run over, I could call on the church. The church would be wonderful. But not this. I could not bear it. Gerald might be excommunicated and I would be humiliated and pitied. Women with problems were encouraged to take them to the bishop or to the Relief Society president. I couldn't go to the bishop, not now. I had promised Gerald I'd do nothing until he got back" (74).

Six main categories of experience seem central to these personal accounts:

1. the emergence of awareness of same-sex attraction
2. mental and physical efforts to avoid, suppress, or deny same-sex attraction
3. efforts to explore or reorient these same-sex feelings by
   a. seeking more knowledge and understanding of the self and others
   b. securing social support and guidance from parents, friends, partners, spouse, and professional authorities
   c. reflecting on self-feelings regarding sexual objects
4. committing oneself to a plan of action to maintain or reorient the self via
   a. "coming out"
   b. seeking further social support
   c. remaining in the closet
5. coming out for good
6. the aftermath

Assessing Mormon Sexuality into the 1990s

A third collection of essays, *Multiply and Replenish: Mormon Essays on Sex and Family* (Corcoran 1994), expanded on these themes. Many of the essays first appeared in *Dialogue* or *Sunstone*. Historical essays by Lawrence Foster and Klaus J. Hansen open this volume. Foster compared Shaker celibacy, on the one hand (which Joseph Smith vehemently rejected), and Oneida community perfectionism, on the other. He then showed how Joseph Smith went beyond biblical literalism by laying claim to continuing revelations, most notably instituting plural marriage as a key feature of the new and everlasting covenant (Doctrine and Covenants 132). Between 1839 and 1844, the Mormon settlement at Nauvoo, Illinois, provided the crucible for this Mormon innovation in the development of new family doctrines "designed to reestablish social cohesion not only on earth, but also throughout all eternity" (8–9).

Hansen, like Foster, noted that nineteenth-century Mormonism was "heavily influenced by pragmatic Puritan notions of the conduct of family and sexual relationships," whereas late-twentieth-century popular church literature and exhortations appear, if anything, "to be more Victorian than the Victorians" (Foster 1994 [1982], 11–12; see also Hansen 1994 [1981], 38–41). "Almost everywhere, from the visitor's center display lauding family home evening to the exhortations in the *Church News* section of the *Deseret News,* the family ideal held up for Mormons conveys the gush and cloying sentimentality of a Hallmark gift card. The images that are suggested for emulation tend to be those of pasteboard saints, supermen and superwomen whose blemishes as well as humanity are blotted out" (Foster 1994 [1982], 12). Foster sees in this transformation and the "preoccupation with a sentimentalized ideal of family life" a danger of idolatry, a defensive Mormon "tribal attitude." He concludes, "Particularly as the Church of Jesus Christ of Latter-day Saints reaches outward across the world in an attempt to become a truly universal church rather than an intermountain American sect, a progressive openness to truth wherever it may be found will be essential" (13–14).

One aspect of this broad transformation was the renewed emphasis on chastity. Marvin Rytting examined leaders' "exhortations for chastity" in church publications over the period from 1951 to 1979. He believed this study underestimated chastity injunctions "since chastity is usually preached in youth firesides, standards nights, and interviews—and possibly the home"—which are not reflected in the published sources (1994 [1982], 86). Furthermore, Rytting found that there was "*an overall increase in … references to chastity* from the end of the 1950s to the end of the 1970s (which was the temporal limit of the study); that "*statements about chastity [became] more explicit*"; and that "*the rhetoric [became] much stronger*" (87; emphasis in original). In addition, he suggested that successive church presidents also affected "*the tone of chastity exhortations*" (96) as either more "Puritan" or more "Victorian." In Rytting's view, Victorianism was a "secular sentiment" and a "social reaction to the anxiety produced by a loss of control.... It is not intrinsic to Mormonism." In his view, what the church needs—both individually and as a culture—is "a well-managed intimacy which values sexuality but also controls it" (100–101).

While teaching undergraduate nursing students at Brigham Young University, clinical social work professor Romel W. Mackelprang noted, "When it came to highly personal questions related to sexuality and church policy, students were extremely anxious to talk privately with someone who shared their religious beliefs but who did not know them personally or was not in an ecclesiastical position over them. As I spoke with these students I was struck by the uncertainty and in some cases guilt [that] some were experiencing as they attempted to fit their sexuality with their religious convictions" (1994 [1992], 47).

In seeking to account for this phenomenon, Mackelprang suggested that "church leaders sometimes convey conflicting messages to members regarding sexuality." He provided several examples: they may forcefully emphasize "that sexual activity is to be reserved for marriage," that "masturbation and other autoerotic activity" are sins, and that "sexual contact outside of marriage can jeopardize membership." These sins require confession to the Lord and one's local ward bishop or other church leader to receive full forgiveness. The same was true for any homosexual activity. Furthermore, "some leaders consider homosexuality to be so grievous a sin that they do not differentiate between sexual orientation and sexual activity in calling for [church] action against gay men and lesbians" (48). At the same time, church members are taught that "sex in marriage is a special way of sharing with one's mate" and that "procreation is as close to being godlike as men and women can become" (49).

In contrast to general American social data showing increasing levels of sexual activity among college students, Harold T. Christensen's comparative study of LDS sociology students revealed a striking persistence of conservative Mormon premarital sex norms among these youth. Christensen categorized his college student samples as intermountain Mormon, intermountain non-Mormon, and midwestern non-Mormon and used measures of sexual attitudes and behavior in 1958, 1968, and 1978. Self-reports showed that approximately three-quarters to four-fifths of the Mormon respondents followed the church standard of chastity at each point in time, whereas the two non-Mormon samples were near the 60 percent mark in 1958, and declined over the twenty-year time period, following the general societal pattern of this era. Having previously examined his 1968 student sample, Christensen focused in this article on the 1978 results comparing men and women in the same three groups noted above, but with respect to censorship of pornography, the expected number of months for dating intimacy to develop, and the extent of disapproval of premarital coitus. In all instances, the Mormon students registered more conservative attitudes than either of the non-Mormon groups and had comparable rates from both men and women. Thus, among LDS students in 1978 there were no gender discrepancies in attitudes or behavior, and these students also showed "the persistence of chastity" as a conservative Mormon norm in striking contrast to the non-Mormon samples (1994 [1982], 70).

Christensen suggested that "religious socialization" is the major variable at work:

> From infancy on Mormons are socialized into viewing unchastity as a sin and chastity as one of the highest virtues. This is continually stressed: in the home, from the pulpit, in programs of the several church organizations, and in articles carried by church publications. Promiscuity carries severe sanctions ranging from disapproval to being denied entrance into the temple to being either disfellowshiped or excommunicated. Of course repentance followed by forgiveness provides a way back into the full graces of the church. But overstepping in the sexual area is not taken lightly and the perspectives the church holds on these matters, together with the pressures that it exerts, provide a powerful means of social control. (80)

He also noted that the Mormon male tends to be especially conservative—"favoring censorship of pornography," "disapproving premarital coitus," and "attending church more frequently" (80) than non-Mormons, with more conservative measures on chastity and preferences for a virginal marriage partner as well. "The norm in Mormon culture is chastity for both sexes. It is a restrictive single standard, approached by means of 'taming' the male, not a permissive single standard, achieved by means of liberalizing the female (such as in Scandinavia, for example)" (81).

One of the problems in LDS family theology is the place of adult never-married persons as examined in a literature review by Marybeth Raynes and Erin Parsons (1994 [1983]). Their findings may be extended to divorced and widowed persons; separated, deserted, or prisoner-of-war spouses; or out-of-wedlock parents. In their view, most of the material on the never married was both limited and judgmental and was based on a pattern of commentaries that Gregory Bateson would have called a "double-bind," in which contradictory messages cannot be challenged or resolved (1972, 206–8).

The authors reported: "We found no positive statements about unmarried men, regardless of circumstance.... In contrast, worthy single women are consoled that, should they not be chosen for the 'most choice career' [celestial marriage], they will yet receive all the blessings of matrimony in the hereafter" (1994, 222). Raynes and Parsons noted some change in the two prior decades in single women's views of themselves, seeing singleness as providing opportunities for personal growth, even as older single women mentioned their pain and struggle to be patient and "endure to the end." The one article about single men they assessed reported that "single men seem to feel chastised, lonely, labeled, left out, and often sexually frustrated" (223). In *Guidelines for Single Adults* issued by the church in 1980, unmarried LDS singles were urged to join singles programs and conferences as a way to expand their sphere of usefulness. Nonetheless, a General Authority speaking at a singles conference at BYU in 1982 suggested that "a single person is not a whole person, and being single—particularly divorced singleness—was described as being unacceptable to the Lord" (224).

The voice of one "single" man was included in *Multiply and Replenish*. Delmont R. Oswald identified himself as a divorced father of two children after eleven years of marriage, who was in good standing in the church but had not remarried in the ten years since his divorce. He received a cancellation of sealing from his ex-wife, so technically he was in the same category as a never-married man. He was, therefore, "not eligible to obtain 'a fullness of glory and exaltation in the celestial kingdom' unless and until [he] remarr[ied]" (1994 [1990], 231).

Oswald reported his inner feelings after listening to President Ezra Taft Benson address the single adult men during the April general conference in 1988, urging these men to take on the responsibilities of marriage. The highest rate of inactivity in the church is among divorced males and the second highest is among never-married males. What troubled him was President Benson's tone.

> I heard his words as those of an adult lecturing a child. Singles are perhaps overly sensitive to this approach because they often find themselves treated as eternal teenagers.... I would have felt more comfortable being addressed as a brother and fellow adult....
>
> It was President Benson's concluding quote from 2 Nephi 1:21 that troubled me most: "Arise from the dust, my sons, and be men." Not only

did I feel that this placed me in [negative] company with Laman and Lemuel, but that my very masculinity and adulthood were being questioned—simply because I was not married.... The message this quote sends to an often already sensitive audience is, "O.K. children, quit playing childish games and grow up. It's time to change your ways." (232–33)

Obviously, this response is complicated by the complexities of divorce.

> The single male must also face the constant specter of homophobia. Male friends from the age of twenty-five on view their unmarried associates with a jaundiced eye. Now that homosexuality is more open, church members are even more suspicious and judgmental....
>
> There is also a growing fear throughout society of child molesters, and singles are always more suspect than married men....
>
> To the single male in the church who is not anticipating marriage, I can only say, "Endure to the end." Make the commitment to take the difficult path of activity [in the church] rather than the easy path to inactivity. (235–38)

Only recently have homosexual members themselves organized to have their voices heard and to provide support to one another. And some have published accounts of their struggles within the church (Blodgett 1999). Several organizations such as Evergreen International and Affirmation offer supportive communities along with Parents of Gays and Lesbians and Family Forum. As Katherine Rosman reported in the *Nation,* some members "have gone from being obedient, God-fearing church members to vocal, angry gay-rights activists who have willingly ostracized themselves from the only community they have ever known" (2002, n.p.). This anger, however, seems unlikely to have much of an effect in the church.

THE FORMATION AND REGULATION OF LDS SEXUALITY OVER THE LIFE COURSE

Training in attitudes, values, and behavior for marriage and family involves at least four developmental stages among the Latter-day Saints, culminating in marriage as the basis for sexual relations. These stages may be labeled as a childhood stage generally beginning well before age eight, an adolescent stage beginning about age twelve, a young adult stage beginning about age eighteen, and marriage itself as the adult stage of full sexual expression, but even then not without limits. A positive and encouraging clinician's view of contemporary sexuality in Mormonism indicates that "leaders now teach that sexual intimacy for physical pleasure, emotional bonding, and relationship enhancement is acceptable and even approved" (Mackelprang 1994 [1992], 59).

Childhood Sexuality

The most comprehensive published LDS account of sexual development is *A Parent's Guide* (1985), which employs the continuous development of intimacy as its interpretative focus. The childhood stage involves the family as the initial social setting for learning about sex under parental guidance, with a primary focus on attitudes and values and the sharing of any information that seems appropriate to a child's questions. In church literature such as the *Friend* (the church's children's magazine), the familial setting is idealized as a nuclear unit of parents and children (husband and wife in their roles as father and mother in relation to their sons and daughters as brothers and sisters). An extended family of bilateral kindreds is implied by this idealization, and is realized in the church through an extensive interest in family history and genealogy. Reunions of extended family kindreds are not at all uncommon.

Latter-day Saints' families are subject to many of the same structural and ideological stresses as other American families and are evaluated accordingly, including a recognition of single-parent families (usually with a negative to neutral evaluation), "hidden" same-gender and polygamous families (hidden because they are either negatively sanctioned or illegal, and are negatively evaluated), part-church families (usually with a neutral to negative evaluation), and most commonly two-working-parent families (also with a neutral to negative evaluation). Only the intact nuclear family of husband (father), wife (mother), and children (sons and daughters; brothers and sisters) is given unambiguous positive evaluation. Adoption through LDS Social Services is also strongly approved as part of family formation for couples biologically unable to have children of their own.

The church defines the parents as those primarily responsible for the sexual education of their children, with strong sanctions against abuse—physical, sexual, psychological—and positive support for warm, firm, nurturing, parent-directed child rearing. In *A Parent's Guide* the "physical aspects of human sexuality" are largely confined to a single page, with the suggestion that "you and your children may want to study a medical text or a quality encyclopedia" (30). The family is represented as having a patriarchal order and hierarchy in which fathers provide for and protect their families and mothers nurture members of the family. Parents lead and children follow in family activities such as "Family Home Evening."

This structuring is coupled with a proposed egalitarian marital ethic—that is, husbands and wives are expected to treat each other as complementary equals, and are therefore to provide for their children the "models" of gender expression. Nonetheless, *A Parent's Guide* advises, "There is much good that comes from drawing a veil between the children and yourself (as parents) regarding private, intimate life. This is not a veil of fear or disgust, but one by which the body and its functions are robed in modesty and honor" (30).

It is worth acknowledging that little is known about child sexuality either in the LDS Church or American society more generally. David L. Weis, a coeditor of *Sexuality in America* (Francoeur, Koch, and Weis 1999), notes that "childhood sexuality remains an area that has been largely unexplored by researchers. Childhood is widely seen as a period of asexual innocence. Strong taboos continue concerning childhood eroticism, and childhood sexual expression and learning are still divisive social issues" (91). One of the few reference books in this area is by a sociologist, Floyd M. Martinson, titled *The Sexual Life of Children* (1995). *A Parent's Guide* (1985) approaches children's sexuality through the eyes of parents and other adults (as reported above) rather than through the "meanings that children attach to their experience" (Francoeur, Koch, and Weis 1999, 93). It is these "meanings" to children, put together in a system of "assemblies," that yield what children come to know and believe through interaction with family members, same-sex peers, cross-sex peers, television, children's books, church, school, and neighborhood friends and leaders. One model from this perspective proposed by sex researchers John H. Gagnon and William Simon suggests the following set of "scripts" or "assemblies" as developing over the life course, beginning in childhood:

1. the emergence of a specific gender identity
2. the learning of a sense of modesty
3. the acquisition of a sexual vocabulary
4. the internalization of mass-media messages about sexuality
5. the learning of specific acts defined as sexual
6. the learning of gender, family, and sexual roles
7. the learning of the mechanisms and processes of sexual arousal
8. the development of sexual fantasies and imagery
9. the development of a sexual value system
10. the emergence of a sexual orientation
11. the adoption of an adult sexual lifestyle (As listed in Francoeur, Koch, and Weis 1999, 94)

The first six of these scripts are well under way during the years of childhood. Because LDS doctrine places such importance on "choice" or "moral agency" as part of human development, it is worth stressing that sexual orientation and identity is not something a person chooses but rather is something of which they become aware at some moment of "emergence" along the path of childhood, adolescence, and adulthood.

Adolescence and Church Standards for Sexuality

At age twelve, LDS boys and girls are gender-segregated into age groups: Aaronic priesthood roles for young men (deacons, twelve to thirteen; teachers, fourteen to fifteen; priests, sixteen to seventeen); and young women organization classes for young women (beehives, twelve to thirteen; Mutual Improvement Association maids, fourteen to fifteen; laurels, sixteen to seventeen). A variety of church settings also provide for gender-mixed activities. But abstention from sexual activity is the absolute rule throughout childhood and adolescence, as taught by the Law of Chastity, while youth are also encouraged to seek and cultivate heterosexual interests and pairings. The church advocates no dating before age sixteen and then group dating that slowly moves toward occasional pair-wise boy-girl dating thereafter, and then dating that is increasingly directed toward marital considerations in young adulthood. Homosexuality is absolutely forbidden and in the past has been harshly criticized. Marriage and childbearing are presented as the penultimate goal of life during adolescence, while the ultimate goal is exaltation in the Kingdom of God, which includes the hope of achieving post-mortal divinity as warranted by lifelong fidelity following a temple (celestial) marriage.

From early adolescence onward the church becomes a partner with parents in directing and sanctioning sexual feelings, beliefs, values, knowledge, and behavior. *A Parent's Guide* is the first and only sexuality guide the church has produced, and a new one is sorely needed. On its basis, parents have been encouraged to monitor public school sex education as supplementary to their own and the church's efforts, but increasingly school-based sexual education is eclipsing what the church provides, even though the church seeks to minimize the impact of what leaders perceive as an overly sexualized, secular general American public culture. In turn, the church promotes the alternative of sexual abstinence and chastity before marriage through a variety of channels, including the church magazine for teens and young adults, *New Era,* weekly evening social activities for young men and young women, regular monthly "fireside" Sunday-evening gatherings for youth featuring inspirational talks by local leaders, "standards" gatherings that emphasize positive interpersonal relationships, and stake-level socials and dances—all the while underscoring the Law of Chastity. A booklet titled *For the Strength of Youth* (Church, First Presidency, 2001) sets forth both the positive goal of chastity and the negative threats posed by sexuality that are faced by youth, providing direct church guidance in support of personal agency and accountability. The opening narrative voice of *For the Strength of Youth* underscores the conditions of agency and accountability, the notion that choices have consequences, and the personal responsibility involved and encourages the internalization of church values:

> Your Heavenly Father has given you agency, the ability to choose right from wrong and to act for yourself. You have been given the Holy Ghost to help you know good from evil. While you are here on earth, you are being proven to see if you will use your agency to show your love for God by keeping his commandments.
>
> While you are free to choose for yourself, you are not free to choose the consequences of your actions. When you make a choice, you will receive the consequences of that choice. The consequences may not be immediate, but they will always follow, for good or bad. Wrong choices delay your [eternal] progression and lead to heartache and misery. Right choices lead to happiness and eternal life. That is why it is so important for you to choose what is right throughout your life.
>
> You are responsible for the choices you make. You should not blame your circumstances, your family, or your friends if you choose to disobey God's commandments. You are a child of God with great strength. You have the ability to choose righteousness and happiness, no matter what your circumstances. (4–5)

This booklet then lists a series of topics for further discussion: gratitude, education, family, friends, dress and appearance, entertainment and the media, music and dancing, language, dating, sexual purity, repentance, honesty, Sabbath-day observance, tithes and offerings, physical health, service to others, faith, and the living Christ, concluding with a testimony of the apostles to the living Christ and the Proclamation on the Family.

Under "dating," the booklet indicates that those who date "are responsible to help each other maintain their standards and to protect each other's honor and virtue." Dating too early (before age sixteen) "can lead to immorality." In an effort to reduce what might be viewed as an early form of "performance pressure," the booklet notes, "Not all teenagers need to date or even want to," and advocates that young people who begin dating should plan "activities that are positive and inexpensive and that will help you get to know each other" (24–25).

The section on sexual purity in *For the Strength of Youth* anticipates the physical intimacy between husband and wife as "ordained of God for the creation of children and for the expression of love between husband and wife." However, the limit is clear: "God has commanded that sexual intimacy be reserved for marriage." This statement underscores the Law of Chastity as a purity code of premarital sexual abstinence. Further discussion provides a rationale for this commandment as preparation "to make and keep sacred covenants in the temple," "to build a strong marriage and…bring children into the world," and to "protect yourself from the emotional damage that always comes from sharing physical intimacies with someone outside of marriage" (26).

The Law of Chastity seeks to counter the ways that "Satan may tempt you to rationalize," and advises: "Do not do anything to arouse the powerful emotions that must be expressed only in marriage. Do not participate in passionate kissing, lie on top of another person, or touch the private, sacred parts of another person's body, with or without clothing. Do not allow anyone to do that with you. Do not arouse these emotions in your own body" (26–27). Detailed summaries of these standards are also provided as wallet- and billfold-size brochures for both young women and young men.

The contrasting pattern of negative avoidance and positive sanctions for sexual behavior implies an underlying threat to young people of moving from those sins of lesser import to those that may threaten access to celestial glory. As former president Spencer W. Kimball noted, "Immorality does not begin in adultery or perversion. It begins with little indiscretions like sex thoughts, sex discussions, passionate kissing, petting and such, growing with every exercise" (1980, 94). In a similar sense, apostle M. Russell Ballard reported:

> Some young men and women in the Church talk openly about sexual transgression. They seem to forget that the Lord forbids all sexual relations before marriage, including petting, sex perversion of any kind, or preoccupation with sex in thought, speech, or action. Some youth foolishly rationalize that it is no big deal to sin now because they can always repent later when they want to go to the temple or on a mission.…The idea of sinning a little is self-deception. Sin is sin! Sin weakens you spiritually, and it always places the sinner at eternal risk. Choosing to sin, even with the intent to repent, is simply turning away from God and violating covenants. (1993, 6)

Young Adulthood: A Time of Transition

In young adulthood in the church, the situation of young men and young women is somewhat different. Young men are obliged to seriously consider undertaking a two-year mission at age nineteen and before age twenty-six. Usually, this timing allows for one year of college study or the initial exploration of a job or career. Taking up a mission then places all other considerations on "hold" for two additional years. Young women are not under obligation to take up a mission but may do so as a privilege once they reach age twenty-one and are still unmarried. This privilege is available until age thirty-nine, and requires an eighteen-month commitment. These differences between young men and young women are related to the strong emphasis on marriage and motherhood for young women as well as priesthood responsibilities among young men. At the same time, the Law of Chastity remains in effect and continues for the duration of the mission, and upon return until the time of marriage. And without a mission commitment, the pressures to marry become increasingly direct.

A recent issue of the church magazine *Ensign* carried a story by apostle Dallin H. Oaks, titled "Dating versus Hanging Out," which counseled eighteen to twenty-five year olds "to channel your associations with the opposite sex into dating patterns that have the potential to mature into marriage" (2006, 16). Oaks quoted *Time* magazine as identifying this age group as "a distinct and separate life stage, a strange, transitional never-never land between adolescence and adulthood in which people stall for a few extra years, [postponing] ... adult responsibility," which suggested to Oaks "the indecision some [LDS] college graduates have in ... accepting the responsibilities of marriage and family" (*Time* is quoted in the *Ensign* article) (12). Clearly, this directive article was designed to light a fire under young men and women to cultivate a desire for marriage, while being expected to remain chaste.

Adult Sexuality within Marriage

Sexuality within marriage is approved without distinction as to civil or temple marriage. And marital sexual activity is given positive sanction using scriptural and prophetic support as justification for heterosexual genital intercourse as the only unambiguously positively defined means by which spouses might become "one flesh" (Gen. 2:24) in expressing their love without necessarily bringing children into the world. Terrance D. Olson, writing on LDS sexuality in the *Encyclopedia of Mormonism: The Church and Society,* quotes President Spencer W. Kimball as follows:

*The union of the sexes, husband and wife (and only husband and wife), was
for the principal purpose of bringing children into the world. Sexual experiences were never intended by the Lord to be a mere plaything or merely to
satisfy passions and lusts. We know of no directive from the Lord that proper
sexual experience between husbands and wives need be limited totally to the
procreation of children, but we find much evidence from Adam until now
that no provision was ever made by the Lord for indiscriminate sex.* (1995,
463; emphasis in the original)

Elsewhere, very pointedly, President Kimball observed, "There are some
people who have said that behind the bedroom doors anything goes. That is
not true and the Lord would not condone it" (464).

Lester E. Bush's earlier examination of the 1969 First Presidency statement on birth control made clear several points about adult sexuality. First,
in the church's view, marriage between a man and a woman is the only approved basis for sexual relations. Second, the statement reaffirms the commandment to multiply and replenish the earth and the church's teachings
against birth control, as modified by important family considerations. Third,
the statement identifies married couples and the Lord as the locus of inspiration, wisdom, and discretion in reaching family planning decisions (1976,
27). He quotes President McKay: "It is also the policy of the Church to
regard marital relations of husband and wife as *their personal problem and
responsibility to be solved and to be established between themselves as a sacred
relationship*" (28; emphasis in the original).

Among the categories of sexual activity, male-female genital sexual intercourse is the highest and most sacred positively approved practice in LDS
marriage, although many other practices are approved without comment or
assumed to be neutral. But some forms of stimulation such as oral or anal
sex receive a negative valuation, while even the neutral and positive practices
are wrapped with expectations of self-control and restraint.

The church's view of temple marriage as a sealing ordinance under priesthood authority also implies a conception of sexual intercourse as a sacred act
essential for exaltation. Sexual intercourse is intended to be a private, sacred,
repeated experience, to be discussed only between spouses who have been
wed in a civil ceremony or sealed in temple marriage. Sexual intercourse in
this conception serves as the central sacred bond through a temple sealing
that celebrates a man and a woman as "one flesh," in order to realize three
other cultural goals: to provide mortal bodies for the waiting spirits who are
the progeny of Heavenly Father and Heavenly Mother, to bind in covenants
of commitment and love a man and a woman in their roles as husband and

wife, and to establish the eternal families that will fill the celestial kingdom in eternity, whose members will meet Heavenly Father and Heavenly Mother face to face and take their place among the gods. They will then be able to procreate further waiting spirits in what is referred to as "one eternal round." Procreation, therefore, means giving rise to bodily tabernacles in mortality and the promise of giving rise to spirit children in the celestial kingdom, if the husband and wife remain worthy to do so. Sexual intercourse, therefore, may be considered the supreme act of mortal and eternal existence that gives to temple marriage its sacred power and significance.

THE PROCLAMATION ON THE FAMILY

The family-centric view espoused by the church and what it means to be "LDS" or "Mormon" is nowhere more evident than in the formal statement issued by church leaders more than a decade ago, *The Family: A Proclamation to the World* (First Presidency and Council of the Twelve Apostles 1995). The initial salutation of the proclamation identifies the authors by their authority to speak on behalf of the LDS Church: "We, the First Presidency and the Council of the Twelve Apostles ... solemnly proclaim ..." Then two essential teachings follow: "that marriage between a man and a woman is ordained of God" and "that the family is central to the Creator's plan for the eternal destiny of His children" (see para. 1). These doctrines are presented as universal statements that the remaining paragraphs are intended to explicate and support. However, a close reading and unpacking of the text clearly indicate the particular LDS religious meanings of "marriage" rather than one with a universal cross-cultural and secular applicability.

The first teaching, "that marriage between a man and a woman is ordained of God," is a straightforward gender-specific definition of marriage, on the one hand, backed by an assertion of divine authority, on the other. Some observers have noted that the use of "a man" and "a woman" in this definition rather than "one man" and "one woman" allows for the practice of plural marriage—as was instituted by the Latter-day Saints from the 1840s until the 1890s and may still be practiced in their vicarious temple sealings for the dead. This definitional phrasing, however, also accommodates a particular understanding of marriage as what the LDS Church calls an ordinance of exaltation for time and eternity and again moves the understanding of marriage in the proclamation from the secular to the religious realm.

The second teaching, "that the family is central to the Creator's plan for the eternal destiny of His children," also is a religious statement particular to the LDS Church that indicates family formation is a vitally important goal related to "the Creator's plan for the eternal destiny of His children."

This plan is known among Latter-day Saints by several names such as "the plan of salvation" (Jarom 1:2; Alma 42:5; Moses 6:62), "the plan of redemption" (Jacob 6:8; Alma 12:25, 42:11), and "the great Plan of Happiness" (Alma 42:8). In this teaching, the meaning of "God" expands to cover "heavenly parents," implying Heavenly Mother as well as Heavenly Father, and specifies a relation of kinship descent in regard to their "beloved spirit son[s] or daughter[s]" (para. 2).

The plan of salvation as part of LDS beliefs unfolds within three different periods of existence: the "premortal, mortal, and eternal." In the Mormon system of belief, the human origin story begins in "the premortal realm," where "spirit sons and daughters knew and worshiped God as their Eternal Father and accepted His plan by which His children" could do four things: "obtain a physical body," "gain earthly experience," "progress toward perfection," and "ultimately realize his or her divine destiny as an heir of eternal life." Thus, the "divine destiny" of each spirit is to become "an heir of eternal life" (para. 3) where this inheritance "enables [one's] family relationships to be perpetuated beyond the grave." Further, the church provides "sacred ordinances and covenants … in holy temples [that] make it possible for individuals to return to the presence of God and for families to be united eternally."

Whereas Heavenly Father and Heavenly Mother are conceived to have begotten spirit sons and daughters in the preexistence, Adam and Eve are treated literally as the first human beings in "their potential for parenthood as husband and wife" in mortality (para. 4). The brethren "declare that God's commandment for His children to multiply and replenish the earth, [directed to Adam and Eve,] remains in force." This command may be taken to apply both individually and socially. Since all human couples are not fertile, the social and biological reproduction of the human species does not require that every couple bear children, as long as the aggregate result provides adequate population replacement without threatening the world's "carrying capacity." Applied to individuals, however, the declaration provides a normative expectation that LDS couples will bear many children, or adopt them. The proclamation continues, "We further declare that God has commanded that the sacred powers of procreation are to be employed only between man and woman, lawfully wedded as husband and wife." Essentially, this assertion of the use of sacred powers as commanded by deity attributes to heterosexual genital sexual intercourse a sacramental quality that the proclamation then seeks to link to the legal system.

Finally, chastity and fidelity as the core ethical positions of the church on sexuality are referred to as "the Lord's law of moral conduct." In the words of

President Gordon B. Hinckley, "We believe in chastity before marriage and total fidelity after marriage. That sums it up. That is the way to happiness in living. That is the way to satisfaction. It brings peace to the heart and peace to the home" (1996, 49). Former president Spencer W. Kimball had offered a more expansive statement, indicating that "any... sexual contact [outside of marriage], including fornication, adultery, and homosexual or lesbian behavior, is sinful" (Church 1999, 249; Doctrine and Covenants 42:24). This ethical core makes marriage the pivotal context for approved sexual activity and leads to the view that marriage allows a man and a woman to be considered "one flesh," a deeply positive view of human sexuality as presented in the book of Genesis (2:21–24). Also, the instructor's manual for the church's course Marriage and Family Relations notes: "The physical relationship between a husband and a wife can be beautiful and sacred. It is ordained of God for the procreation of children and for the expression of love within a marriage: 'Therefore shall a man leave his father and his mother, and shall cleave to his wife: and they shall be one flesh'" (Church 2000, 71, quoting Gen. 2:24; see also Church 1997, chap. 39).

The proclamation leaves unstated the church's distinction between civil marriage for time only, which refers to marriage under secular law, and temple (or celestial) marriage for time and eternity, which is the church's religious sealing ordinance reserved only for "temple worthy" Latter-day Saints. By not stating and maintaining this distinction, the Proclamation on the Family mixes and confuses secular civil marriage with the meanings and criteria that apply only to temple marriage, and thereby seeks to provide a basis for a religious opposition to same-gender civil marriage. Same-gender civil marriage, like opposite-gender civil marriage, has no relation to or effect on temple marriage and its religious meanings. Authority for civil marriage under state and federal law is entirely separate from authority for celestial marriage. And civil marriage allows for full sexual self-expression by Latter-day Saints who do not qualify for temple marriage or who choose the civil form rather than the celestial form for some other reason. By opposing same-gender civil marriage, the LDS Church is forcing its gay members into a double bind that does not apply to its heterosexual members: remain celibate under the Law of Chastity or leave the church (or be excommunicated) if you act on your sexual desires—and do not point out or challenge the discrepancy of attributing to civil marriage the worthiness criteria that apply only to temple (or celestial) marriage. Otherwise, by supporting same-gender civil marriage the church would be affording its homosexual members the same opportunity for sexual access to a marital partner that it offers its heterosexual members.

The Crisis of Homosexuality in the Church

Of all the areas of sexual behavior that LDS leaders have sought to regulate, homosexuality has emerged near the top of the list as the most problematic. A letter from the First Presidency makes the church's position clear:

> The Lord's law of moral conduct is abstinence [from sexual relations] outside of lawful marriage and fidelity within marriage. Sexual relations are proper only between husband and wife appropriately expressed within the bonds of marriage. Any other sexual contact, including fornication, adultery, and homosexual and lesbian behavior, is sinful. Those who persist in such practices or who influence others to do so are subject to Church discipline. (1991)

The Proclamation on the Family provides a public commentary and expansion on the position presented in this letter, offering a justification for the church's opposition to same-gender sexual relationships. Yet it does not directly address many questions that were arising within the church, including the distinction between gender identity and gender orientation.

Immediately following the Proclamation on the Family, Dallin H. Oaks, a member of the Quorum of the Twelve, made a significant effort to address what he called "same-sex attraction" in the church, magazine *Ensign*. He raised a series of questions for members to consider:

> What do we say to a young person who reports that he or she is attracted toward or has erotic thoughts or feelings about persons of the same sex? How should we respond when a person announces that he is a homosexual or she is a lesbian and that scientific evidence "proves" he or she was "born that way"? How do we react when persons who do not share our beliefs accuse us of being intolerant or unmerciful when we insist that erotic feelings toward a person of the same sex are irregular and that any sexual behavior of that nature is sinful? (1995, 7)

In response to the first of his own questions, Oaks cited eleven gospel doctrines that define fundamental LDS beliefs involving gender as a preexistent characteristic of all persons and celestial marriage between a man and a woman in the church's temples as essential for exaltation. By virtue of their "agency," all persons are accountable for their behavior no matter what susceptibilities or feelings they may experience.

In applying these doctrines, Oaks condemned "gay bashing," stressed compassion to those suffering ill health through HIV or AIDS, and marked the distinction between same-gender thoughts and feelings ("which should be resisted and redirected") and homosexual behavior ("which is a serious sin"). He noted, "It is wrong to use these words *[homosexual, lesbian, and gay]* to denote a *condition,* because this implies that a person is consigned by birth to a circumstance in which he or she has no choice in respect to the critically important matter of sexual *behavior"* (9). He then developed a "hypothetical progression" of same-sex attraction from personal susceptibilities to feelings, thoughts, behavior, and addiction, concluding that "we remain responsible for the exercise of our agency in the thoughts we entertain and the behavior we choose," as he had discussed in a prior talk given at Brigham Young University (9).

In response to his second question, he undertook a review of the science of physical inheritance and psychosocial factors in an effort to challenge anyone who might claim they were born with a same-sex orientation. In summary, he suggested, "Some scientists deny that behavior is genetically influenced. Others are advocates of... theories suggesting that 'there is substantial evidence for genetic influence on sexual orientation.'" But "most scientists [have] conceded that the current evidence is insufficient and that firm conclusions must await many additional scientific studies" (10). This assessment would seem to imply that the scientific evidence is less compelling than most scientists believe. In regard to gender orientation endocrinologist John Money wrote:

> The concept of voluntary choice is as much in error here as in its application to handedness, or to native language. You do not choose your native language as a preference, even though you are born without it. You assimilate it into a brain prenatally made ready to receive a native language from those who constitute your primate troop and who speak it to you and listen to you when you speak it. Once assimilated through the ears into the brain, a native language becomes securely locked in—as securely as if it had been phylogenetically preordained to be locked in prenatally by a process of genetic determinism, or by the determinism of fetal hormonal or other brain chemistries. So also with sexual status or orientation, which—whatever its genesis—also may become assimilated and locked into the brain as monosexually homosexual or heterosexual or as bisexually a mixture of both. (1988, 11–12)

Furthermore, sexual orientation is not contagious, and is developing by about age three. It cannot be taught or transmitted from one sibling to another or among friendship circles that arise from other propinquities. As

Money indicates, "A sexual status (or orientation) is not the same as a sexual act. It is possible to participate in homosexual acts, and even to be cajoled or coerced into participation, without becoming predestined to have a permanently homosexual status—and vice versa for heterosexuality" (12).

Oaks concluded his discussion by referring to the responsibility of church officers to call transgressors to repentance, on the one hand, and "to reach out with love and understanding" to members struggling with same-sex attraction, on the other. In support, he quoted current church president Gordon B. Hinckley: "I desire now to say with emphasis that our concern for the bitter fruit of sin is coupled with Christlike sympathy for its victims, innocent or culpable. We advocate the example of the Lord, who condemned the sin, yet loved the sinner. We should reach out with kindness and comfort to the afflicted, ministering to their needs and assisting them with their problems" (1995, 13).

Oaks also quoted the criticism of a member whose letter concluded, "If some of the General Authorities could express more sensitivity to this problem [of same-gender attraction], it would surely help to avoid suicides and schisms that are caused within families." In his comments, Oaks seemed especially aware of the dilemma faced by members as well as church leaders:

> Each member of Christ's church has a clear-cut doctrinal responsibility to show forth love and to extend help and understanding. Sinners, as well as those who are struggling to resist inappropriate feelings, are not people to be cast out but people to be loved and helped (see 3 Ne. 18:22–23, 30, 32). At the same time, Church leaders and members cannot avoid their responsibility to teach correct principles and righteous behavior (on all subjects), even if this causes discomfort for some.
>
> Church leaders are sometimes asked whether there is any place in The Church of Jesus Christ of Latter-day Saints for persons with homosexual or lesbian susceptibilities or feelings. Of course there is. The degree of difficulty and the pattern necessary to forgo behavior and to control thoughts will be different with different individuals, but the message of hope and the hand of fellowship offered by the Church is the same for all who strive. (13)

There is a tone of sympathetic understanding in Oaks's representation of the crisis faced by many church members and families in regard to same-gender attraction, but it is also clear that the church's conceptualization of homosexuality as a sin requires that members who see themselves as homosexual adjust to the church's standard of chastity regarding any expression of their sexuality outside of marriage. In Oaks's words:

The struggles of those who are troubled by same-sex attraction are not unique. There are many kinds of temptations, sexual and otherwise. The duty to resist sin applies to all of them.

The most important help the Church can offer to persons who have surrendered to sin or to those who are struggling to resist it is to fulfill its divine mission to teach true doctrine and administer the divine ordinances of the restored gospel. The gospel applies on the same basis to everyone. Its central truth is our Savior's atonement and resurrection, that we might have immortality and eternal life. To achieve that destiny, an eternal marriage is the divine and prescribed goal for every child of God, in this life or in the life to come. Nevertheless, this sacred goal must come about in the Lord's way. (13)

Oaks concluded with a parable comparing scientific evidence and church doctrine, suggesting that scientific evidence about same-gender relations is like observing the operations of an automobile, and disassembling and analyzing its parts, whereas religious doctrine is similar to "reading the operator's manual written by the manufacturer." "The operator's manual for our bodies and souls is the scriptures, written by the God who created us and [as] interpreted by his prophets" (14).

The effect of Oaks's article was to suggest that church leaders are aware of and understand the largely silent distress over same-gender attraction of a notable segment of church members and their extended families and friends. Nonetheless, to many members in the 1990s it seemed that church leaders had a "tin ear" for their struggles (Christensen 2002).

CHALLENGES TO THE CHURCH'S POSITION ON HOMOSEXUALITY

Challenges among members to the church's conceptualization of homosexuality and gender orientation began in the 1970s with the "Payne letter," an extended commentary on what the writer considered the misrepresentation of homosexuality in an introductory psychology class at Brigham Young University (Jenkins 1978). More disturbing to many gay and lesbian Latter-day Saints was a pattern of suicides through the 1980s and '90s among young Mormon men who often voiced their difficulty in reconciling their gay identity with their LDS faith. In this period Wayne Schow (1995) wrote an important reflection on his relation with his son, Brad, who died of AIDS on December 5, 1986. And *In Quiet Desperation*, Fred and Marilyn Matis reflected on their son's suicide in early 2000 during the church's campaign against same-gender marriage in California (Matis, Matis, and Mansfield 2004). In 2001 the support group Affirmation organized a candlelight vigil in Salt Lake City and elsewhere under the slogan "No more deaths! No more silence!" to draw attention to what they considered "the damaging—and sometimes fatally damaging—power of anti-gay religious teachings." "We want to communicate a message of hope and solace," said vigil organizer Duane Jennings. "We make this effort a plea for education and understanding. We call for people of faith to hold intelligence closer to their hearts than ignorance, prejudice, and intolerance" (2001, n.p.).

Among the speakers at this vigil were David and Carlie Hardy, the parents of a young gay Mormon who had earlier attempted suicide. In 1999 David Eccles Hardy wrote a letter to Elder Boyd K. Packer that Hardy subsequently made public. In it he expressed his frustration with church writings about homosexuality:

> I never thought I would say this, but as a father given the choice between (a) my son's suicide, (b) his complete abandonment of the Church and embracing of the extreme gay culture…, or (c) living in a committed, monogamous [gay] relationship for the rest of his life practicing the Gospel virtues of love, commitment, and fidelity [that] we have taught in our home, I would have to pick the latter. The Church, however, is now doing all in its power to prevent that [possibility].… Parents like us are ultimately forced to make a hopeless decision: abandon our homosexual children, or turn from the Church. (n.p.)

A year and half later, the Hardys held a news briefing during the church's general conference in which they identified four church publications that they said contained "hurtful and damaging language," promoted "fear and entrenched ignorance," and drove "gay [and lesbian] children to self-loathing, despair, and suicide." The pamphlets they identified were *Letter to a Friend,* which referred to homosexuals as "perverts," "abominations," and "servants of Satan"; *To Young Men Only* (Packer 1976), "which [supposedly] admonishes young LDS men to 'protect themselves' by physically assaulting gays when confronted with their homosexuality [consider, for instance, the case of Matthew Shepherd]"; *To the One* (Packer 1978), which taught that the real reason gays are unable to change their sexual orientation is due to selfishness; and *For the Strength of Youth* (Church 2001), which at that time labeled homosexuality as similar to rape and incest. They asked that church leaders either endorse these pamphlets as correct doctrine, revise them, or cease their publication and distribution. They pled with the leaders of the church: "Please hear us." "We represent a multitude of real families … and we have a real need for your help in addressing this issue in a positive and productive way" (2000, n.p.).

Another set of parental voices was raised by Millie and Gary M. Watts. They are the parents of six children, two of whom are gay. At age twenty-three their son Craig confided in his parents his personal feelings that he was homosexual: "I've been trying for several years to get rid of these feelings without success," Gary quoted him as saying. "I feel like I have cancer or cerebral palsy or some incurable disease." Craig said he went on a mission as part of his effort to "get over it" without telling a soul. Later, he wrote to his sister:

> A year after my mission, I told Mom and Dad, went to psychiatrists, worried. Slowly I told friends and collected my self-esteem. Now I don't cry anymore when I tell people. I don't think of it as the worst thing in the world I could possibly tell someone about myself. I think of it as just one more of the quirks in life.... I think it's a shame that sexuality is so hushed up in Mormon culture. I went through a lot of misery that could have been avoided. I worry about the others like me who are stuck there now, unable to tell anyone (that is the most perfect state of loneliness), perhaps contemplating suicide or marriage as the only way out. (1997, 43–44)

Subsequently, Gary Watts argued for the moral neutrality of homosexuality: "As long as there is a generalized, ongoing disagreement over the moral neutrality of homosexuality, the discrimination and disenfranchisement of gays, lesbians, bisexuals, and transgendered individuals will continue" (44). Watts then quoted approvingly Methodist bishop Mel Wheatley Jr.: "Homosexuality, quite like heterosexuality, is neither a virtue nor an accomplishment. It is a mysterious gift of God's grace communicated through an exceedingly complex set of chemical, biological, chromosomal, hormonal, environmental, developmental factors totally outside my homosexual friend's control. His or her homosexuality is a gift—neither a virtue nor a sin. What she or he does with their homosexuality, however, is their personal, moral, and spiritual responsibility" (46).

And speaking for himself, Watts reported,

> The most unchristian thing that has happened to me in my lifetime was the excommunication of my son from the Church. Why excommunication? So the Church could announce to the world that it abhorred homosexuality and could not and would not allow such individuals to remain

members. I still can't understand how allowing gay people in committed relationships to remain members would harm the Church. In fact, present Church policy does considerably more harm. Membership in the Church is so important to so many gay members that they try heterosexual marriage, unwittingly dragging a spouse and any resulting children into a maelstrom. The carnage thus produced is simply incalculable. (49–50)

This pessimistic assessment led Watts, in a subsequent article, to propose a logical, positive next step that would affirm committed, monogamous same-gender relationships. He presumed five "necessary realities" that must be faced:

1. "The church will not amend its law of chastity."
2. "Most gay and lesbian members and their families will continue to see their same-sex attraction as a normal biological variant that is rarely, if ever, chosen and not readily amenable to change."
3. "Current church policy as it relates to homosexuality has and will continue to produce significant pain, anguish, dissent, and consternation among both straight and gay members."
4. "It is irrational to believe that allowing gay members in committed relationships to remain full members will usher in a new era in which heterosexuals will begin to seek homosexual relationships."
5. "Church policy as it relates to homosexuality evolves as our understanding of sexuality increases, and it is vitally important that no one comes to the current debate assuming that current policy is fixed and immutable." (1998, 2–53)

His key observation was this: "Most bishops, without encouragement from the First Presidency and/or general authorities, will continue to be uncomfortable about providing support for gay members who have chosen a committed, monogamous relationship. Such encouragement would not necessitate a change in doctrine, but would require a change in the way the church implements policy regarding sexual intimacy outside the bonds of marriage." What Watts suggested is finding a way "to provide some reward and incentive for gay members to sustain a committed, monogamous relationship that would have value for the church … [and] would enable them to remain members." Then "most of the animosity currently extant would evaporate overnight" (53).

Present policy makes no distinction between committed, monogamous same-sex relationships and promiscuity; no distinction between responsibility and sexual license. It occurs to me that placing no value on committed, monogamous same-sex relationships is at the root of the strained relationship between the church and its gay members, as well as their immediate and extended families. One way to value a committed, monogamous same-sex relationship is to institute a policy that allows gay members in such a relationship to maintain their membership in the church. Temple recommends and attendance could still be restricted to members who are in full compliance with the law of chastity. We have many members of the church who do not qualify for temple recommends for a variety of reasons.... Most members who are unable to live these ideals completely nonetheless remain active, contributing members and benefit from their participation in the church. (54)

Essentially, what Watts proposed is that committed, monogamous same-gender relationships be treated in the same way that committed, monogamous different-gender relationships are treated, except that the latter are recognized in the secular law of marriage.

THE LDS CHURCH ONCE AGAIN
ENTERS THE POLITICAL ARENA

On February 1, 1994, the First Presidency released a letter to General Authorities; regional representatives; stake, mission, and district presidents; temple presidents; bishops; and branch presidents indicating that the church will "oppose any efforts to give legal authorization to marriages between persons of the same gender" (n.p.). On July 7, 2004, LDS Church leaders issued a statement supporting state and federal efforts to ban gay marriages constitutionally. Opponents of the church's support for a federal constitutional amendment argued that such an amendment would write discrimination into the U.S. Constitution (Bulkeley 2004).

In a further series of statements culminating in a news release on June 2, 2006, the First Presidency of the Church of Jesus Christ of Latter-day Saints urged priesthood leaders in the United States to support a proposed amendment to the Constitution defining marriage as consisting "only of the union of a man and a woman" and that "marriage or the legal incidents thereof" should not be "conferred upon any union other than the union of a man and woman." Church members were urged to "express themselves on this urgent matter to their elected representatives in the Senate" (Church, First Presidency, 2006, n.p.). The LDS Church also joined with the Religious

Coalition for Marriage, agreeing that "an amendment to the Constitution ... is necessary to protect and preserve the institution of marriage between a man and a woman." The LDS Church news release on April 24, 2006, also asked participants in public debate "to be respectful of each other," even on "matters of principle" that "may be deeply held" (Church, Newsroom, 2006a, n.p.).

On June 7, 2006, the U.S. Senate for a second time considered a proposed marriage-protection amendment to the Constitution. On a procedural vote to bring this measure to the floor for a direct vote, which would require sixty favorable votes, the Senate voted forty-nine in favor to forty-eight against. This was one more vote in favor than was garnered when the same proposal was presented in 2004. Approval for a constitutional amendment requires a two-thirds vote, sixty-seven out of one hundred. Thus, as Steve Chapman (2006) of the *Chicago Tribune* noted, there had been no change in the Senate in the previous two years, though during the same period fourteen states approved bans on same-sex marriage, raising the total of state legislative or state constitutional bans to forty-five.

As of December 2006, federal law was governed by the Defense of Marriage Act, which defined marriage as being between one man and one woman, signed by President Clinton in 1996. Three states, Vermont, Connecticut, and New Jersey, have legalized civil unions, providing spousal rights to same-gender couples, which, Chapman said, "has taken on the look of a soothing, sensible compromise" (n.p.). At the same time, California, Hawaii, Maine, and the District of Columbia have provided domestic partners with some spousal-like rights to persons of the same gender. Only Massachusetts performs same-gender marriages, now going on four years, without any indications of the wholesale problems that were predicted by opponents.

In Chapman's view, public opinion on issues of discrimination has also shifted in the last generation. The effort to amend the Constitution by inserting a definition of marriage is now seen by many as intolerant of homosexuals as a sexual minority and as writing discrimination into the Constitution. When the Gallup Poll asked if homosexuals should have "equal rights in terms of job opportunities" in 1977, 56 percent said yes and 33 percent said no. The numbers in 2006 had 89 percent favoring equal employment rights, with 9 percent opposed. And Chapman suggested that "attitudes on gay marriage are likely to grow more positive, not less. The battle for tolerance has largely been won among young people, who will be guiding policy in the not-too-distant future" (n.p.). Furthermore, the effort to begin a multistate ban on adoptions by same-sex couples has also failed to make much headway. Chapman also argued that as states enacted their bans on same-sex marriage, there would be less need for a federal constitutional amendment, given the resistance of Americans to tampering with the Constitution. But how these issues will finally play out in the general population is yet unclear.

The first question that arises in this situation with a bearing on LDS sexual ethics is why a homosexual couple would want to have the legal right to marry. The answer is that marriage, or its equivalent in the form of a "civil union," provides particular "benefits" or "rights" that unrelated persons do not possess, such as the right to be present in hospital settings otherwise restricted to family members, to be considered related for purposes of family-based work benefits, for spousal or partner inheritance, and other forms of legal standing. Some research has suggested that more than one thousand benefits accrue to couples who are married (or legally partnered) that do not apply to two unrelated individuals (U.S. Government Accounting Office 1997). Thus, same-sex couples living in committed relationships are asking for fair treatment in terms that are equivalent to heterosexual marriage, and believe their commitments are as binding and important to good social order as are the commitments of heterosexual couples. This "fair treatment" is essentially what the LDS Church recognizes as "civil marriage" for heterosexual couples in contrast to "temple marriage" but seeks to deny to same-gender couples.

The second question asks why the Church of Jesus Christ of Latter-day Saints opposes same-gender marriage, or, alternatively, civil unions. The answer to this question depends fundamentally on understanding how the LDS Church conceives of the temple sealing in marriage for time and eternity. "Celestial marriage" was defined by the prophet Joseph Smith as a divine directive from Heavenly Father within "the new and everlasting covenant" by which members could strive for exaltation in the celestial kingdom. The concept of exaltation envisioned that a worthy man and his wife or wives, sealed in a temple marriage under proper priesthood authority, could raise righteous progeny as an eternal family.

The current distinction within the church between temple (celestial) marriage and civil marriage, not discussed in the Proclamation on the Family, is pertinent. Celestial marriage is a church-sanctioned sealing between a man and a woman that depends on priesthood authority under the church president as the presiding high priest, and may be entered into only by church members who meet worthiness standards. These worthiness standards include following the Law of Chastity, maintaining one's status as a tithe-paying member, following the Word of Wisdom as a health code, and sustaining the prophet as president of the church. Celestial marriage also provides for sexual access between marital partners and through the sealing ordinance creates eternal families for time and eternity, whose eternal validity depends on continued fidelity. Civil marriage, on the other hand, varies among partners as a function of secular law, and generally in the United States affords a number of legal benefits between marital partners that are valid during the lifetime of the spouses, including legitimate sexual access. The church recognizes for its own purposes the validity of civil marriage between opposite-sex partners, not performed in a temple or under church sanction, and considers civilly married partners to be church members in good standing, even though not sealed in a temple celestial marriage. Its only opposition is to same-sex civil marriages, and it lobbies politically to prohibit them. This effort, of course, creates a double bind for gay, lesbian, bisexual, and transsexual members who may claim their homosexual identity as sons and daughters of God and members of the church but may not act upon that identity sexually under the current Law of Chastity and exclusion from civil marriage rights.

The Church's Most Recent "Talking Points"

The most recent attempt to explore several dozen theological and practical questions on same-gender attraction within the church was quietly posted on the church's newsroom Web site in mid-August 2006. It was presented as a structured interview with Elder Dallin H. Oaks, a member of the Quorum of the Twelve, and Elder Lance B. Wickman, a member of the seventy (Oaks and Wickman 2006). These senior church officials responded to a panel of prepared questions from two members of the church's Public Affairs staff. This exchange had about it the feel of "talking points," intended to confront, justify, and defuse some of the more problematic aspects of the church's positions on same-gender marriage and homosexuality. The church leaders sought to present their arguments from the point of view of an LDS parent, in this case a father who, we may assume, holds the Melchizedek priesthood. First, this parent is seen talking with his seventeen-year-old son, somewhat later we may imagine that this son left on a mission at age nineteen and has come home from his mission about age twenty-one, and then again a few years later we may imagine him yet unmarried in his midtwenties. Possibly due to the male priesthood authority structure of the LDS Church, this example focuses exclusively on the relations between a father and a gay son without reference to lesbian daughters, or mother-daughter, mother-son, or sibling-sibling relationships. These would add further depth, additional considerations, and more complexities, but were not part of this discussion.

To begin, Public Affairs broaches a hypothetical but realistic scenario of a seventeen-year-old LDS son coming, with great difficulty, to talk with his father about his belief that he is sexually attracted to men, has no interest in girls, and is probably gay. This son would likely hold the office of a priest in the Aaronic priesthood, having taken seriously his previous offices in the church of deacon and teacher. He has sought to suppress his (same-gender) feelings and remains celibate, but realizes news of his homosexual feelings will be devastating to his family "because we've always talked about his [going on a] Church mission, about his temple marriage and all those kinds of things. He just feels he can't live what he thinks is a lie any longer, and so he comes in this very upset and depressed manner. What do I tell him as a parent?" (n.p.).

Elder Oaks responds first by saying, "You're my son. You will always be my son, and I'll always be there to help you." This is a firm but cool acceptance of his gay son in the familial father-son relationship, but, one hopes, will open the way for further discussion. Still, it is also a relationship between a Melchizedek elder and a young Aaronic priest, and no one in the church can forget the different levels of authority associated with this set of statuses. Elder Oaks, role-playing the father, draws a distinction between inclinations or feelings, on the one hand, and behavior, on the other, and states, "It's no sin to have inclinations that if yielded to would produce behavior that would be a transgression. The sin is in yielding to temptation."

This statement makes clear from the father's point of view (as a Melchizedek elder or high priest) that homosexual behavior is not morally neutral in the church, but is strongly disapproved. Elder Oaks goes on to suggest that his son should simply consider himself "a member of the Church of the Jesus Christ of Latter-day Saints and you're my son, and that you're struggling with challenges." Clearly, these efforts at meaning making are intended to convey empathy for this son without affirming an irrevocable gay identity. At the same time, there is no mistaking the church's position that homosexual practices constitute "serious sin."

The remainder of the first section of this interview is woven of questions and answers largely rehearsed in earlier discussions of church positions, such as whether the church requires lifelong celibacy of its homosexual members (Elder Oaks answers affirmatively), whether gender orientation might be a core characteristic of a person (Elder Wickman suggests that it probably is, but certainly is not the only one, so LDS gays and lesbians should expand the personal horizons of their sense of self), whether temptations to act on homosexual feelings are controllable (both men urge that all human beings have agency and therefore have the power to redirect personal feelings and

control their sexual behavior), and whether someone with same-gender attraction may go on a mission (both say yes, as long as the Law of Chastity is
obeyed). In the midst of these exchanges the "nature versus nurture" debate
is briefly considered, but it is not treated in depth. Yet this may be an area
worth more serious consideration and exploration.

The most complete account of gender development and psychosexual
differentiation ("nature" versus "nurture") of which I am aware was developed by John Money (in Reinisch, Rosenblum, and Sanders 1987, as reported by Francoeur 1991, 74–95). It was "described [metaphorically] as a
road map with a dozen gates arranged along two main paths, one producing
a person of the female gender, the other producing a male-gendered person.
The genetic and anatomical gates mark either/or forks in the road which lock
tightly once we pass through them. Other gates, involving psychological and
social factors, are more complex and flexible because they involve a variety of
options spread out over time" (74). A listing of these "gates" involves the following factors, expressed under an "Eve" plan and an "Adam" plan:

1. chromosomal gender at fertilization
2. gonadal gender during the second and third months of fetal
   development
3. hormonal gender from the third month onward
4. internal sexual anatomical development from the second and third
   months onward
5. external sexual anatomical development from the second and third
   months onward
6. neural encoding and gender brain development from the fourth
   month onward
7. gender assignment at birth by visual inspection of external anatomy
8. gender scripting from infancy onward
9. gender role from infancy onward
10. juvenile gender identity and development
11. gender orientation and love maps from preadolescence and puberty
    onward
12. adult gender identity and personal status during the balance of the
    life course

John Money and Patricia Tucker suggest that

as you approached each gated sex-differentiated point, you could have
gone in either direction, but as you passed through, the gate locked,

fixing the prior period of development as male or female. Your gonads, for example, could have become either testicles or ovaries, but once they became testicles, they lost the option of becoming ovaries, or if they became ovaries they could never again become testicles.

In behavior, however, at first you drove all over the highway, but as you proceeded you tended to stick more and more to the lanes marked out and socially prescribed for your sex. The lines and barriers dividing male from female for each kind of sex-linked [gender-role] behavior vary according to your culture and experience, and the kind of individual you have become makes a difference in the way you feel about crossing them, but you never lose these options entirely. (1975, 73, in Francoeur 1991, 75)

Because the social, cultural, behavioral, and biophysical sciences have been moving our understanding of sexuality forward on a path that suggests heterosexual, homosexual, bisexual, and transgender orientations all have the same "nature and nurture" basis, there is good reason to explore their meanings in relation to President Hinckley's statement that all human beings are "sons and daughters of God." This universalism is very much in keeping with our morally neutral scientific understanding of gender, and both deserve extended consideration among church authorities.

The second scene of interaction represented between a father and gay son presumably occurs when the son has completed a mission as an elder in the Melchizedek priesthood, who now says that "he can't help his [same-gender feelings]," that "he's moving out of the home," and that "he plans to live with a gay friend." What should be the "proper response" of a Latter-day Saint father in this situation?

Elder Oaks responds by "affirming our continued love" for this son while at the same time reminding him of a statement of the First Presidency that "homosexual or lesbian behavior is sinful" and "subject to Church discipline." Then in his role as parent, he says,

My son, if you choose to deliberately engage in this kind of behavior, you're still my son. The Atonement of Jesus Christ is powerful enough to reach out and cleanse you if you are repentant and give up your sinful behavior, but I urge you not to embark on that path because repentance is not easy. You're embarking on a course of action that will weaken you in your ability to repent. It will cloud your perceptions of what is important in life. Finally, it may drag you down so far that you can't come back. Don't go that way. But if you choose to go that way, we will always try to help you and get you back on the path of growth.

Again, this response is a restatement of the church's position regarding individual agency in relation to sexual behavior considered as sinful outside of marriage, with repentance as the only redress that the parents may suggest. But the son does persist and escalates his requests: "Well, if you love me, can I bring my partner to our home to visit? Can we come for the holidays?" To this escalation, Elder Oaks models a response:

> I can imagine that in most circumstances the parents would say, "Please don't do that. Don't put us into that position." Surely, if there are children in the home who would be influenced by this example, the answer would likely be that [one].... I can also imagine some circumstances in which it might be possible to say, "Yes, come, but don't expect to stay overnight. Don't expect to be a lengthy house guest. Don't expect us to take you out and introduce you to our friends, or to deal with you in a public situation that would imply our approval of your 'partnership.'"

In this exchange, there is a sense of discrepancy and the double meanings of approach and avoidance between what is said and the actions implied. But Oaks acknowledges that circumstances vary, and he is trying to keep the door open rather than pronouncing a benediction on "social death."

Elder Wickman suggests that

> it's important [for] a parent to avoid a potential trap, [involved in] a shift from defending the Lord's way to defending the errant child's lifestyle.... It really is true the Lord's way is to love the sinner while condemning the sin. That is to say we continue to open our homes and our hearts and our arms to our children, but that need not be with approval of their lifestyle. Neither does it mean we need to be constantly telling them that their lifestyle is inappropriate. An even bigger error is now to become defensive of the child, because that neither helps the child nor helps the parent.

Elder Oaks adds a statement from the First Presidency: "We encourage Church leaders and members to reach out with love and understanding to those struggling with these issues," an obligation that "rests with particular intensity on parents who have children struggling with these issues... even children who are engaged in sinful behavior."

Public Affairs then asks whether "rejection of a child" is not "to some degree the natural reaction of some parents" whenever "their children fall short of expectations." Elder Oaks counters that church leaders "surely encourage parents not to blame themselves" and "Church members not to blame parents." He encourages "great compassion" for parents whose desire to protect their children has "moved them to some positions that are adversary to the Church. I hope the Lord will be merciful to parents whose love for their children has caused them to get into such traps." These statements clearly "reframe" the issues as a potential "trap" for the parents that may have the possible effect of distancing them from the church due to their love for their child, a result these church leaders seek to avoid.

The third scene of imagining a parent's point of view in the relationship between a father and a gay son arises as the son reaches his midtwenties and clearly is now an adult in the Melchizedek priesthood. Public Affairs sets the scene for a parent as follows:

> My son has now stopped coming to church altogether. There seems no prospect of him returning. Now he tells me he's planning on going to Canada where same-gender marriage is allowed. He insists that he agrees that loving marriage relationships are important. He's not promiscuous; he has one relationship. He and his partner intend to have that relationship for the rest of their lives. He cannot understand that a lifetime commitment can't be accepted by the Church when society seems to be moving that way. Again, if I am a Latter-day Saint father, what would I be expected to tell him?

Elder Wickman responds by saying that "marriage is defined by the Lord himself. It's the one institution that is ceremoniously performed by priesthood authority in the temple [and] transcends the world.... There is no such thing in the Lord's eyes as ... same-gender [temple] marriage. Homosexual behavior is and will always remain before the Lord an abominable sin." Elder Oaks adds that "the Parliament of Canada and the Congress in Washington do not have the authority to revoke the commandments of God, or to modify or amend them in any way." Clearly, these religious arguments against this son's claims and plan assert a "higher law" than the Constitution's provision against the establishment of religion and in other ways fail to address the adult son's concern for a committed, same-gender, lifelong, monogamous, loving relationship that in Canada may receive the blessings of legal marriage.

Elder Oaks adds, "Let's not forget that for thousands of years the institution of marriage has been between a man and a woman. Until quite recently, in a limited number of countries, there has been no such thing as a marriage between persons of the same gender." The problem here is that the anthropological record may be used to refute this claim. Hugo Salinas (2006), associate director for Affirmation, a gay and lesbian support group, notes that

> homosexuality has manifested itself in cultures and nations across history, and that same-sex partnerships have never been the object of universal condemnation.... As recently stated by the American Anthropological Association, "the results of more than a century of anthropological research on households, kinship relationships, and families, across cultures and through time, provide no support whatsoever for the view that either civilization or viable social orders depend upon marriage as an exclusively heterosexual institution. Rather, anthropological research supports the conclusion that a vast array of family types, including families built upon same-sex partnerships, can contribute to stable and humane societies." (2006, n.p., citing American Anthropological Association 2004)

Elder Oaks then asks why a "cohabiting, happy, and committed" same-gender couple would want "to have their relationship called a marriage. "Why do they want to add to it the legal status of marriage...?" The answer, I think, is no different from the answer for heterosexual couples: it gives social expression to their relationship, legitimates the intimacy of sexual access, and provides a wide array of social benefits, including the right of adoption as part of family building. Oaks suggests that the only articulate motive is the desire to rectify discrimination, which, he says, "is not a very good argument."

The real problem in this discussion, as in the Proclamation on the Family, is that the church fails to discuss systematically its own distinction between civil marriage and temple (or celestial) marriage. By all accounts, civil marriage even in the church's view is vetted and performed under the laws of states, nations, and other existing secular legal entities. Civil marriage is a right of citizenship. The church in its Articles of Faith proclaims: "We believe in being subject to kings, presidents, rulers, and magistrates, in obeying, honoring, and sustaining the law" (in the Pearl of Great Price). As an international church and possible world religion, the civil marriage laws of the world that the church must recognize inevitably vary according to the national or civil jurisdictions within which particular civil marriages are performed.

In general, civil marriages under the authority of nation-states give public social recognition to a committed relationship between citizens and provide for legitimate sexual access between partners, the legitimation of children as members of society by birth and adoption, and the allocation of varied social benefits during the course of the marriage until its dissolution by divorce or death. Accordingly, the Latter-day Saints have understood civil marriage as binding its partners "for time only." In contrast, temple (or celestial) marriage is an ordinance of the LDS Church, restricted by its standards of worthiness, that is performed only in an LDS temple under priesthood authority, incorporating elements of civil marriage while adding others, and sealing its members as eternal families "for time and eternity."

The founding prophet, Joseph Smith, viewed "celestial marriage" as part of "the new and everlasting covenant" preparatory to the millennial reign of Christ in the last days, and included plural wives as one of its chief expressions. Latter-day Saints claimed celestial marriage as a "higher law" than any governed by civil authority, which resulted in conflict with the U.S. government, resolved by the Supreme Court in the *Reynolds* decision (Gordon 2002), allowing freedom of religious belief while affirming Congress's right to regulate religious practice and behavior. No longer is plural marriage at the core of temple (celestial) marriage; the core now is the church's priesthood control by virtue of its worthiness standards and the power to selectively bless church members' relationships for time and eternity.

The church's worthiness standards for a temple marriage require obedience to the church's moral laws of chastity and fidelity, payment of an honest tithe, following the Word of Wisdom, recognizing the church president as a living prophet, and honoring the priesthood. Worthiness is assessed and certified through a face-to-face interview with a member's local ward bishop and the stake president, resulting in the issuance of a temple "recommend" (a certification card like a driver's license) for admission to a temple in order to perform ordinance work, first for oneself and then as a vicarious act for others who are deceased. Only worthy Latter-day Saints may be sealed in a temple marriage for time and eternity as part of the plan of salvation. Temple marriage is a rite of the LDS Church, not a right of citizenship.

For LDS members, the normative and ideal standard of marriage is temple (celestial) marriage, which requires sexual abstinence under the Law of Chastity prior to the temple ordinance and fidelity in marital sexual relations after either temple or civil marriage (or with proper confession and repentance if these restrictions have not been followed). Heterosexual couples may enter a civil marriage without these church conditions, legitimating sexual relations between the partners, who may subsequently seek a temple marriage. The church opposes same-gender civil marriages by all church members, and seeks to enact laws or a constitutional amendment to apply this rule to all citizens under civil marriage laws defining civil marriage as being "between a man and a woman." By opposing same-gender civil marriage (or defining civil marriage as only "between a man and a woman"), the church seeks to impose one feature of its worthiness standards of sexual morality for temple marriage on all citizens, namely, abstinence from any homosexual sexual relations. At the same time, by seeking to define civil marriage as legitimate only between a man and a woman, the church also aims to require of its nonheterosexual members that they abstain from sexual relations according to the Law of Chastity without having recourse to civil marriage, while failure to abstain from sexual relations subjects them as members of the church to disfellowshipment or excommunication. This effort to bring civil marriage among citizens under LDS Church rules of worthiness for members is the reason that opponents of the church's political effort claim that the church seeks to "write discrimination into the Constitution."

Some of the implications of this church position become clearer when Public Affairs in conclusion asks whether the church's arguments against same-gender marriage among citizens also apply to civil unions or other relationships that provide "some kind of benefits short of marriage." Elder Wickman answers in the affirmative, noting,

> There are numbers of different types of partnerships or pairings that may exist in society that aren't same-gender sexual relationships that provide some right that we have no objection to. [But] there may be on occasion some specific rights that we would be concerned about being granted to those in a same-gender relationship. Adoption is one that comes to mind, simply because it is a right which has been historically, doctrinally associated so closely with marriage and family,... [and] has to do with the bearing and rearing of children. Our teachings,... expressed most recently in ... the Family Proclamation by living apostles and prophets, is that children deserve to be reared in a home with a father and a mother.

CONCLUSION

When Thomas F. O'Dea examined the sources of strain and conflict within the value system of the Latter-day Saints, he identified the church's encounter with modern secular thought as its major challenge (1957, 222). That challenge remains important as the church enters the twenty-first century, with special relevance to sexuality. There is an increasing scientific consensus that homosexuality and heterosexuality as well as bisexuality and transgendered development are products of the same prenatal and postnatal biocultural processes. These processes are represented scientifically by John Money's linear two-path, twelve-gate model of adult gender identity and status, with six gates passed prenatally and six gates passed postnatally, portrayed most fully in chapter 4 of Robert T. Francoeur's textbook *Becoming a Sexual Person.* In Francoeur's words: "Becoming a sexual person [heterosexual, homosexual, bisexual, or transgendered] is a lifelong challenge. The challenge begins when the egg and sperm first unite in fertilization. It continues before birth with the development of our gonads, sexual hormones, anatomy, and neural patterns. Along the way, environment, social interactions, and learning become increasingly important and influential, interacting always with our nature" (1991, 101). Such a model, of course, does not consider what Latterday Saints envision as premortal existence, represented by Heavenly Father and Heavenly Mother with their host of spirit sons and daughters. Nor does it represent postmortal existence when spirit selves are clothed anew in immortal bodies according to their glory in the celestial kingdom as members of their own celestial families. Given human experience in this life on earth, it is not inconceivable, in LDS terms, that some spirit sisters and brothers, aunts and uncles, nieces and nephews and cousins, as well as sons and daughters and occasional parents and grandparents may represent the full range of genders eternally.

In the meantime, the gender-identity crisis in the church today puts its gay, lesbian, bisexual, and transgendered members in a double bind. On the one hand, President Hinckley and the General Authorities affirm that gay and lesbian persons (and presumably bisexual and transgendered as well) are "the sons and daughters of God" just as fully as are heterosexual persons. Clearly, the LDS Church is moving away from a norm that segregates its members by their gender orientation or gender identity, seeking instead to substitute a behavioral criterion by which prohibition of sexual activity outside of marriage is the norm. In positive terms, human sexual relations should be expressed only within the marriage relationship. But by defining this relationship as heterosexual only, all of those human beings whose sexual sense of self is other than heterosexual are excluded, even if they participate in lifelong, committed, monogamous relationships of fidelity for time, as in the church's view of civil marriage for heterosexuals.

In demographic terms, Tim B. Heaton has suggested that the legitimation of mortal same-gender relationships as constituting a major threat to the family is not supported by compelling demographic evidence, with a modest incidence ranging from less than 6 percent of adults to about 10 percent, though these modest percentages mean large numbers of people ranging in the many millions. He notes:

Legitimization of same-sex relationships clearly challenges the belief that sexual intimacy should only be expressed in heterosexual relationships. Beyond this challenge to sexual norms, it is not clear how legitimization would undermine the family structure of society. Research indicates that some gay men do not adhere to the ideal of monogamy. One argument for legitimizing same-sex relationships is to promote stability. In short, the costs and benefits to legalizing or in other ways legitimizing same-sex relationships have not been empirically demonstrated. Given this lack of clear evidence and the small percentage of the population involved, I would not place same-sex relationships on the list of major threats to family life. (1999, 27–28)

Second, in ideological terms, a behavioral norm prohibiting sexual activity outside of marriage is fully compatible with the extension of the church's view of civil marriage for time only to persons of all genders. On the other hand, in theological terms, temple (celestial) marriage would be the only marriage form that meets the church's normative standards of worthiness and serves as an ordinance of exaltation. To be "religiously neutral," nation-states or other legal jurisdictions might underwrite and legitimate "civil partnerships," reserving "marriage" to supplementary forms of divine sanction provided by any and all religious groups. Temple (celestial) marriage, then, would have a status much more like baptism; it would be a clearly defined religious rite. It could still be wrapped around the minimal sanctioning and legitimating role of the governing nation, state, or locality.

Third, variation in gender orientation and identity will not go away. Human groups will continue to produce children in each generation distributed according to population genetics and cultural attitudes in roughly the same proportions as now. This means that both homosexuality and heterosexuality will continue to involve deeply rooted feelings of personal identity and sexual orientation. Issues of fairness and justice, rooted among the young, will favor long-term democratic consent and reason, and protection and equality for sexual minorities.

Today, church leaders and members face five critical questions:

1. Is homosexuality a choice? The test is this: Write a detailed autobiographical account of how, when, and under what conditions you came to an awareness of your own sexual identity in whatever terms you would describe it. Did you choose this identity or discover it as part of your own emerging self-awareness?

2. Can gay men or lesbians live committed lives as couples blessed by Heavenly Father and Heavenly Mother? The answer to this question is found among those gay and lesbian couples who are living such lives. President Hinckley refers to them as sons and daughters of heavenly parents. The real issue is whether they can live together as committed partners for a lifetime, just as some married heterosexual couples do.

3. In what righteous ways can gay men and lesbian women express their love for one another in sexual terms? Mainly in the same ways that heterosexual couples express their love, through sexual behavior and with very few differences that should be worked out within their committed relationship.

4. How can gay men and lesbian women form multigenerational righteous families, raising their own children? By adoption, artificial insemination, and similar procedures. One of my single colleagues has adopted two infant daughters and a son who are just entering their grade-school years. He is doing this as a loving single parent. It is possible and deserves community support.

5. How can General Authorities fulfill President Hinckley's mandate to avoid disrespect and exhibit love, tolerance, and respect for those he calls "sons and daughters of God"? Given the history of inflammatory oratory and hostile labels in both the LDS Church and American society generally, this will take some doing. It will require support and leadership from all institutional sectors. But so far, only the smallest of steps along this path have been taken.

REFERENCES

American Anthropological Association. 2004. "Broadening the Marriage and Family Debate." *Anthropology News* (April). http://www.aaanet.org/press/an/0404dia-pa.htm.

Ballard, M. Russell. 1993. "Keeping Covenants." *Ensign,* May, 6.

Bateson, Gregory. 1972. *Steps to an Ecology of Mind.* New York: Ballantine.

Blodgett, Alan. 1999. "No Longer Welcome: An Account of My Excommunication from the Church of Jesus Christ of Latter-day Saints." Prepared as a case report for the Mormon Alliance, October 21. http://www.affirmation.org/learning/no_longer_welcome.shtml.

Bulkeley, Deborah. 2004. "LDS Church Supports Gay-Marriage Bans." *Deseret Morning News,* July 8.

Bush, Lester E. 1976. "Birth Control among the Mormons: Introduction to an Insistent Question." *Dialogue: A Journal of Mormon Thought* 10, no. 2: 12–44.

Cameron, Kim S. 1992. "Authority." In *Priesthood and Church Organization: Selections from "The Encyclopedia of Mormonism,"* ed. Daniel H. Ludlow, 25–28. Salt Lake City: Deseret Book.

Carter, David. 2004. *Stonewall: The Riots That Sparked the Gay Revolution*. New York: St. Martin's.

Chapman, Steve. 2006. "Conservatives Are Losing on Gay Rights." http://www. chicagotribune.com/news/columnists/chi.

Christensen, Harold T. 1976. "Mormon Sexuality in Cross-cultural Perspective." *Dialogue: A Journal of Mormon Thought* 10, no. 2: 62–75.

———. 1994 [1982]. "The Persistence of Chastity: Built-in Resistance in Mormon Culture to Secular Trends." In *Multiply and Replenish: Mormon Essays on Sex and Family*, ed. Brent Corcoran, 67–84. Salt Lake City: Signature Books.

Christensen, Harold T., and Marvin B. Rytting. 1976. Introduction to *Dialogue: A Journal of Mormon Thought* 10, no. 2: 9–11.

Christensen, Robert J. 2002. "Tin Ears and Hard Love: A Personal Response to Elder Boyd K. Packer's 'Ye Are the Temple of God.'" Honorable mention, Affirmation Writing Awards. http://www.affirmation.org/learning/tin_ears_and_hard_love.shtml.

Church of Jesus Christ of Latter-day Saints. 1997. *Gospel Principles*. Salt Lake City: Intellectual Reserve.

———. 1999. *Doctrine and Covenants and Church History Gospel Doctrine: Teacher's Manual*. Salt Lake City: Intellectual Reserve.

———. 2000. *Marriage and Family Relations: Instructor's Manual*. Salt Lake City: Intellectual Reserve.

Church of Jesus Christ of Latter-day Saints, Church Educational System. 2001. *Eternal Marriage: Student Manual*. Salt Lake City: Intellectual Reserve.

Church of Jesus Christ of Latter-day Saints, First Presidency. 1991. Letter on standards of morality and fidelity to all members of the Church of Jesus Christ of Latter-day Saints. November 14. Signed by Ezra Taft Benson, Gordon B. Hinckley, and Thomas S. Monson.

———. 1994. Letter on same gender marriages to General Authorities; regional representatives; stake, mission, and district presidents; temple presidents; bishops; and branch presidents. February 1. Signed by Ezra Taft Benson, Gordon B. Hinckley, and Thomas S. Monson.

———. 2001. *For the Strength of Youth*. Salt Lake City: Intellectual Reserve.

———. 2006. Letter to General Authorities, area seventies, and stake presidencies in the United States. May 25.

Church of Jesus Christ of Latter-day Saints, Newsroom. 2006a. "Church Supports Call for Constitutional Amendment." April 24. http://www.lds.org/newsroom.

———. 2006b. "Same Gender Attraction." September 17. http://www.lds.org/newsroom.

Comfort, Alex, ed. 1972. *The Joy of Sex: A Gourmet Guide to Love Making*. New York: Simon and Schuster.

Corcoran, Brent, ed. 1994. *Multiply and Replenish: Mormon Essays on Sex and Family*. Salt Lake City: Signature Books.

First Presidency and Council of the Twelve Apostles of the Church of Jesus Christ of Latter-day Saints. 1995. *The Family: A Proclamation to the World.* Salt Lake City: Intellectual Reserve.

Forrest, Jeannie, and Mark O. Bigler. 1999. "Church of Jesus Christ of Latter-day Saints." In *Sexuality in America: Understanding Our Sexual Values and Behavior,* ed. Robert T. Francoeur et al., 29–42. New York: Continuum.

Foster, Lawrence. 1994 [1982]. "Between Heaven and Earth: Mormon Theology of the Family in Comparative Perspective." In *Multiply and Replenish: Mormon Essays on Sex and Family,* ed. Brent Corcoran, 1–17. Salt Lake City: Signature Books.

Francoeur, Robert T. 1991. *Becoming a Sexual Person.* 2d ed. New York: Macmillan.

Francoeur, Robert T., Patricia Barthalow Koch, and David L. Weis, eds. 1999. *Sexuality in America: Understanding Our Sexual Values and Behavior.* New York: Continuum.

Gordon, Sarah Barringer. 2002. *The Mormon Question: Polygamy and Constitutional Conflict in Nineteenth Century America.* Chapel Hill: University of North Carolina Press.

Hansen, Klaus. 1976. "Mormon Sexuality and American Culture." *Dialogue: A Journal of Mormon Thought* 10, no. 2: 45–56. Revised version reprinted as "Changing Perspectives on Sexuality and Marriage." In *Multiply and Replenish: Mormon Essays on Sex and Family,* ed. Brent Corcoran, 19–46. Salt Lake City: Signature Books, 1994.

———. 1994 [1981]. "Changing Perspectives on Sexuality and Marriage." In *Multiply and Replenish: Mormon Essays on Sex and Family,* ed. Brent Corcoran, 19–46. Salt Lake City: Signature Books. Reprinted from *Mormonism and the American Experience,* 147–78. Chicago: University of Chicago Press.

Hardy, David Eccles. 1999. Letter to Elder Boyd K. Packer. October 7. http://lds-mormon.com/hardy.shtml.

Hardy, David Eccles, and Carlie Hardy. 2000. Press conference statement. http://www.affirmation.org/learning/press_statement_by_david_and_carlie_hardy.shtml.

Heaton, Tim B. 1999. "Social Forces That Imperil the Family." *Dialogue: A Journal of Mormon Thought* 32, no. 4: 19–41.

Hinckley, Gordon B. 1996. "This Thing Was Not Done in a Corner." *Ensign,* November, 48–51.

Hurston, Anna [pseud.]. 1991. "Suffering into Truth." In *Peculiar People: Mormons and Same-Sex Orientation,* ed. Ron Schow, Wayne Schow, and Marybeth Raynes, 14–22. Salt Lake City: Signature Books.

Jenkins, Cloy, et al. 1978. "Prologue: An Examination of the Mormon Attitude towards Homosexuality." http://www.affirmation.org/memorial/prologue.shtml.

Jennings, Duane. 2001. "Affirmation Vigil in Salt Lake City." May 8. https://www.affirmation.org/suicide_info/2001_vigil_salt_lake.shtml.

Johnston, Gordon. 1991. "To Thine Own Self Be True." In *Peculiar People: Mormons and Same-Sex Orientation,* ed. Ron Schow, Wayne Schow, and Marybeth Raynes, 43–48. Salt Lake City: Signature Books.

Kimball, Spencer W. 1969. *The Miracle of Forgiveness*. Salt Lake City: Bookcraft.

———. 1980. "President Kimball Speaks Out on Morality." *Ensign,* November, 94.

Kinsey, Alfred C., et al. 1953. *Sexual Behavior in the Human Female*. Philadelphia: W. B. Saunders.

Kinsey, Alfred C., Wardell B. Pomeroy, and Clyde E. Martin. 1948. *Sexual Behavior in the Human Male*. Philadelphia: W. B. Saunders.

Mackelprang, Romel W. 1994 [1992]. "'They Shall Be One Flesh': Sexuality and Contemporary Mormonism." In *Multiply and Replenish: Mormon Essays on Sex and Family,* ed. Brent Corcoran, 47–66. Salt Lake City: Signature Books.

Martinson, Floyd M. 1995. *The Sexual Life of Children*. Westport, Conn.: Bergin and Garvey Publishers.

Matis, Fred, Marilyn Matis, and Ty Mansfield. 2004. *In Quiet Desperation: Understanding the Challenges of Same-Gender Attraction*. Salt Lake City: Deseret Book.

Mauss, Armand L. 1976. "Shall the Youth of Zion Falter? Mormon Youth and Sex: A Two-City Comparison." *Dialogue: A Journal of Mormon Thought* 10, no. 2: 82–84.

McLaren, Angus. 1999. *Twentieth Century Sexuality: A History*. Oxford: Blackwell Publishers.

Metalious, Grace. 1950. *Peyton Place*. Reprint, Boston: Northeastern University Press, 1999.

Money, John. 1988. *Gay, Straight, and In-between: The Sexology of Erotic Orientation*. New York: Oxford University Press.

Money, John, and Patricia Tucker. 1975. *Sexual Signatures: On Being a Man or Woman*. Boston: Little, Brown.

Oaks, Dallin H. 1995. "Same-Gender Attraction." *Ensign,* October, 7–14.

———. 2006. "Dating versus Hanging Out." *Ensign,* June, 10–16.

Oaks, Dallin H., and Lance B. Wickman. 2006. "Same-Gender Attraction." http://www.lds.org/newsroom/issues/answer.

O'Dea, Thomas F. 1957. *The Mormons*. Chicago: University of Chicago Press.

O'Donovan, Rocky. 1994. "'The Abominable and Detestable Crime against Nature': A Brief History of Homosexuality and Mormonism, 1940–1980." In *Multiply and Replenish: Mormon Essays on Sex and Family,* ed. Brent Corcoran, 123–70. Salt Lake City: Signature Books.

Olson, Terrance D. 1995. "Sexuality." In *Encyclopedia of Mormonism: The Church and Society,* ed. Daniel H. Ludlow, 462–66. Salt Lake City: Deseret Book.

Oswald, Delmont R. 1994 [1990]. "A Lone Man in the Garden." In *Multiply and Replenish: Mormon Essays on Sex and Family,* ed. Brent Corcoran, 231–38. Salt Lake City: Signature Books.

Packer, Boyd K. 1976. "To Young Men Only." LDS general conference address, October.

———. 1978. "To the One." Fireside address given to the twelve stakes, Brigham Young University, March 5.

A Parent's Guide. 1985. Salt Lake City: Church of Jesus Christ of Latter-day Saints.

Pearson, Carol Lynn. 1991. "Good-bye, I Love You." In *Peculiar People: Mormons and Same-Sex Orientation,* ed. Ron Schow, Wayne Schow, and Marybeth Raynes, 71–85. Salt Lake City: Signature Books. Reprinted from *Good-bye, I Love You.* New York: Random House, 1986.

Raynes, Marybeth, and Erin Parsons. 1994 [1983]. "Single Cursedness: An Overview of LDS Authorities' Statements about Unmarried People." In *Multiple and Replenish: Mormon Essays on Sex and Family,* ed. Brent Corcoran, 217–30. Salt Lake City: Signature Books.

Reinisch, June Machover, Leonard A. Rosenblum, and Stephanie A. Sanders, eds. 1987. *Masculinity/Femininity: Basic Perspectives.* New York: Oxford University Press.

Rosman, Katherine. 2002. "Mormon Family Values." *Nation,* February 25. http://www.thenation.com/docprint.mhtml?i=20020225&s=rosman.

Roth, Philip. 1959. *Goodbye Columbus: And Five Short Stories.* New York: Modern Library.

Rytting, Marvin. 1994 [1982]. "Exhortations for Chastity: A Content Analysis of Church Literature." In *Multiply and Replenish: Mormon Essays on Sex and Family,* ed. Brent Corcoran, 85–102. Salt Lake City: Signature Books.

Salinas, Hugo. 2006. "A Response to Elder Dallin H. Oaks and Lance B. Wickman." September. http://www.affirmation.org/media.2006_08.shtml.

Schow, Ron, H. Wayne Schow, and Marybeth Raynes, eds. 1991. *Peculiar People: Mormons and Same-Sex Orientation.* Salt Lake City: Signature Books.

Schow, Wayne. 1995. *Remembering Brad: On the Loss of a Son to AIDS.* Salt Lake City: Signature Books.

Smith, Wilford E. 1976. "Mormon Sex Standards on College Campuses; or, Deal Us Out of the Sexual Revolution!" *Dialogue: A Journal of Mormon Thought* 10, no. 2: 76–81.

Solus [pseud.]. 1976. *Dialogue: A Journal of Mormon Thought* 10, no. 2: 94–99. Reprinted in *Peculiar People: Mormons and Same-Sex Orientation,* ed. Ron Schow, Wayne Schow, and Marybeth Raynes, 5–13. Salt Lake City: Signature Books, 1991.

U.S. Government Accounting Office. 1997. Letter to the honorable Henry J. Hyde. January 31.

Wallace, Anthony F. C. 2003. "Identity Processes in Personality and in Culture." In *Revitalizations and Mazeways: Essays on Culture Change,* ed. Robert S. Grumet, 1:269–309. Lincoln: University of Nebraska Press.

Watts, Gary M. 1997. "Mugged by Reality." *Sunstone* 20, no. 3: 43–51.

———. 1998. "The Logical Next Step: Affirming Same-Sex Relationships." *Dialogue: A Journal of Mormon Thought* 31, no. 3: 49–57.

9

Mormons and the State

~ Michael Nielsen and Barry Balleck ~

In his study of Mormonism and the state, Thomas F. O'Dea notes the Church of Jesus Christ of Latter-day Saint (LDS) belief that America was established in order to facilitate the restoration of the gospel. Despite the importance of this idea, O'Dea observes that Mormons had not yet "worked out consistently the political implications of their religious philosophy." Mormonism's "theocratic and separatist aspects [are] counterbalanced by democratic and patriotic motives which [are] equally genuine and equally well grounded in Mormon doctrine" (1957, 171). This suggests a rich base from which a highly articulated religiopolitical philosophy might grow, but such a philosophy has not yet developed.

The building blocks for such a philosophy seem readily available. O'Dea's broad analysis of Latter-day Saint social life notes such themes as the church's involvement in politics, LDS concepts regarding authority and government, patriotism versus particularism, and the political conservatism shown by most LDS churchgoers. One important element in this analysis is O'Dea's recognition that Mormonism features tensions between hierarchy and congregationalism, or between vertical and horizontal organizational structures. Tension between institutional control and local and individual autonomy shaped the church's historical development (chap. 7) and are highly relevant to a discussion of Mormon religion and politics. The tension continues to affect the relationship of Mormons with the state, but, as the church has become more assimilated into mainstream U.S. society (Mauss 1994), problems associated with this tension have become more noticeable at the individual rather than institutional level. The institutional church has sought to harmonize its relations with the state, with the expectation that its members support state policies. Individuals who see a discrepancy between the gospel message and the state's practices are therefore left with conflicted identities to reconcile.

POLITICS OF THE LDS CHURCH

For much of its early history the LDS Church had a tense relationship with politics. Before its trek to Utah, the church was feared to engage in block voting in order to elect LDS candidates, and the resulting anti-Mormon sentiment sometimes resulted in violent clashes between Mormons and others. The situation intensified once rumors of Mormon polygamy heightened the "us versus them" dynamics among citizens. Following Joseph Smith's death, the majority of Mormons moved with Brigham Young to the isolated Utah Territory, where Young established something of a theocracy despite the presence of a federal governor. A strained relationship with the federal government continued, notwithstanding Salt Lake City's remote frontier location. In 1857, President James Buchanan sent troops to Utah to remove Brigham Young from power. In what became known as the "Utah War," federal troops entered Utah ostensibly to end the practice of polygamy and to remove Brigham Young as governor of the Utah Territory. With the impending Civil War, federal troops left Utah and, though deposed as governor, Brigham Young continued in his role as de facto leader of the Utah Territory for the next two decades while polygamy continued.

As a condition of granting Utah statehood the church announced an end to polygamy in 1890 and disbanded its own political party in 1893. At this time most Mormons were reluctant to support the Republican Party due to its efforts to put an end to Mormon polygamy. Knowing that they needed to achieve some level of political neutrality, the church sent apostle John Henry Smith on the stump to convince congregations that it was possible to be a good Latter-day Saint and a good Republican. In one common version of the story bishops were to assign half of their members to be Republicans and half to be Democrats (Prince and Wright 2005, 334). A few years later, polygamy again became an issue when the U.S. Senate held hearings regarding whether to allow Reed Smoot to represent the state. He was admitted to the Senate, thanks to the large number of senators who abstained from the vote to reject him. Although the church's historic deviance from marital norms marked it as outside mainstream life, the first half of the twentieth century saw the church assimilating to its host culture and seeking greater acceptance from it in politics and other matters, as when a young Hugh B. Brown's stake president asked him and three other LDS men to enlist in a military officer training program (Campbell and Poll 1975, 52).

One noteworthy example of this effort is the prominent role of J. Reuben Clark Jr., who had a significant impact on U.S. foreign policy during the early twentieth century. Clark, with a law degree from Columbia University, served as undersecretary of state for Calvin Coolidge, solicitor to the

Department of State, and counsel before international tribunals and arbitrational commissions and later was appointed ambassador to Mexico. One of the hallmarks of his government service was a lengthy memo known as the "Clark Memorandum on the Monroe Doctrine" that argued for a more isolationist interpretation of the Monroe Doctrine than had been in effect under the administration of Theodore Roosevelt. This was motivated largely by his belief that self-determination should define government and individual identity (Wood and Taylor 1973). Clark's views stemmed from four characteristically Mormon beliefs: the necessity for human freedom, the rejection of power politics, an overwhelming belief in the ultimate triumph of moral truth, and a belief in the special historical mission of the United States. He, like other LDS leaders, considered the Constitution divinely inspired to free people from an oppressive government (Hillam 1983).

Clark's government service ended in 1933, when he was called to serve in the Quorum of the Twelve. He then served as counselor to LDS presidents Heber J. Grant, George Albert Smith, and David O. McKay, who found Clark's experience in government helpful in their efforts to make the church more accepted in society. Clark's desire to see individual people and governments achieve on their own was reflected in McKay's approach to politics. It also may be an important reason "there has been little critical word from church leaders regarding national foreign policy for several decades" (Glass 1993, 65).

To the extent that church authorities did make statements about government and politics during the mid-twentieth century, they tended to pit democracy and self-determination against communism. This is borne out by analyses of general conference addresses, which show that during the period 1950–1979 there was a significant increase in concern about communism, "false" political ideologies, and political tyranny (Shepherd and Shepherd 1984). These themes were not limited to general conferences. Upon returning from his 1952 trip around the world, David O. McKay reported to his fellow General Authorities, "We are facing Satan himself. [Communists] are anti-Christ. They want to destroy Christianity... [and] there is only one way to meet them and that is by force, the only thing they understand" (Prince and Wright 2005, 282). He later told executives of the Boy Scouts of America, "It is a question of God and liberty, or atheism and slavery. The success of Communism means the destruction of Religion" (284).

In the context of the cold war and fierce anticommunist sentiment, Ezra Taft Benson worked hard to promote the John Birch Society among Latter-day Saints. His deeply conservative statements resonated with many LDS, and, given that he served as U.S. secretary of agriculture while a member of the Quorum of the Twelve, his voice carried a special air of authority in such matters (Prince and Wright 2005) that often outweighed Hugh B. Brown's calls for political moderation (Campbell and Poll 1975, 258). McKay's anticommunist belief and his reluctance to disagree publicly with an apostle meant that Benson's conservative message was the most consistent and noticeable political viewpoint expressed by a General Authority, despite Brown's, N. Eldon Tanner's and other apostles' efforts to rein in Benson. Indeed, when McKay died, so did the extremism in Benson's political speech (Prince and Wright 2005).

Following McKay's administration, the church saw a subtle change in how its publications, leaders, and members referred to the General Authorities. Whereas Presidents Grant and McKay were rarely called "prophet," during Spencer Kimball's administration the term was used frequently, a trend that has continued to this day. A side effect of this development is that it is difficult for Mormons to dissent from the political views expressed by church leaders (Quinn 1997). This becomes particularly acute when leaders, who are revered as "prophets, seers and revelators," declare, "We will not lead you astray. We cannot" (368, quoting Ballard 1994) and that the president of the LDS Church "will never mislead the Saints" (ibid., quoting Faust 1996). This has contributed to the increasingly Republican view of LDS members who, when they looked at the political involvement of their church leaders, saw Benson as being the most outspoken and overtly political during the 1950s–1970s. His anticommunist books, with titles such as *The Red Carpet* (1962) and *An Enemy Hath Done This* (1969), were readily available as the most noticeable "LDS" view regarding political or governmental matters.

The effect of this has been long-lasting despite the fact that the official position of the LDS Church is political neutrality in domestic politics. Every U.S. election year LDS leaders read statements that encourage church members to participate in political affairs but note that the church does not endorse any political party, nor does it allow the use of its facilities for election activities. Notwithstanding this apparent neutrality, there is very little semblance of a two-party political system among members of the LDS Church. In Utah, the state with the highest population percentage of Mormons (62 percent, according to Canham 2005), nearly 72 percent of Utahns voted for President George W. Bush in the 2004 election. Utah was the only state in the United States in which a single candidate garnered more than 70 percent of the vote. In 1984, 75 percent of Utah voters voted for Republican Ronald Reagan. The last presidential election in which a Democrat captured the Utah vote was 1964, when nearly 55 percent of voters in

Utah voted for President Lyndon B. Johnson (Leip 2006). Beginning in high school and continuing through adulthood, Mormons are more likely than non-Mormons to describe themselves as politically conservative. Indeed, Mormons have increased their support for conservative political candidates during the past twenty years (Heaton, Bahr, and Jacobson 2004). At the state level, presently only eight of twenty-nine Utah state senators and nineteen of seventy-five members of the house of representatives are Democrats. This represents a marked change from forty years ago, when visitors representing the French government were reportedly impressed by the ability of Mormon Republicans and Democrats to work together (Campbell and Poll 1975, 274).

Utahns' support for Republicans and George W. Bush continues today even in the face of the declining popularity of both the Republican Party and President Bush in national political polls. Despite national public opinion polls that show George W. Bush's popularity remaining fixed below 40 percent, Utahns provide Bush with approval ratings over 60 percent (Bernick 2007). The popularity of Bush extends to his policies, as Utahns overwhelmingly agree with a majority of Bush's policy agenda. Indeed, at least one Mormon has had a hand in shaping the Bush presidency on matters of war, with Jay Bybee as the assistant attorney general who wrote the memo to Attorney General Alberto Gonzales providing a rationale to define *torture* so narrowly that there might be a legal defense for performing acts hitherto considered illegal. Following the memo, church spokesperson Dale Bills commented by saying that the church "condemns inhumane treatment of any person under any circumstances" but that "the church has not taken a position on any proposed legislative or administrative actions regarding torture" (Moore 2005, n.p.). LDS involvement with U.S. politics shows that what began as a radical movement outside the norms of its host culture has transformed itself into a conservative voice supporting those norms.

Although McKay eventually developed a more nuanced view of world politics, realizing distinctions between communism as a system, individual communists, and individual socialists, the effect of staunch political rhetoric continued to affect the church years later on the international scene as well as the domestic. Gregory A. Prince and William Robert Wright describe a 1985 report by East German secret police that stated that the church was "to be classified as representatives of the right wing of American conservatism" and cited connections between the church leadership and the Reagan administration as well as individual Mormons and the U.S. Secret Service (2005, 322). A lingering effect of Benson's anticommunist efforts is that Mormons are significantly more likely than non-Mormons to agree that communism is the worst kind of government (Heaton, Bahr, and Jacobson 2004).

RECENT EFFORTS BEYOND U.S. BORDERS

Interest in the world beyond U.S. borders has long been part of the church worldview, spurred in large part by its missionary emphasis. Shortly after establishing the church, Joseph Smith predicted that it would grow far beyond the borders of the United States, a process O'Dea describes and is revisited in other chapters in the present volume. Missionaries were sent to England and other parts of Europe, and drew thousands of converts who immigrated to "Zion." Since 1977 the church has established missionary training centers in Brazil, Europe, Asia, and the Pacific to train native populations in the teaching of church doctrines (Cowan 2006).

Although early converts to the church immigrated to build Zion, by the 1890s this began to change; converts remained in their home countries, as immigration was not encouraged (Jensen n.d.). The differing needs and experiences of Mormons in various areas of the world highlighted the tension O'Dea speaks of between hierarchy and individuality. Where there were sufficient numbers of Latter-day Saints available, the church began building chapels and temples to serve the congregations. In 1923, the first temple outside of the United States was constructed in Cardston, Alberta, Canada. Of the 124 temples that the church operates today, 60 are found in countries other than the United States. In 1985, the church built a temple behind the Iron Curtain in Freiburg, East Germany. This was the first temple to have been constructed in a communist country, built some six years before the fall of communism in Eastern Europe. These developments are notable for the central role of temples in LDS life; Mormons often see the spread of temples as a marker of the church's growth and health. Many of the faithful viewed the Freiburg temple as heralding a new age in the growth of the church in what was considered an inhospitable region.

In 1983, the David M. Kennedy Center for International Studies was established on the campus of Brigham Young University (BYU) with the goal of increasing international experiences and understanding of BYU students ("Welcome" 2006). David M. Kennedy had impressive careers in both government and banking. His service began on the staff of the Federal Reserve System Board of Governors in 1930, where he remained until 1946, rising through increasingly responsible positions, culminating in his assignment as assistant to the chairman of the Board of Governors. After serving as U.S. secretary of the treasury and carrying out diplomatic assignments for the government, he spent several years as a special representative of the First

Presidency of the church. His efforts were instrumental in gaining recognition of the church in many nations (Hickman 1987).

In 1987 the LDS Church constructed the Brigham Young University Jerusalem Center for Near Eastern Studies in Jerusalem. The academic offerings at the center focus on biblical and contemporary studies, correlated with a study of archaeology, biblical geography, Near Eastern history, Judaism, Islam, Near Eastern languages, and international relations and politics (Galbraith 2007). In addition to its mission of educating students, it is intended to give the church a presence in the Middle East, where proselytizing efforts are often legally prohibited.

The church also maintains LDS Philanthropies, which donate food and other vital necessities to victims of natural and other disasters throughout the world. In addition to its disaster-relief efforts, this arm of the church manages the Perpetual Education Fund (PEF). Announcing the fund at the April 2001 general conference, President Gordon B. Hinckley recognized that many missionaries complete their service but return home to a bleak future because of poverty. The PEF consists of an endowment whose interest is loaned to church members, who use the money to fund education or other self-improvement efforts. The goal is to help reduce the suffering caused by poverty, provide better for their families materially, and improve the likelihood that they will continue in church service and leadership positions (Hinckley 2001).

From the perspective of peace and conflict studies, efforts such as LDS Philanthropies and the Perpetual Education Fund address the problem of structural violence, the structural inequities that foment direct violence. Although war and other forms of direct violence receive much attention, the effects of structural violence can be great despite the fact that their negative results, which accrue over a longer period of time, are often subtle. Structural violence receives comparatively little attention in LDS writings. One exception to this is Hugh Nibley's writing on materialism and social justice (for example, Nibley 1989). More recently, Bradley Walker (2002, 2003a, 2003b) has discussed the possibility of restructuring the church welfare system so that it more efficiently helps the church's least-wealthy people. Walker's tangible suggestions for alleviating the suffering he poignantly documents offer one person's grassroots efforts to direct the church toward recognizing structural violence and moved a self-described "cold war warrior" to action (Jones 2005, 106).

The church's Perpetual Education Fund may be considered an example of an effort to address structural violence. By loaning impoverished Mormons the economic means to accomplish educational self-improvement goals, it directly improves the state of individual members, and indirectly enhances the church in those areas. Potential criticisms of such a strategy are that the PEF may not take into consideration the changing status of borrowers and that the church has sufficient assets to make grants rather than loans. Proponents of the PEF counter that the system builds self-reliance and rewards hard work, values consistent with the Mormon work ethic. Alternatively, one might see all organizational actions in a context of realpolitik, the belief that organizations act in ways that keep, increase, and demonstrate their power. This type of analysis would emphasize the benefit accrued to the church by improving the postmission successes of its returned missionaries. It may well be that the church values the improvements that the PEF generates both to its individual participants and to the institution.

THE LDS CHURCH AND WAR

Perhaps the ultimate responsibility of the state is to provide for the safety of its citizens and to protect them from threats from other states. How does the LDS Church view this function of the state? A starting point would be to consider how the institutional church and its members understand war and the positions the church takes in world affairs.

The importance of war is heightened when one recognizes that its destructive power has increased with improvements in technology. As weapons have become increasingly powerful, we hold the capacity to kill and wound greater numbers of people in a single event. The threat of this happening seems greater as a result of the fact that states use war to achieve their economic and political goals (Barash and Webel 2002). The nature of war also has changed in the sense that the majority of wars occur within the state, and the vast majority of casualties are civilians (Winter et al. 2001). Whereas the war deaths that occurred before the twentieth century were almost exclusively experienced by the soldiers fighting the war, the twentieth century saw a dramatic shift in the nature of warfare. For example, during World War II, fully 50 percent of the casualties were civilians, but, at the beginning of the twenty-first century, more than 90 percent of all casualties in war are civilians (Raymond and Raymond 1999). The nature of warfare has put civilians—children and other innocent bystanders—on the front line of conflicts. When compared to classic warfare with clearly drawn battle lines, today's insurgencies and counterinsurgencies are more difficult to define as being good or bad, as "both insurgents and counterinsurgents are known to employ abhorrent tactics, such as terror, assassination, or the indiscriminate killing of the innocent" (Hillam 1975, 224). Although wars in the past were typically declared on states, the United States is presently engaged in a war against an abstraction, "terror," which makes defining specific opponents, targets, and goals difficult.

Despite admonitions that Mormons be peacemakers and forgive their enemies, the church's position on the conduct of war has always been somewhat ambiguous. Though many passages in LDS scriptures indicate an overall opposition to war, the church also believes in being subject to "kings, presidents, rulers, and magistrates in obeying, honoring, and sustaining the law" (12 Article of Faith). This belief suggests that members of the church follow their political leaders despite the moral or ethical reservations that they may have about the policies those leaders advocate. This tension between peacemaking versus obeying one's leaders accounts for much of the apparent conflict in LDS views regarding war. It has also become more noticeable as Mormonism has moved from being a radical frontier sect to a more accepted part of mainstream life in the United States.

Many discussions of war are found in LDS scripture. In addition to well-known conflicts described in the Bible, war permeates the Book of Mormon and is addressed also in the Pearl of Great Price and the Doctrine and Covenants. The same can be said of the discussions of war presented by LDS leaders. For example, Boyd K. Packer lauds war when he remarks, "From the ugliness of armed conflict have come some of the finest spiritual experiences, moments of spiritual heroism" (1971, 9).

Nibley's analysis of scriptural discussions of war leads him to conclude that "the verses forbidding conflict are of a general and universal nature, while those which countenance it all refer to exceptional cases" and that it is "dangerous and foolish" to generalize from those exceptions to justify war (1971, 53). Applying this approach to the declarations of church leaders, one sees a tendency for church officials to view church teachings as the solution to war. Typical of these are David O. McKay's assertions that "one cause of...war lies deeply rooted in the fact that those highly so-called Christian nations have never applied the gospel of Jesus Christ" (1914, n.p.) and that "permanent peace will be found only in the application of principles of the gospel of peace" (1944, n.p.). Similar statements have been made by virtually all presidents of the church during the past century. In their analysis of general conference themes, Gordon Shepherd and Gary Shepherd note,

> Though modern Mormon leaders strongly identify with national patriotic values and entertain an idealized conception of traditional American virtues, they regularly excoriate what they perceive to be the many permissive, self-indulgent, and licentious currents of modern life presumably encouraged by the spread of secular consciousness. Broken down into their

basic messages, most conference sermons include some kind of appeal for people to forsake worldly ways and to have faith in the simple verities of the old time gospel. (1984, 197)

In this spirit J. Reuben Clark said, "Guns and bayonets will, in the future as in the past, bring truces, long or short, but never the peace that endures.... Peace can only be achieved through the strength and power of moral force in the world, not the strength and power of arms" (Hillam 1983, 25). Clark worried that the military not become too powerful a force in domestic affairs, while at the same time he recognized that some ideals were worth fighting for. He saw the United States as a divinely blessed land whose mission was to be a light and example to the rest of the world (Allen 1973). Clark believed that the United States would one day "bring, through the workings of our own example, the blessings of freedom and liberty to every people, without restraint or imposition or compulsion from us; a conquest that shall weld the whole earth together in one great brotherhood in a reign of mutual patience, forbearance, and charity, in a reign of peace to which we shall lead all others by the persuasion of our own righteous example" (Hillam 1983, 27).

Since the difficulty encountered with polygamy, LDS Church leaders have rarely come out against government policy, including policies regarding war. One example of this, republished several times in church magazines, is the story of Harold B. Lee who, while president of the church, was asked by a reporter from another country what the church's position was on the Vietnam War. In his retelling of the story, Robert E. Wells describes this as a "trap." "If the prophet answered, 'We are against the war,' the international media could state, 'How strange—a religious leader who is against the position of the country he is obliged to sustain in his own church's Articles of Faith.'" If President Lee answered that the church favored the war, Wells expected that the media would report, "'How strange—a religious leader in favor of war.' Either way, the answer could result in serious misunderstandings both inside and outside the Church" (1991, 85). Wells reports Lee as replying that the peace spoken of by Jesus Christ is a personal one that comes through living the commandments. World peace will come when the world's inhabitants individually change their behavior and seek to live more Christian lives.

The "trap" Lee avoided comes from the church's twelfth Article of Faith and its mandate to obey legal authorities. This is a relatively unusual feature of Mormonism, as many other religious groups have no similar mandate, and religious leaders such as Gandhi and Martin Luther King certainly advocated deliberate disobedience. Although some scholars suggest that world conflict is reduced when religions adhere to their ideals, rather than moderate them in order to meet the expectations of state leaders (for example, Appleby 1998), contemporary Mormonism deals with the issue by avoiding conflict with the prevailing government.

One fascinating recent example of this occurred when the Iraq War loomed on the horizon. Elder Russell M. Nelson of the Quorum of the Twelve Apostles stated in the October 2002 general conference, "Now, as members of The Church of Jesus Christ of Latter-day Saints, what does the Lord expect of us? As a Church, we must 'renounce war and proclaim peace.' As individuals, we should 'follow after the things which make for peace.' We should be personal peacemakers. We should ... expand our circle of love to embrace the whole human family" (41). The next day there was a "clarification" of Nelson's position in an editorial by the church-owned *Deseret News*. In the article, the church maintained that Nelson's remarks had been "misconstrued"; it was not the case that the church was speaking out against an attack. This sentiment was echoed by Senator Bob Bennett (R-UT), who told the rival *Salt Lake Tribune* that "Mormons have a duty to promote peace, but also to follow their nation's leaders" ("LDS Church" 2002, n.p.).

Of course, an individual's statement, even if made by someone with the status of elders Nelson or Clark or the church president at the time, carries less institutional weight than does an official statement issued by its officers. This makes the church's opposition to the MX missile system one of the most notable actions it has performed during the past several decades. Proposed by the Reagan administration in 1981 as a deterrent to a Soviet missile threat, the MX system would have a vast complex of silos store nuclear missiles that would rotate from silo to silo, under the premise that the sheer number of missiles and silos would be too many to completely eliminate in a first-strike attack. Initially, the LDS Church was silent on the proposal, but eventually it weighed in against the proposal. Its statement opposed the plan for reasons ranging from the damage caused by its construction to its continuation of the arms race itself ("News of the Church" 1981). The church's statement is widely thought to have been a significant factor in the proposal's defeat (Glass 1993).

As a contrast to the MX missile statement, consider the church's recent statement against a plan to store nuclear waste in Skull Valley, Utah (Church of Jesus Christ of Latter-day Saints 2006). The statement bore at least a superficial similarity to that issued some twenty-five years earlier, citing safety, public health, and environmental concerns, and asking the government to seek other options for the disposal of nuclear waste. Nevertheless, the latter statement was much briefer (three sentences versus thirteen paragraphs) and lacked the supporting rationale that characterized the MX missile statement. Although the Bureau of Land Management has not yet ruled on the proposal, a spokeswoman for Private Fuel Storage, which would benefit from the storage site, doubted that the statement would have an impact on the outcome (Fahys 2006). Without a developed rationale supporting moral objections to the plan, the statement reflects "not in my backyard" objections that generally carry little weight in social debates.

Although it is difficult to say with certainty the percentage of Mormons who support George W. Bush's policies regarding the war in Iraq, the supermajority of Utahns who are both LDS and Republican seem to indicate the general propensity of Mormons to support those policies. Unfortunately, in studies of Utahns it is difficult to separate the effects of the intermountain western culture from that of the LDS religion, and we do not have systematic data that would enable such an analysis. An alternative is to examine institutional and individual statements and behaviors, and glean from them what we can, following the approach taken by O'Dea. Doing this, we shall see conflicting ideals of peace and patriotism.

Religious Identity and War

The previous discussion has dealt with the church as an institution, but it is instructive also to consider these issues as they affect individual Latter-day Saints and their sense of self. By investigating people's allegiances and how they construct their identities, we gain some insight into religion's role in people's lives. This may be particularly true in cases involving direct violence, which heightens the need to protect one's identity and promotes violence toward members of outgroups (Druckman 2001; Niens and Cairns 2001). Similar observations may be made regarding such issues as race and gender roles, but because these issues are discussed elsewhere in this volume, we limit our focus to the military identity and war.

One of the most prominent ways that Mormons integrate their religious and military identities is in the area of missionary service. Observers draw favorable connections between the two, noting similarities ranging from the general purpose (service to others) to the importance of being fit for the task at hand. Although too much can be made of the analogy (Shepherd and Shepherd 1984), the finding that black military veterans serve in higher church lay leadership positions, on average, than do black nonveterans (Jacobson et al. 1994) speaks to the connection.

LDS views about war result from ideals regarding establishing peace and maintaining war, civic loyalty and responsible citizenship, respect for individuals' agency, and a belief in the divine destiny of the United States (Wood 1992). The LDS hymnbook, like many Christian hymnals, includes militaristic themes such as "We Are All Enlisted" and "The Battle Hymn of the Republic"; this extends to music for children (for example, "The Army of Helaman"). The importance of patriotism in one's identity is illustrated in stories Mormons tell about war. Elder A. Theodore Tuttle describes his role in helping deliver the flag that would fly over Mount Suribachi and made famous in the photo depicted in the U.S. Marine Corps Memorial in Arlington, Virginia. The role of religion in interpreting war experiences is illustrated by Kenneth Schubert's account of his final bomber flight over Europe. Using John 15:13, "Greater love hath no man than this, that a man lay down his life for his friends," he cites his appreciation for the pilot's sacrifice of flying their bomber to the end after ordering the rest of the crew off the failing aircraft. He thinks similarly of the family in Belgium who risked their lives by hiding him from the searching Gestapo during the following four months (Saints at War Archive n.d.).

One of the more articulate examples of favorable attitudes toward war was offered in a 1969 *BYU Studies* article (Smith 1969). After demonstrating that he is familiar with the horrors of war, Wilford E. Smith describes several positive functions that war plays in society. War maintains political order and clarifies a society's values, and it has the ability to "cleanse and unify a nation in the presence of hallowed sacrifice" (48). War can offer tangible benefits to the economy, and when soldiers marry women from the war's locale, it can break down barriers between groups of people. Finally, Smith argues, war also reminds people that certain values transcend life.

Religious identity often permeates the reminiscences of LDS soldiers, as illustrated by an eighteen-year-old navy recruit during World War II: "I reconciled myself to the possibility that someday I might have to pull the trigger of a gun aimed at someone.... I was never sure, however, that I could shoot if I knew the other guy was a Mormon. That's how strongly I felt about brotherhood in the gospel." Though taking some measure of comfort in the idea promoted by church authorities that combatants would not be held responsible for their actions while in the military, he "also remembered the story of the Ammonites in the Book of Mormon and still had pangs of conscience. My brooding has gone on ever since, and the more I study the history of any war or see Latter-day Saints involved on both sides of civil strife, the more I am convinced that much of what I was taught as a youth may have been too simplistic" (Allen 1990, 23). James B. Allen reconciles his religious ideals and his personal experience by concluding that his religion will not accomplish civil peace; instead, it will bring personal peace in the midst of conflict.

This theme is echoed in a study of Latter-day Saints in 1980s war-torn Ireland (Harris 1990). Despite the potential unifying force of a shared religion, friendships among Latter-day Saints that cross the line between Northern and Southern Ireland were the exception, and LDS values of patriotism caused Mormons to "stand out dangerously" (8). One elder's quorum president from Belfast said he and others "liked being beaten because it reinforced [our] view of [our]selves as persecuted" (12). On the other side of the struggle in Northern Ireland was an LDS prison guard who discounted claims that hunger strikers fasted in prison for more than a week. Yet after becoming a bishop, he stopped participating in beatings of the prisoners. The church seemed to provide a sense of stability in the midst of conflict, although it did not reconcile easily their sociopolitical and religious identities.

Questions of religious and national identity arise among Latter-day Saints on both sides of the battlefield. During World War II, for example, one LDS American describes being surprised to learn that his German opponents wore belt buckles that declared "God with us." "That kind of shook [me] a little," he explained. "God's with us, and he's with them, too?" (Roy, Skabelund, and Hillam 1990, 4). A soldier in the German Afrika Korps described a similar sentiment when thinking, before the war, that his experience with LDS missionaries and others made it difficult to consider them the enemy (125). His account suggests that religion can have a moderating effect, which is echoed in the disappointment an LDS reporter in Vietnam felt upon hearing that two fellow Latter-day Saints were involved in the senseless My Lai massacre (128).

It is during the Vietnam War that we find one of the more noteworthy illustrations of the tension between religious and national identities among Latter-day Saints, when a small group of Latter-day Saints collected a wide array of resources to assist LDS conscientious objectors in demonstrating their religious rationale for opposing war (Thomasson 1971). Gordon C. Thomasson's book consists of statements by the First Presidency on a variety of war-related issues and articles written by Latter-day Saints who saw conscientious objection as an honorable position to take. Despite the book's small circulation, it gave a voice to Latter-day Saints who objected to war. Indeed, at least one reviewer wondered aloud why the church itself was not promoting the book's contents widely, and suggested that the church may be too closely aligned with a political ideology that is contrary to a gospel of peace (Delogu 1971).

Individuals such as Thomasson may interpret the twelfth Article of Faith in such a way that they feel free to oppose war, but since its decision to abandon polygamy and assimilate into American life, the institutional church has rarely spoken out against U.S. movements toward war. The first occasion it did this was when the First Presidency opposed legislation that would mandate a military draft during World War II and wrote letters to Utah legislators against the draft (Quinn 1997). This opposition seemed most overtly to be a by-product of the isolationism favored by Clark and others at the time, but it might also have been influenced by concern over what it would do to the church's missionary effort, which relies on young men of draft age.

The second, more noteworthy, case involved the proposed MX missile system of the early 1980s. Because the LDS Church initially claimed that it was not a "moral issue" and therefore would not take a position on the matter, fellow churchgoers sometimes labeled Mormons who opposed the missile system "left-wing radicals." In the words of one opponent, "My conscience wouldn't let me do anything else, even though it might not do any good. I couldn't live with myself if I hadn't tried to stop it.... I owed it to my children to find out if there wasn't a better way to promote our national defense" (Glass 1993, 129). Ed Firmage, one of Utah's more high-profile opponents of the MX system, interpreted traditional LDS teachings in a way that used Mormonism as a vehicle to oppose the MX system. For him, an important part of his opposition was a sense of stewardship over the world and our collective responsibility to care for the land for later generations. Firmage and others saw their stewardship both as a duty and as part of their identity (Glass 1993).

Firmage continues to exemplify an atypical view in Mormonism. Motivated clearly by his belief that the world needs religion and the morality that it instills in people, Firmage argues that people who move from being oppressed to empowered often become oppressors. Consequently, religious people approve of weapons employing depleted uranium, with the result that "women give birth to stillborn monsters. Men die from water in wells a thousand years old. Children play in the sand, absorbing their death. Pregnant women with sandled feet, much like Jesus and Mary, walk through the desert sand and absorb radioactivity. The radiation will last until the middle of the next century" (2005, 256). From Firmage's perspective, structural violence has a pervasive effect on society, and religion must work to reduce such violence.

Another well-known figure in contemporary Mormonism, Eugene England (1984), believes that the Book of Mormon and other LDS scripture suggest that the best course of action in conflicts may be a pacifist one. His ideals have been echoed in other Mormon contexts by individuals (for example, Sherlock 2004), and help to motivate Mormons for Equity and Social Justice, a small grassroots organization, in their efforts to promote peace.[1]

These examples illustrate the fact that some Latter-day Saints, in their effort to live their religion, arrive at the conclusion that they must follow their conscience when it diverts from national—and church—directed norms. How common this is remains unknown; there are no data indicating the number of LDS draftees who sought conscientious-objector status during the Vietnam War, for example. But it is clearly a minority, and a relatively marginalized one at that, as illustrated by the fact that a search for the phrase *conscientious objector* in LDS Church publications revealed only one use of the phrase, in a woman's reminiscence of mission life during World War II, published in the *Ensign* (Bradbury 1993).

More common are the messages conveyed in *Let Your Heart Not Be Troubled* (2005), a video recently produced by the church for LDS soldiers involved in Iraq and Afghanistan. Elder Boyd K. Packer describes his military service as having prepared him for leadership positions in the church and as having been instrumental in opening countries to missionary work. Elder Robert C. Oaks sees the war in Iraq as a fight for freedom, which makes it worth fighting. More broadly, he invokes identification of religious and military images, stating that "no matter what war we are a part of, it is important to know that we are on the Lord's side." More explicit still is Elder Lance B. Wickman's observation that Mormon and Moroni were soldiers and that it is a soldier who stands atop the spire of LDS temples. Wickman also invokes the missionary spirit, stating that because of the Iraq War, "for the first time since ancient times men holding the priesthood set foot in that land of the Tigris and the Euphrates, the cradle of civilization." After President Hinckley also reminds viewers of the role LDS servicemen have played in overseas missionary work, the video ends with an emotional musical number by the BYU Men's Chorus accompanying pastoral images of home life. Military service in war is portrayed as a key component of a faithful LDS identity, as a way to reinforce religious values of freedom and home life, and even as a vehicle for spreading the gospel message.

Seeing religion as a vehicle for peace is a classic role that religion plays in individuals' lives (Pargament 1997), and often takes the form illustrated by the soldier who said, "Your faith in God helped soften your fear of death" (Roy, Skabelund, and Hillam 1990, 130). At other times, however, it eases the guilt that might accompany the knowledge that one has killed, as suggested by another soldier's words: "With the knowledge I had that death is no more than walking through another door, the whole idea of death didn't really mean a lot because in reality there was no death. People were just being sent off to other places.... We all go on to the Great Judge and to our reward, whatever that might be. It will all come out in the end, and whether this individual went on to his reward or I did, we all continue to live, so all I did was send this guy on vacation" (126–27).

CONCLUSION

In a thorough analysis of LDS thought and doctrine regarding war, Steven A. Hildreth (1984) concludes that the church's history is characterized by a firm and consistent renunciation of war. When Germany invaded Poland in 1939, the First Presidency sent letters to the Senate Foreign Relations Committee and to the State Department advocating that the United States engage in peaceful negotiations to end the war. In 1940, with LDS Church members on both sides of the battlefield, the First Presidency stated that its members should support their respective governments while they prayed for peace. "The Mormon Church, despite popular belief to the contrary, *is not* 'hawkish.' Not once during its one hundred and fifty-year history has the Church supported a war as 'just'" (240).

In the MX missile case, Hildreth concludes, moral concern for humanity motivated LDS Church opposition, and not parochial self-interest. This continued a long-standing, principled stance. For example, in 1945 when 70 percent or more of Americans favored a mandatory term of one-year military service, the First Presidency opposed it, stating that the increase in militarization would stimulate increased militarization in other countries, burden the citizenry with taxes, and encourage fighting rather than prevent it (243). Indeed, Hildreth presents a strong case that the church has consistently opposed war and spoken out frequently against it. Could the same be true today, some two decades following Hildreth's analysis and five decades following O'Dea's? Perhaps, but the evidence is not clear-cut. Instead, it seems as though the balance has shifted over the past generation or two between the desire to be good citizens, on the one hand, and opposition to war, on the other.

Is there a change in the frequency with which leaders have spoken against war? Or is there perhaps an increase in the need to be good citizens of whatever country one resides in? Systematic data on this question are few, but they do exist. Shepherd and Shepherd's analysis (1984) of general conference themes shows a decline in the frequency with which the threat of war is mentioned, and a simultaneous increased emphasis on the responsibilities of citizenship. This pattern is also consistent with the observation that it was during World War II that church leaders began speaking of "Zion" residing in one's heart, and not as a literal gathering place in Utah with the main concentration of church members (Embry 1993). This is one notable effect of the church's position that members support their government.

Another possibility is that there is now and always has been a distinction between the perspective of general church authorities on such matters and that of average members. Given their different positions in the organizational hierarchy, differences in attitudes might be expected, as one's position in an organization affects one's perception of issues relevant to that organization. Still, this does not account for the fact that a symposium of LDS experts employed in the defense industry disagreed over such basic questions as how we might best define what a good state does and whether U.S. intervention in conflicts is justified (Hudson and Kartchner 1995).

Recent data indicate that 73 percent of Mormons in Utah support the current war in Iraq, whereas 62 percent of non-Mormons oppose it (LaPlante 2006). Although the chair of BYU's Department of Church History and Doctrine is quoted as saying, "I am quite sure that President Hinckley would feel fine about LDS people entertaining variant persuasions on the war," Matthew D. LaPlante also quotes the authors of *Saints at War* (Freeman and Wright 2001), who speculate that Mormon support for the war might result from their desire to be accepted as legitimate U.S. citizens, a suggestion that recalls Armand L. Mauss's thesis (1994).

Although the LDS Church leadership stated that members should be good citizens regardless of where they live, they clearly supported the Allies over the Axis forces during World War II. The church purchased more than seventeen million dollars in war bonds to support the war effort (Embry 1993, citing R. Walker 1982). In effect, the church's neutrality was superficial; it viewed the U.S. Constitution as an inspired document, and believed that the country had a special role in God's eyes. One wonders how long, as the church becomes increasingly international, and as noncombatants bear the brunt of war's casualties, such a pattern may continue. If it became clear that the United States was an aggressor in an unjust war, would the message that Latter-day Saints be good soldiers for their country continue to be preached? In such a situation, which of its professed values—peace versus loyal citizenship—would the church embrace most strongly? The tensions O'Dea noted between individual agency and organizational control remain a part of the Mormon experience, and are likely to remain until LDS political philosophy more successfully addresses these issues.

NOTE

1. See the group's Web site, http://www.mesj.org.

REFERENCES

Allen, James B. 1973. "J. Reuben Clark, Jr.: Views on American Sovereignty and
    International Organization." *BYU Studies* 13, no. 3: 347–72.

———. 1990. "When Our Enemies Are Also Saints." *BYU Studies* 30, no. 4: 20–26.

Appleby, R. Scott. 1998. "Religion and Global Affairs: Religious 'Militants for Peace.'" *SAIS
    Review of International Affairs* 18, no. 2: 38–44.

Ballard, M. Russell. 1994. "Counseling with Our Councils." *Ensign,* May, 24–26.

Barash, David P., and Charles P. Webel. 2002. *Peace and Conflict Studies.* Thousand Oaks,
    Calif.: Sage.

Benson, Ezra T. 1962. *The Red Carpet.* Salt Lake City: Bookcraft.

———. 1969. *An Enemy Hath Done This.* Salt Lake City: Parliament Publishers.

Bernick, Bob, Jr. 2007. "Utah Still the Reddest Red, Poll Finds." *Deseret Morning News.*
    http://www.deseretnews.com/dn/views/0,1249,650220729,00.html.

Bradbury, Lucy R. 1993. "No Money, No Books, Nothing." *Ensign,* October, 43.

Campbell, Eugene E., and Richard D. Poll. 1975. *Hugh B. Brown: His Life and Thought.* Salt
    Lake City: Bookcraft.

Canham, Matt. 2005. "Rise and Fall: Mormon Majority Is Slipping Away." *Salt Lake
    Tribune,* July 24, A10.

Church of Jesus Christ of Latter-day Saints. 2006. "Church Urges Alternatives for Nuclear
    Waste." Press statement, May 4. http://www.lds.org/newsroom/showre-
    lease/0,15503,3881-1-23335,00.html.

Cowan, Richard O. 2006. "Missionary Training Centers." http://www.lightplanet.com/
    mormons/daily/missionary/MTC_EOM.htm.

Delogu, Orlando E. 1971. "In Good Conscience: Mormonism and Conscientious
    Objection." *Dialogue: A Journal of Mormon Thought* 6, no. 1: 69–71.

Druckman, Daniel. 2001. "Nationalism and War: A Social-Psychological Perspective." In
    Peace, Conflict, and Violence, ed. Daniel J. Christie, Richard V. Wagner, and Deborah
    DuNann Winter, 49–65. Upper Saddle River, N.J.: Prentice-Hall.

Embry, Jessie L. 1993. "'The Good War': RLDS and LDS Americans' Responses to World
    War II." *John Whitmer Historical Association Journal* 13: 51–64.

England, Eugene. 1984. "Can Nations Love Their Enemies? An LDS Theology of Peace." In
    Dialogues with Myself: Personal Essays on Mormon Experience, 135–52. Salt Lake City:
    Signature Books.

Fahys, Judy. 2006. "LDS Joins N-storage Foes." *Salt Lake Tribune,* May 5. http://www.sltrib.
    com.

Faust, James E. 1996. "The Prophetic Voice." *Ensign,* May, 4–5.

Firmage, Edwin B. 2005. "Why Did the Watchdogs Never Bark?" In *God and Country: Politics in Utah,* ed. Jeffrey E. Sells, 245–66. Salt Lake City: Signature Books.

Freeman, Robert C., and Dennis A. Wright. 2001. *Saints at War.* Salt Lake City: Covenant Communications.

Galbraith, David B. 2007. "BYU Jerusalem Center." http://www.lightplanet.com/mormons/daily/education/BYU_JC_EOM.htm.

Glass, Matthew. 1993. *Citizens against the MX: Public Language in the Nuclear Age.* Urbana: University of Illinois Press.

Harris, Claudia W. 1990. "Mormons on the Warfront: The Protestant Mormons and Catholic Mormons of Northern Ireland." *BYU Studies* 30, no. 4: 7–19.

Heaton, Tim B., Stephen J. Bahr, and Cardell K. Jacobson. 2004. *A Statistical Profile of Mormons: Health, Wealth, and Social Life.* Lewiston, N.Y.: Edwin Mellen Press.

Hickman, Martin B. 1987. *David Matthew Kennedy: Banker, Statesman, Churchman.* Salt Lake City: Deseret Book.

Hildreth, Steven A. 1984. "Mormon Concern over MX: Parochialism or Enduring Moral Theology?" *Journal of Church and State* 26 (Spring): 227–53.

Hillam, Ray C. 1975. "The Gadianton Robbers and Protracted War." *BYU Studies* 15, no. 2: 215–24.

———, ed. 1983. *J. Reuben Clark and International Relations.* Provo: Brigham Young University Press.

Hinckley, Gordon B. 2001. "The Perpetual Education Fund." *Ensign,* May, 51–53.

Hudson, Valerie M., and Kerry M. Kartchner, eds. 1995. *Moral Perspective on U.S. Security Policy: Views from the LDS Community.* Provo: Brigham Young University Press.

Jacobson, Cardell K., Tim B. Heaton, E. Dale LeBaron, and Trina Louise Hope. 1994. "Black Mormon Converts in the United States and Africa: Social Characteristics and Perceived Acceptance." In *Contemporary Mormonism: Social Science Perspectives,* ed. Marie Cornwall, Tim B. Heaton, and Lawrence A. Young, 326–47. Urbana: University of Illinois Press.

Jensen, Richard L. n.d. *Immigration to Utah.* http://www.media.utah.edu/UHE/i/IMMIGRATION.html.

Jones, Garth N. 2005. "The Making of Grave Community Sin." *Dialogue: A Journal of Mormon Thought* 38, no. 2: 105–8.

LaPlante, Matthew D. 2006. "Utahns and the War: A Religious Divide." *Salt Lake Tribune,* January 30, A1.

"LDS Church Torn on Decision to Fight Iraq." 2002. *Daily Utah Chronicle,* October 11. http://media.www.dailyutahchronicle.com/media/storage/paper244/news/2002/10/11/WorldReport/Lds-Church.Torn.On.Decision.To.Fight.Iraq-295430.shtml?sourcedomain=www.dailyutahchronicle.com&MIIHost=media.collegepublisher.com.

Leip, Dave. 2006. "Dave Leip's Atlas of U.S. Presidential Elections." http://www.uselectionatlas.org/RESULTS/.

Let Your Heart Not Be Troubled: A Message of Peace for Latter-day Saints in Military Service.
    2005. DVD. Salt Lake City: Intellectual Reserve.

Mauss, Armand L. 1994. *The Angel and the Beehive: The Mormon Struggle with Assimilation.*
    Urbana: University of Illinois Press.

McKay, David O. 1914. "Conference Report," p. 88. *New Mormon Studies CD-ROM.* Salt
    Lake City: Smith Research Associates, 1998.

———. 1944. "Conference Report," p. 82. *New Mormon Studies CD-ROM.* Salt Lake City:
    Smith Research Associates, 1998.

Moore, Carrie A. 2005. "Religions Decry Use of Torture: Utah Leaders Sign Petition; LDS
    Issue Own Statement." *Deseret News,* November 24. http://www.deseretnews.com/dn/
    view/9,1249,635163735,00.html.

Nelson, Russell M. 2002. "Blessed Are the Peacemakers." *Ensign,* November, 39–41.

"News of the Church." 1981. *Ensign,* June, 76.

Nibley, Hugh. 1971. "If There Must Needs Be Offense." *Ensign,* July, 53.

———. 1989. *Approaching Zion.* Salt Lake City: Deseret Book.

Niens, Ulrich, and Ed Cairns. 2001. "Intrastate Violence." In *Peace, Conflict, and Violence,*
    ed. Daniel J. Christie, Richard V. Wagner, and Deborah DuNann Winter, 39–48.
    Upper Saddle River, N.J.: Prentice-Hall.

Oaks, Robert C. 2005. "Latter-day Saints and Military Service." In *Let Your Heart Not Be
    Troubled: A Message of Peace for Latter-day Saints in Military Service.* DVD. Salt Lake
    City: Intellectual Reserve.

O'Dea, Thomas F. 1957. *The Mormons.* Chicago: University of Chicago Press.

Packer, Boyd K. 1971. "Our Honored Brethren." *New Era,* August, 9.

———. 2005. Introduction to *Let Your Heart Not Be Troubled: A Message of Peace for Latter-
    day Saints in Military Service.* DVD. Salt Lake City: Intellectual Reserve.

Pargament, Kenneth I. 1997. *The Psychology of Religious Coping.* New York: Guilford.

Prince, Gregory A., and William Robert Wright. 2005. *David O. McKay and the Rise of
    Modern Mormonism.* Salt Lake City: University of Utah Press.

Quinn, D. Michael. 1997. *The Mormon Hierarchy: Extensions of Power.* Salt Lake City:
    Signature Books.

Raymond, Alan, and Susan Raymond. 1999. *Children in War.* Film, Home Box Office.

Roy, Denny, Grant P. Skabelund, and Ray C. Hillam. 1990. *A Time to Kill: Reflections on
    War.* Salt Lake City: Signature Books.

Saints at War Archive. n.d. http://www.saintsatwar.org.

Shepherd, Gordon, and Gary Shepherd. 1984. *A Kingdom Transformed: Themes in the
    Development of Mormonism.* Salt Lake City: University of Utah Press.

———. 1994. "Sustaining a Lay Religion in Modern Society: The Mormon Missionary
    Experience." In *Contemporary Mormonism: Social Science Perspectives,* ed. Marie
    Cornwall, Tim B. Heaton, and Lawrence A. Young, 161–81. Urbana: University of
    Illinois Press.

Sherlock, Richard. 2004. "Rooted in Christian Hope: The Case for Pacifism." *Dialogue: A Journal of Mormon Thought* 37, no. 1: 95–108.

Smith, Wilford E. 1969. "Some Positive Functions of War." *BYU Studies* 10, no. 1: 43–56.

Thomasson, Gordon C., ed. 1971. *War, Conscription, Conscience, and Mormonism.* Santa Barbara: Mormon Heritage.

Walker, Bradley. 2002. "Spreading Zion Southward, Part I: Improving Efficiency and Equity in the Allocation of Church Welfare Resources." *Dialogue: A Journal of Mormon Thought* 35, no. 4: 91–110.

———. 2003a. "First, Mothers and Children: A Postscript to 'Spreading Zion Southward, Parts I and II.'" *Dialogue: A Journal of Mormon Thought* 36, no. 2: 217–24.

———. 2003b. "Spreading Zion Southward, Part II: Sharing Loaves and Fishes." *Dialogue: A Journal of Mormon Thought* 36, no. 1: 33–47.

Walker, Ronald W. 1982. "Sheaves, Bucklers, and the State: Mormon Leaders Respond to the Dilemmas of War." *Sunstone* 7, no. 4: 43–56.

"Welcome to the David M. Kennedy Center for International Studies." 2006. http://www.kennedy.byu.edu/aboutus/welcome.php.

Wells, Robert E. 1991. "Peace." *Ensign,* May, 85.

Wickman, Lance B. 2005. "Like unto Moroni." *Let Your Heart Not Be Troubled: A Message of Peace for Latter-day Saints in Military Service.* DVD. Salt Lake City: Intellectual Reserve.

Winter, Deborah DuNann, Daniel J. Christie, Richard V. Wagner, and L. B. Boston. 2001. "Conclusion: Peace Psychology for the Twenty-first Century." In *Peace, Conflict, and Violence,* ed. Daniel J. Christie, Richard V. Wagner, and Deborah DuNann Winter, 363–71. Upper Saddle River, N.J.: Prentice-Hall.

Wood, Robert S. 1992. "War and Peace." In *Encyclopedia of Mormonism.* 4 vols., ed. Daniel H. Ludlow, 1547–50. New York: Macmillan.

Wood, Robert S., and Stan A. Taylor. 1973. "J. Reuben Clark, Jr., and the American Approach to Foreign Policy." *BYU Studies* 13, no. 3: 441–52.

Preserving Peculiarity as a People

*Mormon Distinctness in Lived Values
and Internal Structure*

~ LOREN MARKS AND BRENT D. BEAL ~

ONE DOES NOT EVEN NEED TO OPEN the paperback version of *The Mormons* to receive Thomas F. O'Dea's (1957) initial thesis. An illustration of the Nauvoo Temple in an arsonist's flames, with scenes of mob violence literally etched in the background, vividly conveys that this faith is a force that evokes a wide range of passionate response, ranging from mobocracy to martyrdom. From its inception in 1830, the peculiar Mormon faith has frequently clashed with its environment. Sociologist John C. Jarvis notes, "The entire [Mormon] community pulled up stakes and relocated farther west *seven* times in its first fourteen years ... [due to] the high tensions that the close-knit Mormon community developed with its [non-Mormon] neighbors in New York, Ohio, Missouri, and Illinois" (2000, 246).

For those who embraced Mormonism, it was viewed as no less than the Church and Kingdom of Christ restored to the earth in purity and power (Bushman 1985). For many who opposed it, it was a danger that seemed to arouse not only profound hatred but also violent action, including mob violence, arson, pillaging, and eventually a state-sanctioned Extermination Order by Governor Boggs of Missouri (Roberts 1930; Young 1994). However, our purpose in this chapter is not to recount nineteenth-century Mormon history but to examine the quite different yet ongoing struggle of American Mormons with their environment over the past fifty years since O'Dea's work was published.

O'DEA'S FASCINATION WITH MORMON PECULIARITY

O'Dea's *The Mormons* is comprised of nine broadly themed chapters and a brief epilogue. Of the thirty-one specific topics O'Dea selectively addresses in these chapters, most are surveyed in a few pages or less. There are two topics, however, that receive considerable attention. The topic O'Dea chooses to address at greatest length is treated in the section "The Mormons Become a 'Peculiar People'" (1957, 53–75). A later section of seventeen pages is called "The Mormon Encounter with Secular Thought." If the reader will pardon the tedium of the above details, the significant point here is that O'Dea seems particularly fascinated by the contrast between Mormons and those around them. In the first section referenced above, O'Dea describes how this contrast was initially created and sharpened. In the second section, he addresses the challenges of Mormons' intellectual reentry into the dominant American culture, a culture that their early prophets (particularly Brigham Young) forcefully eschewed (Roberts 1930). Not only is this juxtaposition of Mormons and the United States the focus of the book's two longest sections, but the contrast is also a recurring theme throughout the volume. In sum, *The Mormons* is not only a scholarly report that combines "intellectual objectivity and intelligent human sympathy" (O'Dea 1957, vii) but also a narrative that clearly (if unintentionally) reflects O'Dea's fascination with the peculiarities of a peculiar people. We now turn to a discussion of the issues of peculiarity, tension, and identity that seem to fascinate O'Dea in connection with the Mormons.

PECULIARITY, TENSION, AND IDENTITY: THE MORMON CASE

O'Dea, by his own report (vii), had seen much of the world before embarking on *The Mormons* study. As a key player in the Harvard Comparative Study of Values in Five Cultures, he likely had considerable say on what group he would examine. *Why the Mormons?* A partial answer may lie in the fact that social scientists in general and sociologists in particular have historically been intrigued by deviants or groups that fall well outside the norm. Further, social scientists tend to engage in the related search for conceptual boundaries that may be used to categorize or study those who fit within or outside these boundaries. The Mormons, at least in the 1950s, still held some exotic appeal as U.S. outsiders.[1]

An additional response to the "why study the Mormons" question may lie in the fact that O'Dea identified the Church of Jesus Christ of Latter-day Saints (LDS) as an anomaly in that it seemed to challenge the classical "sect-to-church" wisdom of the time (see Niebuhr 1929; and Troeltsch 1931). Summarily, this view posited that new religious groups typically tended to move unidirectionally from states of high tension with dominant culture and society to assimilated, compromised, low-tension positions as a price for acceptance (Mauss 1994a; Stark and Bainbridge 1985). A critical reason the Mormons were of interest to O'Dea and others was not simply that they were peculiar, but that they were somewhat anomalous in their manifested ability to *remain* peculiar across time, by (selectively) countering the pull toward assimilation with dominant American culture.

As the Mormons learned throughout their first seventy years as a faith, dominant cultures are not only reluctant to accept but are also prone to actively (even violently) reject groups that are *too* peculiar (Bushman 1985, 2005; Shipps 1994). However, in efforts to become socially acceptable enough to be tolerated, high-tension faiths risk becoming enough like others that they lose a vital characteristic—their unique identity. As Laurence R. Iannaccone and Carrie A. Miles note, "A certain amount of tension with secular society is essential to success—the trick is finding, and maintaining, the right amount" (1994, 283).

The Mormons' perennial peculiarity was likely a force that drew O'Dea from Boston to Utah in 1950. However, has the hallmark peculiarity been retained since that time … or have the Mormons become "not so much a peculiar people [but] a rather common people characterized by a peculiar history?" (Albrecht 1998, 254; see also Vaisey and Heaton 2005). In the balance of this chapter, we will examine how the Mormons have maintained peculiarity in connection with two "important spheres of Mormon distinctness" identified by O'Dea: distinctness in *lived values* and distinctness of the *internal structure* of the Mormon organization (1957, 112).[2] We will further see that these two spheres are closely related. Specific illustrations of each sphere of distinctness will be offered to ground the conceptual in concrete examples. Lived values will be discussed first.

MORMON DISTINCTNESS IN LIVED VALUES

From the potential list of distinct values held by the Mormons, two examples attract our consideration in this chapter due to their high visibility to outsiders and salience to insiders (Dollahite and Marks 2006). First, we turn our attention to the unique Mormon health code known as the Word of Wisdom. This will be followed by a discussion of sexual values and practices, in connection with what Mormons refer to as the Law of Chastity. Before addressing the Word of Wisdom and the Law of Chastity, a critical theological point that links these two ideals needs attention.

LDS theology is strikingly unique (some might say heretical) in teaching that God "the Father has a body of flesh and bones as tangible as man's" (Doctrine and Covenants 130:22). Douglas James Davies emphasizes the pragmatic impact of this doctrine: "Mormonism established the human body as the key religious and ritual focus of life in a much more accentuated way than any other western form of Christianity.… The body is then the site of opportunity for action in the Word of Wisdom and in ethical and sexual control.... The narrower focus on sexual control and [dietary] rules tends to ensure that bodily appetites, as such, serve as perpetual reminders of the need to obey divine rules to be a worthy Saint" (2000, 122, 143). The physical body is viewed not as vile or base but as the sacred and eternal temple of an individual's spirit. The LDS Church expends no small effort in exhorting its members to keep their temples clean through obedience to the two standards discussed next.

The Word of Wisdom

O'Dea offers a concise but accurate view of both the prescriptions (fruits, vegetables, grains, and sparing use of meats) and proscriptions (alcohol, tobacco, coffee, and tea) outlined in the Word of Wisdom (Doctrine and Covenants 89). However, he also captures a significant point that is often overlooked regarding the basis of this counsel, namely, that in Mormon doctrine the physical and spiritual are one (1957, 144).

In connection with the Mormon prohibition of tobacco, it must be remembered that O'Dea was writing in the 1950s when cigarettes were widely held as a harmless pleasure and smoking was normative—more than 50 percent of American men were smoking as late as 1965 (National Center for Health Statistics 2005). Hence, the Word of Wisdom was likely viewed by some as the pinnacle of teetotalism—a health code strict and bizarre enough to prompt O'Dea's comment that obeying "the Word of Wisdom appears to have replaced plural marriage as the [Mormon] badge of Zion" (146). O'Dea further emphasizes that "much effort is expended by the church to show the harmful effects of liquor and tobacco" (145)—although the first surgeon general's report on smoking was not issued until 1964, so scientific evidence supporting the Word of Wisdom was scarce at the time (National Center for Health Statistics 2005).

Fifty years later, there are several studies that shed light on the potential health benefits of the Word of Wisdom. These include the findings of Steven R. Simmerman (1993) and James E. Enstrom (1998a) of substantially (up to 50 percent) lower cancer rates among practicing Mormons, and the finding by Enstrom (1998b) that highly involved Mormons live an average of eight to eleven years longer than the general population. Before Mormons assume a triumphal stance relative to the Word of Wisdom, however, it is noteworthy that shortly after Enstrom made his Mormon longevity-related discovery, another study by Robert A. Hummer and colleagues (1999) with a nationally representative sample of more than twenty-one thousand from a *variety of faiths* indicated a 7.6-year longevity advantage (13.7 years for

African Americans [see Marks et al. 2005]) among those who attend worship services more than once a week, compared with the longevity of nonattenders. In short, longevity appears to be not so much a Mormon anomaly as it is a correlate of high involvement in any faith community (Koenig, McCollough, and Larson 2001; Marks 2005, 2006).

Since O'Dea's book, the smoking trends in the United States have moved markedly in the direction of Mormon-advocated abstinence. The percentage of Americans who smoke roughly halved between 1965 and 2003 (National Center for Health Statistics 2005).[3] However, other developments during the fifty-year interim such as the popularization of certain illicit drugs (especially marijuana) and the current coffeehouse boom have ensured that the Word of Wisdom—although not the exclusive key to Mormon longevity—remains a "badge of Zion" that may mark Mormons as a peculiar people, as keeping kosher distinguishes practicing Jews (Dollahite 2007).

It would be valuable to compare and contrast the LDS Word of Wisdom and its related outcomes with other faiths that have similar health codes (such as the Christian Scientists, Jehovah's Witnesses, and Seventh-Day Adventists). Unfortunately, based on Harold G. Koenig, Michael E. McCollough, and David B. Larson's comprehensive *Handbook of Religion and Health* (2001), empirical studies focusing on Christian Scientists and Jehovah's Witnesses are rare. Although many studies have examined Seventh-Day Adventist health, comparisons are almost uniformly with the general population, not with Mormons. On a conceptual level, however, it is interesting to note that William S. Bainbridge listed the three faiths mentioned above along with Mormonism as the four "really successful distinctly novel American movements [that] remain Christian" (1997, 411). It is probable that for these other three religions, strict health codes serve as badges of identity and strengthen the respective faiths' "boundaries of truth" as they seem to do in the LDS Church (Davies 2000, 242).

The Word of Wisdom: Do Mormons Live It?

In connection with the Word of Wisdom, we now turn to the pragmatic question: "But do the Mormons *live* it?" As we turn to data to respond to this and subsequent questions, we note that reliable data on American Mormons living outside of Utah are limited, whereas data regarding Mormons outside the U.S. borders are almost nonexistent (Bahr and Forste 1998). Even so, sufficient data are available to sketch partial responses.

Among adolescents, several studies employing a variety of surveys and measures indicate that LDS youth as a composite group (including never

and rarely attending youth) use alcohol, tobacco, and illicit drugs less frequently than their non-LDS peers (Amoateng and Bahr 1986; Hawks 1989;
Heaton, Bahr, and Jacobson 2004; Johnston, Bachman, and O'Malley 1993;
Lorch and Hughes 1985). However, when "active," practicing LDS youth
are considered separately (for example, Bahr 1994), or when the sampling
approach favors actively involved, church-attending youth (for instance,
Chadwick and Top 1998; Top and Chadwick 1998), the LDS rates of alcohol, tobacco, and drug use drop to 25–33 percent of the national average.

When considering LDS young adults' and adults' alcohol, tobacco, and
illicit drug use, strong differences remain between LDS and non-LDS samples (Mauss 1994a; Merrill, Folsom, and Christopherson 2005). However, as
with research on LDS youth, when researchers focus on "active," religiously
involved LDS adults, differences are exacerbated (Barry and Nelson 2005;
Enstrom 1998a, 1998b).

It is lamentable that most studies in this area have failed to consider
levels of involvement and activity in the LDS faith in addition to reported
affiliation because, as several scholars have noted, relying on religious self-
identification without also assessing significant variation in commitment
yields less precise data (Carroll et al. 2000; Heaton, Goodman, and Holman
1994; Marks 2004). The effort by some scholars to make active versus inactive distinctions among Mormons enhances our understanding significantly.
A key conclusion in this area drawn by Stephen Bahr is that "the difference
between active and inactive individuals is considerably greater among Mormons than ... in other religions. Being an active Mormon makes more difference in deterring drug use than being active in any other religious groups
does" (1994, 131).

As we return to the core question of whether post-O'Dea Mormons are
peculiar in terms of actually *living* the proscriptive elements of their Word
of Wisdom, we must offer a tripartite answer. If we consider inactive (nominal but nonattending) Mormons as a group, there is little to distinguish
them from the American mainstream. In fact, Tim B. Heaton, Stephen J.
Bahr, and Cardell K. Jacobson (2004), using data from the *Monitoring the
Future* survey, found that "rarely or never" attending LDS youth use cigarettes, marijuana, and illicit drugs at rates *higher* than the U.S. norms for
non-LDS youth. By way of contrast, if all self-identifying Mormons (from
active to inactive) are lumped together, we begin to see differences in terms
of alcohol, tobacco, and drug use, although many of these differences are
moderate. However, when researchers—whether studying youth or adults—
refine their focus to *active,* attending Latter-day Saints, truly striking differences emerge, including years of longevity, much lower cancer rates, and

harmful substance-usage rates that are a fraction of national averages (Bahr 1994; Barry and Nelson 2005; Enstrom 1998a, 1998b). Such differences might well be labeled distinctive and peculiar.

In sum, for active Latter-day Saints, the Word of Wisdom seemingly remains "a badge of Zion" (O'Dea 1957, 146). In some ways, however, the Word of Wisdom may now be a secondary badge of identification, compared to the next distinct value we will discuss: the Law of Chastity.

The Law of Chastity

LDS scripture explains the Law of Chastity as follows: "Thou shalt love thy wife with all thy heart, and shalt cleave unto her and none else. And he that looketh upon a woman to lust after her shall deny the faith, and shall not have the Spirit; and if he repents not he shall be cast out" (Doctrine and Covenants 42:22–23). In practice, this is interpreted to mean that sexual relations of any kind are forbidden outside of traditional marriage (Holland 1998).

To offer context for the Law of Chastity from 1957 to the present, we can turn to Heaton, Bahr, and Jacobson's reflection that "perhaps no cultural change has had a greater impact on...family behavior than has the sexual revolution" (2004, 87). It is noteworthy that O'Dea's *The Mormons* antedated the sexual revolution, the widespread introduction of the birth control pill, and *Roe v. Wade*. In fact, *sex* does not even appear in the book's index, nor do the terms *cohabitation, homosexuality, nonmarital births,* or *abortion*. In this respect, O'Dea's social context preceding the Age of Aquarius may have resembled the Victorian era more than twenty-first-century America, at least in terms of sexual norms. Indeed, other than citing the Mormon belief that sex and marriage are eternal principles and that "improper relationships of the sexes aside from marriage vow [are] censured and punished" by the church (1957, 140–41), O'Dea rarely broaches sexual topics. A key point is that although the Mormon doctrine called the Law of Chastity may be peculiar in contemporary America, it may not have differed sharply from the U.S. cultural mores of the 1950s. Indeed, as late as 1967, 85 percent of Americans condemned premarital sex as morally wrong, although a little more than a decade later the disapproval percentage had dissipated to 39 percent (Yankelovich 1981).

A brief comparison of the 1950s with today indicates some other dramatic shifts in U.S. sexual attitudes and practices. For example, in spite of the current widespread availability of birth control, the nonmarital birthrate was well over 30 percent in the 1990s (compared with 5 percent in 1960); and the plus–30 percent figure for the 1990s does not capture the accompanying escalation of abortions between the 1950s and the present (Popenoe 1996).

Moving from a cultural to religious vantage on sex, it is important to note that most faiths espouse some variation of the Law of Chastity—historically, this is not a unique or Mormon doctrine (see H. Smith 1991). However, in post–sexual revolution America where personal freedom and the right to privacy are supreme values, this ideal of chastity has been partially to severely muted as the tension between the traditional sacred ideal and contemporary secular norm has steadily increased. The Mormons claim to hold precisely the same view on chastity that they did in 1957, complete with frequent statements from church leaders that reinforce the idea that the new morality is nothing more than old-fashioned immorality (Hinckley 2000). Additionally, recent national data indicate that 84 percent of Mormon teens report that their congregation has done a "fairly good" or "excellent" job in helping them understand sex, 17 percent more than any other denomination (Smith and Denton 2005). Based on these data, it would seem that on the whole, the LDS Church is not avoiding the topic of sex (with the accompanying doctrine of abstinence). As we did with the Word of Wisdom, let us move to an investigation of empirical data to answer the question, "Are the Mormons truly a peculiar people in terms of lived values when it comes to sexual *practice?*"

The Law of Chastity: Do Mormons Live It?

Data collected in the late 1980s and early 1990s from American high school seniors indicated that 73 percent of males and 56 percent of females reported having had sexual intercourse (Benson 1990), compared with 10 percent of LDS male high school seniors (one-seventh of the U.S. rate for non-LDS males) and about 16 percent of LDS females (two-sevenths of the U.S. rate for non-LDS females) (Top and Chadwick 1998). However, the Top and Chadwick data were based on samples that favored active LDS youth. Recent NELS and AddHealth survey data (which include a fuller range of activity levels in the LDS Church) offer a much different picture. Both national surveys indicate that 75–80 percent of American youth have premarital sex before age twenty (Heaton, Bahr, and Jacobson 2004). The corresponding rates for premarital sexual experience among LDS youth range from 48 percent on the low end to 60–64 percent on the high end. Although these most recent figures are still well below the national average, they are remarkably higher than those from a decade ago, even accounting for differences in sampling. Based on these data, LDS youth appear to be different but not truly peculiar.

As we shift focus from adolescence to young adulthood, non-LDS versus LDS differences remain. Namely, the percentage of Mormon women and men who have cohabited is roughly half that of non-Mormons (Heaton, Goodman, and Holman 1994; see also Stark 1998). Group differences between Mormons and non-Mormons increase, however, when "active" Mormons are considered as a distinct group. Jason S. Carroll and colleagues, for example, found that highly religious LDS emerging adults (ages eighteen to twenty-five) are significantly less likely to approve of and engage in premarital sex than comparison groups, including highly religious Catholic and Protestant peers (2000, 198, 202). Larry J. Nelson (2003) similarly found in a study with an LDS (Brigham Young University) sample that only 5 percent reported that they had ever had sexual intercourse, a remarkably low figure compared to the 85 percent report of one college sample (Bogaert and Fisher 1995).

In 1957, O'Dea posited that obedience to the Word of Wisdom had replaced polygamy as the leading "badge of Zion." Almost forty years later, Tim B. Heaton, Kristen L. Goodman, and Thomas B. Holman examined National Survey of Families and Households data on a wide array of sexual values and behavior and concluded that *"findings on sexuality differentiate Mormons from non-Mormons more than any other set of variables"* (1994, 100; emphasis added). At the time of this report, sexual abstinence outside of traditional marriage may have replaced the Word of Wisdom as the leading "badge of Zion" for *active* Mormons. However, a little more than a decade later, the "Law of Chastity" appears to be considered as a "Suggestion of Chastity" by many—and perhaps the majority of—LDS youth. When active, highly involved Mormons are considered separately, the distance between them and national norms expands to the degree that active Mormons are identifiable as a peculiar people; however, if sexual activity among LDS youth continues to increase, we may see a critical marker of distinction and peculiarity become a minor difference (see Heaton, Bahr, and Jacobson 2004).

Our chapter began by outlining two key Mormon doctrines that O'Dea identified among the unique teachings that formed an "important sphere [of] Mormon distinctness" (1957, 112). We now turn to the question, "How does the LDS Church strive to *maintain* the peculiar, high-tension doctrines of the Word of Wisdom and the Law of Chastity to the degree that significant, measurable impact is evident—at least in the lives of its actively involved members?" Many answers to this question lie in the second important sphere of Mormon distinctness identified by O'Dea: the church's unique internal structure.

Distinctness of the Internal Structure of the Mormon Church

There are several aspects of the LDS Church's internal structure that are distinct from other religions. Work identifying and describing these unique features is abundant (for example, Dollahite and Marks 2006; Mauss 1994a; Shipps 1985, 1994; Stark 1998). Therefore, our aim will be not to describe these structural features in detail but to illustrate *how* they support Mormon peculiarity, particularly in connection with the Word of Wisdom and the Law of Chastity. The structural elements we will consider are the missionary program; lay priesthood; lay, unpaid clergy (bishops); church service callings; and the temple (and temple recommend interviews).

How Does the LDS Missionary Program Preserve Peculiarity?

In 1957, the year O'Dea's *The Mormons* was published, 2,518 full-time missionaries were "set apart" to officially represent and proselytize for the LDS Church. In 2002, 37,248 full-time missionaries were set apart for service in 160 nations, an increase of nearly fifteenfold (Deseret News 2004; Watson 2005).[4] Moving beyond raw numbers to ratios, in 1957 the LDS Church sent out 1.7 missionaries per 1,000 members (2,518 missionaries out of 1,448,314 members). By 2002, the ratio had nearly doubled to 3.2 per 1,000 (37,248 missionaries out of 11,721,548 members) (Deseret News 2004).

Although some young women elect to serve missions, the vast majority of those currently serving LDS missions are single young men, who typically serve for two years (Stark 1998). Not only are these missionaries volunteers, but it is also expected that the missionary and his family will provide at least a substantial portion (if not all) of the approximately ten thousand dollars needed to sustain him during his two-year service. With this brief profile of the missionary program offered, we discuss some ways the program helps maintain Mormon peculiarity.

One must live church standards in order to serve a mission and enter the temple, the pinnacle of LDS membership (more on this topic later). Subsequently, there is tremendous pressure for LDS youth to live the Word of Wisdom and the Law of Chastity throughout the challenging adolescent years (Dollahite and Marks 2006). Although recent samples that combine inactive and active LDS youth fail to indicate striking differences between LDS youth and national norms (Heaton, Bahr, and Jacobson 2004), studies with active LDS youth do indicate remarkable differences that are especially pronounced for males (Carroll et al. 2000; Nelson 2003; Top and Chadwick 1998). One possible factor in these differences is that the LDS directive that "every young man should serve a mission" is taken seriously by a high percentage of active LDS teenage males who are aware that breaking the Law of Chastity may prevent them from serving a full-time mission.

A second way in which the missionary program may preserve Mormon peculiarity is that is establishes tension with—and a striking contrast to—U.S. cultural norms (Bushman and Bushman 2001). At the point in the life course when many American young men are attending fraternity parties, LDS male youth are exhorted (even commanded) to leave life as they know it in order to proselytize for a faith whose peculiar doctrines include abstinence from premarital sex and proscription of alcohol, illegal drugs, and tobacco (Dollahite and Marks 2006).

Those who serve missions are removed from the "teen scene" and are immersed in a subculture that stringently protects young men from the behaviors antithetical to their faith. The missionary subculture carries its own peculiar but proud identity that many young men and women grow to cherish—thereby helping them to further internalize the unique values they are proclaiming and proselytizing (see Shepherd and Shepherd 1994).

As missionaries are surrounded by and closely affiliate with peers who espouse and live the same peculiar values, they also receive extensive leadership training and leadership opportunities that prepare them for postmission service in the church. In the words of Douglas James Davies, "If Latter-day prophets stand at the apex of the Mormon organization, the missionaries are to be found at the baseline" (2000, 191). It is in large measure the missionary program that develops the next generation of LDS leaders, thereby enabling "the Mormons to rely on a volunteer, unpaid, yet trained, priesthood to staff the church" (Stark 1984, 21). It is to the local leaders in this unpaid, yet trained, priesthood that we now turn our attention.

How Is the Lay Mormon Priesthood Peculiar?

Douglas Davies explains that the "Mormon priesthood, directed by [free] agency and combined with covenant, yields a core spirituality that adds up to more than the sum of its parts and underlies all church and family life" (2003, 213). Marie Cornwall (1994) has further noted that the Mormon priesthood is unique among the religions of the world. What is it, then, that is unique, core, and foundational about the LDS priesthood?

One of the key distinctions of the priesthood in the LDS Church is that it is held not solely by the clergy but by qualifying males ages twelve and above. Although we will not detail priesthood offices and advancements here (for overviews, see Dollahite and Marks 2006; and Shipps 1994), we will emphasize that when the returned missionary transitions into postmission life, he is still a member of the priesthood with specific responsibilities, including the charge to continue to live "worthily." In short, he is to remain temple worthy and prepare for a temple marriage (topics we will return to later). A similar charge is given to the LDS young woman, whether or not she serves a mission.

How Does a Lay Mormon Priesthood Preserve Peculiarity?

Although widespread priesthood ordination is practiced, church founder Joseph Smith emphasized, "There are many who have been ordained among you, whom [the Lord has] called, but few of them are chosen" (Doctrine and Covenants 95:5). Smith later expounded on this theme:

> Behold, there are many called but few are chosen. And why are they not chosen? Because their hearts are set so much upon the things of this world, and aspire to the honors of men, that they do not learn this one lesson—That the rights of the priesthood are inseparably connected with the powers of heaven, and that the powers of heaven cannot be controlled nor handled only upon the principles of righteousness. That [the priesthoods] may be conferred upon us is true; but when we undertake to cover our sins ... [or act in] unrighteousness, behold, the heavens withdraw themselves; the Spirit of the Lord is grieved; and ... Amen to the priesthood or authority of that man. (121:34–37)

The key to priesthood authority in Mormonism, therefore, is not seminary or divinity school training, but behavioral congruence with church doctrine. This doctrine places the burden of responsibility for honoring the priesthood on all those who are called. Honoring the priesthood is roughly equivalent to being peculiar and "not of the world" in that many components of LDS worthiness involve avoiding the dominant culture's sexual, behavioral, and substance-related norms. Other demanding components of worthiness include the payment of a full tithing (10 percent of one's income), a personal testimony of certain tenets of the faith, and fulfillment of priesthood duties (including nonsacramental, service-related responsibilities). To reiterate, even though "many are called" (that is, ordained to the priesthood), only the "chosen" (the righteous) can properly administer church ordinances, including baptisms, confirmations, and ordinations. Furthermore, to perform these ordinances for family members is considered a high privilege by many LDS fathers, a privilege reserved for those living the faith (Dollahite 2003).

Let us tie together three critical points: all worthy male members of the LDS faith (twelve years and over) may hold the priesthood, those who are ordained may utilize their priesthood only when they are *worthy* (that is, peculiar), and in LDS doctrine it is the priesthood holder's right, responsibility, and sacred privilege to administer ordinances, especially in the case of a father performing ordinances for his children. When one considers these three ideas jointly, the peculiarity preservation mechanism is apparent. In sum, to be a worthy LDS father and priesthood holder, one must live in congruence with sacred (peculiar) LDS covenants and in opposition to several "worldly" norms. The importance of parents "practicing what they preach" with respect to religion has been documented in other world faiths (Marks 2004). However, the LDS Church is quite unique in its ability to say to its male members, "If you do not practice, you do not perform the ordinances." For many LDS fathers, the privileges and benefits of the priesthood and the faith are apparently worth the costs (see Stark and Finke 2000).

How Are Mormon Lay Clergy (Bishops) Peculiar?

Perhaps no feature of the Mormon priesthood and clergy is more peculiar and distinct than the office of the unpaid bishop (the pastor or congregational-level leader). Based on his reading of the Book of Mormon, O'Dea concluded, "Radical western religion is seen in the emphasis on clergymen to work [to support themselves], a tenet that later finds permanent expression in the structure of the Mormon church" (1957, 32).

James T. Duke points out, "A church with a lay clergy, as is the LDS Church, is far different from a church led by a paid ministry" (1998, 3). Two key differences in an unpaid local LDS clergy are that the office of bishop does not attract those seeking a secure living, and Mormon bishops are drawn from the ranks of lay, employed, married members, members who subsequently tend to have a great deal of practical, lived experience in the world (Stark 1998). A third difference is that, from the outset, the bishop's assignment is temporary (usually about five years).

In connection with the first distinction above—that bishops receive no housing, pay, or other remuneration for their approximately twenty hours a week of service[5]—Mauss emphasizes that in times past, "church callings or positions in the lay ministry [like that of bishop] were regarded as sacrifices…not badges of prestige" (1994a, xii). In connection with the temporary nature of a bishop's calling, Mauss further emphasizes that in the LDS Church, "yesterday's relatives and college roommates become tomorrow's church superiors ... but the terms of appointment are only temporary ... so there is a fair amount of rotation both vertically and horizontally" (126). Therefore, whereas the *office* of bishop is respected, the man filling it will, in due time, be replaced. It has been posited that this "limited tenure method of organization ... ensures a kind of balance of power" in the church (Davies 2000, 162). Indeed, when he is "released" and his tenure ends, the former bishop will move on to teach a children's class or whatever he is "called" by the new bishop to do. With the nature of the LDS lay clergy position of bishop briefly defined and its peculiarities highlighted, we turn to the substantive question of *how* a bishop helps to maintain congruence among his congregation in terms of promoting the peculiar lived values of the Word of Wisdom and the Law of Chastity.

How Do Mormon Lay Clergy (Bishops) Preserve Peculiarity?

In terms of promoting and maintaining peculiar Mormon doctrines and practices, LDS bishops may be direct and bold in "preach[ing] naught but repentance" (Doctrine and Covenants 19:21). The collection plate will be no lighter if the bishop preaches boldly, for there *is* no pastoral collection plate or democratizing influence of the dollar to factor into sermons. Further, the LDS bishop has no incentive to dilute the peculiar Mormon values to satisfy the wealthy in his congregation—a constant tendency in congregations with paid clergy because *"the privileged pay a higher [social] cost for strictness"* (Stark and Finke 2000, 203).[6] One could subsequently categorize LDS bishops as peculiarity preservationists with nothing to lose (or gain) financially.

A bishop's central charge is to serve and strengthen the youth in his congregation, each of whom he is to interview regularly regarding their personal lives (including whether they are living the peculiar values of the church). This level of individualized attention is made possible by the Mormon practice of keeping congregations small. As Rodney Stark and Roger Finke note, LDS leaders are "so committed to small local fellowships that they will split the local group into two fellowships even when only one building is available" (2000, 155). This practice promotes a familial, close-knit feeling and allows the bishop to build relationships with his congregation, especially the youth.

In maintaining close ties with youth, a bishop's energy and zeal are essential ... particularly as the cultural current against peculiar Mormon values increases (Dollahite and Marks 2006). Similar to those serving full-time missions, bishops have the reassurance of knowing that the accompanying strains and demands of the position are for a finite period. Figuratively, the "distinct" structure of the LDS Church identified by O'Dea allows the bishop to serve as a leg on a relay team, as opposed to a distance runner who labors until death or retirement. While he runs his leg, however, a bishop has a wealth of additional support in promoting and preserving Mormon peculiarity in the way of church callings, as discussed next.

How Do Church Callings Preserve Peculiarity?

Max Weber once described lay-operated, activist Mormonism as "half-way between monastery and factory" (1976, 264; see also Davies 2000). Indeed, sociologist James T. Duke (1997) estimates that the average LDS ward (congregation) receives between four hundred and six hundred hours of volunteer service per week from those serving in "callings," a remarkable pool of human resources at no direct cost to the church. This figure adds context to Gordon Shepherd and Gary Shepherd's statement that "to understand Mormonism, one must understand the lay character of the Mormon religion" (1994, 162). Indeed, the unpaid LDS bishops are not the only laborers who are promoting and preserving lived Mormon values. From the church's origins, "besides being a faith and an ethic, Mormonism [has been] a work" (Bushman 1985, 153).

Stark and Finke, referring to the religious apathy of western Europe, state, "As Adam Smith pointed out, kept clergy are lazy … *kept laity are lazy too,* being trained to regard religion as free" (2000, 228; emphasis added). Compare this point with a correlate presented by LDS Church founder Joseph Smith, who declared that "a religion that does not require the sacrifice of all things never has power sufficient to produce the faith necessary unto life and salvation" (1835, 69). A related doctrine appearing early in the Book of Mormon states, "For we labor diligently … for we know that it is by grace that we are saved, after all we can do" (2 Nephi 25:23). In addition, countless other LDS scriptures and hymns extol the virtue and necessity of faith-based sacrifice and service by *all* members, not just the clergy.

Although unpaid priesthood and clergy serve vital roles in the LDS community, the typical LDS congregation has many—often more than half—of its necessary operating positions staffed by women (Cornwall 1994). Whereas LDS priesthood ordination is for men, women serve in a number of capacities where priesthood is not required, including the Relief Society Women's Organization, the Young Women's Organization (for twelve to eighteen year olds), the Sunday school, and the Primary Children's Organization (Davies 2003). These service "callings" are given to women and men, and—like most responsibilities in the LDS Church—they are assigned and are for a limited but not predetermined duration. Typically, however, one will serve in a calling for anywhere from a few months to a few years (Bushman and Bushman 2001).

Callings facilitate retention of both new and longtime members by encouraging active involvement and by directly and indirectly promoting peculiar, lived LDS values. On a related note, Rodney Stark has pointed out that "authority is regarded as more legitimate and gains in effectiveness to the degree that members perceive themselves as participants in the system of authority" (1998, 52). Stark later emphasizes that the "amazing degree of amateur participation at all levels of [the LDS Church's] formal structure" helps to foster just such legitimation and increased commitment to the faith (53).

Church callings also fill another less evident purpose: a minimization of what economists refer to as the free-rider problem. LDS doctrine from 1832 states this aim explicitly: "Verily I say unto you, that every man...is obliged to provide for his own family...and let him labor in the church. Let every man be diligent in all things. And *the idler shall not have place in the church,* except he repent and mend his ways" (Doctrine and Covenants 75:28–29; emphasis added). One hundred and seventy-five years later, this ethic is still in place. Shepherd and Shepherd indicate, "Mormons virtually equate being a Latter-day Saint in good standing with being 'active' in church callings...the term *inactive* [denoting] deviance or defection from the faith" (1994, 162). Davies similarly concludes, "[In Mormonism] holiness results from activity and not from passivity.... To be properly active is to be on the path to salvation, through temple ordinances and through that holiness gained by practical life in family, work and leisure" (2000, 33).

Economist Laurence R. Iannaccone explains that churches like the LDS Church that require high costs force members and prospective members "to participate fully or not at all" (1994, 1188). Consistent with this point, the time and energy costs inherent in an LDS calling, coupled with the 10 percent tithing expectation, do tend to foster an all-or-nothing ethos.

An additional point is that callings are extended in personal face-to-face interviews with a priesthood leader. For both women and men, personal worthiness is necessary for service in most callings. This mandate imbues service callings with a certain amount of social prestige because those serving are apparently both worthy and willing to serve.

Service callings are costly to individual Latter-day Saints in terms of both time and energy (Duke 1997). Many callings require at least a couple of hours a week (with others requiring many times that) in addition to attendance at three-hour Sabbath meetings. In light of these significant temporal and financial costs, Stark and Finke query, "One of the most important and

disputed issues in the scientific study of religion [is] *Why do they do it?*
Why are people willing to make the very high levels of sacrifice required by
higher-tension religious organizations?" (emphasis in original). In response
to their own question, Stark and Finke argue, "The answer can be found
in elementary economics. Price is only one factor in any exchange; quality
is the other, and combined they yield an estimate of *value*. Herein lies the
secret of the strength of higher-tension religious groups: despite being expensive they offer greater value, indeed, they are able to do so partly *because*
they are expensive" (2000, 145; emphasis in original). Indeed, the large pool
of time, knowledge, skills, and experience available through callings makes it
possible for LDS congregations to provide high-quality programs to persons
across the life course (Dollahite and Marks 2006; Smith and Denton 2005).

Thus, we see that service callings offer several key benefits to the LDS
Church. First, callings help maintain necessary peculiarity (worthiness) in
individual members. Second, most callings necessitate attendance and participation at Sabbath services, thereby promoting both short- and long-term
church involvement. Third, because most members are given at least one
calling, the free-rider problem is minimized (Stark 1998).

As we review the distinct structure and function of the lay-staffed LDS
Church, we note that the faithful Mormon adherent has immediate, tangible, resource-rich programs; an operating structure that includes and integrates her or him as an active contributor (instead of as a passive consumer);
and perceived otherworldly rewards (promises of salvation). These benefits may be substantial enough that even the related stigmatic social costs
of being peculiar may—through allegiance, investment, and pride in the
church—be transformed into badges of Zion for active members (Bloom
1992).

The Costs and Challenges of Peculiarity: A Brief LDS Retrospective

Although much of this chapter has addressed how the LDS Church has employed its peculiarities to its advantage, peculiarity can have high individual
and institutional costs as well. As we noted at the chapter's outset, the first
twenty years of Mormon history on U.S. soil were nothing short of violent—prompting no less a figure than Sir Thomas Huxley (1889) to compare the U.S. treatment of Mormons with the Roman Empire's dealings
with early Christianity (cf. Davies 2003).

The year after Huxley's 1889 piece was published, the fourth president of
the LDS Church, Wilford Woodruff, issued a manifesto ending the greatest
Mormon peculiarity, polygamy. The financial assets of what Leonard J. Arrington (1966) calls the "Great Basin kingdom" were seized, and the church

was faced with the choice to assimilate or die. Woodruff chose the former option, in LDS belief, based on revelation (Doctrine and Covenants, Official Declaration 1), although the church has never renounced the doctrinal foundation of the practice (Bloom 1992).

A second collision between LDS peculiarity and dominant culture arose during the civil rights movement regarding a policy that had been in place since the tenure of Brigham Young to not ordain blacks to the priesthood (Davies 2003; Mauss 1994b). In 1978, the twelfth LDS president, Spencer W. Kimball, announced a revelation indicating that priesthood and temple blessings were to be made available to all races (Doctrine and Covenants, Official Declaration 2).

It is significant to note that in both cases, discontinuous change was instituted by the prophet and president of the church, change that decreased peculiarity and tension with dominant culture. Interestingly, it is the Mormons' somewhat peculiar belief in a modern-day prophet, seer, and revelator that makes major discontinuous changes like these possible without committees or formal councils, and with relatively little dissent, considering the size of the institution.

In spite of these two historic changes that have reduced peculiarity, such changes are conspicuous because they are rare. Doctrinally, at least, the LDS faith remains distinct and peculiar even if some behavioral distinctions seem to be diminishing (Mauss 2005). These doctrinal and programmatic peculiarities are strong enough that—at least in most places outside of the Intermountain West—the costs of peculiarity that accompany membership mean that the "badge of Zion" discussed by O'Dea is a weighty one to wear. Many—even the majority—of those who join the faith later fall into "inactivity." For this group, perhaps the social, financial, or temporal costs of membership in the Church of Jesus Christ of Latter-day Saints are too high. Interestingly, even among those members who are active in the LDS Church, Davies has identified a key division: "a church within a church," or a "committed nucleus" that differs from the rest (2000, 4). Last, it is to this highly committed population and its energizing center that we turn our attention.

How Does the Temple Directly Preserve Mormon Peculiarity?

There is one element of LDS belief and practice that melds immediate benefits of this life with otherworldly rewards in a singular way. LDS theology and practice culminate in the temple, with the establishment (or continuation) of an eternal family. It is, in part, this family theology that makes the temple the *axis mundi* of Mormon life (cf. Eliade 1959), a sacred, fixed point that is strong enough to maintain sacred ideals even though they may be in high tension with the countervailing practices of "the world."

Whereas O'Dea was fascinated with the Mormons in general, Douglas Davies (a leading contemporary non-LDS scholar of Mormonism) is specifically intrigued by the temple in LDS theology and practice. Davies (2000, 2003) has alternatively referred to the temple as Mormonism's "prime source of identity," as "essentially distinctive," as "the medium of [the Mormon] message," and as its "power-generating centre." He even goes so far as to posit that it is "the temple [that carries] the mythological and historical weight of core Mormonism" (2000, 257). What is it about an edifice that prompts such statements?

In Mormonism, the capstone of both faith and family life is found in temple worship, namely, in temple covenants and rituals (Packer 1995; Talmage 1912). Davies has noted that "the whole development of [Mormon] temple rites introduces a scheme that also moves towards the very edge of the Christian ritual spectrum" (2000, 236). Underlying these distinct rites are distinct doctrines that constitute "a veritable theology of the family" (Jarvis 2000, 245). LDS family theology is succinctly expressed in a formal church statement by the First Presidency and Council of the Twelve Apostles titled "The Family: A Proclamation to the World," a portion of which reads: "The divine plan of happiness enables family relationships to be perpetuated beyond the grave. Sacred ordinances and covenants available in holy temples make it possible for individuals to return to the presence of God and for families to be united eternally" (1995, 102).

It is a sacred Mormon belief that in the temple, a man and woman may be married to one another for time and all eternity along with the blessings of having their children eternally sealed to them as well (Davies 2003). After receiving these blessings and the prerequisite washing, anointing, and endowment, an individual may stand as proxy for those from previous generations who did not participate in these ordinances (Packer 1995). In Mormon thought, these proxy efforts do not "convert" the dead to the faith or make them part of the eternal family chain, per se (Davies 2003). However, it is believed that proxy work opens a new realm of opportunity and possibility for the deceased who *do* wish to accept the temple blessings performed in their behalf (baptism, eternal marriage, and so on). The living who devote their time to this effort are taught that the day will come when some of those for whom they have served as proxy will offer their most profound gratitude and view the individuals who enabled them to receive these blessings as "saviors on Mount Zion" (Packer 1995). This doctrine is poignant for many Latter-day Saints who are actively engaged in temple Mormonism. However, as with other LDS privileges described previously, participation in the temple is predicated on worthiness.

How Does the Temple Indirectly Maintain Peculiarity?

The LDS president preceding Hinckley, Howard W. Hunter, admonished LDS members to "look to the temple of the Lord as the great symbol of... [your] membership" (1994, 8). To members of the LDS Church, temples are more than places of worship; they are "a house of God... sanctified and consecrated to be holy" (Doctrine and Covenants 109:8, 12). Although open houses for the public are held prior to a temple dedication, only members who meet a specific list of worthiness-related criteria may enter the temple once it has been dedicated, consistent with the doctrine that "no unclean thing shall be permitted to come into [God's] house and pollute it" (109:20). Indeed, admittance to an LDS temple requires a written temple recommend that can be obtained only through a series of two in-depth interviews (one with a local congregational leader, and one with a regional leader) where personal religious beliefs, practices, and community involvement as well as family-related behavior are explicitly and specifically questioned (cf. Bushman and Bushman 2001). A person who certifies that they qualify receives a recommend deeming her or him temple worthy. Temple recommends are typically valid for two years, after which the member must repeat the two-tier process by personally reporting the requisite level of personal worthiness.

The Temple-Based Expansion of Mormonism

This centrality of the temple for the LDS Church is reflected by a phenomenal recent boom in temple building involving hundreds of millions of dollars. When *The Mormons* was published in 1957, there were 10 LDS temples in operation, 8 of which were in the United States. As recently as 1981, there were only 20 temples globally (Deseret News 2004). By comparison, under current president Gordon B. Hinckley (1995–present) temple building has increased dramatically. At present, there are 124 operating LDS temples, with 6 more under construction and 12 announced.[7]

With this expansion of temples in mind, it is interesting to note that Davies concluded his volume *The Mormon Culture of Salvation* (2000) by speculating whether Salt Lake City, with its iconic temple, might one day become a sacred center comparable to a Jerusalem or a Rome. In his *Introduction to Mormonism* (2003) a few years later, his idea on this topic had evolved. Instead of pursuing the "Salt Lake City as Mormon Mecca" idea, he points out in the more recent work that "Latter-day Saint temples built in each major part of the world would ensure that Zion existed within an architectural context rather than in one specific geographical" location (204). In effect, through temple building, Mormonism allows itself to introduce a global network of sacred *centers*. Mormons from outside the United States will not need to make pilgrimages to the Salt Lake Temple because, increasingly, the temple will be brought to them in their own part of the globe. Davies concludes his latter discussion of Mormon sacred centers by indicating that the temple-building era ensures that "the essential nature of Mormonism [will] be present and distributed throughout the world" (224). Indeed, more than half of currently operating temples (64 of 124) are not in the United States.[8]

We now come to the catch. Davies estimates that whereas "in a small American town with a long Mormon history" 70 percent of attending members might have temple recommends, the figure in areas of "new mission work" (that is, outside of U.S. borders) is likely to be closer to 15 percent (2000, 196). Temples, regardless of how sacred or symbolic, can serve as the "power-generating centre" of Mormonism only if they are being attended and utilized. Church attendance and callings, as previously discussed, are important. However, the LDS meetinghouse is a "halfway house" between Babylon and Zion—the secular world and the temple. It is the temple, and the temple only, that offers exaltation (Davies refers to this as LDS "super-salvation") through eternal marriage.

In the pre-O'Dea era, the geographically compact nature of the church helped promote temple Mormonism, but this task becomes increasingly difficult as the membership expands and diffuses. If the global temple participation rate remains at 15 percent, the likelihood of increased assimilation between Mormonism and host cultures seems high. Conversely, if temple participation increases, so will the hallmark and medium of Mormon peculiarity and distinction.

In sum, the temple, along with the structural features of the missionary program, lay clergy, lay priesthood, and church callings constitute much of what O'Dea referred to as a second sphere of Mormon distinctness...its internal structure. It is this distinct internal structure that, in large measure, supports, sustains, and maintains the first sphere of distinctness: lived values.

Conclusion

In the first section of this chapter, we selected two peculiar LDS values—the Word of Wisdom and the Law of Chastity—and then determined the degree that these values are converted into measurable *behavioral* differences by an ostensibly peculiar people. As we have shown, across age and for both the Word of Wisdom and the Law of Chastity, data indicate that *active* Mormons remain a peculiar people in some respects. However, less active members are not clearly distinguishable from the general population. Further, in terms of sexual practices among LDS youth, there appears to be significant movement toward the cultural norm of premarital sexual activity (Heaton, Bahr, and Jacobson 2004).

In the latter section of the chapter, we have highlighted several facets of the church's distinct internal structure, along with explanations of how and why these features prompt contemporary Mormons to live their unique values. To restate a critical point, the distinct lived values and distinct internal structure of the Mormon Church work synergistically to preserve the peculiarity of the Mormons and their lived faith. In the words of Harold Bloom, "[The] Mormons, like the Jews before them, are a religion that became a people. That … always was Joseph Smith's pragmatic goal, for he had the genius to see that only by becoming a people could the Mormons survive" (1992, 83).

Fifty years after O'Dea's *The Mormons* was published, it may be an overstatement to claim that the Mormons are still "a people." However, if we look to Douglas James Davies's "church within a church"—those who actively participate in *temple Mormonism*—then we still witness a distinctive and peculiar people. Robert Gottlieb and Peter Wiley call the LDS Church a "curious combination of typicality and peculiarity" (1986, 253), and indeed it is (cf. Vaisey and Heaton 2005). However, the combination of typicality and peculiarity may be an impossible one to sustain. On this note, we conclude by shifting to the precarious domain of prediction. Specifically, it seems that whether Mormonism rises to become an authentically peculiar new world faith or increasingly assimilates with secular norms will not be primarily determined by the raw membership numbers that tend to fascinate sociologists of religion. Instead, we think it is likely that the faith's future peculiarity (or assimilation) will be most strongly influenced by the success or failure of the LDS Church to convert new and lukewarm members to the core "church within a church" of temple Mormonism. In this sense, temples (and temple Mormonism) are, and will be, the central markers of Mormon peculiarity, identity, and destiny.

Notes

1. The authors appreciate insight from a reviewer on these points.

2. O'Dea also mentions a third sphere, "the distinctness of Mormon relations with the larger culture," but due to the breadth of this third sphere, only the first two will be discussed in this paper.

3. It is interesting to note that Utah is the only state where less than 10 percent of women smoke (9.3 percent). Further, the figures for men (13.7 percent) and ninth to twelfth grade students (7.4 percent) are the nation's lowest by significant percentages (http://apps. nccd.cdc.gov/brfss/page.asp).

4. If we compare foreign missionary efforts of American Protestant bodies with the LDS missionary effort, we find that the Episcopal Church has 0.2 foreign missionaries per 10,000 members, and the Southern Baptist Convention has 8.9 (Stark and Finke 2000, 152). The 2004 LDS mission figure (if we include domestic full-time missionaries as well) was roughly 200 missionaries per 10,000 members (almost 60,000 missionaries per 12 million members) or one thousand times the Episcopal rate and more than twenty times the Southern Baptist rate.

5. Stark and Finke emphasize, "No one seeks unpaid, costly religious positions from materialistic motives.... [G]iven the sacrifices required of their positions, Mormon bishops ... must be motivated primarily by faith" (2000, 66).

6. Research indicates that in many congregations, most church contributions come from a few large donors (Hoge 1994; Hoge and Yang 1994). Thus, paid clergy do not financially need widespread approval, but they do need approval (financial support) from the wealthy few.

7. Information per the Web site http://www.ldschurchtemples.com, as of July 25, 2007.

8. Ibid.

References

Albrecht, Stan L. 1998. "The Consequential Dimension of Mormon Religiosity." In *Latter-day Saint Social Life: Social Research on the LDS Church and Its Members,* ed. James T. Duke, 253–92. Provo: Religious Studies Center, Brigham Young University.

Amoateng, Acheampong Y., and Stephen J. Bahr. 1986. "Religion, Family, and Adolescent Drug Use." *Sociological Perspectives* 29: 53–76.

Arrington, Leonard J. 1966. *Great Basin Kingdom: An Economic History of the Latter-day Saints, 1830–1900.* Lincoln: University of Nebraska Press.

Bahr, Howard M., and Renata T. Forste. 1998. "Toward a Social Science of Contemporary Mormondom." In *Latter-day Saint Social Life: Social Research on the LDS Church and Its Members,* ed. James T. Duke, 133–201. Provo: Religious Studies Center, Brigham Young University.

Bahr, Stephen. 1994. "Religion and Adolescent Drug Use: A Comparison of Mormons and Other Religions." In *Contemporary Mormonism: Social Science Perspectives,* ed. Marie Cornwall, Tim B. Heaton, and Lawrence A. Young, 118–37. Urbana: University of Illinois Press.

Bainbridge, William S. 1997. *The Sociology of Religious Movements.* London: Routledge.

Barry, Carolyn M., and Larry J. Nelson. 2005. "The Role of Religion in the Transition to Adulthood for Young Emerging Adults." *Journal of Youth and Adolescence* 34: 245–55.

Benson, Peter L. 1990. *The Troubled Journey: A Portrait of 6th–12th Grade Youth.* Minneapolis: Search Institute.

Bloom, Harold. 1992. *The American Religion: The Emergence of the Post-Christian Nation.* New York: Simon and Schuster.

Bogaert, A. F., and W. A. Fisher. 1995. "Predictors of University Men's Number of Sexual Partners." *Journal of Sex Research* 32: 119–30.

Bushman, Claudia Lauper, and Richard Lyman Bushman. 2001. *Building the Kingdom: A History of Mormons in America.* New York: Oxford University Press.

Bushman, Richard Lyman. 1985. *Joseph Smith and the Beginnings of Mormonism.* Urbana: University of Illinois Press.

———. 2005. *Joseph Smith: Rough Stone Rolling.* New York: Alfred A. Knopf.

Carroll, Jason S., Steven T. Linford, Thomas B. Holman, and Dean B. Busby. 2000. "Marital and Family Orientations among Highly Religious Young Adults: Comparing Latter-day Saints with Traditional Christians." *Review of Religious Research* 42: 193–205.

Chadwick, Bruce A., and Brent L. Top. 1998. "Religiosity and Delinquency among LDS Adolescents." In *Latter-day Saint Social Life: Social Research on the LDS Church and Its Members,* ed. James T. Duke, 499–523. Provo: Religious Studies Center, Brigham Young University.

Cornwall, Marie. 1994. "The Institutional Role of Mormon Women." In *Contemporary Mormonism: Social Science Perspectives,* ed. Marie Cornwall, Tim B. Heaton, and Lawrence A. Young, 239–64. Urbana: University of Illinois Press.

Davies, Douglas James. 2000. *The Mormon Culture of Salvation.* Burlington, Vt.: Ashgate.

———. 2003. *An Introduction to Mormonism.* New York: Cambridge University Press.

Deseret News. 2004. *Deseret News 2004 Church Almanac.* Salt Lake City: Deseret News.

Dollahite, David C. 2003. "Fathering for Eternity: Generative Spirituality in Latter-day Saint Fathers of Children with Special Needs." *Review of Religious Research* 44: 237–51.

———. 2007. "Latter-day Saint Marriage and Family Life in Modern America." In *American Religions and the Family: How Faith Traditions Cope with Modernization,* ed. Don S. Browning and David A. Clairmont. New York: Columbia University Press.

Dollahite, David C., and Loren D. Marks. 2006. "Family and Community Nurturing Spirituality in Latter-day Saint Children and Youth." In *Nurturing Childhood and Adolescent Spirituality: Perspectives from the World's Religious Traditions,* ed. Karen-Marie

Yust, Aostre N. Johnson, Sandy E. Sasso, and Eugene C. Roehlkepartain, 394–408. Lanham, Md.: Rowman and Littlefield.

Duke, James T. 1997. "Church Callings as an Organizational Device in the LDS Church." Paper presented at the annual meeting of the Association for the Sociology of Religion.

———. 1998. "Cultural Continuity and Tension: A Test of Stark's Theory of Church Growth." In *Latter-day Saint Social Life: Social Research on the LDS Church and Its Members,* ed. James T. Duke, 71–103. Provo: Religious Studies Center, Brigham Young University.

Eliade, Mircea. 1959. *The Sacred and the Profane: The Nature of Religion.* New York: Harcourt Brace Jovanovich.

Enstrom, James E. 1998a. "Health Practices and Cancer Mortality among Active California Mormons." In *Latter-day Saint Social Life: Social Research on the LDS Church and Its Members,* ed. James T. Duke, 441–60. Provo: Religious Studies Center, Brigham Young University.

———. 1998b. "Health Practices and Mortality among Active California Mormons, 1980–1993." In *Latter-day Saint Social Life: Social Research on the LDS Church and Its Members,* ed. James T. Duke, 461–72. Provo: Religious Studies Center, Brigham Young University.

First Presidency and Council of the Twelve Apostles of the Church of Jesus Christ of Latter-day Saints. 1995. "The Family: A Proclamation to the World." *Ensign,* November, 102.

Gottlieb, Robert, and Peter Wiley. 1986. *America's Saints: The Rise of Mormon Power.* San Diego: Harcourt, Brace, and Jovanovich.

Hawks, Ricky D. 1989. "Alcohol Use Trends among LDS High School Seniors in America from 1982–1986." *AMCAP Journal* 15: 43–51.

Heaton, Tim B., Stephen J. Bahr, and Cardell K. Jacobson. 2004. *A Statistical Profile of Mormons: Health, Wealth, and Social Life.* Lewiston, N.Y.: Edwin Mellen Press.

Heaton, Tim B., Kristen L. Goodman, and Thomas B. Holman. 1994. "In Search of a Peculiar People: Are Mormon Families Really Different?" In *Contemporary Mormonism: Social Science Perspectives,* ed. Marie Cornwall, Tim B. Heaton, and Lawrence A. Young, 87–117. Urbana: University of Illinois Press.

Hinckley, Gordon B. 2000. *Standing for Something.* New York: Three Rivers Press.

Hoge, Dean R. 1994. "Introduction: The Problem of Church Giving." *Review of Religious Research* 36: 101–10.

Hoge, Dean R., and Fenggang Yang. 1994. "Determinants of Religious Giving in American Denominations: Data from Two Nationwide Surveys." *Review of Religious Research* 36: 123–48.

Holland, Jeffrey R. 1998. "Personal Purity." *Ensign,* November, 75–78.

Hummer, Robert A., Richard G. Rogers, Charles B. Nam, and Christopher G. Ellison. 1999. "Religious Involvement and U.S. Adult Mortality." *Demography* 36: 273–85.

Hunter, Howard W. 1994. "Exceeding Great and Precious Promises." *Ensign,* November, 8–9.

Huxley, Thomas H. 1889. "Agnosticism." *Nineteenth Century* 144 (February).

Iannaccone, Laurence R. 1994. "Why Strict Churches Are Strong." *American Journal of Sociology* 99, no. 5: 1180–1211.

Iannaccone, Laurence R., and Carrie A. Miles. 1994. "Dealing with Social Change: The Mormon Church's Response to Change in Women's Roles." In *Contemporary Mormonism: Social Science Perspectives,* ed. Marie Cornwall, Tim B. Heaton, and Lawrence A. Young, 265–86. Urbana: University of Illinois Press.

Jarvis, John C. 2000. "Mormonism in France." In *Family, Religion, and Social Change in Diverse Societies,* ed. Sharon K. Houseknecht and Jerry G. Pankhurst, 237–66. New York: Oxford University Press.

Johnston, Lloyd D., Jerald G. Bachman, and Patrick M. O'Malley. 1993. *Monitoring the Future.* Ann Arbor: University of Michigan Press.

Koenig, Harold G., Michael E. McCollough, and David B. Larson, eds. 2001. *Handbook of Religion and Health.* New York: Oxford University Press.

Lorch, Barbara R., and Robert H. Hughes. 1985. "Religion and Youth Substance Use." *Journal of Religion and Health* 24: 197–208.

Marks, Loren D. 2004. "Sacred Practices in Highly Religious Families: Christian, Jewish, Mormon, and Muslim Perspectives." *Family Process* 43: 217–31.

———. 2005. "Religion and Bio-psycho-social Health: A Review and Conceptual Model." *Journal of Religion and Health* 44: 173–86.

———. 2006. "Religion and Family Relational Health: An Overview and Conceptual Model." *Journal of Religion and Health* 45:603–18.

Marks, Loren D., Olena Nesteruk, Mandy Swanson, Betsy Garrison, and Tanya Davis. 2005. "Religion and Health among African Americans: A Qualitative Examination." *Research on Aging* 27: 447–74.

Mauss, Armand L. 1994a. *The Angel and the Beehive: The Mormon Struggle with Assimilation.* Urbana: University of Illinois Press.

———. 1994b. "Refuge and Retrenchment: The Mormon Quest for Identity." In *Contemporary Mormonism: Social Science Perspectives,* ed. Marie Cornwall, Tim B. Heaton, and Lawrence A. Young, 24–42. Urbana: University of Illinois Press.

———. 2004. Preface to *A Statistical Profile of Mormons: Health, Wealth, and Social Life,* ed. Tim B. Heaton, Stephen J. Bahr, and Cardell K. Jacobson, i–v. Lewiston, N.Y.: Edwin Mellen Press.

Merrill, Ray M., Jeffrey A. Folsom, and Susan S. Christopherson. 2005. "The Influence of Family Religiosity on Adolescent Substance Abuse according to Religious Preference." *Social Behavior and Personality* 33: 821–35.

National Center for Health Statistics. 2005. "Health, United States, 2005, with Chartbook on Trends in the Health of Americans." http://www.cdc.gov/nchs/data/hus/hus05.pdf.

Nelson, Larry J. 2003. "Rites of Passage in Emerging Adulthood: Perspectives of Young Mormons." In special issue, *New Directions for Child and Adolescent Development:*

Cultural Conceptions of the Transition to Adulthood, ed. Jeffrey J. Arnett and Nancy L.
    Galambos, 100: 33–49.

Niebuhr, H. Richard. 1929. *The Social Sources of Denominationalism.* New York: Holt.

O'Dea, Thomas F. 1957. *The Mormons.* Chicago: University of Chicago Press.

Packer, Boyd K. 1995. "The Holy Temple." *Ensign,* February, 32–36.

Popenoe, David. 1996. *Life without Father: Compelling New Evidence That Fatherhood and
    Marriage Are Indispensable for the Good of Children and Society.* New York: Basic Books.

Roberts, B. H. 1930. *A Comprehensive History of the Church of Jesus Christ of Latter-day
    Saints.* 6 vols. Reprint, Provo: Brigham Young University Press, 1976.

Shepherd, Gordon, and Gary Shepherd. 1994. "Sustaining a Lay Religion in a Modern
    Society: The Mormon Missionary Experience." In *Contemporary Mormonism: Social
    Science Perspectives,* ed. Marie Cornwall, Tim B. Heaton, and Lawrence A. Young,
    161–81. Urbana: University of Illinois Press.

Shipps, Jan. 1985. *Mormonism: The Story of a New Religious Tradition.* Urbana: University of
    Illinois Press.

———. 1994. "Making Saints: In the Early Days and the Latter Days." In *Contemporary
    Mormonism: Social Science Perspectives,* ed. Marie Cornwall, Tim B. Heaton, and
    Lawrence A. Young, 64–83. Urbana: University of Illinois Press.

Simmerman, Steven R. 1993. "The Mormon Health Traditions: An Evolving View of
    Modern Medicine." *Journal of Religion and Health* 32: 189–96.

Smith, Christian, and Melinda Lundquist Denton. 2005. *Soul Searching.* New York: Oxford
    University Press.

Smith, Hustin. 1991. *The World's Religions.* San Francisco: Harper.

Smith, Joseph. 1835. *Lectures on Faith.* Salt Lake City: Deseret Book, 1985.

Stark, Rodney. 1984. "The Rise of a New World Faith." *Review of Religious Research* 26:
    18–27.

———. 1998. "The Basis of Mormon Success: A Theoretical Application." In *Latter-day
    Saint Social Life: Social Research on the LDS Church and Its Members,* ed. James T.
    Duke, 29–70. Provo: Religious Studies Center, Brigham Young University.

Stark, Rodney, and William S. Bainbridge. 1985. *The Future of Religion.* Berkeley and Los
    Angeles: University of California Press.

Stark, Rodney, and Roger Finke. 2000. *Acts of Faith.* Berkeley and Los Angeles: University of
    California Press.

Talmage, James E. 1912. *The House of the Lord.* Reprint, Salt Lake City: Bookcraft, 1962.

Top, Brent L., and Bruce A. Chadwick. 1998. *Rearing Righteous Youth of Zion.* Salt Lake
    City: Bookcraft.

Troeltsch, Ernst. 1931. *The Social Teaching of the Christian Churches.* Vol. 2. New York:
    Macmillan.

Vaisey, Steve B., and Tim B. Heaton. 2004. Introduction to *A Statistical Profile of Mormons: Health, Wealth, and Social Life,* ed. Tim B. Heaton, Stephen J. Bahr, and Cardell K. Jacobson, 1–21. Lewiston, N.Y.: Edwin Mellen Press.

Watson, F. Michael. 2005. "Statistical Report, 2004." *Ensign,* May, 25.

Weber, Max. 1976. *The Protestant Ethic and the Spirit of Capitalism.* Trans. Talcott Parsons. London: Allen and Unwin.

Yankelovich, Daniel. 1981. *New Rules: Searching for Self-fulfillment in a House Turned Upside Down.* New York: Random House.

Young, Lawrence A. 1994. "Confronting Turbulent Environments: Issues in the Organizational Growth and Globalization of Mormonism." In *Contemporary Mormonism: Social Science Perspectives,* ed. Marie Cornwall, Tim B. Heaton, and Lawrence A. Young, 43–63. Urbana: University of Illinois Press.

Part III

The International Church

From Near-Nation to
New World Religion?

~ ARMAND L. MAUSS ~

Mormonism had ... gone from "near-sect" to "near-nation"... almost [becom-ing] a separate nationality [and] ... ethnic identity.

—THOMAS F. O'DEA, *The Mormons*

The Mormons will soon achieve a worldwide following comparable to that of Islam, Buddhism, Christianity, Hinduism, and other dominant world faiths ... becoming the first major faith to appear on earth since the Prophet Mohammed rode out of the desert.

—RODNEY STARK, "The Rise of a New World Faith"

WE CAN ONLY WONDER WHAT O'DEA WOULD HAVE THOUGHT of Stark's projection a mere three decades after publication of *The Mormons* in 1957. From his midcentury vantage point, O'Dea had already been somewhat sur-prised to find in the Mormons an anomaly among historic cases. Having studied in the tradition of Max Weber and Ernst Troeltsch, O'Dea would have expected the Mormons to have taken either of the two roads to obliv-ion prescribed in the conventional wisdom: stagnate and shrink into an un-assimilable moribund sect or lose their unique identity altogether by cultural assimilation into the secularized morass of respectable religions. Yet Mor-monism had done neither; instead, the Church of Jesus Christ of Latter-day Saints (LDS) had become almost a separate nation by the end of the nine-teenth century, once admired by economist Richard T. Ely for its organiza-tional vitality.[1] Even half a century later, when O'Dea began his work, the church had still not devolved into either of the two conventional forms of diminished vitality that he would have expected. Why had it not done so, and what were its prospects for the future? These were the questions that seem to have launched O'Dea's landmark 1957 study.

Mormon Protonationality as a Historical Anomaly

O'Dea's interest in the Mormons, then, seems to have derived from his recognition of the anomalies and contradictions that he saw in the Mormons as a historical case study. Among these, he discussed at considerable length the misfit between the Mormon case and the theoretical typology of "church" versus "sect" that had been in vogue among sociologists for at least a half century (Troeltsch 1912).[2] He addressed this anomaly both in his 1957 book and even more pointedly in an earlier 1954 article. The usual pattern, O'Dea explained, was that sects begin as dissatisfied schismatic offshoots from established religious traditions or "churches." Most of them remain small and do not survive even a generation. Those that do survive tend to follow either of two trajectories: they eventually become "churches" in their own rights by making the necessary accommodations to the surrounding culture and lose their unique identity or remain indefinitely as small and stagnant organizations, unable to break out of a self-imposed sectarian narrowness in their appeal.

By the middle of the twentieth century, when O'Dea was writing, the Mormon religion did not really fit either of those patterns. It certainly had not died out, despite considerable persecution and repression. It had developed some of the traits usually associated with a "sect," but not all of them. Nor had it ever really become a "church" in the conventional sense that its membership crossed political and even national boundaries, as (for example) the Methodists had done, and it had never become part of the political and economic establishment of a nation in the way that churches usually do. Nevertheless, even though geographically limited mainly to a rather remote part of the United States, it remained a vibrant and growing organization, thus somehow avoiding the "sectarian stagnation" that might have been expected to overtake it. To O'Dea, this anomaly called for an explanation, which he undertook to provide through a careful analysis of the internal values, culture, organization, and governance of the LDS Church.

In his 1954 article, O'Dea discussed ten factors in particular that militated against the full and permanent development of Mormons as a "typical sect." Some of these factors were overlapping or interrelated, but they included most prominently *some* degree of accommodation (eventually) with the surrounding American society: a centralized, authoritarian structure combined with a certain organizational flexibility learned from having had to start over again so many times in earlier locations; a steady rate of growth, both from natural increase and from the success of its widespread missionary work; and the policy of gathering all the converts to its own remote culture region, unattractive to other settlers, where its unique culture and community could be created apart from the strong assimilationist pressures that it would have faced if it had stayed in its earlier and more easterly locations (O'Dea 1954, 288–90; 1957, 111–14). Because of these unique historical circumstances, Mormons never quite fitted anywhere in the standard typology between "sect" and "church." Instead, said O'Dea, they achieved an "incipient nationality," evolving from a "near-sect" to a "near-nation," occupying their own cultural area and homeland within the larger American nation (1954, 285, 292).[3] The "combination of distinctive values, separate and peculiar social institutions, and geographic segregation" was "strengthened by three 'Mormon wars' and constant...conflict" with the outside to produce a total Mormon cultural environment and worldview that became "progressively more distinct" (1957, 114 and more generally in chaps. 6–8).

O'Dea recognized that after 1890 and the achievement of statehood for Utah, Mormonism had taken a more accommodationist posture toward the world—somewhat more "churchlike"—with its abandonment of polygamy, theocracy, and collectivist economic experimentation, yet it had also retained certain characteristics typical of a "sect" (such as claims of peculiarity, chosenness, aloofness from the world, and chiliastic expectations). Thus, even at midcentury O'Dea could still observe the surviving traits of a distinctive "Mormon people," with almost a separate "ethnicity," if not a separate nationality. He pointed to the interpenetration of church life and community bonds with an extensive kinship matrix (polygamous and otherwise). He still saw in Mormons and their church a continuing self-identification as a people chosen and set apart from the world, even while divinely charged with converting the world. He located the theological rationale for this self-identification in the dual restorationism of the Mormon claims and teachings—that is, in its combined ancient Christian and ancient Hebrew restorationism, both of which had been replicated and acted out in the Mormon experience as the new "chosen people." Both its peoplehood and its chosenness had been forged on the anvil of common suffering, common effort (both in success and in failure), common memory, and common myths of providential guidance and intervention—all in emulation, O'Dea noticed, of the ancient Hebrew Exodus and Chronicles (1954, 291; 1957, 115–16). Such was the nature of the culture still surviving among the Mormons even at midcentury.

The "Hebraic layer" in the Mormon heritage and self-conception has also been noted, inter alios, by Jan Shipps (1998), who identified it as a distinctive overlay that the founding prophet, Joseph Smith, himself added to the Christian restorationism and primitivism with which he began. Considering all the implications of that overlay, one might fairly claim that O'Dea actually *underestimated* its impact on the development of the Mormon "ethnicity." Subsequent research has spelled out in greater detail than O'Dea did just how important the Hebraic element was in the Mormons' construction of their own identity during the nineteenth and early twentieth centuries.[4] This element might not have been so conspicuous by the time O'Dea was writing. However, it is clear from authoritative Mormon teaching, even as late as midcentury, that the Mormons had constructed an ethnic identity for themselves that combined their own scriptural claim, emerging in the 1830s, of literal Israelite genealogy and genetics ("blood") with the mythology of "British Israelism" so popular in England and the United States later in that century (Mauss 1999, 134–48).

This synthesized identity eventually took the form of a widely held Mormon belief that descendants of the ancient Israelite tribes, particularly the tribe of Ephraim, had been providentially led in ancient times to occupy much of northwestern Europe, especially the British Isles and North America. Even though these British and Germanic peoples had lost track of their original Israelite identity, they were still the covenant people of Abraham and thus had "in their blood," as it were, a natural inclination to heed the promptings of the Spirit of God, making them especially receptive to the "Restored Gospel," as the Mormon message was often called. This kind of "spiritual genetics" helped to explain why the gospel was restored in the United States, and why its first and most numerous converts were American, British, Scandinavian, and German (147–58). It also helped to explain why the cultures and institutions of those Northwest European peoples were so "superior" to those of other peoples and thus destined from the beginning to spread ever westward. This was obviously a Mormon version of good old American "Manifest Destiny," with all the same potential for racism (159–65). From at least the 1860s onward, however, it combined with the other elements recognized by O'Dea to provide a powerful reinforcement to the emerging ethnic identity of the Mormons. In other words, the Mormon identity had been even more "ethnic" than O'Dea realized. By the end of the twentieth century, the racialized element had been deliberately muted and had largely disappeared from Mormon discourse, but in O'Dea's time it was still important (165–72).

Yet despite the quasi ethnicity and separateness that O'Dea saw in the Mormons still at midcentury, he nevertheless recognized also a great paradox: if from one perspective Mormon history had replicated the Hebrew experience, from yet a different perspective, it had also replicated the main outlines of *American* history. "Despite the marked and general peculiarity of Mormonism,... its typical American quality is no less real; for here is one of the great paradoxes of the Mormon experience," which in many ways actually replicated, in miniature, the more general American historical experience of colonization in the wilderness: "political self-government [in] conflict with the mother political institutions... group self-consciousness associated with the new continent," and the impact of westward movement (as per Frederick Jackson Turner) on the "formation of Mormon character, culture, and institutions." Thus, the "spectacle of distinction and similarity, the strange combination of peculiarity and typicality, stands out as the most striking Mormon characteristic.... [I]n many respects the most American of religions, [Mormonism] is also the only one to carry out a prolonged conflict with American institutions and to have displayed potentialities for separate national development" (1957, 116–17).[5]

AMERICAN ASSIMILATION VERSUS SECTARIAN RETRENCHMENT

It was, indeed, the "striking characteristic" of combined "peculiarity and typicality" in the American cultural and political environment that was to provide the dynamic for the Mormon future in ways that O'Dea did not foresee. He had been so preoccupied by the looming Mormon struggle with "modern secular thought" (which we shall discuss below) that he apparently failed to recognize the future implications of the enduring "sectarian" tendencies that still remained in Mormonism. Indeed, if he had considered those implications *over against* the growing engagement of the church with modern secular culture, he might have reconsidered his prescription for the Mormon future. That he did not fully appreciate the surviving sectarian dynamic in Mormonism is perhaps understandable, given the epistemological limitations of the paradigm of irresistible secularization within which O'Dea and nearly all other social scientists operated in those days. However, the emergence of a "new paradigm" in the sociology of religion during recent decades has rendered highly problematic the traditional prediction that new religious "sects" that survive will inevitably be somewhat secularized as they are transformed into "churches" and join the cultural and political establishment (see Warner 1993).

Inevitable Secularization versus the New Paradigm

This new paradigm is associated primarily with the work of Rodney Stark and his colleagues.[6] Emerging in the professional literature a few years after O'Dea's demise in 1974, the new paradigm evolved largely in response to the apparent anomaly of the new religious movements proliferating in Europe and the United States during an era of ostensibly rampant secularization (the 1960s and '70s). Confronting that anomaly led Stark to reject the time-honored thesis of inevitable secularization in favor of a theory based on the argument that in a free religious environment, secularization will always be a self-limiting process. No society can meet the varied and endemic human needs for meaning and fulfillment merely with the rewards of this world, so there will always be a quest for promises to be fulfilled in the next world. Since this quest is not about material rewards or fulfillment, it does not derive from the "opiate of the masses," as Marx would have it. Rather, the appeal of religion depends on a rationalistic assessment of the promises made by a religious community for *spiritual* rewards, primarily in the next world, to those who would embrace its particular religious program or regimen.[7] Believers, potential or actual, tend to value the claims and promises of a religion in proportion to the "costs" of membership. Accordingly, the more and higher the costs (social, economic, and emotional), the higher the value placed on the religious "products" that are offered—at least up to a point. This accounts for another apparent anomaly recently recognized, namely, that religious communities that make fairly strenuous demands on their members (again, up to a point) are the ones that tend to grow and thrive. Furthermore, the most *secularized* societies are the ones *least* likely to fulfill nonmaterial human needs, so the popular demand for religion in all its varieties will be greatest precisely in those societies (assuming religious freedom). Thus is secularization a *self-limiting process.*[8]

Whether or not by design, the new paradigm has obvious connections with earlier theoretical currents in sociology, social psychology, and economics.[9] As it has developed during the past two decades or so, it has become increasingly comprehensive theoretically, and much of it has been subjected to empirical tests, explicitly or implicitly. It has been applied comparatively across times and cultures, often with confirming if counterintuitive results—though not without some controversy. Indeed, the new paradigm has virtually set the agenda for much of the research in the sociology of religion since at least 1985. Stark has even applied it in various ways to the case of the Mormons, whom he occasionally cites as an example (among many others) of a religious movement that has thrived by making *demands* on its members and thereby increasing the "costs" of Mormon membership (see, for example, Stark 2005, chap. 4; 1996b). In fact, under the influence of Laurence R. Iannaccone, the new paradigm has increasingly taken on the theoretical trappings and terminology of market economics, with concepts such as "cost," "religious products," "firms," "market niche," "religious capital," and so on.[10]

This synthesis of economics and sociology appears to be a productive one, as (for example) when we understand that the "tension" between a religious movement and its surrounding culture exacts a "cost," both for the movement and for the individual members. The tension (and therefore the costs) can be either increased or decreased through the tactics and strategies employed by the movement to seek a modicum of accommodation with the surrounding culture while simultaneously attempting to maintain its unique and separate identity. *Too much* tension (for example, through seemingly extreme teachings or practices in the movement) will bring costly repression and threaten the viability of the movement. On the other hand, *too little* tension (through general assimilation) will threaten the separate identity of the movement and its *raison d'être.* From this new theoretical perspective, a "sect" can be redefined as a relatively high-tension religious organization and a "church" as a relatively low-tension religious organization. Furthermore, this redefinition gives the traditional church-sect typology the dynamic potential for explaining the *differential* success of new religious movements and organizations across time; that is, the durability of a religious movement depends on making the necessary adjustments to maintain the *optimum* level of tension with the surrounding and evolving culture.

Of course, the traditional expectation (apparently shared by O'Dea) was that sects almost inexorably make their accommodations with society and evolve into churches, or else they just "stagnate" and eventually die. Given the conventional secularization model that had dominated social science thinking until recent times, this expectation would have seemed logical. However, once we recognize that religious organizations, like other social systems, are dynamic *tension-management systems,* it becomes apparent that they can move as logically to increase tension as to reduce it, that is, toward more *sect*like postures as well as in the conventional churchlike direction. Already in 1963, Benton Johnson had recognized in passing the possibility of this kind of "reversal," and the logic of such a prospect was formalized some years later by Iannaccone (Johnson 1963, 543n15; 1971; Iannaccone 1988).[11] Eventually, in a later book by Rodney Stark and Roger Finke, the phenomenon of churchlike to sectlike development was integrated into the "new paradigm" more generally and documented with several case studies (2000, chap. 10).[12]

The New Paradigm and the Mormon Case

However, the first application of this "reversal" idea to the general history of a religious denomination was my own 1994 study of the transformation of the modern Mormon Church.[13] In many ways, this book picked up from where O'Dea's book had left off. His book had discussed and analyzed mainly the nineteenth century and the first half of the twentieth century of Mormon history. O'Dea had been especially interested in the process of Mormon assimilation into American society, and the extent to which the trajectory of accommodation would continue after midcentury.[14] My book, by contrast, was a study of the *counter*accommodation processes that became evident in the Mormon Church after O'Dea's book. My general thesis was that during the mid-twentieth century, church leaders became increasingly uncomfortable with the extent to which Mormonism had sacrificed its unique identity for national respectability. To use the language of the "new paradigm" discussed above, the leaders began to worry about the implications of "reduced tension" with the surrounding culture and decided to *increase that tension* by selectively reemphasizing certain traditional Mormon doctrines and by renewing demands for conformity to traditional religious observances and moral standards.[15]

I called this process *retrenchment,* and it clearly reflected a generalized church policy of greater tension between the surrounding culture and the Mormons, both individually and institutionally.[16] This retrenchment took several forms: renewed emphasis on following the prophet as God's current mouthpiece in even mundane matters; renewed reliance on the Book of Mormon in church teaching and discourse, combined with a retroactive "Mormonizing" hermeneutic for the King James Bible; a large increase in the missionary corps and a call for universal missionary service by male youth; increased commitment to genealogical research (for vicarious postmortem rites on behalf of ancestors); proliferation of new temples around the globe for performing such rites; and renewed emphasis on the importance of the family institution, defined primarily in conservative, neo-Victorian terms. In addition, rapid postwar growth had threatened the orderly management and control of the leadership over auxiliary organizations and over the content of church meetings, classes, and lesson manuals. The leadership response, starting in the 1960s, was the implementation of an organizational restructuring called "correlation," which greatly centralized the control of all ecclesiastical functions and teaching materials into the hands of the top priesthood leaders in Salt Lake City (or, operationally, into the hands of an extensive paid professional staff) (Mauss 1994, 163–67; Shipps 2000, 374–81; Prince and Wright 2005, 142–58).[17]

This is not the place to recapitulate at length the explanations and evidence for all of this, as detailed in my book *The Angel and the Beehive*.[18] Suffice it to say that according to my findings, the actual path chosen by church leaders for the Mormon future was drastically different from that suggested by O'Dea's diagnosis and prescription. Under the influence of the secularization paradigm dominant in his time, O'Dea, in effect, had fretted about whether the Mormons would be able to accommodate adequately to "modern secular thought" in order to survive and grow. By contrast, I applied the logic of the *new* paradigm to explain why the viability and growth of the church actually depended on moving in the *opposite* direction from that which O'Dea had envisioned. Not that "modern secular thought" could be ignored altogether, but that the precise relationship to modernity achieved by the church would reflect its own *quest for optimum tension* with modern society in various ways. The rapid growth of the church around the world since O'Dea's time, to say nothing of its considerable accumulated wealth, would seem to have vindicated the decision by the church leaders (however that decision was made) to *increase* tension with the world, rather than to decrease it, in seeking a *new optimum level* for the second half of the twentieth century.[19]

O'Dea's Prognosis for the Mormon Future

If, as I argue here, the modern history of the Mormon Church has reflected a policy more of retrenchment than of assimilation, how well has such a policy enabled the Mormons to deal with the challenges that O'Dea saw lying ahead? Even as he was reflecting on the processes and institutions that had created the Mormon people as a unique historical phenomenon, O'Dea could see the signs of drastic change at midcentury, despite the efforts of the church "to preserve its separate identity and to remain unobtrusively 'gathered' while still a part of the larger nation": Mormon outmigration to the cities on both coasts and the construction of churches and temples outside the traditional Mormon heartland both pointed, said O'Dea, to a "more abstract, more spiritualized, conception of the gathering" and of other traditional Mormon ideas (1957, 118). The success and spread of the church during the second half of the twentieth century, however, he warned, would bring new and important challenges to the very viability of Mormonism: "Perhaps Mormonism's greatest and most significant problem is its encounter with modern secular thought," a challenge to which O'Dea then takes an entire chapter to analyze in detail (222, chap. 9).

His analysis of the Mormons is guided by his underlying assumption of the inevitability of secularization for the survival and relevance of religious traditions in general. He identifies which aspects of "modern secular thought" that he expects to "test the ... viability" of Mormonism, and then he considers the derivative sources of "strain and conflict" inherent in many of the very values and institutions that had proved historically so important in creating the Mormon culture and people (224–25, 242–57). O'Dea concludes his study with an epilogue that has some ambivalence but generally offers an optimistic prognosis for the Mormon future: "It is my suspicion that those who emphasize the obsolescence of Mormonism, ... who see the end of the movement in a stereotyped lack of creativity and a routine running down, ... are wrong. There is still too much vitality—the characteristic Mormon vitality—remaining for such a prognosis to be likely.... Its flexibility in the past, and its viability under the most adverse conditions, do not augur badly for its future" (262–63). Clearly, this was a tentative optimism, however, and as O'Dea looked to the future, he focused correctly on an important predicament with which Mormon leaders would have to contend, namely, the powerful impact of modern secular influences. He did not, however, anticipate the magnitude of a second major predicament, namely, the rapid growth of the LDS religion in the United States and globally, which would greatly complicate the relationship of the church with the world.[20]

The LDS Encounter with Modern Secular Thought

In his wide-ranging discussion of the "strains and contradictions" in mid-century Mormonism, O'Dea first reviewed the general impact of "modern secular thought" on traditional religious communities, and then he went on to discuss in detail each of *nine* such contradictions that had developed across time in Mormonism particularly. Clearly and implicitly, he considered the future viability of the church and religion to depend on a successful resolution of these strains and contradictions (222–57). Fifteen years after completion of *The Mormons*, O'Dea was invited to reflect again on the "sources of strain and conflict" in Mormonism (1972). By this time, he had become considerably less sanguine about his prognosis. What had intervened, besides time, to change O'Dea's assessment? We cannot be sure, of course, exactly what he had seen and experienced that would have made the difference. We know that his original experience in Utah had lasted only a matter of weeks during his research for *The Mormons* but that he had later returned to live in Utah for five years (1959–1964) as part of a faculty stint at the University of Utah (Michaelsen 1978). Had this more extensive personal experience during those five years revealed to him some aspects of Mormon culture that undermined his optimism about the "characteristic Mormon vitality" that had seemed so important to him earlier? Perhaps.

Yet O'Dea's 1972 assessment was clearly preoccupied with the race question as the great "diagnostic issue" testing the Mormon prospects for viability and vitality. Despite considerable outside pressure for "progressive change," the Mormons (or at least their leadership) were found wanting by O'Dea on that crucial diagnostic issue, and thus apparently he saw a need to revise his earlier prognosis in a more pessimistic direction. Besides its special focus on the race issue, O'Dea's 1972 essay is clearly intended as a more general update of the concluding observations in his 1957 book about the organizational predicaments of the LDS Church at midcentury. Given his own intellectual biases, it is not particularly surprising that O'Dea would have found the response of the church on the race issue to be inadequate by the early 1970s.[21] What is less clear is why he had come to see the race issue in particular almost as a surrogate in general for "the church's most profound problem ... [namely,] [h]ow to renew the original democratic and ethical spirit of Mormonism ... and thereby provide the basis for a more contemporary and more vital understanding of Mormon values." For him, this one issue seemed to carry almost the entire burden of testing the "church's adequacy to handle ... its encounter with modernity [more generally].... [The church would] eventually be judged by ... its response to the problem of racial justice." O'Dea's 1972 verdict was almost ominous: "The Mormon church in its defensive and stand pat position reveals itself as responding inadequately to [this] diagnostic issue." Indeed, the church "stands before enlightened American opinion at worst as guilty of unchristian behavior, or at best as being tied up in obsolete provincial American and Mormon racist attitudes and unable to shed them" (162–65).

Although O'Dea's revised expectations about the future of Mormonism occurred in the context of Mormonism's then unresolved race issue, they must be considered also in the light of a much broader cultural transformation in the country—namely, the arrival of the Age of Aquarius in the 1960s and 1970s, when the entire nation had to contend with the rise of a youthful counterculture that challenged many values taken for granted in the country up to midcentury. This development, along with the rapid church growth beginning about the same time, had enormous effects on how the church leadership and membership came to view the Mormon relationship with the outside world, where "modern secular thought" was beginning to take on a meaning far more threatening to traditional LDS values than anything O'Dea had envisioned at midcentury. Countercultural influences, especially in matters of female autonomy, sexual behavior, drug use, and certain other so-called lifestyle matters, had come to be seen as serious challenges to traditional moral strictures even in the nation as a whole, but particularly within the Mormon community. Indeed, the retrenchment posture taken by the church, as explained above, was in large part a response precisely to this more general cultural crisis (Mauss 1994, 67, 123–24). As Mormon leaders grappled with the "strains and contradictions" identified by O'Dea, they had to do so against this entire background. Fortuitously, and perhaps fortunately as well, certain inexorable historical developments in Mormonism itself had already drained many of O'Dea's nine "contradictions" of their immediacy and salience, even by the time of his 1972 essay—and certainly by the arrival of the new century.

Largely Resolved Strains and Contradictions

Among those that remain less salient ones today, I have in mind particularly the strains or contradictions between rationality and charisma, plural marriage and changing doctrine, modern progress and agrarianism, patriotism and particularism, and belief and environment—the latter term used by O'Dea to refer mainly to the realities of the non-Mormon outside world and its peoples (1957, 256–57 and more generally 241–57). All five of these particular contradictions have become quite "academic"—literally so, in the sense that although they have been the object of a fair amount of scholarly attention, they have lost nearly all their salience as problems with which church members and leaders feel the need to contend in the ordinary life of the religious community. To the extent that such historical issues do come up, they might be discussed by scholars and teachers, or cited from the pulpit for pedagogical purposes, but most modern Mormons would consider these as "problems solved."

For example, the first, *rationality versus charisma,* has given way to a thoroughgoing routinization of charisma with a highly rationalized and coordinated control over the process of revelation (Mauss 1994, 210–12; Stark 2005, chap. 2). In the second case, though *plural marriage* remains unabated among schismatic groups, the church has simply turned the problem over to the state, and the "change of doctrine" issue, which was so important when the church repudiated polygamy, has become even more moot with the change of policy toward blacks (see Van Wagoner 1986; and Driggs 1990, 1991). It is hard to see much strain between *progress and agrarianism* when Utah is one of the most urbanized states in the nation, home to modern electronic industries such as Novell and WordPerfect (now part of Corell) (Heaton, Hirschi, and Chadwick 1996, esp. 3–18). As for *patriotism,* it has largely replaced the Mormon particularism of the pre–World War II era, as American Mormons have become increasingly conservative and nationalistic in their politics, are overrepresented in Congress, and (at this writing) seeing another Romney as a presidential candidate (Heaton, Bahr, and Ja-cobson 2004, chap. 7).[22] Finally, as a religious denomination with the ma-jority of its members now living outside not only of Utah but of the United States, there seems little doubt about a successful *engagement with the out-side "environment"* (in which O'Dea saw a potential problem for Utah out-migrants) (Heaton, Hirschi, and Chadwick 1996, 59–67).

Unresolved Strains and Contradictions

Despite an apparent mitigation across time of the contradictions in those five cases, however, some of the other strains and contradictions identified by O'Dea in 1957 remain salient in modern Mormonism, most notably, per-haps, the strains between *authority and democracy* (or obedience and indi-vidualism) and between *consent and coercion*. One might also add two other contradictions not yet entirely resolved from O'Dea's original list: that be-tween *family ideals and equality of women* and between *political conservatism and social idealism*. All four of these contradictions continue to complicate the Mormon encounter with modern secular thought. However, in his dis-cussions of all these dichotomies, O'Dea drew primarily on *historical* exam-ples, especially from the nineteenth century, and his examples were to be-come considerably less relevant with the passage of time. Indeed, as we look at the issues faced by the LDS Church in the twenty-first century, the di-chotomies or contradictions still vexing the church often seem to converge, in one way or another, upon O'Dea's *consent versus coercion*—which might be rephrased in modern Mormonism as *loyalty to the church versus individ-ual agency* (usually dubbed "free agency" in Mormon parlance).

O'Dea had observed in 1957, probably correctly, that the traditional Mormon tensions between consent and coercion, obedience and individu-alism, and authority and democracy had been pretty well managed by the church historically. In church polity and governance, he found "a democracy of participation ... [along with] ... hierarchical organization and authori-tarian operation." Such participation, he pointed out, requires "at least pas-sive loyalty," which "must ultimately rest upon consent." He recognized that the "exact proportion of consent to coercion" in the operation of any or-ganization "is difficult to gauge and does not permit of quantitative mea-surement." Furthermore, some coercion is and was, in the mid-nineteenth century, "a part of any constitutional government ... in ... established com-munities," including the U.S. government itself, but the Mormon leader-ship typically used "coercion as a supplement, [and] ... in this it does not ap-pear to have differed in its fundamental working from all leadership and all government." He acknowledged that such organizational imperatives might be "a source of difficulty" for intellectuals, as it was for dissident movements such as the Godbeites, but "all communities draw a line against dissent somewhere" (243–45).

Just where to draw such a line has been a recurrent quandary for the LDS leadership since O'Dea wrote these words. Indeed, in many ways the quandary has been more vexing in recent years, when the main outside pressures have come almost entirely from the "modern secular thought" that was O'Dea's main focus already in 1957 (and even more so in 1972). In the nineteenth century, when survival had depended on solidarity in the face of a politically hostile American nation and government, consent and obedience were less debatable in the ranks of the church. Within a theocratic framework called "the political kingdom of God," a strong Mormon tradition had developed of subordinating individual ideas and preferences to the greater good, as revealed through the church leaders, particularly the prophet-president. That tradition had attenuated somewhat by O'Dea's time, but it was clearly still relevant (Hansen 1966; Williams 1966).

During the second half of the twentieth century, however, the chief enemy, as O'Dea foresaw, did indeed become modern secular culture, with its relentless challenges to traditional institutions and religious truths of all kinds, and its seductive moral and cultural relativism (Mauss 1994, chaps. 5–6, pp. 85–86, 126–30). To contend with these new challenges, LDS leaders began more strenuously than earlier in the century to call for loyalty and obedience to authority and for agency to be exercised in support of the church both ecclesiastically (within) and politically (without). The resulting *retrenchment* has been accompanied by some apostasy, as O'Dea would have expected, which has "creat[ed] enemies without [but] acted as a purgative within" (O'Dea 1957, 244). In the United States, at least, the recurrent injunction to "follow the prophet" has brought a degree of compliance with moral and lifestyle strictures and a commitment of both time and money among most members that are unusual even for a relatively religious American population. To the consternation of many other Americans, furthermore, grassroots Mormon compliance with the *political* preferences of church leaders also remains conspicuous, at least in the United States.

Such compliance has expressed itself during the past few decades primarily in the increasingly conservative voting tendencies of the Mormon electorate, especially (but not only) where moral or countercultural issues are involved; the resistance of Mormons, including leaders and members of both sexes, to the feminist political agenda; and a similar resistance to the gay-rights agenda, especially where it involves broadening the definition of "marriage" or "family" to include same-sex spouses (Mauss 1994, 112–22; see also Heaton, Bahr, and Jacobson 2004, chap. 7). Political interventions by Mormon leaders, sometimes surreptitious and sometimes public and strident, have been particularly conspicuous in all the most controversial issues, and American Mormons have mostly followed their leaders. The usual explanation given for official church intervention in such matters is that they are "moral" rather than "political" issues—an artificial distinction, of course, since all these issues involve contention over *public policy* within the *political* arena. For the most part, these conservative tendencies are justified by Mormon spokespersons as upholding *traditional personal and family values* in the face of an onslaught of modern secular liberalism, agnosticism, and relativism.

As noted in chapter 7, the generally conservative tendency among Mormons that has dominated in recent decades can be seen, furthermore, in Republican presidential and congressional preferences; a "patriotic," if somewhat ambivalent, view of militarism in foreign policy; conservative views on abortion; and a strong if losing rearguard resistance to liberalizing laws on alcohol and drug use. In gender politics, the feminist agenda was overtly resisted, with church resources and political mobilization, during the International Women's Year campaign and the Equal Rights Amendment struggle of the 1970s (Bradley 2005). In the statewide controversies and campaigns over legitimating same-sex marriages, the LDS Church has again asserted itself strongly against any such developments.[23] Such political interventions in the service of the LDS moral outlook have been an important part of the retrenchment process that has increased the tension between the Mormon community and the secular national culture. Accordingly, the church has paid some price in its public image but has been glad to do so, considering the values that it has seen to be at stake.

Beyond these political initiatives toward the *outside,* which have conspicuously brought Mormons and their church to the attention of the nation as a whole, the church has also struggled with a more *internal* strain between *loyalty to the Church and individual agency.* This struggle too was intensified by the retrenchment process *inside* the church after the 1950s, which for some members, especially those of a more intellectual bent, increased the "cost" of membership by demanding loyalty in certain respects that seemed to impinge on individual agency. On a more collective basis, the retrenchment took the form of the organizational restructuring called "correlation," which centralized the control of programs, religious instruction, and religious literature into the hands of a paid professional staff charged by the apostles with standardizing and simplifying the discourse and pedagogy of the entire church to the "lowest common denominator," as it were. Local leaders and teachers, furthermore, were generally cautioned not to resort to any supplementary literature or programs that might have permitted some enhancements in accordance with local needs (Mauss 1994, 163–67; Shipps 2000, 374–81).[24]

Seemingly in response to this homogenization, a vibrant "unsponsored sector" of intellectual conferences, books, journals, and independent organizations has emerged outside the control of the church leaders.[25] These grassroots institutions, some now more than forty years old, scarcely existed at all in O'Dea's time, when the few Mormon intellectuals were often critical nonbelievers or else felt obliged to exile themselves from Utah altogether in order to escape community and family pressures or reprisals (Geary 1977). At present, the intellectuals within Mormonism (a growing but still relatively small proportion of the membership) cover a range from apostates to apologists, with perhaps a bimodal tendency but a fairly full distribution across the entire range.[26] A few spontaneous local "study groups" around the country have also always existed at the grassroots, based in one or a few stakes of the church, where speakers and discussions on Mormon-related topics occur monthly or a few times a year. These are outside official church auspices but are generally tolerated (if not embraced) by at least the local church leadership.[27] By the 1980s, these independent conferences, publications, and study groups had become worrisome to some of the church leaders, who responded with admonitions about giving too much credence to "alternate voices" (see Oaks 1989; and Mauss 1990). Some of the more critical and strident of these alternate voices were, indeed, eventually excommunicated from the church for "conduct unbecoming" faithful members.[28]

New Strains and Contradictions

Indeed, by examining the conference proceedings and the publications of these organizations outside church control, one can see the emergence of new issues that O'Dea did not include among the strains and contradictions he discussed. At least three deserve some discussion here : *patriarchal tradition versus equality of women; chastity outside marriage versus conjugal aspirations of homosexuals;* and *modern scientific evidence versus the historicity of the Book of Mormon.*[29] The first two of these have recently been sharpened by the Proclamation on the Family, issued by the First Presidency and Council of the Twelve Apostles in 1995, the provisions of which would seem to have added a new canonical reinforcement to traditional LDS doctrines about marriage, heterosexuality, and women's roles.[30] In contrast, although O'Dea had considered "family ideals versus equality of women" as one of his strains and conflicts, his analysis was largely historical (pointing especially to the polygamy era). In looking at the contemporaneous church, however, O'Dea proved no more prescient about the women's issue than he had been about the race issue, for he assured his readers that this "apparent contradiction…has become unimportant.…Today, practically no difficulty arises from this problem,… [for] auxiliary organizations activate women to an extent that makes them feel very much a part of the church" (1957, 250).

That rather sanguine assessment was, of course, made before the rise of the new feminist movement, which challenged the neo-Victorian definition of women's roles still operative in O'Dea's time, both in the nation and in the LDS Church. This surrounding cultural change, furthermore, occurred just as the LDS organizational restructuring (priesthood correlation) destroyed the autonomy of church auxiliaries, particularly the women's Relief Society. In light of such external and internal changes, one wonders if it could still be true, as O'Dea had found it to be, that there is but little discontent among grassroots Mormon women. Such discontent as there might be is rarely, if ever, expressed openly in church settings but rather in the independent Mormon forums and publications; yet the church does appear to face a growing dropout rate by girls and young women. There is little evidence that Mormon women are any more eager to have the priesthood than they were in O'Dea's time.[31] However, at least in North America, as they continue to enjoy more access to advanced education, more career options, more autonomy in family life, and longer periods of singleness (all of which are strongly apparent in the twenty-first century), some Mormon women are coming to feel increasingly marginalized by their lack of control over their own programs and policies, and by the strongly male ecclesiastical culture of contemporary Mormonism. A strain is still there among the granddaughters of O'Dea's Mormons.[32]

The emergence in recent decades of a public homosexual presence seems to have taken the Mormons somewhat by surprise, and it has quickly become among the most vexing issues to face the church since O'Dea's time. No one knows how many homosexual ("gay") Mormons there are, but the number is probably around 5 percent in the United States, if proportional to the population as a whole.[33] Originally, the church's definition of the homosexual orientation was guided by the conventional wisdom in psychiatry, namely, that it was some sort of psychological disorder that could be "cured" by appropriate treatment. However, as psychiatry changed its diagnosis (under political as much as under scientific influences), the LDS Church once again found that the surrounding secular environment had presented a new challenge to its core values.[34] As homosexual relationships (or at least their accommodation) have increasingly been normalized in public policy, the LDS moral standard of celibacy outside of traditional marriage has come increasingly under pressure, especially, of course, for those homosexual Mormons who have "come out of the closet" and wish to retain their standing in the church despite their homosexual relationships—often with the sympathy, if not outright support, of their devout LDS families.[35] Such a desire contravenes both the long-standing demand on LDS members for chastity (celibacy) outside the bounds of heterosexual marriage and the important theological role of the family institution in Mormon soteriology (recently emphasized in the Proclamation on the Family). The resulting conflict for church members is heightened by the periodic intervention of their leaders into political campaigns that would legally and constitutionally reinforce the traditional marriage institution in the nation or would prevent any further legitimating of homosexual relationships or both.

The predicament for church policy, whether internal or external, is all the more difficult because of the ambiguity in the scientific evidence about the etiology of homosexuality. On the one hand is the recurrent claim by homosexuals that they did not choose their sexual orientation, for it goes back as far as they can remember. On the other hand, in neither medicine (psychiatry), psychology, nor the social sciences have theories been developed that can explain the origin of the homosexual orientation. Even the few studies that have found neurological or other physical differences between homosexuals and heterosexuals have depended on post-onset data, so causal direction cannot be determined. Most Mormons seem mystified by the situation, and, as one might suspect, some believe that homosexuality simply has to be accommodated as a reality, whereas others (including even a few with homosexual experience) claim that the homosexual orientation can be changed.[36] As the scientific and political controversies have swirled about the nation, LDS leaders have continued to insist on chastity for the unmarried as a condition of membership in good standing, combined with occasional expressions of love and acceptance for LDS homosexuals who remain celibate. Especially in view of the paucity of scientific knowledge on the ultimate origins of sexual orientation per se, church leaders have increasingly left that as a moot question, preferring instead to reiterate the traditional standard of chastity outside of marriage, whether for heterosexuals or homosexuals, and to remonstrate against homosexual behavior as a violation of church standards.[37] It is difficult to see an end to the conflict between the LDS moral strictures in this matter and the increasing accommodation of homosexual relationships in the surrounding society—and even in other religious denominations.[38]

Finally, a third relatively new source of strain and conflict in the LDS Church derives from a resurgent controversy over the historicity of the Book of Mormon.[39] O'Dea, of course, had taken for granted that the book was a product of the nineteenth century and that Joseph Smith himself had been the principal (if not the only) author. However, O'Dea had also taken the book seriously as a legitimate work of religious literature revered as divinely inspired scripture by Mormons. He acknowledged the theories of non-Mormon critics about the actual origin of the book, most of whom he did not find very convincing, noting in passing, with some irony, that "the *Book of Mormon* has not been universally considered by its critics as one of those books that must be read in order to have an opinion of it" (1957, 26)![40] During most of the time intervening since O'Dea wrote, very little occurred in the analysis or commentary on the Book of Mormon that would have given the upper hand either to apologists or to critics. Throughout a mid-century period (the 1940s to the 1960s), a rather ambitious and sustained effort was made by Mormon archaeologists, both professional and amateur, to uncover evidence from various sites in Mexico and Central America that might support claims about the ancient American origins of the book, but to very little avail (Mauss 2003, 139–42). If O'Dea knew of such efforts, he made no comments about them.

After O'Dea, little critical attention was paid to the Book of Mormon, either by apologists or by critics and scoffers, until the 1980s, when the Foundation for Ancient Research and Mormon Studies (FARMS) came into existence.[41] Largely eschewing archaeological research as its mission, FARMS has instead devoted itself to textual analysis, scouring the text of the Book of Mormon for parallels, connections, and even allusions to ancient Semitic scriptures, peoples, and cultures from which the book is believed to be derivative. This methodology was inspired by the late and celebrated Mormon scholar Hugh Nibley (1910–2005), an expert in ancient languages, who devoted his career at Brigham Young University (BYU) to establishing the historical authenticity of the Book of Mormon by inference from his putative discoveries of its textual and cultural ties to the ancient world.[42] In this endeavor, FARMS was soon joined by Mormon anthropologist John L. Sorenson, who had decided that archaeological digs were not very likely to yield the kind of evidence that would convince non-Mormon scholars. Accordingly, Sorenson turned instead to an intriguing search for geographic and topographical evidence from the Book of Mormon text that might make it possible to identify, with reasonable precision, the location in ancient America where the story of the book had actually taken place. The combined investigations of Sorenson, other FARMS scholars, and their disciples have produced a fairly strong consensus at FARMS that the Book of Mormon is ultimately the product of an ancient people or peoples who lived in a limited area of Mesoamerica and were probably the ancestors of today's Mayan people (Sorenson 1985).

The work of Sorenson and numerous other FARMS scholars has become voluminous and persuasive enough during the past two decades that it has generated a critical counterliterature, most of it from other Mormons who no longer accept the traditional claims of the church about the book (for example, Metcalf 1993; and Vogel and Metcalf 2002). There are quite a variety of approaches in this literature, much of which is devoted to criticizing the evidence and reasoning advanced by the scholars at FARMS. Most recently, however, the critics have found their ammunition chiefly from molecular biology, where surveys of DNA samples from various parts of the Western Hemisphere have failed to turn up any evidence that today's aboriginal peoples of the hemisphere include descendants of Israelite or other Semitic origin who might have written the Book of Mormon as the church claims (Southerton 2004; Murphy 2003). Scholars at FARMS and other Mormon scientists have responded with theories and evidence of varying persuasiveness to argue for alternative ways of explaining the DNA record that might still allow for the presence of a relatively small colony of Israelites during certain periods in the ancient history of the hemisphere (Whiting 2003; Leavitt, Marshall, and Campbell 2003). Neither side in this DNA controversy has succeeded in moving the other very far, so something of a standoff remains.

Interestingly enough, the church leaders themselves have remained almost entirely aloof from the arguments between FARMS and its critics, perhaps because few of them, if any, have the academic or technical expertise to engage the arguments at a scholarly level. There can be little doubt that they find the literature of FARMS, and of scholarly apologists more generally, to be helpful, and occasionally some of that literature will be included in official church publications, at least on a selective and condensed basis. Yet some of the positions taken by FARMS have been at odds with traditional Mormon understandings of the Book of Mormon and its claims. For example, in promulgating the idea that the Book of Mormon story took place in the limited geographic setting of Mayan Mesoamerica, FARMS is, in effect, repudiating the traditional Mormon assumption, at both the official and the grassroots levels, that the protagonists in the Book of Mormon story once populated the entire hemisphere.[43] This traditional view is certainly the one that O'Dea assumed to be the standard Mormon teaching, and it has been reiterated even in very recent years by the president of the church himself at dedications of Mormon temples in Latin America. How-ever, in general, church leaders have confined themselves to testifying of the divine origin of the Book of Mormon and its teachings, matters in which they are the presumptive experts, as though leaving the scientific quandaries to sort themselves out. To the extent that this sorting out takes place accord-ing to the canons and evidence of secular scholarship, in which FARMS seems committed to engage, there is an inherent risk that church leaders will not be happy with the scientific verdicts on the Book of Mormon, if and when they are ever conclusive.[44]

The Uneasy Rapprochement with Secular Scholarship

Beyond the Book of Mormon controversy, the church leadership has also tried, with mixed success, to accommodate some intellectuals and to enlist their help in dealing with other theological and historical issues that have created the most serious threats to traditional truth claims and to the church's public image. I refer to this success as "mixed" because the top church lead-ership itself, taken collectively, is not always of one mind about the kind of relationship it wants with Mormon intellectuals. Many scholars and academ-ics, including some very competent and talented ones, are employed by the church itself, not only on the BYU faculties but also as religion teachers in the massive Church Educational System, and as historians and archivists on research projects at church headquarters. Church leaders keep an eye on these scholars, but in general they are considered safe and loyal because they are in church employ and thus subject to dismissal if their work or public comments are perceived as harmful to church interests. A number of intel-lectuals, both inside and outside church employment, have made their disaf-fection or apostasy public enough that they have been ignored by church leaders as essentially outsiders; in a few aggravated cases, some have even been excommunicated. Still others, privately employed but public in their written and oral treatments of Mormonism, are scattered along the contin-uum at various positions between apologists, on the one end, and dissenters, on the other (Duffy 2004). It is this middle group that receives mixed reac-tions from church leaders: sometimes they are cultivated and used to good effect, and at other times they are treated with benign neglect, depending sometimes on their personal relationships with certain leaders.

Early in the twenty-first century, it is often difficult to characterize just what the "official" posture of the church is toward its own intellectu-als. This is so partly because the church leadership itself, though conserva-tive, is not monolithic in its outlook, either toward intellectuals or toward O'Dea's "modern secular thought," and partly because the sheer number of

Mormon intellectuals today is so much larger and more varied than it was in 1957 (Walker, Whittaker, and Allen 2001, 60–112). Organizational developments during the past few decades, starting with "correlation," suggest a certain amount of ambivalence in how much the leaders are willing to accommodate intellectual independence.[45] Even the correlation program was long resisted in high places, and there are still periodic grassroots pressures to customize and stylize the church program to meet local needs perceived in some congregations and classrooms (Prince and Wright 2005, 151–58). The collective ambivalence of the leaders toward modern scholarship in history and religion can perhaps best be seen through developments within the LDS Church Historical Department itself since 1970.

Prior to the 1970s, the office of church historian had always been in the hands of an apostle, who had usually considered his charge to be more that of a gatekeeper than of a guide to church historical materials. Then, during the early 1970s, when a series of ill and aging prophets occupied the office of president, a group of apostles, led apparently by Spencer W. Kimball and Howard W. Hunter, saw the need to modernize and professionalize the writing of Mormon history. They recruited the first church historian ever to have been professionally trained in academic historiography, Leonard J. Arrington, a professor of economic history at Utah State University, who had founded the Mormon History Association in 1965 as a fully independent scholarly society and had distinguished himself as an exponent of the "new Mormon history." Arrington surrounded himself with a cadre of similarly trained younger scholars from academe, and together they were responsible for an unprecedented output of historical books and articles that were sympathetic without being apologetic and guided by the canons and methodology of academic historiography (Walker, Whittaker, and Allen 2001, 61–68, 87–89).

Within five years, however, a more conservative group of apostles had become highly critical of what they saw as a lack of spiritual, faith-promoting qualities in the work of Arrington and his colleagues, so they moved to curtail or close down the production of "new Mormon history" at church headquarters. A resolution of the disparate apostolic views took the form of a compromise, in which Arrington and his staff would be re-created as a new historical research institute at BYU, the Joseph Fielding Smith Institute for LDS History, where they would continue to write academic history (within some clearly understood constraints). Meanwhile, the office of church historian reverted permanently to a full-time church leader at church headquarters, and the LDS Church Historical Department became more selective in granting access to its archives.[46] In 2005, the "other shoe dropped," as it were, and the Arrington legacy ended altogether with the closing of the Smith Institute. At the same time, however, many of the professional historians from that institute were brought back to church headquarters to carry on the kinds of major research and publication projects envisioned by Arrington, only now less conspicuously.

Church leaders have traditionally been uncomfortable with scholarly research, writing, and conferences on Mormons that are independent of church control. However, during the past forty years or so, a civil if somewhat uneasy relationship has been maintained between the church leadership and historians or other intellectuals more generally, whether or not the latter are employed by the church. In addition, there are some recent signs that church leaders have become more desirous of seeing the academic study of the Mormon religion and culture acquire some respectability even outside of church control. Recent examples of this trend can be seen in the conferences on Mormonism held at Yale Divinity School in 2003 and at the Library of Congress in 2005, which were convoked mainly under non-Mormon auspices but drew the full participation of church-employed scholars and even of apostles or other general authorities (Parry 2006).[47]

A more extensive and enduring indication of some rapprochement between the LDS leadership and modern intellectual developments can be seen also in the rise of new academic programs in Mormon studies at a few universities—so far, most notably, at Utah State University and the Claremont Graduate University in southern California.[48] The church leadership in general has remained quite aloof from such developments, offering only the most tacit and tentative approval to date. This is certainly not yet the kind of embrace of "modern secular thought" that O'Dea might have advocated, but it does seem to herald some reduction in "cultural tension" by today's leadership, and a new confidence that the church now has the intellectual resources to manage a constructive relationship with both the secular world and the world's various religious traditions.

CONCLUSION:
OF PARADIGMS AND PROSPECTS FOR GLOBAL GROWTH

In his study of the Mormons and their Church of Jesus Christ of Latter-day Saints, Thomas F. O'Dea offered an essentially sympathetic portrait of a unique American institution. His assessment of its future was mainly optimistic, both in his 1957 book and in his 1954 article, yet he pointed to a number of "strains and conflicts" that would have to be resolved somehow in order for the church to avoid reverting to "sectarian stagnation" and to continue to thrive on the American religious landscape. In the context of the dominant paradigm in the social sciences of that era, O'Dea assumed and, in effect, prescribed that most of the strains and conflicts he saw could best be resolved by coming to terms with "modern secular thought," just as most mainstream Protestant churches had done by that time. When he looked at the Mormons again in 1972, he was not encouraged by what he saw, for in his view the nagging race issue in the church did not portend a readiness for the embrace of modernity that he had prescribed.

Instead, the church moved in just the opposite direction—away from the fashionable secular nostrums of the time that might have hastened its assimilation into the dominant culture's respectable churchlike religion. In choosing a policy of retrenchment after about 1960, the church sought to increase, rather than decrease, its tension with American culture and to accept the social and political "costs of doing business" in the American religious marketplace. Thereby, the church highlighted its *differences* in that marketplace that made its "products" more valuable than those of its competitors, especially those competitors promoting the products of this secular world, rather than those of the next world. In opting for this retrenchment strategy, the leaders of the church were not, of course, consulting social scientists, but, as matters developed, it became apparent that this Mormon strategy for viability and growth converged nicely with the "new paradigm" that eventually emerged in the sociology and economics of religion during the 1980s and 1990s.[49]

What seems to have resulted from this strategy was a renewed vitality that greatly increased not only the human and material capital inside the church but also its ability to deploy those resources both at home and in extensive worldwide proselyting. The retrenchment mode underlying this strategy included an organizational "correlation" or restructuring borrowed largely from the corporate business world, which eliminated, on a cost-benefit basis, many programs, policies, and customary activities that generations of American Mormons had found enriching to their community lives.[50] The standardization and centralized control over the literature of the church alienated many of the new generation of intellectuals, who had grown up expecting their adventurous thinking and writing to be more widely appreciated by church leaders. So not everyone coming of age after midcentury was comfortable with the growing retrenchment mode, but if and when any departed in disaffection, their ranks were quickly filled with new converts who had never known any other kind of LDS Church.[51] Most American Mormons, at least, whether converts or lifelong members, have continued to demonstrate their commitment to the church with fairly high rates of church attendance and tithe paying, and the Mormon "market share" has reached fourth place by now (Heaton, Bahr, and Jacobson 2004, chap. 3; Stark 2005, chap. 4; Phillips 1998; Ostling and Ostling 1999, chap. 21, esp. 374–75).[52] Presumably, even O'Dea would thus have to concede that Mormonism in the United States is a more thriving enterprise than he might have expected, given his prognosis and prescription.

Yet most Mormons are no longer Americans. Of the world's 13 million Mormons in 2007, slightly more than half now live outside the United States. One suspects that O'Dea would have been astonished at both the total and the non-American proportion, considering that when *The Mormons* was published, there were only 1.5 million Mormons, most of whom lived in Utah and almost all the rest of whom lived in the western United States (Stark 2005, 144). The growth of the church can be attributed almost entirely to its enormous missionary corps, which itself has grown steadily during the past half century and numbers between 50,000 and 60,000 at the beginning of the twenty-first century (129). The wide distribution of Mormon congregations around the globe has necessitated the building of some 124 Mormon temples (at the end of 2006) for the sacred and vicarious rituals so important to Mormons, a twelvefold increase since O'Dea's time.[53] Many thousands of chapels and churches have been built for regular Sunday worship around the world as well, and many of the Mormon congregations are in the less industrialized parts of the world, where the church must also fight disease and malnutrition. All of this has required outlays of church funds in the many billions of dollars, which itself testifies to the effectiveness of the church's strategy for success (Ostling and Ostling 1999, chap. 7). The Church of Jesus Christ of Latter-day Saints has therefore certainly become a *global* church, but whether or not it can be considered a "world church"—to say nothing of "world religion"—would be a matter of semantics and definition. Surely, it is not a "world church" in the sense of having a significant presence in most parts of the world as, for example, Catholicism has. Nor can Mormonism be considered a "world religion" in the sense that it is one of the largest religions in the world, which clearly it is not (Mauss 1996, 1994, chap. 12; Neilson 2005).

To put the reality most accurately, perhaps we should say that the LDS Church is almost entirely a Western Hemisphere church, with 85 percent of its membership living in either North or South America. Furthermore, its continued growth is itself problematic, at least at the relatively high rates that we have seen so far. In much of the world, especially the less industrialized parts, such as Latin America, the Mormons receive vigorous competition from the Jehovah's Witnesses and the Pentecostals, who seem to work in the same "market niche" as the Mormons and do at least as well, if not better.[54] In Europe, Mormon growth is especially slow, and in some countries it depends disproportionately on the conversion of immigrant populations, which are already marginal to the indigenous cultures of Europe (Lobb 2000). In most countries, Mormon converts have proved difficult to retain (especially the men), partly because the sheer numbers have overwhelmed the resources of the local congregation to integrate them culturally, socially, and intellectually (Bennion and Young 1996; Shepherd and Shepherd 1996). In almost all of the world, the Mormon religion has been perceived (not without reason) as an American religion, and its appeal has waxed and waned with the popular attitudes toward the United States, its foreign policies, and its cultural exports. As with all "exported" religions, furthermore, Mormonism faces the quandary of how to achieve the *optimum tension* in each new cultural setting—or, in other words, how best accommodate itself to that culture without suffering unacceptable kinds of syncretic corruption (Mauss 1994, 208–12).[55]

For all of these reasons, and certain others, the Mormon growth rate has started to level off, especially outside the United States. Indeed, if we were to consider *retention rates,* some might conclude that *actual* growth is *negative* (Heaton 1992, 1527; Shepherd and Shepherd 1996, 45–48). Observers inside and outside the church have long known that in most of the world the retention rate in Mormon congregations has been running at between 20 percent and 30 percent. That is the general range of the proportion in a congregation attending Sunday worship services with any regularity, and similar proportions of the Mormons on official church records identify themselves as LDS on national census records (Knowlton 2005; Phillips 2005). This predicament has actually led to the merging and closing of some Mormon missions, wards (congregations), and stakes (small dioceses) in a few countries, especially in Latin America. The male lay priesthood on which the LDS Church depends around the world is a mixed blessing in this respect. On the one hand, every man is a potential priest or elder, who can be called on for leadership. On the other hand, his ordination or appointment as a leader is conditional upon conforming to certain church norms, such as regular attendance; abstaining from alcohol, tobacco, and drugs; strict marital fidelity; and making family life a priority. Apparently, fewer male than female converts are willing to stand these "costs" of membership. As a result, there is not enough male leadership in many places to keep wards and stakes at manageable sizes, a situation that, of course, just exacerbates the difficulty of integrating and retaining new converts (Shepherd and Shepherd 1996, 45–52).

Church leaders are well aware of all these issues, although they have not yet developed adequate strategies for dealing with all of them. Considering how the church has thrived during the past half century, it would seem that the revelatory process among LDS prophets (however that process works) is alive and well (Stark 1999). Or, to repeat O'Dea's understated assessment from fifty years ago: "Its flexibility in the past, and its viability under the most adverse conditions, do not augur badly for its future" (1957, 263).

How would a twenty-first-century O'Dea interpret another century of Mormon history in 2057, and what would be his or her prognosis for the future? Would still another theoretical paradigm be necessary? If Rodney Stark's most optimistic projections were to be realized, despite all the constraints reviewed just above, the world would have 120 million Mormons by 2057 (2005, 145).[56] What impact would such growth and distribution of LDS membership have on the doctrines and practices of the church? The massive Mormon proselytizing program after 1957 had the unintended consequence of transforming the Mormons' view of their enterprise from an ethnic, almost tribal religion into a universalistic faith community with a global vision and aspirations.[57] How will scholars of the future interpret and understand the significance of Mormonism in the history of the world's religions?

NOTES

1. After an extended visit to Utah, Ely had famously commented that the "organization of the Mormons is the most nearly perfect piece of social mechanism with which I have ever ... come into contact, excepting alone the German army" (1903, 668).

2. Troeltsch is explicitly cited by O'Dea (1957, 266), along with a number of other scholars in the same tradition.

3. With some chagrin, O'Dea reports in a footnote (293) that having come to this conclusion independently, he later discovered that it had already appeared a generation earlier in a classic sociology textbook, which noted that the Mormons in Utah had achieved "something approaching" a separate "nationality" (Park and Burgess 1921, 872–73).

4. This is a matter that receives considerable attention in my article "In Search of Ephraim: Traditional Mormon Conceptions of Lineage and Race" (1999).

5. O'Dea's reference to Turner was meant to evoke the historiographic theory, in vogue during much of the twentieth century, that analyzed (and in some ways celebrated) the formative influence of constant frontier living on the distinctive American character (see Turner 1920). The ultimate "Americanness" of the Mormon religion has been more recently discussed—one could even say celebrated—in the work of literary critic Harold Bloom (1992).

6. These colleagues are primarily William S. Bainbridge, Roger Finke, and Laurence Iannaccone. In its most recent, comprehensive, and accessible form, this "new paradigm" is exemplified in Stark and Finke 2000.

7. Interestingly enough, even O'Dea, toward the end of *The Mormons,* seemed to anticipate a basic premise of the "new paradigm." It would be a grave mistake, he said, "for a religious movement to concentrate its attention on this-worldly activities, since it is precisely this-worldliness and activism that modern man appears to be finding inadequate. For organized religion to offer competition in spheres of life in which non-religious organizations do better—spheres themselves inadequate to the facing of deeper human problems—is to be found wanting" (1957, 262).

8. This highly truncated general outline of the "new paradigm," as it had developed by the mid-1980s, is well and persuasively developed in Stark and Bainbridge 1985 and presented in a formal theoretical framework in Stark and Bainbridge 1987. It should be noted also that this paradigm has had a somewhat mixed reception among European scholars, some of whom find that it does not fit their data very well. This controversy is reviewed in Stark and Finke 2000, chap. 3.

9. In the sociological literature, see, for example, Kanter 1972; Homans 1974; and Emerson 1976. In economics, Nobel Prize winner Gary S. Becker's theory (often called "rational choice" theory) is applied to religion as part of a more comprehensive economic framework in his works *The Economic Approach to Human Behavior* (1976) and *Accounting for Tastes* (1996).

10. Laurence R. Iannaccone, once a student of Becker, is chiefly responsible for the synthesis of sociology and economics in the "new paradigm." See, for example, Iannaccone 1988, 1990, and 1994.

11. I take the idea of a "tension-management system" from Moore 1963; see also Mauss 1994, 4–14. I have inferred the idea of "optimum tension" from my reading of the work of Rodney Stark and colleagues, originally from Stark and Bainbridge 1985, esp. 50–60, 149–67, 363–65.

12. Some of the case studies in this chapter were based on articles that had been published somewhat earlier.

13. This case study would have strongly supported the argument in chapter 10 of *Acts of Faith,* though curiously the authors did not cite it among the literature on which they based their argument.

14. It must be noted that since O'Dea wrote, a much fuller literature has appeared on the subject of Mormon assimilation, or "Americanization," as it is sometimes called. Aside from a variety of journal articles, the first book-length treatment to deal with the *religious* assimilation of the Mormons was Shepherd and Shepherd 1984, which used an intriguing analysis of general conference sermons to trace changing Mormon religious beliefs across time. The *political* process of Americanization is fully documented in Larson 1971; and Flake 2004. The most general and comprehensive study of the assimilation process will be found in Alexander 1986. A more recent study using an innovative and provocative theory is Yorgason 2003. Historian Jan Shipps has also had much to say about twentieth-century Mormonism (see esp. Shipps 2000).

15. More recently, the various efforts of LDS leaders to cope with this changing situation in the modern church were discussed in a series of papers presented at the twenty-ninth annual Sidney B. Sperry Symposium on the BYU campus. The papers were published in a collection titled *Out of Obscurity: The LDS Church in the Twentieth Century* (2000).

16. There is no intention here to claim that this retrenchment process issued from some sort of explicit recognition by church leaders of the need for increased "tension" in line with social science theories. Their response was far more intuitive and pragmatic, based on their own observations and experiences.

17. Organizational changes accompanying the "retrenchment" process receive a certain amount of attention also in E. Kimball 2005, starting especially in chapter 8.

18. Several articles by other authors since *The Angel and the Beehive* appeared have seemingly vindicated the basic thesis of this book when it has been more widely applied. It is a theme running implicitly, and in some cases explicitly, through a recent collection of summer seminar papers on the changing conditions for women in the LDS Church (see Bushman 2004). My retrenchment thesis is particularly applicable to the papers by Katie Clark Blakesley, "A Style of Our Own: Modesty and Mormon Women, 1951–2003"; Kristine Haglund Harris, "Who Shall Sing If Not the Children? Primary Songbooks, 1880–1989"; and Tina Hatch, "Changing Times Bring Changing Conditions: Relief Society, 1960–Present." On the same theme, see also Kear 2001.

19. Critics of *The Angel and the Beehive* (Mauss 1994) have noted that in some ways the church has taken a *more accommodationist* posture in recent years than it had done in O'Dea's time, particularly in its use of public relations to present itself as a legitimate part of the Christian family of denominations (contra the claims of many Christian evangelicals). I acknowledge that kind of public relations strategy, but I argue that the retrenchment motif in the church is found mainly in what the church says about itself to the members on the *inside,* rather than in what it says about itself to the *outside,* which will always be calculated to curry favor. *Inside* discourse, I argue, is overwhelmingly *retrenchment oriented* (for example, there is only one true church, and it is ours; follow the prophet; study the scriptures; keep the commandments; go on missions; go to the temple; keep mothers at home with their children, and so on, all of which received much less emphasis before 1950).

20. On the rapid growth of the LDS Church, see Stark 1984, 1996a, and 2005, especially chapter 7.

21. See my essay on O'Dea and the race issue in this same collection (Chapter 7).

22. On the potential presidential candidacy of Mitt Romney, see Bunzel 2006.

23. See the comprehensive (if indignant) account in Quinn 2000, followed by my response, pp. 53–65.

24. Of course, "enhancements" to some church leaders might be considered "corruptions" to others!

25. The phrase "unsponsored sector" was first used in Arrington and Bitton 1992, 308 and chapter 16 more generally. The most visible products of the unsponsored sector, in

order of their origin, are the Mormon History Association (1965), which began publishing the *Journal of Mormon History* in 1974 (http://www.mhahome.org); *Dialogue: A Journal of Mormon Thought,* a quarterly published beginning in 1966 by the Dialogue Foundation (http://www.dialoguejournal.com); and *Sunstone* magazine, published four to six times a year since 1975 by the Sunstone Foundation (http://www.sunstoneonline.com). There are a few others of later origin. *BYU Studies,* published at BYU since 1959, is a fully respectable scholarly journal but not independent of church auspices (http://www.byustudies.byu.edu). The Foundation for Apologetic Information and Research (FAIR), founded in 2001, holds annual conferences and makes available electronically a rich variety of apologetic literature in defense especially against the numerous anti-Mormon Web sites that have emerged in recent years. Its electronic publications are generally quite scholarly and have so far retained the tacit approval, though not the sponsorship, of church leaders (http://www.fairlds.org).

26. See Duffy 2004 for a review of the range of positions among contemporary LDS intellectuals.

27. Some of these study groups have been thriving for decades. See http://www.mesg. tierranet.com for information on the Miller-Eccles Study Group of southern California, one of the longest running of these.

28. News accounts of these excommunications can be found in *Sunstone* magazine for November 1993 ("Six Intellectuals Disciplined for Apostasy") and December 1993 ("Disciplinary Actions Generate More Heat"), as well as in numerous press accounts during the fall of 1993. Several more excommunications of publicly critical Mormon scholars occurred in the immediately succeeding years, but few, if any, have occurred during the administration of President Hinckley.

29. A list of references to these topics, both polemical and analytical, would be far too large for even a long endnote. In any bibliographic database for literature on the Mormons, keywords such as *women* (especially if paired with *priesthood*), *feminism, homosexual, same-sex, Book of Mormon, historicity,* and related terms would turn up numerous articles and books, including both those published under church auspices and those published independently. See, for example, the huge reference work by James B. Allen, Ronald W. Walker, and David J. Whittaker, *Studies in Mormon History, 1830–1997* (an indexed bibliography covering historical and published social science literature) (2000), which fortunately is still being regularly updated electronically by Allen via http://mormonhistory.byu.edu. Via the same kinds of key words, access to cumulative back issues of *Dialogue, Sunstone,* the *Journal of Mormon History,* and *BYU Studies* can also be obtained via their respective Web sites.

30. See the LDS Church's formal "The Family: A Proclamation to the World" (http://www.lds.org>newsroom, then search for "families and children"). See the informative discussion of the proclamation in Bushman 2006, 38–42.

31. Also, more generally, by the 1990s social scientists and commentators were finding data that raised considerable doubt about feminist assumptions that modern, educated women were chafing under traditional gender roles. This is not the place to review all that

literature, but see, for example, Allen 2006, which cites research by University of Virginia sociologists W. Bradford Wilcox and Stephen L. Nock in the journal *Social Forces.*

32. See the balanced discussion of this question in Bushman 2006, 111–24. The enormous range in the attitudes of Mormon women on such matters is illustrated in Beaman 2001; Hatch 2004; and Bennion 2006.

33. In recurrent national polls such as the General Social Survey, this is the proportion of the population, men and women combined, that claims recent homosexual activity (Heaton 1999; the homosexual percentage is on p. 26).

34. On the politics of psychiatric diagnoses, see Bayer 1981; and Scott 1990. The reference to the changing diagnoses of homosexuality is on p. 304 of the Scott article.

35. Indeed, Affirmation, a thriving support group for homosexuals and their families, has formed among the Mormons. See its Web site at http://www.affirmation.org.

36. The latter view is represented by the efforts of Evergreen International, an organization devoted to helping people who wish to diminish their homosexual feelings or overcome homosexual behavior. See its Web site at http://www.evergreeninternational.org. The Association of Mormon Counselors and Psychotherapists (AMCAP) questions the conventional diagnosis of homosexuality in the *Diagnostic and Statistical Manual IV* of the American Psychiatric Association and calls for values-centered counseling that remains open to the possibility that a client might seek to change his or her homosexual behavior, if not orientation. See its Web site at http://www.amcap.net. Neither Evergreen nor AMCAP is affiliated with the LDS Church.

37. The authoritative view of the church leaders on the issues of etiology versus behavioral conformity will be found in a fairly extensive article by Elder Dallin H. Oaks (1995).

38. A useful and wide-ranging discussion of the homosexual predicament among Mormons will be found in Schow, Schow, and Raynes 1991. See also the briefer consideration of this predicament in Bushman 2006, 124–29.

39. That is, whether the book is a miraculous translation of an ancient text, as it claims to be, or a product of one or more nineteenth-century authors writing as though they were ancients.

40. See also O'Dea's entire discussion of the Book of Mormon in 1957, chap. 2, plus 266–67nn1–3.

41. Founded in 1980, FARMS enjoyed the status of an independent research foundation until 2001, when, more or less amicably, it was brought under the administration of BYU. In 2006, it was further subsumed under the Maxwell Institute for Religious Scholarship at BYU (http://farms.byu.edu), but it continues to produce many publications under the FARMS imprint.

42. See the overview in Mauss 2003, 142–46. Nibley's first books on this theme were originally used as official instruction manuals for the LDS lay priesthood: *Lehi in the Desert* (1950) and *The World of the Jaredites* (1951).

43. The introduction to the officially published Book of Mormon has, in effect,

canonized this traditional understanding by referring to the book as the history of the "principal ancestors" of American Indians.

44. It should be noted that these controversies touch the grassroots church membership scarcely at all. The active and believing members simply put their faith in the divine origin of the Book of Mormon and tend to shrug off questions about geographic or biological quandaries. Inactive members also shrug off such questions as not particularly salient in their religious lives. However, among active members of an intellectual bent, the controversies have had some effect: A 2005 survey of the readers of *Dialogue* found that only 36 percent considered the book a "literal historical document," although another 23 percent considered its teachings to be "of divine origin." A similar survey twenty years earlier had found that 63 percent believed the book to be literal history. At least in the 2005 survey, however, this difference in how the Book of Mormon is perceived seems *unrelated to church attendance:* 97 percent of those who see the book as literal history attend church every week or "most weeks," but even among the 23 percent who accept its divine teachings *without* believing that it is literal history, 93 percent go to church every week or "most weeks." See Reynolds, Remy, and Mauss 2006.

45. See a rather candid treatment of this matter in Bushman 2006, chap. 9.

46. A rather full account of the rise and fall of the brief Arrington era will be found in Bitton 1983. See also Walker, Whittaker, and Allen 2001; and Arrington 1998, esp. 139–74, 209–26.

47. For details on the conference at the Library of Congress, go to http://www.lds. org and search "The Worlds of Joseph Smith," where MP3 broadcasts can also be downloaded. The proceedings of this conference were eventually published in *BYU Studies* 44, no. 4 (2005).

48. On the Claremont program (and certain others), see the rather critical portrayal by journalist Daniel Golden (2006). Utah Valley State College in Provo has had a Mormon-studies component in its religious-studies program for several years, but not a separate program. The programs at Utah State University and Claremont Graduate University are just starting, and both expect to have selected occupants for endowed chairs in Mormon studies, as well as relevant curricula, by the fall of 2007. Neither of these chairs has actually been fully endowed as of this writing. Utah State University has completed an endowment for a chair in religious studies (see Koerner 2004), but not yet the funding for a special chair in Mormon studies (to be named for Leonard J. Arrington). See the Web sites http://www.cgu.edu> Schools>Religion>Councils>LDS and http://www.usu.edu>HASS, then search "Religious Studies."

49. This is, of course, the theme of my entire book *The Angel and the Beehive* (1994).

50. The streamlining involved in "correlation" had the effect of closing down many beloved auxiliary programs and professionalizing others (for example, the welfare program and the construction of new churches), obviating the need for volunteers. Some of these institutions remembered so nostalgically by Mormons of my generation are highlighted

briefly by O'Dea in *The Mormons* (1957, 146–50, 215–21), but discussed in much greater detail in Alexander 1986, chap. 8. See also R. Kimball 2003; and Mangum and Blumell 1993. The influence of a corporate model borrowed from the business world (including the use of outside consultants) is apparent from the treatments in Allen and Leonard 1992, chap. 20, esp. 599–606; and Prince and Wright 2005, chap. 7.

51. Most Mormon growth has come from new converts in recent years. In O'Dea's time, the overwhelming majority of those newly baptized in the LDS Church were the children of members, as contrasted to new converts. Since about 1960, the ratio has gradually turned around, and convert baptisms have long outnumbered child baptisms by three or four to one—even more in some years. See Heaton 1992.

52. The 2005 edition of the *Yearbook of American and Canadian Churches* lists the LDS as the fourth largest in the nation (see "Recent News" for July 12, 2006, in the National Council of Churches Newsletter [*NCC Newsletter*] at http://www.ncccusa.org).

53. Prior to 1960, only 12 temples were in use by the church, 8 in North America, 2 in Europe, and 2 in Polynesia. By now, 136 are in use or under construction (Deseret News 2000, 453–54).

54. This generalization is apparent from Gooren 2001, 2007; Grover 2005; and Knowlton 1996.

55. Two fascinating recent essays on Mormonism in Haiti and in East Africa reveal this quandary in bold relief (Basquiat 2004; Huxford 2006).

56. *Deseret News Church Almanac* estimates are a more modest seventy-plus million (Deseret News 2000, 151).

57. This is the underlying theme of my 2003 book, *All Abraham's Children.*

References

Alexander, Thomas G. 1986. *Mormonism in Transition: A History of the Latter-day Saints, 1890–1930.* Urbana: University of Illinois Press.

Allen, Charlotte. 2006. "The Return of the Happy Housewife." *Los Angeles Times,* March 5, M1.

Allen, James B., and Glen M. Leonard. 1992. *The Story of the Latter-day Saints.* 2d ed. Salt Lake City: Deseret Book.

Allen, James B., Ronald W. Walker, and David J. Whittaker. 2000. *Studies in Mormon History, 1830–1997.* Urbana: University of Illinois Press.

Arrington, Leonard J. 1998. *The Adventures of a Church Historian.* Urbana: University of Illinois Press.

Arrington, Leonard J., and Davis Bitton. 1992. *The Mormon Experience: A History of the Latter-day Saints.* 2d ed. Urbana: University of Illinois Press.

Basquiat, Jennifer Huss. 2004. "Embodied Mormonism: Performance, Vodou, and the LDS Faith in Haiti." *Dialogue: A Journal of Mormon Thought* 37, no. 4: 1–33.

Bayer, Ronald. 1981. *Homosexuality and American Psychiatry: The Politics of Diagnosis.* New York: Basic Books.

Beaman, Lori G. 2001. "Molly Mormons, Mormon Feminists, and Moderates: Religious Diversity and the Latter Day Saints Church." *Sociology of Religion* 62, no. 1: 65–86.

Becker, Gary S. 1976. *The Economic Approach to Human Behavior.* Chicago: University of Chicago Press.

———. 1996. *Accounting for Tastes.* Cambridge: Harvard University Press.

Bennion, Lowell C., and Lawrence A. Young. 1996. "The Uncertain Dynamics of LDS Expansion, 1950–2020." *Dialogue: A Journal of Mormon Thought* 29, no. 1: 8–32.

Bennion, Molly M. 2006. "A Lament." *Dialogue: A Journal of Mormon Thought* 39, no. 2: 115–22.

Bitton, Davis. 1983. "Ten Years in Camelot: A Personal Memoir." *Dialogue: A Journal of Mormon Thought* 16, no. 3: 9–33.

Blakesley, Katie Clark. 2004. "A Style of Our Own: Modesty and Mormon Women, 1951–2003." In *Latter-day Saint Women in the Twentieth Century,* ed. Claudia L. Bushman. Summer Fellows' Papers, 2003. Provo, UT: Joseph Fielding Smith Institute for LDS History, Brigham Young University.

Bloom, Harold. 1992. *The American Religion: The Emergence of a Post-Christian Nation.* New York: Simon and Schuster.

Bradley, Martha Sonntag. 2005. *Pedestals and Podiums: Utah Women, Religious Authority, and Equal Rights.* Salt Lake City: Signature Books.

Bunzel, John H. 2006. "Is America Ready for a Mormon President?" *Boston Globe,* February 19, op-ed page.

Bushman, Claudia L., ed. 2004. *Latter-day Saint Women in the Twentieth Century.* Summer Fellows' Papers, 2003. Provo: Joseph Fielding Smith Institute for LDS History, Brigham Young University.

———. 2006. *Contemporary Mormonism: Latter-day Saints in Modern America.* Westport, Conn.: Praeger.

Deseret News. 2000. *Deseret News 2001–2002 Church Almanac.* Salt Lake City: Deseret News.

"Disciplinary Actions Generate More Heat." 1993. *Sunstone* 93 (December): 67–68.

Driggs, Kenneth D. 1990. "After the Manifesto: Modern Polygamy and Fundamentalist Mormons." *Journal of Church and State* 32 (Spring): 367–89.

———. 1991. "Twentieth Century Polygamy and Fundamentalist Mormons in Southern Utah." *Dialogue: A Journal of Mormon Thought* 24 , no. 4: 44–58.

Duffy, John-Charles. 2004. "Defending the Kingdom, Rethinking the Faith: How Apologetics Is Reshaping Mormon Orthodoxy." *Sunstone* 132 (May): 22–51.

Ely, Richard T. 1903. "Economic Aspects of Mormonism." *Harper's Monthly* 106 (April): 668.

Emerson, Richard. 1976. "Social Exchange Theory." *Annual Review of Sociology* 2: 335–62.

Flake, Kathleen. 2004. *The Politics of American Religious Identity: The Seating of Senator Reed Smoot, Mormon Apostle.* Chapel Hill: University of North Carolina Press.

Geary, Edward A. 1977. "Mormondom's Lost Generation: The Novelists of the 1940s." *BYU Studies* 18, no. 1: 89–107.

Golden, Daniel. 2006. "In Religious Studies, Universities Bend to Views of Faithful." *Wall Street Journal,* April 6, A1.

Gooren, Henri. 2001. "The Dynamics of LDS Growth in Guatemala, 1948–1998." *Dialogue: A Journal of Mormon Thought* 34, nos. 3–4: 55–75.

———. 2007. "Latter-day Saints under Siege: The Unique Experience of Nicaraguan Mormons." *Dialogue: A Journal of Mormon Thought* 40, no. 3 (Fall): 131–55.

Grover, Mark L. 2005. "The Maturing of the Oak: The Dynamics of LDS Growth in Latin America." *Dialogue: A Journal of Mormon Thought* 38, no. 2: 79–104.

Hansen, Klaus J. 1966. "The Metamorphosis of the Kingdom of God." *Dialogue: A Journal of Mormon Thought* 1, no. 3: 63–83.

Harris, Kristine Haglund. 2004. "Who Shall Sing If Not the Children? Primary Songbooks, 1880–1989." In *Latter-day Saint Women in the Twentieth Century,* ed. Claudia L. Bushman, 23–42. Summer Fellows' Papers, 2003. Provo, UT: Joseph Fielding Smith Institute for LDS History, Brigham Young University. Later published in *Dialogue* 37, no. 4: 90–127 (Winter 2004).

Hatch, Tina. 2004. "Changing Times Bring Changing Conditions: Relief Society, 1960–Present." In *Latter-day Saint Women in the Twentieth Century,* ed. Claudia L. Bushman. Summer Fellows' Papers, 2003. Provo, UT: Joseph Fielding Smith Institute for LDS History, Brigham Young University. Later published in *Dialogue* 37, no. 3: 65–98 (Fall 2004).

Heaton, Tim B. 1992. "Vital Statistics." In *Encyclopedia of Mormonism.* 4 vols., ed. Daniel H. Ludlow, 4:1525–31. New York: Macmillan.

———. 1999. "Social Forces That Imperil the Family." *Dialogue: A Journal of Mormon Thought* 32, no. 4: 19–41.

Heaton, Tim B., Stephen J. Bahr, and Cardell K. Jacobson. 2004. *A Statistical Profile of Mormons: Health, Wealth, and Social Life.* Lewiston, N.Y.: Edwin Mellen Press.

Heaton, Tim B., Thomas A. Hirschi, and Bruce A. Chadwick. 1996. *Utah in the 1990s: A Demographic Perspective.* Salt Lake City: Signature Books.

Homans, George C. 1974. *Social Behavior: Its Elementary Forms.* 2d ed. New York: Harcourt Brace.

Huxford, Gary. 2006. "Yesterday's People." *Dialogue: A Journal of Mormon Thought* 39, no. 1: 82–93.

Iannaccone, Laurence R. 1988. "A Formal Model of Church and Sect." *American Journal of Sociology* 94, supp., S241–68.

———. 1990. "Religious Practice: A Human Capital Approach." *Journal for the Scientific Study of Religion* 29: 297–314.

———. 1994. "Why Strict Churches Are Strong." *American Journal of Sociology* 99, no. 5: 1180–1211.

Johnson, Benton. 1963. "On Church and Sect." *American Sociological Review* 28: 543.

———. 1971. "Church and Sect Revisited." *Journal for the Scientific Study of Religion* 10, no. 2: 131.

Kanter, Rosabeth Moss. 1972. *Commitment and Community: Communes and Utopias in Sociological Perspective.* Cambridge: Harvard University Press.

Kear, Warrick. 2001. "The LDS Sound World and Global Mormonism." *Dialogue: A Journal of Mormon Thought* 34, nos. 3–4: 77–93.

Kimball, Edward L. 2005. *Lengthen Your Stride: The Presidency of Spencer W. Kimball.* Salt Lake City: Deseret Book.

Kimball, Richard L. 2003. *Sports in Zion: Mormon Recreation.* Urbana: University of Illinois Press.

Knowlton, David C. 1996. "Mormonism in Latin America: Towards the Twenty-first Century." *Dialogue: A Journal of Mormon Thought* 29, no. 1: 159–76.

———. 2005. "How Many Members Are There Really? Two Censuses and the Meaning of LDS Membership in Chile and Mexico." *Dialogue: A Journal of Mormon Thought* 38, no. 2: 53–78.

Koerner, Jane. 2004. "Teaching about Religion." *Utah State Magazine* (Summer). http://www.utahstate.usu.edu/issues/summer04/index.html.

Larson, Gustive O. 1971. *The "Americanization" of Utah for Statehood.* San Marino, Calif.: Huntington Library.

Leavitt, Dean H., Jonathan C. Marshall, and Keith A. Campbell. 2003. "The Search for the Seed of Lehi: How Defining Alternative Models Helps in the Interpretation of Genetic Data." *Dialogue: A Journal of Mormon Thought* 36, no. 4: 133–50.

Library of Congress. 2005. "The Worlds of Joseph Smith." *BYU Studies* 44, no. 4.

Lobb, C. Gary. 2000. "Mormon Membership Trends in Europe among People of Color: Present and Future Assessment." *Dialogue: A Journal of Mormon Thought* 33, no. 4: 55–68.

Lyman, E. Leo. 1986. *Political Deliverance: The Mormon Quest for Utah Statehood.* Urbana: University of Illinois Press.

Mangum, Garth L., and Bruce D. Blumell. 1993. *The Mormons' War on Poverty, 1830–1990.* Salt Lake City: University of Utah Press.

Mauss, Armand L. 1990. "Alternate Voices: The Calling and Its Implications." *Sunstone* 76 (Spring): 7–10.

———. 1994. *The Angel and the Beehive: The Mormon Struggle with Assimilation.* Urbana: University of Illinois Press.

———. 1996. "Mormonism in the Twenty-first Century: Marketing for Miracles." *Dialogue: A Journal of Mormon Thought* 29, no. 1: 236–49.

———. 1999. "In Search of Ephraim: Traditional Mormon Conceptions of Lineage and Race." *Journal of Mormon History* 35, no. 1: 131–73.

———. 2003. *All Abraham's Children: Changing Mormon Conceptions of Race and Lineage.* Urbana: University of Illinois Press.

Metcalf, Brent L. 1993. *New Approaches to the Book of Mormon: Explorations in Critical Methodology.* Salt Lake City: Signature Books.

Michaelsen, Robert S. 1978. "Thomas F. O'Dea on the Mormons: Retrospect and Assessment." *Dialogue: A Journal of Mormon Thought* 11, no. 1: 44–57.

Moore, Wilbert E. 1963. *Social Change.* Englewood Cliffs, N.J.: Prentice-Hall.

Murphy, Thomas W. 2003. "Simply Implausible: DNA and a Meso-American Setting for the Book of Mormon." *Dialogue: A Journal of Mormon Thought* 36, no. 4: 109–31.

Neilson, Reid L. 2005. Introduction to *The Rise of Mormonism*, by Rodney Stark. New York: Columbia University Press.

Nibley, Hugh. 1950. *Lehi in the Desert.* Salt Lake City: Bookcraft.

———. 1951. *The World of the Jaredites.* Salt Lake City: Bookcraft.

Oaks, Dallin H. 1989. "Alternate Voices." *Ensign,* May, 27–30.

———. 1995. "Same-Gender Attraction." *Ensign,* October, 7–13.

O'Dea, Thomas F. 1954. "Mormonism and the Avoidance of Sectarian Stagnation: A Study of Church, Sect, and Incipient Nationality." *American Journal of Sociology* 60, no. 3: 285–93.

———. 1957. *The Mormons.* Chicago: University of Chicago Press.

———. 1972. "Sources of Strain in Mormon History Reconsidered." In *Mormonism and American Culture,* ed. Marvin S. Hill and James B. Allen, 147–67. New York: Harper and Row.

Ostling, Richard N., and Joan K. Ostling. 1999. *Mormon America: The Power and the Promise.* New York: HarperCollins.

Out of Obscurity: The LDS Church in the Twentieth Century. 2000. Twenty-ninth annual Sidney B. Sperry Symposium. Salt Lake City: Deseret Book.

Park, Robert R., and Ernest W. Burgess. 1921. *Introduction to the Science of Sociology.* Chicago: University of Chicago Press.

Parry, Seth. 2006. "An Outsider Looks at Mormonism." *Chronicle of Higher Education* 52, no. 22: B9.

Phillips, Rick. 1998. "Religious Market Share and Mormon Church Activity." *Sociology of Religion* 59, no. 1: 117–30.

———. 2005. "Rethinking the International Expansion of Mormonism." *Nova Religio* (October).

Prince, Gregory A., and William Robert Wright. 2005. *David O. McKay and the Rise of Modern Mormonism.* Salt Lake City: University of Utah Press.

Quinn, D. Michael. 2000. "Prelude to the National 'Defense of Marriage' Campaign: Civil Discrimination against Feared or Despised Minorities." *Dialogue: A Journal of Mormon Thought* 33, no. 3: 1–52.

Reynolds, Robert W, John D. Remy, and Armand L. Mauss. 2006. "Maturing and

Enduring: *Dialogue* and Its Readers after Forty Years." *Dialogue: A Journal of Mormon Thought* 39, no. 4 (Winter): 82–106.

Schow, Ron, Wayne Schow, and Marybeth Raynes, eds. 1991. *Peculiar People: Mormons and Same-Sex Orientation.* Salt Lake City: Signature Books.

Scott, Wilbur J. 1990. "PTSD in DSM III: A Case in the Politics of Diagnosis and Disease." *Social Problems* 37, no. 3: 294–310.

Shepherd, Gordon, and Gary Shepherd. 1984. *A Kingdom Transformed: Themes in the Development of Mormonism.* Salt Lake City: University of Utah Press.

———. 1996. "Membership Growth, Church Activity, and Missionary Recruitment." *Dialogue: A Journal of Mormon Thought* 29, no. 1: 33–57.

Shipps, Jan. 1998. "Difference and Otherness: Mormonism and the American Religious Mainstream." In *Minority Faiths and the American Protestant Mainstream,* ed. Jonathan Sarna, 21–109. Urbana: University of Illinois Press.

———. 2000. *Sojourner in the Promised Land: Forty Years among the Mormons.* Urbana: University of Illinois Press.

"Six Intellectuals Disciplined for Apostasy." 1993. *Sunstone.* 92 (November): 65–73.

Sorenson, John L. 1985. *An Ancient American Setting for the Book of Mormon.* Salt Lake City: Deseret Book.

Southerton, Simon G. 2004. *Losing a Lost Tribe: Native Americans, DNA, and the Mormon Church.* Salt Lake City: Signature Books.

Stark, Rodney. 1984. "The Rise of a New World Faith." *Review of Religious Research* 26, no. 1: 18–27.

———. 1996a. "So Far, So Good: A Brief Assessment of Mormon Membership Projections." *Review of Religious Research* 38, no. 1: 175–78.

———. 1996b. "Why Religious Movements Succeed or Fail: A Revised General Model." *Journal of Contemporary Religion* 11, no. 2: 133–46.

———. 1999. "A Theory of Revelations." *Journal for the Scientific Study of Religion* 38, no. 2: 287–308.

———. 2005. *The Rise of Mormonism,* ed. by Reid L. Neilson. New York: Columbia University Press.

Stark, Rodney, and William S. Bainbridge. 1985. *The Future of Religion: Secularization, Revival, and Cult Formation.* Berkeley and Los Angeles: University of California Press.

———. 1987. *A Theory of Religion.* Reprint, New Brunswick: Rutgers University Press, 1996.

Stark, Rodney, and Roger Finke. 2000. *Acts of Faith: Explaining the Human Side of Religion.* Berkeley and Los Angeles: University of California Press.

Troeltsch, Ernst. 1912. *The Social Teaching of the Christian Churches.* Trans. Olive Whyon. 2 vols. New York: Macmillan, 1931.

Turner, Frederick Jackson. 1906. *The Rise of the New West.* New York: Henry Holt.

———. 1920. *The Significance of the Frontier in American History.* New York: Henry Holt.

Van Wagoner, Richard S. 1986. *Mormon Polygamy: A History.* Salt Lake City: Signature Books.

Vogel, Dan, and Brent L. Metcalf. 2002. *American Apocrypha.* Salt Lake City: Signature Books.

Walker, Ronald W., David J. Whittaker, and James B. Allen. 2001. *Mormon History.* Urbana: University of Illinois Press.

Warner, R. Stephen. 1993. "Work in Progress toward a New Paradigm for the Sociological Study of Religion in the United States." *American Journal of Sociology* 98: 1044–93.

Whiting, Michael F. 2003. "DNA and the Book of Mormon: A Phylogenetic Perspective." *Journal of Book of Mormon Studies* 12, no. 1: 24–35.

Williams, J. D. 1966. "The Separation of Church and State in Mormon Theory and Practice." *Dialogue: A Journal of Mormon Thought* 1, no. 2: 30–54.

Yorgason, Ethan R. 2003. *Transformation of the Mormon Culture Region.* Urbana: University of Illinois Press.

12

Growth, Retention, and Internationalization

~ David G. Stewart Jr. ~

Thomas O'Dea's work focused primarily on the U.S. Church of Jesus Christ of Latter-day Saints, reflecting LDS demographics of his time. However, O'Dea foresaw a shift in the center of gravity of the LDS faith from the Utah Zion to international areas and anticipated both the significance and the challenges this shift would bring. He wrote:

> The recent dedication of a Swiss temple testifies to the first stage in the separation of the Mormon notion of Zion and the gathering from a definite peace [*sic*] of land and from the New World. A more abstract, more spiritualized, conception of the gathering, in which a Mormon way of life is seen as possible without physical removal to and residence in a Mormon community in America, is developing. A unique concatenation of circumstances and aspects of its won values and structure enabled Mormonism to escape the common sectarian fate of reaching early stabilization and stagnating in isolation. (1957, 118)

He recognized that the LDS Church stood at the threshold of a new era in its history: "The Mormon movement may be on the eve of its Diaspora, which would not mean that its central city would cease to be central but that belongingness would no longer be exclusively identified with a specific place.... In the Mormon case, such a shift in emphasis implies a recognition of the more intangible and more contemplative aspects of the religious life. Such a turn would be of the utmost importance for Mormonism" (261).

Many of the same issues that Thomas O'Dea recognized in the U.S. church also apply to international settings. The transplantation of church structures and programs developed in Utah into international cultural settings has produced both challenges and opportunities. The international expansion of the church has contributed to increased awareness of needs worldwide and has produced an exceptional era of giving to charitable and humanitarian causes. Temples have been built in many nations, family history work has expanded, and the church has enjoyed increasing respect. However, the combination of circumstances that O'Dea recognized as formative elements in the development of the U.S. Mormon identity has often been difficult to achieve in international settings, and most long-established international LDS communities continue to rely heavily on North American resources, missionaries, and leaders for both maintenance and growth. The church has experienced remarkable success in some areas, such as West Africa and Mongolia, whereas it has struggled with low activity and convert retention rates in most other regions.

Membership Growth: Size and Regional Distribution

Internationalization and Growth of the Church

O'Dea pointed out that the practice of leaving secular society to gather to Zion in the mountains created an isolated and distinctive environment in which Mormonism could flourish. Attempts to establish a more spiritual worldwide Zion with members in their native lands have achieved measured success, with difficulties posed by both internal and external challenges. In 1911, the First Presidency wrote, "The establishment of the latter-day Zion on the American continent occasions the gathering of the Saints from all nations. This is not compulsory, and particularly under present conditions, is not urged, because it is desirable that our people shall remain in their native lands and form congregations of a permanent character to aid in the work of proselyting" (Clark 1970, 222). Since that time, the church's international presence has continued to expand. Today, the majority of Latter-day Saints live outside of the United States. As part of the gospel mandate to "teach all nations" (Matt. 28:19), the LDS Church entered 59 new nations in the 1990s alone (Duke 1999) and currently operates in more than 140 countries and territories.

Though sometimes reported as the "world's fastest growing church" (Lobdell 2003; Smith 2002; "Atlanta Suburb" 2002; "Utah's Wheel" 1999) or as the "fastest growing church in the United States," the Church of Jesus Christ of Latter-day Saints has experienced a progressive decline in annual growth rates, from more than 5 percent annually in the late 1980s to less than 3 percent from 2000 to 2005, although the number of full-time missionaries serving over this period increased considerably (*Ensign* May 1973–

May 2005). The average LDS missionary experienced 8 baptisms in 1989, and 6–6.5 baptisms annually throughout the 1990s. From 2000 to 2004, the annual number of converts per missionary had fallen to 4.5, of which only one-quarter to one-third became regularly participating members. The LDS Church continues to grow more rapidly than Orthodox, Catholic, and most mainline Protestant faiths. However, many U.S.-based faiths organized after the LDS Church, including the Seventh-Day Adventists (7–10 percent annual growth), the entire Pentecostal movement (5–7 percent annual growth), and many evangelical faiths (3–6 percent annual growth), have experienced more rapid growth and internationalization.

O'Dea's description of the LDS Church as an "American Zion" has remained relevant even as continued international expansion has occurred. The Mormon Church remains primarily a hemispheric church. Approximately 85 percent of LDS members live in North and South Americas, and another 10 percent live in island nations (Bennion and Young 1996; Babbit 2000). Only 5 percent of LDS members live in the vast continental landmass of Europe, Asia, and Africa that is home to 80 percent of the world's population. Although substantial international growth has taken place and 80 percent of LDS convert baptisms now occur outside of North America (primarily in Latin America), the LDS Church has not been as successful at leveraging its affluent, high-missionary-sending U.S. population into committed international members at the same rate as many other outreach-oriented faiths. Just over 50 percent of the nominal 12 million Latter-day Saints live outside of the United States. In contrast, 12 of the 13 million Seventh-Day Adventists, 5 of 6 million active adult Jehovah's Witnesses (and 12.5 of 14.5 million affiliates), and 33 million of 35 million Assemblies of God members live outside of the United States. In 1960, there were approximately 60 million evangelicals in Western nations and 25 million in non-Western nations (Johnstone and Mandryk 2005, 3). By 2000, there were 110 million evangelicals in Western nations and more than 310 million in non-Western nations. Lawrence A. Young notes, "The Mormon church, which was established nearly eighty-five years before the Assemblies of God, has only one-fifth as large of a presence in Latin America" (1994, 60).

Despite considerable international expansion, the LDS Church continues to draw most of its strength from North America. Approximately 80 percent of full-time LDS missionaries come from North America, with another 16 percent coming from Latin America. Other faiths have experienced a more rapid shift of their missionary force to an international base. Of the 202,000 Protestant missionaries serving worldwide in 2004, 71,000 came from North America (35 percent), 70,000 came from Asia (35 percent, including 41,000 from India), 22,000 came from Europe (11 percent), 12,000 came from Africa (6 percent), 10,000 came from Latin America (5 percent), and 9,500 (5 percent) came from Pacific nations (Johnstone and Mandryk 2005). Although O'Dea observed the strong focus on self-sufficiency and pragmatism in the early U.S. church, most international congregations are still dependent on the U.S. church for both funds and missionary manpower.

LDS missionary allocation also reflects Americentric dynamics. Nearly one-third of LDS missions cover North America (5 percent of the world's population), almost one-third are based in Latin America (8 percent of the world population), and the remaining one-third cover the remaining 87 percent of the world population. Protestant missionaries are more evenly distributed in the world's major population centers: in 2004, 85,000 missionaries served in Asia (42 percent), 27,000 in Africa (13 percent), and 23,000 each in Europe, Latin America, and North America (11 percent each) (ibid.).

As O'Dea anticipated, the LDS center of gravity is changing as the church becomes more internationalized. Native Latin American, Asian, African, and European missionaries represent an increasing proportion of the LDS missionary force. Of the more than 130 LDS missions organized between 1990 and 2005, 37 percent are in the Eastern Hemisphere, and only one-quarter are in North America. By 2005, the Book of Mormon was available in full or part in 105 languages, including 77 of the 273 languages spoken by more than 1 million people, and half of the world's 100 most spoken languages. The Book of Mormon was translated into approximately 80 of these languages between 1976 and 2005. Whereas O'Dea spoke with wonder and anticipation of the construction of the Swiss temple, today there are 124 operating LDS temples worldwide and another 12 under construction.

NOMINAL, PARTICIPATING, AND SELF-IDENTIFIED MEMBERSHIP

LDS Member Activity and Convert Retention

Thomas O'Dea anticipated the challenge of establishing a more universal identity, if not an indigenous identity, for the international church, recognizing the related needs of church adaptation to local cultures and of international convert assimilation into the Latter-day Saint community. He noted, "Mormonism today faces the problem of prosperity and of assimilation in a new form. Yet so far, Mormonism in winning a new respectability has managed to preserve its genuine peculiarity" (1957, 262). Though he recognized the spectrum of participating and disengaged individuals among nominal members, it is not clear whether he fully anticipated the sheer magnitude of the problem, or the wide regional variations in member activity and convert retention seen today. Low international convert retention has become a defining challenge of the contemporary LDS Church that has not been adequately resolved. Although the church makes no claims about member activity rates and no official LDS activity rates are published, the *Encyclopedia of Mormonism* reported, "Attendance at sacrament meeting varies substantially. Canada, the South Pacific, and the United States average between 40 percent and 50 percent. Europe and Africa average about 35 percent. Asia and Latin America have weekly attendance rates of about 25 percent" (Ludlow 1992, 1527–28). An Associated Press article noted, "While the church doesn't release statistics on church activity rates, some research suggests participation in the church is as low as 30 percent" (Henetz 2003). Compiled research and census data suggest that approximately 30–35 percent of LDS members worldwide, or about 4 million, may participate regularly. Since some members are part-active and do not attend every week, or may face extenuating hardships, the total number of LDS members who participate at least occasionally may be slightly more, although census data and other research suggest that the total is unlikely to be much higher. Sociologist Armand Mauss states that "75 percent of foreign [LDS] converts are not attending church within a year of conversion. In the United States, 50 percent of the converts fail to attend after a year" (Willis 2001). It is particularly concerning that the areas with the most rapid numerical membership increase, Latin America and the Philippines, are areas with extremely low convert retention.

North America

Even in its heartland, the LDS faith has struggled with slowing growth and high turnover. The 1990–2000 Glenmary study (Glenmary Research Center 2002) reported that the LDS Church ranks twenty-third among the 149 participating denominations in overall U.S. growth rate but first among denominations reporting more than 1 million adherents. This study was widely misreported in both the popular press and the LDS media as finding that the LDS Church was the "fastest growing church in the United States" (Zoll 2002).[1] The U.S. LDS growth rate over the period of 1990–2000 was 19 percent, or 1.76 percent per year compounded, a respectable figure in an industrialized nation with a low birthrate, but hardly a dynamic one. Data were based solely on the number of adherents claimed by religious bodies and did not examine rates of member participation or self-identified religious affiliation.

The City University of New York (CUNY) American Religious Identification Survey (ARIS) queried the self-identified religious affiliation of a large cohort of U.S. citizens in 1990 and 2001 (Mayer, Kosmin, and Keysar

2001). The study found that the LDS Church had one of the highest turn-over rates of any U.S. faith. Because of high turnover, the actual growth rate in the number of Americans identifying themselves as Latter-day Saints between 1990 and 2001 was found to be similar to the overall U.S. population growth rate. The study found that just under 2.8 million Americans ages eighteen and over identified themselves as Latter-day Saints. There are 5.3 million U.S. citizens officially on LDS membership rolls, although this includes a declining percentage of minors under age eighteen and many inactive and disengaged adults. The ARIS survey cited 1.33 million adults in the United States who identify themselves as Jehovah's Witnesses, though the Jehovah's Witnesses claimed only 980,000 official members in the United States. The CUNY authors observed, "Some groups such as Mormons... appear to attract a large number of converts ('in-switchers'), but also nearly as large a number of apostates ('out-switchers')." An independent survey of self-reported religious identification conducted by *USA Today* in 2002 demonstrates that the percentage of individuals identifying themselves as Latter-day Saints is significantly lower than official membership figures in almost every state (Grossman 2002).

In Utah, approximately 10 percent of LDS membership, or 180,000 individuals, are listed in the "address unknown file" (Canham 2005). Elder Merrill Bateman noted that approximately 50,000 individuals in Utah are added to the lost-address file each year, and that 90 percent of those added are found within the next year. Those on the list longer than a year (and located less frequently) constitute more than 70 percent of lost address–file members and almost invariably represent inactive members. Overall U.S. "lost address–file" statistics have not been disclosed, but are unlikely to be less than the 10 percent of membership reported in Utah.

The 2001 Canadian census reported a 3.9 percent increase in self-identified LDS members over the decade, from 100,700 in 1991 to 104,750 in 2001, compared to an official membership increase of 25 percent (125,000 to 156,575) from 1990 to 2000 ("Selected Protestant Denominations" 2003). During this same period, the number of Seventh-Day Adventists identified on the census increased by 20.4 percent, and the Evangelical Missionary Church increased self-identified membership by 48.4 percent. The LDS increase of 3.9 percent for an entire decade represents an annual increase in self-identified LDS membership of less than 0.4 percent. This is well below the national growth rate of 0.96 percent, suggesting that self-identified LDS membership may be losing ground in proportion to the total Canadian population. A total of 67 percent of Canadian members claimed by the church identify themselves as Latter-day Saints, down from 80 percent in 1991.

Latin America

LDS growth and retention in Latin America provide a study in challenges anticipated by O'Dea, including the establishment of a Mormon Zion outside of North America and the assimilation of new converts without existing social or cultural ties to the church. Mexico, Brazil, and Chile have the second, third, and fourth largest LDS populations in the world, respectively, although Brazil is expected to surpass Mexico in the near future. Of LDS convert retention in Latin America, Carrie Moore writes, "Although the church does not provide statistics on activity rates, the number of inactive members in some areas eventually outpaced those who were active by a substantial margin" (2002b, A1). Peggy Fletcher Stack points out, "Baptizing Chileans is easy. People have little trouble finding Jesus among the Mormons, shifting allegiance from the pope to prophet, or seeing visions of church founder Joseph Smith rather than the Virgin Mary. But making them into lifelong Latter-day Saints is another thing. Less than a third of those baptized stay in the Mormon fold" (2006, A1). Brigham Young University (BYU) professor Ted Lyon, who served as a Chilean mission president and the president of the Chilean Missionary Training Center (MTC), notes that only 57,000 of the nominal 535,000 Latter-day Saints in Chile attend church on an average week, and 200,000 names are in the lost-address file. Dr. Lyon observes that low activity rates arose at least in part because "too many people were baptized before they had made the commitments to pay tithing or to attend church" (ibid.). John Hawkins, who has studied LDS growth in Guatemala, states:

> There has, in the past, been this notion (among missionaries) that if they are not willing to commit to baptism in two weeks, you drop them and keep going.... Members found that oppressive because conversions were happening so rapidly that once the missionaries moved on to other areas, the people they baptized were left without a support system and the local members were overloaded trying to keep up with all the new converts. Many simply gave up and waited to see "who the good ones were" that would come to church on their own and make a contribution without a lot of nurturing from the congregation. (Moore 2002b, A1)

Latin American studies professor Mark Grover acknowledges "a wide gap between the number of people baptized and the number attending church" (Walch 2003, A1).

There are 205,229 individuals ages five and above who identified themselves as Latter-day Saints on the 2000 Mexican census, compared to

850,000 members claimed by the church at the time (Borden 2001a; see also 2001b). Peggy Fletcher Stack reports, "According to several Brazilian leaders, the LDS activity rate here is between 25 percent and 35 percent. That means for every three or four converts, only one stays" (2003, A1). The 2000 Brazilian census reported 199,645 individuals identifying the Church of Jesus Christ of Latter-day Saints as their faith of preference, or 26.8 percent of the 743,182 claimed by the church at year-end 1999. This included 92,197 men and 107,448 women. On the 2002 Chilean census, 103,735 Chileans identified themselves as Latter-day Saints, or 20 percent of the 520,202 members claimed by the church. Of youth ages fifteen to twenty-nine, 1.1 percent identify themselves as Latter-day Saints, compared to 0.5 percent of the population over age seventy-five. The census did not report religious affiliation for individuals under age fifteen, which represented 25.7 percent of the total Chilean population in 2002.

Recent institutional adjustments are beginning to demonstrate the institutional resiliency and flexibility of the LDS Church in enduring and overcoming challenges noted by O'Dea. In April 1999, President Gordon B. Hinckley stated, "The days are past, the days are gone, the days are no longer here when we will baptize hundreds of thousands of people in Chile and then they will drift away from the church.... When you begin to count those who are not active, you are almost driven to tears over the terrible losses we have suffered in this nation." Apostle Jeffrey R. Holland confirmed that combating low activity and convert retention rates was a major goal of his assignment in Chile (Moore 2002a, B1). While overseeing church efforts in Chile from 2002 to 2004, Elder Holland "revised policy to insist that converts attend church three weeks in succession" and taught missionaries to focus on building the church rather than simply adding numbers (Stack 2006, A1). He noted that these efforts have led to substantial improvement, with more converts remaining active and greater numbers of Chileans serving missions.

Europe

European LDS activity rates appear to have fallen below the earlier 35 percent figure cited in the *Encyclopedia of Mormonism* due to low convert retention rates, reflecting ongoing struggles with assimilation and with maintaining an LDS lifestyle in increasingly secular societies. Wilfried Decoo writes that in 1996, the "estimated Church membership in Western Europe [is] ... 347,000 members represent[ing] 0.09 percent of the total population.... [A]bout one out of four members is active. Our effective membership in Europe [including the United Kingdom is] ... about 87,000 or 0.02 percent"

(1997, 164). The 2001 Austrian census reports 2,236 citizens who identify the LDS Church as their faith of preference, compared to 3,917 members listed in the *Deseret News 2003 Church Almanac* at year-end 2000 (57 percent). Local members report that actual LDS activity in Austria runs at about 43 percent, one of the highest rates in Europe. Gary Lobb (2000) has documented that activity rates of members in large cities of Western Europe vary from 20 to 30 percent. These data correlate with my personal research gathered from traveling to twenty nations. Data from 1999 from mission offices, local members, and full-time missionaries report activity rates of 28 percent in Hungary, 25 percent in the Czech Republic, 20 percent in Estonia, and 20 percent in Poland.

Africa

African missions have generated some of the highest LDS growth and retention rates. Former African mission president Dale LeBaron notes that "during the year 2000 sacrament meeting attendance in the West Africa Area was 54 percent, second only to the Utah South Area" (2001, n.p.). The fact that an activity rate just above 50 percent rates as the second highest among the church's twenty-nine areas underscores that activity rates are very low in many other areas. The West Africa Area represents the only convert-based area in the church reporting more than 50 percent member activity today. However, a paucity of active adult males in some areas has created logistical and administrative difficulties. Peggy Fletcher Stack reported on a black branch in South Africa: "Of 23 people baptized into Guguletu Branch of The Church of Jesus Christ of Latter-day Saints during 1997, only three were men age 18 or older. Of these three, only one remains active in the church. The branch has 253 members on the rolls, but an average weekly attendance of about 65. Seldom are there more than two married couples. Five married men attend regularly, four have jobs" (1998, A1). In contrast, some branches in Kenya report a large preponderance of adult male attendees, primarily because many men are unable to afford transportation for their wives and children.

Asia

Asian missions demonstrate similar challenges of fractional convert retention rates and declining growth. Jiro Numano, an experienced LDS leader in Japan and editor of a pro-LDS Japanese-language publication, analyzed official membership data:

Several problems are not apparent from these favorable numbers. First, the active membership of the church is only a fraction of the official membership. As recently as 1992, after forty-five years of post-war missionary effort, only 20,000 members could be counted as active out of a total membership of more than 87,000, or about 23 percent. Depending on how strict a definition one uses of "active member," the figure could range from 15 percent active, with a strict definition, to as much as 30 percent.... I estimate 25 percent active as a realistic figure for the country in general. This means that three-fourths of church members in Japan are inactive, having nothing to do with the church. A second problem is the decreasing rates in recent years both of baptisms themselves and of activity on the parts of new converts. As an illustration, although 50,000 people were baptized from 1978 through 1990 (including some children of members), the increase in active membership was only 10,000, with virtually no growth in Melchizedek priesthood holders. Since 1981, furthermore, attendance at sacrament meetings, priesthood meetings, and Relief Society meetings have all remained fairly level, despite thousands of new convert baptisms. In general, the growth in nominal membership has outstripped the growth in activity by either men or women. (Numano 1996, 24–25)

Philippine member activity and convert retention rates have traditionally not exceeded 20–25 percent. Apostle Dallin H. Oaks was assigned to serve in the Philippines from 2002 to 2004 to combat the challenges of low retention and inactivity. During his stay, Oaks insisted that prospective converts attend church at least four weeks and firmly overcome substance addictions prior to baptism. Although only a minority of mission presidents implemented the standards set by Elder Oaks, those who did experienced dramatic improvements in convert retention rates.

Pacific Nations

Pacific data also demonstrate wide discrepancy between official membership and self-identified religious affiliation. Marjorie Newton, wife of a former bishop, notes:

While the official membership figure was 78,000 in 1991, the Australian census that year showed only 38,372 Latter-day Saints. A letter from the area presidency urging members to respond to the voluntary census question on religious affiliation was read in every ward sacrament meeting before the census, making it unlikely that many active Latter-day Saints would have refused to answer. When we consider that the census figure also includes those of the 4,000 RLDS members who responded, the conclusion seems inescapable that well over half the nominal Mormons in Australia no longer regard themselves as Latter-day Saints. (1996, 194)

In 1996, the church claimed 87,000 Australian members, compared to 42,158 individuals reporting the LDS Church as their faith of preference on the census (which did distinguish between the LDS and RLDS Churches) that year. In 2001, the church reported 102,773 Australian members at year-end, compared to 48,775 individuals identifying themselves as Latter-day Saints on the census (47 percent of official membership).

From 1991 to 2001, the official membership numbers in New Zealand increased from 77,000 to 91,373. Over this same period, the number of individuals identifying themselves as Latter-day Saints or Mormons on the New Zealand census fell from 48,009 in 1991 to 41,166 in 1996 and 39,915 in 2001, with almost all regions of the country showing decline. Other faiths, such as Pentecostal Christians, showed census increases during this same period. As the 2001 census allowed individuals to specify up to four religious affiliations and those reporting multiple affiliations were counted in each group, it is unlikely that any significant number of participating Latter-day Saints were not counted. The decline in the correlation between official LDS membership figures and census data from 62 percent in 1991 to 43.7 percent in 2001 suggests that over this period, the church accumulated many nominal members but retained few, and may even have experienced a net loss of previously active members.

Are Census Data Valid?

Official reports of LDS growth present nominal membership figures without consideration of member activity or participation. The large disparities between official and participating membership figures have often made it difficult for members and leaders to identify, let alone correct, the root problems. The church has been understandably reluctant to label individuals as "inactive," instead using the euphemism "less active" to describe those who do not attend church at all. A 2005 general conference talk claimed that research demonstrated that "almost all less-active members interviewed believe that God exists, that Jesus is the Christ, that Joseph Smith was a prophet, and that the Church is true" (Whetten 2005, 91). However, I am aware of no independent, transparent, large-scale studies or censuses to date that have demonstrated LDS self-identification rates anywhere close to official membership figures.

Census reports and other sociologic studies are subject to varying margins of error and potential methodological problems. Nonetheless, there are many reasons to believe that census data accurately reflect the respondents' religious preferences. Only a small number of individuals in each census refused to answer questions about religious affiliation. Strong official requests by LDS Church leaders for local members to register the LDS Church as their faith of preference have been made in virtually every nation where the census has included religious affiliation data. Comparison between census data and official membership claims of other religious groups in these same nations can also provide a validity check. In contrast to the 20 percent (Chile), 24 percent (Mexico), and 27 percent (Brazil) correlation between LDS membership claims and census data on religious affiliation, the number of individuals identifying the Jehovah's Witness organization as their faith of preference weighs in at between 175 percent and 206 percent of official membership figures in these countries, representing both baptized adult members and a large number of affiliates. More individuals identified themselves as Seventh-Day Adventists than are officially claimed in each country. The LDS Church enjoys a relatively positive reputation in these nations, so it is unlikely that Mormons would be less likely than Adventists or Jehovah's Witnesses to express their true religious preferences. The consistently low correlation between LDS membership claims and self-identified census data across many nations, the high correlation between membership and census data for other denominations, and the close correspondence between census data and other research on member self-identification and participation all suggest that census data are reliable.

Although census and other sociologic studies face innate limitations, data on self-identified religious preference likely provide more meaningful indicators of church growth and strength than official membership figures, which have no obligatory correlation to member participation or identification. Nominally identifying oneself as a Latter-day Saint does necessarily imply church activity, but it would be difficult to claim that those who do not identify themselves as Latter-day Saints are active or contributing members. Indeed, the comparison between 103,735 self-identified Latter-day Saints reported on the Chilean census and the 57,000 Chileans attending LDS meetings each Sunday suggests that far from shortchanging the strength of the church, census data may generously overestimate the quantity of participating, committed international members. Fractional rates of self-identification document that most individuals outside of North America officially claimed on LDS membership rolls do not consider themselves members of the LDS Church, demonstrating that the challenge of inactivity runs far deeper than inadequate socialization, economic hardship, or transportation problems.

Implications of Activity and Retention Data

Whereas Thomas O'Dea observed a relatively high level of member participation in the U.S. church, world LDS activity rates have drifted progressively downward, with the majority of membership increase coming in international areas with high numbers of baptisms but poor retention rates. Most disengaged individuals claimed as members by the church do not report the LDS Church as their faith of preference. Declining member participation rates raise three major issues for the church's future. First, a clear and consistent focus on baptizing genuinely committed, actively participating converts rather than merely achieving baptisms will be central to future institutional vitality. Many other groups, including the Seventh-Day Adventists and Jehovah's Witnesses, have consistently achieved very high convert retention and member participation rates in the same cultures where LDS missions have experienced only fractional retention, so LDS retention difficulties cannot be attributed to deficiencies of local culture. Second, the home and visiting teaching and outreach programs are being increasingly stretched with unfavorable ratios of "lost sheep" to faithful members, with member participation becoming the exception rather than the rule in most areas. Third, chronically low member activity rates raise the question of what it means to be a Mormon. When a minority of members attend church, less attention can be devoted to the degree to which participating members observe other church teachings. The expanding challenge of member nonparticipation threatens to erode many unique elements of the Mormon faith that have figured prominently in its past successes. In this sense, the challenge described by O'Dea of redefining Mormon identity from that of a Utah-based Zion to a more spiritual and universal concept of an indigenously strong international church is perhaps even more important than when he described it fifty years ago.

GROWTH IN STRUCTURE

Congregational Growth

Armand Mauss has noted, "The key to the church's future growth will be at least as much a function of retention as conversion. While our numbers continue to grow, the rate at which we are creating new stakes has noticeably slowed down. That is a clear indication of a retention problem" (Stack 1996, A1). From 1998 to 2003, the church gained a total of 119 stakes, or an average of 24 stakes per year. There were 4,838 new LDS wards and branches organized between 1994 and 2004, or 1.32 congregations per day. The low number of congregations and stakes being formed reflects fractional retention of converts. As wards and branches require active, contributing members in order to function, ward and branch growth may represent a more meaningful indicator of the actual strength and growth of the church than raw membership numbers. Slow congregational growth rates provide additional evidence of marginal rates of LDS member participation and demonstrate that the challenges of establishing the LDS faith in international settings anticipated by O'Dea remain highly relevant and have not been fully resolved.

In comparison to the 26,670 congregations serving the 12.3 million nominal LDS members at year-end 2004, the Seventh-Day Adventist Church reported 12,894,000 baptized adult members in 117,020 Sabbath schools (congregations) meeting in 53,502 churches (2003 Seventh-Day Adventist Statistical Report), whereas the Jehovah's Witnesses cited 6.5 million members in 96,894 congregations in their August 2004 membership annual report (Jehovah's Witnesses 2004). The Seventh-Day Adventist Church experienced a 70 percent increase in the number of congregations during the 1990s and is anticipated to exceed that rate during the present decade ("Number of Adventist Congregations" 2000). K. P. Yohannan's Protestant Gospel for Asia group organizes more than 6 new congregations in India and South Asia each day, over twice as many as the entire LDS Church worldwide. The phenomenon of LDS congregations that have four to eight times as many official members as Adventist and Jehovah's Witness congregations reflects the reality that only a fraction of nominal LDS members attend or participate, that these other groups do not report children in their membership, and that they focus on medium and small congregations to keep travel distances short.

The "building from centers of strength" policy introduced in the early 1990s has slowed the rate of LDS congregational growth and missionary assignment to new areas, instead focusing on strengthening members in existing units. Hundreds of existing congregations have been consolidated into larger units, especially in South America, and the rate of unit expansion has noticeably slowed. This practice at least in theory focuses on building strong indigenous units that will be less dependent on foreign missionaries. However, few areas have experienced major improvements in convert retention

or member activity rates, and prolonged proselytization in a single area typically leads to diminishing returns. As studies repeatedly document that new
congregations grow faster than old congregations (see Wagner 1990; and
Garrison 1999), this shift in policy has likely been responsible for part of the
decline in LDS growth rates. It is premature to fully assess the legacy of the
"centers of strength" program, although it will undoubtedly be mixed.

O'Dea noted the unique opportunity for development and strength
that the American Zion provided to historical Mormonism. The "centers of
strength" policy appears to be an attempt to foster such an environment, yet
attempts to achieve concentrations of international members in specific geographic areas differ from the nineteenth-century Utah Zion in salient ways.
Whereas early LDS missionaries preached itinerantly across large areas and
gathered converts to specific gathering points, modern proselytizing involves
not the relocation of converts but rather the restriction of missionaries to the
cities designated as "centers of strength." International congregations function within the context of larger secular society, rather than experiencing the
more homogenous and isolated environment of the early Utah Zion.

The emphasis on having a few large congregations rather than greater
numbers of smaller, locally accessible ones can require transportation over
large distances. Programs developed by the Utah church and exported to
other areas often make assumptions of short distances, low cost, and readily accessible personal transportation that often do not hold in the developing world. One LDS humanitarian reported on his research in Africa and
Asia: "I do informal surveys of Church members in developing countries
of the cost of transportation to get to church.... Many times, I have found
that members are spending 20–30% of their monthly income to pay for
transportation costs to get to church." When weekday church activities and
home and visiting teaching responsibilities are added, the time and expense
of travel for members who rely on public transportation can be prohibitive.
The sacrifices of international Mormons are often not fully appreciated by
U.S. members, many of whom are accustomed to having LDS chapels only
a few minutes away.

From Agrarian to Urban Church

O'Dea observed the conflict between modernization and agrarianism in the
mid-twentieth-century LDS Church. The LDS Church was founded in an
agrarian setting. Dan Jones, Wilford Woodruff, and other highly successful
nineteenth-century LDS missionaries itinerantly proselytized in small towns
and villages alike, gathering receptive converts to centers of strength. Mormon settlers founded hundreds of small communities across the western

United States. The agrarian values of the church's early years contributed to ideals of practicality and thrift.

Outside of the Americas, the contemporary LDS Church is almost exclusively a large city church, with forays into a few medium-size towns in close proximity to major hub cities and mission headquarters. LDS missionaries are attached to defined geographic areas constituting the boundaries of established church units and typically do not proselytize outside of their assigned areas. Cities offer advantages in logistics, infrastructure, and communications, while providing access to a larger potentially receptive population. The transition from rural America to major world cities has had profound implications for the Mormon identity.

Although Latter-day Saint planners cite a mandate to reach all people, the question of how rural areas will be reached has received little attention. In India, the 50 LDS missionaries serve in approximately 15 cities, yet there are an estimated 500,000 small towns and villages, and only 12 percent of Indians live in the 300 most populous cities. Indonesia has more than 220 million inhabitants living in more than 100,000 villages and towns on 5,500 hundred islands, but only 22 LDS congregations, all but 3 of which are on the island of Java. In Ukraine, there are 40,000 small towns and villages, but just 60 LDS congregations in 28 cities. While the world urban population is gradually climbing, much of Africa and Asia remain rural: only 28.5 percent of Chinese, 21 percent of Pakistanis, 6.3 percent of Nigerians, 5.8 percent of Ethiopians, 3.4 percent of Cambodians, and 1 percent of Nepalis live in cities of more than 100,000 (Central Intelligence Agency 2003). Given the church's agrarian roots and generally favorable views of rural peoples as "the salt of the earth" compared to more negative stereotypes of widespread sinful activity in large cities, it seems surprising that the LDS Church has not utilized itinerant missionaries, radio and satellite broadcasts, or other approaches to reach rural peoples.

Humanitarian Work

In the church's humanitarian programs, we can see that the pragmatic and utilitarian spirit of the Latter-day Saints noted by O'Dea is still very much alive. The international expansion of the church has contributed to increased awareness of needs worldwide and has contributed to an exceptional era of giving, with the humanitarian work of the modern church gaining new significance because of its scale. The LDS Church has been one of the first humanitarian responders to many crises, from the Asian tsunami to Hurricane Katrina. The LDS Church is one of the most giving churches, donating tens of millions of dollars annually to non-LDS charitable causes.

The church's renowned welfare programs provide for needy members and assist in meeting the needs of the larger community. LDS humanitarian priorities established by the presiding bishop have focused on emergency response and on programs that foster education, increase skills, and improve quality of life. Such programs produce striking parallels with O'Dea's observations of cooperation and mastery among the mid-twentieth-century Utah Saints, as well as the continued focus on helping members to become self-sufficient.

The Perpetual Education Fund (PEF), created in 2002, provides low-interest loans for education primarily to returned international missionaries. The program was created to assist with the transition that many international LDS missionaries face when they return home and find that they have little opportunity to utilize their skills, receive an education, or find employment. President Gordon B. Hinckley stated, "Where there is widespread poverty among our people, we must do all we can to help them to lift themselves, to establish their lives upon a foundation of self-reliance that can come of training. Education is the key to opportunity" (2001, 51). By the end of 2004, more than fifteen thousand individuals had received PEF loans, 85 percent of them from Latin America. Church programs have also allowed a limited number of young adults with proficiency in English from mission areas around the world to attend church universities.

CHANGING SOURCES OF MEMBERS AND IMPLICATIONS

Families and Growth

The challenge noted by O'Dea of building successful "Zion societies" in regions without the isolation and member concentration of the Utah church has introduced new sources of strain. O'Dea observed that although Latter-day Saints emphasize the role of men as leaders in the home and in the priesthood, "Mormon women have a great degree of equality," and that "practically no difficulty" arose from gender issues following the abandonment of polygamy (1957, 250). However, LDS congregational structure depends on active adult men to fill leadership roles, and the paucity of participating adult men in many international LDS congregations has led to organizational and logistic difficulties.

Many single members, especially international women, have difficulty finding a faithful LDS spouse, and either remain single throughout life or marry a nonmember, which in most cases leads to the children being raised outside of the church. In 1986, Kristen L. Goodman and Tim B. Heaton noted that "for every 100 [North American] LDS women in the prime marriage ages (20–29 years) there [were] 89 LDS men." They further noted that the gender disparity between active church attendees among single adults was even more out of balance: "For all singles over 30 there are 19 active men [who attend church weekly] for every 100 active women" (89). The discrepancy among young singles is even greater outside of North America. Church universities provide meccas for English-speaking LDS young single adults to learn and socialize, yet non-English speakers have no such comparable gathering points. The *Encyclopedia of Mormonism* asserted, "The percentage of adults in a temple marriage varies from about 45 percent in Utah to less than 2 percent in Mexico and Central America.... For all of South America, with 2.25 million members, less than 1.8% of the total adult membership has been married in the temple" (Ludlow 1992, 1531–32). Although the construction of smaller temples throughout the world may make temple marriage somewhat more accessible, the problems of inactivity and few eligible potential partners remain.

Declining Family Size

Thomas O'Dea noted the conflicts between traditional LDS values and secular society as a source of strain. Although Latter-day Saints are traditionally known for having large families, the influence of secular society has led to smaller LDS families, with declining birthrates paralleling—although still slightly above—U.S. non-LDS populations. Lowell C. Bennion and Lawrence Young contend, "Although Mormons reject infant baptism, they count as members any 'children of record' blessed and named soon after birth. Thus unbaptized children of members (until age eight) make up an important share of the LDS population (about 15 percent among Americans)" (1996, 9). For the past two decades, the annual number of children of record added to church rolls has progressively declined in spite of increasing LDS membership in high-birthrate regions of the world, particularly Latin America. Today, there are approximately twice as many LDS members as in 1982, but the annual increase in children of record has declined in both relative and absolute terms. Recent years demonstrate annual increases of children of record in the range of 0.6 percent to 0.8 percent of total LDS membership. These figures, which are well below the reproductive level necessary to maintain current membership levels, reflect the fact that the majority of LDS members are inactive and raising their children outside of the church.

The average U.S. LDS family has approximately three children, or one more child than the average non-LDS family. LDS families in Mexico and Japan have fewer children than the national average (Heaton, Goodman, and Holman 1994), and similar trends may exist in many other nations.

Although in the 1970s and 1980s LDS leaders spoke against the use of contraceptives (with some exceptions for personal hardships), this topic has subsequently been almost entirely abandoned from the pulpit. Dr. Tim Heaton (2002) documented that rates of contraceptive use between U.S. LDS and non-LDS populations are virtually identical, at 80.5 percent. Gynecologist Robert Romney noted that at least 80 percent of young women seen at the Brigham Young University health center for premarital exams request some form of contraception (Farnsworth 2004). The U.S. LDS divorce rate lags only 5–10 percent behind the 50 percent national average (Moore 2002c), and the average non-LDS couple thirty years ago had more children and was more likely to stay married than the average LDS couple today.

Although the LDS Church was historically able to achieve significant membership increases through a high birthrate, it has now become primarily dependent on convert baptisms for growth and, in international areas, even for maintenance. As member participation rates are significantly lower for new converts than for children of record raised in Mormon families, the task of improving convert retention and establishing strong indigenous congregations worldwide has become central to the church's prospects for future growth.

Missionary Service

The decline in the number of full-time missionaries from 60,850 at year-end 2001 to 52,060 at year-end 2005 reflects both falling LDS birthrates and tighter standards for missionaries under the "raising the bar" program. The "raising the bar" policy introduced in 2003 focuses on ensuring that prospective missionaries are worthy and embody church standards. Church educational programs, such as seminary and institute, have played a central role in keeping international LDS youth active and promoting missionary service. Although missionary numbers have started to rebound slightly from their nadir in 2004, the rate of increase is slower than in past years when Latter-day Saints had larger families. Missionary service rates among North American LDS young men (25–30 percent) continue to be much higher than among international members (typically below 10 percent). The church has been very successful at mobilizing native missionaries in West Africa and Mongolia (which in 2001 provided 40 percent of the missionaries serving from the Asia North Area [Stewart 2001]), but less successful in most other international areas.

Many nations with vast population bases, such as India, allow native missionaries much wider freedom to proselytize than foreign missionaries, yet there has been only a token LDS presence. The growth of the LDS missionary force is coming to depend increasingly on missionary recruitment of new converts and international members, and greater effectiveness at mobilizing native missionaries will be necessary if the LDS Church is ever to become a major faith in populous Asian nations.

Member-Missionary Participation

LDS Missionary Department studies have reported that only 3–5 percent of active LDS members in North America are regularly involved in missionary work (Ballard 2000).[2] The average Jehovah's Witness spends more than sixteen hours a month proselyting (2005 Report of Jehovah's Witnesses), whereas the Seventh-Day Adventist "Go One Million, Sow One Billion" member-missionary initiatives have resulted in the formation of thousands of new congregations worldwide. The records of these groups stand in stark contrast to that of Latter-day Saints, of whom barely a quarter report making a single attempt to initiate a gospel discussion with a nonmember during the prior year (Barna 2001b). The percentage of member referrals in a cross-section of North American investigators fell from 42 percent in 1987 to 20 percent in 1997, with the average congregation providing two referrals per month (Ballard 2000). These trends are of particular concern in light of Missionary Department research that 86 percent of new converts who remain active have close personal ties to other LDS members (Hart 1991). With the number of annual convert baptisms falling below 2 percent of total LDS membership in 2004 and 2005, efforts to involve increasing numbers of members in outreach will be a major determinant of the church's future growth.

The Utah-based Zion provided an environment where Mormonism could flourish, but this isolation has also presented new difficulties. Whereas Thomas O'Dea noted relatively high levels of member participation and considerable sacrifice made by members of the Mormon faith, contemporary data demonstrate levels of social involvement that far exceed member performance in other core areas. Isolation can foster strength and cohesiveness of a community as O'Dea observed, yet it also imposes barriers. Groups such as the Adventists and Jehovah's Witnesses that have existed as minorities within a larger secular society from their inception have consistently achieved much higher member-missionary participation rates than Latter-day Saints. LDS apostle M. Russell Ballard (2003) has cited research that LDS members are generally much more uptight in gospel discussions than nonmembers.

CULTURAL ISSUES

The American World Church

Thomas O'Dea observed that nineteenth-century European converts who immigrated to Utah were rapidly assimilated, with minimal impact on the culture of the U.S. church (1957, 92). The vast initial nineteenth-century Mormon success in preaching in England and Scandinavia with little adaptation to local culture may have established precedents of exporting U.S.-based missionary paradigms that have been less successful in building a strong indigenous church in other areas. In 1987, Elder Boyd K. Packer reminded a group of church leaders that "we can't move [into various countries] with a 1947 Utah Church! Could it be that we are not prepared to take the gospel because we are not prepared to take (and they are not prepared to receive) all of the things we have wrapped up with it as extra baggage?" (97). In spite of a growing community of international believers, the LDS Church is widely viewed even by its own members in other countries, even in English-speaking nations such as the United Kingdom and Australia, as primarily an American religion (Newton 1996).

The international LDS Church has adapted to its environment in some ways, while retaining strong American cultural elements. Careful correlation meetings ensure that official church manuals and materials are relevant and suitable for a U.S. audience, yet U.S.-based materials are ported over to other languages with no such correlation. German Latter-day Saint Peter Wollauer wrote of church videos: "The videos intellectually bring the message, but emotionally there is a lack of identification—high school, problems with dating, a teaching moment in the desert. The young people are not able to feel the situation, because the school system is very different, the tradition of dating is very different, and there is no desert in Germany" (Stack 1994). The North American trappings of the international church are unmistakably obvious to most international observers, though many U.S. members are unable to recognize them. Perhaps the most difficult challenge for the individual viewing the world through the lens of his own cultural glasses is that he often does not realize that he is wearing glasses at all.

Sociologist Armand Mauss "posed several questions about what kinds of cultural traditions the church could assimilate without assimilating too much. For example, people in India have a totally different idea about what type of music is reverent and inspirational; Mauss questioned whether it would ever be considered appropriate for these members to sing Indian music in church instead of the traditional LDS hymns" (Babbit 2000, A1).

Though such questions have not been definitively answered, it is likely that considerable adaptation will be needed for the church to become an indigenously strong and socially attractive institution in nations where the cultural elements of the American church clash with local culture.

Thomas O'Dea cited Mormon flexibility and ingenuity as key factors in the nineteenth- and early-twentieth-century church's ability to thrive under adverse circumstances. The contemporary church has sought to achieve standardization of protocols without unduly compromising its local flexibility, although this ideal has yet to be fully achieved. The development of missionary paradigms under uniquely favorable North American conditions that often do not reflect international realities has often led to conclusions and programs that are less effective in other cultures and settings. Although the LDS Church has traditionally demonstrated considerable responsiveness and flexibility in English-speaking areas, its international approach has been more reactive than proactive. The assignment of apostles Holland and Oaks to areas of the developing world to troubleshoot problems of low convert retention and member participation was greatly needed, but these areas have experienced very low retention rates for nearly a half century. Mission presidents who introduce needed local changes often see their policies completely reversed after their departure, and current policies allow little mechanism for institutional learning or quality-improvement processes.

The *Preach My Gospel* missionary manual published in 2004 offers no specific cultural insights, yet it avoids many of the U.S. culture-based tactics found in past missionary guides that posed difficulties in other cultures, and encourages missionaries to develop and use their own cultural insights rather than following a formula. In recent years, international leaders have also experienced greater degrees of autonomy. Wollauer noted, "German missionary work was slow for a long time because mission presidents from the United States used American methods of contacting and teaching potential converts. With more German mission presidents, stake and ward leaders 'emancipated' from U.S. leaders, the conversion rate has picked up. That does not mean that we ignore the counsel and suggestions of General Authorities, but it does mean that we feel free to find our own German and Austrian way to put these suggestions into practice" (Stack 1994).

English versus Non-English

The LDS Church operates on a tiered linguistic system between English and other languages. Other languages are assigned to one of three "phases" depending on the number of LDS speakers and maturity of the church, with each phase corresponding to a set of resources designated for translation. Scriptures and curriculum resources are translated, whereas many other resources are not. Fluency in English is a practical prerequisite for advancement in church hierarchy beyond the level of mission president or area authority.

The church has made great efforts in recent years to bridge the gap between English speakers and non-English speakers in the church. Foreign audio translations of general conference addresses have been made available live online in many languages, and recent general conference addresses and church manuals are now available in other languages on the church Web sites.

Culture and Indigenous Identity

Perhaps the greatest linguistic gap between English-speaking and non-English-speaking Latter-day Saints lies in the lack of indigenous non-English Mormon literature. Publishers like Deseret Book have been indispensable in defining contemporary U.S. Mormon culture. The vast array of resources, from "historical fiction" to capture the interest of teens challenged by archaic scriptural vocabulary to self-help books on parenting, adds an immersive element to Mormon life. Indigenous church literature—whether official or unofficial—plays an important role in developing a sense of community and identity within the church and in fostering the perception of the church as an acceptable local religion rather than a foreign one. There are two Seventh-Day Adventist publishing houses in the United Kingdom alone, yet no nation outside of the Americas has a single publishing house dedicated to printing indigenously produced LDS literature.

U.S. members often fail to fully appreciate the challenges faced by non-English-speaking Saints. Former Belgian bishop Wilfried Decoo observed:

> I well remember a leadership meeting at which a local leader asked a visiting general authority if it would be possible for the church distribution center in Frankfurt to make available books from the Deseret and Bookcraft companies, even in English for local English-speaking members, with permission perhaps to translate some of the more popular books into other languages. The visiting authority responded categorically that the scriptures should be enough for any of the Saints. Yet in the foyer I observed his wife reading a book by Hugh Nibley and his daughter a novel by Jack Weyland. (1996, 118)

Although most non-English-speaking members are appreciative of the resources they have, most also acknowledge a desire for more.

The desire of U.S. leaders to maintain central control of international units has often hindered the autonomy necessary to develop a strong indigenous Mormon identity. In the challenge of standardization versus indigenous identity, or of hierarchal structure versus congregationalism in O'Dea's terms, standardization and hierarchy have typically claimed the upper hand. Non-English publications by local members have often been officially discouraged (Decoo 1997; Numano 1996), or, at best, not encouraged, although international Saints hunger for greater involvement. Even in the LDS international magazine, the overwhelming majority of articles are written by U.S. authors, perpetuating the perception of an American church looking out at the world rather than a truly integrated world faith. Decoo points out that the result is an informational and cultural religious void in societies that place a high value on information and culture. Japanese Mormon Jiro Numano wrote, "If Japanese members were given the editorial responsibility for the international church magazine in Japan, *Seito no Michi,* members might read the entire magazine with the enthusiasm now reserved for the few pages devoted to local news" (1996, 228–29). The church's English-speaking leadership has been concerned that it would not be able to ensure the same level of orthodoxy in indigenous non-English literature. Nonetheless, the importance of such resources to North American Mormon culture should be acknowledged, as well as the cultural void in non-English communities in their absence.

External Conflicts

The differences between Latter-day Saint values and secular culture cited by Thomas O'Dea encompass many areas, but three major societal trends—decreasing church attendance, increasing substance abuse, and the decline of chastity—typify this conflict. The growth of such contrasts highlights the distinctiveness of Latter-day Saints observed by O'Dea. These differences have been a source of internal strength for Latter-day Saints, while at the same time presenting external challenges to growth. These differences highlight challenges faced by many potential Mormon converts that require diligent effort and preparation over sustained periods to overcome.

Church Attendance

Western societies have experienced increasing nominalism and decreasing Christian church attendance. Declining national trends exist in self-reported rates of weekly church attendance among adults worldwide: 2 percent in Russia, 4–5 percent in Scandinavia, 14 percent in Germany, 21 percent in France, 27 percent in the United Kingdom, 25–46 percent in various nations of Latin

America, 44 percent in the United States, and more than 80 percent in Ireland and Nigeria ("Study of Worldwide Rates" 1997). These rates trended down to the present levels during the twentieth century. Even modest self-reported attendance rates are often exaggerated. U.S. research suggests that only about half of Christians who report being in church each week actually attend (Hadaway and Marler 1998). Although overall trends demonstrate increasing secularization, this phenomenon of decreasing participation among mainline Protestant and Catholic denominations has occurred concurrently with the increasing growth of other faiths, particularly Islam: studies now show that more people attend mosques than Anglican churches in the United Kingdom each week (Hellen and Morgan 2004). Among Christians, most growth has occurred among Pentecostal, evangelical, and independent churches. Weekly church attendance has not been part of the upbringing of most prospective LDS converts, making the convert preparation process more difficult.

Substance Abuse

Few areas demonstrate the conflict between LDS teachings and secular trends as dramatically as substance abuse. In an 1833 revelation prohibiting the use of alcohol, tobacco, and other forbidden substances, the Lord warned Joseph Smith "of evils and designs which do and will exist in the hearts of conspiring men in the last days." Substance abuse has become one of the foremost economic, political, medical, and social problems of the twenty-first century. Although tobacco use is on the decline in the United States, the prevalence of smoking among adult males has reached epidemic proportions in eastern Europe, Asia, and Africa. United Nations data suggest that 40–50 percent of male mortality in eastern Europe is directly connected to tobacco-related diseases, whereas alcohol abuse accounts for another 10–15 percent. Industrial distilling processes have made alcohol more readily available and in more potent forms than ever before in history. Alcohol is a major contributor to homicides, suicides, and motor vehicle accident deaths, as well as contributing to domestic abuse and the breakup of many families. Illegal drug abuse has spawned a host of criminal behaviors and has become a prime medium for the spread of HIV and hepatitis B and C. Tea is a national drink in many nations of Europe and Asia, creating a cultural barrier to receptivity of the LDS message.

The baptism of prospective converts who have not fully overcome addictions to substances forbidden by the Word of Wisdom remains a major cause of high relapse rates and low convert retention. Elder Dallin Oaks notes, "According to one study, 75 percent of adult converts in North America had to give up at least one of these substances mentioned in the Word of Wisdom—tobacco, alcohol, coffee, or tea—and 31 percent had to give up smoking, a very addictive habit.... One third to one half of them reported that they had experienced 'occasional,' 'frequent,' or 'complete' lapses into their abstinence" (2003, 57).

Chastity

The church, which requires that members refrain from any sexual relations outside of marriage, faces a widening gulf between scriptural standards and secular values that presents obstacles for outreach, as well as challenging some existing members. Studies report that in the United States, 60 percent of all adults (Barna 2003), including 54 percent of mainline Christians, 42 percent of weekly church attenders, and 36 percent of born-again Christians, believe that premarital cohabitation is morally acceptable (Barna 2001a). Sociologist Stephanie Coontz observes, "People's behavior about marriage changed more in the past 30 years than in the last 3,000" (Roberts 2006, sec. 4, p. 3). One recent study reported that 95 percent of Americans born from the 1940s onward had engaged in premarital sexual relations by age forty-four, with the median age of first premarital relations creeping down to seventeen for those born after 1970 (Finer 2007). Promiscuity is also spreading rapidly, even in nations that have traditionally fostered strong family values. In China, 70 percent of Beijing residents reported sex before marriage in 2005, compared to just 15 percent in 1989 (Beech 2006). Similar trends of growing permissiveness and promiscuity are seen in many other nations, both presenting challenges for the receptivity of nonmembers as well as contributing to attrition among Latter-day Saints. Latter-day Saints continue to be relatively successful in maintaining moral values, at least among highly active and involved members. Brent L. Top and Bruce A. Chadwick (1999) report that 10 percent of male senior LDS seminary students and 17 percent of female senior seminary students in the United States report having had premarital sexual relations, compared to 77 percent of male and 66 percent of female senior high school students nationwide. Although there is still much room for improvement, these statistics demonstrate that Latter-day Saints are maintaining much of their distinctiveness in an increasingly secular world.

STANDARDS, GROWTH, AND RETENTION

While the LDS faith experiences significant external challenges, declining LDS growth and low convert retention in an era of unprecedented opportunities when other denominations are experiencing accelerating growth suggest that internal factors also play an important role in church growth and member retention. Internal challenges to church growth previously discussed include declining LDS family size, low member participation in missionary outreach, slowing rates of missionary increase, and U.S. programs transplanted into cultures for which they are often mismatched. Additional challenges include varying standards for baptism that are often unclear or are not consistently enforced.

Thomas O'Dea correctly identified LDS standards as a source of strength. Some critics have assumed that high membership expectations are detrimental to LDS growth, claiming that the church is "incapable of growing exponentially" because "the strict lifestyle that the church promotes, eschew[ing] alcohol, premarital sex and even coffee, prompts many converts to drift away" (Gerstein 2005, 1186). In fact, the world's rapidly growing missionary churches are not those that require little (Catholic, Orthodox, and mainline Protestant churches experience few conversions), but faiths with high membership requirements, such as the Seventh-Day Adventists and Jehovah's Witnesses. The Hartsem Faith Communities Today study, the largest study of religious congregations in U.S. history, found that strictness of member expectations contributes to high growth rather than dissuading prospective converts (Hartsem Institute for Religious Research n.d.), as individuals receive the benefits of faith only as they put forth effort. Laurence R. Iannaccone documented that free-riders who maintain nominal membership while failing to contribute weaken any religious body and result in the fruitless dissipation of resources. "Any attempt to directly subsidize the observable aspects of religious participation (such as church attendance) will almost certainly backfire" (1994, A3). Low standards and subsidization of requirements foster maladaptive dynamics that hamper church growth. Converts who join with the expectation of giving active service strengthen a church, whereas those who join expecting to be passively served weaken it.

The insightful recognition of O'Dea and Iannaccone that high expectations make stronger members has been abundantly demonstrated. From 1840 to 1890, more than 97 percent of LDS converts in Britain (89,625 of 92,465) left their lands, homes, and families to undertake the perilous transatlantic journey and emigrate to the U.S. Zion (Stark 1998). The self-selection threshold of commitment and sacrifice that characterized the early LDS Church is present in only a very limited degree today. In contrast to the unpressured, nonstandardized, and often lengthy prebaptismal process of O'Dea's time, a standardized missionary program was introduced in 1959 through the efforts of Elder Henry Moyle and then modified by others. This standardized worldwide program attempted to bring individuals from their first contact with the missionaries to baptism within a period of two to three weeks. The pressure to baptize investigators as soon as possible led in many cases to loose standards that were based more on acknowledgment of LDS beliefs and future promises than on observance of LDS teachings for any meaningful period prior to baptism. As suggested by Iannaccone, the lower entry standards backfired, perpetuating very low convert retention rates.

Postbaptismal attrition is heavily front-loaded. Elder Dallin H. Oaks notes that "among those converts who fall away, attrition is sharpest in the two months after baptism" (2003, 56), and missionaries report being told in the MTC that up to 80 percent of inactivity occurs within two months of baptism. In the context of the church's long-term commitment to its members, such data highlight the need for more rigorous teaching, preparation, and qualification of prospective converts before baptism, as the baptism of uncommitted or insincere individuals who do not remain active presents a lifetime liability to the church. My research has found that in many areas, the average LDS investigator has read fewer than ten pages in the Book of Mormon and has attended church twice or less at the time of baptism (2007, 256). Not surprisingly, the large majority of such converts are completely lost to the church within two months of baptism. Repeated churchwide exhortations for members to fellowship new converts resulted in little improvement in retention, as the problem of low entry requirements remained largely unaddressed. In contrast, converts in higher-retaining missions typically have been reading scriptures daily, have attended church weekly for at least a month, and have established friendships with active members before baptism.

The problem of inactivity has had profound consequences for the international church. With unfavorable ratios of active to inactive members, many international congregations face chronic difficulties in meeting their own internal shepherding needs and are poorly able to reach out to the larger community. Low activity rates have also made it difficult for the church to establish a strong indigenous identity in many nations. As most international LDS inactives lack even nominal belief or identification with the LDS Church, the social programs and changes that led to a dramatic increase in member participation in the early twentieth century Utah church are having only a minor impact on international activity rates today.

Growing awareness of the problem of low convert retention resulting from the rushed baptism of inadequately prepared individuals has received greater attention in recent years and has sparked institutional change. Elder M. Russell Ballard noted, "We cannot establish the Church unless we have real growth—not simply numbers on paper" (1999, n.d.). President James E.

Faust taught, "Should we not baptize all those who want to or are willing to be baptized? The answer is not that simple. It is a great responsibility to bring someone into this Church who has not been adequately taught and who has not received of the Spirit so that through baptism they may become a new person through repentance.... We must be certain the repentance process is at work" (Dockstander 1996, 3). Some progress resulted from the assignment of apostles Jeffrey R. Holland to Chile and Dallin H. Oaks to the Philippines to study and address the challenges of low member retention. The First Presidency issued a statement in 2002 requiring all prospective converts to attend church several times and keep all commitments regularly before baptism (Church of Jesus Christ of Latter-day Saints 2002). *Preach My Gospel,* a missionary manual for both full-time and member missionaries, was published in 2004. This manual introduces many major missionary-program changes and educates missionaries for the first time about their essential role in ensuring convert retention. *Preach My Gospel* also reinforces that converts must keep all commitments consistently to be baptized.

With awareness of retention problems at an all-time high, the LDS Church currently has a better opportunity to improve convert retention rates worldwide than it has had since the standardized missionary program was introduced in the late 1950s. Although the new standards have significantly improved convert retention rates in the limited areas where they have been consistently adhered to, I have found wide variation in their implementation, with most missions demonstrating considerable degrees of noncompliance. Some missions have reported substantial improvements, whereas many other mission and area leaders have continued to push rush-baptize tactics, leading to continued high convert attrition. Time will tell whether the discipline exists among missionaries and leaders to enforce standards helping prospective converts to consistently develop the habits of faith that are crucial to their long-term activity before baptism, or whether such guidelines will be viewed merely as nice ideals that are rarely applied.

Conclusion

Thomas O'Dea recognized many key issues that have become defining challenges of the contemporary LDS Church. The challenge posed by O'Dea of developing a more universal and spiritual identity beyond the concept of an American Zion, and more specifically a strong indigenous identity in each land, has not yet been fully navigated and remains just as relevant—and perhaps even more crucial—than at the time of O'Dea's writing fifty years ago. The external conflicts O'Dea noted between Mormon values and secular culture, as well as internal challenges such as hierarchal structure versus congregationalism, have continued to manifest themselves in the international church. The distinctive values of the LDS faith, even in the setting of very different cultures, serve as a reservoir of strength. Latter-day Saints continue to assist each other and their non-LDS neighbors in humanitarian ways. The contemporary relevance of many of O'Dea's initial observations is remarkable.

The dynamics of the LDS faith have remained similar in some ways, whereas in other aspects they have changed dramatically from O'Dea's era. North American LDS birthrates have declined, and the challenge of becoming a multigenerational family church outside the United States remains in its nascent stages. Proselytizing has become the major mechanism of Mormon growth, with most of that growth occurring internationally. Slowing growth and low convert retention have become major institutional challenges. Certain internal difficulties must be overcome for the LDS Church to once again become a fast-growing faith where member activity is the norm rather than the exception.

Thomas O'Dea acknowledged that "strains and conflicts are both signs and sources of vitality.... That its values provide a meaningful context to great numbers of its adherents cannot be denied. Its flexibility in the past and its viability under the most adverse conditions do not augur badly for its future" (1957, 263). The increasing size of the church, widespread standardization of policies, and the highly centralized nature of church administration have made it difficult for the church to demonstrate the same degree of local resourcefulness and responsiveness seen a century ago, especially in non-U.S. cultures. Nonetheless, there are definite and encouraging signs of a faithful, committed, and increasingly large body of international Latter-day Saints. The resourcefulness of a large base of highly committed membership and continued institutional adjustments suggest that current difficulties are surmountable.

The next fifty years will likely see a continued shift in the center of gravity of the LDS faith to international areas. The day may come when speakers of Spanish, and perhaps additional languages, outnumber English speakers. International Saints are likely to achieve greater representation in leadership positions as the church in their native lands matures. New steps, both official and unofficial, will likely be implemented to develop the identity and cohesion of international LDS communities. All of these trends suggest that gradual and continuing institutional adjustments to meet the needs of the international flock are inevitable.

Notes

1. The erroneous claim of the "fastest growing church in the United States" was also made in the LDS *Church News,* the *Ensign,* and other official publications.

2. I have verified with the Missionary Department that the 3–5 percent figure cited in the August 1999 Conversion and Retention broadcast is correct, and that the 35 percent figure cited in the *Ensign* is an error.

References

"Atlanta Suburb Flourishes with Church Membership." 2002. *The Church in the News* (referring to the *Atlanta Constitution Journal*), April 11.

Austrian Census. 2001. http://www.statistik.at/presse2002/religion.pdf.

Babbit, Christi C. 2000. "Growth of LDS Church as Upside, Downside." *Deseret News,* November 25.

Ballard, M. Russell. 1999. "Conversion and Retention" satellite broadcast, August 29.

———. 2000. "Members Are the Key." *Ensign,* September, 8.

———. 2003. "The Essential Role of Member Missionary Work." *Ensign,* May, 37.

Barna, George. 2001a. "Practical Outcomes Replace Biblical Principles as the Moral Standard. September 10. http://www.barna.org/cgi-bin/PagePressRelease.asp?PressReleaseID=97&Reference=F.

———. 2001b. "Protestants, Catholics, and Mormons Reflect Diverse Levels of Religious Activity." Barna Press Release, July 9.

———. 2003. "Morality Continues to Decay." November 10. http://www.barna.org/FlexPage.aspx?Page=BarnaUpdate&BarnaUpdateID=152.

Beech, Hannah. 2006. "Sex Please—We're Young and Chinese." *Time Asia,* January 23.

Bennion, Lowell C., and Lawrence A. Young. 1996. "The Uncertain Dynamics of LDS Expansion, 1950–2020." *Dialogue: A Journal of Mormon Thought* 29, no. 1: 8–32.

Borden, Tessie. 2001a. "Mexico Mormon Flock Grows." *Arizona Republic,* July 10.

———. 2001b. "Mexico Mormon Flock Grows." *Spokesman Review,* July 22.

Brazilian Census. 2000. Instituto Brasileiro de Geografia e Estatistica, Censo Demographico.

Canham, Matt. 2005. "Church Won't Give Up on 'Lost Members.'" *Salt Lake Tribune,* October 17.

Central Intelligence Agency. 2003. *CIA World Factbook.* Available online at http://www.cia.gov/library/publications/the-world-factbook.html.

Chilean Census. 2002. Chilean National Institute of Statistics. http://www.ine.cl/cd2002/religion.pdf.

Church of Jesus Christ of Latter-day Saints. 2002. First Presidency letter, December 11.

Clark, James R., comp. 1970. *Messages of the First Presidency.* Vol. 4. Salt Lake City: Bookcraft.

Decoo, Wilfried. 1996. "Feeding the Fleeing Flock: Reflections on the Struggle to Retain Church Members in Europe" *Dialogue: A Journal of Mormon Thought* 29, no. 1: 97–118.

———. 1997. "Issues in Writing European History and in Building the Church in Europe." *Journal of Mormon History* 23, no. 1: 139–76.

Dockstander, Julie A. 1996. "President Faust: 'Time-Tested Principles of Conversion.'" *Church News,* June 29.

Duke, James T. 1999. "Latter-day Saints in a Secular World: What We Have Learned about Latter-day Saints from Social Research." BYU Hickman Lecture, March 4. http://fhss.byu.edu/adm/hickman_lecture.htm.

Farnsworth, Kira. 2004. "LDS Church Not Opposed to Birth Control." *BYU Newsnet,* January 21.

Finer, Lawrence B. 2007. "Trends in Premarital Sex in the United States, 1954–2003." *Public Health Reports* 122 (January–February): 73–77.

Garrison, David. 1999. *Church Planting Movements.* Southern Baptist International Mission Board, October. E-book, available at http://www.churchplantingmovements.com/documents_pdf/englishcpm.pdf.

Gerstein, Josh. 2005. "Mormons Rising in Government, Business, Schools." *New York Sun,* October 18.

Glenmary Research Center. 2002. "Religious Congregations and Membership, 2000." September 20. http://www.glenmary.org/grc/RCMS_2000/findings.htm.

Goodman, Kristen L., and Tim B. Heaton. 1986. "LDS Church Members in the U.S. and Canada: A Demographic Profile." *Association of Mormon Counselors and Psychotherapists* 12, no. 1: 88–107.

Grossman, Cathy Lynn. 2002. "Charting the Unchurched America." *USA Today,* March 7.

Hadaway, C. Kirk, and P. L. Marler. 1998. "Did You Really Go to Church This Week? Behind the Poll Data." *Christian Century,* May 6, 472–75. http://www.religion-online.org/shoarticle.asp?title=237.

Hart, John L. 1991. "LDS Mission Presidents Embark on a Work of Love." *Church News,* June 22.

Hartsem Institute for Religious Research. n.d. "Faith Communities in the U.S. Today." http://fact.hartsem.edu.

Heaton, Tim B. 2002. "Dealing with Demographics." Paper presented at the 2002 FAIR conference.

Heaton, Tim B., Kristen L. Goodman, and Thomas B. Holman. 1994. "In Search of a Peculiar People: Are Mormon Families Really Different?" In *Contemporary Mormonism: Social Science Perspectives,* ed. Marie Cornwall, Tim B. Heaton, and Lawrence A. Young, 87–117. Urbana: University of Illinois Press.

Hellen, Nicholas, and Christopher Morgan. 2004. "Muslims Outpace Anglicans in UK." *The Times* (London), January 25. http://www.timesonline.co.uk/article/0,,2087-976226,00.html.

Henetz, Patty. 2003. "Latter-day Saints Urged to Help Retain New Converts." *San Francisco Chronicle,* April 5.

Hinckley, Gordon B. 2001. "The Perpetual Education Fund." *Ensign,* May, 51.

Iannaccone, Lawrence R. 1994. "Why Strict Churches Are Strong." *American Journal of Sociology* 99, no. 5: 1180–1211.

Jehovah's Witnesses. 2004. "Membership and Publishing Statistics, 2004." http://www.jw.media.org/people/statistics.htm.

Johnstone, Patrick, and Jason Mandryk. 2005. *Operation World.* Carlisle, Calif.: Paternoster Press.

LeBaron, Dale E. 2001. "The Inspiring Story of the Gospel Going to Black Africa." Devotional, Ricks College. News release, April 5.

Lobb, Gary C. 2000. "Mormon Membership Trends in Europe among People of Color: Present and Future Assessment. *Dialogue: A Journal of Mormon Thought* 33, no. 4: 55–68.

Lobdell, William. 2003. "New Mormon Aim: Reach Out to Blacks." *Los Angeles Times,* September 21.

Ludlow, Daniel H., ed. 1992. *Encyclopedia of Mormonism.* Vol. 4. New York: Macmillan.

Mayer, Ergon, Barry A. Kosmin, and Ariela Keysar. 2001. *American Religious Identification Survey.* New York: City University of New York.

Moore, Carrie A. 2002a. "Elder Holland 'a Student' in Chile." *Deseret News,* October 13, B1.

———. 2002b. "Flood of Converts Alters the Face of the LDS Church." *Deseret News,* October 5, A1.

———. 2002c. "Statistics Offer Good and Bad News for LDS." *Deseret News,* August 11, B5.

Newton, Marjorie. 1996. "Towards 2000: Mormonism in Australia." *Dialogue: A Journal of Mormon Thought* 29, no. 1: 193–206.

Numano, Jiro. 1996. "Mormonism in Modern Japan." *Dialogue: A Journal of Mormon Thought* 29, no. 1: 224–25.

"Number of Adventist Congregations Worldwide Increases 70 Percent, Says Office of Global Mission." 2000. Adventist News Network, October 24.

Oaks, Dallin H. 2003. "The Role of Members in Conversion." *Ensign,* March, 52–58.

O'Dea, Thomas F. 1957. *The Mormons.* Chicago: University of Chicago Press.

Packer, Boyd K. 1987. "Address to the Church Coordinating Committee Meeting, 8 September." Copy in Historical Department Library, Church of Jesus Christ of Latter-day Saints. Quoted in Lee Copeland, "From Calcutta to Kaysville: Is Righteousness Color-Coded?" *Dialogue: A Journal of Mormon Thought* 21 (Autumn 1988): 89–99.

"Report of Jehovah's Witnesses Worldwide." 2005. http://www.watchtower.org/statistics/worldwide_report.htm.

Roberts, Sam. 2006. "So Many Men, So Few Women." *New York Times,* February 12, sec. 4, p. 3.

"Selected Protestant Denominations, Canada, 2001 and 1991." 2003. Statcan Press Release, May.

"Seventh-day Adventist Statistical Report." 2003. http://www.adventiststatistics.org.

Smith, Christopher. 2002. "Saints in Las Vegas: LDS Church Thriving in the Glow of Sin City." *Salt Lake Tribune,* April 6.

Stack, Peggy Fletcher. 1994. "As Mormon Church Grows, Global Challenges Arise." *Salt Lake Tribune,* August 20.

———. 1996. "Growing LDS Church Goes Global. *Salt Lake Tribune,* February 10.

———. 1998. "African Culture Presents Challenges for Mormon Converts." *Salt Lake Tribune,* April 4.

———. 2003. "Brazil Leaves Impression on LDS Church." *Salt Lake Tribune,* April 5.

———. 2006. "Building Faith, a Special Report: The LDS Church in Chile." *Salt Lake Tribune,* March 31.

Stark, Rodney. 1998. "The Basis of Mormon Success: A Theoretical Application." In *Latter-day Saint Social Life: Social Research on the LDS Church and Its Members,* ed. James T. Duke, 29–70. Provo: Religious Studies Center, Brigham Young University.

Stewart, David G., Jr. 2001. "The Mongolian Miracle." http://www.cumorah.com.

———. 2007. *Law of the Harvest: Practical Principles of Effective Missionary Work.* Henderson, Nev.: Cumorah Foundation.

"Study of Worldwide Rates of Religiosity, Church Attendance." 1997. Press release, University of Michigan, Institute for Social Research, December 10.

Top, Brent L., and Bruce A. Chadwick. 1999. "Helping Teens Stay Strong." *Ensign,* March, 27.

"Utah's Wheel Greasing History." 1999. *The Guardian* (United Kingdom), January 25.

Wagner, C. Peter. 1990. *Church Planting for a Greater Harvest.* Ventura, Calif.: Regal Books.

Walch, Tad. 2003. "LDS Surge in Latin America." *Deseret News,* March 21.

Whetten, Robert J. 2005. "Strengthen Thy Brethren." *Ensign,* May, 91.

Willis, Stacy A. 2001. "Mormon Church Is Funding Its Future." *Las Vegas Sun,* May 4.

Yohannan, K. P. n.d. "Revolution in World Missions." http://www.gfa.org.

Young, Lawrence A. 1994. "Confronting Turbulent Environments." In *Contemporary Mormonism: Social Science Perspectives,* ed. Marie Cornwall, Tim B. Heaton, and Lawrence A. Young, 43–63. Urbana: University of Illinois Press.

Zoll, Rachel. 2002. "Mormon, Evangelical Christian Churches Growing Fastest, Study Says." *Anchorage Daily News,* September 17.

13

The Mormons of the World

The Meaning of LDS Membership
in Central America

~ HENRI GOOREN ~

THE MEMBERSHIP GROWTH OF THE CHURCH of Jesus Christ of Latter-day Saints (LDS) is impressive, growing from six Latter-day Saints in 1830 to approaching thirteen million by 2006.[1] The LDS Church boasts a very strong top-down organization, which is analyzed in detail by Thomas F. O'Dea (1957, 174–85; see also Gooren 1999, 64–65). Especially since the 1950s, the Mormon Church is gradually becoming an international church. Rodney Stark may be exaggerating in calling Mormonism the next world religion (Stark 1984, 1990, 1996, 1998; see also Decoo 1996, 98; Gooren 1991, 51; 1999, 66; Grover 1985, 137–39; Knowlton 2005, 54; and O'Dea 1957, 185),[2] but there is no doubt that the LDS Church is gaining many new members worldwide. Growth has been strong in some Pacific islands (such as Tonga) and especially in Latin America.

Nowadays, more than 35 percent of the worldwide membership is concentrated in Latin America, compared to about 45 percent in the United States and Canada. Growth in Latin America has been particularly strong in Chile, Uruguay, the Andean countries, and Central America as a whole (Gooren 2007). By 2020, if the current growth rates continue, the majority of Mormons in the world will be Latin Americans (Grover 2005, 85). This would have surprised Thomas O'Dea and other scholars of Mormonism in the 1950s.

The success of the Latter-day Saints in Latin America begs two questions. What is the meaning of LDS Church membership for the multitudes of Latin Americans who converted to the church? And what does the future majority of Latin American Mormons mean for the organization and functioning of the LDS Church itself? This article will deal mostly with the first question, the meaning of LDS Church membership for Latin Americans. It will also analyze the supposed rational and intellectual appeal (O'Dea 1957, 241–42; Widtsoe 1998) of the LDS doctrine for Central Americans and contrast it with the more emotional—and certainly less intellectual—tendencies of the main religious competitors of the Mormon Church in Central America, the Pentecostals.

As in Pentecostalism, the attractions of Mormonism are not sufficient to keep more than half of the new converts active in the church after the first year. David C. Knowlton (2005, 54) shows that only about one-quarter of all baptized Mormons identify themselves as such in the national censuses of Mexico and Chile. These are the core members, "the church within the Church" (Davies 2000, 4). I shall argue here that perhaps another one-quarter are still (occasionally) active as members, although membership does not form an essential element of their lives and identities.

Some of the initial attractions of Mormonism turn out to be its principal obstacles to sustained commitment, especially the church's organization and its strict rules of conduct, which are difficult to maintain for some people. I first analyze the recruitment process of Mormons in Central America. Following O'Dea (1957, 222ff), I then analyze three principal sources of strain and conflict for Mormons in Central America: callings, machismo, and inactivity. All three are connected to local leadership performance. A final section probes the meaning of LDS membership in contemporary Central America. What is the relevance of Thomas O'Dea's 1957 book on the LDS way of life in the United States for analyzing Mormonism in contemporary Central America?

Mormon Success in Central America

Following O'Dea, I focus especially on the supposed rational and intellectual appeal of Mormonism in Central America. O'Dea wrote in *The Mormons*, "Mormonism has been inclined toward rationality from the start, and this has long been related to a certain utilitarianism in the general Mormon outlook.... Argument rather than emotion plays an important part in Mormon proselytizing" (1957, 241).

In my 1990 study of an LDS ward in San José, Costa Rica, I closely observed how the missionaries tried to convince the *investigators,* or potential converts (Gooren 1991, 29–32). Most of the investigators came from the upper lower classes and the lower middle class; the majority of them were women. These investigators were invariably young, usually between fifteen and twenty-five, and intellectually very curious. But they were not critical: almost all accepted everything the elders told them at face value. The high literacy rate in Costa Rica of 92 percent aided the missionary work, because investigators were required to read many texts (30). Giving away the Book of Mormon in Spanish for free was an important part of the mission strategy.[3] The missionaries would subtly pressure people to make the next appointment soon, usually in a few days. But the investigators often complained that they had no time to do their "homework": to read texts from the Bible, Book of Mormon, Doctrine and Covenants, and brochures containing the *Discussions* (called *Charlas* in Spanish).

There were six *Discussion* brochures, which were officially called *Study Guides (Guías de estudio).*[4] The missionaries practiced a verbatim rendering of the *Charlas* at the Missionary Training Center in Provo, Utah. As their Spanish improved, they sometimes improvised more—or "trusted the Holy Spirit," as they described it (30). The elders would take turns in giving the talks. A discussion was supposed to take about a half hour, but they usually took more than an hour in Costa Rica because of frequent digressions and interruptions (unexpected visitors, children demanding attention, and general noise).

A typical *Charla* meeting always started with an opening prayer by an elder, followed by the singing of one or two hymns, and then the talk. The first *Discussion* explained *Our Heavenly Father's Plan* for humanity and included the story of how Joseph Smith was guided by God to find the gold plates of the Book of Mormon and found a new church, the only true church. The second *Charla, The Gospel of Christ,* discussed the resurrection of Christ. The key *Discussions* were 3 and 4, *The Restoration* and *Eternal Progress.* Number 3 dealt with the corruption of the church in the centuries after Christ, resulting in the loss of the "keys to the authority of the lay priesthood." Joseph Smith was told by God in his First Vision that all churches were false. Around this time, the missionaries would urge investigators not only to read the Book of Mormon but also to pray about its contents and ask the Holy Spirit for a confirmation that it is true. The reasoning is as follows: if the Book of Mormon is authentic, then Joseph Smith is a true prophet of God, and then the Mormon Church must be the true church of Christ. Again, I would like to stress that it is a form of reasoning that is mostly intellectual. *Discussion* 4 dealt with the *preexistence,* where spirits exist before they are born with a body. The missionaries explained the importance of the law of chastity to maintain pure bodies. They then asked the investigator in a very direct manner if he or she complied with this God-given law. The answer was always accepted at face value. The *Discussion* ended with an explanation of Joseph Smith's revelation on the Word of Wisdom: "We shouldn't consume alcohol, tobacco, coffee, tea, or harm-

TABLE 13.1. Key LDS indicators for Guatemala, Costa Rica, and Nicaragua, 2005

	GUATEMALA	COSTA RICA	NICARAGUA
Year of arrival	1947	1946	1953
Registered members	200,537	34,036	52,184
LDS population percentage	1.37	0.85	0.95
Number of stakes	40	5	7
Number of wards	236	42	44
Annual growth percentage, 2004-2005	1.9	1.6	9.0
High growth years	1982-1990	1988-1992	1990-1998

Sources: Deseret News 2006; Gooren 2001, 2007.

ful drugs." *Charla* 5 talked about the importance of leading a Christ-like life; afterward, the missionaries inquired after a possible date for baptism. The final discussion was called *Members of God's Kingdom* and discussed Christ's roles as creator, savior, example, and judge in our final judgment. The conditions to accept Christ in our lives were explicitly mentioned: baptism by immersion, faith, repentance, accepting the gifts of the Holy Spirit, following God's commandments, and serving his true church. A date must be set for baptism after the final *Discussion,* unless the investigator had not yet been to church on a Sunday. But this was rare. Out of the thirty investigators I followed in Costa Rica, only two failed to be baptized (32).

The missionaries aimed to have at least one *Discussion* every week with the investigator, which they usually accomplished. Investigators hardly ever cried or showed other emotions, except curiosity. They typically said that Mormonism made sense to them; it was "logical," and it "could answer the questions they'd had for a long time." We see traces of what O'Dea called the intellectual appeal of Mormonism and its use of logical argument as a conversion method. The most eager investigators went through all six *Charlas* in two weeks. This meant that their knowledge of the Mormon Church was rudimentary at best. But the Utah-born LDS mission president in Costa Rica did not consider this a problem: "The most important thing is that they get baptized. After that they still have a lot to learn" (32).

How successful are the LDS missionaries in the region? Table 13.1 gives an overview of key indicators of the Mormon Church in three key countries in Central America. I analyze LDS growth here by referring to my current fieldwork on religious competition in Managua, Nicaragua, and to my earlier studies of representative urban LDS wards in Guatemala City and San José, Costa Rica (1991, 1999, 2007).[5]

Guatemala has the largest number of Mormons, the result of explosive growth throughout the 1980s, as well as the highest LDS population percentage. But Guatemala's current annual growth rate is barely 2 percent, which is similar to Costa Rica. Since LDS Church growth equals the general population growth in these countries, there is a relative stasis of membership occurring here. Only in Nicaragua is there still strong growth, exceeding 9 percent a year. The growth explosion in Nicaragua took place in the 1990s and was actually a catching-up process. The war and government harassment by the ruling left-wing Sandinistas severely limited the missionary work of the church. Between 1982 and 1990, several Mormon Church buildings were confiscated and used by Sandinista youth groups and the Sandinista army. For about eight years, the LDS Church functioned underground in Nicaragua (see Gooren 2007 for details).

Various authors (Gooren 1999, 2000; Grover 1985, 2005; Knowlton 1996, 2005; Stark 1998)[6] conclude that the main general attractions of LDS membership in Latin America are its smooth organization that radiates success and middle-class values, style of worship and hymns, lay priesthood, strict rules of conduct, huge missionary force, practical teachings (for example, on household budgeting and on raising children), social networks, and doctrine or "spirituality." Guatemalan members themselves mentioned the church's strict morality (Gooren 1999, 2, 153, 155, 161, 186), learning new things (156, 161), feeling the joy of God's love (155, 162), being blessed with miracles (160, 166–68), and receiving support from other members (155, 169).

However, Guatemalan Mormons mentioned *not* receiving support from other members—especially leaders—as the main factor in becoming inactive. Hence, I have concluded that successful integration in church depended mainly on acquiring a testimony of its truthfulness and building up relations with other members (Gooren 1999, 207). During my studies in Costa Rica and Guatemala in the 1990s, I observed that there were many new baptisms, but not nearly as many new members. Half of all new converts left the religion within a year—a figure that seems to be constant all over Latin America (Gooren 1991, 58; 1999, 66; Grover 1985, 137–39; Knowlton 2005, 54).

O'Dea already pointed out that "close personal integration into the church community lent a heightened intensity to the Mormon experience and gave it added personal relevance" (1957, 120). After baptism, the new members hardly had contact anymore with the missionaries, who occupied a marginal position in the ward and stake structure. New members had to deal with the bishop and the stake president—or usually with their counselors. They were reminded to pay their tithing. Occasionally, they would be asked to give an opening or closing prayer or share their testimony on fast Sunday. They would be invited to come to various sorts of meetings. Most new converts would receive a time-consuming *calling*, a voluntary church assignment, within weeks of their baptism. For some, a calling raised their self-esteem, integrated them in the church community, and thus became a mechanism for commitment. But for others, receiving a calling was the first step on the road to inactivity (as discussed later in the section on callings).

In summary, the typical Mormon *conversion career* (Gooren 2005, Gooren 2006b) in Central America went as follows.[7] After the first contact with Mormon members or missionaries, the investigator received the *Discussions*. She or he was invited to study the *Charla Study Guides* and the Book of Mormon—the rational elements of conversion—and to ask the Holy Spirit for a confirmation of its veracity. In about half of the cases, a testimony of the truthfulness of the Book of Mormon and hence Joseph Smith and the Mormon Church was gradually built up. With the testimony came acceptance of the church organization and its hierarchical lay priesthood for men. If new members built up a good relationship with the leaders and members, they were more likely to accept a calling and thus became more integrated in the local church community: the ward and stake. In turn, this integration strengthened their commitment.

PENTECOSTAL SUCCESS IN CENTRAL AMERICA

In the current context of strong Pentecostal growth all over Latin America (Bonino 1997; Chesnut 2003; Chiquete and Orellana 2003; Corten and Marshall-Fratani 2001; Garrard-Burnett and Stoll 1993; Martin 1990, 2002; Samandú 2001; Schaefer 1992; Stoll 1990), it is interesting to contrast the supposed intellectual appeal of Mormonism with the more emotional and experiential appeal of the Pentecostal churches. The early literature analyzed the growth of Pentecostal churches in the context of processes of modernization and especially urbanization (Lalive d'Epinay 1969; Roberts 1968; Willems 1967). Pentecostalism offered people social networks, a close-knit community, a strict code of conduct, the possibility of increased self-esteem through empowerment, and "free social space" (Martin 1990, 180) for cultural innovations. Above all, the heterogeneous Pentecostal churches offer some unique "products," which ultimately allows them to dominate—at least for the time being—the religious market in almost all Latin American countries (Chesnut 2003; Gooren 2006a; Stark and Finke 2000).[8]

Some of the products that Pentecostalism offers are not unique. I already mentioned that people were attracted to Mormonism because of its social networks, sense of community, strict rules of conduct, and potential for empowerment. All of these elements can also be found in Pentecostalism. But the myriad Pentecostal churches—most of them, anyway—offer a few elements that are truly unique and form the basis for their success. Pentecostalism is about experience more than tradition or study.[9] Pentecostal churches offer direct access to the *charismata,* the gifts of the Holy Spirit: healing, prophesying, and speaking in tongues. Pentecostalism allows room for emotional catharsis: the electric band rocks, people sing their lungs out, some believers dance themselves into a trance, and famous international preachers can render hundreds of people unconscious ("falling in the Spirit"). In short, Pentecostalism is about experience and emotion; Mormonism is about study and work: serving others in a voluntary calling as teacher, counselor, and so on. The myriad Pentecostal churches are still mostly—though certainly not all—in the early stages of institutionalization. The routinization of charisma is only just beginning, and the institutionalization process is causing conflicts in some Pentecostal churches. Mormonism, on the other hand, has been thoroughly institutionalized, rationalized, and even bureaucratized—in classical Weberian (1922) form—at least since the 1950s.

People looking for intense religious experiences and emotions may thus find that Pentecostalism caters better to their needs. These people might join the Mormon Church for a while, but they will almost certainly become inactive within a few months. Conversely, people with a more intellectual approach to religion might become disillusioned after some months of singing and joyous clapping in a Pentecostal church. Should they happen to come into contact with Mormon members or missionaries, they might find out that the LDS Church is better suited to their preferences. People pursuing their options on the religious market may not try out one church and another as if test-driving a Ford or Chrysler (Gooren 2006a, 57), but if they do not like the church they are in, they will certainly look for another one better suited to what they consider important in a church. This explains why the desertion rates in Pentecostal churches all over Latin America are very similar to the 50 percent dropout rates of Mormon converts after the first year.

In Mexico, for example, "68 percent of those baptized in Evangelical churches in the 1980s had dropped out by the end of the decade" (Bowen 1996, 225). Based on Kurt Bowen's extensive surveys in more than forty Mexican congregations, the total disaffiliation rate in Pentecostal churches was 43 percent, meaning that a little more than half of all those who once belonged to a Pentecostal church actually stayed in it (70–71, 218–19).

In summary, Pentecostalism offers intense religious experiences and emotions in a context of urbanization and (often) political turmoil. Pentecostal churches offer direct access to the gifts of the Holy Spirit: healing, prophesying, and speaking in tongues. As with Mormonism, people are also attracted to Pentecostalism because of its social networks, sense of community, strict rules of conduct, and potential for empowerment. The high inactivity rates in Pentecostal churches of up to almost 50 percent are quite similar to Mormonism in the region.

Following O'Dea, the subsequent sections will explore the connections between sources of strain and conflict in Mormonism—callings, machismo, and inactivity—and local leadership performance in Central America.

Sources of Strain and Conflict, Part I: Callings

O'Dea (1957, 222ff) identified various sources of strain and conflict in the North American Mormon Church of the 1950s, which will obviously be different in contemporary Central America. Influenced by the secularization thesis, O'Dea wrote that "Mormonism's greatest and most significant problem is its encounter with modern secular thought" (222). The rising levels of education among LDS members would create a strong current of intellectuals, who would inevitably get into conflict with the church leadership. Mormon orthodoxy would ultimately drive more liberal intellectuals away or into a less active membership status (222–40). O'Dea foresaw events that would happen fifty years later. The September 1993 excommunication of six prominent intellectuals discouraged active LDS scholars from studying the Mormon Church with methods from the social sciences or humanities.[10] No such disputes exist as yet in Latin America, where there are still very few LDS scholars—especially in these disciplines anyway.

O'Dea (241–42, 242–45, 253–55) was also prophetic by foreseeing already the tensions between rationality and charisma, political conservatism and social idealism, and authority and individualism. These tensions were also visible in the interaction between members and the church organization in Central America. The main problems, in Central America and all over the world, seemed to be the church's demands on its members and, partly connected with this issue, the performance of local church leaders (Brown 1978; Craig 1970; Gooren 1999; Hawkins 1988; Knowlton 1996; Tullis 1980).

In a later work on the sociology of religion, O'Dea (1966, 90ff) noted that the institutionalization of religion always faced "a set of structurally inherent dilemmas," which subsequently caused "internal strains and functional problems" in the churches concerned (90). O'Dea identified five such *dilemmas of institutionalization* (90–97).

I argue that the *dilemma of power* is important for the LDS Church in Latin America. O'Dea (96–97) noted that the routinization of religious charisma invariably led religions to seek protection from worldly authorities and thus to accumulate worldly power. This is essentially what happened in Deseret in the nineteenth century and why Joseph Smith entered state and even national politics after the 1840s (O'Dea 1957, 63). In Latin America, however, the Mormon Church has little hope of making an alliance with worldly governments: the Roman Catholic Church beat them to it. Instead, the institutional dilemma of power has consequences for local LDS congregations in Central America. I will demonstrate below that there is a direct link between bad leadership performance, especially at local ward and stake levels, and the high inactivity rates in Central America.

The dilemma of *mixed motivation,* as church offices gradually become paid jobs, is addressed by Mormonism through its lay priesthood and volunteer assignments (that is, callings). In O'Dea's own words: "Institutionalization involves a stable set of statuses and roles, defined in terms of functions, upon which are incumbent rights and obligations" (1966, 91). Because the Mormon Church generally uses volunteers and usually rotates callings after three to five years, there is no established clergy. But the church bureaucracy could cause problems for its leaders (as discussed later) and could foster alienation among its members, much more than the supposed alienation caused by the wearing-out of religious symbols over time (92).

The Mormon Church requires from its (active) members a very strict morality. Only members "in good standing," about one-fourth of all registered members in the Central American LDS wards I studied, will receive a *temple recommend.* This is a card that allows one to enter the temple and participate in essential rituals. Faithful members are required to pay their tithes, follow the Word of Wisdom (abstaining from coffee, tea, and alcohol), and obey the commandments (especially the Law of Chastity, which condemns sex before marriage). The church also demands that members spend many hours a week in church meetings, study the scriptures and the manuals, and fulfill the obligations of their callings.

Three-quarters of all active members in the La Florida ward I studied in Guatemala City had a calling. Bishop Mario of this ward said, "Any calling in church provides the opportunity to serve. The whole point is that the person who's called finds the way to serve the others in his calling.... Any assignment, any calling in church, gives this blessing of knowing that you're useful for other people.... It gives you life experience" (Gooren 1999, 169).

In most cases, receiving a calling will strengthen a member's church commitment. In Guatemala, Patricio returned to the Mormon Church after God helped him to stop drinking. He received a warm welcome in his ward after many years of backsliding and inactivity: "About two days later the bishop came and asked if I'd accept a calling as second counselor of the bishop. I even started to cry. How was it possible that I'd moved away and there's so many who deserve it more than I, and I even failed.... When I was in church before I never had a calling. Nothing.... Never. But he told me this would help me and really: it did!" (162). But "Bishop A" in San José, Costa Rica, also uttered a warning: "A calling is not a guarantee for instantaneous success. Many people have to grow into it, that's exactly how it's meant to be" (25).

The situation of most LDS members in Central America was very different from the United States. Hence, performance in callings was often problematic in Guatemala:

> The top-down authority model with rotating voluntary callings is probably very well suited to the United States, with its high levels of organization, education, and prosperity. However, the situation of LDS members in a Guatemalan low-income neighborhood like La Florida is radically different. A hard life, marked by poverty and health problems and low schooling, makes performance in callings generally sub-standard. New members often find it hard to handle a calling and many shirk responsibility. (85)

Growing into a calling was supposed to raise commitment and bring life experience to new members; church leaders were responsible for encouragement and coaching during this process. Although most members had a calling, there are only a dozen or so really important leadership positions at the ward level. The church seemed to prefer to recruit young leaders in Central America and other growth areas such as Africa (Gooren 1991, 58). Young leaders were expected to be more open to instruction.[11] Former church president Spencer W. Kimball succinctly summarized what was expected of good church leaders:

> This kind of leader must have a strong feeling of responsibility, moral courage, and a will to complete his responsibilities against all odds. He will need to develop good judgment and effective administration, always as guided by the spirit.
>
> He recognizes and acknowledges the work and the worth of others. He has a warm personal relationship with people and he commands their

respect by his treatment of them. He exerts influence with, rather than power over, his people. He listens attentively and sympathetically.... He encourages self-responsibility in others. (Brown 1978, 108)

In a nice understatement, church authority Harold Brown recognized that President Kimball's standard was a high one.[12] In truth, the members' performance in a calling was always directly linked to leadership performance. Local LDS leaders in Central America were generally young, inexperienced, and often quite authoritarian.

Bishops and stake presidents are simply unable to imitate the North American managerial leadership model.[13] Young people lack the necessary experience and maturity to perform as leaders. Those few leaders who do function well often stay in office too long, because there is nobody to replace them. This sometimes makes good leaders complacent, thus destroying leadership dynamism. Good leaders often find it hard to delegate responsibilities to church organizations like the Quorum of Elders or the stake High Council. They lack confidence in ordinary members. (Gooren 1999, 85)

Local LDS leaders preferred to handle almost all issues themselves, instead of delegating them to groups, like the Elders Quorum. Hence, the role of the bishopric, consisting of the bishop and his two counselors, was vastly inflated in Costa Rica, Guatemala, and Nicaragua. The same process was visible for the stake council: although the high council was very active, most members preferred to deal directly with the stake president (Gooren 1991, 35; 1999, 85, 90, 93).[14]

A lack of self-confidence among teachers made most Sunday-school classes boring and thus reduced the participation of visitors. Insecure leaders and members preferred to follow the manuals to make sure they got things right. A lack of self-confidence among many (new) members strengthened the authoritarian attitudes of some leaders: many new converts simply wanted to be *told* what to do, instead of finding out for themselves.

The LDS leadership in Costa Rica, Guatemala, and Nicaragua was certainly more authoritarian than in the United States (although the Utah-born mission president in Costa Rica was quite authoritarian as well). Authoritarian leaders in Central America often presented their orders as divinely inspired messages, making it hard for members to question them (Gooren 1991, 36).[15] But where did this authoritarianism come from in the first place?

SOURCES OF STRAIN AND CONFLICT, PART II: MACHISMO

F. Lamond Tullis identifies hierarchical and *machista* elements in the local cultures of Latin America as important factors in the problems surrounding leadership performance:

> Cultural inclinations... have led to some ecclesiastical and leadership atrocities in Latin America.... As it is the most prepared and qualified people who tend to speak up against abuses..., they find their own membership status placed in question. They are either cowed or driven underground. The Church is therefore not able to enjoy the benefit of its most able people because they are afraid to become involved. Such behavior turns counselors and advisors into "yes men" who refuse to voice a disagreement with their leader even in private counsel. (1980, 72)

The highest church leaders are well aware of the cultural conflicts that are caused by conversion to Mormonism, especially the problem of machismo. This is a quote from regional representative Harold Brown, from the Brigham Young University (BYU) Centennial Conference in 1976:

> Paternal or maternal authority as exercised in Latin America ranges from tender understanding to despotic paternalism.... A male child frequently is given a position of deference and privilege within the family relative to his sisters. Indeed, he often grows up "spoiled." Thus begins the attitude of male dominance, rather widespread in Latin America, popularly called *machismo*. In its traditional packaging, this element of self-esteem is incompatible with the gospel and LDS culture because it relates more to privilege than to responsibility, more to self-assertion than to cooperative action. (1978, 111)

The LDS mission president in Costa Rica identified the training of capable leaders as the biggest challenge for the Mormon Church in Latin America. He thought pride was the main problem for men in the region. An LDS missionary from California told me, "Men have big egos here" (Gooren 1991, 45).

Machismo is easier to describe than to analyze. Roger N. Lancaster's first description in his classic study of machismo presents it as the mirror image of appropriate *women's* behavior in Nicaragua: "Feminine action emphasizes planning over risk, self-abnegation over self-promotion, domesticity over worldliness, action in and through networks rather than interpersonal competition" (1992, 93). From this passage, it logically follows that men influenced by machismo will like risks, indulge in self-promotion, enjoy "the world," and above all like to compete with other men. The main elements of this male competition seem to be the number of women they can have sex with, the number of children they can father (usually with different women), the amount of alcohol they can stomach, and—occasionally—the number of fights they can win. Machismo is primarily about power relations with other men and not so much with women (236).

This may sound like a caricature, but consider another passage from Lancaster's fascinating study of machismo and power in Nicaragua: "What is machismo? Why do Nicaraguan men behave as they do (as Nicaraguan women vigorously complain): beating their wives, simultaneously fathering children in multiple households, abandoning compañeras and children, gambling away hard-earned money, and drinking to excess?" (235). Lancaster's answer is that men are afraid to lose their dignity, their honor. They are afraid to be seen as a homosexual and thus to be ridiculed by other men and women. Machismo keeps both men and women locked in conduct that negatively affects family welfare. Conversion to evangelical churches, or to Mormonism, provides one possible way out of this conduct:

> [Evangelism] strengthens the social and economic base of the family by prohibiting competing activities such as drinking, dancing, and (directly and indirectly) contact with other women. Perhaps more important, Evangelism [or Mormonism] provides a social alternative to male "street culture."… Men who lead virtuous lives can gain recognition and respect from the congregation when they participate in preaching and leading the hymns at the nightly meetings. (Bossen 1984, 175)

The connections between gender roles, machismo, conversion, and the household are most thoroughly analyzed, although perhaps slightly idealized as well, in the classic study by Elizabeth E. Brusco on evangelicals in Colombia:

> With conversion, machismo is replaced by evangelical belief as the main determinant of husband-wife relations. The machismo role and the male role defined by evangelicalism are almost diametrical opposites. Aggression, violence, pride, self-indulgence, and an individualistic orientation in the public sphere are replaced by peace seeking, humility, self-restraint, and a collective orientation and identity with the church and the home.… In evangelical households the husband may still occupy the position of head,

but his relative aspirations have changed to coincide with those of his wife. (1995, 137)

Ramiro provided a good example of this process happening in the Mormon Church in Guatemala City. Ramiro was a second-generation Mormon who had drifted away from church and became inactive during his adolescence. He led a very *machista* life and continued with this in part after his marriage at twenty-five:

> After we got married I still drank for a time. Maybe what made me reflect was when my first daughter was born and the responsibilities of the home became greater. We needed more money to live on and sometimes there wasn't enough and I felt a bit irresponsible. All of this made me reflect and think about improving my situation. Because when you're in this environment you waste a lot of money. You're not particularly interested in the state of your family.... But I tried to correct this error by becoming active in church. So there I started to improve my situation. (Gooren 1999, 156–57)

In many of the lower-class Mormon families I studied in Costa Rica and Guatemala, however, the men were not active in church. They had dropped out because of conflicts with other members—like Miguel in Guatemala City (Gooren 1999, 164)—or they stopped going to church because they valued their freedom too much. That is, many men initially came to church and got involved in a calling. But after a while, they found church life tedious and resented the many hours a week they had to spend on church affairs. They started neglecting their callings. If they still had many nonmember friends, they might be invited to go out together. Mormons are not forbidden to see a film or go to a bar, but the temptations are routinely stressed: non-Mormons drink and flirt in these places. If they experienced marital problems, many men found it easier to follow the patterns of machismo—spending most of their time outside the home—than to talk openly about these problems with their wives.

If active male members persisted in leading a life of drinking, gambling, and womanizing, they were censured and—if failing to repent—ultimately excommunicated by their bishop. This happened to fifty-year-old "C," the father of a big and highly active Mormon family with three daughters and one son in San José, Costa Rica (Gooren 1991, 22–23). C cared nothing for the church and ridiculed his wife and children, who spent many hours a week there.

Active Mormons "in good standing" (that is, core members) are not supposed to cheat on their spouses or drink alcohol. The social control in the ward strongly discouraged even flirting between people who were not married (47). Mormon machismo in matrimony was expressed mainly in another way: the husband would force his views on his wife. This often resulted in a lack of communication and a tense situation.

A typical example could be found in Costa Rica with husband "K" (bank employee, twenty-eight) and spouse "L" (housewife, thirty-two) and their two children. K was a second-generation Mormon whose parents divorced when he was twelve. His mother subsequently dropped out of church, but his father was an important leader in the Paseo Colón ward on the other side of San José. K was a lukewarm member in the *affiliated* category, until he served his mission in Panama in 1981–1983. There he met his future wife, L. Their seven years of marriage were not easy: K was a congenial man, but he could go into a temper when he felt dominated by his wife. L had a strong character. As the secretary of the stake high council, K was away from home on most nights, which suited both well.

But K was determined that they leave their rented home in Curridabat, near the homes of L's mother and sister, and move in with his father in Moravia. L was resisting him, because living in Moravia meant going to another LDS ward and thus losing contact with her friends and her brother in her current ward. She also feared seeing her mother and sister less. L became disillusioned when she saw that some church leaders, such as the bishop, supported her husband. When she told her bishop of her marriage problems, he told her to talk it out with her husband. But the bishop told K in private that he should find a psychologist to treat his wife. L was very upset about this breach of confidence; the stake president seemed to agree with her. But since her husband was adamant, L had no choice but to accept the move (25, 53).

The hierarchical, top-down organization of the LDS Church would seem to strengthen some elements of machismo (like the authoritarianism), while helping to weaken other elements (like adultery and alcohol abuse). The LDS Church manuals and magazines stress family harmony and counseled couples to talk openly, respect each other's opinions, and share responsibilities (47). In Central America, this strengthens women's capability for empowerment.[16] In some cases, the marriage problems were structural and ended in a divorce. Although Mormons are not forbidden to go through a civil divorce, and LDS divorce rates are similar to mainstream U.S. society,[17] dissolving a marriage sealed "for time and eternity" in a temple was extremely difficult. Additionally, divorce after civil marriage carried a stigma and social consequences in the religion. If the husband left, so did the priesthood holder of the family (unless there were adult sons). Male Mormons often lost their leadership calling after divorce, although the church usually allowed them to finish their regular "term" of three to five years. In some cases, a divorce eventually led to inactivity of either husband or wife.[18]

SOURCES OF STRAIN AND CONFLICT, PART III: INACTIVITY

I noted above that for some new converts, such as Patricio in Guatemala, receiving a calling helped them to become integrated in the ward organization. But for others, receiving a calling was a pressure they were not able to deal with, so they dropped out (Gooren 1999, 170). If the testimony of the new member was (still) relatively weak, if outside pressure from nonmember relatives was strong, or if no good rapport was established with leaders, the new converts would most likely drop out. Other important disaffiliation factors were the time and money demands the church made (Gooren 2007, 134–55; Mauss 1996, 240) and backsliding into alcohol problems (Gooren 1999, 163–65). Since many new converts were attracted to the smooth church organization, many dropped out when it proved to be anything but smooth. David C. Knowlton (1996) mentions the weak church organization as the main factor in the high inactivity rates. I noted earlier that inactivity was often directly related to bad leadership performance (Gooren 1999, 85; Tullis 1980, 72).

However, inactivity was also related to the new converts' experiences with the older members in general. "Veteran" members were supposed to coach new members and even to become friends with them. But I noticed in Costa Rica that only a handful of the most active members would regularly devote attention to the new members. Most of the older members showed a definite *lack* of interest in the newcomers, which came as a cold shower after all the attention the (North American) missionaries devoted to them (Gooren 1991, 33). The LDS wards in Costa Rica and Guatemala had campaigns to visit inactive members and ask why they had dropped out. However, only a handful of these people returned to church. LDS leaders put more emphasis on prevention: they wanted the older members to coach the converts through the whole recruitment process. Bishop A in Costa Rica mentioned older members setting bad examples—cheating, gossiping, radiating pride and arrogance—as the prime reason new members became disillusioned in the church and dropped out. But the bishop also acknowledged that some people took the step of getting baptized into the church too lightly and without sufficient preparation or instruction. The new converts, the older members, and the missionaries were *all* failing here, he thought (34).

The Utah-born LDS mission president in Costa Rica mentioned four factors causing inactivity, which partly overlapped with the bishop's assessment (34). First, new converts often felt excluded by older members, who were aloof and uninterested in their problems. Second, many new converts never understood the information in the six *Charlas* well: they underestimated the severe responsibilities connected to baptism. Third, a lack of knowledge and a lack of commitment caused people to have a weak testimony of the church. Fourth, the mission president mentioned "a lack of responsibility among Latins": he thought that many Latinos in general had a hard time fulfilling the promises they made.

All of the above factors contributed to the high dropout rate of 50 percent in the first year after joining. New members found it hard to follow the Word of Wisdom, especially when non-Mormon friends and relatives would offer them coffee. When many new members did not show up regularly in church on Sundays, social control was minimized. But new members who did go to church faithfully and made a genuine effort to perform well in their calling soon found out that they had to devote many hours a week to church matters. People who lacked the skills or resources for effective time management would be unable to meet the church's demands and hence gradually dropped out (34).

In San José, I was able to follow twenty-eight people after their conversion to Mormonism. Only nine people, or about one-third, became well integrated in the church organization during the seven months I could observe them. Four others occasionally showed up in church; two people I saw in church only once more. Out of twenty-eight people I monitored, only nine remained active according to the strictest definition and perhaps a total of fifteen—a little more than one-half—in the broadest definition (34). These data again confirm that the Mormon Church in Central America is better at *bringing* people in than in *keeping* people in.

So what does it mean to be a Mormon in Central America for those members who remained active in the Mormon Church?

The Meaning of Being a Mormon in Central America

Curious as it may seem, the rather obvious question of what it means to be a Mormon—whether in Latin America or in the United States—has hardly been addressed *directly* in the literature on Mormonism. O'Dea identified four important elements of early Mormonism: a new definition of God, new forms of religious expression (the baptism for the dead, endowment rituals, and sealed marriages), the gathering of Zion, and—until 1890—polygamy (1957, 54–60).

This section probes the meaning of LDS membership in contemporary Central America by comparing experiences from members in Costa Rica, Guatemala, and Nicaragua. The Mormon Church has operated freely in Guatemala and Costa Rica since the 1950s and experienced a boom in the 1980s. By contrast, the left-wing Sandinistas in Nicaragua occupied Mormon buildings and forced the church organization to go underground between 1982 and 1990 (Gooren 2007). A subsequent membership boom followed in the 1990s.

The question of what it means to be a Mormon in a certain country is obviously related to the original attractions that Mormonism offered people in the first place. People initially felt attracted to Mormonism because of its organization, doctrine and spirituality, practical teachings, strict rules of conduct, and social networks. Studying another subject, I analyzed three further meanings of LDS membership in Guatemala: achieving a closeness to God, providing a framework for personal growth and empowerment, and maintaining commitment as an ongoing struggle against backsliding (2000, 109–11).

Especially during my fieldwork in Guatemala I could closely observe what being a Mormon meant for people. My Guatemalan LDS informants mentioned the following elements most often:

1. a strong focus on the family (cf. O'Dea 1957, 140–42)
2. a focus on spiritual progress, including going to the temple and the temple marriage (cf. ibid., 133)
3. being part of God's kingdom through belonging to the church community and obeying its rules
4. being different from other people by complying with the Word of Wisdom (try drinking no coffee in Central America!) and the strict moral code of conduct (cf. ibid., 146)[19]
5. spending many hours (between four and nineteen hours a week!) on church affairs, ranging from the three Sunday meetings, weeknight meetings, proselytizing activities, and preparations for callings and speeches (Gooren 1999, 2, 154–56, 159, 160, 161–62, 169, 173)

The emphases in Nicaragua were slightly different, judging from my recent fieldwork there. The sense of being part of God's kingdom and the sense of being different from others were stronger under the influence of harassment by the Sandinista government (1982–1990). The strong focus on the family was always there, but perhaps the focus on spiritual progress and spending many hours on church affairs were of relatively lesser importance. In Costa Rica, the focus on spiritual progress was important, but it was less connected to going to the temple, as this was a lengthy and costly process, the closest temple at that time still being in Guatemala City, two thousand miles away.[20] Being part of God's kingdom and hence being different from other people were just as important in Costa Rica as in Guatemala or Nicaragua. The focus on family was always strong, as was the social control on spending many hours on church affairs.

Apart from these country differences, which were mostly connected to the political context, the main differences in how people experienced being a Mormon in daily life were related to their church commitment. Looking closely, an increasing order of importance was visible in the five key elements I identified as relevant to the Mormon identity.

The focus on the family was visible even among *inactive* members, including those who no longer identified with the LDS Church at all. Many inactive Mormons would probably become Pentecostals in the long run. The local culture in Central America idealized family life, although the role of the husband was considered secondary to the wife, especially in the education of the children. In Mormonism, both parents share this responsibility. Only the affiliated and core members connected this focus on the family to the idea of spiritual progress. Although most informants typically talked about their *individual* spiritual progress, Mormon teachings closely connected this element to their spouses and their children (Gooren 1991, 46).

The third element, being part of God's kingdom through belonging to the church community and obeying rules, also worked out differently for different sorts of members. *Affiliated* members still felt part of God's kingdom, even though they did not always show up on Sunday for sacrament and priesthood (or Relief Society) meetings. But these affiliated members did not know much about the unique history of the Mormon Church, after Joseph Smith's First Vision and the foundation of the church's "charismatic bureaucracy" (Bushman 2005, 258). Affiliated members who still complied with the Word of Wisdom doubtless felt a stronger connection with the church. Church leaders and members expressed confidence that following the church rules concerning morality, sexuality, and food helped people in their spiritual progress. Besides, it also strengthened their family life.

Complying with the many church rules also heightened the sense of separation of *core members* from nonmembers in mainstream Costa Rican, Nicaraguan, and Guatemalan society. Through machismo, sexuality was strongly present in the street life in all of these countries. By *not* engaging in looking, flirting, or talking to members of the opposite sex, committed Mormons enhanced their sense of being different from other people. Every day, Mormons were challenged to prove their worth, to assess their spiritual progress, to fight the possibility of backsliding.[21] Many of the affiliated members found it impossible to comply with all of the church's demands, especially the taboos on coffee and tea (and alcohol).

Finally, it should be clear by now that only the core members spent an average of between five and twenty hours a week on church matters (Gooren 1999, 173, 196). This included not only the three hours they spent each Sunday in church but also activities to prepare for their calling responsibilities, doing church administration work (that is, filling out forms), and participating in church meetings. People with administrative or teaching callings needed five to ten hours a week, but leaders in Guatemala routinely needed between eight (bishopric counselors) and eighteen (the bishop himself) hours a week. Mormon commitment required great amounts of time to be dedicated to the church. In the form of tithing, people were also expected to donate money to the church. I concluded that almost everybody in Guatemala City occasionally skipped paying their tithing, whereas those who did comply rarely donated a full 10 percent of their income (196). The bishop was the only one in the ward who really knew how much everybody was paying. He awarded the temple recommend to all members who regularly tithed. These were the members in good standing, the core members.

CONCLUSION

I have shown that the number of registered members was actually a poor indicator of LDS penetration in Central America, since the inactivity rate hovered around 50 percent (or higher). I have argued that inactivity and the meaning of LDS membership in Central America were closely related; they are like two sides of the same coin. Many new members were unable to make Mormonism an important element of their lives. In this conclusion I elaborate my typology of LDS members to help analyze the meaning of membership in Central America.[22] I think that the meaning of being a Mormon was ultimately connected to the question of what type of Mormon member we were talking about. I think there were at least four "ideal typical" membership categories in Central America.

Apostates were former members who no longer considered themselves Mormons and who had often joined another church. They came into contact with the LDS missionaries, received the *Charlas (Discussions),* and were baptized, but Mormonism did not offer what they were looking for. Most of these people were now active in a Pentecostal church; others may have

returned to the Catholic Church or became disaffiliated from organized religion altogether. Hence, calling all of these people "inactive members" is a
meaningless euphemism.

A second category consisted of *inactive members,* who still considered
themselves Mormons, although they never went to church. They formed
at maximum about half of all registered members. All of the disaffiliation
factors mentioned above—bad experiences with leaders and members, a
weak testimony, insufficient knowledge of the church, insecurity, bad performance in callings—applied to them. However, they were sufficiently so-
cialized into the church to maintain an identity as Mormons. Some still
obeyed the Word of Wisdom, which was at odds with the *machista* mentality. They shared Mormonism's focus on the family and its emphasis on
spiritual growth. Many of them still felt part of the Mormon community,
even though they were inactive. Miguel in Guatemala was a good example
(Gooren 1999, 164).

Affiliated members, the third group, regularly went to church, but they
did not comply with all of the membership requirements. Not all of them
tithed. If they had a calling at all, their performance was probably often sub-
standard. For affiliated members, especially those with friends who were not
Mormons, backsliding into machismo always formed a risk. Most obeyed
the Word of Wisdom, although for a sizable minority this was a problem:
they were occasionally backsliding into drinking a cup of coffee or a glass
of *guaro.* Hence, the bishopric did not consider them to be "members in
good standing" and would not award them a temple recommend. A central
feature of Mormonism, temple work, was thus beyond their reach. Sixty-
five-year-old carpenter Bernardo in Guatemala City was a typical affiliated
Mormon. He did not have a calling, because he said he was "too old" (168).
He admitted having struggled with his alcohol problem for all of his life
and claimed that only through the support of the church rules and church
members had he managed to stop drinking (167–68). He was focused on
his family and—less so—on spiritual progress, but he had never been to a
temple. He spent only about four hours a week on church matters, the lowest score for all active Mormon informants (173).

Finally, the *core members* conformed to all the expectations of LDS
membership and were thus eligible for a temple recommend.[23] They made
up no more than about one-quarter of all registered members. All of them
had a calling and carried it out as was expected of them. All church leaders—that is, anyone with an important leadership calling at the ward, stake,
branch, or district level—could be found in this group. They were strongly
focused on their family and on their spiritual progress. They strongly felt a

part of God's kingdom and were deeply aware that they were different from inactive Mormons and nonmembers. Machismo was a taboo, although its remnants could be found in leaders' authoritarian attitudes. All core members spent between five and eighteen hours a week on church matters.

Stan L. Albrecht (1998, 270) distinguished no fewer than nine types of Mormon members in the United States, based on the markers of identification, belief, and community outlined by Merlin Brinkerhoff and K. L. Burke (1980). In Albrecht's scheme, my *core members* would all fall in the categories of "fervent followers" or "ritualists," who combined a high identification with Mormonism with a high or low belief. The *affiliated members* could be placed in the properly termed categories of "outsiders" or "marginal Saints." They fostered a low identification of Mormonism, paired with a high or low belief. The *inactive members* could be either a "splinter Saint" or a "social apostate." Both rejected the LDS community; the "splinter Saint" had a high belief and the "social apostate" a low belief. The members I designated *apostates* myself, since they now rejected their former LDS identity entirely, formed a combination of "splinter Saints" and "social or doctrinal apostates." These people all rejected the LDS community and maintained at best a low belief or else no belief at all.

The conversion-careers typology offers an alternative perspective to analyze the four Mormon membership categories I found in Central America. However, LDS members in Central America seemed to fit in only three categories of the conversion-careers typology. The core members were situated at the level of *confession,* involving a high level of participation inside the church and a strong evangelism on the outside. Apostates and inactive members were at the level of *disaffiliation,* affiliated members at the level of *affiliation,* and core members combined elements of *confession* (the highest level of church participation) and *conversion. Conversion* in the limited sense of the conversion-careers approach refers to a (radical) personal change of identity and worldview (Gooren 2005, 154).

The typical conversion careers of LDS members in Central America are easy to sketch. People's involvement in church is typically connected to their moving through the life course. Anyone joining the LDS Church in Central America had a 50 percent chance of becoming inactive in the first year.[24] The odds of becoming an affiliated member were 25 percent. These affiliated members got along with members and leaders, but their social networks were mostly situated outside of the LDS Church. The new Mormon also had a 25 percent chance of becoming a core member, who got along well with members and leaders and whose social networks were dominated by fellow Mormons. The key distinguishing trait for core members was their ability to developing friendship ties with other Mormons. After all, most people perform best when interacting with their own kind.

NOTES

1. I would like to thank Ryan Cragun, André Droogers, Quirine Eijkman, Mark Grover, Imke Harbers, Anton Houtepen, Miranda Klaver, Armand Mauss, Elisabet Rasch, João Rickli, Regien Smit, Saskia van Drunen, Peter Versteeg, and the three editors for their valuable comments on an earlier draft of this article.

2. Stark (1984, 1990, 1996, 1998) ignores that the dropout rate for Mormon converts in the first year is at least 50 percent (Decoo 1996, 98; Gooren 1991, 58; 1999, 66; Grover 1985, 137; Knowlton 2005, 54). O'Dea estimated that "between one-third and one-half of the church membership" in the United States was active (1957, 185).

3. Giving away copies of the Book of Mormon remains an important strategy. A Nicaraguan Mormon gave me a copy with a long handwritten message, including an earnest appeal to me: read it and pray to the Holy Spirit for guidance (research notes, Managua, June 21, 2005).

4. In 1990, there were still six *Discussions*. Since 2004, there are only four *Charlas,* which are conducted jointly by the missionaries and ward elders (LDS bishop Las Palmas, interview with author, Managua, February 6, 2005).

5. My 1991 master's thesis explored the reasons for LDS growth in San José, Costa Rica. My 1999 dissertation analyzed the connections between church membership and having a microenterprise among Mormons, Pentecostals, and Catholics in Guatemala City. My current research focuses on competition between charismatic Catholics, Pentecostals, and Mormons in Managua, Nicaragua. All three were ethnographic studies with an emphasis on qualitative methods (participant observation and formal and informal interviews).

6. This is Stark's full list of attractions: medium tension with society, legitimate authority, lay priesthood, labor force (callings, missionaries), ethic, fertility, success among the unchurched, network ties, and effective socialization (1998, 47–66).

7. See Gooren 2005, 2006b, for an elaboration of the conversion-careers approach and its five levels of religious commitment: preaffiliation, affiliation, conversion, confession, and disaffiliation.

8. The religious-market perspective is developed most clearly in Stark and Finke 2000. However, I find their conceptualizations of both rational choice and interreligious competition quite problematic (Gooren 2006a).

9. During my 2005 and 2006 fieldwork in Nicaragua I was surprised that hardly any Pentecostal church, whether the classic Assemblies of God or a megachurch like Hosanna, offered Sunday-school study classes anymore.

10. For an illuminating look at the "September Six," see Shipps 2000, 198–203. See also Annus 2006, 109–11.

11. "Being teachable" is the expression that is often used (Gooren 1991, 17).

12. As you might imagine, not all stake presidents and leaders, either in the United States or in Latin America, meet the ideal criteria set forth by President Kimball (Brown 1978).

13. See also Reynolds 1978, 16.

14. Ryan Cragun noted in an e-mail (June 21, 2006) that this also happens to some degree in the United States.

15. The authoritarianism of LDS leaders in Central America reminds me of O'Dea's characterization of early Mormonism: "What had developed was a democracy of participation and an oligarchy of decision-making and command" (1957, 165).

16. O'Dea thought that early Mormonism "came very close to accepting the equality of women with men" (1957, 249). Women in Utah received the right to vote in 1870. Typically, the increasing institutionalization of the church weakened the position of women in the LDS Church (250).

17. O'Dea already noted in the 1950s, "The rate of divorce is high in Utah and among Latter-day Saints" (1957, 141).

18. For the United States, see also Bahr and Albrecht 1989 and Heaton, Goodman, and Holman 1994. For Belgium, see Decoo 1996, 102, 108.

19. According to O'Dea, the Word of Wisdom "has become for Mormons a most salient mark of their membership in the church. Together with tithing, it separates the loyal and fervent from the Jack Mormon and the half-hearted" (1957, 146).

20. The LDS temple in Costa Rica has been functioning since June 2000 (Deseret News 2006, 548).

21. The parallel with Pentecostalism is obvious here. I am also reminded of Max Weber's Protestant-ethic thesis: individual action becomes rationalized, because continuous evaluation of each act is necessary to probe its possible effects on one's salvation (Gooren 1999, 6–7; Weber 1904–1905, 117, 136).

22. My dissertation distinguished four types of members: inactive members, less active members, more active members, and voluntary leaders (1999, 84–85). LDS missionaries in Costa Rica had their own membership classification. Article 6 from the apocryphal articles of faith for missionaries read: "We believe in the same organization that existed in the primitive church, viz.: active members, inactive members, disfellowshipped members, excommunicated members, dead members" (Gooren 1991, 64).

23. Core members were thus the only members in Central America who were influenced by what O'Dea succinctly identified and analyzed as the LDS "work, health, recreation, and education complex" (1957, 143–50).

24. O'Dea's estimate of between 33 and 50 percent active Mormons in the United States suggests that this (in)activity rate is very stable and should perhaps be considered normal for the LDS Church (1957, 185).

References

Albrecht, Stan L. 1998. "The Consequential Dimension of Mormon Religiosity." In *Latter-day Saint Social Life: Social Research on the LDS Church and Its Members,* ed. James T. Duke, 253–92. Provo: Religious Studies Center, Brigham Young University.

Annus, Iren E. 2006. "Review Essay: New Studies in Mormonism." *Nova Religio* 9, no. 4: 98–111.

Bahr, Howard M., and Stan L. Albrecht. 1989. "Strangers Once More: Patterns of Disaffiliation from Mormonism." *Journal for the Scientific Study of Religion* 28, no. 2: 180–200.

Bonino, José Míguez. 1997. *Faces of Latin American Protestantism.* Grand Rapids, Mich.: Eerdmans.

Bossen, Laurel. 1984. *The Redivision of Labor.* Albany: State University of New York Press.

Bowen, Kurt. 1996. *Evangelism and Apostasy: The Evolution and Impact of Evangelicals in Mexico.* Montreal: McGill-Queen's University Press.

Brinkerhoff, Merlin, and K. L. Burke. 1980. "Disaffiliation: Some Notes on Falling Away from the Faith." *Sociological Analysis* 41: 1–54.

Brown, Harold. 1978. "Gospel, Culture, and Leadership Development in Latin America." In *Mormonism: A Faith for All Cultures,* ed. F. LaMond Tullis, 106–15. Provo: Brigham Young University Press.

Brusco, Elizabeth E. 1995. *The Reformation of Machismo: Evangelical Conversion and Gender in Colombia.* Austin: University of Texas Press.

Bushman, Richard L. 2005. *Joseph Smith: Rough Stone Rolling.* New York: Alfred A. Knopf.

Chestnut, R. Andrew. 2003. *Competitive Spirits: Latin America's New Religious Economy.* New York: Oxford University Press.

Chiquete, Daniel, and Luis Orellana, eds. 2003. *Voces del Pentecostalismo Latinoamericano: Identidad, teología, e historia.* Concepción de Chile: RELEP/CETELA/ASSETT.

Corten, André, and Ruth Marshall-Fratani, eds. 2001. *Between Babel and Pentecost: Transnational Pentecostalism in Africa and Latin America.* Bloomington: Indiana University Press.

Craig, Wesley W., Jr. 1970. "The Church in Latin America: Progress and Challenge." *Dialogue: A Journal of Mormon Thought* 5, no. 3: 66–74.

Davies, Douglas J. 2000. *The Mormon Culture of Salvation.* Burlington, Vt.: Ashgate.

Decoo, Wilfried. 1996. "Feeding the Fleeting Flock: Reflections on the Struggle to Retain Church Members in Europe." *Dialogue: A Journal of Mormon Thought* 29, no. 1: 97–118.

Deseret News. 2006. *2007 Church Almanac.* Salt Lake City: Deseret News.

Garrard-Burnett, Virginia, and David Stoll, eds. 1993. *Rethinking Protestantism in Latin America.* Philadelphia: Temple University Press.

Gooren, Henri. 1991. "De expanderende mormoonse kerk in Latijns Amerika: Schetsen uit een wijk in San José, Costa Rica" [The Expanding Mormon Church in Latin America: Sketches from a Ward in San José, Costa Rica]. Master's thesis, Utrecht University.

———. 1999. *Rich among the Poor: Church, Firm, and Household among Small-Scale Entrepreneurs in Guatemala City.* Latin America Series, no. 13. Amsterdam: Thela.

———. 2000. "Analyzing LDS Growth in Guatemala: Report from a *Barrio.*" *Dialogue: A Journal of Mormon Thought* 33, no. 2: 97–115.

———. 2005. "Towards a New Model of Conversion Careers: The Impact of Personality and Situational Factors." *Exchange* 34, no. 2: 149–66.

———. 2006a. "Religious Market Theory and Conversion: Towards a New Approach." *Exchange* 35, no. 1: 39–60.

———. 2006b. "Towards a New Model of Religious Conversion Careers: The Impact of Social and Institutional Factors." In *Paradigms, Poetics, and Politics of Conversion,* ed. Wout J. van Bakkum, Jan N. Bremmar, and Arie Molendijk, 25–40. Leuven and Dudley, Mass.: Peeters.

———. 2007. "Latter-day Saints under Siege: The Unique Experience of Nicaraguan Mormons." *Dialogue: A Journal of Mormon Thought* 40, no. 3: 134–55.

Grover, Mark L. 1985. "Mormonism in Brazil: Religion and Dependency in Latin America." Ph.D. diss., Indiana University.

———. 2005. "The Maturing of the Oak: The Dynamics of LDS Growth in Latin America." *Dialogue: A Journal of Mormon Thought* 38, no. 2: 79–104.

Hawkins, John P. 1988. "Behavioral Differences Are Like Language Differences; or, 'Oh Say, What Is Truth' vs. 'Do as I'm Doing.'" In *A Heritage of Faith: Talks Selected from the BYU Women's Conferences,* ed. Mary E. Stovall and Carol Cornwall Madsen, 157–70. Salt Lake City: Deseret Book.

Heaton, Tim B., Kristen L. Goodman, and Thomas B. Holman. 1994. "In Search of a Peculiar People: Are Mormon Families Really Different?" In *Contemporary Mormonism: Social Science Perspectives,* ed. Marie Cornwall, Tim B. Heaton, and Lawrence A. Young, 87–117. Urbana: University of Illinois Press.

Knowlton, David C. 1996. "Mormonism in Latin America: Towards the Twenty-first Century." *Dialogue: A Journal of Mormon Thought* 29, no. 1: 159–76.

———. 2005. "How Many Members Are There Really? Two Censuses and the Meaning of LDS Membership in Chile and Mexico." *Dialogue: A Journal of Mormon Thought* 38, no. 2: 53–78.

Lalive d'Epinay, Christian. 1969. *Haven of the Masses.* London: Lutterworth.

Lancaster, Roger N. 1992. *Life Is Hard: Machismo, Danger, and the Intimacy of Power in Nicaragua.* Berkeley and Los Angeles: University of California Press.

Martin, David. 1990. *Tongues of Fire: The Explosion of Protestantism in Latin America.* Oxford: Blackwell.

———. 2002. *Pentecostalism: The World Their Parish.* Oxford: Blackwell.

Mauss, Armand L. 1996. "Mormonism in the Twenty-first Century: Marketing for Miracles." *Dialogue: A Journal of Mormon Thought* 29, no. 1: 236–49.

O'Dea, Thomas F. 1957. *The Mormons.* Chicago: University of Chicago Press.

————. 1966. *The Sociology of Religion.* Englewood Cliffs, N.J.: Prentice-Hall.

Reynolds, Noel B. 1978. "Cultural Diversity in the Universal Church." In *Mormonism: A Faith for All Cultures,* ed. F. LaMond Tullis, 7–22. Provo: Brigham Young University Press.

Roberts, Bryan R. 1968. "Protestant Groups and Coping with Urban Life in Guatemala." *American Journal of Sociology* 73, no. 6: 753–67.

Samandú, Luis E., ed. 2001. *Protestantismos y procesos socials en Centroamérica.* San José: CSUCA.

Schaefer, Heinrich. 1992. *Protestantismo y crisis social en América Central.* San José: DEI.

Shipps, Jan. 2000. *Sojourner in the Promised Land: Forty Years among the Mormons.* Urbana: University of Illinois Press.

Stoll, David. 1990. *Is Latin America Turning Protestant? The Politics of Evangelical Growth.* Berkeley and Los Angeles: University of California Press.

Stark, Rodney. 1984. "The Rise of a New World Faith." *Review of Religious Research* 26, no. 1: 18–27.

————. 1990. "Modernization, Secularization, and Mormon Success." In *In Gods We Trust,* ed. Thomas Robbins and Dick Anthony, 201–18. 2d ed. New Brunswick, N.J.: Transaction Publishers.

————. 1996. "So Far, So Good: A Brief Assessment of Mormon Membership Projections." *Review of Religious Research* 38, no. 2: 175–78.

————. 1998. "The Basis of Mormon Success: A Theoretical Application." In *Latter-day Saint Social Life: Social Research on the LDS Church and Its Members,* ed. James T. Duke, 27–70. Provo: Religious Studies Center, Brigham Young University.

Stark, Rodney, and Roger Finke. 2000. *Acts of Faith: Explaining the Human Side of Religion.* Berkeley and Los Angeles: University of California Press.

Tullis, F. LaMond. 1980. "The Church Moves Outside the United States: Some Observations from Latin America." *Dialogue: A Journal of Mormon Thought* 13, no. 1: 62–73.

Weber, Max. 1904–1905. *The Protestant Ethic and the Spirit of Capitalism.* New York: Scribner, 1958.

————. 1922. *Economy and Society: An Outline of Interpretive Sociology.* 2 vols. Berkeley and Los Angeles: University of California Press, 1978.

Widtsoe, John A. 1998. *Rational Theology: As Taught by the Church of Jesus Christ of Latter-day Saints.* Salt Lake City: Signature Books.

Willems, Emilio. 1967. *Followers of the New Faith: Culture Change and the Rise of Protestantism in Brazil and Chile.* Nashville: Vanderbilt University Press.

14

Go Ye to All the World

*The LDS Church and the Organization
of International Society*

~ David Clark Knowlton ~

In the mid-twentieth century Thomas F. O'Dea (1957) noticed that the relationship between the United States and the Church of Jesus Christ of Latter-day Saints (LDS) was evolving. His explanatory task had encompassed the church's beginnings and its evolution up to that moment. Nevertheless, he mentioned transformations he saw in the church and issues it might face in a simultaneously changing world.

Mormons were migrating outward from the core geographical region they had pioneered to distant areas of the country, following possibilities for mobility built into the evolving relationships among a society, a people, and a church, themselves in motion. The church had changed from a primarily village-based organization, where wards were intimately involved in agricultural and social reproduction, to a suburban congregation-based faith, focused on the maintenance of religious life in a strongly non-Mormon world (see also Mauss 1994; Leone 1979; and Swedin 2003).

Since O'Dea wrote, Mormons have continued migrating, following work, even outside the boundaries of their country, in the massive post–World War II expansion of U.S. society into the world. As a result of that and the simultaneous growth of the LDS missionary effort, millions of people in other countries have become Mormon. A majority of Latter-day Saints now reside outside the United States, scattered among the countries of the world.

Although not his topic, nevertheless O'Dea provided a key to how we can look at this international church. Instead of simply seeing Mormonism in its own terms, with its growth and change explained by its internal dynamics alone, O'Dea's analysis of Mormonism built on a core principle of historical sociology. This is the idea that organizations, like the church, are both enabled and constrained by the changing relationship they have with their host society that itself is in constant motion.

The relationship between the United States and the church, in these terms, is the foundation on which O'Dea built his understanding. Yet as Mormonism moves into the world, there is the question of how its ongoing relationship with the United States engages its developing relationship with hundreds of other nation-states. Which is the society that can serve as the basis of analysis? The United States, while still the place where close to half of all Mormons live, is no longer the single, and increasingly not the main, host society. But then neither are the other individual, local nation-states. Instead, the church now finds itself in a supranational society that itself has been growing in the postwar period. This society enables and constrains church growth, just as it enables and constrains the nation-states, including the United States, within which the church builds chapels and finds members.

This chapter will continue O'Dea's analytical effort by exploring the relationship between Mormonism and this international society. It will first compare international Mormonism with other religious bodies arising from American societies in a specific place as a means of demonstrating the importance of looking at supranational social organization. It will explore the evolution of this supranational society and then speak to issues that arise from it for understanding Mormon society.

INTERNATIONAL MORMONISM IN COMPARISON

Before discussing the nature of this social context in which Mormonism is now both constrained and enabled, it will be useful to compare the Church of Jesus Christ of Latter-day Saints with other religious organizations that were born in the United States.

Along with the Latter-day Saints Church, the U.S.-born religions that have survived and spread most in the international arena are arguably Pentecostalism (here we look at the Assemblies of God, the largest single Pentecostal organization), the Seventh-Day Adventists, and Jehovah's Witnesses (see table 14.1).[1] Immediately, we notice several things that are of relevance to O'Dea's earlier analysis.

First, although the others have relatively similar percentages of their membership in their society of origin, the Church of Jesus Christ of Latter-day Saints stands out for still having almost half of its members in the United States. None of the others come even close. This factor is particularly significant. It points to the different relationships with the United

TABLE 14.1. U.S.-origin religious bodies compared: Membership by world region

	ANGLO-AMERICA	LATIN AMERICA	EUROPE	ASIA	AFRICA
Assemblies of God	17%	45%	5%	9%	23%
Jehovah's Witnesses	18%	32%	24%	10%	16%
Latter-day Saints	47%	37%	4%	10%	2%
Seventh-Day Adventists	10%	32%	3%	22%	33%

Sources: Assemblies of God unpublished data provided to the author on his request and in his possession; Jehovah's Witnesses data from Worldwide Report of Statistics; LDS Church data from the Deseret News 2003 Church Almanac; Adventist data from the 138th Annual Statistics Report, General Conference of the Seventh-Day Adventists, 2003.

States that the different groups have, and how it served as a platform or an impediment, at different times, to international expansion.

Second, although the Assemblies of God exceeds the others in percentage of members in Latin America, all of them have large percentages of their membership in this Spanish- and Portuguese-speaking region of the Western Hemisphere. It has been a key place for Christian religious change in the past century. The social evolution of the some twenty Latin American countries in an evolving global order is key to understanding each of these groups. Although most analyses focus on the internal nature of Latin American society to explain the growth of these imported non-Catholic organizations, or on bilateral relations between the United States and Latin American society, the changing nature of religion in the supranational arena is an important factor, seldom discussed, that we will tackle here.[2]

Third, the Jehovah's Witnesses have almost five times more of their membership in Europe than the other groups. This again has to do with the particularities of their presence in Europe during the war and afterward.

Fourth, although the rest have relatively equal percentages in Asia, the Adventists have doubled the percentage of any of the others.

Finally, they differ in their percentage of members in Africa, but the LDS number is negligible when compared with the others. Although these last three points have relevance, in the interest of space I will not develop them below.

The distribution of members indicates that each of the religious groups has a different relationship with its host society and has not moved into the international arena in the same way. Indeed, on the basis of this distribution alone, one can argue that they occupy different social niches in the global society. And the supranational society impacts each one of them some-what differently because their historical backgrounds set the stage for their present.

Mormonism stands out because it suffered far more tension with its host society. It was the only religious body to combine colonization of a geographical area (with resultant protonationalism and a racial policy favor-ing northern Europeans and indigenous Amerindians or mixed bloods while excluding Africans); an immigration policy built on conversion and migra-tion of members from abroad, especially northern Europe; a relative with-drawal from international missionary work at the same time the others were actively moving outward; a relatively late return to missionary work; and a strong reliance on the institutions of its primary host, the United States, which were expanding globally, for the church's own growth. The incipient development of a framework for transnational religions to develop, separate from the umbrella of empire or of nation-states, is an important shadow en-tangled in these factors, as a perusal of Mormon proselytizing in the United Kingdom, Scandinavia, or Polynesia will show (Underwood 1999, 2005; Thompson 1963; Martin 1990; Davies 1987; Mulder 2000; Shumway 1991; Sahlins 1992). Though these factors help explain the relative distribution of Mormons around the world, they also mean that the LDS Church faced a different structure of opportunities and costs than did the other groups.

LOCAL SOCIAL TRACES OF SUPRANATIONAL CONCERNS

The implications of this differentiation of niches for the specific religious bodies can further be seen in a comparison of traces of these historical dif-ferences. In 2000 Mexico required its people to identify their religious mem-bership for the decennial national census. This count affords us one snap-shot of the different religions' relationship with socioeconomic status and hence a global political economy (see table 14.2).

Mormons stand out for having the lowest percentage of their members (that is, those who claimed that status to the census takers) from the poorer segments of society and the largest, by far, in the upper income bracket. To further show this difference between Mormons and the other groups, one can look at educational attainment. Again, Mormons stand out for having the highest levels of educational attainment among their member-ship (see table 14.3). Mormonism follows a different pattern from the other American-born groups. These data from Mexico are not isolated or repre-sentative of Mexico alone; rather, they indicate global strategies of prosely-tizing and the ways the different groups found a place in the world order (see Lawson 2005).[3]

TABLE 14.2. Income of members of selected religious groups in Mexico, 2000

	<1 AND 1 MINIMUM WAGE	>1 AND <3 MINIMUM WAGE	3 AND >3 MINIMUM WAGE
Pentecostals	39.4	42.2	14.5
Seventh-Day Adventists	49.5	32.4	14.0
Latter-day Saints	13.2	45.6	36.2
Jehovah's Witnesses	25.4	50.3	19.6

TABLE 14.3. Educational attainment of selected religious groups' membership according to the 2000 Mexican census

	PENTECOSTAL	SEVENTH-DAY ADVENTISTS	LATTER-DAY SAINTS	JEHOVAH'S WITNESSES
Not specified	0.8	0.8	0.9	0.9
No education	12.0	12.0	2.1	5.3
Preschool	0.5	0.6	0.2	0.3
Primary school	47.5	48.5	20.0	39.8
Secondary school/ technical school	22.4	18.6	25.9	30.0
Medium level	11.1	10.9	28.2	17.5
Advanced level	6.0	8.4	22.7	6.1

This kind of profile, in which each of the American-born religious bodies is located somewhat differently in the structure of Mexican society, is related to O'Dea's analysis. It represents conscious choices by church administrators in terms of deployment of proselytizing resources and the development of a religious structure favorable to the people who most strongly adhere to it. But it also represents a relationship with the society of origin and the new host society, as well as the evolving global order.

Mormonism chose, although the choice was overdetermined, to emphasize a particular social segment where it has found success.[4] Adventists, in contrast, work with the very, very poor, especially the rural poor. Among them they have pioneered education and schools, hospitals, and other development institutions. The Adventists came in at a time when state institutions of this nature were very weak and it was controversial to provide them to many rural peoples (Knowlton 1982; Lewellen 1978). As a result, in some areas, they have helped institutionalize the modern, liberal state for rural peoples.

In contrast, Mormons have not been successful, on the whole, in rural areas in Latin America, because of a poor fit between the LDS ward structure and the realities of rural life. These different stances show up in the numbers and are in turn conditioned by the time and place the organizations began proselytizing—the Adventists moved very strongly into rural Latin America in the early twentieth century, whereas Mormons were turned inward and were recovering from their conflict with U.S. society. When Mormons began massive proselytizing in Latin America, their dominant model was no longer the Mormon village ward of the nineteenth century but the suburban congregation ward. Instead of the informal networks of a village society institutionalized in village wards, we have formal societies enshrined in laws, policies to be implemented, and bureaucratic distance and control, typical of the social framework of the suburban ward. Furthermore, given the LDS emphasis on education, the Mormon diaspora took a strongly middle-class or upper-middle-class character. It is no surprise that Mormonism, as a result, found more success in the areas of urbanization and suburbanization in Latin America than it has elsewhere. Adventists, in contrast, did not begin their proselytizing at a time of ascendant American power following World War II. They began much earlier, while Mormons were withdrawing and turning inward. As a result, they not did move into places such as Latin America in conjunction with the spread of American military, cultural, and economic missions, as well as American multinational businesses, in the way Mormonism did. Nor have the Adventists shrouded themselves in American culture and the American flag in the way Mormonism has.

Mormons and Adventists, as well as the Assemblies of God, are simply located differently in Mexican and in global society. This gives them different interests and concerns and plays itself out in theology, social organization, and interventions in social and political concerns.

The strong presence of the well educated and the well off among Mormons indicates a connection between Mormon growth and the development of formal national economies in Latin America, and in global society. One can see this in the members who stay in the church and claim that status to census takers, in the architectural style and location of buildings and offices, as well as in the theological emphases of contemporary church teachings.

Whereas Mormonism seems to have drawn its membership most heavily from those Mexicans whose educational and social backgrounds place them within the formal society and its paradigms of national economic growth, in contrast Pentecostals and Seventh-Day Adventists are more located among social segments that tend to be more marginal to formal society, such as rural peoples and low-level workers in the cities.[5] These sectors have faced different social and economic struggles than those of the more formal group. The formal sectors are not only located more firmly in the official structure of national society but also are more involved in processes that today connect national societies with the formal supranational global order.

This gives them a different position in the Mexican national project. A key part of the Mormon place has been the church's elective affinity with formal economic enterprises and the expansion of regimes of business and governmental management, which is part of its location within the broader American postwar expansion into the world. The social changes wrought by the global, and local, growth of this social form provided the requisite social niche for Mormon growth.

Transnational Religion and National Sovereignty

In the early days of Mormonism in Mexico, issues of its U.S. base proved problematic in ways that are telling for our argument. The LDS Church attempted to work as a transnational church, but issues of Mexican national sovereignty versus control over church affairs by its foreign hierarchy, which happened to be Anglo-American, split the church in Mexico and created concerns over national sovereignty.[6] These issues have played themselves out very differently for the other groups. Nevertheless, every American-born religion has faced the problem of its society of origin and implied entanglements with the U.S. foreign presence versus problems of national sovereignty. But most have long since been able to separate themselves from that issue to a very large extent. Mormons have had particularly difficult problems because of their insistence on control and leadership by the General Authorities, instead of national ones. Until recently, the structure of global religious society did not favor that kind of church structure, despite careful legal work to enable the church to function under the laws and conditions of different countries while maintaining its own unitarian structure.[7]

Although the LDS Church now makes a strong public relations insistence that it is a local and an international church, not a U.S. church, two things have been most important in minimizing this difficulty and allowing the church to function more freely. First, Mexican national understandings of the role of plural religious bodies in relationship to national sovereignty have evolved. This is the case not only in Mexico but in most other nations as well. Second, in addition to these changing national understandings, international conventions on religion have changed, and these have opened a door for seeing a church like the Latter-day Saints as international, rather than national. It allows for religious multinationals to have a presence in various countries without necessarily triggering concerns over sovereignty. This is further made possible and legitimate because of the growth and development of a host of supranational agencies, nongovernmental organizations, businesses, and legal structures, which become part of the supranational social context of Mormon growth.

When Mormonism first began in Mexico, in 1875, almost none of those existed. Religion, as a result, occupied a very different place. For example, the relationship of Catholicism to the Mexican nation was a matter of severe struggle because the church was not clearly subordinate to the state, among other things, and could claim the loyalty of and had the ability to mobilize a large portion of the population. As a result, severe limits were placed on religion, in order to guarantee and protect the Mexican state and Mexican sovereignty following the Mexican Revolution and the Cristero revolt (a conservative prochurch rebellion that shook Mexico) in the first decades of the twentieth century.[8] However, in 1992, as part of a much broader liberalization of the Mexican society and economy, Mexican president Carlos Salinas de Gortari began a rapprochement with the Catholic Church by pushing through congress the lifting of legal restrictions on religious activity. In part, this was a recognition of the important role Catholicism still had in the country's society. But, in part, it was also a recognition of the importance of new international conventions around religion, and their relationship with other neoliberal policies demanded by multilateral institutions, to which Mexico would have to subscribe to continue living in the international world's good graces. Opening to the global economy was an important part of this technocrat's vision of the Mexican future, and it included a new religious order. This new openness around religion relaxed the strictures the LDS Church had faced in Mexico and allowed it greater freedom of movement as an openly supranational church.

Although this is true for Mexico, it is also true for other countries of the world as well. They too have been influenced by the supranational order that led to Salinas's change of religious policy. Thus, when we look at LDS Church history in Mexico, it is important to see it in the matrix of broader political, economic relationships with which the church and the nation were enmeshed, as well as the evolution of new compacts and structures governing relationships among nations and thereby providing regulations for nongovernmental organizations such as transnational churches. This requires we look at the evolution of supranational society.

The Growth and Structure of Supranational Society

In the late nineteenth century the first truly supranational social organizations were founded. Before that time there was no legal structure to allow for the flow of communications and commerce around the globe, to which we are now accustomed, other than through imperial organization or imposition or bilateral agreement among nations. Nevertheless, out of these came the first forms of global institutions. For example, the International Telecommunications Union and the Universal Postal Union were founded in 1865 and 1874, respectively (International Telecommunication Union n.d.; Universal Postal Union n.d.; United Nations n.d.a). The next major step, the development of global financial institutions, was delayed by the existence of a common gold standard. Its demise, in part, led to the Bretton Woods Conference in 1944, after World War II, out of which came the International Monetary Fund and the World Bank.

Despite the relatively tentative beginning of global institutions, in the twenty-first century we have increasingly important multilateral organizations that enable and regulate much of the communication and commerce among nations, as well as increasingly within them. We also have an incipient international judicial system, including a criminal court, and a growing body of international law.[9] Around these have developed strongly multinational bodies, such as businesses—the income of the larger corporations is greater than the gross domestic product of most nations—nongovernmental organizations, and religions (De Grauwe and Camerman 2002; Anderson and Cavanagh n.d.). Their existence within nations, since the nation is still the legal foundation of the international order, as well as outside of them and in some ways above them, is a key part of the contemporary global social order.

One hundred years ago religion was mostly local or more connected with society and with the local sociopolitical order (Martin 1990). Although there were missionary organizations, enabled by the imperial powers or challengers to them, nevertheless most religion was local and was generally an important part of local social reproduction. We did not have the strong global religious organizations, such as translocal, supranational churches, that we have today. This argument includes Catholicism.

Although called the universal church because of its widespread existence, among other things, the Catholic Church still had a strong and primary relationship with local societies. This is most evident in Latin America, where local religious sodalities and feasts, as well as popular religion, have until recently been far more important to the church than the Vatican or even national hierarchs (Parker 1993). Through them, the hierarchy built and legitimated its power. Over the past century the Catholic Church has seen the Vatican's power increase, a process known as Romanization (Meyer 1989; Klaiber 1992). At the turn of the twentieth century, the various countries of Latin America, where almost half of the world's Catholics are located today, still claimed the right for their governments to name local bishops. Throughout the nineteenth century and the twentieth the place of the Catholic Church, and hence the space of religion, in those societies has been fought over and redefined, allowing for religious pluralism and for some kind of separation of church and state. These agreements have been formalized in treaties with the Vatican, called concordats, and they allow for the Vatican to control the naming of local hierarchs. One should notice, however, as a residue of historic social organization, that the Vatican is not only a way of referring to the centralized church hierarchy of Catholicism; it is also a state in a world of states. As a result, the concordats are treaties between states. Other religious bodies did not have this sociopolitical status. Instead, they functioned under, and as dependencies of, states and empires.

The twentieth century was a century of major religious change. As the legal structure of the world changed, allowing for the development of a kind of universal system of communication as well as economic exchange, it also allowed for the development of kinds of universal religious ideas and organizations that were not deeply entrenched in local societies in the same way. Indeed, this is part of why Mexican and other liberals in the nineteenth and twentieth centuries have welcomed proselytizing by transnational religious bodies, such as Mormonism, even when they have been resisted by nationalists. Both the global and the local natures of religious organizations have been reworked.

Something as complex as a growing supranational sphere of religion is due to many, conjoined, social pressures, including those that have led to the multilateral organizations described above. One way of approaching the supranational religious structure is to look at the changing legal environment that enabled the development of this new level of religious organization. In this sense, the supranational space develops from the new political and legal language articulated in the Universal Declaration of Human Rights, declared in 1948 by the General Assembly of the United Nations. This document, as it has become institutionalized in the world, both as a legal tool and as a tool of political pressure, is a critical beginning point for seeing major change in religion. To be sure, it responded to changes already afoot, but it then enabled much greater change.

In Article 18 the Universal Declaration states, "Everyone has the right to freedom of thought, conscience and religion; this right includes freedom to change his religion or belief, and freedom, either alone or in community with others and in public or private, to manifest his religion or belief in teaching, practice, worship and observance" (United Nations n.d.b). This clause in the declaration enunciated, and enabled, a major change in the relationship among state, society, people, and religion. Religion became a separate domain that had no necessary conjugation with these others. It became a property and right of individuals, indeed a universal right. Individuals, the darlings of the liberal and neoliberal thinker as the primary social actor, claimed the right to freedom of thought, conscience, and religion. Religion was no longer a necessary property of societies, especially of national societies, although it could still be conceived as a property of ethnic societies, but not national societies.[10] This is consonant with modernization theory and development theory, and their policies have preferred secularization and individualization. These latter were an important part of post–World War II social policy.

By freeing religion from local social control, the declaration opened the door for global religions composed of individuals in many countries sharing a common belief, from which organizations could develop, although they are not considered in this body of law. They follow as a consequence of individual belief and right of adherence. Affiliation with the global faith could become the measure of social belonging, rather than localized religious practices. This is a critically important transformation.

Nation-states have further become judgeable vis-à-vis one another, and vis-à-vis multilateral agencies, in terms of how they allow individuals to practice this right to religion. As a result, this changed idea of freedom of conscience in public and private has become important in international affairs. Although not binding, the Universal Declaration has served as a powerful moral and political force. It has become part of a system of pressure on countries to accept the legal framework that defines religion in this way, no matter the preexisting social and national dependencies. In order to qualify fully for international social legitimacy and material benefit, nations must accept this new religious form.

In 1966 the United Nations adopted two covenants that became binding as nations ratified them and included them in their national laws. They were implemented by the UN as of 1976. These are the International Covenant on Civil and Political Rights, adopted and opened for ratification in 1966, and the International Covenant on Economic, Social, and Cultural Rights. Both covenants explicitly prohibit the derogation of human rights solely on the basis of religion. The Covenant on Civil and Political Rights, Article 18, states:

Everyone shall have the right to freedom of thought, conscience and religion. This right shall include freedom to have or to adopt a religion or
belief of his choice, and freedom, either individually or in community
with others and in public or private, to manifest his religion or belief in
worship, observance, practice and teaching. No one shall be subject to
coercion which would impair his freedom to have or to adopt a religion
or belief of his choice. Freedom to manifest one's religion or beliefs may
be subject only to such limitations as are prescribed by law and are necessary to protect public safety, order, health, or morals or the fundamental
rights and freedoms of others. (Office of the United Nations High Commissioner for Human Rights n.d., n.p.)

On the basis of this covenant comes the recognition that religion may be
practiced in groups. The covenant further recognizes that religion, like language, may be a property of minority groups. Nevertheless, this legal structure does not provide a definition of how religion might be organized into
groups nor the legal basis on which they can be so organized. It specifically
does not explore how religious bodies as legal persons might be formed.

As a result, religious groups are organized according to the legal requirements for associations of individuals under the various national legal structures. However, the opening of the door for associations of people of common conscience and belief to operate in more than one country allowed
supranational religious organizations to develop. The rights of these groups
to operate, or, more specifically, of their members to exercise their membership in these supranational religious groups, are policed by the United
Nations, which reports on religious freedom; by various nongovernmental
organizations; and by states such as the United States, which has made reporting on the respect for religious rights in other countries part of its foreign policy and a potential condition for aid.

Social Organization of Supranational Religious Order

The legal issues are but one concern in the development of the supranational level of religious organization. Among other concerns are those of religions that work in multiple countries developing economies of scale and
appropriate administration as they manage their transnational interests.
Given the increasing globalization of the economy, media, and social movements, religious groups increasingly require equally global coordination of
efforts and reflections in order to develop and carry out meaningful responses. Furthermore, they have a need to defend themselves, seek advantage, and respond to actions and possibilities by the multilateral agencies.

These include the United Nations and its various agencies, the World Bank, and the International Labor Organization. Also, the existence of supranational religious organizations tends to give a premium to groups that themselves are organized supranationally.

We can see the complexity of supranational organization that is developing, and the pressures for it, in almost any religious group. Nevertheless, supranational religious organizations are not cut from the same organizational cloth. A comparison of Anglican, Lutheran, Catholic, Evangelical, Pentecostal, Mormon, Jehovah's Witness, Seventh-Day Adventist, or even multidenominational organizations such as the World Council of Churches structures easily illustrates the variety. We have a range from strict associations of independent members with little centralization to strongly centralized groups. We also have a range from those that build on agglomerations of independent national churches to those that depend on the strongly centralized and hierarchized models more typical of the multinational corporation.

One way of bringing order to this is to look for typologies of social organizations that can help us make sense of the variety we see in the transnational religious arena. In an exploration of autopoiesis Richard Adams proposes a typology that provides a useful framework: "Individuals are the initial creators of social organization but the growth of regulatory elements inherently takes control away from their hands" (1988, 177). His concern with self-regulation of the resultant organizations and their relationships with their constituents provides an important framework for us.

Adams's classification depends on a separation between centralized organizations and those that simply stem from the coordinated actions of members, without any central organization. The latter are called "coordinated units." Once a center is established, Adams distinguishes whether the center can exercise power independently from its base members and whether it can independently delegate power to others, such as agencies that it creates. The simple existence of a center makes the groups "consensus units," in Adams's terms, followed by "majority units" and "corporate units" sequentially. Finally, Adams distinguishes groups that have a strong center that has capacities of separate, independent power. These are called "administered units" because of the relative strength and independent power of the center. As a result, the key variable here is precisely this independent power of the center, such that it becomes more powerful than its constituent parts (Adams 1975) (see table 14.4).

The LDS Church is an example of an administered unit. It has a strong center, the Corporation of the First Presidency, which exercises independent power and delegates power to lower social levels. There is little ability of the

TABLE 14.4. Typology of supranational religious organization

| | TYPE OF OPERATING UNIT | | | | |
| | INFORMAL UNITS | | | FORMAL UNITS | |
	COORDINATED UNITS	CONSENSUS UNITS	MAJORITY UNITS	CORPORATE UNITS	ADMINISTERED UNITS
Separate, independent power	Yes	Yes	Yes	Yes	Variable
Identify common membership	Yes	Yes	Yes	Yes	Variable
Grant power reciprocally	Yes	Yes	Yes	Yes	Variable
Allocate power centrally		Yes	Yes	Yes	Variable
Center exercises power independently			Yes	Yes	Yes
Center delegates power				Yes	Yes

Source: Adams 1975.

lower social levels to pressure or allocate power to the First Presidency. Not only is this a matter of theology, but it is also built into the legal, organizational structure. In this, it is like the modern multinational corporation, where upper management has substantial independent power beyond that of lower levels of the organization or even stockholders.

In contrast, the World Assemblies of God Federation exists on the interface between a consensus unit and a majority unit. The issue for these Pentecostals is the development of a center while being very concerned to limit the independent exercise of power of that center. Given their theological focus of congregational independence and the rights of believers to have a direct relationship with God and his spirit, yet given the needs for larger-scale social organization, this tension makes sense.

In a world organized into nations, where they are understood to be the sovereign units from which other organizations stem, religious groups by definition stem from those national legal and social structures that grant them existence and recognize them. However, the increasing importance of supranational religious groups is giving them a power that is beyond that of nation-states. Furthermore, by existing as a transnational organization, beyond the control of any single nation-state, religious groups are able to accumulate capital and power that they can bring to bear against nation-states if there is ever a conflict, and they can use this power to keep control over local church entities.

The period since the human rights covenants have been promulgated has seen astounding religious change around the world. Though driven by the massive social and economic changes consonant with social change during this time of massive urbanization and liberalization of economies and societies, nevertheless this developing global religious order has also played an important role.

IMPACT OF THE SUPRANATIONAL ORDER ON MORMONISM

This section will explore several of the major ways in which this new order has in part led to important changes in Mormonism, as part of an initial foray into understanding Mormonism's relationship with this developing host society in which it now moves.

Universalism

As has been mentioned, these supranational religious groups involve some important changes in the relationship between religion and society. Religious groups are now far less context dependent than earlier forms of religious life. They tend to be much less involved in local society. Rather, they are focused on the relationship of the believer to the translocal body of believers, or to God, with the body being a representative of that. Religion is now a separate social domain that has no necessary conjugation with others, such as kinship, politics, economics, and so on. Affiliation with the global faith can become the measure of social belonging, rather than localized religious practices.

For example, Mormonism may have claimed a certain absolute truth and universality from its beginnings, but in the nineteenth century it was strongly committed to building up Zion, a specific locale and place. Mormon theology was filled with the particulars of place and the role of religion in that place. These notions motivated the migration of converts to a particular place, the Mormon West in the United States.

The LDS Church has now developed a different sense and institutionalization of universality as it has built congregations abroad, especially in the postwar missionary push, at a time when the universal ideals of religion as an individual right were being articulated. Mormonism has now reworked its sense of Zion and the church in order to encompass a global religious society and organization. The connection of these two movements—a new Mormon universality at a time of changing understandings of the place of religion vis-à-vis local societies—is directly related.

New Subjectivities

The literature on globalization has strongly emphasized the ways in which identity, for many people, is no longer connected with specific local communities, but indeed is translocal (see Appadurai 1996). To understand this, one must note how in the various projects of nation building, loyalty to the nation and an identity as a national subject were obligatory and primary. Indeed, part of the conflict the Latter-day Saints had with the United States was around this primary loyalty. Many Americans suspected the Saints' loyalty lay with their religion and their prophet and not with the nation. There was concern over the immigration of Saints from Europe directly to Utah without having passed through national processes of vetting and Americanizing. As a result of this conflict, it is not surprising that Latter-day Saints became strongly patriotic as Americans.

In Mexico this was a problem for the Anglo colonists of the North who have been so important for Mormon growth throughout Latin America. Even after a century in Mexico, and substantial Mexicanization, American identity is strong and an integral part of their religious identity. Among the Mexican national population that became Mormon, this was a difficult problem. They sought ways to Mexicanize their Mormon identity, even though the bulk of their fellows were American. One example of this is the writings of Margarito Bautista (1935) that locate the Book of Mormon story strongly in Mexican history. But his writings make sense only against the backdrop of the strong American ideology he was resisting.

With the changes in international understandings on religion, this is no longer quite as much a problem. Though local ideologies connecting Mormonism with specific local societies still develop, more interesting is how strongly the identity of Latter-day Saints now seems translocal and indeed supranational. They are connected with an international, multiethnic, and multiracial people who are the children of God. This has involved an intense cultural project of separating, winnowing, what could be called the gospel from what could be called culture, such that the gospel could require equally people along the Wasatch Front and fourth-generation Mormons in Buenos Aires to leave behind their cultures for this new, more focused gospel culture, or to see it in tension with the ways of the Lord.

This means that the subjectivities of Latter-day Saints everywhere, although the church encourages them to respect and honor their nation, are still religiously outside or beyond any nationality. In some areas these are already developing ethnic characteristics like those held by long-term Mormons in the core geographical region. It remains to be seen to what extent this ethnicization of Mormons as a distinctive kind of people will continue.

Administrative Centralization and Bureaucratic Complexity

As noted above, the Church of Jesus Christ of Latter-day Saints is distinctive in that it has a strongly centralized structure, such that it fits Richard N. Adams's criteria for an administrative unit. This form of organization is much more common in multinational businesses than in religious forms of transnational social organization. Although the LDS Church strongly emphasizes its prophet and his role in the divine organization of the church, it is also important to notice that this structure has evolved in response, in part, to the exigencies of becoming a supranational church.

Generally, this process of centralization and unification of authority under the priesthood is called "correlation." One of the major changes the church underwent in the latter half of the twentieth century, correlation involved developing a central line of authority under which all the auxiliaries and other portions of the church were to function. As the recent biographies of church presidents David O. McKay and Spencer W. Kimball make clear, pressures stemming from the international church were an important motivator for this change (Prince and Wright 2005; Kimball 2005). This development is not singular to the Latter-day Saints but is consonant with changes many other religious groups are making as the supernational sphere of religion develops. The singularity is the strength of centralization and the resultant autonomy of the organizational top.

Another portion of this international growth involves the greater development of organizational complexity. In Mormonism this has included the growth of the church bureaucracy with its different agencies and thousands of employees, as well as a parallel growth in complexity of Mormon society. In the latter, one also sees the growth of supranational organization. Although separate from, and at times in tension with, the unified authority of the church, nonetheless this Mormon society is also part of the international growth of Mormonism. An interesting example of this is the development of chapters of Affirmation, an organization of gay and lesbian Mormons throughout Latin America (Knowlton 2006b).

Engagement in International Politics

Given the strong emphasis by Mormon leaders on disengagement from politics, addressing the place of the LDS Church in international politics might seem strange. However, increasingly, international agencies, such as UNESCO, the World Bank, and so on, are places where issues are debated and policies implemented that affect things that Latter-day Saint leaders consider to have moral weight. A key example of this is the family and policies around the family.

The Proclamation on the Family arguably is a strong response to debates and changes around the nature and place of the family, the place of women, and sexuality throughout the world. These debates are not simply a matter or interest to Americans. Feminism is a global social movement and has had a strong impact on societies around the globe. Gay rights is a similar social movement, with gay-pride parades appearing in major cities the world over. As a result, it is no surprise, given its position, that the LDS Church should organize a center at Brigham Young University to engage in these debates and should promulgate itself a policy that would be the basis of teaching and political action the world over.

Organizing Its Members into a Militant Cadre

Again, this point may seem surprising, but in its activities in defense of so-called traditional marriage, the church has organized U.S. members as a strong political force that has had an impact. In its teachings from the pulpit, the brethren encourage members everywhere to become politically involved in important moral causes. The definition of these causes is primarily from the leadership of the church, and little public disagreement is tolerated.

Mormonism is not alone in this. One sees this attempt to develop members into a militant social and political voice in other religious groups. The Catholic Church is an important example.

Focus on the Formal Authority Structure

Earlier we discussed the Mormon emphasis on formal society. When the LDS Church enters a country, it is careful to establish formal, legal status to enable it to build its structure of hierarchy, from supranational leadership to congregations and members. This hierarchy is critical. Although there are many instances of congregations forming on their own and then asking for church sanction, such as happened in West Africa, among other places, the church is generally careful, and indeed somewhat skeptical of such movements. People must demonstrate their loyalty to the formal structure to be acceptable.

This is important. Pentecostalism has grown to be one of the world's largest religious phenomena over a relatively short period because of its ability to take advantage of people movements. It requires a very simple organizational structure where the focus is primarily on the relationship between the believer and God and then on the minimal aggregation of people into congregations. Mormonism self-limits by requiring people to accept an authority structure to which the individual must submit. This limits its ability to respond quickly to the needs and possibilities afforded by movements of people.

The formal structure has proved to be an organizational problem in the less developed world. Official society has shown itself unable to organize the large demographic growth and the movement of peoples away from traditional structures of authority and into new rural movements and urban spaces. Instead, what has been called informal society—whether in economy or religion—has filled this gap. The main difference is the relationship to the formal legal and governmental structure.

Mormonism has been on the side of formality. Although this has not provided for the immense growth of Pentecostalism, it still has afforded a certain growth. Social scientists have emphasized the massive development of informality in much of the world, but nonetheless there has also been an expansion of formal society during the same period. Mormonism is unique in its strong anchoring in this expansion of formal society, with its requirements of education and hierarchy. As a result, there is an elective affinity between this social form, with its emphasis on management, formal rationality, and bureaucratic authority and Mormonism. This is key for understanding the place of Mormonism in the supranational religious structure.

Sacralization of Management and Formal Rationality

Given the importance of the formal sector and its logic for Mormonism, it should not surprise us that an elective affinity has been established between a Mormon focus on eternal progress and the need to gain merit in good actions on earth to attain earthly as well as eternal position. Techniques and logic of management have become a common and almost commonsense tool for understanding and planning eternal progress. They also are means by which Mormon leaders are trained for the management of quorums and congregations. As a result, management logics have been sacralized within Mormonism. Following this, Marcus Martins (1996) points to a predilection among Brazilian Mormons for education and careers in management.

Interestingly, the science of management developed and became popular at the same time the supranational sphere of religion was developing. Had Mormonism proselytized widely in the early twentieth century, as did the Seventh-Day Adventists and Pentecostals, this social logic would not have been available to the same degree. By the mid-twentieth century, when Mormonism began its massive international push, management was well developed as an idea and practice. Not only did it become the style in operating the church's bureaucracy—although it was not a natural style for some General Authorities of the time—but it also developed as a means of understanding how members should work for their salvation. And it became available for an elective affinity with the expansion of management professions and a managerial class in Latin America at the same time. As a result, at the moment, this relationship between management and Mormonism is solidly consolidated.

International Mobility Structures

As a result of Mormon growth, international structures of social mobility are appearing. One way of seeing this is within the church's bureaucracy, given that church employment has been an important means of anchoring the church in a leadership connected to it by employment. However, another way is to notice the church members who work in international and multinational businesses who find openings within their corporations for other Latter-day Saints. If nothing else, this strengthens peoples' connection to an LDS identity at the same time weakens national identification.

Counterweight to Pressures from Nation-States

As we have discussed, the importance of the human rights conventions brings international pressure to bear on nations that would limit what can be considered religious freedom. It has given the church an additional tool when, for one reason or another, a national government might resist its presence and activities. Though not absolutely incisive, the new international legal structure does provide a powerful tool guaranteeing an openness toward the LDS Church and others that otherwise might run against the interests of the national or religious society. One publicly well-known example of this took place in Russia as it, under what was called an onslaught of sects, tried to determine what was legitimate and what was illegitimate religion. The human right to religious freedom provided the legal instruments that allowed prominent Latter-day Saints in the U.S. government to promote the issue as an important one in bilateral and multilateral issues with the new Russian state, such that Mormonism became an acceptable religion to the Russian state.

This is not historically unique or new. Only the legal tools are new. In Mexico we see the clear struggle over the role of the church's central organization and its Anglo leadership in the face of nationalist pressures. Furthermore, mission growth, the renting of buildings for congregations to meet in, the buying of property for chapels to be built, the registration of itself as a legal person under the laws of the nation-state for transactions to occur, the obtaining of visas for missionaries from the United States, and the shipment of religious materials all had to be performed with the instructions of the church's system of hierarchy. At times, this has been difficult and has required substantial work from within the church to overcome barriers.

Similarly, when terrorists bombed Mormon chapels in Bolivia and assassinated two missionaries, foreign pressure on the Bolivian government led it to break the main group attacking the church (Knowlton, 2007).

CONCLUSION

As the LDS Church moves forward in the twenty-first century, the influence of the supranational society will become ever more important as its primary host society. The United States, whose relationship with Mormonism was such an important part of O'Dea's analysis, will continue to have an impact, but as the membership of the church grows more outside the United States and as the membership within it declines as a relative percentage of its total, its influence will weaken. No other nation-state will replace it as the major host. Those days are gone. Instead, given the number of countries in which it is found, the church will move more and more in that supranational space, and its evolution will enable as well as constrain church growth. Within it, the church is one of the main citizens, as one of the most ubiquitous and most centrally organized. As a result, it is likely to influence the ongoing evolution of the supranational space of religion. In a global society it will be an influential organization.

NOTES

1. On the sociology of Pentecostalism's substantial growth, see Martin 2001.

2. For access to the voluminous literature on religious change in Latin America, see Bastian 1994; Burdick 1993; Martin 1990; Smith 1999; Stoll 1991; and others.

3. The Chilean census confirms this pattern in a very different country and context. See Knowlton 2006a.

4. Although Mormons have proselytized the very poor, they generally have not built social service institutions among them, nor do they provide a supportive framework for them. It is likely they abandon the church at far greater rates than more well-off converts. Marcus Martins (1996) observes that church leaders in Brazil are reluctant to proselytize the poor. The important trope of looking for "leaders" demonstrates the class position Mormons have chosen. But as we note, this choice is highly constrained by the position Mormons occupied in U.S. and global society as they moved out into the world following World War II.

5. The literature on formality and informality is voluminous. As paths into the thicket, see de Soto 1989; and Hart 1987.

6. Tullis 1987 is an excellent introduction to the complex history and social dynamics of Mormonism in Mexico.

7. The recent David O. McKay and Spencer W. Kimball biographies contain examples of this (Prince and Wright 2005; and Kimball 2005, respectively).

8. As entries to the literature on the Mexican Revolution as well as the Cristero movement, see Meyer 1997; and Katz 1998.

9. There are, nevertheless, disputes around this and a strong feeling that it has created a new colonial world replete with a new imperialism. See Anghie 2005.

10. As I wrote this chapter in Bolivia in June 2006, there was a conflict over this in terms of a proposed constitutional convention that might rearticulate the rights of religion under the national constitution. At least two questions were contained therein. First, was the state's special, historical relationship with Catholicism to be abandoned as a matter of law, and, second, how does indigenous Andean religion fit in a system written for Christianity, when Indians are the majority of the country and wish to develop institutions that recognize their ethnic culture?

References

Adams, Richard N. 1975. *Energy and Structure: A Theory of Social Power.* Austin: University of Texas Press.

———. 1988. *The Eighth Day: Social Evolution as the Self Organization of Energy.* Austin: University of Texas Press.

Anderson, Sarah, and John Cavanagh. n.d. "Top 200: The Rise of Corporate Global Power." The Institute for Policy Studies. http://www.ips-dc.org/reports/top200text.htm#II.%20 OVERVIEW%20OF%20THE%20TOP%20200.

Anghie, Antony. 2005. *Imperialism, Sovereignty, and the Making of International Law.* New York: Cambridge University Press.

Appadurai, Arjun. 1996. *Modernity at Large: Cultural Dimensions of Globalization.* Minneapolis: University of Minnesota Press.

Bastian, Jean Pierre. 1994. *Protestantismos y modernidad Latinoamericana: Historia de unas minorias religiosas en América Latina.* Mexico City: Fondo de Cultura Económica.

Bautista, Margarito. 1935. *La evolucion de Mexico: Sus verdadaderos progenitores y su origen; el destino de America y Europa.* Mexico: Talleres Gráficos Laguna.

Burdick, John. 1993. *Looking for God in Brazil: The Progressive Catholic Church in Urban Brazil's Religious Arena.* Berkeley and Los Angeles: University of California Press.

Davies, Douglas. 1987. *Mormon Spirituality: The Latter-day Saints in Wales and Zion.* Nottingham: University of Nottingham.

De Grauwe, Paul, and Filip Camerman. 2002. "How Big Are the Big Multinational Corporations?" *Tijdschrift voor Economie en Management* 47, no. 3: 311–26.

Deseret News. 2002. *2003 Church Almanac.* Salt Lake City: Deseret News.

de Soto, Hernado. 1989. *The Other Path: The Invisible Revolution in Latin America.* New York: Harper and Row.

Hart, Keith. 1987. "The Informal Economy." In *The New Palgrave Dictionary of Economic*

Theory and Doctrine, ed. John Eatwell, Murray Milgate, and Peter Newman. Vol. 2. New York: Macmillan.

International Telecommunications Union. n.d. "I.T.U. Overview: History." http://www.itu. int/aboutitu/overview/history.html.

Jehovah's Witnesses. 2000. "Worldwide Report of Statistics." http://www.watchtower.org.

Katz, Friedrich. 1998. *The Life and Times of Pancho Villa.* Palo Alto: Stanford University Press.

Kimball, Edward L. 2005. *Lengthen Your Stride: The Presidency of Spencer W. Kimball.* Salt Lake City: Deseret Book.

Klaiber, Jeffrey. 1992. *The Catholic Church in Peru, 1821–1985: A Social History.* Washington, D.C.: Catholic University of America Press.

Knowlton, David Clark. 1982. "Conversion to Mormonism and Social Change in a Rural Bolivian Aymara Community." Master's thesis, University of Texas at Austin.

———. 2006a. "Unto the Least of These: The Political Economic Profile of Mormons in Latin America." Paper presented at the meetings of the Asociación Latinoamericana para el Estudio de la Religión, July, São Paulo, Brazil.

———. 2006b. "Vivir en el espíritu: Vidas interiores mormonas, género, sexualidad, y tensión religiosa" [Living by the Spirit: Mormon Inner Lives, Gender, Sexuality, and Religious Tension]. *Mandrágora* (journal of the Brazilian Research Group on Gender and Religion).

———. 2007. "Mormonism and Guerillas in Bolivia." *Journal of Mormon History.* 32, no. 3: 180–208

Lawson, Ron. 2005. "Comparing the Global Growth Rates and Distribution of Adventists, Mormons, and Witnesses." Paper presented at the Society for the Scientific Study of Religion Meetings, Rochester, New York.

Leone, Mark P. 1979. *The Roots of Modern Mormonism.* Cambridge: Harvard University Press.

Lewellen, Ted C. 1978. *Peasants in Transition: The Changing Economy of the Peruvian Aymara: A General Systems Approach.* Jackson, Tenn.: Westview Press.

Martin, David. 1990. *Tongues of Fire: The Explosion of Protestantism in Latin America.* Boston: Blackwell Publishing.

———. 2001. *Pentecostalism: The World Their Parish.* Boston: Blackwell Publishing.

Martins, Marcus. 1996. "The Oak Tree Revisited: Brazilian Leaders' Insights on the Growth of the Church in Brazil." Ph.D. diss., Brigham Young University.

Mauss, Armand L. 1994. *The Angel and the Beehive: The Mormon Struggle with Assimilation.* Urbana: University of Illinois Press.

Meyer, Jean. 1989. *Historia de los cristianos en América Latina: Siglos XIX y XX.* Mexico City: Vueta.

———. 1997. *La Cristiada.* Mexico City: Clio.

Mulder, William. 2000. *Homeward to Zion: The Mormon Migration from Scandinavia.* Minneapolis: University of Minnesota Press.

O'Dea, Thomas. 1957. *The Mormons.* Chicago: University of Chicago Press.

Office of Archives and Statistics. 2003. "138th Annual Statistics Report, General Conference of the Seventh-day Adventists." http://www.adventist.org/ast/general_statistics.shtml.

Office of the United Nations High Commissioner for Human Rights. n.d. "International Covenant on Civil and Political Rights." http://www.ohchr.org/english/law/ccpr.htm.

Parker, Cristian. 1993. *Otra lógica en América Latina: Religión popular y modernización capitalista.* Mexico City: Fondo de Cultura Económica.

Prince, Gregory A., and William Robert Wright. 2005. *David O. McKay and the Rise of Modern Mormonism.* Salt Lake City: University of Utah Press.

Sahlins, Marshal. 1992. *Anahulu: The Anthropology of History in the Kingdom of Hawaii.* Chicago: University of Chicago Press.

Shumway, Eric. 1991. *Tongan Saints: Legacy of Faith.* Provo: Institute for Polynesian Studies, Brigham Young University.

Smith, Christian. 1999. *Latin American "Religión" in Motion.* New York: Routledge.

Stoll, David. 1991. *Is Latin America Turning Protestant? The Politics of Evangelical Growth.* Berkeley and Los Angeles: University of California Press.

Swedin, Eric G. 2003. *Healing Souls: Psychotherapy in the Latter-day Saint Community.* Urbana: University of Illinois Press.

Thompson, E. P. 1963. *The Making of the English Working Class.* New York: Vintage Books.

Tullis, F. LaMond. 1987. *Mormons in Mexico.* Logan: Utah State University Press.

Underwood, Grant. 1999. *Millenarianism and Nineteenth Century New Religions: The Mormon Example.* Urbana: University of Illinois Press.

———. 2005. *Pioneers in the Pacific: Memory, History and Cultural Identity among the Latter-day Saints.* Provo: Religious Studies Center, Brigham Young University.

United Nations. n.d.a. "About the United Nations/History." http://www.un.org/aboutun/history.htm.

———. n.d.b. "Fiftieth Anniversary of the Universal Declaration of Human Rights." http://www.un.org/rights/50/decla.htm.

Universal Postal Union. n.d. "About Us." http://www.upu.int/about_us/en/glance.html.

15

"That Same Sociality"

Mormons and Globalization in the Twenty-first Century

~ Sarah Busse Spencer ~

The establishment and maintenance of a certain kind of sociality (or sociability) have been part of Mormonism since the beginning. Joseph Smith described an early ideal of heaven when he wrote, "That same sociality which exists among us here will exist among us there" (Doctrine and Covenants 130:2). For a variety of social, financial, and religious reasons, Mormon converts were initially urged to congregate in one place, to "gather to Zion," demonstrating a type of sociality that required living together and frequent interaction, based on a rural lifestyle, agricultural occupations, and small-town gemeinschaft. In *The Mormons*, O'Dea noted that this "gathered" condition provided a base for the "further development of Mormon distinctiveness in three important spheres: in that of values, in the internal structure of the Mormon fellowship, and in the relations between Mormonism and the larger community" (1957, 112). Mormons desired others who "gathered to Zion" to share a set of theological beliefs, a communal and congregational structure, and also "that same sociality" that they strove to create in their new community.

During the twentieth century, Mormon leaders began encouraging converts to remain in their homes and "build Zion" in their native lands rather than gathering to one location in the United States. The request for foreign converts to stay and build Mormonism in their home countries has led to the growth of Mormon congregations in non-U.S. settings. Although O'Dea merely noted this change in passing, fifty years after O'Dea's study, the internationalization of Mormonism is one of the most salient features of the church and its people in the twenty-first century. Many aspects of contemporary church structure, teaching style, and interaction with outsiders have been shaped by this international growth. In the process of becoming a worldwide church, Mormonism has also become a force for globalization.

This chapter explores issues involved in the growth of Mormonism in international settings through a case study of a recently established Mormon congregation in a location O'Dea could perhaps never have foreseen—the Russian Federation. The choice of setting and methodology are described below. Data for this chapter come from a larger research project on changing social conditions conducted in Novosibirsk, Russia, in 2000 and 2002.[1] This chapter looks at the implications of three aspects of Mormonism—church structure, church doctrine, and Mormon behaviors, including sociability—for local Russian congregations. Ultimately, this chapter argues that by insisting on uniformity in such different contexts, the Mormon Church represents not simply a particular American church but also a process of globalization by what has been called a "new religious tradition" (Shipps 1985) and a "new world religion" (Givens 2003).

O'DEA ON INTERNATIONAL MORMONS

In *The Mormons,* O'Dea describes key sources of strain in the Mormonism of his day: rationality versus charisma, authority versus individualism, agrarianism versus progress, and belief versus environment, or a tension between the religion and the host society. In describing these tensions, O'Dea demonstrates his connection to other sociological theories. The discussion of rationality versus charisma and the tension of belief versus environment are issues earlier raised in Max Weber's sociology of religion (1963). The influence of Talcott Parsons is particularly noticeable in O'Dea's work (as indeed could be expected from much sociology of that era), as O'Dea echoes Parsons's dimensions of particularism versus universalism and collective versus individualistic orientation (1951).

O'Dea referred to Mormonism as a "peculiarly American religion" (1957, 258). He called Mormonism an "American religion" even while describing the dramatic contrasts of Mormon religious and social values with those of the broader American society. He described the "typical American quality" (116) of Mormonism, and of the Mormon experience as "an America in miniature" (117)—for example, in the pioneering efforts and belief in success through hard work. Mormonism, in O'Dea's description, seems to have wholeheartedly embraced the individualism that at the time was presumed to characterize American society.

O'Dea spent relatively little time describing the Mormon missionary program, which seems unusual given its theological significance and its central role in the dramatic growth of the church since its inception. O'Dea merely suggested the custom for Mormon young men "to go on missions to foreign countries" and how this served as a stepping-stone in young men's lay leadership careers in the church (177), but did not discuss the implications of missionary work in foreign settings.

O'Dea did note in passing the early stages of growth of the Mormon Church outside the United States in the building of the Swiss temple and other non-U.S. temples. In contrast to the early history of gathering and separation, O'Dea argued that the trend of maintaining Mormon outposts elsewhere represents "the first stage in the separation of the Mormon notion of Zion and the gathering from a definite piece of land and from the New World." For O'Dea, this implied that "a more abstract, more spiritualized, conception of the gathering, in which a Mormon way of life is seen as possible without physical removal to and residence in a Mormon community in America, is developing" (118).

Given these two facts—the description of Mormonism as an "American religion" and noting the growth outside the United States—it seems strange that O'Dea did not take the next logical step and describe the potentials for tension between these "American" Mormon beliefs and non-American social and cultural environments. As other authors have noted, the interaction of "American Mormonism" with other cultures and traditions poses the greatest challenge for the contemporary Mormon Church (Tullis 1979). Other scholars have noted the contrasts with other cultures, such as that in Latin America (Knowlton 1994; see chapters 13–14); this chapter describes the tensions specific to the introduction of Mormonism to the Russian Federation.

METHODOLOGY AND CHOICE OF LOCATION

The reception of Mormonism in Russia is of central importance in extending O'Dea's study into the twenty-first century because, of all the nations in which Mormonism has been introduced since the 1950s, the Soviet Union in that era would have seemed the least-likely location. A greater antithesis of the ideals of American society than the Soviet Union could hardly have been imagined during the cold war. Accounts of Soviet society stressed the differences between American and Soviet societies, from the latter's state-sponsored atheism and central planning to collectivist child-rearing practices that encouraged docility and submission to group influence (Bronfenbrenner 1972) or the pressures on citizens of a totalitarian regime (Inkeles and Bauer 1959). Many of Parsons's famous dichotomies can be read as a contrast between American society with authoritarian societies such as Soviet society. He associates modern Western society, including the United States, with individualism, universalism, functional specificity, and affect neutrality (1954, 160–61). In contrast, Soviet society, not unlike authoritarian Nazi Germany, could be associated with Parsons's opposite characteristics of collectivism and particularism (1951, 67).

Thus, when the collapse of the Soviet regime provided an opportunity to study Russia firsthand, it seemed also logical to include an exploration of the reception of this church with "American" characteristics in what many presumed to be an "un-American" setting. Ethnography or participant observation relies on a study of individuals in their own settings, and has been called a "natural" form of sociology and a "paradigmatic way of studying the social world" (Burawoy et al. 1991, 2–3). Early research on post-Soviet or postsocialist society has been pioneered by ethnographers in Russia (Humphrey 2002), Romania (Verdery 2003), and Hungary (Burawoy and Lukacs 1992). Though the sociology of religion, like the larger field, relies heavily on survey research, ethnographies have been instrumental in studies of religious congregations, such as recent work on black churches in Boston (McRoberts 2003) or immigrant Chinese churches (Guest 2003). This chapter draws on material gained through ethnographic research, including but not limited to participant observation in a case study of a Mormon congregation in urban Siberia.

When choosing a location in which to conduct an ethnography of Russian society, it was apparent that Moscow was not a suitable setting because, as the capital city, it has long been distinct from the rest of the country, especially during Soviet years with the concentration of economic and political resources and power. St. Petersburg has its own unique historical reasons; it is not typical of the rest of Russia, but like Moscow it has had greater contact with the West for a longer period of time than other areas of the country. To represent the majority of Russians who live in urban areas, it was necessary to conduct the research in a city, and the search for a city where Mormon missionaries have been active for several years coupled with a research university to host a foreign scholar led to the selection of Novosibirsk.

Founded in 1893, Novosibirsk straddles the Ob' River where the trans-Siberian railroad crosses this major Siberian waterway 1,750 miles east of Moscow. Midway between Moscow and Vladivostok, and the largest city in Siberia, Novosibirsk serves as the official seat of the Novosibirsk *okrug* (federal district) of the Russian Federation and as the unofficial commercial capital of Siberia. The city's geography and position in the Soviet economic infrastructure continue to shape the impact of global flows of finance and individuals (Spencer 2004).

Like other urban areas in Russia, this city of more than 1.5 million inhabitants has its share of "winners" and "losers" in the transition to capitalism (Silverman and Yanowitch 1997) and a labor market (Gimpelson and Lippoldt 2001). Winners include owners of local businesses and the college graduates hired by local or Western newly created firms. Losers include many former employees of the military-industrial production, once a central feature of Novosibirsk's economy, and the teachers and doctors whose state salaries are barely above the poverty level. Distinctive to Novosibirsk are the numerous research scientists and professors connected with the Siberian branch of the Russian Academy of Sciences. Like elsewhere in Russia, the social legacy of communism (Millar and Wolchik 1994b) is palpable in Novosibirsk, especially considering its lack of pre-Soviet history and its construction as a quintessential "socialist city" (French and Hamilton 1979). On the whole, social, economic, and political conditions in Novosibirsk approximate those in other medium-size cities in Russia.

When I arrived in Novosibirsk, the mission president, a Canadian, mentioned one congregation in this city as having particular challenges with growth and retention, despite an extra allotment of missionary and financial resources. Because I was looking to understand the tensions between the host society and Mormonism, it seemed an obvious choice to begin with a congregation that was struggling to make inroads in the local population. For nine months, I attended this branch as a church member. Though I made no secret of my identity as a sociologist who came to research Russian society and culture, I did not announce to members that the congregation as such was the focus of my research, since it was not the only organization I was studying. Though I did interview some members of this and other Mormon congregations about their education and employment histories, formal interviews in 1999–2000 did not include direct questions about the church or challenges of church growth or cultural differences. Instead, the following insights and descriptions of attitudes and events emerged naturally over the year as I participated in church life and became acquainted with members. This informal, naturalistic approach allowed for an authentic understanding of the perceptions of local members on their own terms.

The Globalization of Russian Society

Russian exposure to global influences has been recent and overwhelmingly rapid: in nearly twenty years Russia has gone from near total isolation to sudden inundation with Western culture, consumerism, and commerce. Prior to 1991, socialist nations followed their own trajectory of development, insulated by their relative economic, political, and social autarky from changes that swept other industrialized nations, including the rise of the information society (Castells and Kiselyova 1995). When the Soviet Union collapsed, a population accustomed to social and commercial isolation was suddenly bombarded with consumer goods (such as McDonald's or Levi's), cultural products (movies and TV programs), and economic and political advice (from USAID, the International Monetary Fund, and so on) from the West.

Establishing this American church represents globalization not only through introducing a new theology but also through re-creating local units identical to units of this church around the world, tied together by a rule-bound bureaucratic administration. Bringing bureaucratic organization to an industrialized nation might at first glance seem to be bringing nothing new, merely continuing a pattern of Soviet modernization. After all, principles of "scientific management" (Taylor 1911) were imported into the Soviet Union in its earliest years, and the Soviet government managed politics and the economy by means of a massive bureaucracy. However, appearances aside, the Soviet Union was never a fully "modern" state but, as one scholar terms it, an "anti-modern" society (Rose 1999). The Soviet government, termed later an imperfect bureaucracy (Millar and Wolchik 1994a), represented not an ideal-type impersonal rational bureaucracy (Weber 1968) but rather a bureaucracy of clientelism (Mendras 1998) and an economic and political setting characterized by personalism and "neotraditionalism" (Walder 1986) rather than impersonal rationality. Thus, administration through rational principles such as those O'Dea described in Mormonism is at odds with the administrative tradition and culture of Russia.

RELIGION IN RUSSIA

Mormon doctrine and evangelizing represent a departure from both traditional views of Russian Orthodoxy and state-sponsored atheism for several reasons. For many Russians, religiosity is linked to ethnicity rather than to a specific theology. From a survey conducted in 2000, Russian researchers reported that "the percentage of respondents who reported an affiliation with a specific religion (60.5 percent) turned out to be substantially higher than the percentage of those who believed in God (43.4 percent)." In this same survey, "more than half of the respondents (55.9 percent) classified themselves as followers of the Orthodox faith" (Mchedlov, Gavrilov, and Shevchenko 2003, 59), with only about 3 percent identifying themselves as Muslim. Summarizing similar research, another scholar argues that "religious self-identification frequently reflects neither a personal belief system nor a regular religious practice"; in contrast, it is "often perceived as part of the traditional cultural environment or as an ethnic style of life: 'I am Russian, and therefore Orthodox' or 'I am Tartar, and therefore Muslim'" (Krindatch 2004, 126).

Many Russians believe that religious feeling belongs to certain categories of people: the elderly and very young, the poor, and the poorly educated. Contemporary research by Russian scholars suggests that "the majority of believers consists of women, the elderly, and people who do not have a high level of education," as was noted during the Soviet period. In contrast, "nonbelievers" are predominantly "men, relatively young people, and those with a high level of education." Believers are also, according to these scholars, "inclined to be conservative in their economic views," and express a preference for state planning and have little enthusiasm for price liberalization or privatization (Elbakian and Medvedko 2003, 12). Other researchers describe a "a persistent tendency for religious commitment to 'become younger,'" pointing to the fact that people ages twenty-one and younger are slightly more represented among those claiming a belief in God (6.3 percent) than of the respondents as a whole (5.3 percent) (Mchedlov, Gavrilov, and Shevchenko 2003, 59). These researchers also expressed concern that "the religious quest of many young people is not institutionally formalized" (61), which, they fear, might lead to the dangers of what they call "pseudoreligious speculation." By this they mean "magic and the occult" and other "destructive pseudoreligious trends" (60–61).

Many observers have noted a gap between the large number of Russians who identify as Russian Orthodox and the very small number who have a correct idea of Russian Orthodox teachings or dogma. In response to this concern, one Russian scholar argues that this is not a new phenomenon: in the czarist era, peasants were not literate, and very little effort was made to teach them doctrine, stemming from a ruling by Russian Orthodox leaders that the "masses of common people could be saved without any theology." Even for the elites, a complete translation of the Bible was not available in Russian until 1875 (Sinelina 2003, 30). In the Russian Orthodox tradition, aristocracy and peasants alike valued faith over doctrinal knowledge. "There is nothing surprising in today's Russian believers," Tuliia Tu Sinelina continues, "deprived as they are of religious education, finding it difficult to understand such dogmas as the personhood of God ... the immortality of the soul ... and so on" (31).

Of course, whatever religious teachings were once available in czarist-era Russia have been long buried under seventy-five years of state-sponsored atheism. One of the legacies of this attempt to eradicate religion is that nearly twenty years after the collapse of communism, and despite a dramatic upsurge in the activity of the Russian Orthodox Church, there are not enough Russian Orthodox Church buildings for even the proportion of the population self-identifying as Russian Orthodox (37). This is more true of the far East and thinly settled areas in the eastern part of the country than of the traditional heart of Russia (Krindatch 2004, 127–28). Foreign Protestant missionary activity has, in contrast, been more represented in these eastern areas of Siberia and the far East than in the western portion of the country, illustrating a "territorial distribution of the new religious organizations ... inversely proportional to the geography of those religions and churches that are considered 'traditional' for Russia" (134). This has been less the case for Mormons, who concentrate their mission offices in large cities regardless of traditional religious patterns. According to one survey of registered "religious communities" (including offices and worship locations), Mormons had forty-six such groups in January 2003, which represented 2 percent of all registered religious communities in the country (132).

The reception of a foreign religion in Russia depends in part on attitudes toward "foreignness" (such as the nationalism inspiring rejection of foreign food products [Caldwell 2002]) and in part on Russian attitudes to religion in general and foreign religion in particular. Attitudes to foreign churches in Russia are affected by perceptions of Western culture that are not overwhelmingly positive. When asked in a survey whether "western culture" has had a "negative impact" on Russia, most respondents generally agreed: 48 percent in 1996 and 67 percent in 2002. Asked about the "western model of society," most respondents in 2000 either doubted its relevance for Russia (30 percent) or agreed outright that it is "not suitable for Russia" and "contradicts" the Russian way of life (37 percent) (Krindatch 2004, 133). In a 1997 survey in Russia, almost all respondents "agreed with the general principle of freedom of personal choice of belief," whereas "only 40 percent supported the full legal equality of all religions and churches" (135).

The law on religion of 1990, "passed in the liberal spirit of perestroika and glasnost," accorded equal rights to all religions under the law and guaranteed freedom of conscience (Davis 1997, 645). Derek H. Davis suggests that this law "was perhaps an idealistic vision of what Russia might be in theory but nevertheless an overestimate of what Russia was prepared to be in practice" (650). The religious pluralism suggested in this document proved too dramatic for a population accustomed in the czarist era to a single religion (Russian Orthodoxy) or the atheism of the Soviet Union. In contrast, the 1997 law on religion, though paying lip service to the idea of religious freedom, recognizes the "special status of Orthodoxy over all other religious traditions" (649) and sets strict criteria for all other religions. The law recognizes "religious groups," which may meet but not own property, and registered "religious organizations," which may own property and invite foreign guests to the location in which they are registered. A very few foreign churches, including the Mormon Church, have been granted the preferred status of a "centralized religious organization" (Elliott and Corrado 1999, 111), allowing them to own property, invite foreigners, and establish congregations throughout the entire country.

The Russian Social Context

Understanding the social and cultural environment that the Mormon Church faces in Russia also requires recognition of several social structural features of contemporary Russian society described through ethnographic research (Spencer 2003). In general, most Russians have small numbers of friends and acquaintances whom they have known for many years and with whom they share many aspects of their lives. Because every close relationship takes time and energy to cultivate, most Russians think of good social relations as a finite quantity, limited in number. A typical social network consists of family, work colleagues, schoolmates, two or three close friends, neighbors, and perhaps a few "useful acquaintances" in shops, services, or government offices. This is not to say that Russians do not seek to have more social ties, and many Russians are constantly engaged in making "useful" connections (Ledeneva 1998), but these are usually one connection at a time, through a known acquaintance. Some observers might say that Russians have a low "propensity to socialize" (Unger 1998) with outsiders or strangers.

However, this perceived unwillingness to socialize with strangers may simply be lack of practice. Russians have traditionally had few opportunities to increase the size or diversity of their networks. With no history of voluntary associations, with sports or hobby clubs sponsored only by the Communist Party, and no bars or pubs for "hanging out" in the Soviet Union, most Russians once had few opportunities to strike up casual acquaintances. Because the Soviet Union restricted mobility, travel, and contact with foreigners, Russians have in the past had little experience interacting with strangers or people with widely different backgrounds. Life in a totalitarian police state gave Russians sufficient cause to distrust strangers, and habits of distrust are difficult to break, resulting in low levels of "generalized trust" (Misztal 1996). Thus, not socializing with strangers can be seen as a result of social isolation (Wilson 1987), that is, without opportunities to meet outsiders, people have few skills for being friendly with strangers.

Another essential element of Russian society is the importance of the collective *(kollektiv)* (Ashwin 1996). Because employment in the Soviet Union
tends to be long-term, most adults have been at the same workplace for most
of their adult lives. Experiencing regular association with a fixed group of
well-known colleagues in a stable collective has been a significant and valued experience for most people who grew up in the Soviet era. Though attitudes are changing, most Russians still value the sense of belonging to a collective. Though traditionally this was found in the workplace, some people
are now seeking substitutes elsewhere for collectives they no longer have at
work (through unemployment, factory closures, and so on). Good relations
(khoroshie otnosheniia) within a collective are considered important by most,
and in addition many prefer groups that can be characterized as comfortable *(udobno, uiutno)*, warm *(serdechno)*, or family-like. In many workplace
collectives, birthdays, holiday celebrations, and teatime are as important as
family celebrations. These characteristics of Russian society—difficulty meeting strangers, comfort in small circles, and lack of generalized trust—are especially problematic for the Mormon Church that expects a continual influx
of new members and a certain level of sociability among its members.

Church Structure: Standardized and Globalizing

One of the spheres of "Mormon distinctiveness" that O'Dea mentioned is
the "internal structure of the Mormon fellowship." This includes both church
structure and what O'Dea referred to as Mormonism's "socioeconomic and
familial ethic" (1957, 112). O'Dea described early church organization and its
gradual evolution to something more comparable with contemporary Mormon hierarchy, without, however, describing the evolution of that structure
in non-U.S. settings. Whereas in the early years there may have been a structural distinction between congregations "in Zion" and members "in the mission field," in the twentieth and twenty-first centuries there has been a move
to homogenize church structure first among the Mormons who migrated
eastward (118) and then in the establishment of congregations outside the
United States.

Scholars have suggested that the activity of Protestant missionaries in
spreading Christianity around the globe has been a source of globalization
(Dunch 2002). Unlike many Protestant missionary efforts, Mormon missionaries no longer set up missions intended to be permanently subordinate
to and distinct from the sending congregations. Part of the "spiritual gathering" O'Dea described can be seen in the goal to eventually establish wards
and stakes (with the right of patriarchs, a measure of local self-government,
and the possibility of a temple) in each country where Mormons send mis-

sionaries, rather than units permanently dependent on outside leadership. Current Mormon efforts are thus much more comparable to earlier efforts of the Catholic Church of establishing congregations under control from Rome, insisting on a common language and liturgy.

As historian Robert Bartlett has argued, the Catholic Church in the tenth through twelfth centuries A.D. was the unifying force in the creation of modern Europe. Roman Catholic priests and bishops went beyond spreading the Christian faith to the corners of Europe; they also sought to bring every village under diocesan control. Bishops insisted on obedience to the pope, specific rites (including the use of Latin for church worship and all church matters), and even a specific social order, based in part on Roman law (Bartlett 1993). By seeking to recast outlying regions in a particular mold connected to a center, the medieval Catholic Church contributed to the homogenization and interconnectedness of western Europe, laying the foundation for its eventual unification and globalization. This process over centuries has led Roland Robertson to argue that the Roman Catholic Church "can surely lay claim to being the oldest significant globe-oriented organization" (1992, 81).

Today, Mormon missionaries establish a mission with the goal of growing small branches into wards and groups of wards into stakes, to be identical to the structure and equal in status with wards and stakes around the world. Administratively, the Mormon bureaucracy treats all wards and branches identical regardless of location: each receives an operating-budget allotment based on attendance figures, and similar operating instructions are issued to all unit leaders. Administration is based on routine procedures, the "rationality" O'Dea described, with the *Church Handbook of Instructions* translated into most of the languages of countries where the church operates. Because of this pattern of uniform church structure and organization, creating equal outposts of "one church" in many locations, the impact of the Mormon Church has been more comparable to that of the Catholic Church in its history, and thus it serves as an agent of globalization.

Mormon Structure in Russia

The Mormon Church has operated in Russia since 1992 (Browning 1997), beginning in St. Petersburg and Moscow, and by 2000 had seven mission headquarters in the country, four in the traditional heartland of Russia, with outlying areas covered by mission headquarters in Yekaterinburg (covering the Ural Mountains), Vladivostok (for the far East), and Novosibirsk. Missionaries have worked since 1994 in Novosibirsk, which serves as the headquarters for missionary efforts across the vastness of Siberia, an area approximately the size of the continental United States. Approximately ninety missionaries served in six Siberian cities in 2000, about half the number of missionaries the church uses in other missions. Under the limits that Russian law and its implementation impose on their missionary efforts, local leaders are restricted to fewer full-time missionaries than the church would otherwise supply to the area. The church kept on average between twenty-four and thirty full-time missionaries in Novosibirsk at any one time during 2000.

In Russia, the church has followed its standard practice of initially authorizing missionaries to establish and lead congregations, while identifying and training local members to staff all local congregations. In 2000, a few key leadership positions were still filled by missionaries, but local members staffed most leadership roles. Most congregations began by meeting in local schools or cultural halls *(dom kul'turi)* in which missionaries rented space for Sunday meetings. As congregations grew and the church became more established, the church arranged for full-time rental or purchase of a floor or wing of a building, then renovating the interior space to resemble Mormon Church buildings in other parts of the world.

Small Congregations

In 1999–2000, there were approximately two hundred Russians attending five small congregations (or branches) in the city of Novosibirsk. These branches represented five major regions of the city and were named for neighborhoods they served. In 1999–2000 I attended the Sunrise congregation, with average attendance at Sunday services about twenty-five of a membership list of about eighty. The neighborhoods from which this branch drew suffered higher unemployment, alcoholism, and poverty than other areas of the city. The Sunrise congregation began by meeting in a Sunday-only rental, first in a music school and then in 2000 in a local agricultural college. Sacrament meeting was held in the school auditorium, and Sunday school met in a room that had originally been designed to show students how to defend their collective farms against nuclear or chemical warfare, sporting a life-size mannequin in full combat gear and a picture of Lenin above the chalkboard. Activities or midweek events were held originally at a member's apartment, and later at one of the other full-time rental locations in the city.

In 2000, the church was new enough and the branches small enough that there was often confusion between a view of the congregation as part of a larger religious organization, subject to hierarchical leadership, and a view of the congregation as a local social institution, directed by local members for local interests. In some ways, the small branches faced challenges like those faced by "house churches" in other settings (Kong 2002).

For example, some members wanted the church to have more social events, when those were held in members' homes and represented the "cozy" and "warm" feelings Russians treasure. One time a member advocated holding "branch family home evenings" every Monday night at someone's home. Other members, however, repeated the church's formal, universal admonition that Monday nights were to be used for family events and not for church socials. The disagreement represented the conflict between the idea of a local social group running itself and a congregation of a larger organization that could dictate what kinds of events to have. Gradually, as the church has grown in Russia, those who catch the vision of a larger, centrally directed church continue attending, whereas many of those who prefer the small, personal groups stop attending as church congregations grow beyond the size that can hold social events in someone's apartment. Some early members, having joined when the church was very small, preferred the small, intimate groups and did not relish the growth into a large institutional church.

Challenges of Growth

Growth rates are of significant concern to both central leadership in Salt Lake City and their authorized representative mission presidents. Regional church leadership was concerned with the lack of growth in the small branches and in 2001 decided to combine the five small branches into three larger branches. Although this was meant to help encourage growth, this arrangement has also aided and required local congregations to develop more formal patterns of interaction.

A congregation where sixty or seventy attend on Sunday can hold social events only at a church building, not in someone's apartment. All social events are now held in permanent church buildings, whether rented or owned, which have been renovated to appear similar to other Mormon facilities, and are most similar to those in the crowded cities of western Europe. Standard Mormon pictures—scenes from the Book of Mormon and pictures of Joseph Smith and of current church leaders—hang on the walls. Church leaders strive for uniformity of design when renovating buildings and choosing pictures, and as these members in Novosibirsk attend larger church-owned buildings, they come increasingly to recognize the church's style of decoration and norms of design. Both permanent locations have a kitchenette and social hall, meaning that the branches, though larger, can seat everyone when events involve food. The overall effect of the change to church-managed property has been that both meetings and socials feel less like a "home church" and more like an institutional church.

On a revisit to Novosibirsk in 2002, I expected members to still express concern for the disruption the new congregational boundaries had brought to associational patterns. However, of far more concern to many Russian members was the recent rotation in mission presidents. The president serving from 1999 to 2001 had a very hands-on, involved approach, making sure that certain programs such as youth camp occurred even if that meant extra work for the full-time missionaries. The president serving from 2001 to 2004 had a much more hands-off attitude, preferring to delegate as much as possible to local leaders. He believed in allowing them to take the consequences of their own efforts more directly, preferring a program to be canceled when local members did not adequately plan rather than stepping in and saving the day. Used to a long tradition of personalistic rule, some Russian members experienced this "hands-off" approach as withdrawal, or abandonment, and waxed nostalgic for the previous president.

The new South branch covers all of Sunrise and part of another former branch and meets at the church's building in the city center, an hour's travel each way from the heart of the Sunrise neighborhood. Some members in this area have stopped attending because of the distance and time involved, whereas others ceased coming because they cannot afford the rising bus and trolley fares to make the trip, especially when several family members are involved. For some, the proximity and closeness of the neighborhood had been important in church attendance. Though certain individuals stopped attending because of these changes, organizationally the redistricting has proved to be a huge success for the two branches that meet in the city center. South branch saw more members join in one month (June 2002) than had joined in the entire year of 2000. Sunday attendance averaged about fifty-five members out of more than one hundred on the rolls.

Administrative changes and length of time associating at church had begun to work on the practices of local members by 2002. Ludmilla, previously the Relief Society president of Sunrise branch, now an assistant to the Relief Society leader for South branch, made a point of verbally welcoming visitors and newcomers to the Sunday Relief Society meeting, which she had never done before. All the women who take turns conducting Relief Society now ask visitors to introduce themselves in the meeting, as is common practice in Mormon meetings in other locations but a new practice for many Russians. In one exchange, I observed a first-time visitor explain that she had just come from Kazakhstan, and several women in the group asked if she needed help with housing, furniture, a job, and other essentials. The concern for temporal affairs that I observed the women to have among their own group in 1999 had extended to concern for visitors and newcomers in 2002. A permanent meeting location has also allowed the branches to have a stable location for items that local members donate to be shared among the less fortunate in the congregations.

STANDARDIZED MORMON DOCTRINE

One purpose of uniform church administration has been to ensure that the teachings of the church are uniformly proclaimed and practiced throughout the world. In the past forty years, local congregations, even in Utah, have been subjected to numerous changes in organization and meeting schedule and formats in order to unify the entire church under a single format. The "Correlation Committee" at church headquarters is responsible for issuing teaching materials that present doctrines in a unified manner, independent of locale. In contrast to Sunday lessons in the 1950s that O'Dea might have seen, Sunday school, Relief Society, priesthood, and even primary lessons of the contemporary church are now "correlated," that is, thoroughly routinized and bureaucratized. These materials are translated in their entirety and issued simultaneously in nearly twenty languages, including Russian. The uniformity in doctrine and predictability of meeting format are frequently remarked upon by Mormons who visit other congregations in their travels. Returning to their own congregations, Mormons proudly testify that "the church is the same wherever you go."

Mormon Doctrine in Russia

As elsewhere in the Mormon Church, new members in Russia are accepted into the church only if they agree to basic doctrinal principles, including belief in modern-day prophets. An emphasis is placed not only on believing the Book of Mormon and other books as scripture but also on reading and studying them on a regular basis at home and in church meetings. Although this fits the "revivalistic Protestantism" O'Dea saw at the root of Mormonism (1957, 5), it represents a contrast from Orthodox theology and czarist-era practice. Most Russians today, however, know little of the pre-Soviet period of Orthodoxy and see Mormonism only against the background of the current Orthodox efforts to educate Russians about basic religious concepts or the Soviet era of anathematizing all religion. Currently, some Russian Mormons embrace the Mormon emphasis on doctrine and scripture reading, but the attitude of other Russians who do not join the church is similar to suspicious or dismissive attitudes of many outside the church to Mormon doctrine and scripture.

When missionaries first came to Russia, only some of the church materials were available in Russian, and even the Doctrine and Covenants was not yet translated into Russian in 1994. Missionaries often found themselves providing ad hoc translations for phrases they used at home, and early members sang Mormon hymns as translated by missionaries in various cities. Just over ten years later, all necessary church materials are available in Russian, including all scriptures, manuals for teachers, and the *Church Handbook of Instructions.* The most recent change bringing the Russian church experience more in line with the U.S. experience was the 2005 publication of a hymnal in Russian, containing approximately two-thirds of the hymns of the English-language edition. General conference talks are provided via recordings shipped from Salt Lake with voice-over translation, and later published in the Russian-language edition of the *Liahona,* the church's international magazine. By 2002, the *Liahona* in Russian went from four to twelve issues per year and, like other foreign-language editions, has become more uniform with the English-language edition. The *Liahona* combines articles directly translated from the three English-language periodicals *Ensign, New Era,* and *Friend,* with some of the focus of the *Church News,* providing news about the church for eastern Europe and Russia. In the doctrine proclaimed and espoused, the church in Russia is living up to the formal and informal expectations of being "the same wherever you go."

The increasing availability of Mormon materials in Russian and the increased experience of local Russian church leaders has led to an increasing standardization in the way Russians talk about Mormon doctrinal concepts. As with any situation requiring translation, some doctrinal precepts might be rendered one way or another way in Russian. In 2000, I heard some concepts referred to in more than one way, or even by inconsistently borrowing the English word. However, by 2005, stable linguistic patterns had emerged in referring to a particular doctrinal construct; stable patterns had also emerged in the language used ritually in conducting Sunday meetings. Thus, the longer members attend church, the more the language becomes standardized, routinized, and the ideas and concepts "the same everywhere you go."

Universal Ideal Mormon Behaviors

A list of encouraged beliefs and actions (including accepting modern-day prophets and additional scripture and paying tithes) and forbidden activities (immorality, drinking alcohol, smoking, and use of illegal drugs) puts the Mormon Church in tension with its original host culture of American society and with every other society into which it has expanded. The well-known prohibition against coffee and alcohol in the Word of Wisdom does present challenges and social difficulties for Mormons everywhere. However, American society today generally tolerates a wide variation of eating practices such as vegetarianism, and Mormons are but one group with different eating habits. In Russia, in contrast, drinking alcohol at social events, and drinking black tea every day, is a ubiquitous part of the social landscape (Patico 2002), so much so that refusing vodka or tea is considered offensive, and the complete abstinence from these substances is for many incomprehensible. Thus, the beliefs that O'Dea included in the "health" complex of Mormon values are much more in tension with the social and cultural environment of Russia than they are in the United States.

As O'Dea also suggested, Mormonism contained not only values of health (alongside those of hard work and recreation) but also values of how people should relate, giving Mormonism "its own socioeconomic and familial ethic" (112). Like other aspects of the Mormon way of life, O'Dea argued that this has its roots in their specific history, in this case of self-reliance in the wilderness of Utah. O'Dea wrote, "The Mormons, as a result of their own history and the general forms of church teaching, possess what may be called an 'agrarian ideology'; that is, they perceive and define social problems and personal goals with an outlook that took concrete shape in terms of a way of life based upon farming" (1957, 251). Though O'Dea applied this "agrarian ideology" to policies of self-reliance and hard work, it might also be extended to describe the attitude Mormons are expected to take toward each other—that is, even in urban settings to have a type of small-town, farmer friendliness with each other.

A key source of popular ideology as well as doctrine of the contemporary Mormon Church can be found in talks given by church leaders at the semiannual general conference broadcast around the world from Salt Lake City. Among the many topics addressed in "conference talks" are practical advice such as storing food for emergencies, the exhortation to read scriptures and pray, and emphasis on the importance of "spreading the gospel." As part of this last mandate, members are expected to "fellowship" new converts, visitors, and "friends of the church" (or nonmembers). Many speakers assume that the members listening know what "fellowshipping" means, but occasionally the behavioral advice is quite specific.

In one address, M. Russell Ballard, one of the church's twelve apostles, reminded listeners that new members must "receive a loving and warm welcome by the members of the church." He continued, "Every member of the church should foster the attributes of warmth, sincerity and love for the newcomers, as the missionaries are taught to do." He exhorted members to "help with the conversion process by making our wards and branches friendly places, with no exclusivity, where all people feel welcome and comfortable." Someone returning to the church after a period of nonattendance, he suggested, "should feel the warmth of being wanted and being welcomed into full fellowship." He reminded listeners that "being warm and friendly are Christ-like qualities," that "our hearts should be open to everyone," and that "the warmth of a radiant smile and friendly greeting can go far in smoothing the way for good... relations" (1988, 28). This warm smile and friendly greeting correspond more to American stereotypes of "small-town" or "farmer" rather than to stereotypes of the cold, distant, or blasé attitudes of urban dwellers (Hummon 1990).

Most prominent church leaders and American missionaries can be relied upon to follow this advice to be outgoing and "friendly" at least during their term of service. Being outgoing and friendly and offering a hand to a stranger are often considered important signals of "being Mormon." Missionaries and church leaders from the United States model these types of religious behaviors in their interactions around the world, including Russia. For many in Russia, this type of friendliness, particularly shaking hands with everyone, is associated with American culture. In Russia, this overt friendliness to strangers seems very "foreign," since Russians had not previously developed the skills and norms for meeting strangers that are more prevalent in American society. Thus, the friendliness enjoined by Mormon leaders seems at great odds with Russian cultural norms.

Mormon Norms Meet Russian Practices

Thus, not only the prohibition against alcohol, black tea, and smoking runs counter to activities that Russians see as integral to their culture (Patico 2002), but also this admonition to be "friendly" to everyone is foreign to a culture with a strong sense of close-knit, deep friendships (Pesmen 2000). Other actions that Mormons encourage, including reading scriptures, believing in God, and following a modern-day prophet in Salt Lake City, also seem very "foreign" in the daily lives of most Russians. Even the idea of belonging to a "foreign" church is an unusual event when Russian Orthodoxy is so closely aligned with Russian identity. Yet some Russians choose to join the Mormon Church, renounce vodka and black tea, and agree to follow an American prophet.

For local residents of Novosibirsk (where there are not many Americans, unlike Moscow or St. Petersburg), meeting a Mormon missionary is usually their first and only face-to-face meeting with an American. When I first attended the Sunrise branch, in October 1999, members completely ignored me until they discovered that I was a member from the United States. "Well, that is different," one woman exclaimed in disgust. "We thought they were 'listeners'!"[2] "Why didn't they announce it before the meetings?" another older woman exclaimed in dismay, referring to the practice of announcing from the pulpit when church officials visit congregations. At the time, the Russian members had a long way to go before they would come close to the ideal of "warmth" and "love" that Ballard exhorted members to show. Even in 2002, visiting branches where I was unknown produced similarly cold receptions. Yet this experience is similar to a story Ballard recounts as having occurred in Utah, so even American Mormons do not always follow his advice. To some extent, therefore, even while falling short of a proclaimed ideal, Russians Mormons are much like Mormons in other settings, though perhaps for different reasons.

Yet Russians retain a sense of their own cultural norms and sometimes demand that American missionaries conform to their local sense of appropriate behavior. Missionaries around the world give away copies of the Book of Mormon to anyone interested in reading the book. American missionaries in Novosibirsk were initially puzzled by local reluctance to accept a free book. The difficulty for Russians was sometimes not a lack of curiosity but a hesitation to accept what they perceived as a "gift" from someone they did not know. In contrast, once a person had established ties with missionaries and other members, they were ready to accept such a "gift." Missionaries adopted the local practice of making a presentation of this book, as well as other church literature, when someone chose to become a member through baptism into the church. Baptism is treated by many locals as an occasion like a birthday, to celebrate with visiting, cake, and well wishes. Gifts, though not necessary, are socially appropriate markers of relationships (Mauss 1990), and many recipients are disappointed if the book is not personalized through an inscription from the giver.

Mormonism as a Global Religion

Insofar as individuals adopt behaviors they would not otherwise have adopted because of their affiliation with a global church, behaviors may be thought of as "transnational practices" (Sklair 2002) and to some extent an indication of a "global" *habitus* (Illouz and John 2003). Russians who become Mormons adopt many new practices and are exposed to new doctrines and behaviors that they initially consider to be "foreign." Yet their insistence on "gifting" copies of the Book of Mormon demonstrates one of the ways that Russians adapt Mormon practices to be more consistent with their traditional Russian *habitus* (Bourdieu 1977).

American missionaries in Novosibirsk have taught free English conversation lessons for several years as a means of reaching out to the community. Originally held in the central public library (a less accessible building than Americans might imagine), these classes are now held once a week at the church building in the city center. Russians who meet missionaries through these lessons think of them primarily as cultural ambassadors of the United States, not unlike Peace Corps volunteers who were briefly stationed in Novosibirsk and taught English classes in local colleges.

Russians who express an interest in the missionaries' religion, or even join the church, come to see them in their primary function as religious messengers, but along with doctrine expect missionaries also to tell about their lives in the United States. Other American visitors, including myself, are often mistaken for some type of missionary, and I was often appealed to on questions of doctrine or procedure, illustrating that many Russians believe that Americans must have a better understanding of this American church. In 2000, an investigator who lived with her aged parents could not invite missionaries to her home because her father refused to see them as religious emissaries and saw them only as Americans, against whom he still retained prejudices learned during the cold war. Generally, Russians perceive Mormonism as an American church, despite the fact that it is represented as a worldwide church in church magazines such as the *Liahona*.

Many young adult Russian Mormons express increased interest in learning English after some time in the church. Senior missionary couples and mission presidents and their wives typically speak little Russian and interact with members and give talks through the aid of a translator. Though young missionaries often translate for them, Russian young adults with a good command of English are increasingly called upon to assist these senior leaders. Perhaps such events lead young adults to view English proficiency as a means for visibility at church. Everyone in Novosibirsk knows the story of the few locals who obtained paid work with the church because among their other qualifications they could speak English. This, along with the increasing standardization of doctrines and building styles, is a possible reason Russian members think of this church not as a local product but as a distinctly foreign, American church.

CONCLUSION

This chapter has examined an area left unexamined by O'Dea in *The Mormons,* namely, the reception of this "American" religion in international settings. O'Dea pointed out the ways in which Mormonism could be seen as an "American religion" while also emphasizing the tension between Mormon belief and the American environment. O'Dea noted that the Mormons' experience had led them to develop a distinctiveness marked by "its own ideas and values, its own theological innovations, and its own socioeconomic and familial ethic" (1957, 112). Though he mentioned the beginnings of true international growth of the Mormon Church, as seen in the establishment of temples in Switzerland and other non-U.S. locations, he did not discuss the implications of this growth, namely, the double tension between religion-secular and American-local that arises when Mormons "gather" in other settings.

This chapter has suggested ways in which Mormon distinctiveness and the tension between belief and environment are manifest in the establishment of permanent congregations in one city in the Russian Federation. In the internal structure of church organization, leaders strive to reproduce in Russia the same hierarchical administration found in the United States and elsewhere. In doctrine, Mormon leaders and missionaries are careful to stick to the approved, routinized curriculum now standard worldwide. In behaviors, Mormons in Russia are expected not only to forgo alcohol and other harmful substances but also to share "that same sociality" of friendly handshakes and warm smiles expected of Mormons everywhere. All of these aspects represent a double tension between Mormonism and the Russian environment—the tension of religious tenets with a secular society plus the tension of American missionaries preaching what is perceived as American ideals with Russian cultural norms. However, longitudinal, ethnographic experience in one congregation in Novosibirsk, Russia, suggests that many Russians are managing this tension and choosing to accept the changes that becoming Mormon entails. In the process, they retain some Russian cultural elements such as gift giving but gradually adapt to become part of a church that is proud to be "the same wherever you go." With forces for uniformity spread throughout the world with such success, Mormonism is truly a "world religion" and represents a powerful force for globalization in the twenty-first century.

NOTES

1. Research for the larger project conducted in 2000 from which this chapter draws data was supported in part by a grant from the International Research and Exchanges Board (IREX) with funds provided by the National Endowment for the Humanities, the U.S. Department of State that administers the Title VIII Program, and the IREX Scholar Support Fund. None of these organizations is responsible for the views expressed.

2. The term most often used in English for visitors brought by missionaries is *investigator,* that is, one who is "investigating" the doctrines of the church by meeting with missionaries and attending services. For translation into Russian, church officials wisely chose the more neutral term *listener (slushitel'),* that is, one who is listening to the missionaries' message and listening to church services. This translation was chosen to avoid the obvious association of the word *investigator* with the police or secret service. Even Gordon B. Hinckley, current church president, avoids the term *investigator,* preferring the more appealing term *friend of the church.*

References

Ashwin, Sarah. 1996. "Forms of Collectivity in a Non-monetary Society." *Sociology: The Journal of the British Sociological Association* 30, no. 1: 21–39.

Ballard, M. Russell. 1988. "The Hand of Fellowship." *Ensign,* November, 28.

Bartlett, Robert. 1993. *The Making of Europe: Conquest, Colonization, and Cultural Change, 950–1350.* Princeton: Princeton University Press.

Bourdieu, Pierre. 1977. *Outline of a Theory of Practice.* Cambridge: Cambridge University Press.

Bronfenbrenner, Urie. 1972. *Two Worlds of Childhood: U.S. and U.S.S.R.* New York: Pocket Books.

Browning, Gary. 1997. *Russia and the Restored Gospel.* Salt Lake City: Deseret Book.

Burawoy, Michael, Alice Burton, Ann Arnett Ferguson, Kathryn J. Fox, Joshua Gamson, Nadine Gartrell, Leslie Hurst, et al. 1991. *Ethnography Unbound: Power and Resistance in the Modern Metropolis.* Berkeley and Los Angeles: University of California Press.

Burawoy, Michael, and Janos Lukacs. 1992. *The Radiant Past: Ideology and Reality in Hungary's Road to Capitalism.* Chicago: University of Chicago Press.

Caldwell, Melissa L. 2002. "The Taste of Nationalism: Food Politics in Post-socialist Moscow." *Ethnos* 67, no. 3: 295–319.

Castells, Manuel, and Emma Kiselyova. 1995. *The Collapse of Soviet Communism: A View from the Information Society.* Berkeley and Los Angeles: University of California Press.

Davis, Derek H. 1997. "Russia's New Law on Religion: Progress or Regress?" *Journal of Church and State* 39, no. 4: 645–56.

Dunch, Ryan. 2002. "Beyond Cultural Imperialism: Cultural Theory, Christian Missions, and Global Modernity." *History and Theory* 41, no. 3: 301–26.

Elbakian, Ekaterina S., and Stepan V. Medvedko. 2003. "The Impact of Religious Values on the Economic Preferences of Russian Believers." *Sociological Research* 42, no. 5: 7–23.

Elliott, Mark, and Sharyl Corrado. 1999. "The 1997 Russian Law on Religion: The Impact on Protestants." *Religion, State, and Society* 27, no. 1: 109–34.

French, Richard Anthony, and F. E. Ian Hamilton, eds. 1979. *The Socialist City: Spatial Structure and Urban Policy.* Chichester, N.Y.: Wiley and Sons.

Gimpelson, Vladimir, and Douglas Lippoldt. 2001. *The Russian Labor Market: Between Transition and Turmoil.* Lanham, Md.: Rowman and Littlefield.

Givens, Terryl L. 2003. *By the Hand of Mormon: The American Scripture That Launched a New World Religion.* New York: Oxford University Press.

Guest, Kenneth J. 2003. *God in Chinatown: Religion and Survival in New York's Evolving Immigrant Community.* New York: New York University Press.

Hummon, David M. 1990. *Commonplaces: Community Ideology and Identity in American Culture.* Albany: State University of New York Press.

Humphrey, Caroline. 2002. *The Unmaking of Soviet life: Everyday Economies after Socialism.* Ithaca: Cornell University Press.

Illouz, Eva, and Nicholas John. 2003. "Global Habitus, Local Stratification, and Symbolic Struggles over Identity." *American Behavioral Scientist* 47, no. 2: 201–29.

Inkeles, Alex, and Raymond Bauer. 1959. *The Soviet Citizen: Daily Life in a Totalitarian Society.* Cambridge: Harvard University Press.

Knowlton, David. 1994. "'Gringo, Jeringo': Anglo Mormon Missionary Culture in Bolivia." In *Contemporary Mormonism: Social Science Perspectives,* eds. Marie Cornwall, Tim B. Heaton, and Lawrence A. Young. Urbana: University of Illinois Press.

Kong, Lily. 2002. "In Search of Permanent Homes: Singapore's House Churches and the Politics of Space." *Urban Studies* 39, no. 9: 1573–86.

Krindatch, Alexey D. 2004. "Patterns of Religious Change in Post-Soviet Russia: Major Trends from 1998 to 2003." *Religion, State, and Society* 32, no. 2: 115–36.

Ledeneva, Alena. 1998. *Russia's Economy of Favours: "Blat," Networking, and Informal Exchanges.* New York: Cambridge University Press.

Mauss, Marcel. 1990. *The Gift: The Form and Reason for Exchange in Archaic Societies.* New York: W. W. Norton.

Mchedlov, Mikail, Turii A. Gavrilov, and Aleksandr G. Shevchenko. 2003. "A Social Portrait of Today's Religious Believer." *Sociological Research* 42, no. 5: 57–73.

McRoberts, Omar. 2003. *Streets of Glory: Church and Community in a Black Urban Neighborhood.* Chicago: University of Chicago Press.

Mendras, Marie. 1998. "State, Money, Clientelism" (L'état, l'argent, la clientele)." *Tocqueville Review (La Revue Tocqueville)* 19, no. 1: 35–54.

Millar, James R., and Sharon L. Wolchik. 1994a. "Introduction: The Social Legacies and the Aftermath of Communism." In *The Social Legacy of Communism,* ed. James R. Millar and Sharon L. Wolchik, 1–30. Cambridge: Cambridge University Press.

———, eds. 1994b. *The Social Legacy of Communism.* Cambridge: Cambridge University Press.

Misztal, Barbara A. 1996. *Trust in Modern Societies.* Cambridge: Polity Press.

O'Dea, Thomas F. 1957. *The Mormons.* Chicago: University of Chicago Press.

Parsons, Talcott. 1951. *The Social System.* New York: Free Press.

———. 1954. *Essays in Sociological Theory.* New York: Free Press.

Patico, Jennifer. 2002. Chocolate and Cognac: Gifts and Recognition of Social Worlds in Post-Soviet Russia. *Ethnos* 67, no. 3: 345–68.

Pesmen, Dale. 2000. *Russia and Soul: An Exploration.* Ithaca, N.Y.: Cornell University Press.

Robertson, Roland. 1992. *Globalization: Social theory and global culture.* Thousand Oaks, Calif.: Sage Publications.

Rose, Richard. 1999. "Living in an Antimodern Society." *East European Constitutional Review* 8, nos. 1–2: 68–75.

Shipps, Jan. 1985. *Mormonism: The Story of a New Religious Tradition.* Urbana: University of Illinois Press.

Silverman, Bertram, and Murray Yanowitch. 1997. *New Rich, New Poor, New Russia: Winners and Losers on the Russian Road to Capitalism.* Armonk, N.Y.: M. E. Sharpe.

Sinelina, Tuliia Tu. 2003. "On Criteria for Determining Religious Commitment." *Sociological Research* 42, no. 5: 24–39.

Sklair, Leslie. 2002. *Globalization: Capitalism and Its Alternatives.* Oxford: Oxford University Press.

Spencer, Sarah Busse. 2003. "Social Relations in Post-Soviet Society: Russian Capitalism Embedded." Ph.D. diss., University of Chicago.

———. 2004. "Novosibirsk: The Globalization of Siberia." In *Russian Transformations: Challenging the Global Narrative,* ed. Leo McCann, 128–47. London: Routledge Curzon.

Taylor, Frederick Winslow. 1911. *The Principles of Scientific Management.* Mineola, N.Y.: Dover Publications, 1998.

Tullis, F. LaMond, ed. 1979. *Mormonism: A Faith for All Cultures.* Provo: Brigham Young University Press.

Unger, Danny. 1998. *Building Social Capital in Thailand: Fibers, Finance, and Infrastructure.* New York: Cambridge University Press.

Verdery, Katherine. 2003. *The Vanishing Hectare: Property and Value in Post-socialist Transylvania.* Ithaca, N.Y.: Cornell University Press.

Walder, Andrew G. 1986. *Communist Neo-traditionalism: Work and Authority in Chinese Industry.* Berkeley and Los Angeles: University of California Press.

Weber, Max. 1963. *The Sociology of Religion.* Boston: Beacon Press.

———. 1968. *Economy and Society: An Outline of Interpretive Sociology.* Berkeley and Los Angeles: University of California Press.

Wilson, William Julius. 1987. *The Truly Disadvantaged: The Inner City, the Underclass, and Public Policy.* Chicago: University of Chicago Press.

Biography of Thomas F. O'Dea

Thomas F. O'Dea was born on December 1, 1915, in Massachusetts and grew up during the Great Depression, part of an Irish Catholic immigrant family. As a young man he became involved in the labor movement, the Socialist Party, and the Young Communist League. In 1938 he was called by the U.S. House Un-American Activities Committee to give testimony about the Young Communist League at Harvard. He was cited for contempt in 1940 as a result of his refusal to testify. Despite these activities, he spent time in the military during World War II in North Africa, India, China, Australia, and the Mariana Islands. After the war he returned to Harvard, where he graduated summa cum laude in 1949, at the age of thirty-three. For his undergraduate honors thesis he examined conflicts between the local Catholic center and Catholic Church authorities. Soon after, he produced "A Study of Mormon Values," a large literature review on Mormon history and beliefs. He was then invited to join Harvard University's Comparative

PICTURED ABOVE: Thomas F. O'Dea, author of *The Mormons,* first published in 1957. Courtesy Thomas F. O'Dea photographs, MSS P-255, L. Tom Perry Special Collections, Harold B. Lee Library, Brigham Young University, Provo, Utah.

Study of Values in Five Cultures, headed by Clyde Kluckhohn and a number of other prominent social scientists. The five cultures that this project investigated were the Hopi, the Navajo, Mexican Americans, white Texas settlers, and the Mormons. His bibliographic study and his time in both Salt Lake City and Ramah, New Mexico, as part of the cultural study formed the basis of his first book, *The Mormons*, published in 1957. During his fieldwork, O'Dea participated fully in the LDS community and ward activities. He helped write a skit that was presented at the local LDS church, and he was invited and spoke in an LDS sacrament meeting.

O'Dea completed his M.A. and Ph.D. at Harvard in 1951 and 1952. His education at Harvard was influenced not only by the five-cultures project but also by the notable presence of Talcott Parsons. This influence can be seen in the functionalist-values approach that O'Dea used throughout much of his career. Following the completion of a Ph.D., he began his formal academic career as a research fellow at the Massachusetts Institute of Technology (1951-1953), where he later taught as an assistant professor (1954-1956). He also spent part of the 1955-1956 academic year at the Center for Advanced Study in the Behavioral Sciences at Stanford University. The following three years, during which *The Mormons* was published, he taught at Fordham University. He also spent summers at Boston College in 1954 and Utah State University in 1956. In the summer of 1958 he spent time at the University of Utah before being employed there from 1959 to 1965. His two final academic appointments were at Columbia University (1965-1966) and the University of California at Santa Barbara, where he held appointments in the Department of Sociology and the Department of Religious Studies. He also spent time traveling in the Middle East, where he began studies of different religious faiths, focusing on comparative research among Christianity, Judaism, and Islam. One side research project resulted in a 130-page single-spaced document titled "Social Change in Saudi Arabia: Problems and Prospect." The rights to the document were owned by the Arabia American Oil Company and were not released publicly.

O'Dea died on November 13, 1974, at the age of fifty-eight. His death at a relatively young age was a great loss to the academic community, particularly to the sociological study of religion that he had championed most of his academic life.

WRITINGS ON THE CHURCH OF JESUS CHRIST OF LATTER-DAY SAINTS BY THOMAS F. O'DEA

"A Study of Mormon Values." *Comparative Study of Values: Working Papers* (Laboratory of Social Relations, Harvard University), no. 2 (October 1949).

Miscellaneous field notes from interviews in Salt Lake City and Ramah, New Mexico, 1950.

"A Comparative Study of the Role of Values in Social Action in Two Southwestern
Communities," with Evon Z. Vogt. *American Sociological Review* 18 (1953): 645-54.

"Mormon Values: The Significance of a Religious Outlook for Social Action." Ph.D. thesis,
Harvard University, 1953.

"The Effects of Geographical Position on Belief and Behavior in a Rural Mormon Village."
Rural Sociology 19 (1954): 358-64.

"Mormonism and the American Experience of Time." *Western Humanities Review* 8 (1954):
181-90.

"Mormonism and the Avoidance of Sectarian Stagnation: A Study of Church, Sect, and
Incipient Nationality." *American Journal of Sociology* 40 (1954): 285-93.

The Sociology of Mormonism: Four Studies. Publications in the Humanities, no. 1.4.
Cambridge: Department of Humanities, Massachusetts Institute of Technology, 1955.
(This is a reprinting of four previously published articles.)

The Mormons. Chicago: University of Chicago Press, 1957; paperback ed., 1964.

"The Mormons: Strong Voice in the West." *Information: The Catholic Church in American
Life* (March 1961): 15-20.

"Mormonism Today." *Desert: Magazine of the Southwest* 26 (June 1962): 23-27.

Foreword to the Phoenix edition of *Desert Saints,* by Nels Anderson. Chicago: University of
Chicago Press, 1966.

"Latter-day Saints." In *The Catholic Encyclopedia* (1967 ed.), 8:525-29.

"Sects and Cults." In *International Encyclopedia of the Social Sciences* (1968 ed.), 14:130-36.

"The Mormons: Church and People." In *Plural Society in the Southwest,* ed. Edward H.
Spicer and Raymond H. Thomson, 115-66. New York: Interbook, 1972.

"Sources of Strain in Mormon History Reconsidered." In *Mormonism and American Culture,*
ed. Marvin S. Hill and James B. Allen, 147-67. New York: Harper and Row, 1972.

"Mormon Values: The Mutual Dependence of Belief, Action, and Social Structure."
Undated manuscript.

Selected Other Important Works

The Sociology of Religion. Englewood Cliffs, N.J.: Prentice-Hall, 1966.

American Catholic Dilemma: An Inquiry into the Intellectual Life. New York: New American
Library, 1958; republished in 1962.

The Catholic Crisis. Boston: Beacon Press, 1968.

Alienation, Atheism, and the Religious Crisis. New York: Sheed and Ward, 1969.

Sociology and the Study of Religion: Theory, Research, Interpretation. New York: Basic Books,
1970.

"Youth in Protest: Revolution or Revelation?" American West Lecture, University of Utah,
November 24, 1970.

Religion and Man (with others). New York: Harper, 1972.

Readings on the Sociology of Religion (compiled with Janet K. O'Dea). Englewood Cliffs, N.J.: Prentice-Hall, 1973.

Sources of Information

Karlenzig, Bruce. "O'Dea, Thomas F." In *Encyclopedia of Religion and Society,* ed. William H. Swatos Jr. Walnut Creek, Calif.: Altamira Press, 1998.

Michaelson, Robert S. "Enigmas in Interpreting Mormonism." *Sociological Analysis* 38 (1977): 145-53.

———. "Thomas F. O'Dea on the Mormons: Retrospect and Assessment." *Dialogue: A Journal of Mormon Thought* 11, no. 1 (Spring 1978): 44-57.

Contributors

Barry Balleck is an associate professor of political science at Georgia Southern University. He teaches courses in international studies and terrorism. He received his Ph.D. from the University of Colorado.

Brent D. Beal is an assistant professor in the Rucks Department of Management in the Ourso College of Business at Louisiana State University. He received his Ph.D. in business administration from Texas A&M University. His research interests include corporate social responsibility, intellectual property and knowledge management, and the sociology of knowledge and philosophy of science.

Janet Bennion is an associate professor of anthropology and chair of the Social Science Department at Lyndon State, specializing in alternative sexuality and nontraditional religious movements. She has written two books on women in polygamous fundamentalist movements in Montana (*Women of Principle*, 1997) and in Mexico (*Desert Patriarchy*, 2003).

Douglas J. Davies, an anthropologist and theologian, is professor in the study of religion at Durham University, UK. Recent publications include *The Mormon Culture of Salvation* (2000), *Introduction to Mormonism* (2003), *A Brief History of Death* (2004), *The Encyclopedia of Cremation* (with Lewis Mates, 2005), and *Bishops, Wives and Children: A Study of the Church of England* (with Mathew Guest, 2007). He is an Oxford D.Litt., and an Honorary Dr. Theol. of Uppsala University.

LYNN ENGLAND received his Ph.D. from the University of Pittsburgh. He taught in the Sociology Department at Brigham Young University for thirty-six years and served as chair. His work focuses on the ways in which rural communities are able to sustain themselves in the face of the forces of globalization and modernity. His studies have also involved research among the Raramuri peoples of Mexico. England's recent writing has focused on the sociological contributions of W. E. B. Du Bois.

TERRYL L. GIVENS is professor of religion and literature and holds the James A. Bostwick Chair in English at the University of Richmond. His several books include *By the Hand of Mormon: The American Scripture That Launched a New World Religion* (2003) and *"When Souls Had Wings": The Idea of Pre-existence in Western Thought* (2007).

HENRI GOOREN is an assistant professor in the Department of Sociology and Anthropology at Oakland University in Rochester, Michigan. A cultural anthropologist, he specializes in religion in Latin America and conversion to Pentecostalism, charismatic Catholicism, and Mormonism in particular He recently finished a book called *Conversion Careers: Why People Become and Remain Religiously Active*. After conducting fieldwork in Nicaragua in 2005–2006, he is now writing a book that deals with competition for members between churches in Nicaragua.

MELVYN HAMMARBERG is associate professor of anthropology and Graduate Group Chair in American Civilization at the University of Pennsylvania and a consulting curator in the University Museum. He is the author of *The Indiana Voter: Historical Dynamics of Party Allegiance during the 1870s* (1977), editor of *Interpreting American Culture: A Regional Approach* (1992), and author of the *Penn Inventory for Posttraumatic Stress Disorder* (1991). He is currently completing a cultural study of the Latter-day Saints with the working title "Quest for Glory: The World of the Latter-day Saints."

TIM B. HEATON is a professor of sociology at Brigham Young University. He recently published *The Health, Wealth, and Social Life of Mormons* with Cardell Jacobson and Stephen Bahr (2004).

JOHN P. HOFFMANN is a professor of sociology at Brigham Young University. His research addresses adolescent behavior, criminology, and the sociology of religion. His book *Japanese Saints* was published in 2007.

CARDELL K. JACOBSON is a professor of sociology at Brigham Young University. His recent research has focused on intergroup marriage in the United States and other countries. Recent books are *All God's Children: Racial and Ethnic Voices in the LDS Church* (2004) and, with Tim B. Heaton and Stephen J. Bahr, *The Health, Wealth, and Social Life of Mormons* (2004).

DAVID CLARK KNOWLTON is an associate professor of anthropology at Utah Valley State College where he specializes in the study of religion in Latin America as well as international Mormonism.

ARMAND L. MAUSS is professor emeritus of sociology and religious studies at Washington State University, now living in Irvine, California. He is past editor of the *Journal for the Scientific Study of Religion* and past president of the Mormon History Association. His most recent books on the Mormons are *The Angel and the Beehive: The Mormon Struggle with Assimilation* (1994) and *All Abraham's Children: Changing Mormon Conceptions of Race and Lineage* (2003).

LOREN MARKS is an assistant professor in the School of Human Ecology at Louisiana State University. He received his Ph.D. in family studies from the University of Delaware. He is conducting a national study that examines the connection between religious faith involvement and family relationships.

CARRIE A. MILES is a senior research fellow at the Center for the Economic Study of Religion at George Mason University and a nonresident scholar at the Institute for the Studies of Religion at Baylor University. She is the author of *The Redemption of Love: Rescuing Marriage and Sexuality from the Economics of a Fallen World* (2006). She is presently doing research on family, economics, and religion in Africa.

MICHAEL NIELSEN is an associate professor of psychology at Georgia Southern University. He teaches courses in social psychology and the psychology of religion. He received his Ph.D. from Northern Illinois University.

SARAH BUSSE SPENCER received her Ph.D. in sociology from the University of Chicago in 2003. Her research interests include change in postsocialist societies, the role of social capital in inertia and social change, and the intersection of religion and globalization. She currently teaches at the College of New Jersey.

DAVID G. STEWART JR. is a pediatric orthopedic surgeon practicing in the Las Vegas area. He has researched LDS growth and retention in more than twenty countries, and is the author of *Law of the Harvest: Practical Principles of Effective Missionary Work* (2007). He received his M.D. from the University of Colorado.

O. KENDALL WHITE JR. is the William P. Ames Jr. Professor of Sociology and Anthropology at Washington and Lee University. As a former student of O'Dea, his book *Mormon Neo-orthodoxy: A Crisis Theology* (1987) and various articles in the sociology of religion have O'Dea's footprints all over them.

Index

DATE DUE
